The Best Of t

WINE COUNTRY

A witty, opinionated and remarkably useful guide to California's vinelands

By Don W. Martin and Betty Woo Martin

Pine Cone Press, Inc. • **Columbia, California**

This book is dedicated—with deep gratitude—to the authors of the Twenty-first Amendment to the Constitution of the United States of America.

BOOKS BY DON AND BETTY MARTIN

Adventure Cruising • 1996
Arizona Discovery Guide • 1990, 1993, 1994, 1996
Arizona in Your Future • 1991, 1993, 1998
The Best of the Gold Country •1987, 1990, 1992
The Best of San Francisco •1986, 1990, 1994, 1997
The Best of the Wine Country •1991, 1994, 1995, 1997
Inside San Francisco • 1991
Las Vegas: The Best of Glitter City • 1998
Nevada Discovery Guide • 1992, 1997
Northern California Discovery Guide • 1993
Oregon Discovery Guide • 1993, 1995, 1996
San Francisco's Ultimate Dining Guide • 1988
The Toll-free Traveler • 1997
The Ultimate Wine Book • 1993, 1997
Utah Discovery Guide • 1995
Washington Discovery Guide • 1994, 1997

Library of Congress Cataloging-in-Publication Data
Martin, Don and Betty—
   The Best of the Wine Country.
   Includes index.
   1. California—Description & Travel (California Wine Country)—Guidebooks. 2. California—History (California wine industry).

ISBN:0-942053-17-6
Library of Congress catalog card number 95-92024

Wine country maps • **Dave Bonnot**, Columbine Type and Design, Sonora, Calif.
   Illustrations • **Bob Shockley**
   Photography • **Don W. Martin**

THE COVER • *Tasting rooms convey much of the color and romance of California's wine country. Here, travelers can absorb the winery's atmosphere and sample its products. The cover captures a portion of a stained glass window in the Sebastiani Vineyards tasting room in Sonoma.*

CONTENTS

MAPS

FOREWORD

Don Martin and I have been friends for more than two decades, and we have seen many changes in the wine industry through the years. However, one thing remains unchanged: an interest in visiting the Wine Country.

There was a time when this interest was focused mostly on the Napa Valley, when the only food available was from a few old family restaurants. If you wanted to stay overnight, you had better have a friend with an extra room, or be willing to put up with a second-rate motel.

Well, those are from the not-so-good old days, as far as winery visitors are concerned. The number of places to eat and stay has multiplied and moved upscale dramatically. And the number of visitors has increased geometrically.

The Wine Country now offers everything from fancy resorts and convention facilities to some of the best restaurants in California. We now have our share of foreign ownership in the wine industry, which has brought wine and food flavors never dreamed of twenty years ago. And people have a choice of many wine producing regions, which offer not only interesting wineries but some great wines.

There was a time when I could boast of having been in the door of the great majority of California's wineries. Today there are wineries that I may have heard of, but I'd have to check a phone book to find them—even some in Sonoma and Napa. There were about 240 wineries in California in 1970; today there are more than 800.

With all of these changes, how can winery visitors find their way around without some help? This book takes an honest approach to the problem, giving people direction and choices as they visit the state's many Wine Countries. I live here, and I plan to keep it within reach.

By the way, here's another important thing about *The Best of the Wine Country.* The authors have kept the tempo light, and they poke a little fun at people who take wine too seriously. Wine should add enjoyment to a meal, not complicate it.

Life is complicated enough. A glass of wine, as well as Don and Betty's guidebook, will help ease the pressure.

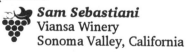 *Sam Sebastiani*
Viansa Winery
Sonoma Valley, California

INTRODUCTION

"Fine fruit flavors over a steely base. It's a serious wine that secretly just wants to have fun."

—Winetaster's description of a Domaine de la Bousquette Blanc de Noir

Like that silly taster's description above, this is a serious book about wine that just wants to have a little fun. What you hold in your hand is a completely revised version of the original 1991 edition, so it should be even more fun and—of course—more useful.

It was written for people who want to explore California's wine country and learn more about wine. It was not written for wine writers. In fact, it might offend some of those Colombard commentators, since it has a little fun at their expense.

In flooding their tasting descriptions with silly adjectives, some of these Riesling reporters peddle more confusion than useful information.

Really. Can you imagine a Cabernet that is "heavy on the tongue with a leathery finish and a slight hint of basil?" Try to picture a Pinot Noir with a big nose. (A late harvest Jimmy Durante?)

Betty and I chuckle when these Riesling reporters try to bury us in a hailstorm of hyperbole. So, we begin each chapter of this book by quoting one of their more memorable tasting descriptions. Each is authentic, found in the rich repository of contemporary wine writing.

These Semillon scribes *do* have a lot to tell us. By reading their newspaper columns or reviews in *The Wine Spectator*, we can learn what interesting wines have been released, which vintner is winning all the medals and what dynamite Zinfandel is priced under ten dollars. But many of these writers, it seems, get paid by the adjective.

We *are* earnest about wine, incidentally. I've been a student of the California wine industry for thirty-five years, and I've sipped Sirah with serious intent since the age of consent. I was an active wine writer briefly, peddling my prose to *Vintage Magazine* and significant other publications. But I soon tired of searching for the ultimate adjective to properly portray the pedigree of a Pinot. I decided that it was much more fun to drink wines than to talk about them.

And that's the subject of this book: discovering California wineries and drinking their wines—from Sonoma Sirah to Paso Robles Pinot.

There's no scarcity of books about the state's wine industry. However, some tell us more about the winemaker's relatives than we ever wanted to know. Others offer encyclopedic listings of every winery in the state. Many focus on the Napa and Sonoma valleys, although major California winelands stretch from Mendocino to Temecula.

This is a wine country *guidebook*, designed to steer you to nearly 300 of the state's wineries and tasting rooms. Like our other guides, it's selective. Instead of covering every far-flung tasting room, we focus on areas with wineries in reasonable concentration. We won't send you to a remote corner of the San Joaquin Valley for a sip of generic chablis.

Further, we include only wineries offering tasting and/or tours without prior arrangement. Thus, you can toss this book into the glove compartment of your Belchfire V-Six and head for the nearest vineyard. We also suggest nearby restaurants and lodgings, and other area attractions.

In researching this book, we solicited nothing but information. We visited tasting rooms as tourists, sipped the wine, took the tours, asked a few questions and left. We dined covertly, made our own sleeping arrangements and paid our admission at attractions and museums. Thus, *The Best of the Wine Country* is full of opinions—but they're all ours.

THE WINERIES

We offer a wide choice of wineries in each area, listing virtually all of those with tasting rooms that have set hours. These range from fascinating to funky, from regal to rustic. Our judgments are personal and arbitrary; exclusion from this book should not be regarded as an affront or an oversight.

You'll note initials or little symbols beside each winery listing. They mean just what you think they mean:

T ● Tasting: the winery offers gratis sips of its product; a dollar sign following the symbol indicates a charge for wine samples.

GT ● Guided tours are offered, generally on a specific schedule.

GTA ● Appointment needed for guided tours.

ST ● Self-guiding tours: signs, arrows and/or graphics will lead you through the winery.

CT ● Casual tours, which can range from a peek into the aging cellars to an invitation to browse about on your own. Ask the tasting room host or hostess for specifics.

✕ ● Picnic area is located near the winery. Most tasting rooms are licensed to sell and uncork a bottle for your lunch. It definitely *gauche* to bring your own from elsewhere.

👜 ● A **gift shop** or a good selection of giftwares and/or specialty foods is located in or near the tasting room. Most tasting rooms sell a few wine related logo items, but we don't use the 👜 symbol unless the assortment is reasonably extensive.

R ● A **restaurant** is part of the winery or immediately adjacent.

At the end of each listing, under **Tasting notes,** we discuss the variety and general style of wines produced at the winery. We attempt no in-depth critiques, since quality will vary from one vintage to the next. And under **Vintners choice,** we let the winemakers have their say, asking them to select their favorites. When they insist on saying "All of our wines are great," or they decline to make a choice, we omit this listing.

Since we're talking about "the best" of the wine country, we have a little presumptuous fun by listing—at the end of each winery section—places that offer the most interesting tasting rooms, nicest picnic areas, best gift shops, most informative tours and best wine values.

DINING & RECLINING AMONG THE VINES

Since this is a winery guide, we list restaurants and lodgings that are near the vineyards, or in towns bordering the wine country. In areas where winery touring is secondary to other tourist pursuits, such as Monterey and Santa Cruz, we don't list specific lodgings or restaurants. However, we do refer readers to local chambers of commerce, who can provide information.

Wine country dining

Our intent here is to provide a selective dining sampler, not a complete list. We used several methods to select café candidates for possible inclusion: inquiry among locals, suggestions from friends and from other guidebooks, and our own dining experiences. Comments are based more on overviews of food and service, not on the proper doneness of a specific pork chop.

Of course, one has to be careful about recommending restaurants. Obviously, people's tastes differ, and it's difficult to judge a café by a single meal. A chef might have a bad night, or a waitress might be recovering from one. Thus, your dining experience may be quite different from ours. Restaurants seem to suffer a rather high attrition rate, so don't be crushed if one that we recommended has become a laundromat by the time you get there. Also, some change their hours and closing days frequently, often cutting back during the slow season, so call before you go.

We graded the restaurants with one to four stars, for food quality, service and ambiance.

☆ **Adequate**—A reasonably clean café with basic but edible food.

☆☆ **Good**—A well-run place that offers a fine meal and good service.

☆☆☆ **Very good**—Substantially above average; excellent fare, served with a smile in a fine dining atmosphere.

☆☆☆☆ **Excellent**—We've found heaven, and it has a great wine list!

Price ranges are based on the tab for an average dinner, including soup or salad (but not wine or dessert). Obviously, places serving only breakfast and/or lunch are priced accordingly.

$—Average dinner for one is $9 or less

$$—$10 to $14

$$$—$15 to $24

$$$$—$25 and beyond

Incidentally, many chefs go to bed with the chickens in the wine country, so restaurants may close earlier than those in urban areas. Some upscale designer cafés in Sonoma or the Napa Valley serve their souffles until suitable hours (and they charge San Francisco prices), but don't plan on pork chops much past 9 p.m. in Gilroy or Murphys.

Wineland lodgings

We've checked most lodgings to insure that they're reasonably neat, clean and well run. We often rely on the judgment of the California State Automobile Association (AAA) because we respect its high standards. We also include some budget places that may fall short of Triple A ideals, but still offer a clean room for a respite from wine sipping. Of course we can't anticipate changes in management or the maid's day off, but hopefully your surprises will be good ones.

Some of California's earliest bed and breakfast inns were established in the wine country, and their homey intimacy fits easily into the ambiance of the vinelands. We generally offer a good selection of them. We list only true B&Bs, not merely family homes with an extra room because the oldest son is out stomping grapes. Again, we reach for the stars to rate lodgings:

☆ **Adequate**—Clean and basic; don't expect anything fancy.

☆☆ **Good**—A well-run place with comfortable beds and most essentials.

☆☆☆ **Very good**—Substantially above average, with facilities such as a pool and spa.

☆☆☆☆ **Excellent**—An exceptional lodging with beautifully-appointed rooms, often with a restaurant and resort facilities.

Ø **Non-smoking rooms** available, or the entire facility is smoke free. This is almost universal in bed & breakfast inns. (We no longer use the non-smoking symbol in restaurant listings, since virtually all restaurants in California have non-smoking sections and many are smoke free. All tasting rooms are smoke free as well.)

Price ranges reflect the cost for two people in a single room. Specific prices were furnished to us by the lodgings and of course are subject to change. Use them only as a rough guide and call the hotel, motel or B&B for current rates.

$—a double for under $25
$$—$25 to $49
$$$—$50 to $74
$$$$—$75 to $99
$$$$$—$100 or more

It's always wise to make advance reservations. If you don't like the place and you're staying more than a day, you can always shop around after the first night and exchange lodgings.

FURTHER READING

If you find this book useful and would like to learn more about wine, try our companion sippers' guide, *The Ultimate Wine Book*. Its focus is wine appreciation, wine with food and the latest health findings regarding nature's noblest beverage. For more detail on attractions other than wineries in the northern half of the state, our *Northern California Discovery Guide* may be useful. Both are available at book stores and *Ultimate Wine* is sold at many tasting rooms and wine shops. These and other *Pine Cone Press* books can be ordered directly from the publisher; see the back of this book.

Enough talk. Let's go find a decent Zinfandel.

"Quickly, bring me a beaker of wine, so that I may wet my brain and say something clever." — **Aristophanes**

THANK YOU...

Nancy A. Light, director of communications, **Elizabeth Holmgren,** director or research and education, and **Pat McKelvey,** librarian, all staff members of California's **Wine Institute**. Their assistance was invaluable as we compiled data for the first edition of this book and for our other grape-focused publication, *The Ultimate Wine Book.* We add a special thanks to Nancy for catching some of our mistakes.

Norm Roby, former west coast editor of *Vintage Magazine* and now a *Wine Spectator* contributing editor, for publishing some of my first wine articles.

Lindy Lindquist, who once hired me to write winery newsletters, thus convincing me that I wasn't cut out for that sort of thing.

Kathleen Elizabeth Martin, former wine and gourmet foods specialist for Macy's California, for sharing her wine knowledge.

Robert Mondavi for his efforts to convince America that wine should be regarded—not with awe or trepidation—but with simple respect. To quote Bob: "We view wine as an integral part of our culture, heritage and gracious way of life."

Justin Meyer, Napa Valley winemaker, for having the good sense to write a sensible book: *Plain Talk about Fine Wine.*

David Darlington for authoring an eminently readable and informative book about our favorite wine: *Angels' Visits: An Inquiry into the Mystery of Zinfandel*.

Millie Howie for steering us around northern Sonoma County in years past and helping us discover its fine wines and winemakers.

John and **Jim Pedroncelli**, northern Sonoma County winemakers, and their former tasting room host **John Soule**, for introducing us to the simple honesty of Zinfandel.

Sam Sebastiani of Sonoma Valley's Viansa Winery for taking the time to sit with us on a ditch bank, bottle in hand, to talk about life, wine and the Sebastiani family legend. Further thanks for writing the foreword to this book.

The **Ernie Fortino family,** the "new immigrants" of Gilroy, for sharing their friendship, their enthusiasm and their honest wines.

Margaret Smith for establishing a rather sensible organization called *Zinfandel Advocates and Producers*, to help folks appreciate and enjoy this fine wine. Should you want to get ZAP-ped, contact her at 118 Hillside Drive, Woodside, CA 94062; (415) 851-2319.

Nobody's perfect, but we try
Keeping up with the changes

This book is packed with thousands of facts, and a few of them are probably wrong. If you find an error in fact, or discover a great little place that deserves to be in the next edition, we'd like to know. We'd also like to learn your opinions of this book: What you liked and didn't like; what should have been included or ignored.

All who provide useful information will earn a free copy of any other book on our list. (See the back of this book.)

Address your cards and letters to:

Pine Cone Press, Inc.
P.O. Box 1494
Columbia, California 95310

A BIT ABOUT THE AUTHORS

Don and Betty Martin have written more than a dozen books on travel and wine. When not seeking the ultimate Zinfandel, Don devotes his waking hours to writing, photography and the operation of Pine Cone Press, Inc. He's been writing since he was 16, starting with a weekly newspaper in Idaho while still in high school. Choosing the U.S. Marine Corps instead of college, he served as a military correspondent at various posts in the Orient and in California. Back in civvies, he worked for assorted West Coast newspapers and served several years as associate editor of the travel magazine for the San Francisco-based California State Automobile Association. A member of the Society of American Travel Writers, he has contributed travel and wine articles and photos to assorted magazines and newspapers.

Wife Betty, whose varied credentials have included a doctorate in pharmacy and a California real estate broker's license, does much of the research for their books and she helps manage Pine Cone Press. She also has sold travel articles and photos to newspapers and magazines. Exhibiting a scholarly interest in wine, she has taken courses through the hospitality management program of Columbia (California) College and the Napa Valley Wine Library Association. Even though she has an excellent palate, she's not much of a wine drinker—thus leaving more Zinfandel for Don.

The Martins make their home in Columbia State Historic Park, in the heart of the California gold country—and not far from some of the best of the wine country.

THE CALIFORNIA WINE COUNTRY

Mendocino/Lake Counties
■ UKIAH

Northern
Sonoma
County ■ SANTA ROSA

Napa—Up Valley

SONOMA
■
Sonoma Valley

Napa—
Down
Valley

The Gold Country
■ PLACERVILLE
■ PLYMOUTH
■ MURPHYS
■ COLUMBIA

SACRA-
MENTO

SAN
FRANCISCO
■

LIVERMORE
■ South Bay Areas
■ SAN JOSE

Santa Clara
County ■ SANTA CRUZ
■ GILROY
Southern Santa Clara

MONTEREY ■
■ GONZALES
Monterey County

■ MADERA
■ FRESNO

■ PASO ROBLES
South
Central Coast

■ SAN LUIS OBISPO
■ BAKERSFIELD

■ SOLVANG

■ SANTA BARBARA

■ LOS ANGELES

■ TEMECULA
■ ESCONDIDO
Temecula

■ SAN DIEGO

"The wine is powerful but sleek; it expands across the palate like a fast car cruising a moonlit road, and disappears slowly, its tail-lights crimson in the pulsing summer night."
— Winetaster's description of a Beringer Vineyards Cabernet Sauvignon.

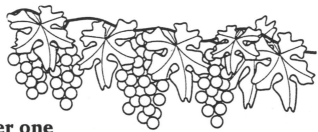

Chapter one
AMERICA'S WINELAND
It all started with *vitis vinifera*

By every measure, California is America's wineland. Several other states produce wine and we've heard rave reviews about Oregon Pinot Noir and Washington Chardonnay. Yet, more than 80 percent of America's wine is produced in California. Wineries are found in 45 of the state's 58 counties. Further, judging from national and international competitions, California's wines are among the world's finest.

In this book, we take you by the hand and lead you through the Golden State's fabled winelands, where you can meet the vintners and taste their wines. As you tour, you'll learn more about this noble beverage.

If you haven't toured one of California's wine regions in recent years, you'll find significant changes—as we did when we worked on a major revision of this book. When **The Best of the Wine Country** was first published in 1991, most vintners were preoccupied with producing varietals—wines made from specific grape varieties. And many worked from a rather short list—Chardonnay, Sauvignon Blanc, Chenin Blanc, Gewürztraminer and Semillon among the whites and such red standard-bearers as Cabernet Sauvignon, Pinot Noir, Merlot and of course that California classic, Zinfandel.

Today, more winemakers are doing what has been done for centuries in Europe—blending a variety of grapes to make styles distinctive to their winery. It began with the red and white Meritage movement, as a few vintners began blending Cabernet Sauvignon and Chardonnay with other wines from their Bordeaux and Burgundy homelands. Other vintners began blending wines from these regions of France without using the lofty Meritage label. (Gundlatch-Bundschu, the Sonoma Valley's good humor winery, came up with "Bearitage".)

Then came the "Rhône Rangers," employing a variety of Rhône Valley reds to make soft, full-flavored wines. The most recent trend is toward Italian varietals. Thus, when you step into a tasting room today you may encounter—in addition to the usual Cabs and Chards—blended wines or varietals made from grapes with unfamiliar names: Cinsault, Mourvèdre, Viognier, Sangiovese, Nebbiolo, Refosco and Aleatico.

The odds are that they won't remain unfamiliar.

Another change since our 1991 edition is the continued growth of new wineries, adding more variety to California's winelands. The first printing of *The Best of the Wine Country* featured more than 250 wineries with tasting rooms that kept regular hours. Now, well into the Decade of the Nineties, that list is crowding 300.

If you want to sleep close to some of these wineries, we've noted another pleasing change—the emergence of several bed and breakfast inns right among the vineyards. Some are extensions of the wineries.

Where's most of this new activity happening? The fastest growing region—in numbers of wineries—is the south central coast of Santa Barbara and San Luis Obispo counties (Chapter 11). Another active area is the Gold Country (Chapter 12), particularly El Dorado and Amador counties, and northern Sonoma County (Chapter 3) has added a few new wineries in recent years. The Livermore Valley (Chapter 7) has stopped suburban intrusion with an agricultural protective zone and gained several wineries.

Napa Valley remains the champion in total winery count, with so many that we needed two chapters—5 and 6—to hold them. Some wineries have changed owners, notably the Frances Ford Coppola purchase of Inglenook. A few wineries have closed while others have opened, for a small overall increase. Interestingly, southern Santa Clara County—the Gilroy-Morgan Hill area in Chapter 8—has remained static since we first published this book, with the same number of wineries under the same ownerships.

The accidental sipper

My affair with wine began by accident, more than thirty-five years ago. While handling publicity for U.S. Marine Corps recruiting in San Francisco, I was invited along with other PR types to a tasting by California's Wine Institute. In my mind at the time, wine was just another beverage—something that occupied shelf space at the corner liquor store. My parents never drank alcohol, nor were they prohibitionists, so my attitude toward wine was neutral. I recall being a serious Scotch drinker at the time.

However, that wine tasting whetted both my appetite and my curiosity.

Although I couldn't tell a Chardonnay from a Charbono, I was intrigued by the almost reverent attitude that wine enthusiasts held for the stuff. With all that swirling and sipping and studied frowning, they seemed part of a mysterious cult. They used words like "nose", "finish" and "balance" in ways foreign to me. I wanted to learn more. Further, the idea of matching a particular beverage to food interested me, because I love good food.

My wife and I began visiting San Francisco Bay Area wineries, and we took wine study courses to learn more about this product. For a time, I was a freelance wine writer, but I ran out of adjectives long before I ran out of interesting wines.

The mystery is gone now, and we've learned to respect and appreciate this civilized beverage. And certainly, we've learned that the best place to become friends with wine is at the winery.

There, you can meet the winemaker, or at least a learned employee, who can discuss wine and unravel its mysteries. You can learn how they make the stuff, how and why they age it and how to best enjoy it with food. You'll also learn that most vintners are friendly, down-to-earth folk who don't worship their wines. They merely respect and enjoy them.

Wineries love to sell their products at retail; thus the popularity of tasting rooms. Large wineries probably don't care where you buy their product, so long as you buy it. However, most of the smaller vintners' high quality wines aren't available at liquor outlets or supermarkets, so you'd best do your shopping at the source. Some sell their wines only at their wineries. Besides, a tasting room nestled among the vines is a lot more appealing than a wine shelf nestled among the cabbages at Safeway.

The greatest advantage of touring is obvious—you can try a variety of wines and decide which are most agreeable to your palate and your budget. And where better to tour than in California, with its vast and widespread vineyards? Wine grapes rank sixth among the state's agricultural products. Grapes of all types comprise its second most valuable crop, exceeded only by dairy products. Wineries are a major tourist draw, as well. Some large Napa Valley establishments attract 300,000 sippers a year.

Overall, however, Americans are wimps when it comes to drinking wine. U.S. per capita consumption is 2.5 gallons a year, compared with about 20 in France and Italy. Wine drinking increased rapidly during the 1970s and 1980s as more Americans came to appreciate its value with food. However, caught in the wave of an anti-alcohol movement, wine use has dropped in recent years. Incidentally, per capita wine consumption in California is more than double the national average.

Where's the grapes?

And just where is California's wine country? Vineyards are scattered over most of the state, from the north coast to San Diego. However, premium grapes—those sensitive little fellows that require warm days, cool nights and well-drained soil—occupy more limited areas.

Historically, most of California's premier wines have been produced in vineyards encircling the San Francisco Bay Area. North bay counties of Napa,

WINERIES OFFER CASE DISCOUNTS

Sonoma and Mendocino, and the Livermore and Santa Clara valleys to the south offer the proper conditions.

The north bay counties are still major producers, although many south bay grapes have been squeezed out by the population crush, so vintners have sought new horizons. They're finding them in the Sierra Nevada foothills, in Monterey County, the south central coast area of Paso Robles and Santa Barbara counties, and the Temecula Valley, north of San Diego.

These so-called premium growing areas produce only about 15 percent of California's total wine output. Most of the rest comes from the dry, hot and huge San Joaquin Valley. There, more hardy vines thrive to produce the large—and generally drinkable—flood of jug wines. A single winery, E. & J. Gallo of Modesto, bottles more than half of America's total wine output. Neither Gallo nor most of the other valley giants have tasting rooms, so that region is not included in this book.

In the beginning, someone stepped on a grape

Historians debate which came first—wine or beer. Some scholars insist that beer was the first alcoholic beverage, since grain was cultivated before grapes. Others say wine came first because grapes are self-contained little alcohol factories. While beer has to be brewed from yeast and grain, grapes are coated with wild yeast and will ferment naturally when the skin is broken.

Stomp some grapes, step back, and you'll soon have wine. (Most winemakers, however, use cultured yeast to better control fermentation.)

"The wine industry certainly dates from at least 3000 B.C.," according to Maynard A. Amerine and Vernon L. Singleton's *Wine: An Introduction for Americans*. "Some housewife probably left crushed grapes in a jar and found, a few days later, that an alcoholic product had been formed."

The discovery, in early 1991, of wine stains on the shards of a pre-Bronze Age Sumerian jar pushes the date back even further, to 3500 B.C. Fossilized grape seeds found in Stone Age middens suggest that folks may have been sipping wine 10,000 years ago. The Tigris-Euphrates Valley in Iran, Iraq and Turkey is regarded by historians as the cradle of agriculture and therefore of civilization. It's also the area where Noah supposedly parked his ark—on Turkey's Mount Ararat. According to Genesis 9:20-21, he "began to be a husbandman, and he planted a vineyard; and he drank of the wine and was drunken." Thus, the Bible may have recorded history's first hangover.

Grapes grew wild in California, but early-day padres found them unsuitable for wine making. They had to rely on unreliable shipments from New Spain (Mexico) for their essential altar wines.

Father Junipero Serra established the first mission in present day California at San Diego in 1769. However, some years passed before suitable grape vines, brought in from Mexico by way of Spain, were planted. The good padre wrote in 1781: "I hope that...the corn prospers and that the grape vines are living and thriving, for this lack of altar wine is becoming unbearable."

The vine in question, now called the mission grape, is a descendant of *vitis vinifera*. It's also the parent of Europe's premium grapes, but these had not yet found their way to California. Although some regard Sonoma/Napa as the root of California viticulture, large scale winemaking actually began in Los Angeles. Plantings were so common early in the 19th century that it was called "The City of Vineyards."

California's first fulltime winemaker was Jean Louis Vignes, a Frenchman from Bordeaux. He arrived in Monterey by ship in 1831 and soon adjourned

HOW TO APPRECIATE A FINE WINE

All that sloshing and sniffing practiced by wine-tasters isn't supercilious foolishness. Many subtleties lurk in a bottle of fine wine. Only

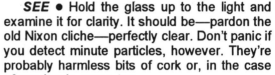

by following these steps can you discern all of the nuances of the essence of the grape.

SEE ● Hold the glass up to the light and examine it for clarity. It should be—pardon the old Nixon cliche—perfectly clear. Don't panic if you detect minute particles, however. They're probably harmless bits of cork or, in the case of aged reds, some tannin residue that was stirred up when the wine was poured.

SLOSH ● Coat the inside of the glass by swirling the wine vigorously (being careful, of course, that you don't slosh it all over the individual next to you).

SNIFF ● Hold the glass up to your nose and inhale deeply, drawing in all the wine's smells—referred to as the *nose* by the pros. The fruity fragrance of the grape is described as the *aroma*, while the more subtle dusky smell is the *bouquet*—the essence of fermentation and aging.

SIP AND SLURP ● Your mother said this was bad manners, but it's the best way to taste wine. Take a sip, cradle it on your tongue, draw air over it, exhale through your nose, then swallow. This aeration—despite its odd sound—releases the wine's complex flavors. Your little taste buds can detect only sweet, sour, salty and bitter. All the nuances of taste are in your nose, and mixing air with the wine helps bring out its subtleties.

A young white wine should taste fresh, crisp and fruity, while reds will be more complex and berry-like, perhaps with hints of wood from barrel-aging.

Some wine writers insist that they can detect cedar, cigar boxes, licorice, pencil shavings, pineapples, apricots, cassis, chocolate, pears, peaches, plums, eucalyptus and—good grief—even the suggestion of a sweaty saddle. We suspect, however, that they've just run short of adjectives. Or, perhaps they sampled too many wines.

to Los Angeles, where he planted vineyards and established a major commercial operation. History reports that he was the first to import European wine grapes. Equally important, he is credited with planting some of the first orange trees in California.

Vignes sold his orange and wine estate in 1855 to his nephews, Pierre and Jean Louis Sansevain. They became the state's leading wine merchants and established its first commercial sparkling wine operation. Then in 1862, the brothers quit their business and California's pioneer vineyards disappeared under spreading Los Angeles suburbs.

While not the first, Sonoma was the most important seat of the state's early wine industry. The story involves an unlikely pair—an energetic young Mexican lieutenant and a flamboyant Hungarian of questionable lineage.

In the years following Father Serra's arrival, the missions became vast agricultural empires. They were governed by the padres and worked by Indians who had been converted to Christianity—often unwillingly. Mexico won its independence from Spain in the 1820s and, some years later, it de-commissioned the missions. Their great landholdings were parceled out to favored soldiers and politicians.

Lieutenant Mariano Guadalupe Vallejo was sent to the most northern of the missions, San Francisco Solano in present-day Sonoma, to oversee its dissolution. The ambitious young officer established a military garrison and laid out a townsite. A good politician, he quickly attained the rank of military *commandante* of all northern California. And he picked up thousands of acres in Mexican land grants. The assertive Vallejo soon became a major producer of California wines.

The man from Hungary

Enter the visionary gentleman of dubious lineage. Agoston Haraszthy (*Har-RAS-they*) arrived in Sonoma in 1856, met General Vallejo and purchased land to start a vineyard. He had come to America in 1840 after fleeing his native Hungary, perhaps for choosing the wrong side of a revolution. He was variously known as Colonel Haraszthy or Count Haraszthy, although the source of either title is vague.

He certainly was an ambitious fellow, and a gad-about promoter. In the sixteen years since touching American soil, he had founded the town of Sauk City, Wisconsin, crossed by wagon train to San Diego, dabbled in real estate, become a state assemblyman and later director of the U.S. Mint in San Francisco. He had attempted to raise wine grapes in Wisconsin, San Diego, San Francisco and San Mateo before finally finding the proper land and climate in Sonoma. The count and General Vallejo became fast friends. Two Haraszthy sons, in fact, married two Vallejo daughters.

Haraszthy's Buena Vista Farm became America's most prosperous wine empire. He lived regally in a Pompeiian villa cresting a knoll above his vineyards. His greatest contribution to California viticulture was the importation of hundreds of thousands of premium European grape cuttings. Many of these were made available to growers throughout the state.

The free-wheeling count's departure was appropriately bizarre. In 1868, restless for a new challenge, he went to Nicaragua to start a sugar cane plantation. Attempting to cross a stream, he fell into the water and vanished. Apparently, he was devoured by alligators.

The wine industry which Haraszthy helped set into motion had to struggle during its formative years. Over-production and the depression of the

1870s dropped wine prices to ten cents a gallon. Then the industry was nearly ruined by the invasion of *phylloxera,* a louse that destroys grapevine roots. Toward the end of the century, an ironic solution was found. The roots of wild American grapes, which the European varieties had replaced, were resistant to the little bug. By grafting *vitis vinifera* cuttings onto *vitis californica* root stock, the wine industry was saved. For the moment, at least.

The 1906 San Francisco earthquake dealt the business a serious blow, in and out of the wine country. Many Sonoma and Napa County wineries were ruined by the temblor, which in fact was centered north of San Francisco. The city was the production and distribution center for much of California's wine, and the fire following the earthquake destroyed millions of gallons.

Then on January 16, 1920, the infamous Volstead Act further brutalized what was left of the industry. We know it as Prohibition, with a capital "P." Repeal, with a capital "R," came on December 5, 1933, when Utah became the 36th state to ratify the Twenty-First Amendment to the Constitution.

During that long dry spell, California wineries had struggled mightily, and two-thirds of them closed. The rest survived by making sacramental wines and by selling grapes, since home winemaking was still legal. Particularly popular was a product with the wonderful name of Vine-Glo. It was a barrel of grape juice, complete with instructions for converting it to wine. Another product, a brick of compressed grape pomace, could be dissolved in water to create grape juice. A warning label stated:

"This beverage should be consumed within five days; otherwise it might ferment and become alcoholic."

The industry recovered slowly after Repeal. Thousands of acres of premium vines had been torn out and replaced with common grapes better suited to the production of Vine-Glo and wine bricks. Many Americans had gotten out of the wine-and-food habit. Further, the country was in the middle of the Depression. In 1934, several growers led by Napa's Louis Martini formed the Wine Institute to improve the quality of wine and promote its use. It's still the industry's leading voice.

World War II brought some financial respite to vintners. European wines were no longer available and the price of California grapes went from $15 to $50 a ton. However a shortage of labor, containers and rail cars hampered

California's vinelands offer particularly pleasing vistas. Here, young vines dance over a steep ridge near the Silverado Trail in the Napa Valley.

growth. The industry didn't really get back on its feet until the Fifties. By the Seventies, it had become fashionable to serve wine with dinner and California's winemakers were off and running.

They haven't looked back, except to see if their competitor had somehow produced a better Chardonnay.

Types of wine, premium and otherwise

For a glossary of wine terminology, see Chapter 14, page 324

To give you an idea of what you'll be sipping at tasting rooms, we present a list of the more common wine types, both varietal (which just means a specific variety) and generic.

Aleatico (*ah-lee-AHT-TEE-co*) — Common Italian red of the Muscat family with that grapy Muscat aroma and flavor, one of the "new varietals" now being planted in California.

Angelica — Sweet, ordinary dessert wine that originated in California, probably named for Los Angeles; sometimes made from the mission grape.

Barbera (*bar-BEAR-ah*) — A full-flavored red wine grape grown in northern Italy and now becoming popular in California.

Beaujolais (*BO-sho-lay*) — In France, a wine from a specific district, near Burgundy. In California, the name refers to wine made from the Gamay grape, often labeled Gamay Beaujolais.

Burgundy — In France, it refers to a specific wine producing region, famous for the Pinot Noir grape. In California, it means anything red.

Cabernet Sauvignon (*cab-air-nay sou-vin-YAWN*) — Considered the noblest of red wine grapes; the primary wine of a fine Bordeaux.

Carignane (*car-reen-YAN*) — Commonly planted red grape of medium quality; of southern French origin. Sometimes spelled "Carignan."

Chablis — Generic term in the U.S., referring to any white wine. A specific growing region in France.

Champagne — A term describing sparkling wine in the United States. In the rest of the civilized world, it's applied only to effervescent wine produced in France's Champagne district. Some American winemakers honor this tradition and call their product sparkling wine.

Charbono (*shar-BO-NO*) — Red grape of Italian origin producing full bodied, sometimes rough wine.

Chardonnay (*SHAR-doe-NAY*) — One of the premiere white grapes, grown in the Burgundy region of France and extensively planted in California. A good Chardonnay is dry, yet rich and full, sometimes spicy or nutty and with a hint of wood, since it's often barrel-aged. Sometimes called Pinot Chardonnay in California, although that reference is now quite rare.

Chenin Blanc (*SHAY-nan blawn*) — White grape, producing a typically fruity wine.

Chianti (*kay-AN-tee*) — Italian red wine usually made from the Sangiovese grape (see below), typified by full, berry-like flavor. Usually drunk young. In America, the term is loosely applied to any full flavored, low-tannin wine. Spaghetti wine, if you will.

Cinsaut (*SAN-so*) — Red grape producing full-bodied wine, common in France and South Africa, and now among the "new wines" of California.

Colombard (*COL-lum-bahr*) — A rather ordinary French white grape, producing a full-bodied, usually high-acid wine.

Fumé Blanc (*FU-may blawn*) — Literally "White Smoke," a name first used by Napa Valley's Robert Mondavi to describe a lush, subtly smoky-flavored white wine produced from the Sauvignon Blanc grape.

Gewürztraminer (*Ge-WURZ-tra-mee-ner*) The world's most difficult-to-spell wine grape. Common in Germany, France's Alsace district and California. It's typically fruity, spicy and sometimes a bit sweet.

Green Hungarian — An ordinary white wine of unknown parentage, once common in California but now deservedly falling from favor.

Grenache (*greh-NAHSH*) — Fruity southern French grape commonly used to make rosé wine in California. Sometimes labeled Grenache Rosé.

Gray Riesling — White wine grape of unknown parentage, since it isn't a Riesling; first reference may have been at Wente Brothers Estate winery in the Livermore Valley.

Johannisberg Riesling — German white wine grape from the Rhine Valley. Typically fruity, usually fermented dry. It's a true Riesling, while many other grapes bearing that name are not.

Meritage — A term adopted by a group of California wineries to designate red or white premium wines blended from classic French grape varieties. Red Meritage seems to be more common. A winery must join the

Meritage Association to use the label, and must meet strict blending criteria. Fewer than 25 wineries qualify.

Merlot (*Mair-lo*) — Red grape producing a lush, full-flavored wine; often blended with Cabernet Sauvignon to ease its tannic edge, both in California and Bordeaux.

Mourvèdre (*moor-VED-dre*) — Another of the newly popular grapes in California; a widely traveled medium-bodied French red with a nice berry nose; it's often called Mataró in other countries.

Muscat (*MUS-kat*) — Grape commonly planted throughout the world, usually white although there are red versions within its more than 200 varieties. Muscat wines are noted for their "grapey" flavor, whether made dry or sweet. The grape often is used to produce dessert wines.

Nebbiolo (*ne-bee-OH-lo*) — Classic Italian red grape, now finding its place in California vineyards, either as a varietal or for blending.

Petit Syrah or **Sirah** (*Puh-TEE see-RAW*) — Rather high tannin red grape grown in California; of French origin.

Pinot Gris (*PEE-no gree*) — A cousin of Pinot Noir, not as complex or robust; now being planted in California vineyards, mostly for blending.

Pinot Noir (*PEE-no nawahr*) — Classic French red grape; right up there with Cabernet; commonly grown in Burgundy. Thus in France, a great Burgundy is a great Pinot Noir.

Port — Sweet, fortified wine named for Orporto, the city in Portugal that is the center of the Port trade.

Riesling (*REESE-ling*) — Noble white German grape predominately grown in the Rhine Valley. The name has come to be loosely associated with an assortment of white wines.

Sangiovese (*sawn-jo-VAY-SAY*) — Full-bodied Italian red common to the Chianti region and used in the wines of that name; now gaining favor in California; often called Sangioveto in Italy.

Sauternes (*saw-TAIRN*) — French white wine, often sweet and usually golden. The term also is used to describe any number of generic sweet California wines; often spelled "Sauterne" here.

Sauvignon Blanc (*SO-veen-yawn blawn*) — It ranks with Chardonnay as one of the great French white wine grapes. Full bodied with a distinctive fruity bouquet.

Sherry — Sweet or dry fortified wine whose name is derived from the Jerez district of Spain, where it originated.

Sylvaner (*sil-VAN-er*) — Premium white grape originating in Germany or Austria.

Trebbiano (*treb-be-AH-no* or *treb-YAWN-no*) — Italian grape that's the world's most common producer of white wine, yet its just now gaining favor in California; produces full-bodied wine with a rather light bouquet.

Viognier (*vee-ON-yay*) — Excellent white French grape producing wine with complex fruity taste; virtually unknown in California until recently and now gaining popularity.

Zinfandel — California's most widely planted premium red grape, sometimes called the mystery grape because of its uncertain origin. The wine is typically fruity and can range from light and soft to complex and full-bodied; Zins usually have light to medium tannin, although those from older vines can be quite robust. Zinfandel is a clonal twin to Italy's Primitivo grape and no one is quite sure how it came to America. (See box on page 72.)

DECIPHERING A TYPICAL
CALIFORNIA WINE LABEL

CHIPMUNK
CELLARS

1991
ESTATE BOTTLED
Shenandoah Valley
ZINFANDEL
Pinecone Vineyard

Produced & bottled by Chipmunk Cellars, Ltd.
Plymouth, California
Alcohol 13% by volume ● contains sulfites

1991: A wine can be vintage dated only if 95% of the grapes were crushed in that year.

Estate Bottled means that all the grapes used in the wine came from vineyards owned or controlled by the winery.

Shenandoah Valley is an appellation or Approved Viticultural Area (AVA), an officially designated growing region; 85% of the grapes must be grown within that area.

Zinfandel: A varietal name can be used only if at least 75% of the wine came from that grape.

Pinecone Vineyard is a "designated vineyard." To be listed, at least 95% of the grapes must have come from that vineyard, which must be located in an AVA.

Produced and bottled indicates that at least 75% of the grapes were fermented by the bottling winery. "Made and bottled" requires that only 10% of the grapes be fermented by that winery. Such terms as "Vinted and bottled" or "Cellared and bottled" are non-specific. They don't require the bottler to have produced any of the wine.

Alcohol 13% by volume: This can vary 1.5% either way. To be sold as a table wine, the alcohol content must be between 7 and 14 percent.

Contains sulfites: This statement is required on American wine labels if sulfite content (naturally produced during fermentation and/or added to prevent spoilage) exceeds 10 parts per million. It does in most wines.

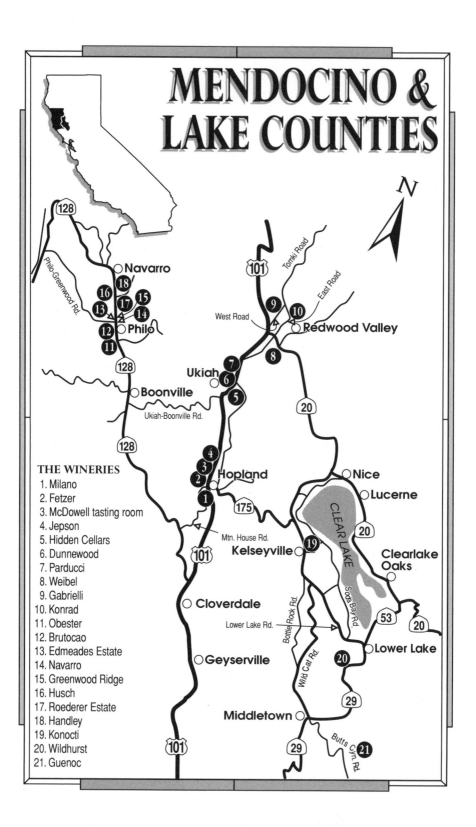

MENDOCINO & LAKE COUNTIES

N

THE WINERIES

1. Milano
2. Fetzer
3. McDowell tasting room
4. Jepson
5. Hidden Cellars
6. Dunnewood
7. Parducci
8. Weibel
9. Gabrielli
10. Konrad
11. Obester
12. Brutocao
13. Edmeades Estate
14. Navarro
15. Greenwood Ridge
16. Husch
17. Roederer Estate
18. Handley
19. Konocti
20. Wildhurst
21. Guenoc

Navarro
Philo
Boonville
Ukiah
Redwood Valley
Hopland
Nice
Lucerne
CLEAR LAKE
Clearlake Oaks
Kelseyville
Cloverdale
Lower Lake
Geyserville
Middletown

Philo-Greenwood Rd.
Toriki Road
East Road
West Road
Ukiah-Boonville Rd.
Mtn. House Rd.
Lower Lake Rd.
Bottle Rock Rd.
Soda Bay Rd.
Wild Cat Rd.
Butt's Cyn. Rd.

128
101
20
175
101
20
53
20
29
29

"Tannins in the background, flavors waiting to explode, a lady-like refinement poised to make a statement."
— Wine taster's description of a Monogram Cabernet Sauvignon from Guenoc Winery, Middletown, Lake County

Chapter Two
MENDOCINO & LAKE COUNTIES
The wine country's northern rim

Poised but not necessarily lady-like and certainly not ready to explode, we begin making our statement—about winery touring—at the top of the California Wine Country.

A few wineries are scattered farther north; one even resides in the redwoods around Arcata, north of Eureka. But that area is better known for clams and sawdust. For touring and tasting purposes, Mendocino and Lake counties offer California's northernmost grouping of vineyards and wineries. The two areas are particularly appealing, for many of the wineries are in some of California's prettiest pastoral settings. Further, wines here have won more than their share of medals. In fact, Lake County boosters insist that their wineries have gleaned more awards per vineyard acre than any other region in the country.

MENDOCINO COUNTY

This area has been creating wines for more than a century, although most of it was bulk production in the early days. However, one Charles Wetmore sailed off to the Paris Exposition of 1899 with some of his Mendocino wines and sailed away with *le grand prix.*

Tryfon Lolonis and Adolph Parducci were two other Mendocino wine pioneers. Greek immigrant Lolonis planted vineyards in Redwood Valley in 1920; Italy's Parducci opened a Cloverdale winery in neighboring Sonoma County in 1916, then moved north to Mendocino's county seat of Ukiah in 1931. A Lolonis descendant is still making premium wines. The Parducci Winery thrives as one of the county's largest, sharing that position with latecomer Fetzer, established in 1968 and now the nation's sixth largest premium winery.

Winemaking didn't become a serious growth industry until the early 1970s. Initially, most growers sold fruits of their labors to established Sonoma County wineries. Then, realizing that the Sonomans kept winning medals with Mendocino grapes, several producers began bottling their own wines. Weibel Vineyards provided a major growth incentive in 1973 when it shifted much of its operation from crowded Alameda County to Mendocino and opened a tasting room beside the freeway north of Ukiah. (It originally was at the end of the freeway, but that swatch of asphalt was extended.)

Currently, about thirty Mendocino County wineries slap labels on their own bottles, and roughly half of these offer tasting to the passing public. Only Parducci offers a tour without prior arrangement. Most wineries are clustered in three different areas—Ukiah-Hopland, Anderson Valley and Redwood Valley. All are in the central to southern reaches of the county.

Ukiah-Hopland

Ukiah calls itself the home of Masonite, but this town of about 13,000 residents is more interesting than that. It offers the excellent Sun House Historical Museum, a few fine old Victorians along tree shaded streets and some serviceable restaurants. The county seat, Ukiah provides a good selection of shops and motels. Nearby Lake Mendocino is popular with boaters and campers.

Twelve miles south, tiny Hopland is turning its weathered storefronts into a charming tourist stop, offering several antique shops, boutiques and interesting cafés. The Hopland micro-brewery and Thatcher Hotel and Restaurant are particularly worth a visit. As you might imagine, hops were once the main crop here and one winery—Milano—occupies an old hop drying shed.

The former land of hops is now surrounded by vineyards. More vines are scattered among green and golden contoured hills between Hopland and Ukiah, presenting a rather pleasant picture. Hopland has two winery tasting rooms and another two wineries open to the public are just off U.S. 101 between the communities. You'll find another pair in Ukiah.

UKIAH-HOPLAND WINERY TOUR ● Assuming you're driving north from the San Francisco Bay Area on U.S. 101, you'll encounter Hopland shortly after entering Mendocino County. Before you do, watch on your left for **Milano Winery,** just beyond the end of the freeway. From there, continue into Hopland for the tasting rooms of **Fetzer Vineyards** in an old vine covered school building on your left and the **McDowell Tasting Room** on the right.

Pressing north from Hopland, you'll soon see **Jepson** on your left. A few miles beyond, after Highway 101 has regained its freeway status, take the Talmage exit, just short of Ukiah. Follow it east less than a mile, turn right onto Ruddick-Cunningham Road and take it to **Hidden Cellars,** which is in

---

WINERY CODES ● *T* = Tasting with no fee; *T$* = Tasting for a fee; *GT* = Guided tours; *GTA* = Guided tours by appointment; *ST* = Self-guiding tours; *CT* = casual tours or a peek into the winery; ✕ = picnic area; 📷 = Gift shop or good giftware selection. Price ranges listed in tasting notes are for varietals; jug wines may be available for less.

Six simple steps to winery touring success

1 • Plan your route in advance (which is why you bought this book) and set practical goals. Don't try to cover more than four or five wineries in a day. There is much to enjoy, to learn and to see in California's winelands. Why rush through them? Be selective. That's another reason you bought this book.

2 • If possible, hit the wine country on weekdays. This should be no great trick if you're on vacation. If you're limited to weekend visits, get an early start. It may go against your grain to start sipping at 10 a.m., but you're here to sample wines, not engage in social drinking. Most tasting rooms—even in busy Napa Valley—are virtually empty in the morning. The crowds hit after lunch and build until closing time.

3 • Plan for a picnic, since many wineries have picnic areas, often among the vines. Usually, you can find a deli in or near California's vinelands, and many tasting rooms also sell picnic fare. And don't be a plebeian; buy your picnic wine at the winery.

4 • Try to visit the wine country during the crush—again on weekdays. You can watch the proceedings and perhaps sample some of the grapes. At small wineries, you may even get to sip a little "must," the freshly crushed juice. The grape harvest ranges from late August through October, so call ahead to see what's being picked where. You'll find phone numbers with the winery listings in this bookt.

5 • Limit the number of samples you try at each winery. If you taste too many wines, their differences will blur. So will your vision.

6 • Although the small amounts of wine poured in tasting rooms shouldn't be a problem, it's still a good idea to select a designated driver. If that's your role, save the urge to party until you're safely back home, off the highway and close to the floor. Nationally, only about two percent of people arrested for driving while intoxicated were drinking wine. Please try to keep it that way.

plain view, smack in the middle of a vineyard. Hop back onto the freeway, drive through Ukiah and take the north State Street exit at the far edge of town. Continue north on State (paralleling the freeway) for half a mile to the **Dunnewood** tasting room. From there, stay with north State Street another 1.2 miles to Parducci Road, turn left and follow it under the freeway to—where else?—**Parducci Wine Cellars.**

Milano Vineyards & Winery • T ✗

❑ *14594 S. Highway 101, Hopland, CA 95449; (707) 744-1396. Daily 10 to 5; MC/VISA, AMEX. Most varieties tasted. A few wine related gift and craft items. Picnic area under arbor.* ❑

The Milone family's small winery is housed in one of the weathered hop kilns that once peppered this rural landscape. The winery dates only from 1977 but the Milones have long been a part of this land. Winemaker Frank's grandfather started farming here early in this century, raising hops, fruit and grapes. The family built the hop kiln in 1947. Through the years, emphasis shifted from hops and orchards to wine grapes.

Frank is an unpretentious, outgoing man and his wines are similar----honest and straightforward. The weathered hop kiln winery is dressed up a bit with a couple of leaded glass windows. The tasting room is in a cozy little upstairs shed attached to the main structure. There's room for about five folks at the counter.

Tasting notes: Milano wines were hearty and full bodied, with pronounced varietal character. The list is simple: several vintage Chardonnays, a couple of fine Cabernets and Zinfandels and some rich late harvest wines. Prices are from the teens to mid twenties. Red, white and blush table wines are drinkable and a good buy at under $5.

Vintners choice: "Cabernet, Chardonnay, Zinfandel and late harvest wines, all reserves," says Frank with simple candor.

Fetzer Vineyards • T ✕ 🍶

⊡ *13500 S. Highway 101, Hopland, CA 95449; (707) 744-1737. Daily 10 to 5; MC/VISA, DISC. Most varieties tasted. Large gift shop with extensive offerings of wine related items, crystal and gourmet foods; deli and picnic area.* ⊡

One of the area's largest wineries with an annual output of 2.4 million cases, Fetzer hosts the public in the ivy shrouded former Hopland High School. The sturdy masonry structure has been fashioned into an impressive visitor complex with a tasting room and gift shops. It's cavernous but attractive, embellished with polished woods, brick columns and stacks upon stacks of wine cases.

The facility draws 100,000 visitors a year and comes close to being crowded on summer weekends. But we had no trouble finding a spot at the large tasting bar on an October Sunday. The late Bernard Fetzer founded the winery in 1968. Later, ten of his eleven children took over and expanded it to 200,000 cases. The family sold the operation to Brown-Forman of Louisville, Kentucky, although they still grow grapes for the winery.

Tasting notes: Fetzer offers an extensive list of reds and whites, from premium to jug, and virtually all are available for tasting. The overall style is light and fruity, although some of the Cabernets show good tannin strength. Many of the wines are remarkably good buys, ranging well below $5 for some very drinkable varietals.

Vintners Choice: Winemaker Dennis Martin favors his Sundial Chardonnay, Valley Oaks Cabernet Sauvignon and Eagle Peak Merlot.

McDowell Tasting Room • T ✕ 🍶

⊡ *Downtown Hopland; (707) 744-1516. May through December: daily from 11 to 5; the rest of the year: noon to 5 on weekdays and 11 to 5 on weekends; major credit cards. All current releases available for tasting. Good selection of wine related gift and specialty food items. (McDowell Valley Vineyards address: P.O. Box 449, Hopland, CA 95449.)* ⊡

This downtown Hopland tasting room looks a bit like a real estate office, with its offset pitched roof, but step inside and you're rewarded by a comfy chalet look with a cathedral ceiling and arched windows. A few picnic tables are placed about outside. The source of its wines is McDowell Valley Vineyards, four miles away at 14100 Mountain House Road, and open by appointment only. The operation was established by Richard and Karen Keehn and Karen's son William Crawford. They sold their building to Associated Vintage Group in 1993, but still make their wine there. Their specialty is Rhône style Syrah and Grenache from ancient vines.

Tasting notes: We liked the hearty, rich Cabernet and Zinfandel with a wonderful berry like flavor. Wines are moderately priced, ranging from $4.50 for good table wines to the low teens for estate Zinfandels, Cabs and premium whites. Also on the list are Chardonnay, Fumé Blanc, Grenache, Cabernet Franc and Petite Syrah.

Vintners choice: "We are industry leaders in the Rhône variety category, and known for world class Fumé Blanc, outstanding Zinfandel and great value Cabernet and Chardonnay," says McDowell's tasting room manager Kat Larue.

Jepson Vineyards ● T GTA ✗

◻ *10400 S. Highway 101, Ukiah, CA 95482; (707) 468-8936. Daily 10 to 5; MC/VISA. Most varieties tasted. Wine related gift items, picnic tables near tasting room. Tours weekends 11 to 4 or by appointment only on weekdays.* ◻

The first thing you notice, after spotting the Jepson Vineyards sign on U.S. 101, is an imposing century old two-story farmhouse, now housing offices and meeting space for the facility. The winery, in a sturdy white painted stone and wooden structure, is a short distance away. The tasting room occupies a prim little bungalow fused to the main winery, looking something like a New England cottage built into the side of a warehouse.

Although small, the tasting room is spacious and light, accented by a gleaming brass chandelier hanging from a finished cedar plank ceiling. A couple of umbrella tables out front extend a silent invitation to picnickers to linger with lunches and newly purchased bottles.

The winery complex and 100-plus acres of vineyards were purchased virtually intact a decade ago by Robert S. Jepson, Jr. This is no mom and pop operation. Jepson obviously has invested generously to create an upscale, state of the art winery, which issues equally upscale premium wines.

Tasting notes: Jepson's limited list includes an excellent Chardonnay with a superb nutty finish, a crisp and fruit filled Sauvignon Blanc, plus a sparkling wine and a Colombard with the fruit evident in the nose and taste. Prices are modest, ranging from $5 upward. The winery also produces brandy, distilled from French Colombard in the classic French pot-still method. It's not available for tasting, of course.

Hidden Cellars ● T CT ✗

◻ *1500 Ruddick-Cunningham Road (Box 448), Ukiah, CA 95482; (707) 462-0301. Weekdays 10 to 4; no credit cards. Most varieties tasted. Some wine logo items; small picnic area; informal tours.* ◻

A functional insulated redwood structure perched beneath a gnarled oak at the edge of a vineyard serves as the winery for small Hidden Cellars. An equally functional counter in a corner of the winery will handle about four tasters at a time. The tasting room may not always be staffed during the off season, but visitors generally can find someone to pour a sip or two. The tour consists of a glance around the room, taking in a collection of oak and redwood barrels, a single temperature controlled stainless steel tank, a small crusher, the usual tangle of hoses and a couple of bicycles.

What all this suggests is that vintner-owner Dennis Patton focuses his energies on winemaking, not tasting room frills. Nearly all the wines on his list are regular award winners. The only thing hidden about the winery, which sits in full view on the historic Hildreth Ranch, is the origin of the name. Patton used that title when he began home winemaking in a sheltered valley of

Mendocino's Mill Creek. He emerged into the open in 1981 and his annual output has increased from a few hundred gallons to about 10,000 cases.

Tasting notes: Winemaker John Buechsenstein creates rich Chardonnay and Sauvignon Blanc and a remarkable Zinfandel that is pleasantly mellow and fruity, yet complex, with a crisp finish. Others on the list are Gewürztraminer, Johannisberg Riesling and some dessert wines. Prices start below $10 and range into the teens.

Vintners choice: "Chardonnay, Sauvignon Blanc and Zinfandel—due to our access to some small but excellent Mendocino vineyards," says the winery's Toni Klein.

Dunnewood Vineyards and Winery • T ✕ 🜄

◻ *2399 N. State Street, Ukiah, CA 95482; (707) 462-2985. Daily 10 to 5; MC/VISA, DISC. Most varieties tasted. Good selection of wine related items. Picnic tables under arbor.* ◻

Old timer tasters will remember this facility as Cresta Blanca, part of the large Guild Winery co-op based in Lodi. Its Ukiah operation was changed to Mendocino Vineyards in 1988 and the tasting room was moved to Hopland. In 1992, it was purchased by Canandaigua Wine Company of New York, one of the world's largest wine producers. The new owners closed the Hopland tasting room and return it to this old winery.

The old winery grounds are nicely landscaped, and visitors can retreat to a shady arbor for a picnic lunch, perhaps accompanied by a bottle from the tasting room. Although Ukiah's business district has grown out to meet the winery, a few vineyards survive near the winery to remind visitors that they're in grape country.

Tasting notes: The Dunnewood style is light and fruity, with little wood and we found them to be quite refreshing. They're also remarkably inexpensive for varietals, beginning around $5.50 and not going much beyond $7.50. Available for tasting when we visited were Chardonnay, Sauvignon Blanc, a jug white, Cabernet Sauvignon and Merlot. All were properly dry and crisp; honest wines for the price.

Parducci Wine Cellars • T GT ✕ 🜄

◻ *501 Parducci Road, Ukiah, CA 95482; (707) 462-9463. Daily 9 to 5; MC/VISA, AMEX. All varieties except champagne are tasted. Gift shop with good selections of wine related items and some specialty foods. Guided tours hourly from 10 to 3. Picnic tables near tasting room.* ◻

One of the two largest of Mendocino's active wineries, this venerable facility was founded by Adolph Parducci in 1931. It is now operated by second and third generations, with son John Parducci in charge. A major interest was sold recently to a teachers' retirement investment group.

The large winery facility backs into low hills above the northern end of Ukiah, a sanctuary from tract homes that march threateningly in its direction. The tasting room is California Mission eclectic—white stucco with Spanish arches and a shake roof. The interior is richly adorned with dark walnut, terrazzo tile and leaded glass. A gift shop specializing in crystal and china glitters from a room opposite the large tasting area.

The hour long tour through both vintage and modern facilities is quite thorough. We recommend it to those unfamiliar with the winemaking art.

Tasting notes: The extensive list covers most varietals, plus a range of jug and dessert wines; most are available for tasting. We favored a crisp and fruity Sauvignon Blanc; a nutty, lush Chardonnay; a full bodied yet soft and rich Cellermaster Zinfandel and a Bordeaux style Cellermaster Cab Merlot. Prices are moderate, with some fine varietals going for as little as $6, and ranging up to the mid teens.

Redwood Valley

This is California's northernmost major wine producing area. For trivia fans, Gabrielli is the state's most northern winery tasting room open to the public. The region is a rolling mix of oak thatched hills, shallow valleys and benchland ridges. Vineyards are scattered in the depressions and on the ridges, offering micro climates where a surprising variety of premium wine grapes thrive. Among notable bottlings are Chardonnay, Sauvignon Blanc, Cabernet Sauvignon and Zinfandel. Much of the foothill area is chopped into country abodes that range from rustically elegant to scruffy. The higher reaches of the valley offer visions of tawny hills, moss draped oaks and an occasional artistically rustic Earl Thollander barn.

Only three of Redwood Valley's several wineries are open to tasting without prior arrangement. Potter Valley, a spur of Redwood Valley, has a few vineyards, but at this writing, it had no wineries accessible without an appointment.

REDWOOD VALLEY WINERY TOUR • This tour dovetails nicely into the Hopland-Ukiah safari. However, a bit of maneuvering is involved, since the trio of wineries form three points of a triangle. From Parducci, return to State Street and drive about three and a half miles north, until you see the see the impressive spired tasting room of **Weibel Vineyards** on your right. It's just beyond the hamlet of Capella. If you take freeway instead of north State Street, you must overshoot the tasting room and double back, since it's between interchanges. Take the West Road exit and return south along the east side frontage road, which is the tail end of north State Street.

From Weibel, continue north on the aforementioned frontage road to a stop sign, turn right and you're on West Road, leading into the heart of Redwood Valley. It's a pleasant drive through a mix of vineyards, pasturelands, ranchettes and rural homes. About three miles of this will deliver you to **Gabrielli Winery,** in an imposing brown structure on your left, uphill behind a young vineyard. (If you hit a T-intersection of Tompki and East roads, you just missed it; look for the large mail box with the number 10950.) Now, return to the freeway, head south and take the Highway 20 exit east. Follow it about a mile and a half to Road A, turn left and drive steeply and briefly uphill to Road B and turn right. It makes a sharp left within a short distance, but continue straight ahead onto the lane marked "Private road; use at your own risk." It's more inviting than it sounds and leads you—within a few hundred feet—to **Konrad Vineyards.**

Weibel Vineyards • T ✕ 🏠

☐ *7051 N. State Street, Redwood Valley, CA 95470; (707) 485-0321. Tasting daily 9 to 5; MC/VISA. All varieties tasted. Nice gift selection; landscaped picnic area; no tours.* ☐

Weibel's tasting room, with its upcurved laminated beams, supposedly forms an inverted champagne glass. Inside, a fountain bubbles appropriately as centerpiece to a dramatic sweep of open space. A curved tasting counter occupies one side. Gift items and wine displays are placed elsewhere about the roomy, circular tasting room.

The grounds are equally attractive, featuring a picnic garden rimmed with grape vines and shaded by ancient oaks with white painted trunks. A burst of petunias emerges from an old barrel slat wine press. Beyond are foam covered stainless steel tanks and utilitarian buildings of Weibel's crushing and fermenting facilities.

Tasting notes: Weibel's wines run the gamut from a few noteworthy varietals and serviceable sparkling wines to ordinary but honest jug wines, assorted sherries, ports and brandy. All but brandy are available for tasting. Overall, prices range from inexpensive to moderate.

Vintners choice: "Chardonnay, white Zinfandel, Green Hungarian, dry sherry and Chenin Blanc," says a winery spokesman.

Gabrielli Winery ● T CT ✗

🞏 *10950 West Road, Redwood Valley, CA 95470; (707) 485-1221. Daily 10 to 5; major credit cards. Most varieties tasted. Picnic area.* 🞏

Shaded by mature trees on the brow of a hill above the vineyards, the new Gabrielli facility occupies a straightforward wood frame winery building, with an attractive, airy cedar sided tasting room fused to the front. The tasting counter exhibits a rustic touch of class: two wine barrels topped by a cloth draped plank. The operation was started in 1989 by Sam Gabrielli, his wife Bernadette Yamada-Gabrielli, her father Tom Yamada, and Jefferson Hinchliffe. They released their first wines and opened their tasting room in 1991. Their focus is on complex barrel fermented wines that are lightly processed to retain their strong varietal character. They have won considerable critical praise for such a young winery.

Tasting notes: The simplicity of handling comes through in the strong flavor of the fruit in the Gabrielli wines. Their flagship is Ascenza, a proprietary blend of five varietals; it was lush yet crisp and brimming with fruit. The Chardonnay was nicely balanced with accents of fruit and spice and hints of wood from its barrel aging. Perhaps the strongest offering was a Zinfandel, high in alcohol and yet soft with good berry flavors and a slight touch of wood. Prices range from $15 to $20.

Konrad Vineyards ● T CT ✗

🞏 *3620 Road B, Redwood Valley, CA 95470; (707) 485-0323. Tasting daily 10 to 5 in summer, 10 to 4 the rest of the year; MC/VISA. Most varieties tasted. A few wine related gift items; lakeview picnic area. Visitors can peek into the adjacent winery.* 🞏

Retired Rear Admiral E.G. Konrad and his wife Anne bought this facility in 1989 from founder Donald Olson, produced wines briefly under the Konrad/Olson label and have now completed the transition to Konrad. The wood sided winery sits atop a ridge, offering pleasing views of the Redwood Valley on one side and Lake Mendocino reservoir and the distant cloud capped Coast Range on the other. The small tasting room is as comfortable as a family living room. A pleasant garden offers picnickers a lakeview lunch site.

Tasting notes: Konrad produces full flavored wines with strong varietal character—particularly the reds. Prices range from $9 for Zinfandel to $12 for Chardonnay and a Bordeaux style blend called Melange a Trois. The Chardonnay was balanced nicely between spice and fruit, with a subtle acid finish. Zinfandel was full berried and drinkable, with gentle tannins and the

Melange a Trois had a soft Cabernet-Merlot nose and spicy-berry flavors, with hints of wood and tannin. Estate bottled Merlot, Petit Sirah, Johannisberg Riesling and a Petite Sirah port complete the list.

Vintners choice: The winery focuses on its estate bottled Zinfandels and Petit Sirah, says a spokesperson.

Anderson Valley

This is exemplary rural northern California, a shallow valley rimmed by hills the color and shape of fresh baked rolls. It's garnished by shady clusters of oaks, madrones and pines and accented by sloping vineyards and emerald pastures.

Grizzled old Boonville is the best known of the valley's hamlets, popular for its grandly rustic turn of the century Boonville Hotel, the appealing Buckhorn Saloon brew pub and a couple of boutiques. Philo, with a population of 273, isn't much bigger than some of the winery complexes surrounding it.

The valley is relatively new as a vineyard area. Although pioneers may have stomped a grape or two, current activity dates from 1971 when the Husch family established a winery near Philo. Most of the valley's vineyards and wineries line Highway 128 between Philo and Navarro. This is one of the cooler and wetter of California's vinelands, so grapes from northern Europe such as Chardonnay, assorted Rieslings and Gewürztraminers do best. However, we did encounter some good Cabernet and Pinot Noir.

ANDERSON VALLEY WINERY TOUR • Take your pick of approaches. State Highway 253 from Ukiah, Highway 128 from Cloverdale or a combination of Mountain House Road and 128 from Hopland are equally twisty and scenic. None of the routes miss any wineries, which don't start cropping up until you pass Boonville.

Touring Anderson Valley winery tasting rooms is no great trick. Although some of the wineries are on side roads, all of their tasting rooms are neatly aligned along Highway 128 between Boonville and Navarro.

You'll first find **Obester Winery,** on your left just short of the small town of **Philo**. Immediately beyond Philo is **Brutocao Cellars,** also on the left. A few miles farther along, you'll encounter a handy cluster of facilities, Kendall-Jackson's **Edmeades Estate** crowning a low hill on the left, and **Navarro Vineyards** and **Greenwood Ridge Vineyards,** side by side on the right. **Husch Vineyards** is a short distance beyond on the left, and the imposing new **Roederer Estate** is across the highway, on a vineyard upslope. Just down the road is **Handley Cellars** on the right, near tiny **Navarro**.

This brief stretch from Edmeades to Handley is one of the more appealing in all of California's wine country—a fetching blend of handsome wineries and sloping vineyards rising behind split rail fences, with softly rounded oak thatched hills on the horizon.

Obester Winery • *T CT* ✕ 🏚

☐ *9200 Highway 128, Philo, CA 95466; (707) 895-2328. Daily 10 to 5; major credit cards. Gift area with wine related articles, books and Obester's line of mustards, dressings and other specialty food items. Picnic tables shaded by lath house. Informal tours when winemaker is free.* ☐

A clump of cheerful mustard colored ranch structures mark this appealing tasting facility just south of Philo. Paul and Sandy Obester began making wine in Half Moon Bay south of San Francisco. That area is better known for pumpkins, but they won their share of awards, using grapes brought in from various wine producing areas. In 1989, they bought an old apple farm near Philo and began planting their own vineyards.

Tasting notes: The Obester list is small, leaning toward lush, full fruited, medium dry whites. Our favorites were a nutty and complex Chardonnay, a Mendocino Sauvignon Blanc and a Gewürztraminer with a nice floral aroma and fruity taste. The winery also produces a full bodied Zinfandel and a rich, complex Pinot Noir. Prices are moderate, from $7 to $13.

Vintners choice: "Sauvignon Blanc, Johannisberg Riesling and Gewürztraminer. Whites are fruity and well balanced," says Lynne Sawyer.

Brutocao Cellars ● T ✕ 📷

◻ *7000 Highway 128, Philo, CA 95466; (707) 895-2152. Daily 10 a.m. to 5 p.m.; MC/VISA. Most varieties tasted. Good wine related gift selection. Picnic tables adjacent to tasting room.* ◻

For decades, Anderson Valley grower Leonard Brutocao sold his grapes to producers such as Fetzer and Beringer, then he began building his own winery in 1990. To reach the public, he purchased the attractive tasting room of the former Scharffenberger Cellars. Although Leonard lives in Los Angeles, the winery operation is a family affair. Tony Stephen is the vineyard manager and his wife Nancy Walker, who he met at the University of California at Davis, is the winemaker. Her parents, retired school teachers Bob and Dolores Walker, manage the tasting room. The Scharffenberger-turned-Brutocao tasting room is one of the more appealing in the Anderson Valley—an attractive sweep of space radiating out from a curved tasting bar. A cathedral ceiling accents the facility's openness.

Tasting notes: The Brutocao list is mostly red, unusual for the cool Anderson Valley, but one could hardly complain. The unfiltered Zinfandel, Merlot, Cabernet Sauvignon and Pinot Noir were full flavored and complex, displaying classic varietal character. On the white side, a Chardonnay was lush, with a pleasing flowery nose. Prices range from $8.50 to the early teens; higher for some reserves.

Edmeades Estate/Kendall-Jackson ● T 📷

◻ *5500 Highway 128, Philo, CA 95466; (707) 895-3009. Daily 10 to 5 April to December (shorter hours in winter); MC/VISA. A variety of Kendall-Jackson wines tasted, plus a few wine focused gift items.* ◻

Highly successful and fast growing Kendall-Jackson of Lake County recently purchased the old Edmeades winery and turned one of the outbuildings—a former garage—into a tasting room. The complex is appealingly rustic, crowning a tree thatched hill above the valley.

The winery has enjoyed remarkable success in recent years, winning a "winery of the year" award and dozens of medals for its products. The original tasting room in Lake County is closed, however, so area visitors must adjourn to this pleasantly funky little tasting room to sip the goodies. A tasting room also is located in Healdsburg, which you'll encounter in the next chapter. Expanding rapidly, the firm also offers wines under the Cambria, Lakewood, Stonestreet and La Crema labels.

Tasting notes: One enters this former garage like an adult kid in a candy store, since selections from several Kendall-Jackson wineries are available for tasting. They run the full gamut of tasting—too much for us to handle, so we focused on the Kendall-Jackson label. A Vintner's Reserve Chardonnay was spicy, full flavored and lush, a Merlot was full of berries with a nippy tannic finish and a Durell Vineyard Syrah was surprisingly soft for this varietal. Prices are mostly in the mid teens.

Navarro Vineyards • T GTA & CT ✗

☐ *5601 Highway 128 (P.O. Box 47), Philo, CA 95466; (707) 895-3686. Daily 10 to 5; MC/VISA. Most varieties tasted. A few T-shirts and such; picnic tables on a deck overlooking vineyard. Ask to peek into the winery, or arrange for a tour by calling in advance.* ☐

Only a few vines separate Navarro and Greenwood Ridge tasting rooms; both are surrounded by vineyards that sweep toward forested hills. We'd recommend either for fine picnicking views.

A cozy tasting room that might accommodate half a dozen people (provided they're feeling friendly) occupies a corner of one of Navarro's modern, wood faced structures. Visitors can adjourn to an outside deck to sip their wine while drinking in the vineland-mountain view. Upscale barn might be the proper architectural definition for this appealing complex. Ted Bennett and Deborah Cahn established the winery in 1975 to focus on what Anderson Valley grows best—Gewürztraminer, Riesling and Chardonnay.

Tasting notes At the risk of repetition, we found the whites to be typically Anderson Valley: lush, high in fruit, with a nice acid finish. Navarro also produces a rather soft, well balanced Pinot Noir. Prices range from $8 for a dry Gewürztraminer to $15 for Chardonnay and Pinot.

Vintners choice: Owner Ted Bennett leans toward his dry, late harvest Gewürztraminer, late harvest Riesling and Chardonnay.

Greenwood Ridge Vineyards • T ✗

☐ *5501 Highway 128., Philo, CA 95466; (707) 895-2002. Daily 10 to 6 in summer, 10 to 5 in the off season; major credit cards. Most varieties tasted. Picnic tables on a deck overlooking vineyards and nearby hills.* ☐

Greenwood's tasting room is an intriguing hexagonal tepee, with a skylight to brighten the spacious interior. Decks with a few picnicking tables overlook the vineyards and a sign on a nearby pond advises visitors not to feed the alligators. The main winery is a few miles away, perched on a ridge above Greenwood Road. It's just six miles inshore from the coastal hamlet of Elk. Owned by Allan Green, the winery produces Sauvignon Blanc, Pinot Noir, Riesling, Chardonnay, Cabernet, Merlot and Zinfandel, with a limited production of 6,000 cases a year. His varietals have earned prestigious awards, including four "Best of Show" in recent years.

Green hosts the annual California Wine Tasting Championship the last weekend of July, with prizes for novice, amateur and professional sippers who can identify specific wines. If you feel you have a competitive palate, contact the winery for details.

Tasting notes: Five wines appeared on Greenwood's list when we visited the tasting room, comprising four varieties—Sauvignon Blanc, Riesling, Pinot Noir and Cabernet, with prices from $9 to $18. The whites were nicely balanced with good fruit flavor and a crisp acid finish. The Cabernet, mellowed by a hint of Merlot, tasted like a fine Bordeaux.

Husch Vineyards • T GTA & CT ✗

☐ *4400 Highway 128, Philo, CA 95466; (800) 55-HUSCH or (707) 895-3216. Daily 10 to 6 in summer and 10 to 5 the rest of the year; MC/VISA. All varieties tasted. A few gift shop items; picnic area under a grape arbor. Informal peek into the winery, or tours by appointment.* ❑

Husch is the valley's only winery senior enough to offer a bit of funky charm. Established in 1971, it occupies an old farm complex that predates the winery itself. The tasting room is in a cute, weatherbeaten granary that could pass for a miner's shack. Here, amiable wine hosts pour from a fair sized list of ten wines. The H.A. Oswald family bought the winery from the Husch clan in 1979. They produce only estate bottled wines, drawing from the Husch vineyards and their La Ribera Vineyards near Ukiah.

Tasting notes: We found the wines to be pleasantly light—dry and fruity for the Chardonnay, Sauvignon Blanc, Gewürztraminer and Chenin Blanc; soft and herbal for the Pinot Noir and Cabernet Sauvignon. Prices wander from $6.50 to $16.

Roederer Estate ● T$ GTA

❑ *4501 Highway 128 (P.O. Box 67), Philo, CA 95466; (707) 895-2288. Tasting daily 11 to 5; MC/VISA. Three sparkling wines sampled for a $3 fee, which is applied toward bottle purchase. Guided tours by appointment; call (415) 652-4900.* ❑

The term "country elegance" may occur as you approach Roederer's sparkling wine facility, nestled into a knoll above the vineyards. The exterior of the low lying redwood structure is upscale American barn; inside, polished tile floors and brass chandeliers add touches of refinement. Visitors can—glass in hand—enjoy a fine Anderson Valley view from a sunny patio beside the winery. Most of the operational facilities are underground to maintain the structure's low profile.

Although new to the Anderson Valley, the House of Roederer dates back to 1776, when it was established in France's Champagne district. Current company chairman Jean-Claude Rouzaud, a descendant of the founders, selected this area for an American expansion in the late 1970s. The climate and soils, he determined, were ideal for Chardonnay and Pinot Noir, the classic blend for Champagne. Vineyards were planted and the first wines were released in 1988.

Tasting notes: Three sparkling wines are tasted—a vintage L'Ermitage, a multi-vintage brut and brut rosé. (The brut is tasted from both .750 and 1.5 bottles to demonstrate the softer effects of aging in larger bottles.) All the Roederer wines were nicely complex, exhibiting subtle flavors of the fruit; they're among California's best sparkling wines. To provide further complexity, some of the wines from each crush are held in reserve, aged in oak and added to later vintages. Prices range from $17 to $35.

Handley Cellars ● T GTA ✗

❑ *3151 Highway 128, (P.O. Box 66) Philo, CA 95466; (707) 895-2190. Tasting 11 a.m. to 6 p.m. daily in summer and 11 to 5 the rest of the year; MC/VISA, AMEX. Most varieties tasted. Some wine related gift objects; two picnic areas on a lawn and a garden courtyard. Tours by appointment only.* ❑

Step into the Handley's comfortably stylish tasting room and admire its international art, folkcraft and Persian carpets; note particularly the carved tasting bar from England. You might think this to be the haven of a long established, much traveled winery dynasty. Yet all of this—and a list of premium wines—was assembled within a few years by dynamic young Milla Handley and her husband Rex McClellan.

After graduating from the University of California at Davis in 1975, she worked for several other winemakers. Then she and Rex established this winery at an old ranch complex in 1987. Of course, Milla's heritage didn't hold her back. She's the great-great granddaughter of Oregon brewmaster Henry Weinhard.

Tasting notes: Eight wines appear on Milla Handley's small but eclectic list, ranging from varietal whites to Pinot Noir to a sparkling rosé. We found the dry whites to be the best of the lot, strong on the fruit, crisp and clean with a bit of acid at the end. Prices range from $7.50 to the mid teens. A $6.50 semi-sweet Brightligher White would be a good hot weather quaffing wine.

Vintners choice: "Our barrel fermented Chardonnays have won many gold medals; our Gewürztraminer is recognized as one of the best in California," boasted spokeswoman Gretchen O'Bergin.

Lake County

Wrapped around California's largest natural freshwater lake, touched by no freeway or railroad, Lake County is noted for its serene rural setting. One of the state's most thinly populated counties, it has barely enough residents to fill an average ball park—about 50,000. The county seat of Lakeport numbers under 5,000.

Lake County would be an island in time, ignored by the world outside, except that the pale blue rough cut gem of Clear Lake draws thousands of summer visitors. They come to angle for bass, hurry across the lake's calm surface behind speedboat tow ropes and lie on its sandy shores. When summer ends, they leave the place to residents, who all seem to know one another as they go about their business in hamlets with ordinary names like Upper Lake and Kelseyville, or optimistic names like Lucerne and Glenhaven.

Viticulture here dates back to 1872 and more than thirty wineries once functioned. But the area's isolation made marketing difficult. Ironically, one of the county's early freight wagon roads led across the flanks of Mount St. Helena to the wine-rich Napa Valley. Lake County's wineries began to falter during a turn of the century wine glut, then Prohibition closed the rest. Commercial crushing didn't resume until 1977. At last count, this rural enclave had only half a dozen wineries; three offer tastings without prior arrangements.

A visit to Lake County's vinelands is certainly worth the brief right-hand detour from neighboring Mendocino. For one thing, the rolling drive over the Mayacamas Mountains that divide the two counties is a remarkably scenic one. For another, the wineries are appealing and uncrowded, and the wines are excellent. In fact, Lake County claims to win more awards per vineyard acre than any other wineland in the world. However, you'll have to go elsewhere to taste the products of the county's most award winning winery. Kendall-Jackson closed its Lake County tasting room recently, and now operates public sipping facilities in the Anderson Valley (see above) and in Healdsburg (see next chapter).

LAKE COUNTY WINERY TOUR ● Drive east from Hopland on State Highway 175 (Hopland Summit Road). It takes you through hillside vineyards, then up a corkscrew route to the crest of the Mayacamas Mountains. Enjoy views both east and west, then roller-coaster down to the Lake County floor. The scenery, a mix of wooded slopes, farmlands and vineyards, isn't as awesome as Mendocino County's vinelands, but it's pleasantly bucolic.

If you're pulling a trailer or driving a long-tailed motorhome, you may prefer a less twisting route by taking Highway 20 south from Redwood Valley above Ukiah. You'll even catch a bit of freeway—gawd knows why it was built—between Upper Lake and Lakeport.

If you've taken the Highway 175 route, swing south onto Highway 29 and follow it about four miles to **Konocti Winery** on your left, just short of the town of Kelseyville. From there, drive about ten miles south on Highway 29 and you'll find **Wildhurst Vineyards** set back off the road on the right. It's just beyond the Highway 29/53 junction at the dinky hamlet of Lower Lake. Continue south on Highway 29 and turn right on Butts Canyon Road in **Middletown.** After about six miles, you'll happen upon the third Lake County facility that keeps regular visiting hours, **Guenoc.** The turnoff to the ridge top winery is opposite a small lake.

Konocti Winery • T CT ✕ 🍶

☐ *Highway 29 at Thomas Drive (P.O. Box 890), Kelseyville, CA 95451; (707) 279-8861. Monday-Saturday 10 to 5 and Sunday 11 to 5; MC/VISA. All varieties tasted. Wine related gift items; picnic tables near tasting room. Casual tours; guided tours by prior arrangement.* ☐

Konocti, a winegrowers' co-op, is housed in a no-nonsense fabricated metal building fronted by a wooden bungalow tasting room. A fair selection of wine focused gift items and picnic fare and specialty foods is offered.

The winery uses only Lake County grapes, drawing from vineyards of 25 member-growers. Active socially, Konocti Winery folk sponsor monthly wine and food pairings and an October harvest festival, open to the public.

Tasting notes: The list is brief but busy—Chardonnay, Fumé Blanc, Riesling, Cabernet Franc, Cabernet Sauvignon and Merlot, plus a blush Cabernet, jug white and red, and a sweet Muscat Canelli. We felt the Chardonnay and Cabernet were best—lush and complex with powerful varietal character. The red table wine is an excellent buy at $5, with strong Cabernet underpinnings. Other prices range into the early teens.

Wildhurst Vineyards • T CT ✕

☐ *11171 Highway 29 (P.O. Box 1223), Lower Lake, CA 95457; (707) 994-4069. Daily 10:30 to 4:30 in summer, Thursday-Monday the rest of the year; MC/VISA. A few wine logo items in the cozy tasting room. Casual winery tours; picnic tables nearby.* ☐

Earlier visitors will remember the small attractive redwood structure tucked into a grove of trees as Stuermer Winery. It's now the new kid on the winery block, leased in 1991 by the Collins and Holdenreid families, both longtime Lake County growers. Myron Holdenreid was one of the first to bring varietals back to the county, planting his first vineyards in the 1960s.

While Myron minds the grapes, a winsome blue eyed winemaker from South Africa, Kathlene Redman, creates fresh and quite drinkable wines. She likes to get them into the bottles early—particularly the whites—to capture the fresh, fruity character.

Tasting notes: Two words—soft and fruity—sum up Kathy's wines, followed by another attractive word: inexpensive. Prices range from $9 to $12 for some of the best Lake County wines we've tasted. The Chardonnay exhibited fine fruit with a subtle touch of wood; Sauvignon Blanc was lushly tasty and the Cabernet Franc was outstanding, gentle yet nippy with a great spicy edge. Others on the list include a dry Riesling, Cabernet, Zinfandel and Pinot Noir. A couple of tasty white blends are Matillaha, a Bordeaux style mix of Sauvignon Blanc and Semillon; and MacKinaw, which is Chardonnay touched with Semillon and Sauvignon Blanc.

Guenoc Winery ● T CT ✕

☐ *21000 Butts Canyon Road (P.O. Box 1146), Middletown, CA 95461; (707) 987-2385. Tasting Thursday-Sunday 10 to 4:30; MC/VISA. Most varieties tasted. Picnic area beneath an arbor; informal tours of the winery.* ☐

"Am delighted. Words don't express my complete satisfaction. Join me in Paradise." Flamboyant British actress Lillie Langtry cabled this enthusiasm to her San Francisco attorney, W.H.L. Barnes, after inspecting vineyard property she'd purchased in Guenoc Valley in 1888. She imported a winemaker from Bordeaux, with the intention of creating "the greatest claret in the country." However, the operation was never a financial success, and she departed in 1906, leaving behind a stately Victorian home overlooking her vineyards. It's now occupied by present owners Orville Magoon and his family. To mark her passage, Lillie's cameo graces the Guenoc label. The winery had the distinction of being the first single vineyard appellation in America.

The facility—an attractive rural rectangle—perches on a ridge, offering visitors views of vinelands, a small lake and tree-thatched mountains. Picnic tables under an arbor provide the same pleasing vista.

Tasting notes: The Magoons' list embraces most classic varietals. We sipped a lush, buttery Guenoc Estate Chardonnay, a fruity Estate Sauvignon Blanc with a hint of oak and a gentle yet complex Zinfandel. Others on the list include a red Meritage (Cabernet Sauvignon and Merlot Bordeaux style blend), Cabernet Sauvignon, Cabernet Franc and Petite Sirah, plus Langtry red and white. Prices range from $10 to $15; more for some reserves.

THE BEST OF THE BUNCH

The best wine buys ● Fetzer Vineyards, Parducci Wine Cellars and Dunnewood Vineyards in Mendocino County and Wildhurst Vineyards in Lake County.

The most attractive wineries ● Roederer Estates, Navarro and Greenwood Ridge in Anderson Valley, and Guenoc in Lake County.

The most attractive tasting rooms ● Weibel Vineyards in Redwood Valley, Fetzer in Hopland, and Roederer Estates and Handley Cellars in Anderson Valley.

The funkiest tasting room ● Husch Vineyards in Anderson Valley.

The best gift shops ● Parducci Wine Cellars in Ukiah and Fetzer Vineyards in Hopland.

The nicest picnic areas ● Konrad Vineyards and Weibel Vineyards in Redwood Valley, Navarro and Greenwood Ridge in Anderson Valley, and Guenoc Winery in Lake County.

Wineland activities and such

Wineland events ● Lake County Spring Wine Adventure, late April; (707) 263-0911. California Wine Tasting Championships, late July at Greenwood Ridge Vineyards; (707) 877-3262. A Taste of Redwood Valley open house at Redwood Valley wineries, Father's Day weekend; (707) 485-1221.

Redwood Empire Fair and Wine Festival, August; (707) 462-4705. Individual wineries also sponsor events throughout the year.

Winery maps and guides • **Lake County Wineries**, available from Lake County Grape Growers Association, 65 Soda Bay Road, Lakeport, CA 95453; (707) 263-0911. **Mendocino County Wine and Unwind** brochure-map, available at area wineries or from Mendocino County Vintner's Association, P.O. Box 1409, Ukiah, CA 95482; (707) 468-1343. **Anderson Valley Winegrowers** map, available at valley vintners or from the Anderson Valley Winegrowers Association, P.O. Box 63, Philo, CA 95466.

BEYOND THE VINEYARDS
Mendocino County

Escapees from the thickly populated San Francisco Bay Area flee to Mendocino to admire the bucolic land forms and play in the water. They fish in the Russian River, swim and boat in Lake Mendocino and scuff seaweed along the wild and handsomely rugged seacoast. For more details on Mendocino—particularly the Mendocino Coast—pick up a copy of our **Northern California Discovery Guide**, available at bookstores everywhere, or it can be ordered directly from the source; see the back of this book.

A very popular Mendocino tourist drive is Highway 128 from Cloverdale to the sea, which passes through the vinelands of Anderson Valley. In **Boonville,** check out the old **Boonville Hotel**, the **Buckhorn Saloon** brewpub and the **Anderson Valley Historical Museum** in the Conn Creek School just beyond town.

The Boonville area is home to a curious language called "Boontling," a rural slang developed by locals a century ago and still used by some. A tourist, for instance, is called a *brightlighter* and good restaurant food is *bahl gorms*. Some Boonville shops sell Boontling dictionaries, should you wish to converse with the natives.

In addition to funny talk and wineries, Anderson Valley offers a couple of hushed redwood groves. Twisting Fish Rock Road above Yorkville takes you to the solemnly beautiful **Mailliard Redwood State Reserve**. Beyond Philo, follow Greenwood Road to **Hendy Woods State Park**, with hiking trails, picnic areas and campsites.

If you persist along Highway 128 or Greenwood Road, you'll encounter the Mendocino coast, on one of the prettiest stretches of seashore in America. Wind-graced meadows and redwood groves march down to a tumbled coastline of seastacks and hidden coves. Drive north to **Mendocino**, an old style New England town that somehow wound up on the Pacific Coast. The picture-perfect village is busy with galleries, antique shops, boutiques, bed and breakfast inns and some remarkably good restaurants.

Meanwhile, back in **Ukiah,** visit the **Grace Hudson Museum and Sun House** with Indian lore and changing historic exhibits. The town also is noted for its collection of Victorian homes; a tour map is available at the chamber of commerce. A launch ramp, campground, picnic area and hiking trail at **Lake Mendocino** can be reached by driving north on Main Street, then going east on Lake Mendocino Drive. Lake Mendocino camping facilities are just off westbound Highway 20, north of town.

From Ukiah, drive three miles east along Vichy Springs Road to **Vichy Springs Resort,** where Mark Twain, Ulysses S. Grant and ordinary folks have been soaking in mineral waters since 1854. You can rent a cozy cabin or ranch style room or pay a "use fee" and have the run of the springs and the 700-acre grounds. (See listing under "Wineland lodgings.")

Hopland shelters a pair of winery tasting rooms, as we noted before, along with a couple of interesting yesterday buildings. The nicely restored **Thatcher Inn** offers rooms and a visually elegant dining room. The brick-front **Hopland Brewery** is a properly funky brewpub with a tree-shaded beer garden. (See listings below.)

If you head north on Highway 101 to **Willits**, you can ride the chuffing little **Skunk Train** through the redwoods to the old fishing village of **Fort Bragg**, home to a few decent seafood restaurants.

Lake County

Clear Lake is the largest freshwater pond entirely within California. Its shores are lined with marinas, fishing piers, swimming beaches and resorts. Some of these old resort towns, like **Lower Lake** and **Clearlake**, are a bit on the scruffy side. However, **Lakeport** is downright cute, with several restored Victorians, false front stores in its tidy downtown area and a nicely groomed waterfront park.

Clear Lake State Park near Kelseyville offers hiking, swimming, a boat launch, camping and picnicking. **Anderson Marsh State Park** is a wetland on the lake's lower tip, encompassing a bird watching area and a pioneer farm complex.

In the pleasantly dusty town of **Lower Lake,** take a peek at the old **stone jail.** Measuring 12 by 17 feet, it's one of the smallest lockups in America. Lower Lake came to life during a brief quicksilver rush and the jail was built by brothers Theodore and John Copsey to house the town's rowdies. Apparently the Copsey brothers over-celebrated its completion and became its first occupants. They also became its first escapees, since they'd neglected to bolt down the roof.

Mendocino/Lake attractions and activities

Anderson Valley Historical Museum ● Highway 128, Boonville; (707) 895-3207. Friday-Sunday 1 to 4 (longer summer hours). Historical exhibits of Anderson Valley and Boonville, including stuff on "Boontling" language; housed in old Conn Creek School.

Boating, swimming ● Lake Mendocino recreation area; (707) 462-7581. Clear Lake recreation areas, 263-5092.

Boat rentals ● Lake Mendocino Marina; (707) 485-8644 or 485-0481.

Excursion train rides ● California Western Railroad (Skunk Trains) through the redwoods from Willits to Fort Bragg; 964-6371 or 459-5248.

Grace Hudson Museum and Sun House ● 431 S. Main St., Ukiah; (707) 462-3370. Wednesday-Saturday, 10 to 4:30 and Sunday noon to 4:30; donations requested. Indian artifacts and area history exhibits.

WINE COUNTRY DINING

Mendocino County

Bluebird Café ● ☆☆ **$$**

◻ *13340 S. Highway 101, Hopland; (707) 744-1633. Monday-Tuesday 6 a.m. to 2:30 p.m., Wednesday-Thursday 6 to 8, Friday 6 to 9, Saturday 8 to 9 and Sunday 8 to 8. Major credit cards.* ◻ Cheerful little country style café with natural woods, ceiling fans, lace curtains and hanging plants. Busy menu ranges from sandwiches, soup and salad to grilled teriyaki chicken breast and vegetarian meals.

Boonville Hotel Restaurant ● ☆☆☆ $$$

☐ *Highway 128 at Lambert Lane, Boonville; (707) 895-2210. California-American; wine and beer. Wednesday-Monday 6 p.m. to 9 p.m., lunch Sunday 11 to 2. MC/VISA.* ☐ Modern restaurant in the old fashioned Boonville Hotel, featuring light California *nouveau* fare such as sea scallop brochette with avocado salsa, and creative pizzas with leeks, grilled peppers and goat cheese. Locally done desserts are noteworthy. (Hotel listed below.)

Broiler Steak House ● ☆☆ $$$

☐ *8400 Uva Dr., Redwood Valley (just north of Ukiah; West Road exit west from U.S. 101, then north on Uva Road); (707) 485-7301. Basic American; mostly steaks; full bar service. Sunday 3 to 10, Monday-Thursday 4 to 10, Friday-Saturday 4 to 11. MC/VISA, AMEX.* ☐ Noisy, friendly restaurant with steaks, accompanied by a huge salad and a melon-sized baked potato buried under a dollop of sour cream; also chicken, chops and seafood; good local wine list. Décor consists of acoustical ceiling tile, potted plants and little else.

Buckhorn Saloon (Anderson Valley Brewing Co.) ● ☆☆☆ $

☐ *14081 Highway 128, Boonville; (707) 895-BEER. Light pub grub; beer and wine. Daily except Wednesday from 11 a.m. MC/VISA.* ☐ Stylish Western saloon styled in natural wood and leaded glass, accented by a large brew kettle out front. The place serves light fare such as sausages, piroshki, teriyaki chicken and fish and chips. Anderson Valley Brewing Company's hearty beers featured; try a pint of hearty, malt-rich High Rollers and you'll *know* you're drinking beer. Smoke-free dining.

El Sombrero ● ☆☆☆ $$

☐ *131 E. Mill St. (Main Street), Ukiah; (707) 463-1818. Mexican; full bar service. Tuesday-Saturday 11:30 to 2 and 5 to 9; Sunday brunch 10 to 2 and dinner 2 to 8. MC/VISA, DISC.* ☐ Appealing Mexican restaurant in a refurbished old farmhouse, with rough-hewn ceiling beams, high back chairs and wrought iron lamps. Traditional Mexican fare, plus specialties such as *camarones* (garlic prawns). Cozy attic cocktail lounge; outdoor dining in season.

The Green Barn ● ☆☆ $$

☐ *1109 S. State St. (Lewis Lane), Ukiah; (707) 462-5555. American; full bar service. Monday-Thursday 11 a.m. to 10 p.m., Friday-Saturday 11 to 11, Sunday 4 to 10. MC/VISA, AMEX.* ☐ Farm style restaurant in a vintage two-story house. The menu also is typically down home: steaks, prime ribs, liver and onions and—good grief—even chicken fried steaks.

Hopland Brewery ● ☆☆ $

☐ *13351 Highway 101 South, Hopland; (707) 744-1015. Light pub grub; beer and wine. Sunday-Thursday 11 a.m. to 10 p.m., Friday 11 to midnight, Saturday 11 to 1:30 a.m. MC/VISA.* ☐ An old style brewpub serving beer sausages, seafood, salads and other light snacks with its micro- brews; in a sturdy century-old red brick tavern with pressed tin walls and early American furnishings; beer garden shaded by a grape trellis.

Hopland Farms ● ☆ $

☐ *Highway 101, Hopland; (707) 744-1298. Light deli fare; wine and beer. Monday-Saturday 6 a.m. to 8 p.m., Sunday 6:30 to 8. MC/VISA.* ☐ Mini- mart with a deli counter; handy stop for a quick lunch; serving daily specials and large sandwiches at modest prices.

Lotus Restaurant ● ☆☆ $

❑ 403 S. State St. (Clay Street), Ukiah; (707) 463-2288. Chinese-Japanese; wine and beer. Monday-Thursday 11 a.m. to 3 and 5:30 to 9:30 p.m., Friday 11 to 3 and 5 to 10, Saturday noon to 10, closed Sunday. MC/VISA. ❑ Storefront restaurant trimmed by an occasional paper lantern serves huge portions at modest prices. Versatile menu lists both Chinese and Japanese fare; sushi bar.

The Maple Restaurant ● ☆☆ $

❑ 295 S. State St., Ukiah; (707) 462-5221. American; meals $5 to $10; wine and beer. Monday-Friday 7 to 3:30, Saturday noon to 10m, closed Sunday. MC/VISA. ❑ Simple American diner with a basic Formica interior; inexpensive fare in generous portions. It's the kind of place where the waitress approaches your table with a smile and a coffee pot.

Thatcher Inn Restaurant ● ☆☆☆☆ $$$

❑ 13401 S. Highway 101 (Center Street), Hopland; (707) 744-1890. American-continental; full bar service. Breakfast Monday-Saturday 8 to 10, Sunday brunch 9 to 2; lunch Monday- Saturday 11:30 to 2, dinner daily 5:30 to 9:30. Major credit cards. ❑ Housed in a restored stagecoach stop, featuring typical American and some classic continental dishes. Handsomely restored dining room with floral wallpaper, tin ceilings and marble-topped candle-lit tables. Stately, clubby bar adjacent.

Lake County

Anthony's Restaurant ● ☆☆☆ $$

❑ 2509 Lakeshore Blvd., Lakeport; (707) 263-4905. Italian-American; full bar service. Friday-Tuesday 5 to 10 p.m., closed Wednesday-Thursday. Major credit cards. ❑ Attractive restaurant across street from the lake, dressed up in white lace tablecloths, black velvet drapes and red carpets. Varied menu with Italian specialties, a large seafood selection and typical steaks, chicken and chops.

Lakeside Restaurant & Bar ● ☆☆☆ $$

❑ 6330 Soda Bay Road, Kelseyville; (707) 279-9450. French-Continental; full bar service. Dinner nightly from 5:30. Reservations suggested; MC/VISA. ❑ Attractive small restaurant on Clear Lake. Menu features include escargot, rack of lamb Persille and fresh seafood. Good wine list.

Park Place ● ☆☆ $$

❑ 50 Third Street, Lakeport; (707) 263-0444. American; wine and beer. Daily 11 to 9. MC/VISA. ❑ Pleasantly casual early American style establishment opposite Lakeport's lakefront park; outdoor patio and a roof garden with views of the lake. The menu focuses on pasta, with a few chickens and chops. The chicken margarita marinated in lime and topped with salsa is somewhat tasty.

WINELAND LODGINGS

NOTE: Prices were provided by the establishments and are subject to change. Use the price ranges only as a rough guideline and call the places listed to confirm their current rates.

Wine Country Referrals is a reservation service for hotels, motels, inns, B&Bs and vacation homes in Lake, Mendocino, Napa and Sonoma counties; P.O. Box 543, Calistoga, CA 94515; (707) 942-2186, FAX (707) 942-4681.

Mendocino County

Boonville Hotel ● ☆☆☆ $$$$ Ø

◻ *Highway 128 at Lambert Lane (P.O. Box 326), Boonville, CA 95415; (707) 895-2210. Rooms $65 to $145. MC/VISA.* ◻ Refurbished historic hotel with Early American style rooms featuring down comforters, fresh flowers and other amenities; free continental breakfast. All rooms are non-smoking. **Boonville Hotel Restaurant** listed above.

Days Inn ● ☆☆ $$$

◻ *950 N. State Street (Low Gap Road), Ukiah, CA 95482; (707) 462-7584. Couples $46 to $65, singles $42 to $48. Major credit cards.* ◻ Room phones, TV, pool; some old fashioned refurbished rooms with high ceilings and polished woods. **Sweetwood Barbecue** serves dinners from $8.95 to $14.95; full bar service. Non-smoking areas.

Super Eight Motel ● ☆☆ $$$ Ø

◻ *1070 S. State St. (Talmage), Ukiah, CA 95482; (707) 462-1221. Couples $48 to $62, singles $38 to $48. Major credit cards.* ◻ Thirty-one room motel with TV movies, room phones and pool; some in-room spa tubs. **Ukiah Garden Café** serves Tuesday-Saturday 11 to 2 and 5 to 9, Sunday brunch 9:30 to 2; closed Monday. American-Greek; dinners $9 to $20; full bar service; non-smoking areas.

Vichy Springs Resort ● ☆☆☆☆ $$$$$

◻ *2605 Vichy Springs Rd. (three miles east of U.S. 101), Ukiah, CA 95482; (707) 462-9515. Couples $125 to $160, singles $85 to $135. All major credit cards.* ◻ A refurbished 1854 hot springs resort with naturally carbonated mineral baths, Swedish massage, Olympic sized swimming pool, hot therapy pool and other amenities. Modern furnished rooms in a ranch style building, plus two guest cottages with fireplaces. Rates include breakfast and the use of mineral baths and pools. Seven hundred acres for hiking, picnicking and mountain biking.

Lake County

Best Western El Grande Inn ● ☆☆ $$$

◻ *15135 Lakeside Dr. (P.O. Box 4598), Clear Lake, CA 95422; (800) 528-1234 or (707) 994-2000. Couples $73, singles $67. Major credit cards.* ◻ In-room phones, TV with fee movies; some suites with refrigerators; pool, hot tub. **Restaurant** serves Monday-Friday 6 a.m. to 10 p.m. and Sunday from 8 to 10. American fare; $8 to $15; full bar service.

Konocti Harbor Resort & Spa ● ☆☆☆☆ $$$$

◻ *8727 Soda Bay Rd., Kelseyville, CA 95451; (707) 279-4281. Couples $69 to $90, singles $59 to $90, kitchen apartments $150 to $225. Major credit cards.* ◻ Large lakeside resort with extensive landscaped grounds; marina, rental boats, two pools, playground, miniature golf, health spa, tennis; planned activities in summer. Rooms have TV, radios and phones. **Dining Room** and coffee shop serves 7 a.m. to 10 p.m.; American; meals $10 to $20; full bar service.

Skylark Shores Motel and Resort ● ☆☆ $$$

◻ *1120 N. Main St. (11th Street), Lakeport, CA 95453; (707) 263-6151. Couples $58 to $90, singles $50 to $62, kitchenettes $80 to $95. All major credit cards.* ◻ Forty-five room motel on the lake with boat launches and docks; TV, room phones, pool.

BED & BREAKFAST INNS
Mendocino County

Philo Pottery Inn ● ☆☆ *$$$$* Ø

☐ *8550 Highway 128 (P.O. Box 166), Philo, CA 95466; (707) 895-3069. Couples $80 to $95, singles $77 to $90. Five rooms, three with private baths; full breakfast. MC/VISA.* ☐ Restored 1888 redwood farmhouse that once served as a stage stop. Rooms furnished with American antiques, old fashioned beds with patchwork quilts and down comforters. Wood stove and library in living room; airy front porch with English garden. Twelve-mile mountain bike trail adjacent; Anderson Valley wineries nearby.

Toll House Inn ● ☆☆☆☆ *$$$$$* Ø

☐ *15301 Highway 253 (P.O. Box 268), Boonville, CA 95415; (707) 895-3630. Couples $125 to $150, riverfront chalet with kitchen in organic garden for $190. Four rooms; private baths; full breakfast. MC/VISA, DISC.* ☐ Elegantly restored 1912 toll house on a 360-acre ranch; hiking, picnicking. Rooms furnished with an antique-modern mix; artworks adorn the walls. Some units with fireplaces and spa tubs.

Thatcher Inn ● ☆☆☆☆ *$$$$* Ø

☐ *13401 S. Highway 101 (Center Street), Hopland, CA 95449; (707) 744-1890. Couples and singles $90 to $150. Twenty rooms with private baths; full breakfast and Sunday champagne brunch. MC/VISA, AMEX.* ☐ Impeccably restored inn, housed in an 1890 stage stop hotel. Victorian and American antiques, floral print wallpaper, brass beds and armoires. Comfortable library with easy chairs and fireplace. Lounge and **restaurant** (see listing above).

Lake County

Forbestown Inn ● ☆☆☆ *$$$$* Ø

☐ *825 Forbes St. (Ninth Street), Lakeport, CA 95453; (707) 263-7858. Couples $85 to $110, singles $75 to $85. Four rooms, one with private bath; full country breakfast. MC/VISA, AMEX.* ☐ Attractive 1869 Victorian in downtown Lakeport. Rooms nicely furnished with American oak antiques, floral drapes, king and queen beds. Landscaped grounds; pool and spa.

Mendocino-Lake county information sources

The Greater Ukiah Chamber of Commerce, 495 E. Perkins St., Ukiah, CA 95482; (707) 462-4705.

Mendocino County Convention & Visitors Bureau, P.O. Box 244, Ukiah, CA 95482; (707) 462-3091.

Lake County Chamber of Commerce, 875 Lakeport Blvd., Lakeport, CA 95453; (707) 263-5092.

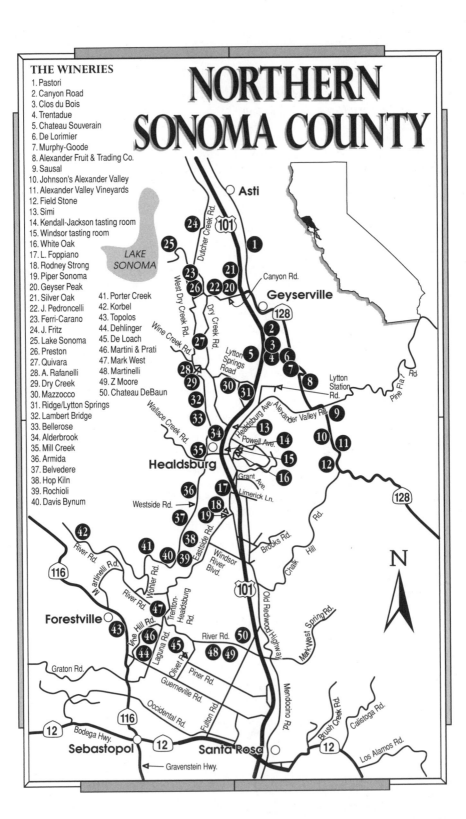

NORTHERN SONOMA COUNTY

THE WINERIES

1. Pastori
2. Canyon Road
3. Clos du Bois
4. Trentadue
5. Chateau Souverain
6. De Lorimier
7. Murphy-Goode
8. Alexander Fruit & Trading Co.
9. Sausal
10. Johnson's Alexander Valley
11. Alexander Valley Vineyards
12. Field Stone
13. Simi
14. Kendall-Jackson tasting room
15. Windsor tasting room
16. White Oak
17. L. Foppiano
18. Rodney Strong
19. Piper Sonoma
20. Geyser Peak
21. Silver Oak
22. J. Pedroncelli
23. Ferri-Carano
24. J. Fritz
25. Lake Sonoma
26. Preston
27. Quivara
28. A. Rafanelli
29. Dry Creek
30. Mazzocco
31. Ridge/Lytton Springs
32. Lambert Bridge
33. Bellerose
34. Alderbrook
35. Mill Creek
36. Armida
37. Belvedere
38. Hop Kiln
39. Rochioli
40. Davis Bynum

41. Porter Creek
42. Korbel
43. Topolos
44. Dehlinger
45. De Loach
46. Martini & Prati
47. Mark West
48. Martinelli
49. Z Moore
50. Chateau DeBaun

Asti

Geyserville

LAKE SONOMA

Canyon Rd.

Dutcher Creek Rd.

West Dry Creek Rd.

Wine Creek Rd.

Dry Creek Rd.

Lytton Springs Road

Lytton Station Rd.

Pine Flat Rd.

Wallace Creek Rd.

Healdsburg Ave.

Alexander Valley Rd.

Powell Ave.

Grant Ave.

Healdsburg

Limerick Ln.

Westside Rd.

Eastside Rd.

Brooks Rd.

Chalk Hill Rd.

Windsor River Blvd.

River Rd.

Martinelli Rd.

Wohler Rd.

Vine Hill Rd.

Trenton-Healdsburg Rd.

Forestville

Laguna Rd.

Olivet Rd.

Piner Rd.

River Rd.

Graton Rd.

Guerneville Rd.

Occidental Rd.

Fulton Rd.

Old Redwood Highway

Mendocino Rd.

Mark West Spring Rd.

Brush Creek Rd.

Calistoga Rd.

Los Alamos Rd.

Bodega Hwy.

Sebastopol

Santa Rosa

Gravenstein Hwy.

N

"...Fresh, clean, elegant and lively, with a ripe black-current edge to the plum and cherry flavors. The tannins are firm, but rounded, and the flavors have amplitude, echoing fruit on and on."
—Description of a Guenoc Cabernet Sauvignon Lake County

Chapter Three
NORTHERN SONOMA COUNTY
From Zin vineyards to redwood forests

Mention Sonoma and some wine enthusiasts think of the Sonoma Valley and winery pioneers General Vallejo and Count Haraszthy. That's chronologically correct, since the California wine industry's roots go deep into Sonoma Valley soil.

Today, however, northern Sonoma County has more wineries, more vineyard acres and produces more wine than its better known neighbor. In all of California, it's second only to the Napa Valley in total premium wine grape acreage, with more than 30,000 acres of vines.

A scenic southern extension of Mendocino County, northern Sonoma is a mix of tawny hills, redwood groves in hidden canyons and shady oak clusters bearded with Spanish moss. More than 1,400 miles of rural roads invite aimless wandering and spontaneous picnics beside trickling creeks. The Sonoma Coast, like the Mendocino Coast above it, is a spectacular sweep of sea stacks, velvety green headlands and charming yesterday towns weathered—like old men of the sea—by ocean breezes.

Let's not forget the main reason we came here. The north county's gravelly, loamy soils along the flanks of the Russian River and Dry Creek produce some of America's premier wines. The region offers a further advantage for the winetasting crowd—uncrowded wineries ranging from tiny and rustic to historic and grandiloquently modern.

A few decades ago, this area was busy with hop yards and orchards. Some unused hop kilns survive, marked by their distinctive conical towers; a couple have been converted to wineries. Plums once were so profuse that the Healdsburg Chamber of Commerce sponsored annual tours to view the pretty pink-white blossoms. The area still blooms with springtime color, but

47

it's wild mustard, California poppies and the tender green buds of awakening grapevines.

The first settlers in this area were not pious mission padres or grape stompers. They were Russian fur hunters, working down the coast from Alaska. Seeking the slippery sea otter, they established a colony called Romazov on the Sonoma Coast in 1809, followed three years later by the fortress of Rossiya—now Fort Ross State Historic Park. Concerned by this intrusion, Mexican officials began moving north from San Francisco in the 1820s. They granted huge tracts of land to favored soldiers and politicians who had helped in their recent war for independence from Spain.

The Russians eventually withdrew and northern Sonoma County became the domain of contented *rancheros* who ran their cattle over the grassy hills. The first American to settle here was Cyrus Alexander. Arriving in the 1840s, he managed one of the Mexican land grants for several years in exchange for 9,000 acres of land. He never produced wine but he did plant some of the area's first grapes. The valley enclosing his ranch now bears his name.

The first vintners of significance were the brothers Korbel. Francis, Joseph and Anton settled along the Russian River in 1882, logged off the redwoods and began planting vineyards. The Korbel winery survives to this day as the largest facility in the area. More European vintners followed and hundreds of acres were soon graced by vines. Unhappily, Sonoma County was one of the first areas in the country to be hit by phylloxera. Even Luther Burbank, recently settled in Santa Rosa, joined the fight against the deadly scourge. Several wineries closed before root grafting ended the crisis. Then many of the survivors were finished off by Prohibition.

One, however, was started right in the middle of Prohibition by an Italian optimist. John Pedroncelli bought a defunct winery in Dry Creek Valley in 1927, gambling that the foolish law soon would be repealed. His gamble paid off and his sons John, Jr., and Jim still run the place.

Generally warmer than Mendocino and the Sonoma Valley, northern Sonoma County produces excellent reds, particularly Zinfandel (see box on page 72). It's also noted for its award winning Cabernet Sauvignon, Pinot Noir and Chardonnay.

We'll tour wineries in the area's three major viticultural regions. Alexander Valley lies alongside U.S. 101, extending from the Mendocino County border south to Geyserville, and east toward the Mayacamas Mountains. Dry Creek Valley is southwest and the Russian River Valley is below that, lying west of Santa Rosa.

Several towns along our routes offer restaurants and other respite. Burgeoning Santa Rosa, with more than 114,000 residents and growing, forms a suburban plug for the lower end of north county. Although it has ample cafés and motels and a good museum or two, we don't regard it as a wine country town. It is instead the northern outpost for San Francisco Bay Area sprawl, the seat of much of the county's recent population spurt. However, the area to the north becomes quickly rural.

Although you haven't quite hit the northern wine country as you approach Santa Rosa, you will encounter an excellent new visitor center that will tell you all you need to know about the wineries ahead. The **Sonoma County Wine & Visitors Center** is an attractive Spanish style complex just off U.S. 101 in Rohnert Park, south of Santa Rosa. To reach it, take the Country Club Drive exit and head toward the Red Lion Inn on a frontage road east of the freeway; the new facility is on the north end of the Red Lion complex. Within this handsome facility, you'll find displays concerning wineries of the northern county and Sonoma Valley, which we visit in the next chapter. Wines from two county vintners are tasted each day, on a rotating alphabetical basis. The center sells wine from most county vintners, plus logo and other wine related gift items. The modern facility also has wine country videos and computer access to 3,600 books and 80 magazines of the Sonoma County Wine Library. The center is open daily 10 to 5 with tasting from 11 to 4. For information call (707) 527-7701.

Continuing north from Rohnert Park through Santa Rosa, you'll shortly encounter pleasantly rustic Healdsburg, which *is* a wine country town. It's surrounded by vineyards and has a few downtown tasting rooms. Citizens of this town of 10,000 are doing a fine job facelifting their downtown area to preserve its vintage look. Its tree shaded, landscaped plaza is rimmed by a bevy of boutiques, antique shops and a good restaurant or two. Several motels and inns permit wineland wanderers to bed down near the vineyards.

North of Healdsburg, Geyserville and Cloverdale also are amidst the vines although they offer fewer facilities. Tiny Geyserville is noted for a couple of good restaurants and two fine Victorian era B&Bs, while Cloverdale has a handful of small motels and cafés.

Alexander Valley

Old Cyrus would be pleased to learn that the valley bearing his name still is essentially agricultural. No city disturbs its bucolic tranquility. Geyserville sits between Alexander and Dry Creek valleys. However, the closest thing to a community within the valley itself is the grizzled **Alexander Valley Store,** a general mercantile in the classic sense.

Less hilly than Dry Creek or Russian River valleys, Alexander is a patchwork of vineyards and pasturelands, flanking the upper reaches of the Russian River. The land climbs gently eastward toward low hills, giving way to clusters of oaks and groves of madroñas.

ALEXANDER VALLEY WINERY TOUR • If you drive to the top of Sonoma County on U.S. 101, you'll see hundreds of acres of vineyards but no tasting rooms. The Italian Swiss Colony in the tiny town of Asti—one of the area's earliest wineries—is no more, although the historic landmark sign survives. The facility was purchased by Wine World, Inc., and the tasting room is closed. Also closed is the tasting room of Pat Paulsen Vineyards, which was located in the former Asti village.

Your first opportunity to sample northern Sonoma wine comes just north of **Geyserville.** Take the Canyon Road exit and follow the east side frontage road a bit over a mile north to **Pastori Winery** in an old metal sided barn on the right. (At the Canyon Road interchange, you'll see Geyser Peak Winery across the freeway, but ignore it for now. It marks the start of our Dry Creek Valley Tour. After visiting Pastori, reverse your route on the frontage road, which becomes Geyserville Avenue and drive through this pleasant little hamlet. Zig under the freeway twice and you'll encounter three wineries, all on the left—**Canyon Road Cellars** on the site of the former Nervo Vineyards, **Clos du Bois** and **Trentadue**. Just south of Trentadue, cross under the freeway on Independence Lane and follow it to the architecturally striking **Château Souverain**.

Having played tag with the freeway, backtrack on Geyserville Avenue and turn right (east) onto Highway 128. You'll shortly encounter the new **De Lorimier Winery and Vineyards** in a shingle sided barn on your right. A couple of miles beyond is **Murphy-Goode Estate Winery**, also on the right. Staying on 128 (which does a couple of rural 90-degree turns), you next reach **Alexander Valley Fruit and Trading Company** (yes, folks, it's a winery) and **Sausal Winery**, both on the left. Between them is the earlier mentioned **Alexander Valley Store** at the junction of 128 and Alexander Valley Road. This century-old general store provides necessities and a small bar for locals, plus picnic fare and a selection of regional wines.

A bit farther along is **Johnson's Alexander Valley Winery** on the right and **Alexander Valley Winery** on the left. Finally, as the valley approaches Mount St. Helena and starts becoming attractively rumpled, you'll hit **Field Stone Winery** on the right. From there, retrace your route a bit, turn left onto Alexander Valley Road and follow it past the general store to Healdsburg.

Pastori Winery • T

☐ *23189 Geyserville Ave., Cloverdale, CA 95425; (707) 857-3418. Tasting daily 9 to 5; no credit cards; personal checks accepted. All varieties tasted.* ☐

Frank Pastori will tell you, in his big booming voice, that he's been making wine for half a century and he has operated his small Pastori Winery since 1970. If you have plenty of time, he'll tell you his kiwi wine story—spiced with a lot of old fashioned four-letter words. About six friendly people or four strangers can fit in the small, austere tasting room, situated in a corner of his metal-sided barn of a winery. Fortunately, since this small family winery is a bit off the beaten winetasting path (although easy to find), it's rarely crowded. Frank's generally there to greet visitors "unless I'm on a tractor." In that case, he says, blow your horn or go up to the house.

Tasting notes: Frank makes big, robust reds with little wood and lots of fruit; "black wines," he calls them. The small list consists of Zinfandel, burgundy (a blend of Zin, Pinot Noir and Petit Sirah) and white Zin. All are estate grown. Prices are remarkably modest, with nothing over $8. When you've made your selection, he totes up your bill on one of those little receipt slips used by corner cafés, consulting a printed card for the state sales tax.

Canyon Road Cellars • T ✕ 📦

☐ *19550 Geyserville Ave., Geyserville, CA 95441; (707) 857-3417. Tasting daily 10 to 5; MC/VISA. Most varieties tasted. Good selection of gift and specialty items, plus a deli offering picnic fare; landscaped picnic area beneath a grape arbor.* ☐

This facility is one of the county's oldest wineries and it has the rustic look to prove it, although it's now part of a modern wine complex. Started by the Nervo family in 1908, it was sold to by Frank Nervo to owners of nearby Geyser Peak Winery in 1974. Geyser, in turn, was purchased by the Trione family, whose home base is Santa Rosa. The new owners continued using the Nervo Winery name until it was changed to Canyon Roads a few years ago.

The weathered farm style complex is easy to spot, occupying a fieldstone, hip-roofed structure. The attractive tasting room is in a remodeled bungalow that once served as a storage facility. The original tasting room, comfortably funky with thousands of calling cards tacked to walls and ceilings, is now an extension of the new.

Tasting notes: Both Nervo and Canyon Road wines are offered, and they're rather inexpensive. The list includes Merlot, Sequoia Red, Chardonnay, Sauvignon Blanc and Semillon, all under $10. The whites are quite fruity and the Chardonnay had a nice nutty finish. Reds are light and drinkable, mostly from young vines. Sequoia Red, a blend of Cabernet Sauvignon, Cabernet Franc and Ruby Cabernet, is quite tasty, a good buy at $6.

Vintners choice: "Sequoia Red won a sweepstakes award at our regional wine classic; also our Canyon Road Sauvignon Blanc won gold at the New World International Wine Competition," says public relations person Ann Rizzo.

Clos du Bois • T 🍷

☐ *19410 Geyserville Ave. (P.O. Box 940), Geyserville, CA 95441; (800) 222-3189 or (707) 857-3100. Daily 10 to 4:30; major credit cards. Most varieties tasted. Good selection of gift and wine logo items.* ☐

Founded in 1974 by wine grower Frank Woods, Clos du Bois has grown rapidly to become one of the largest producers in northern Sonoma County, with an annual output of half a million cases. For years the tasting room and winery occupied leased warehouse space in Healdsburg, then it moved recently to a new—and considerably more appealing—state of the art winery on Geyserville Avenue, off U.S. 101 between Healdsburg and Geyserville.

Tasting notes: The wines were uniformly excellent—with numerous medals to prove it. The Sauvignon Blanc, early harvest Gewürztraminer and Chardonnay had exemplary varietal characteristics, fruity and dry with a hint of spice. A Cabernet was lush and berry-like with a gentle tannin finish. If you like a soft Bordeaux style, try the Marlstone, a blend of Cabernet Sauvignon, Cabernet Franc, Merlot and Malbec.

Vintners choice: "We're best known for producing richly sculpted Chardonnays and velvety smooth Bordeaux style varietals," says the winery's Debra Price.

Trentadue Winery • T ✕ 🍷

☐ *19170 Geyserville Ave., Geyserville, CA 95441; (707) 433-3104. Daily 10 to 5 spring through fall and 10 to 4 in winter; MC/VISA, DISC. All wines sampled. Nice giftware selection and deli items; shaded picnic area.* ☐

You'll likely be greeted by a tail-wagging dog or two at this family-owned ranch complex amidst the vines. The combined tasting room and gift shop is upstairs in a masonry block winery building. A long list of wines and a good selection of glassware, wine related items and other giftwares will tempt the visitor. Leo Trentadue started the winery in 1969 and has expanded his operation considerably, with 170 acres now in vines. The family built the main winery in 1972.

Tasting notes: Trentadue's wines are uniformly excellent and moderately priced. The primary focus here is reds. The list includes some mature Zins and Cabs ready for drinking, yet with enough body to be put down for a

---

WINERY CODES • **T** = Tasting with no fee; **T$** = Tasting for a fee; **GT** = Guided tours; **GTA** = Guided tours by appointment; **ST** = Self-guiding tours; **CT** = casual tours or a peek into the winery; ✕ = picnic area; 🍷 = Gift shop or good giftware selection. Price ranges listed in tasting notes are for varietals; jug wines may be available for less.

few more years. Among our favorites were a robust Zinfandel for $10, a hearty Old Patch Red blend for $11, full-flavored Petit Sirah for $11 and—from the list of whites—a crisply dry Semillon for $7.50. Prices range from $5 to the mid teens. Trentadue also offers some fine ports, which can be sampled for a dollar a nip.

Vintners choice: "Merlot, Petit Sirah, Carignane and Old Patch Red," says Cindy Trentadue.

Château Souverain • T R

☐ *Independence Lane at Highway 101 (P.O. Box 528), Geyserville, CA 95441; (707) 433-8281. Tastings at a tasting bar or café tables, daily 10 to 5; all current releases available. Good selection of wine-related gift items and apparel. See listing under "Wine country dining" for Château Souverain Restaurant.* ☐

One of the county's more striking winery structures, Château Souverain is an architectural blend of hop kiln and French manor house. The tasting room is trimmed with bright splashes of color and hanging tapestries. The adjoining restaurant with a panoramic vineyard vista, is done in pink and beige, accented by chandeliers and embroidered panels.

Tasting notes: Tastings are conducted either at an attractive bar or at café tables. The list includes Sauvignon Blanc, Chardonnay, Pinot Noir, Zinfandel, Merlot and Cabernet Sauvignon, with prices ranging from $7.50 to $13; each has strong varietal character—good buys for the modest prices.

Vintners choice: "My favorites include our Alexander Valley Cabernet Sauvignon and Sonoma County Chardonnay," says winemaker Tom Peterson.

De Lorimier Vineyards and Winery • T CT & GTA ✗

☐ *2001 Highway 128 (P.O. Box 487), Geyserville, CA 95441; (707) 857-2000. Thursday-Sunday 10 to 4:30. Most varieties tasted. Picnic area and informal self guided tours; guided tours by appointment.* ☐

Established in 1985, this attractive family-owned winery occupies a shingle-sided redwood structure nestled among the vineyards. The small tasting room is upstairs above the winery and a single picnic table sits out front.

Tasting notes: Good fruit and strong varietal character are evident in De Lorimier's select list, consisting of a white and red Meritage, Chardonnay, Merlot and several proprietary blends.

Vintners choice: "Mosaic, red Meritage, Spectrum and white Meritage," says the winery's Kimberly Wright. "Our Bordeaux style blends add more interest and complexity to the wines."

Murphy-Goode Estate Winery • T

☐ *4001 Highway 128 (P.O. Box 158), Geyserville, CA 95441; (707) 431-7644. Daily 10:30 to 4:30; MC/VISA. Select varieties tasted. A few wine related gift items.* ☐

Tim Murphy and Dale Goode planted their first grapes in the Alexander Valley in the 1960s, then they joined with marketing specialist Dave Ready to establish the winery in 1985. The modern, medium-sized no-frills winery is fronted by an appealing cathedral-ceiling tasting room.

Tasting notes: Visitors may choose from Fumé Blanc, reserve Fumé, Chardonnay, reserve Chardonnay, Pinot Blanc, Merlot and Cabernet Sauvignon. They tend to be light with pronounced fruit flavor, low in tannin and easy on the wood. A fruity Fumé Blanc and lush, soft Chardonnay were particularly tasty. Prices range from $9 to $12.50; higher for some aged "Library wines" that aren't tasted.

Vintners choice: "The reserve Fumé Blanc is our signature wine; much of our effort goes into it," said our tasting room hostess.

Alexander Valley Fruit and Trading Company ● T ✗ ▮

◻ 5110 Highway 128, Geyserville, CA 95441; (707) 433-1944. Daily 10 to 5; MC/VISA. Most varieties tasted. Interesting selection of gift items, focusing on wine and food gift packs. Picnic area on a knoll with a vineyard view. ◻

Steve and Candy Sommer started their winery in 1984 with a sense of creativity. In addition to producing wines that win a fair share of medals, they assemble gift packs of wine and gourmet food items. Then Steve made *People Magazine* in 1990 when he came up with an unusual packing material—popcorn.

"It's organic, biodegradable, provides good packing protection and it isn't much heavier than styrofoam," Candy told us with honest enthusiasm.

You can buy it at the winery in 14-cubic-foot bags, should you decide to forsake styrofoam pebbles. One of their popular gift packs is wine, popping corn and gourmet seasoning. The name's great: "Hot to Pop."

All this creativity occurs in a tasting room with a country store theme, sitting amidst vineyards on an upslope from the highway. The winery, with a modest capacity of 15,000 cases, is out back. The owners have added a series of summer music events; call the winery for information and reservations.

Tasting notes: The Sommers are traditionalists when it comes to wines: crisp whites and hearty reds. The prices, inside or outside the gift packs, are moderate—$6 to $10; a bit more for some late harvest stuff. Zinfandel revealed the Sommer touch—big berry flavor and soft tannins. Carignane, Sauvignon Blanc, Chenin Blanc, Chardonnay and a couple of late harvest wines complete the list.

Vintners choice: "Our style of wine is light and fruity, as if it was just picked off the vines," says Candy, who apparently likes them all.

Sausal Winery ● T ✗

◻ 7370 Highway 128, Healdsburg, CA 95448; (707) 433-2285. Daily 10 to 4; MC/VISA. Selected wines tasted. Few wine related gift items; small picnic area. ◻

Prim landscaping and an arbor-shaded picnic area accent this small complex, perched on an upslope, half a mile off Highway 128. The small, simple tasting room is fused to the end of the handsome redwood winery.

The facility dates from 1973 although the Demostene family has been growing grapes in the Alexander Valley since 1925. Some of their vines are older still, dating back to the turn of the century. Four children of pioneer grape grower Leo Demostene operate the winery today.

Tasting notes: Sausal's repertoire is small—about six or eight wines and three of these are open for tasting on a given day. We sipped excellent Zinfandel and Cabernet which, typical of Sausal wines, were well-rounded with little hint of tannin or wood. Prices range from $5 for a white Zin to $14 for Zins and Cabs. One can purchase six-bottle packs of "verticals," with three vintages each of aged Zinfandel and Cabernet.

Vintners choice: "We specialize in Zinfandels—all estate grown, some from vineyard more than a hundred years old," reports the winery's Peachie Dunlavy.

Johnson's Alexander Valley Winery • T CT ✕

☐ *8333 Highway 128, Healdsburg, CA 95448; (707) 433-2319. Daily 10 to 5; MC/VISA, AMEX. Most varieties tasted. Some wine related gift items; small picnic area. Visitors can peek into the winery.* ☐

A century-old barn on this family ranch complex holds a couple of surprises: modern winemaking equipment and a pair of grand theater organs. Ranks of pipes fill much of the winery, standing alongside stainless steel fermenters and aging casks. The tasting room itself is a simple affair—a wooden counter in a corner. Johnson family members have been organ buffs for years and they've assembled an antique from Sacramento's old Capitol Theater. Which is all very strange, because no one in the family plays. However, they often host organ concerts with guest performers. The new addition is computer-driven, so resonate tones can filter through the weather-worn old barn at the flip of a switch.

The small, century-old winery is presently owned by Tom and Gail Johnson; their daughter Ellen is the enologist.

Tasting notes: Wines are available only at the winery and a few local outlets. The list is small and the wines are uniformly tasty and fair priced, from $7 to the middle teens. Our favorites were a wonderfully fruity non-barrel Chardonnay and a powerful, complex late harvest Zinfandel with 15.4 percent alcohol. Pinot Noir, Cabernet, white Zin and Johannisberg Riesling complete the selection.

Vintners choice: "Year in and year out, Pinot Noir is our best seller," says Tom. "We do well with our Cabs and Chardonnay, too."

Alexander Valley Vineyards • T GTA ✕

☐ *8644 Highway 128, Healdsburg, CA 95448; (707) 433-7209. Daily 10 to 5; MC/VISA, AMEX. Most varieties tasted. Some wine related gift items; picnic area. Tours by appointment.* ☐

This facility is as modern as neighboring Johnson's is rustic. The adobe brick winery is set in rumpled foothills above Highway 128, rimmed by landscaped grounds, sheltered by moss-bearded oaks. With vineyards in the foreground and a meadow rising beyond, it's one of the valley's most pleasing spots. It's also an historic spot, occupying lands settled by Cyrus Alexander a century and a half ago. His grave site is on a hill above the winery.

The Wetzel family purchased this land in 1963, planted vines and began producing premium varietals in 1975. All are estate produced and vintage dated.

Tasting notes: Winemaker Hank Wetzel's reds are full-bodied yet light in tannin, with a touch of wood. We noted a pleasant spiciness in the Merlot and Zinfandel, and the Gewürztraminer was complex and dry with a strong acid finish. Cabernets were big wines, suitable for aging. Prices range from $7.50 to the mid teens.

Vintners choice: "Cabernets," said Hank. "They're very stylistic, and older wines are available on request."

Field Stone Winery • T CT ✕

☐ *10075 Highway 128, Healdsburg, CA 95448; (800) 54-GRAPE or (707) 433-7266. Daily 10 to 5. All varieties tasted; MC/VISA. A few wine related gift items; picnic area; casual winery tours.* ☐

Your casual tour begins the moment you step through the doorway of the distinctive bunker-style winery. The stroll to the small corner tasting room takes you past ranks of stainless steel fermenters and aging barrels. The winery is fashioned like a root cellar—dug into a hillside, then faced with local stone. Outside, properly gnarled old oaks and picnic tables made from wine barrels complete the earthy setting.

Producing only 8,000 cases a year, this family-owned winery focuses on Cabernets and Petit Sirahs, which have won an assortment of gold medals. Former Berkeley mayor Wallace Johnson established the firm in 1977. It's now operated by his daughter Katrina and her husband John Staten.

Tasting comments: The style is soft and fruity, with a subtly acidic finish in the whites and a touch of wood and tannin in the reds. Among our choices were a crisp, fruity Sauvignon Blanc, a gentle Chardonnay with a hint of oak, a complex Cabernet Sauvignon and a well-rounded Petit Sirah with enough tannin to keep it honest. Prices range from $9 to the low twenties.

Healdsburg & surrounds

Not only is Healdsburg in the heart of the wine country, some wine outlets are in the heart of Healdsburg. A few tasting rooms, orphaned from their wineries, are situated here.

We're not much drawn to storefront tasting rooms. Without the vineyards, picnic areas and embracing sights and smells of their wineries, they're rather sterile. It's like walking into a wine shop that carries only one brand, and you're often dealing with a clerk, not a winery employee. Of course, you do have the advantage of sampling before you buy.

As we mentioned earlier, this town of 10,000 is worth a stop for its venerable plaza, boutiques, antique stores, restaurants and bed and breakfast inns. Neighborhood streets are shaded by mature trees, some sheltering century-old Victorian homes.

HEALDSBURG AREA WINERY TOUR ● Downtown's tasting room count has been reduced to three in recent years, and possibly two. The former William Wheeler Winery tasting room has been replaced by the a wine shop called the Russian River Wine Company and Clos du Bois has moved to the country; see the listing above. Also, White Oak may have moved into the Alexander Valley by the time you arrive; see below for the new address.

Coming into town from your Alexander Valley trek, you'll blend onto Healdsburg Avenue and encounter the nicely landscaped **Simi Winery** complex, on your right. Continue into Healdsburg to the Spanish colonial **Swenson Building** with its domed clock tower on your right, opposite Healdsburg Plaza. It contains the **Kendall-Jackson Tasting Room**, plus an assortment of boutiques and cafés.

From here, follow Plaza Street (along the edge of the plaza) two blocks to the **Russian River Wine Company** at 132 Plaza Street. It's not a winery but a fine wine shop featuring about 200 selections from 80 California wineries—often hard-to-find specialty items. "We taste over 2,000 premium wines to select the few that we offer in our shop," says wine broker George Bato. The shop is open daily 9 to 5 and the address is 132 Plaza St.; call (800) 477-0490 or (707) 433-0490.

Backtrack a block to Center Street, turn left and go two blocks south to **Windsor Vineyards** tasting room on Center just short of Mill Street. Then take three one-block turns—left onto Mill, right onto East and left onto Haydon. With luck, you'll wind up at **White Oak**, a downtown winery at Haydon and Fitch streets. (However, by the time you visit, it may have moved to a new location at 7505 Highway 128 between Sausal and Johnson's Alexander Valley wineries.)

That last paragraph can best be accomplished by walking. You can poke into the shops along the way.

Three other wineries, on the outer fringe of Russian River Valley, are near Healdsburg. Return to Healdsburg Avenue and persist south, ducking under the freeway a time or two, until your route becomes Old Redwood Highway. Just beyond town, you come to **Foppiano Wine Company** on your right; a short distance beyond are **Rodney Strong Vineyards** and **Piper Sonoma Cellars,** also on the right; the two wineries sit side by side among the vines.

Simi Winery • T GT ✕ 📦

☐ *16275 Healdsburg Ave., Healdsburg, CA 95448; (707) 433-6981. Daily 10 to 4:30; MC/VISA, AMEX, DISC. Most varieties tasted free; small charge for some reserve wines. Good gift shop selection. Guided tours daily at 11, 1 and 3. Redwood-shaded picnic areas.* ☐

Venerable Simi is an island of yesterday, surrounded—but not altered—by the swelling city of Healdsburg. Its massive rough-cut stone winery with three-foot-thick walls was built by Chinese laborers in 1890. More practiced Italian stonemasons later added a smoother section. A modern octagonal tasting room stands nearby. The park-like complex—even the parking lot—is carefully landscaped and shaded by redwoods. (If we had a category for most attractive winery carpark, Simi would win.)

The one-hour tour provides a look at modern winemaking in an ancient, pleasantly musty yet spotlessly clean environment. Wine ferments in glossy stainless steel and sleeps in six thousand barrels in a time-worn loft. The sight would send a Dominican monk into ecstasy.

Established in 1876 by Giuseppe and Pietro Simi, the winery was inherited by Giuseppe's daughter in 1904. In an era when women were expected to tend to the stove and their knitting, the remarkable Isobel Simi Haigh took charge. She ran the operation for 66 years, surviving Prohibition, Depression and male chauvinism. She sold the winery in 1969. It has since gone through several owners, finally becoming a part of France's Moet-Hennessy/Louis Vuitton conglomerate.

Tasting notes: Although it's one of northern Sonoma's largest wineries with an output of 140,000 cases, Simi focuses on a few select varietals. The whites we tasted—Semillon, Sauvignon Blanc, Chenin Blanc and Chardonnay—were properly lush and fruity. The sole red is Cabernet Sauvignon, not a big wine but full-flavored with soft tannins. Prices are moderate, ranging from $7 to $16. Vertical tastings of Chardonnay and Cabernet may be arranged for a small fee.

Vintners choice: "Chardonnay, Cabernet and Sauvignon Blanc," says the visitor center manager, a person of few words.

Kendall-Jackson Tasting Room • T 📦

☐ *337 Healdsburg Ave., Healdsburg, CA 95448; (707) 433-7102. Daily 10 to 5; MC/VISA. A downtown tasting room just off the plaza, with gifts and wine logo items. See the Edmeades Estate/Kendall-Jackson listing for Mendocino County in Chapter two, page 34.* ☐

Windsor Vineyards Tasting Room and Gift Shop • T 🎁

☐ *239 Center Street, Healdsburg, CA 95448; (707) 433-2822. Tasting Monday-Friday 10 to 5, weekends 10 to 6. Good selection of wine-related gift items.* ☐

Although Windsor has won its share of medals, it's noted mostly for its marketing gimmickry. The firm specializes in mail order catalog sales and personalized labeling. If you want to serve Fumé Blanc labeled "Bottoms up to Beverly and Bill" at your next wedding reception, this is the place.

Tasting notes: The list includes the usual premium varietals, including Chardonnay, Cabernet Sauvignon, Johannisberg Reisling, Merlot, Pinot Noir, Petit Sirah, Sauvignon Blanc and Zinfandel. The style is drink-it-now fruity with light wood and the wines have won a fair share of medals. They're available only at the tasting room or by mail order. Prices are rather moderate, ranging from around $6 to the early teens.

White Oak Vineyards & Winery • T CT

☐ *208 Haydon St., Healdsburg, CA 95448; (707) 433-8429. Open Friday, Saturday and Sunday from 10 to 4; MC/VISA. Most varieties tasted.* ☐

White Oak functions in a warehouse in the Healdsburg industrial area. The small combined tasting room and office occupies a small cottage nearby. Founded in 1981 by former fisherman and building contractor Bill Meyers, the winery draws from local hillside vineyards. (It was tentatively scheduled to moved to 7505 Highway 128 in 1995 or 1996, between Sausal and Johnson's Alexander Valley wineries.)

Tasting notes: Meyers' Zinfandel, Cabernet Sauvignon, Chardonnay. Chenin Blanc and Sauvignon Blanc are quite good, with strong varietal character. We particularly liked the Zin's nice berry-like flavor and subtle touch of wood; in fact, we bought a few for the cellar. Prices range from around $7 to the middle teens.

Vintner's choice: Among the winemakers favorites are Myers Chardonnay and Zinfandel, plus a "fabulous Sauvignon Blanc."

L. Foppiano Wine Co. • T CT ✗

☐ *12707 Old Redwood Highway (P.O. Box 606), Healdsburg, CA 95448; (707) 433-7272. Daily 10 to 4:30; MC/VISA, AMEX, DISC. Most varieties tasted. Some wine related gift items. Casual tours by appointment. Shaded picnic areas.* ☐

One of the county's pioneer wineries, the Foppiano facility looks its age, although modern equipment lurks beneath its weathered exterior. It was established by John Foppiano in 1896 and the family made jug wines for decades. Leaders of the third and fourth generations, both named Louis, have shifted the focus to premium varieties.

An unadorned, square-shouldered stucco building houses the century-old winery and a cottage-style hospitality center invites tasting. A few picnic tables are parked under shade trees around the farmyard.

Tasting notes: Although the winery is unpretentious, the wines are excellent. We encountered two outstanding reds: a lush, spicy Cabernet Sauvignon and a near-perfect Zinfandel. Other varieties offered under the family label are Sauvignon Blanc, Chardonnay and Petite Sirah, with prices from $7.50 to $10. Older vintages are available at predictably higher cost. Foppiano also markets honest, drinkable varietals under the Riverside Vineyards label; they're good buys at $5.75 to $6.75.

Vintners choice: The Foppianos have been making red wines for a century, explained our tasting room hostess, and they're particularly proud of the Petit Sirah and Zinfandel. "We're mostly a red wine winery."

Rodney Strong Vineyards • T CT ⚔

☐ *11455 Old Redwood Highway, Healdsburg, CA 95448; (707) 433-6511. Daily 10 to 5; major credit cards. Most varieties tasted. Some wine related gift items. Nice picnic area on "The Green," a lawn area near the vineyards; informal tours. The winery also hosts concerts during the summer; call for schedule and ticket information.* ☐

This is one of the area's more interesting architectural creations—an earth-hugging structure of laminated beams and textured concrete. Before entering the tasting room, take a left or right just inside the winery door and stroll around the suspended walkway. You'll get a bird's eye view of the operation, from fermentation tanks to huge oak casts for aging. The tasting room is cantilevered above it all.

Rodney Strong started in the wine business 30 years ago, peddling mail-order wines out of a tasting room in Tiburon. The operation expanded to an old winery in Windsor and has gone through assorted ownerships. In 1889 it was purchased by the Kleins, a three-generation California agricultural family. Many of its wine grapes are drawn from the original vineyards selected by Strong decades ago.

Tasting notes: The winery offers an interesting mix of wines, from slightly sweet Gewürztraminer (available only at the winery) to full-bodied Old Vines Zinfandel from a 90-year-old vineyard. The overall style is soft and fruity with low tannins. Prices range from $7 to the mid teens; more for the Alexander's Crown Cabernet and Reserve Cab.

Vintners choice: "Vineyard designated and estate bottled Sauvignon Blanc, Pinot Noir, Cabernet Sauvignon and Chardonnay," says the winery's Bill Holland.

Piper Sonoma Cellars • T & T$ GTA ⚔ 📷

☐ *11447 Old Redwood Hwy., Healdsburg, CA 95448; (707) 433-8843. Daily 10 to 5. Complimentary tasting or sparkling wine by the glass for $3.50 and $4; MC/VISA, AMEX. Good selection of giftwares; picnic terrace. Self-guided tours or conducted tours by appointment.* ☐

Piper Sonoma speaks of European elegance and properly so, since it's owned by Piper Heidsiek, the champagne subsidiary of France's Remy Martín. The winery and high-style tasting room are in a textured concrete structure fronted by a terrace, formal gardens and a lily pond. Artwork and fancy furnishings grace the hospitality center; a burgundy canopy accents the tasting bar.

Self-guiding tours of this modern facility take visitors along an elevated balcony for vistas of the fermentation room with its steel tank forest, barrel aging cellars, riddling racks and bottling line. Graphics in English and French describe what you're seeing

Piper Sonoma of course follows the traditional *méthode champenoise*, in which the champagne never leaves the original bottle until you drink it. (The slick brochure says "*méthode champenoise* process" which, any first year French student will tell you, is redundant.)

Tasting notes: Piper Sonoma produces three sparkling wines—brut, blanc de noirs and brut reserve. Gratis sips are offered our you can buy full servings in properly slim glasses. All are fine examples of the sparkling art: crisp and dry with a clean finish, yet with strong hints of the Chardonnay, Pinot Blanc and/or Pinot Noir that went into their making.

Dry Creek Valley

Dry Creek Valley is one of our favorite winetasting haunts. We challenge any wineland to match this pastorale. Vineyards carpet the narrow valley floor and ascend its benchlands. Live oak thickets crown rounded knolls and redwood groves are tucked into secret ravines. Ancient Zinfandel vines cover steep hillsides like knotted fists. Family farms with rusty pick-ups sitting out front share the valley with sleek new wineries built by urban millionaires who seek solace under a rural sun.

There's even a rustic Dry Creek country store to confirm the valley's rural heritage. Never mind that it sells *foi gras* and camembert in its deli.

The broad shoulders of Warm Springs Dam plug the upper end of the valley. Built in the mid-80s, the dam provides—ironically—a year-around trickle for the once seasonal Dry Creek. Since it's an earthen dam covered with grass, its dominance of the upper valley is subtle. The reservoir, Lake Sonoma, provides water sports, fishing, shoreside hiking, camping and picnicking.

The valley is noted for producing big, perfectly-balanced Zinfandel from vines predating Prohibition. Zin is the valley's most widely planted grape. The moderate ocean-tempered climate is ideal for Chardonnay, Pinot Noir and Cabernet Sauvignon as well.

DRY CREEK VALLEY WINERY TOUR • If you haven't visited the Dry Creek Valley recently, you'll discover several new wineries ranging from modest to stylishly elegant. The tour is rather complex because of the valley's winding roads, a couple of dead ends and scattered locations of wineries. They aren't far apart, but they're not in orderly rows. Dry Creek and West Dry Creek roads run parallel through the valley, linked by ladder rungs of crossroads.

Start just north of **Geyserville,** taking the Canyon Road exit from U.S. 101 west to long-established **Geyser Peak Winery,** within sight of the freeway. From Geyser Peak, follow the frontage road (Chianti Road) three miles to the new **Silver Oak Cellars**. Backtrack to the freeway interchange, turn right (west) onto Canyon Road and you soon encounter **J. Pedroncelli Winery** on the right. The route T-bones into Dry Creek Road just beyond; turn right, drive about half a mile and you'll see the impressive **Ferrari-Carano** facility, near the junction with Dutcher Creek Road.

Head northeast up Dutcher Creek Road a mile and a half to the new **J. Fritz Winery** at the end of a steep wooded lane. Return to Dry Creek Road and follow it north toward Warm Springs Dam to **Lake Sonoma Winery,** up a lane to your right. Backtrack on Dry Creek to Yoakim Bridge Road (just short of Canyon Road), turn right and cross over to West Dry Creek Road. Go right again and follow this scenically twisting road to **Preston Vineyards and Winery.** Next, head south on West Dry Creek Road to the new **Quivira Vineyards** on the left and **A. Rafanelli** on the right. Turn left (east) onto Lambert Bridge Road and you soon see **Dry Creek Vineyard** on the right and Robert Stemmler Winery—now open by appointment only—on the left.

Just beyond, at Lambert Bridge and Dry Creek Road, you'll encounter **Dry Creek General Store.** It comprises the total "town" of Dry Creek, claiming a population of four. The inviting old store offers a deli, local wine selections and essentials such as food, clothing and fishing worms. Local boys sip their Coors at a tiny bar in a corner of the store. Picnic tables out front encourage visitors to linger. Since most people ask, that palatial mansion on the hill behind the store is not the residence of a wine baron. It was built by an area doctor.

Continue south a short distance to Lytton Springs Road, turn left and climb rolling hills to **Mazzocco Vineyards** and **Ridge/Lytton Springs Winery,** both on the right. Now, you must backtrack a bit. Return to Dry Creek Road, go back to the general store and turn left onto Lambert Bridge Road, return to West Dry Creek Road and turn left. Are we lost yet?

Head south on West Dry Creek over gently rumpled foothills to **Lambert Bridge Vineyards** and **Bellerose Vineyard,** both on the right. West Dry Creek is an exceptionally scenic route, lined with oak thickets, occasional redwoods, vineyards and small family farms.

Just below Bellerose, West Dry Creek bumps into Westside Road near the bold arched gateway to Madrona Manor. Once the home of wealthy pioneer John Alexander Paxton, it's now an opulent inn and restaurant. Turn left onto Westside Road, heading east toward Healdsburg. Just short of the freeway, go right onto Kinley Drive then right again on Magnolia and follow it a short distance to **Alderbrook Winery.**

Geyser Peak Winery • T ✕ 🏠

☐ *22281 Chianti Rd., Geyserville, CA 95441; 857-9463. Daily 10 to 5; MC/VISA. Most varieties tasted. Extensive gift selection; covered picnic area.* ☐

The large Geyser Peak complex sits at the gateway to Dry Creek Valley although the winery itself is on the Alexander Valley side. It's a comely facility with landscaped grounds, terraced patios and a stone-faced ivy-covered winery built against a wooded hillside. It's difficult to believe that freeway traffic is but an exhaust belch away.

Geyser Peak traces its heritage back to 1880, when it was established by pioneer Sonoma County winemaker Augustus Quitzow. Part of an old wooden structure still survives from those days. The winery has gone through a variety of proprietors through the decades, alternately producing bulk wine, jug wines, varietals and brandy. Major expansion came after Schlitz Brewery bought the facility in 1972. Under Schlitz, the Summit brand wine-in-a-box was born, although the label has since been sold to another winery. Schlitz was purchased by in 1982 by Stroh's Brewing, which had no interest in winemaking so the winery was sold to the Henry Trione family of Santa Rosa.

Tasting comments: Among the interesting items we sipped were a "Semchard" (ugly name, but nice blend of Semillon and Chardonnay), a soft and gentle Merlot and a rich yet soft Reserve Syrah. Wine prices are moderate, ranging to the middle teens, with a special Meritage selling for $25.

Vintners choice: "Our limited (estate-bottled) reserve Chardonnay and Cabernet Sauvignon and Meritage," says spokeswoman Ann Rizzo.

Silver Oak Cellars • T$ GTA

☐ *24625 Chianti Rd., Geyserville, CA 95448; (707) 857-3562. Monday-Friday 9 to 4:30, Saturday 10 to 4:30, closed Sunday; MC/VISA. Tasting for a*

$5 fee, which applies toward wine purchase. A few wine logo items. Tours by appointment weekdays at 1:30. ☐

The Napa Valley's master of Cabernet, Justin Meyer, expanded to northern Sonoma County with the purchase of the former Lyeth Winery in 1992. Although his first winery was in the Napa Valley, he has always used Alexander Valley grapes. This new winery acquisition, a Normandy style gray and white structure, sits elegantly behind wrought iron gates, and the classic look continues inside. The original Silver Oak was founded by Meyer and Ray Duncan in the Napa Valley in 1972 and that operation continues to thrive; see listing in Chapter five. The northern Sonoma extension is primarily a production facility for Silver Oak's Alexander Valley appellation. Incidentally, Meyer also is the author of one of our favorite books about the grape, *Plain Talk About Fine Wine.*

Tasting notes: Silver Oak produces only 100 percent varietal Cabernet Sauvignon, drawing grapes from the Alexander Valley and Napa Valley. They're aged in American oak instead of the classic French, giving them a distinct spicy-soft finish. The Alexander Valley Cabernet, grown and produced here, is excellent—gently complex and piquant with a light tannic finish. None are released until they have matured for several years. Prepare for sticker shock: Silver Oak's wines are in the $32 range and up. The array of accolades earned by Silver Oak suggests that they're worth the price.

J. Pedroncelli Winery • T GTA ✗

☐ *1220 Canyon Road, Geyserville, CA 95441; (707) 857-3531. Daily 10 to 5; MC/VISA, AMEX. Most varieties tasted. A few wine logo gift items; small deck with picnic tables. Guided tours by reservation.* ☐

Founded during Prohibition by John Pedroncelli, the winery has grown considerably under his sons' guidance. It now turns out about 100,000 cases annually. Jim handles much of the business and John is the primary winemaker.

We've watched the Pedroncelli complex grow for a quarter of a century. The tasting room, once a counter in a cinderblock storage building, is now an attractive, airy space with high ceilings and a curving bar. Picnic tables near the vineyards encourage visitors to linger in this bucolic setting. It's all part of a pleasing, ranch-style complex of redwood buildings cradled among vine and oak-thatched hills between the Alexander and Dry Creek valleys.

Tasting notes: The Pedroncellis like their whites crisp and lean, and it was evident in their spicy Chardonnay and fruity Chenin Blanc. The Pinot Noir was soft and berry-like and a Cabernet Reserve was outstanding—big, powerful and complex. The Zinfandel was predictably excellent; *The Wine Spectator* has rated it a best buy for under $10 a bottle. Overall, prices range from $6 to $10; a few reserves go to the mid teens.

Vintners Choice: "Zinfandel, which we've been making for 40 years," says third-generation Julie Pedroncelli. "We can draw from excellent Dry Creek Valley grapes."

Ferrari-Carano Vineyards and Winery • T GTA 📦

☐ *8761 Dry Creek Rd., Healdsburg, CA 95448; (707) 433-6700. Daily 10 to 5; MC/VISA, AMEX. Selected wines tasted. Tasteful line of giftwares and clothing. Tours by appointment.* ☐

From old family tradition we move to new opulence. Ferrari-Carano is a striking blend of manor house, castle and leading edge winery. The large facility, fronted by a formal entryway and rimmed by billiard-green lawns, is the most palatial of the Dry Creek operations. Villa Fiore, *House of Flowers,* the new hospitality center, is quite imposing—20,000 square feet of old world Italian elegance. It's surrounded by five acres of theme gardens.

All this largess comes from the coffers of Don and Rhonda Carano, owners of the El Dorado Hotel and Casino in Reno. The double-jointed winery name pays homage to Rhonda's grandmother, who inspired her interest in wine and food.

Tasting notes: The Ferrari-Carano roster is brief but first rate—Fumé Blanc, Chardonnay, Merlot, Cabernet and a rich late harvest Sauvignon Blanc. Premium varietals start around $10 and travel to the middle teens; reserve selections go higher.

J. Fritz Winery • T GTA ✕

☐ 24691 Dutcher Creek Rd., Cloverdale, CA 95425; (707) 894-3389. Daily 10:30 to 4:30; MC/VISA. Most varieties tasted. Nice selection of wine oriented giftwares; picnic area; tours by appointment. ☐

Bunkered rather dramatically into a wooded hillside, this is one of the area's more appealing wineries. Terraced landscaping steps up to a white stucco facility with tall Spanish arch windows. Most of the three-tiered winery is built into the earth and it's surrounded by redwoods instead of vines. The tasting room is dramatically simple, with a high curved ceiling and warmed—when needed—by a friendly Franklin stove. When you enter, say hello to Fritzie the cat, who'll likely be playing with a wine cork. Barbara and Jay Fritz started their winery in 1979, with a focus on conservation, winemaking technology and informality.

"J. Fritz Winery does not belong to the la-de-da school of winemaking. We believe that fine wine discoveries are about pleasure, not intimidation." We don't normally quote from brochures, but we like the Fritz attitude.

Tasting notes: An outstanding Zinfandel caught our attention—light and peppery with a great raspberry taste. Other worthies were a light Chardonnay with a nice hint of acid, crisp and fruity Pinot Blanc wine called Melòn, and a soft and dry Sauvignon Blanc. Prices range from $8 to $13.50; a fine barrel select Chardonnay goes for $18.

Vintners choice: "Sauvignon Blanc and Zinfandel," says the winery's Denise Gill. "Dry Creek Valley has a perfect climate for these."

Lake Sonoma Winery • T CT ✕ 📷

☐ 9990 Dry Creek Rd., Geyserville, CA 95441; (707) 431-1550. Daily 10 to 5. Most varieties tasted; MC/VISA. Wine oriented collectibles and deli with picnic fare and specialty food items. Shaded picnic areas; informal tours of the winery. ☐

A gravel road pitches steeply upward through hillside vineyards to this small and pleasant family winery, completed in 1990. It's the closest winery to Warm Springs Dam. The view of the dam and the valley from the cheerful, airy tasting room and its wraparound balcony is impressive. Founders Bob and Mary Lou Polson and their son Don chose this site for the view, hoping to lure folks headed for the Lake Sonoma Recreation Area.

It's a fine picnic spot, and the Polsons offer all the essentials from their tasting room deli, including bread baked fresh daily.

Unlike some high rollers who've built glitzy wineries in the area, the Polsons are ordinary working folk. They struggled for two decades to make their

A ROSÉ BY ANY OTHER NAME?

Rosé is no longer the Rodney Dangerfield of American wines. For years, many wine enthusiasts—including this one—regarded pink wine as a poor compromise between red and white. Marketing strategies by some firms suggested that rosé "goes with anything," which didn't help its status. Diners intimidated by long wine lists would seek refuge in rosé.

Traditionally, most pink wine was made from Grenache, a sweet, high-yield grape from southern France. Rosé originated there and the word is French for "pink." You probably know that it's made from red grapes by withdrawing the skins early during fermentation. Since most of the color and body come from the skins, this produces a light, fruity wine. (On rare occasion, it's made by blending red and white wine.) France has made some great rosés but most of that produced in California was considered rather ordinary.

Then in 1958, Sonoma County's Pedroncelli family bottled and marketed a rosé made from high-quality Zinfandel grapes, labeling it "Zin Rosé." The raspberry-like complexity of Zinfandel produced a much more pleasing pink wine, and it began winning awards. Others followed, with names like Rosé of Cabernet, Rouge Noir and the notorious "white Zinfandel" (which is actually pink). August Sebastiani produced a pink Gewürztraminer and called it Eye of the Swan.

In the 1970s, wine writer Jerry Mead coined the term "blush wine" to describe a premium rosé produced at northern Sonoma's Mill Creek Vineyards, and the floodgates were opened.

Soon, Zinfandel Blush, Cabernet Blush, Pinot Blush and white Zinfandel were among America's best-selling wines. Pink Zin led the pack, particularly after Sutter Home's Bob Trinchero got into the act. Buying up every loose grape he could find and mass producing white Zin, he practically cornered that market. By the early 1990s, he was selling 2.5 million cases of his white Zinfandel, catapulting Sutter Home from one of Napa Valley's smallest wineries to one of its largest. Pink wine now comprises 38 percent of America's wine sales, and at least half of that is white Zin.

Pedroncelli's Zin Rosé is still an excellent wine, and it's still winning awards. It and other "blush" wines continue to be leading sellers. Finally, California's rosés are getting some respect.

hillside dream come true. Most of their output of about 3,000 cases a year is sold at the winery and through local outlets.

Tasting notes: Winemaker Don Polson's small list consists of Merlot, Zinfandel and Cinsault, a grape from France's Rhône Valley. His Zinfandel—we tasted two vintages—were fruity and soft with a touch of tannin. Prices range from $6 to the mid teens. In addition to tasting, one can buy most of their wines by the glass.

Vintners choice: "Our Dry Creek Valley Zinfandel is full flavored and very berry-like," says Don.

Preston Vineyards and Winery • T ✕ 📦

◻ *9282 West Dry Creek Rd., Healdsburg, CA 95448; (707) 433-3372. Daily 11 to 4:30; MC/VISA. Most varieties tasted. Wine logo items and books; picnic area under an arbor.* ◻

How could we not like a winery that greets you with a neon "Drink Zin" sign. The place is simple and the setting is pleasingly woodsy—a multi-gabled barn beside a creek, with polished wooden floors, drop lamps and a small counter in the tasting room. Although it's built into the main winery building, the tasting room has a pleasant cottage effect, complete with a brick floored porch. Check about the grounds and you'll see a Spanish style *forno* outdoor oven and a bocce ball court. This small and informal winery, established by Lou and Susan Preston, is that kind of place.

Tasting notes: The list contains some interesting wines, such as Viognier, Marsanne and *Faux* (a red Rhône blend), plus tasty versions of Chenin Blanc, Gamay Beaujolais, Barbera, Zinfandel, Cabernet Sauvignon and Syrah. On the dessert side resides Muscat Brûlé and Moscato Curioso. The Chenin Blanc and its close cousin Cuvée de Fumé were soft and spicy with a crisp edge. Most of the reds were rather herbal, a pleasant effect. The Barbera had a nice berry taste and the Cabernet was light, yet with a proper chili pepper nip.

Quivira Vineyards • T GTA ✕ 📦

◻ *4900 W. Dry Creek Rd., Healdsburg, CA 95448; (800) 292-8339 or (707) 431-8333. Daily 10 to 4:30; MC/VISA. Most varieties tasted for no fee, and wine may be purchased by the glass. Wine-related gift items; picnic arbor. Informal peeks into the winery or tours by appointment.* ◻

Housed in an appealing ivy-entwined modern barn, Quivira presents a pleasantly bucolic picture, with picnic tables under olive trees and a wisteria-entwined arbor out front. The winery was established in 1987 by Holly and Henry Wendt, specializing in a small list of estate grown wines. There's a legend behind the winery's name. In 1540, 30-year-old Francisco Vásquez de Coronado was sent from Mexico City into the American southwest in search of the seven golden cities of Cíbola. He found no gold and he was further led astray by a clever Indian who told him of a fabulous city of Quivira, far to the north. It was a ploy to divert Coronado from raiding his village. Returning to Mexico frustrated and with no riches, he nevertheless named the new country he'd explored Quivira.

Tasting notes: The Wendt's brief list won't lead wine tasters astray. Sauvignon Blanc, both regular and reserve, are nicely complex with lots of fruit. The Zinfandel, a frequent medal winner, is excellent, with plenty of raspberry taste and a nip of tannin. Merlot, with a touch of Cabernet, is soft with gentle tannins. The Wendts offer a couple of tasty proprietary wines. Dry Creek Cuvée is a blend of Greenish, Mourvèdre and Syrah, with little Zin; Cabernet Cuvée is a typical Bordeaux blend of Cabernet Sauvignon, Cabernet Franc and Merlot. Prices range from $9.50 to the middle teens.

"We are known for Zinfandel, Sauvignon Blanc and other red wines," reports Jan Mettler.

A. Rafanelli Winery • T

◻ *4685 West Dry Creek Rd., Healdsburg, CA 95448; (707) 433-1385. Daily 10 to 4 in summer; in winter by appointment. No credit cards. All varieties tasted. Guided tours by appointment.* ◻

This small, attractive barnboard style winery is tucked into a wooded grove, reached by a narrow lane framed in a split-rail fence. Trees and landscaping accent the setting. The winery was established three generations ago by the Rafanelli family and is currently operated by David and his wife Patty.

Tasting notes: The tasting ritual is simple and brief, since this 8,000-case winery produces only two varietals—Zinfandel and Cabernet. Both are palate-pleasers, exhibiting strong varietal character. Prices are $12.75 for the Zin and $16.75 for the Cab.

Dry Creek Vineyard • T ✗

☐ 3770 Lambert Bridge Rd. (P.O. Box T), Healdsburg, CA 95448; (707) 433-1000. Daily 10:30 to 4:30; MC/VISA. Most varieties tasted. A few wine related gift items; picnic area on a lawn near the tasting room. ☐

David Stare is one of Dry Creek's first new generation vintners, arriving in 1972. For some reason, my clearest recollection of Dave—from an early interview—was that he was California's first vintner to get personalized license plate. Naturally, it read: WINERY. It's still on one of the pickups.

He's better known as a producer of consistent award-winning wines, notably Fumé Blanc and Zinfandel. Through the years, he has built his winery's capacity to 100,000 cases. The tasting room is in a nice setting—a sturdy structure suggestive of a manor house, climbing with ivy and rimmed by old trees and new lawns.

Tasting notes: Although we're red wine fans and this is red wine country, we were impressed with Dry Creek's crisp, fruity and perfectly balanced Chenin Blanc and Fumé Blanc. A nutty flavored reserve Chardonnay was excellent as well; one of the valley's best. A classic Cabernet Sauvignon with a proper chili pepper nose, Cabernet Franc, Zinfandel and red Meritage round out Dave's list. Reserve Zinfandel and Cabernets are released periodically. Prices range from $7 to the early twenties.

Vintners choice: "Our Fumé Blanc is considered the benchmark of this variety," says winemaker Larry Levin. "We've developed a reputation for Dry Creek Valley appellation Zinfandel, reserve Chardonnay and Meritage, as well."

Mazzocco Vineyards • T ✗

☐ 1400 Lytton Springs Road, Healdsburg, CA 95448; (707) 431-8159. Daily 10 to 4:30; MC/VISA. Most varieties tasted. Small number of wine related items. Tables on balcony overlooking airport. ☐

Mazzocco's location on a vineyard slope overlooking the Healdsburg Airport is no accident. Its founder, Dr. Thomas Mazzocco of Van Nuys, Calif., is a private pilot. He selected this spot for a quick commute when he built the winery in 1985. Visitors to the small facility can enjoy the view of vines and planes from a picnic deck outside the cottage-style tasting room.

Tasting notes: The hilly slopes along Lytton Springs Road are Zinfandel country. Thousands of vines—some a century old—line this pleasantly winding route. So it's no surprise that Mazzocco produces excellent full-bodied Zins. Two to three varieties are generally available, although the supply is sometimes exhausted. Merlot and Cabernet Franc give a Mazzocco's Cabernets a Bordeaux style. We found them to be soft and lush yet full flavored. Other choices include Cabernet, Merlot, Chardonnay and Matrix, a Meritage blend of Cabernet, Merlot, Cabernet Franc, Petit Verdot and Malbec. Prices range from $12 to $20.

Vintners choice: "We're famous for the big, hearty style of our Zinfandel," said a voice from the winery.

Ridge/Lytton Springs Winery • T ✗

☐ *650 Lytton Springs Rd., Healdsburg, CA 95448; (707) 433-7721. Daily 10 to 4; MC/VISA. A few wine related items; some picnic tables near the winery.* ☐

This one of the more appealing of northern Sonoma County's small wineries. The hillside setting is impressive, amidst ancient Zinfandels with trunks the size of young oaks. The tasting room, a counter at the rear of the winery, is at the same time funky and classy. It's set amidst barrels and tanks, with a Persian rug on the floor. There is an implied invitation to relax and linger here.

Established in 1977 as Lytton Springs Winery, the facility recently became part of Ridge Vineyards of Santa Clara County's Montebello Ridge, another winery famous for its Zins. This new northern extension of Ridge draws from the surrounding ancient vines to produce some of the finest Zinfandels in California.

Tasting notes: These are *big* Zins—lush, complex, full of berries, with a good tannin finish. Reach for your checkbook or VISA if you're a Zin lover, for prices range from $15 to $35. Bear in mind that the yield from ancient vines is very low, and the wine is worth it. Also on the list are a private reserve Cabernet at $18 and a Cab-Merlot-Zin blend at $10.

Vintners choice: "We specialize in hearty red wines; big in style, forward, fruity and with jammy textures," says a winery voice.

Lambert Bridge Vineyards • T GTA ✗

☐ *4085 W. Dry Creek Rd., Healdsburg, CA 95448; (800) 634-2680 or (707) 433-5855. Daily 10 to 5; major credit cards. Select wines tasted. Gazebo and picnic area overlooking Dry Creek Valley. A few wine related items; tours by appointment.* ☐

Perched in a wooden glen above scenic Dry Creek Valley, Lambert Bridge is one of the area's more attractive small wineries. It's in a shingle-sided redwood structure accented by a wisteria trellis. The tasting room, with an interesting counter made of oak barrel staves, is within the working winery, surrounded by tiered barrels. A fireplace occupies one end of the structure.

Tasting notes: Lambert's list is short and first rate. Chardonnay was excellent, full and spicy with oak accents from extended barrel aging. The Merlot and Cabernet Sauvignon are soft and full flavored, with a tannin finish that will stand up to aging. Several wines, including Fumé, Zinfandel and Pinot Noir, are available only at the winery. Prices range from $7 to $16.

Vintners choice: "Chardonnay is what we're best known for, although our Cabernet Sauvignon has been getting some great reviews lately," said sales manager Adam Lee.

Bellerose Vineyard • T ✗

☐ *435 W. Dry Creek Rd., Healdsburg, CA 95448; (707) 433-1637. Daily 11 to 4:30; MC/VISA, DISC. Most varieties tasted. Picnic area. Group tours only, by appointment.* ☐

We've found one of Dry Creek Valley's most earthy winery and simplest tasting rooms here. Bucolic, organic Bellerose more resembles an old farmyard than a modern winery. There's even a rusting piece of farm equipment or two, as if to prove the point.

The winery was started in 1978 by Charles and Nancy Richard, who originally worked a pair of draft horses named Rowdy and Curly. The critters, who contributed generously to the organic concept, were honored with their portraits on Bellerose' Workhorse Red Cabernet Sauvignon. Visitors sip wines in a tasting room that consists of a basic plank counter, not far from a cluttered office desk.

Tasting notes: Cuvée Bellerose, a Cabernet Sauvignon-Merlot blend done in the Bordeaux style, is an excellent, outspoken wine that will improve with age. Merlot and a barrel fermented Sauvignon Blanc finish off the short list. Prices range from $9 through the teens and beyond for some of the reserves.

Alderbrook Winery • T GTA ✕

◻ *2306 Magnolia Dr., Healdsburg, CA 95448; (707) 433-9154. Daily 10 to 5; MC/VISA. Most varieties tasted. Wine related gift items; picnic tables overlooking the vineyards. Guided tours by appointment.* ◻

Although close to the freeway, Alderbrook is sheltered by vineyards and it's attractive within. Lots of windows and white painted knotty pine accent the cheerful, open tasting room, housed in a primly attractive, gray and white-trimmed bungalow. The nicely landscaped grounds are popular for picnicking.

The winery itself is housed in a refurbished 80-year-old redwood barn nearby. The facility was started in 1981 by a partnership of Mark Rafanelli, John Clark and Philip Staley. It was purchased recently by George Gillemot of Glenbrook, Nevada.

Tasting notes: The Alderbook focus, unusual for Dry Creek but tasty in the result, is white wines. The Sauvignon Blanc and Semillon were lush and fruity, low in acid but with a pleasant finish. The Chardonnay also was gentle on the acid, while full flavored and spicy. Prices are moderate, from $7.50 to $10.

Vintners choice: "We're best known for our Semillon and Chardonnay," says the winery's Kathleen Mooney.

Russian River Valley

The Russian River flows the length of northern Sonoma County, passing through the Alexander Valley before reaching the Russian River Valley. However, the Russian River appellation refers specifically to the lower part of the stream, from the point where it's joined by Dry Creek.

Initially, the terrain differences are subtle, and the lower Russian River Valley rivals Dry Creek in natural beauty. Farther west, the river swings away from the vineyards. It flows through an old fashioned riverbank resort area that has been popular since the 1920s.

Russian River vineyards occur in two distinct areas. The first group is clustered in rolling hills along Westside Road between Healdsburg and Rio Nido. The second gathering is south of the river, in a mix of farmlands and evergreen clusters. Both areas are accented here and there by redwoods. As in Dry Creek Valley, gentle and forest-clad mountains are never far away and side roads invite wandering into concealed canyons.

One side trip in this area is particularly inviting. From Westside Road near Hop Kiln Winery, turn right onto Sweetwater Springs Road. Follow its winding course uphill, past a cheerful creek, into darkened redwood groves, through the tiny old town of Sweetwater Springs and up to a high point of-

Ancient vines and an old farm house create a pastoral scene along Westside Road in the Russian River Valley.

fering views of half the county. Staying on its corkscrew course, you'll emerge below the redwood groves and hiking trails of Austin Creek State Recreation Area.

RUSSIAN RIVER WINERY TOUR ● From Alderbrook Winery, where you've just finished a final sip of Semillon, retrace your route southwest along Westside Road. Or retire for the night in next-door **Healdsburg** and start afresh tomorrow.

Your first winery encounter will be **Mill Creek** on the right. It's technically in the Dry Creek Valley, but for tour purposes, we're including it with other Westside Road vintners. From there, you'll hit a string of wineries, beginning with the new **Armida**, a short distance beyond Mill Creek and up a hill to your right. Continuing on Westside Road, you'll encounter **Belvedere** on the right, then **Hop Kiln** and next-door **Rochioli**, both on the left, **Davis Bynum** on the right and finally, tiny **Porter Creek,** a short distance up a side road on the right.

As Westside Road blends into River Road, continue west to the baronial wine estate of **Korbel**. Then back-track on River Road for about two and a half miles and turn right onto Martinelli Road. Cross the Russian River, wind through a mix of thick woods and vineyards for a couple of miles until you hit the Gravenstein Highway (Route 116). Go left and follow it briefly to Forestville. About half a mile beyond the tiny town, you'll see **Topolos at Russian River** on the right.

Pay attention from this point, because it gets complicated. Interesting wineries are scattered along a webwork of farm roads in this flatter part of the valley. Continuing southeast from Topolos on Highway 116, turn right into **Kozlowski Farms** at 5566 Gravenstein Highway. It's not a winery but a farm foods outlet specializing in organically produced jams, sauces, chutneys, relishes, homemade pies and other goodies. Dozens of items are available for tasting, and the place has a picnic area. The stuff isn't cheap, but it's excellent. Hours are 9 to 5 daily.

Just beyond Kozlowski, turn left onto Guerneville Road and you'll find **Dehlinger Winery** at Guerneville and Vine Hill roads. Follow Guerneville to Olivet Road, turn left and drive a short distance to **De Loach Vineyards** which is on your left. Now, backtrack on Guerneville Road, turn right onto Laguna Road and follow it to **Martini & Prati,** cresting a hill on the left, and marked by a tall water tower.

You lost yet? Continue on Laguna Road for about a mile and then—at a T-intersection of sorts—swing to the right, which puts you at a stop sign at River Road. Cross River Road onto Trenton-Healdsburg Road and continue half a mile to **Mark West Vineyards**, on your left.

Now, it gets easier. Return to River Road, turn left and follow it some miles to **Martinelli Ranch** on your right. It's both a winery and a farm products outlet, specializing in apples and apple products, jams, dried fruits and nuts. It offers samples of fruit and specialty foods, as well as wine.

Next door is **Z Moore Winery,** also on the right. Now you're approaching the freeway. Before surrendering to civilization's traffic, turn left onto Fulton Road and follow it to the glamorous **Château De Baun,** one of the county's most opulent wineries.

Mill Creek Vineyards • T ✕

☐ *1401 Westside Rd. (P.O. Box 758), Healdsburg, CA 95448; (707) 433-5098. Daily noon to 4:30; MC/VISA. Most varieties tasted. A few wine related items; picnic area in a grove above the tasting room.* ☐

The water wheel on Mill Creek's tasting room, useful only as an ornament, appears to have earned landmark status. It was featured on the 1991 cover of *The Californias,* the state's tourist promotion magazine. The simple tasting room—with wheel attached—*does* look convincingly rustic, although it was built in the 1970s.

The small winery is owned by the Kreck family; its members built much of the tasting room and winery by hand, using logs from their property. It sits among hillside vineyards above Westside Road.

Tasting notes: If you're attracted by the ornamental water wheel, you may stay for the wines, which we found to be very good, and fair priced. The Chardonnay was complex and spicy with gentle acid. A Cabernet Sauvignon was soft and ready to drink, with a nice chili pepper nose and herbal flavor. The Krecks also produce an excellent Cabernet Blush (winner of a dozen medals in 1990) and a late harvest Sauvignon Blanc that's deliciously sweet without being cloying. Zinfandel, Merlot and other premiums also appear on their list. Prices range from $6.75 to $10.

Their Cabernet rosé, incidentally, is part of vineland history. It was this wine, according to Vera Kreck, upon which wine writer Jerry Mead first bestowed the term "blush." (See box on page 63.)

Vintners Choice: "Our Merlot was served in the White House and we've been famous for it ever since," Vera reported proudly.

Armida • T CT GTA ✕

◻ *2201 Westside Rd., Healdsburg, CA 95448; (707) 433-2222. Daily 11 to 4; MC/VISA. Most varieties tasted; a few wine logo gift items. Nice picnic deck overlooking the valley.* ◻

Three eye-catching geodesic domes on the wooded brow of a hill mark one of the Russian River Valley's newest wineries. Founder Bob Armida isn't new to the wine industry, however. An executive with E.F Hutton, he purchased some Russian River vineyards in 1979, with an eye on early retirement and a second career as a vintner. Going back further, he spent summers in this area with his Italian grandparents, who settled here in 1906. He and his wife Rita started Armida—named for his grandmother—when he purchased a defunct winery in 1989.

However, he didn't "go public" with his tasting room until mid-1994. A simple space with atrium ceilings and a tile floor, the tasting room's most impressive feature is its picture window views of the Russian River and Dry Creek valleys. The looks gets better when visitors adjourn to a picnic deck above a pond.

Tasting notes: Since all Armida wines are estate bottled, Armida and his winemaker Frank Churchill can control the product from start to finish. They have won an impressive array of awards. Chardonnays we tasted were excellent—full-mouthed, nutty and lush. A Pinot Noir was light and yet full flavored with a hint of tannin, and a Merlot was richly mellow, with a good berry flavor and—again—that light tannin finish. Prices range from $11 to $17.50.

Vintners choice: "My favorite wine?" Bob grins. "It depends on what I'm eating. Chardonnay is our most popular."

Belvedere Winery • T ✕ 👜

◻ *4035 Westside Rd., Healdsburg, CA 95448; (707) 433-8236. Daily 10 to 4:30; MC/VISA. All varieties available for tasting (limit of four samples). Nice selection of wine related gift items and works by local artists; picnic area.* ◻

Belvedere is a comely winery in a nice locale, set amongst hillside vineyards. A short drive up a gravel lane takes you to a pair of neat wooden buildings, carefully set into the sloping landscape. Lawns and blooming flowers give the place a park-like quality. Honeysuckle droops from a porch overhanging the tasting room.

Winery founder Peter Friedman selects grapes from a variety of county vineyards to produce his reserve wines, which are sometimes issued with thematic labels. For instance, proceeds from his recent "Gifts of the Land Series," bearing wildlife labels done by noted artist Rod Frederick, went to conservation causes. Despite its prim, compact look, this is not a small operation. Belvedere produces half a million cases a year.

Tasting notes: Belvedere's reserve list carries four wines just over $10—a fruity, crisp Chardonnay; a spicy, nicely acidic Merlot; a full-bodied

Cabernet with a gentle tannin finish; and a rich, late harvest Muscat Canelli. The "Discovery" wines also are excellent buys, ranging from $4 to $6.50. That series includes Chardonnay, Sauvignon Blanc, Cabernet Sauvignon, white Zinfandel and a jug white and red.

Vintners choice: "Reserve Russian River Valley Chardonnay and Robert Young Alexander Valley Merlot," says the winery's La Vonne Holmes.

Hop Kiln Winery at Griffin Vineyards • T CT ✕

☐ 6050 Westside Rd., Healdsburg, CA 95448; (707) 433-6491. Daily 10 to 5; MC/VISA, AMEX. Most varieties tasted. Some wine related gift items; art exhibits. Picnic tables under sheltering fig tree, others near a pond. ☐

After visiting a pretend water wheel, we go to a real hop kiln—at least a former one. Dr. L. Martin Griffin succeeded in preserving the esthetics of a century-old hop dryer when he converted it into a winery in the 1970s. Some of the original equipment is intact and the tasting room is fashioned of aged wood, in keeping with the antiquity of the place. His triple towered Hop Kiln is a registered historical landmark. Adorned with the works of local artists, it occupies a mezzanine above the winery. A tour thus consists of walking to a railing and peering down at stainless steel vats and wooden barrels. The grounds are casual, pleasant and bucolic, with trellised gates, informal landscaping and a pond where waterfowl like to hang out.

Tasting notes: The list is surprisingly long for a winery that issues only 10,000 cases a year, but Marty Griffin likes to work with small lots. His Gewürztraminer was the best we tasted in the county, and the Zinfandel was full, complex and acidic, yet comfortably soft. A Petite Sirah was lush with a nice berry-acid finish. Others on the list are white Zinfandel, Chardonnay, Johannisberg Riesling, a fruity white called A Thousand Flowers, Cabernet Sauvignon and a good jug red. Prices are moderate, ranging from $7.50 to the mid teens.

Vintners Choice: "Zinfandel, Marty Griffin's Big Red, Gewürztraminer," said Jo Anne Strobl. "Our red wines are known for being robust and fruity."

J. Rochioli Vineyard and Winery • T GTA ✕

☐ 6192 Westside Rd., Healdsburg, CA 95448; (707) 433-2305. Daily 10 to 5; MC/VISA, AMEX. Selected wines tasted. Shaded picnic area overlooking the vineyards. Tours for small groups by appointment. ☐

Next door to Hop Kiln, Rochioli has the look of comfortable rural prosperity. Passing through a stone gate, you enter a tidy farm complex shaded by ancient trees and accented by gardens. A trim little tasting room overlooking the vines is brightened by art and photo exhibits. Picnic tables occupy a vineyard-view patio. This estate winery, producing about 70,000 case a year, has been owned by the Rochioli family since the end of Prohibition.

Tasting notes: We felt that some Rochioli's least expensive wines were their best—Gewürztraminer and Sauvignon Blanc at $8 and $10 respectively. Others on the list are noteworthy, particularly a lush Chardonnay and a soft, full flavored estate Pinot Noir. Prices range into the high teens.

Vintners choice: "We're known for our Chardonnay and Pinot Noir," said Theresa Rochioli. "We have fine soils and micro-climates that bring out the best flavors in these grapes."

Davis Bynum Winery • T CT ✕

☐ 8075 Westside Rd., Healdsburg, CA 95448; (707) 433-5852. Daily 10 to 5; MC/VISA. Most varieties tasted free; small fee for some limited release wines.

ZINFANDEL: A VINE WITHOUT A COUNTRY?

Imagine this: California wine pioneer Agoston Haraszthy eagerly sorts through the latest batch of grape cuttings he'd shipped from Europe. He picks up a bundle of slips and squints at them curiously.

"Hmmm, can't read the label...all smudged. Must've gotten wet in the hold of the ship." He ponders for a moment, then says: "I think I'll call it 'Zinfandel.' That's a nice European-sounding name."

Some historians say Haraszthy introduced California's most widely planted premium red. They claim that it arrived, fuzzy label and all, with thousands of cuttings he shipped from Europe during the 1860s.

New research has defrocked that theory. Author David Darlington devoted an entire book, **Angels' Visits**, to Zinfandel and its origins. He points out that it was being grown as a table grape in New England in the 1830s, before Haraszthy ever touched American soil.

What, then, *is* the source of the so-called mystery grape? Like the best of mysteries, this one may never be solved. Researchers find no reference to the word "zinfandel" in European documents. However a clonal copy, *Primitivo*, was discovered in southern Italy in 1967 by plant pathologist Austin Goheen of the U.S. Department of Agriculture. Lab tests proved that the Primitivo is indeed a twin to our Zin.

And where did *that* come from? Possibly from the Mideast, according to wine historian Charles Sullivan. Italy was a crossroads of the earliest civilizations, and Greeks or Albanians fleeing the Ottoman Turks might have introduced the vine. However, with 2,000 grapes growing in Italy today, it's impossible to trace their sources.

American Zinfandel *has* been traced—to those 19th century New England nurserymen. Long Island's Robert Prince listed a black "Zinfardel" of Hungary in his 1850 botanical catalog. Other sources mention "Zinfindel," obviously having trouble agreeing on the spelling. Captain F. W. Macondray of Massachusetts may have introduced Zinfandel to California when he came to San Francisco in 1848.

We like to regard Zinfandel as "California's grape," since it came here during the Gold Rush, by way of New England. Unlike its more genteel European ancestors, it's sassy and lively on the palate. It's versatile, suitable for everything from light, fruity blush wines to rich, heavy ports. Young plants produce soft Beaujolais-style reds; old vines yield huge, complex wines rivaling venerable Cabernets.

As author Darlington suggests, Zin is a slightly flawed beauty, like Meryl Streep. It's more intriguing and approachable than some paragon of perfection. Those who venerate Cabernet and Chardonnay are considered aficionados. We Zinfandel enthusiasts are more of a cult.

Speaking of cults, Woodside's Margaret Smith has formed ZAP—Zinfandel Advocates and Producers. Its members, comprised of Zin lovers and Zin vintners, gathers for tastings and other activities focused on California's grape. For membership information, contact ZAP, 118 Hillside Dr., Woodside, CA 94062-3521; (415) 851-2319.

The Dry Creek Valley, Gilroy's Hecker Pass region, Santa Clara County's Montebello Ridge, the Sierra Nevada foothills and San Luis Obispo County are the state's best Zinfandel areas.

A few wine related gift items; picnic patio beside winery. Informal tours when time permits. ⊓

Sitting just above a prim farm complex off Westside Road, the straightforward masonry block structures of the Davis Bynum Winery are dressed in attractive new landscaping. The tasting room is small, neat and simple, with wine price list written on a chalkboard above tiled counter.

Former newspaperman Davis Bynum started his winery in 1965 in a warehouse and store front in Albany, a town near Oakland and far from the nearest serious grapevine. He moved to this former hop ranch in 1973. Wine grapes are drawn from several premium vineyard areas.

Tasting notes: Bynum's list is weighted toward whites, which are moderately priced, from $7 to $12.50. The overall style is rather soft, light and crisp. Of those whites, we tilted toward a lush and softly spicy Chardonnay. The Fumé is particularly impressive; a 1993 version was listed by *Bon Appetit* as one of the world's top ten wine values. Reds include a light, peppery Cabernet and gentle, spicy and subtly acidic Pinot Noir. This is always a nice feature—palate-clearing bits of bread are available between tastes.

Porter Creek Vineyards • T

⊓ *8735 Westside Rd., Healdsburg, CA 95448; (707) 433-6321. Daily 10:30 to 4:30 in summer, weekends only the rest of the year; MC/VISA. Selected wines tasted.* ⊓

You've heard of home winemakers operating out of their garage. Soft-spoken George R. Davis is a *professional* winemaker doing that. Actually, only the tasting room is garaged, and it's a rustic classic: a plank laid over wine barrels. The small winery is up a dusty lane in Porter Creek Valley, just beyond a 1920s-style cottage. The setting hearkens back to the wine country's earlier days, when one stopped by the local vintner with an empty jar to have it filled. George's operation is hardly archaic, however, and his wines have won several awards. He's been doing business here since 1978, drawing grapes mostly from his hillside vineyards of Pinot Noir and Chardonnay.

Tasting notes: From George's small list, we discovered an excellent Chardonnay, full and complex, crisp and perfectly balanced; a light yet full-flavored Estate Pinot Noir and a lush, berry-like Hillside Pinot. Prices range from $10.50 to $18; a tasty Pinot Blanc goes for $6.50.

Vintners choice: "Pinot Noir from our own hillside vines produces a flavorful, nicely concentrated wine," said George.

Korbel Champagne Cellars • T GT ✕ 👜

⊓ *13250 River Rd., Guerneville, CA 95446; (707) 887-2294. Daily 9 to 5; MC/VISA. All varieties except brandy tasted. Extensive gift selection; landscaped picnic areas. Winery tours daily at various times; garden tours mid-April through September, Tuesday-Sunday at 11 and 3.* ⊓

This isn't just a winery; it's an institution. From a visitor standpoint, it's one of the most interesting such institutions in California. Started in 1882, it evolved into a baronial estate with great stone, vine-covered buildings, a tower right out of medieval Germany and old style European gardens. The setting is equally impressive, in a narrowing of the Russian River Valley, rimmed by wooded hills on one side and a vineyard tilting toward the redwood-bordered river on the other.

The setting so resembles central Europe that television's *Combat* series was filmed here for two years. During the shooting, the obliging special effects people blew up old redwood stumps that had been cluttering up the vineyards for decades.

The Korbel tour is one of the most complete in the business. Guests gather at a tiny railway station that once served the valley, visit a formal garden, then stroll into the ancient, wonderfully musty stone cellar. There, a well-done mini-museum recalls the Korbel story with old photos, documents and artifacts. Visitors move from the museum to a theater for a nicely photographed slide show, then they're led through the champagne cellars where the complex process is explained. Finally, eager to sample what they've been studying, they're escorted to the plush, carpeted hospitality center for a tasting conducted by their guide. One learns a remarkable statistic on this tour: Korbel produces seventy percent of all the *méthode champenoise* made in this country—more than one million cases annually.

Assorted Korbels operated the winery until 1954, when it was purchased by the present owners, Gary B. and Richie C. Heck.

Tasting notes: The sparkling wines, ranging from semi-dry to dry, are clean, crisp and a good buy for under $10. Although it has been producing primarily sparkling wine and brandy for several years, the firm has expanded to include a line of still wines.

Topolos at Russian River Vineyard • T GTA 📦 R

◻ *5700 Gravenstein Highway N., Forestville, CA 95436; (707) 887-1575. Daily 11 to 5; major credit cards. Most varieties tasted. Good giftware selection; guided tours by appointment. Restaurant; see listing under "Wine country dining" below.* ◻

This pleasantly rural winery complex looks like it was designed by 1960s flower children. The tasting room is small and cozy, fashioned of old wood; its giftwares lean toward folk crafts. Weather-darkened buildings hold assorted winemaking gear. A nearby garden is planted with native flowers and grasses. Above all this, the soft clink of glassware announces the presence of a restaurant, which features a *nouveau*-tilted menu.

The earthy operation—started in 1963—is the work of Michael, Jerry and Christine Topolos. They produce tasty wines in small, carefully nurtured lots. Not surprisingly, the grape picking, winemaking and even labeling are done by hand. They use, whenever possible, pesticide-free grapes.

Tasting notes: This is serious Zin country. From this bucolic setting emerge some excellent wine buys—particularly if you like big, assertive Zinfandels. You'll generally find four or five on the tasting list, with full, berry-like and peppery flavors. Also on the list is a full-flavored Grand Noir, spicy Petit Sirah, a soft and herbal Sauvignon Blanc and Alicante Bouschet. Rarely bottled in California, Alicante is a French cross breed of Grenache, Tenturier du Cher and Aramond grapes, producing an inky dark, full-bodied red.

Vintners choice: "Our Zinfandel from old vines, Petite Sirah, Grand Noir and Alicante Bouschet," reports a voice from Topolos.

Dehlinger Winery • T CT ✕

◻ *6300 Guerneville Rd., Sebastopol, CA 95472; (707) 823-2378. Friday through Monday 10 to 5; closed during January; MC/VISA. Most varieties tasted. A few wine logo gift items; picnic area.* ◻

We like tasting rooms located inside the winery, surrounded by the feel, sight and good earthy smells of the winemaking process. When you step through the double doors of the small barn style Dehlinger Winery, arrows direct you past vats and barrels to a simple counter. The arrows are redundant, since the place is cozily small. Tasting room décor consists mostly of ribbons that virtually cover a wall behind the counter.

Outside, an old house crouches on a hill above the vineyards, ominously suggestive of the set for *Psycho*. Its role isn't sinister all; it's used by the winery owner for entertaining, according to our tasting room host. Dan Dehlinger established this small winery in 1976, and bottles about 8,000 cases a year.

Tasting notes: The list is short and, fortunately, not sweet. The Chardonnay was crisp, dry and wonderfully nutty; one of the better we've sampled. Cabernet Franc and Cabernet Sauvignon were both light with soft acids, yet spicy with excellent bouquets. Prices range from $12 to $14.

De Loach Vineyards • T GT ✕

◻ *1791 Olivet Rd., Santa Rosa, CA 95401; (707) 526-9111. Daily 10 to 4:30; MC/VISA, AMEX. All current releases tasted. Lawn picnic area; guided tours weekdays at 2 p.m. and weekends at 11 a.m. and 2 p.m.* ◻

A Japanese courtyard marks the entry to this modern redwood ranch-style winery, offering an interesting architectural mix. Art decorates the walls of the tasting room and glossy ceramic tile covers the floor and tasting bar. After sipping, visitors can adjourn to a lawn picnic area near the vineyards and—something unique for wineries—pitch a game of horseshoes.

Located on a plain between the Russian River Valley and Santa Rosa, the winery was established by the De Loach family in 1975. Many of its wines are estate bottled.

Tasting notes: "Uniformly excellent" reads the note I'd scratched on my steno pad. The Chardonnay was fruity and well balanced; the Sauvignon Blanc soft and rich. Both the Zinfandel and white Zin displayed pleasant, peppery noses; flavors were rich and properly berry-like. Pinot Noir, Fumé Blanc, an estate bottled Cabernet and Merlot, plus early and late harvest Gewürztraminers complete the list. Prices range from $7.36 into the mid-twenties. Some limited selection wines go higher.

Vintners choice: "We're especially proud of our Chardonnays and Zinfandels," says a winery voice.

Martini & Prati Winery • T

◻ *2191 Laguna Rd., Santa Rosa, CA 95401; (707) 575-8064. Daily 11 to 4; MC/VISA. Four samples offered from several varieties. A few wine related gift items.* ◻

Amidst operations ranging from upscale to deliberately funky, we've found an old fashion winery making old fashioned wines. As if to prove the point, the tasting room hostess serves it in a traditional thick little Italian drinking glass, which is fitting since the operation is run by traditional Italians. They regard their heritage with pride and with good humor. Look on the tasting room wall for the "Italian chain saw."

A water tower crowns this complex, which looks more like an industrialized farmyard than a winery, with its cluster of pitched-roof warehouses and scatter of equipment. It's obviously been "added-to" as the winery grew since its founding in the 1880s. Present owners Elmo Martini and Edward Prati have run the place since 1951, although assorted Martinis go back to 1902. This is a big operation, producing two million gallons of wine sold in bulk, plus 15,000 or so cases for Martini & Prati labels.

Tasting notes: The list is long and the wines are—well—not bad for the price, which starts around $5 and doesn't go too much higher. Sippers can select four from a list of about ten wines. The best items we tasted were an inexpensive port blend of Zinfandel, Petit Sirah and Carignane and an equally inexpensive and surprisingly spicy and complex Vino Rosso. The "Ravioli Red" (great name) was rich and just short of sweet, which some will like. Assorted varietals, sherries and even a vermouth complete the list, which comes in two labels—Martini & Prati and Fountain Grove. Since this is primarily a bulk operation, bottled wines are sold only at the winery.

Vintners Choice: "We're known for our dessert wines," reports Jeani Martini.

Mark West Vineyards and Winery • T CT ✗ 🏠

◻ *7010 Trenton-Healdsburg Rd., Forestville, CA 95436; (707) 544-4813. Daily 10 to 5; MC/VISA. Most varieties tasted. Gift area with selection of wine country items, Sonoma County gift baskets, specialty foods and picnic fare. Two picnic areas. Parties, luncheons, and VIP tours and tastings by appointment.* ◻

Mark West accords one of the valley's more hospitable winery settings. The shingle-sided tasting room and winery occupy a landscaped yard rimmed on three sides by vineyards. Wooded hills of the Coast Range offer a scenic backdrop to the landscaped grounds, which features a pond and greenhouse of "California carnivores"—insect eating plants.

Speaking of eating, two lawn areas beckon picnickers, who can assemble lunch at the tasting room deli. The place is popular for weddings and other functions encouraged by the sociable owners, Joan and Robert Ellis. The Ellis family created Mark West in the early 1970s, planting three classic varietals—Pinot Noir, Chardonnay and Gewürztraminer—for their estate-bottled wines.

Tasting notes: Mark West produces big, full-flavored wines suitable for immediate sipping or laying away. The three estate wines are rich with varietal character. A Zinfandel from a 90-year-old vineyard was powerful and complex, finished in oak; a three-year-old Pinot Noir was soft with good berry flavor; and a barrel-fermented Chardonnay Reserve was properly toasty and buttery. Gewürztraminer, Johannesburg Riesling and a hand-riddled Blanc de Noir sparkling wine completes the list. Wines are moderately priced for their quality, ranging from $8.50 to the high teens.

Vintners choice: Says CarolAnn Heyden of Public Relations: "Mark West Estate is noted for the perfection of their Chardonnays, smooth, rich Pinot Noir and Alsatian style Gewürztraminer."

Z Moore Winery • T ✗

◻ *3364 River Road, Windsor, CA 95492; (707) 544-3555. Daily 10 to 5. Most varieties tasted. Some wine related gift items. Picnic area under a huge, gnarled oak.* ◻

Housed in a triple-towered hop kiln, Z Moore Winery (without the period) offers sanctuary from busy River Road traffic hurrying toward Freeway 101. The weathered farm buildings seem miles removed from encroaching Santa Rosa suburbs.

"We'd have more visitors," our host said, glancing out the window at the teeming highway, "but they whiz by so fast, they miss the place."

The place shouldn't be missed. The distinctive tasting room occupies one of the drying towers of the hop kilns, affording views of vineyards, ancient apple orchards and distant peaks—as well as the highway. Started in 1985 by Daniel Moore and wife Natalie Zuccarelli-Moore (now we find the Z), it specializes in small lots of carefully crafted wines. Output is about 5,000 cases.

Tasting notes: Those hurried motorists are missing some excellent whites, particularly Z Moore Chardonnay, barrel fermented Gewürztraminer and flower petal rich late harvest Gewürztraminer. An everyday wine is better than ordinary and we love the name: Quaff Gewürztraminer. Prices range from $7.25 for quaffing to the early teens for premiums; limited edition Chardonnays are $18.

Vintners choice: "Gewürztraminer," says Natalie. "We offer three distinctly differently styles of dry Gewürztraminer—barrel fermented dry, puncheon select dry and new barrel select dry. The new barrel select breaks all traditions with its buttery and toasty vanilla oak flavors."

Martinelli Vineyard and Orchards ● T$ ✕ 📷

⬜ 3360 River Rd., Windsor, CA 95492; (800) 346-1627 or (707) 525-0570. Daily 10 to 5; MC/VISA. Most varieties tasted for a $1 fee. Extensive gift and specialty foods selection and art gallery; picnic area. ⬜

The sign says Martinelli Apple Bar, although it's located in an old hop barn that's been kept properly rustic. The tasting counter is surrounded by a virtual country store of giftwares, wine logo items, specialty clothing and foods, with an emphasis on Sonoma County products, even fresh produce. Artworks—most for sale—adorns the weathered walls. An inviting picnic arbor is out front.

Tasting notes: The Martinelli Apple Barn is a longtime fixture here, and wines were added a few years ago. Wines on the small list are moderately priced, ranging from $7.25 into the teens. Zinfandels were nice and peppery the Chardonnay was on the light side, crisp and slightly smoky; the Sauvignon Blanc had pleasant melon and grapefruit flavors—one of the better Martinelli offerings.

Château De Baun ● T CT ✕

⬜ 5007 Fulton Rd., Fulton, CA 95439; (800) 956-WINE or (707) 571-7500. Daily 10 to 5; major credit cards. Most varieties tasted. Wine related gift items; landscaped picnic area; vineyard tours by appointment. ⬜

Château indeed. This opulent French style wine estate begs to be nestled alongside a meandering stream in Burgundy. It sits instead near busy Freeway 101, loftily trying to dismiss the constant growl of traffic.

Inside, sheltered from the freeway noise, one can wrap oneself in old world opulence, surrounded by brass chandeliers, etched glass and carefully-select artworks. We're tempted to call this a tasting *salon*, with its curved brass-trimmed counter and other posh touches. A banquet hall is next door; the winery is elsewhere. The grounds, appropriate to a château, feature formal gardens, a fountain and a gazebo, of course. A new and quite fascinating edition is the *California Viticultural Exhibit,* a planting of 26 types of wine grapes representing most important California varietals, plus 19 trellising styles. Pick up a brochure at the Hospitality Center; it describes the origin and characteristics of each grape variety.

Château De Baun comes within an inch of being overdone, particularly when the wines are labeled "Overture" and "Prelude" and the garden is described as the *jardin symphoné.* Music lovers and successful entrepreneurs

Ken and Grace De Baun finished this symphonic facility in 1989. Here, they seek to compose sparkling wine from the U.C. Davis-developed Symphony grape. They weave that melodic theme throughout the operation. So of course, the wine presses are called Gilbert and Sullivan.

Tasting notes: Considering the obvious investment, wines are moderately priced. The Symphony series of sparkling wines, quite crisp and fruity, start at $6, with predictable names like *Stellé* and *Finalé*. For Romance and Rhapsody, the price goes to $12. Among still wines are a soft and buttery Chardonnay with a hint of wood, light and refreshing Château Rouge and a light, berry-flavored Pinot Noir.

THE BEST OF THE BUNCH

The best wine buys ● Pastori, Canyon Road Cellars and Trentadue wineries in Alexander Valley; J. Pedroncelli Winery in Dry Creek Valley; Simi Winery and Foppiano Wine Company in Healdsburg; Belvedere, Topolos and Martini & Prati in the Russian River Valley.

The most attractive wineries ● Simi Winery in Healdsburg; Ferrari-Carano Winery and Lambert Bridge Vineyards in Dry Creek Valley; Château Souverain in Alexander Valley; Hop Kiln Winery, Korbel Champagne Cellars, Mark West Vineyard and Château De Baun, all in the Russian River Valley.

The most interesting tasting rooms ● Clos du Bois, Alexander Valley Fruit and Trading Company, Johnson's Alexander Valley Winery and Field Stone Winery in the Alexander Valley; Ferrari-Carano Winery and J. Fritz Winery in Dry Creek Valley; Mill Creek Vineyards, Hop Kiln Winery, Korbel Champagne Cellars, Z Moore Winery and Château De Baun, all in the Russian River Valley.

The funkiest tasting rooms ● Pastori Winery and original Nervo tasting room at Canyon Road Cellars in Alexander Valley; Porter Creek Vineyards and Topolos in the Russian River Valley.

The best gift shops ● Canyon Road Cellars and Alexander Valley Fruit and Trading Company in Alexander Valley; Kendall-Jackson and Windsor tasting rooms in Healdsburg; Ferrari-Carano Winery and Lake Sonoma Winery in Dry Creek Valley; and Korbel in the Russian River Valley.

The best picnic areas ● Field Stone Winery in Alexander Valley; Simi Winery, Rodney Strong Vineyards and Piper Sonoma Cellars in Healdsburg area; Lake Sonoma Winery and Lambert Bridge Vineyards in Dry Creek Valley; Hop Kiln Winery, Armida and Korbel Champagne Cellars in the Russian River Valley.

The best tour ● Korbel Champagne Cellars in the Russian River Valley.

Wineland activities and such

Wineland events ● Sonoma County Wine & Visitors Center sponsors a series of culinary and wine events throughout the year; call (707) 586-3795 or write to 5000 Roberts Lake Rd., Rohnert Park, CA 94928. Russian River Wine Road Barrel Tasting, early March; (707) 433-6782. Russian River Wine Festival, mid-May, $10; (800) 648-9922 or (707) 433-6782. Sonoma County Showcase and Wine Auction, early August; (707) 586-3795. Sonoma County Harvest Fair, early October; (707) 545-4203. Individual wineries also sponsor various events throughout the year.

Winery maps and guides ● Free *Russian River Wine Road* map of wineries, restaurants and lodgings, available throughout the area, or contact

Russian River Wine Road, P.O. Box 46, Healdsburg, CA 95448; (800) 648-9922 (California only) or (707) 433-6782. ***Sonoma County Farm Trails*** maps list many wineries as well as direct-to-consumer produce outlets. Pick up a free copy at member outlets or send a self-addressed envelope with 55 cents postage to: Sonoma County Farm Trails, P.O. Box 6032, Santa Rosa, CA 95406; for information call (707) 996-2154. ***Sonoma County Guide*** with winery maps and listings of activities, restaurants and lodgings, available at many wineries and gift shops for $4.95 or $7 by mail from Vintage Publications, 764 Adobe Dr., Santa Rosa, CA 95404; (707) 538-8981.

Wine country tours ● Pure Luxury Limousines offer limo tours; 5750-A Labath Ave., Rohnert Park, CA 94928; (800) 626-5466 or (707) 795-1615. Convertible Cruising offers chauffeured tours with picnics; (707) 935-0110. VinTours features personalized tours of smaller wineries in Sonoma and Napa counties; 536 Orchard St., Santa Rosa, CA 95404; (707) 546-9483. Sonoma Chardonnay Limousine Service offers wine country tours and airport transit; 22455 Broadway, Sonoma, CA 95476; (707) 938-4248. Sonoma Thunder offers van tours and hot air balloon rides; 6984 McKinley St., Sebastopol, CA 95472; (800) 759-5638 or (707) 538-7359. Wine Country Wagons offers tours of the wine country with lunches; (707) 833-2724. VinTours features personalized tours of smaller wineries in Sonoma and Napa counties; 536 Orchard St., Santa Rosa, CA 95404; (707) 546-9483.

BEYOND THE VINEYARDS

Lake Sonoma, created by the construction of Warm Springs Dam in the mid-1980s, out-draws the wineries. Hundreds of thousands of the beer and boating set flock here each summer. Facilities include a visitor center, fish hatchery, boat launches, marina, hiking trails, picnicking, and camping on a knoll with a view of the lake and surrounding countryside.

In Healdsburg, you can visit the **Healdsburg Historical Museum** in the 1911 Andrew Carnegie Library building at 221 Matheson Street. Books and documents relating to the California wine industry and a few early-day wine artifacts are featured in the **Sonoma County Wine Library Collection** in the Healdsburg library at 139 Piper Street.

Earlier in this century, the lower **Russian River Valley** was home to posh and glitzy riverside resorts. At lantern-lit dance pavilions, revelers swayed under the stars to the swinging sounds of Harry James and Jimmy Dorsey. Those days are gone, but many resorts survive in a scaled down and sometimes funky fashion. Canoeing and swimming are popular; be advised that you're likely to encounter a nudie beach or two.

A winding drive north from Guerneville on Armstrong Woods Road takes you to the hushed redwood groves of **Armstrong Redwoods State Reserve** and **Austin Creek State Recreation Area**, with hiking, picnicking and such. If you head downstream on State Highway 116, you can explore the stunning sea stack vistas of the **Sonoma Coast**. Prowl about New England-style **Jenner**, then go south to **Bodega** and **Bodega Bay**, forever marked as the bucolic setting for Alfred Hitchcock's *The Birds*. Much of the ocean front is part of **Sonoma Coast State Beach** with hiking, picnicking, camping, swimming (on rare warm days) and beach-bundling.

If you head north from Jenner, your route will twist along the splendid coastline to **Fort Ross State Historic Park,** a faithful reconstruction of an early Russian fortress and fur trading post. Beyond is **Salt Point State**

Park, a classic ecological wedge of coastal environment, stair-stepping from rough-hewn surf to evergreen highlands. **Kruse Rhododendron State Reserve** is just above that, a stunning study in color when the flowers bloom in spring. For more details on the Sonoma Coast, pick up a copy of our *Northern California Discovery Guide*, available at bookstores, or it can be ordered directly from the source; see the back of this book.

Northern Sonoma activities

Bicycle rentals • Spoke Folk Cyclery, 249 Center St., Healdsburg; (707) 433-7171.

Canoeing • Bob Trowbridge Canoe trips, one to four days with return shuttle; (707) 433-7247.

Farm products • For a map and guide to direct-outlet farms selling fresh and prepared fruits, vegetables, meats, dairy products and wines, pick up a *Sonoma County Farm Trails* map, available at most member outlets. Or send a self-addressed envelope with 55 cents postage to: Sonoma County Farm Trails, P.O. Box 6032, Santa Rosa, CA 95406; for information call (707) 996-2154.

Hot-air ballooning • Air Flamboyant, (800) 456-4711 or (707) 838-8500; Once in a Lifetime, (800) 799-9133 or (707) 578-0580. Sonoma Thunder; (800) 759-5638 or (707) 538-7359.

Water sports • Healdsburg Veterans Memorial Beach Park, (707) 433-1625; Lake Sonoma, 433-9483; Russian River resorts, 869-2584.

Attractions

The Healdsburg Museum • 221 Matheson Street, Healdsburg; (707) 431-3325. Tuesday-Sunday noon to 5; free admission. Local history exhibits in a classic Carnegie library building.

Sonoma County Wine Library Collection • City Library, 139 Piper St., Healdsburg; (707) 433-3772. A few early winery artifacts and extensive collection of wine oriented books and documents; hours vary.

WINE COUNTRY DINING

Catelli's The Rex • ☆☆ *$$*

☐ *21047 Geyserville Ave., Geyserville; (707) 433-6000. Italian-American; full bar service. Lunch Monday-Friday 11:30 to 2, dinner nightly 5 to 9. Casual; reservations for six or more. MC/VISA.* ☐ The local hangout; expect to see a couple of vintners and their spouses seriously discussing the Zinfandel crop. A plain front shields an ordinary interior with ceiling fans, tables and a few booths. The menu, heavily Italian, is busy with pastas, parmigiana, steaks, seafoods and chops. Outdoor patio and banquet facilities.

Château Souverain Café • ☆☆☆ *$$$$*

☐ *400 Souverain Rd. (Highway 101 at Independence Lane), Geyserville; (707) 433-3141. Country French; wine. Open Friday-Sunday, lunch from 11:30, dinner 5 to 8. Reservations recommended. MC/VISA, AMEX.* ☐ Elegant French style café with a dining room and patio, offering impressive views of the Alexander Valley. All smoke-free.

El Farolito Mexican Restaurant • ☆ *$*

☐ *128 Plaza St., Healdsburg; (707) 433-2807. Mexican; wine, beer and margaritas. Daily 10 to 8:30. MC/VISA.* ☐ Simply attired Latino café near the plaza with typical smashed beans and rice fare. Sauces are homemade and chili rellenos are a specialty.

Healdsburg Coffee Company • ☆ $

☐ *312 Center St., Healdsburg; (707) 431-7941. American; light fare; wine and beer. Weekdays 7 to 6, weekends 8 to 6. MC/VISA.* ☐ A cheerful place offering soup, salad, sandwiches, quiche, espresso and local wine; 30 varieties of coffee beans available. On Healdsburg Plaza, with homey oak-antique decé; smoke-free.

John Ash & Co. • ☆☆☆☆ $$$

☐ *4330 Barnes Road (River Road), Santa Rosa; (707) 527-7687. "Wine country regional cuisine"; full bar service. Lunch and dinner daily except Monday. MC/VISA.* ☐ Award-winning restaurant with creative fare assembled by chef-owner John Ash, with a focus on local ingredients. The menu features such innovative savories poached salmon with a beet and horseradish *beurre-blanc*, roast duck breast with rhubarb chutney, and creative pastas. Extensive wine list. On the edge of the wine country with a vineyard view, near River Road and U.S. 101.

Madrona Manor Restaurant • ☆☆☆☆ $$$$

☐ *1001 Westside Rd., Healdsburg; (800) 258-4003. California nouveau; wine and beer. Dinner nightly 6 to 9, Sunday brunch 11 to 2. Reservations advised; required on Saturdays; major credit cards.* ☐ A Victorian mansion with three elegant little dining rooms. North County's most opulent restaurant, featuring entrées such as Peking duck with almond coconut rice, stuffed mild chilies, and salmon steak with mixed herbs. Smoke-free dining room.

Russian River Vineyards Restaurant • ☆☆ $$$

☐ *5700 Gravenstein Highway N., Forestville; (707) 887-1562. Continental with a Greek tilt; wine only. Lunch 11:30 to 2:30, dinner 5:30 to 9:30, Sunday brunch 10:30 to 2:30. Major credit cards.* ☐ Cheerful place with eclectic décor and menu, perched atop tasting room of Topolos winery. Fare includes Mediterranean dishes such as *Souvlaki* (spicy lamb brochette), prawns Santorini, roast duckling in Madeira and black current sauce, and essential American New York peppercorn steak. Patio dining; live music nightly.

Salame Tree Deli • ☆☆ $

☐ *304 Center St. (at Matheson), Healdsburg; (707) 433-7224. Deli fare; wine and beer. Open daily. MC/VISA, DISC.* ☐ Busy corner deli just off the plaza, with a few café tables; offering a wide assortment of sandwiches, salads and such, with a good local wine selection. It's a handy lunch stop.

Southside Saloon & Dining Hall • ☆☆ $$

☐ *106 Matheson St., Healdsburg; (707) 433-4466. American; full bar service. Lunch daily 11:30 to 2:30, dinner 5:30 to 9:30. MC/VISA, AMEX.* ☐ Lively and airy restaurant on the plaza, with a Western-Spanish look. Among its interesting offerings are rock shrimp with linguine, smoked pork chops, garlic/rosemary chicken and turkey *schnitzel*.

WINELAND LODGINGS

NOTE: Prices were provided by the establishments and are subject to change. Use the price ranges only as a rough guideline and call the places listed to confirm their current rates.

The list below represents lodgings near north Sonoma County's vinelands. There's a considerably larger selection of motels, bed and breakfast inns and a few hotels in Santa Rosa. Small resorts line the Russian River and more are in communities along the Sonoma Coast. For information on these places, contact chambers of commerce listed at the end of this chapter.

Wine Country Referrals is a reservation service for hotels, motels, inns, B&Bs and vacation homes in Lake, Mendocino, Napa and Sonoma counties; P.O. Box 543, Calistoga, CA 94515; (707) 942-2186.

Hotels and motels

Best Western Dry Creek Inn ● ☆☆ $$$ Ø

☐ *198 Dry Creek Rd. (at U.S. 101), Healdsburg, CA 95448; (800) 222-5784 or (707) 433-0300. Couples and singles $50 to $79. Major credit cards.* ☐ A 102-room motel with TV movies, room phones and in-room coffee service. Pool, spa; gift bottle of wine and free continental breakfast. Near Lake Sonoma and the Russian River.

Fairview Motel ● ☆ $$ Ø

☐ *74 Healdsburg Ave. (at U.S. 101), Healdsburg, CA 95448; (707) 433-5548. Couples $52 to $56, singles $42. Major credit cards.* ☐ Eighteen rooms with TV movies and phones; pool, spa and playground.

Hotel La Rose ● ☆☆ $$$ Ø

☐ *308 Wilson St. (Highway 101 downtown exit), Santa Rosa, CA 95401; (707) 579-3200. Couples $70 to $95, singles $60 to $85. MC/VISA, AMEX.* ☐ National historic landmark Art Deco reconstructed in 1985, with an English country décor. On northern edge of Santa Rosa near the wine country. All rooms non-smoking. **Joseph's Restaurant & Bar** serves lunch Tuesday-Friday 11:30 to 2 and dinner Tuesday-Saturday 5:30 to 9:30. French-continental fare; full bar service.

Huckleberry Springs ● ☆☆☆ $$$$$

☐ *8105 Old Beedle Rd. (end of Tyrone Road; P.O. Box 400), Monte Rio, CA 95462; (707) 865-2683. Cottages $145, including a full breakfast. Five units with private baths. MC/VISA, AMEX.* ☐ Rustic, luxurious country lodge on 56 acres. Contemporary furnishings in cottages; old style lodge with antiques, folk art and graphics collection. Landscaped Japanese-style spa.

Madrona Manor ● ☆☆☆☆ $$$$$ Ø

☐ *1001 Westside Rd. (P.O. Box 818), Healdsburg, CA 95448; (707) 433-4231. Rooms $135 to $185. Major credit cards.* ☐ Beautifully restored 1881 Victorian mansion. Twenty-one rooms with antique and modern furnishings, fireplaces in many. Nine rooms in the mansion, others in cottages about the grounds. Music room lounge with fireplace, books; piano and light food service. Located on eight wooded, landscaped acres. **Madrona Manor Restaurant** listed above.

Bed & breakfast inns

Applewood ● ☆☆☆☆ $$$$$ Ø

☐ *13555 Highway 116 (Mayes Canyon Road), Guerneville, CA 95446; (707) 869-9093. Rooms $115 to $200. Sixteen rooms, all with TV, room phones and private baths; seven with fireplaces and spa tubs; full breakfast. MC/VISA, AMEX.* ☐ Opulent Mission revival mansion surrounded by lush landscaping, built in 1922 during the salad days of the Russian River resorts. Furnished with European and American antiques and original artwork. Pool, spa, formal gardens. Wine country **dinners** available for guests and the general public, $25 to $35.

Belle de Jour Inn ● ☆☆☆ $$$$$ Ø

☐ 16276 Healdsburg Ave. (opposite Simi Winery), Healdsburg, CA 95448; (707) 433-7892. Couples $115 to $185, singles $110 to $180. MC/VISA. ☐ Posh accommodations in a ranch style complex near downtown Healdsburg. Antique and contemporary furnishings; fireplaces, spas and refrigerators in rooms. Breakfast served in the dining room of an 1869 Italianate ranch home.

Camellia Inn ● ☆☆ $$$$ Ø

☐ 211 North St., Healdsburg, CA 95448; (800) 727-8182 or (707) 433-8182. Couples $70 to $135, singles $60 to $125. Nine rooms, seven with private baths; full breakfast. MC/VISA, DISC. ☐ Nicely appointed rooms in 1869 Italianate Victorian that served as Healdsburg's first hospital. Furnished with Victorian and American antiques. Spas and fireplaces in some rooms. Heated pool, gardens.

Campbell Ranch Inn ● ☆☆☆ $$$$ Ø

☐ 1475 Canyon Rd. (1.6 miles west of 101), Geyserville, CA 95441; (800) 959-3878 or (707) 857-3476. Couples $100 to $165, singles $90 to $155. Five rooms with private baths; full breakfast. MC/VISA, DISC. ☐ Modern ranch style B&B on a wooded knoll with vineyard views. Spa, tennis court, bicycles, pool and gardens. Four rooms in main house, one cottage; modern furnishings, king beds. Living room and family room with TV and fireplace.

Frampton House ● ☆☆☆ $$$$ Ø

☐ 489 Powell Ave. (one mile north of the Plaza), Healdsburg, CA 95448; (707) 433-5084. Couples $70 to $90, singles $60 to $80. Three rooms with private baths; full breakfast, MC/VISA. ☐ Restored early American home sheltered by mature trees; American antique furnishings with accent on oak. Pool, spa, sauna, bicycles; fireplace in sitting room. Breakfast served in solarium above pool.

Grape Leaf Inn ● ☆☆☆ $$$$ Ø

☐ 539 Johnson St. (Grant Street), Healdsburg, CA 95448; (707) 433-8140. Couples $90 to $145, singles $60 to $105. Seven rooms with private baths; full breakfast. MC/VISA. ☐ Beautifully restored 1900 Queen Anne Victorian. Nicely appointed rooms with whirlpool tubs and showers for two, skylight roofs, air conditioning. Wraparound porch and landscaped, tree-shaded yard. Within walking distance of restaurants and shops.

Healdsburg Inn on the Plaza ● ☆☆☆ $$$$ Ø

☐ 110 Matheson St. (Healdsburg Avenue), Healdsburg, CA 95448; (707) 433-6991. Couples and singles $135 to $175. Nine rooms, all with TV and VCRs, phones and private baths; full breakfast; free champagne brunch on weekends. MC/VISA. ☐ Stylish old inn with Victorian furnishings and original art works. Bright, cheerful rooms, all with fireplaces and balconies; some have old fashioned clawfoot tubs for two and some overlooking Healdsburg Plaza. Solarium and roof garden, gift shop and gallery with works of California artists. Former Wells Fargo Express office.

Hope-Bosworth & Hope-Merrill houses ● ☆☆☆ $$$$ Ø

☐ 21238 and 21253 Geyserville Ave. (P.O. Box 42), Geyserville, CA 95441; (707) 857-3356. Bosworth—$95 to $115, four rooms; Merrill—$95 to $140, eight rooms; all with private baths; full breakfast. MC/VISA. ☐ Two turn of the century Victorians across the street from one another in downtown Geyserville. Completely refurbished, furnished with antiques. The 1904 Hope-

Bosworth is American country style; 1870s Hope-Merrill is Victorian with European antiques. Some rooms with fireplaces and spas. Library, gardens, grape arbor. Wine country picnic lunches prepared; $30 for two including wine and gift wicker basket.

Ridenhour Ranch House Inn ● ☆☆ $$$$ Ø

◻ *12850 River Rd. (next to Korbel), Guerneville, CA 95446; (707) 887-1033. Couples and singles $95 to $130. Eight rooms with private baths, full breakfast. MC/VISA, AMEX.* ◻ Ranch style redwood home furnished with American and English antiques and Oriental rugs. Six rooms in ranch house and two cottages; some units with TV. Hot tubs, gardens and meadows on more than two acres.

Santa Nella House ● ☆☆ $$$$ Ø

◻ *12130 Highway 116 (Odd Fellows Park Road), Guerneville, CA 95446; (707) 869-9488. Couples and singles $90 to $95. Four rooms with private baths; champagne brunch. MC/VISA.* ◻ An attractively refurbished Victorian-Italianate farm house. Hot tub, spa; near Russian River beaches. Rooms furnished with English antiques.

Ye Olde Shelford House ● ☆☆ $$$$ Ø

◻ *29955 River Rd. (a mile east of U.S. 101), Cloverdale, CA 95245; (800) 833-6479 or (707) 894-5956. Couples and singles $85 to $110. Six rooms with private baths; full breakfast. MC/VISA.* ◻ Imposing 1885 Victorian country home overlooking the vineyards and wooded hills. Victorian and American antiques; hot tub, pool, bicycles. Sitting room; front porch with old-fashioned swing.

Northern Sonoma County information sources

Healdsburg Chamber of Commerce, 217 Healdsburg Ave., Healdsburg, CA 95448; (800) 648-9922 or (707) 433-6935.

Lake Sonoma Recreation Area, 3333 Skaggs Springs Rd., Geyserville, CA 95441-9644; (707) 433-9483.

Russian River Chamber of Commerce, 14034 Armstrong Woods Rd. (P.O. Box 331), Guerneville, CA 95446; (707) 869-2584.

Santa Rosa Chamber of Commerce, 637 First St., Santa Rosa, CA 95404; (707) 547-1414.

Sonoma County Wine Library Associates, P.O. Box 15225, Santa Rosa, CA 95402; (707) 433-5349.

Sonoma County Convention & Visitors Bureau, 5000 Roberts Lake Rd., Suite A, Rohnert Park, CA 94928; (800) 326-7666 or (707) 586-8100, FAX (707) 586-8111.

Sonoma County Wine & Visitors Center, 5000 Roberts Lake Rd., Rohnert Park, CA 94928; (707) 586-3795.

Windsor Chamber of Commerce, P.O. Box 367, Windsor, CA 95492; (707) 838-4323.

"Lean and silky, with nice, toasty orange peel shades to the plum and to-mato aromas and flavors, echoing spice notes on the finish."
— **Winetaster's description of a Buena Vista Carneros Pinot Noir**

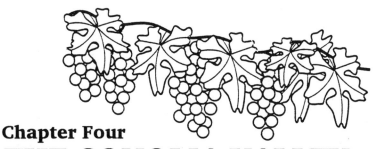

Chapter Four
THE SONOMA VALLEY
Where California wine and history blend

About twenty-five years ago, as I was wrapping up an interview with vint-ner Sam Sebastiani, his father August poked his head through the doorway.

"You got any plans tonight?" he asked.

I shook my head.

"The hell you don't. You and I are going to dinner."

"Sure." I welcomed the prospect of an evening with this Sonoma Valley wine legend. "But, why the sudden invitation?"

August frowned. "I've got one of those fancy New York wine writers in my office and I need an excuse to get rid of him."

We adjourned to the Sonoma Grove Restaurant, where Gus addressed the waitress with his usual gentle gruffness: "Bring my friend here the second best steak in the house. I'll take the best one and bring us a bottle of Zinfan-del."

"Of course, Mister Sebastiani." The waitress grinned wickedly. "What brand?"

August's death in 1980 closed a significant chapter in the Sonoma Valley wine history book. Friendly but incisive, folksy yet astute, he turned a bulk winery into Sonoma's largest producer of varietals. When a wine glut hit in the 1970s, he introduced "jug varietals," marketing premium wines in over-sized bottles at affordable prices. He was the first American winemaker to produce *nouveau* style Gamay Beaujolais and release it within weeks of bot-tling, in the French tradition.

At home in bib overalls, ill at ease in suit and tie, he hosted elegant har-vest dinners in San Francisco to exhibit Sonoma Valley wines to the press and to the world. Not to be overshadowed, wife Sylvia earned a reputation as an outstanding chef and authored a best-selling cookbook, *Mangiamo.*

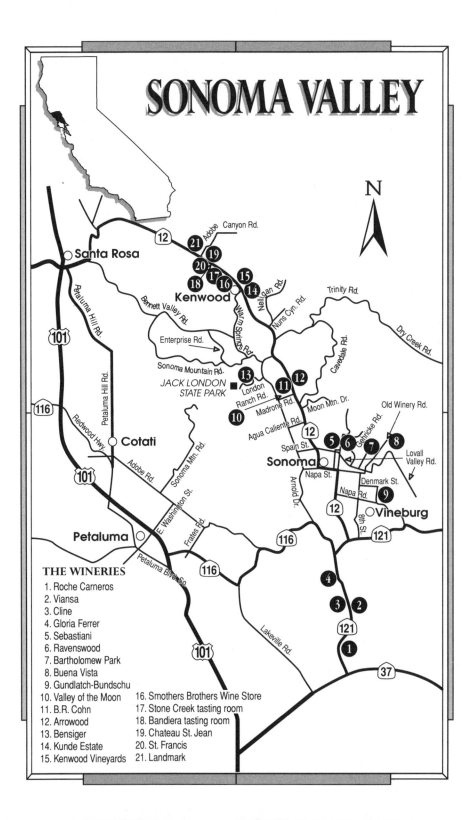

SONOMA VALLEY

N

Canyon Rd.

12 — Adobe

21

19

20

17

18   16   15

Kenwood   14

Santa Rosa

Nelligan Rd.

Trinity Rd.

Petaluma Hill Rd.

Bennett Valley Rd.

Nuns Cyn. Rd.

Cavedale Rd.

Dry Creek Rd.

101

Enterprise Rd.

Warm Springs Rd.

Sonoma Mountain Rd.

116

JACK LONDON
STATE PARK

13

London
Ranch Rd.

11

12

Madrone Rd.

Moon Mtn. Dr.

Old Winery Rd.

Cotati

Sonoma Mtn. Rd.

10

Agua Caliente Rd.

Genricke Rd.

12

5   6   7   8

Lovall
Valley Rd.

101

Adobe Rd.

Spain St.

Sonoma

Napa St.

Denmark St.

9

Arnold Dr.

Napa Rd.

12

8th St.

Vineburg

E. Washington St.

Frates Rd.

Petaluma

Petaluma Blvd. So.

116

121

116

101

Lakeville Rd.

4

3   2

121

1

37

THE WINERIES

1. Roche Carneros
2. Viansa
3. Cline
4. Gloria Ferrer
5. Sebastiani
6. Ravenswood
7. Bartholomew Park
8. Buena Vista
9. Gundlatch-Bundschu
10. Valley of the Moon
11. B.R. Cohn
12. Arrowood
13. Bensiger
14. Kunde Estate
15. Kenwood Vineyards

16. Smothers Brothers Wine Store
17. Stone Creek tasting room
18. Bandiera tasting room
19. Chateau St. Jean
20. St. Francis
21. Landmark

Although Sonoma Valley is famous for its wine legends of Haraszthy and Vallejo, the Sebastiani family has written much of its current history. The saga began in 1904 when Italian immigrant Samuele Sebastiani began producing bulk wines. His son August joined him in the business in 1934. When Samuele died in 1946, August changed the focus to varietals and built the winery into one of the largest in America. Sebastiani and Sonoma are almost synonymous. The name reaches beyond the winery to appear on a theater, a depot and on street signs.

The family remains the valley's largest wine producer, shipping four million cases a year. Sylvia, her youngest son Don, daughter Maryanne and her husband Dick Cuneo run the operation today. After a 1986 family feud resembling a script from the old *Falcon Crest* TV series, eldest son Sam left to form his own winery, Viansa, which continues to thrive in the Carneros district. This is a gently hilly appellation just north of the San Pablo arm of San Francisco Bay, shared by the Napa and Sonoma valleys.

If that family spat resembles a TV script, the rest of Sonoma's history reads like a Gothic novel. In 1823, a year after Mexico freed itself from Spain, maverick priest Jose Altimira bolted from San Francisco's cold and damp Mission Dolores to form a new branch north of the bay. Although the church condemned his action, he was supported by the Mexican California governor and the mission survived. It was the only California mission established under Mexican rule. Altimira named it San Francisco Solano, in honor of a missionary to the Peruvian Indians.

In the 1830s, when the Mexican government stripped the missions of their vast landholdings, young Army official Mariano Guadalupe Vallejo was given the task of dissolving Mission Solano. In doing so, he laid out a town with a classic plaza as its focal point. He called it Sonoma, a name local Indians had given the valley. The plaza remains as its historic centerpiece.

As more Americans arrived, Mexico began losing its grip on its northern outpost of California. On June 14, 1846, a rag-tag bunch of Sacramento Valley gringos marched on Sonoma, imprisoned an angry, sputtering Vallejo in his own barracks and proclaimed California as an independent republic. The group fashioned a crude flag with the outline of a bear (which looked more like a pig), and raised it over the plaza. These "Bear-Flaggers" were later described by Vallejo's sister as a "group of rough-looking desperados."

It was the shortest republic on record. On July 9, a U.S. Naval force led by Commodore John Sloat captured Monterey and annexed California to the United States.

From that point forward, Sonoma's history is concerned mostly with wine. Vallejo, an American supporter even before his imprisonment, became the town's leading citizen and its first major grape grower. Wayfaring Hungarian "Count" Agoston Haraszthy arrived in 1856. (See page 18.) A year later, he established Buena Vista, which ultimately became the largest winery in America. Traveling to Europe under state legislative sanction in the early 1860s, he imported hundreds of thousands of varietal grape cuttings. They formed the foundation for today's premium California wines. It's not an exaggeration to call Haraszthy the father of California viniculture and Sonoma the cradle of the state's premium wine industry.

Like other California winelands, the valley suffered from a wine glut, then phylloxera and finally Prohibition. Haraszthy's failing Buena Vista Winery was shut down when the 1906 earthquake caved in its cellars.

Three wineries preserve the shards of Sonoma Valley's vineland history. Buena Vista was re-opened in 1943 by news executive Frank Bartholomew and it continues to thrive under its current owners, the Moller-Racke family of Germany. Sebastiani owns many of the original mission and Vallejo vineyards. Bartholomew Park Winery (formerly Hacienda Wine Cellars) has some of Haraszthy's old vineyards and a replica of his Pompeiian style villa.

Another historical figure left his mark on the Sonoma Valley, but he blended words, not wine. Jack London, fresh from his literary triumphs, bought land above Glen Ellen in 1905 and devoted the last eleven years of his life to building his "Beauty Ranch." The Valley of the Moon, an Indian description of this scenic land, was popularized in London's book by that name.

Sonoma Valley's wineries are grouped in two areas—from the town of Sonoma south through the Carneros district to San Pablo Bay, and farther up the valley around Glen Ellen and Kenwood. Signposts on street and highway intersections help direct you to the valley's assorted tasting rooms.

SONOMA-CARNEROS WINERY TOUR • To approach Sonoma
from the San Francisco Bay Area, go east on State Highway 37 from U.S. 101 above San Rafael, then turn north onto State Highway 121 at **Sears Point Raceway.** You've entered the Carneros appellation, and this route is appropriately called the Carneros Highway. You'll soon encounter two modern wineries perched on upslopes and surrounded by vineyards: **Roche Carneros Estate Winery** and **Viansa**, both on the right. A Sonoma Valley Visitor Information Center sits near the entrance to Viansa, occupying and Italianate pink stucco structure.

Just beyond Viansa, **Cline Winery** sits back among the vineyards on the highway's left side. The **Fruit Basket**, not a winery but a well-stocked produce and pasta venue, appears next and beyond that, a narrow lane leads uphill through vineyards to **Gloria Ferrer Champagne Cellars**; both are on the left. Just above the Gloria Ferrer entrance, you'll see the **Schellville Airport,** where you can admire some vintage planes and book a flight in an open-cockpit biplane (listed under "Sonoma Valley activities" below).

Continue on Highway 121, then swing left onto Highway 12 at the Sonoma sign; the route becomes Broadway and bumps into **Sonoma Plaza**. Take a right at the stop sign, drive to Fourth Street, turn left and follow it to **Sebastiani Vineyards.** Its extensive facilities border the corner of Fourth and Spain Street. Go east on Spain a few blocks, then turn north (left) onto Gehricke Road and follow it uphill to **Ravenswood,** tucked among the trees.

Return to Spain Street and continue east until it becomes Lovall Valley Road. At a kink in Lovall Valley, head northeast on Castle Road to **Bartholomew Park Winery**. Note the reconstructed Haraszthy villa crowning a low hill as you approach. Retreat to Lovall Valley Road, stay with it a short distance and turn left onto Old Winery Road, lined with giant eucalyptus

---

WINERY CODES • *T* = Tasting with no fee; *T$* = Tasting for a fee; *GT* = Guided tours; *GTA* = Guided tours by appointment; *ST* = Self-guiding tours; *CT* = casual tours or a peek into the winery; ✕ = picnic area; 🏠 = Gift shop or good giftware selection. Price ranges listed in tasting notes are for varietals; jug wines may be available for less.

trees. This takes you to historic **Buena Vista Winery Carneros** at the end of the road.

Your final Sonora-area stop is **Gundlach-Bundschu Winery** and a sign pointed the wrong direction the last time we looked. To get there, follow Old Winery Road south from Buena Vista, turn right onto Napa Street then quickly left onto Eighth Street and follow it two-thirds of a mile to Denmark Street, go left and travel about three-fourths of a mile and turn left into a lane marked by ornamental stone walls.

Roche Carneros Estate Winery • T GTA ✕

⊡ *28700 Arnold Dr. (Hwy. 121), Sonoma, CA 95476; (707) 935-7115. Daily 10 to 5 (to 6 in summer); MC/VISA, AMEX. Most wines tasted free, fee for some reserves. Gifts and specialty food selection. Picnic area; tours by appointment.* ⊡

Perched on a hilltop and housed in a double-pitched roof structure suggestive of an urban barn, Roche offers a pleasing view of the Carneros region, San Pablo Bay, and Sonoma Valley. Picnickers can enjoy the view from tables near the winery. The tasting room is spacious and inviting, like an oversized living room. Samples of Sonoma Valley specialty foods are featured in the gift area.

Joseph and Genevieve Roche planted their vineyards in 1982, intending to concentrate on Chardonnay and Pinot Noir, which do well in the Carneros Appellation. They're still the best of Roche's wines. The small, stylish family winery produces about 4,500 cases a year.

Tasting notes: Roche wines come in two price ranges. A pair of Chardonnays and Pinot Noir Blanc are from $5.95 to $12.95. Both Chards exhibited good varietal character, rich and long on fruit. The higher end Pinot Noir and Merlot, priced from $16.95 to $19.95, also were outstanding, complex and full flavored. The unfiltered Pinot Noir was excellent.

Viansa Winery • T & T$ CT & GTA ✕ 🍴

⊡ *25200 Arnold Dr. (Highway 121), Sonoma, CA 95476; (707) 935-4700. Daily 10 to 5; MC/VISA. Choice of four wines offered for tasting, plus "connoisseur tasting" for a fee. Large gift selection; complete kitchen with deli, picnic and gourmet food items. Valley-view picnic area; informal tours through the oak aging cellar, or guided tours by appointment.* ⊡

When Sam J. Sebastiani left the family business in 1986, he and his wife Vicki combined their names and came up with "Viansa." Their $7 million winery reflects Sam's touch of elegance and Vicki's flair for wine and food.

Tucked high into the brow of a hill above the Carneros, it's now old enough to begin weathering a bit, appropriate to its appearance as a tile-roofed villa in old Tuscany. A nearby picnic area offers a 360-degree view. The tasting room, aptly described by Sam and Vicki as their "Italian marketplace," is one of the valley's most appealing, offering an extensive giftware, cook book, wine book and specialty food shop. The Viansa kitchen issues pastas, *foccacia* bread sandwiches, salads, deli items, desserts and other "California-Italian" fare. Assorted sauces and dips are available for tasting.

It may be our imagination, but a figure in one of the murals—a reclining Roman aristocrat immersed in the good life—bears a passing resemblance to Sam.

Appropriate to the memory of his father, Sonoma Valley wine pioneer August Sebastiani, Sam has created a 90-acre wetland on the property for migrating waterfowl. More than 30 species of waterfowl hang out there, and tours are conducted periodically. ("Gus" was an accomplished amateur ornithologist and had his own duck pond among his vineyards.)

Tasting notes: In addition to some lush and fruity Chardonnays and Sauvignon Blanc and excellent full flavored Cabernets, Viansa produces several interesting blends, drawing on some classic Italian and French grapes. Perhaps the best is a smooth, berry-rich *Prindelo,* a blend of Primitivo, Zinfandel and Charbono. It has a rich Zinfandel-like berry flavor as well it should; Primitivo is the Italian ancestor of Zinfandel. *RiservaAntra Rosso,* a Cabernet Sauvignon-Cabernet Franc blend has a nice herbal overtone with a hint of chili peppers. Prices range from $9 to the middle teens, and beyond for some limited reserves.

Vintners choice: "Our Cabernet Sauvignon is currently the highlight because of the blend of vineyards from Napa and Sonoma, with a touch of Cabernet Franc to add more fruit to the taste," according to Sam.

Cline Cellars • T & T$ GTA ✕

❑ *24737 Arnold Drive, Sonoma, CA 95476; (707) 935-4310. Daily 10 to 6. Choice of four wines tastes free, plus reserve and limited bottling tasting for a fee. Few wine logo and deli items; picnic area on a lawn. Guided tours by appointment.* ❑

Fred Cline got into the wine business in 1982 by using a small inheritance from his grandfather Jacuzzi—that's right; the inventor of the whirlpool bath—to buy the old Firpo Winery on the California delta east of San Francisco. He parlayed that $12,000 into a $3 million debt, but his wines won awards and sold well, and he was able to buy an historic Carneros region ranch in 1991. Younger brother Matt joined the operation in 1986; both are graduates of the University of California at Davis.

Their Carneros tasting room occupies a handsome 19th century white clapboard farmhouse with a wrap-around porch. Low stone walls, a grassy picnic area and landscaping complete a pleasantly bucolic setting.

Tasting notes: We'll avoid the "Rhône Ranger" cliché that other wine writers have used, although the Clines have excelled with lesser known Rhône wines such as Mourvèdre, Syrah (not to be confused with Australia's Sirah), Carignane and Alicante Bouchet. Matt earned a "winemaker of the year" title in 1993 and the Clines have won a considerable collection of awards. Their Côtes D'Oakley and Oakley Cuvée—blends of Mourvèdre, Carignane, Zinfandel and Alicante Bouschet—are soft and light yet full- flavored. The Oakley Cuvée has a nice tannic nip at the end. The Carignane varietal also had a pleasant tannic finish, with a rich berry flavor and the Mourvèdre varietal offered a pleasant herbal taste. Others on the Cline list include a soft and spicy Semillon, and varietal Syrah, Zinfandel and late harvest Zinfandel.

Vintners choice: "Our Zinfandel and Mourvèdre varietals and Oakley Cuvée are particularly appealing," said a Cline team member.

Gloria Ferrer Champagne Caves • T$ GT

❑ *23555 Highway 121, Sonoma, CA 95476; (707) 996-7256. Daily 10:30 to 5:30; Major credit cards. Sparkling wines by the glass from $2.75 to $4.50. Some wine related gift items. Guided tours hourly from 11 to 4.* ❑

From Viansa's Tuscany, we are ferried to the hills of Spain, where the Ferrer family has produced sparkling wine for five centuries. In 1986, they transported the essence of rural Barcelona to this hillside niche in the Carneros. The tile-roofed winery with its graceful Spanish arches shields an underground *cava*, where sparkling wines are coaxed into graceful maturity.

Plan to arrive at tour time to take the full measure of this elegant facility. You'll view fermenting tanks and a bottling line from a gallery, then descend into gunnited caves under 20 feet of earth. Here, great tiers of sparkling wine glisten dully in the subdued light. Along the way, you absorb a quick course in *méthode champenoise* as practiced by the Ferrer family. The tour adjourns to the stylish *Sala de Catadores* (Hall of the Tasters) for a bit of the bubbly.

Tasting notes: Three sparkling wines are sold by the glass—Gloria Ferrer Brut, Royal Cuvée and Carneros Cuvée. Our Ferrer Brut was crisp and faultlessly clean, with subtle aromas and tastes of the fruit. The wines have won numerous awards, including a best in show at a San Francisco Wine Expo. Bottle prices are in the mid teens. Pinot Noir and Chardonnay table wines have been added to the Ferrer list; they are, of course, the classic ingredients for sparkling wines.

Sebastiani Vineyards ● T GT ✕ 🏠

◻ *389 E. Fourth St., Sonoma, CA 95476; (707) 938-5532. Daily 10 to 5. Most varieties tasted. Good giftware selection. Picnic areas near the winery and along the vineyards on Spain Street. Tours every half hour from 10:30 to 4; reservations required for groups of 12 or more.* ◻

Sebastiani Vineyards, whose history we've already covered, forms a transition between town and country. The ancient cut-stone winery is on the edge of a tidy old residential area, while vineyards stretch toward low hills. Nearly 150,000 people a year throng through the winery. The tours are quick and efficient, spilling their happy cargo into the large, earthy tasting room.

The place is permeated with old wine and family history. Ancient beams hold up the ceiling; the arc of a huge wine cask anchors one corner of the room. Faded photos adorn cut-stone walls, Samuele's original basket press and vintage winemaking equipment fills odd niches. A stained glass window depicts the winery logo, and a portion of it glitters from this book's cover. A remarkable gentleman named Earle Brown took up woodcarving when most men retire, and spent the next decade or so inscribing images on every door, barrel top, cask and other exposed wood surface he could find in the winery. The display is perhaps one of the largest wood carving exhibits in America.

Tasting notes: The Sebastiani list is broad-based, ranging from premium varietals to jug wines, including varietal jugs introduced by August. The premium whites are fruity and crisp, not overly filtered and fined—a fate often suffered by high-volume wines. Most of the reds are soft and lush, ready to drink, although some Merlots, Cabernets and Zinfandels are suitable for cellaring. Zinfandel, to my mind, is their best product. A spicy, soft and fruity version recently won a gold, and it's priced at only $8. The long list covers nearly every varietal produced in California, with prices ranging from $6 to the early teens.

Vintners choice: "Chardonnay, Symphony, Merlot and Cabernet, using local grapes with which we've worked for many years," says hospitality manager Margaret Rowell.

Ravenswood ● T GTA ✕ 🏠

◻ *18701 Gehricke Rd., Sonoma, CA 95476; (707) 938-1960. Daily 10 to 4:30; MC/VISA, DISC. Selected wines tasted. Good selection of giftwares and*

Decades of ivy lace the rough stone walls of Buena Vista Carneros Winery, established in 1857 by Agoston Haraszthy.

wine logo items. Picnic area with hillside and vineyard views; guided tours by appointment. ⬜

This is where you go for a little Zin. Or perhaps a lot, if you love the "mystery grape" as we do. This winery, tucked into a wooded slope and besiege by vineyards, specializes in Zinfandel. And most are BIG Zins. We came away with a mixed case. The rustic, stone fronted tasting room looks properly ancient, yet it was opened in early 1991. A picnic terrace offers fine views of vines, pines, giant eucalyptus, wooded slopes and the edges of Sonoma below.

Ravenswood began life in the mid-70s in a prefab warehouse in Sonoma and moved recently to this more enticing spot. Winemaker Joel E. Peterson is obsessed with the notion of bringing out all the earthy, powerful character of Zinfandel, and he usually succeeds. Tasters who like big red wines give his Zin high marks.

"No wimpy wines allowed," reads a sign in the small tasting room.

Tasting notes: Although Zinfandel still rules, the proprietors have shifted toward some interesting Bordeaux style blends of Cabernet Sauvignon, Cabernet Franc and Merlot to expand their list. Most are lush and mellow, yet with enough tannin to encourage aging. A Vintners Blend Merlot is soft and ready to drink, and a couple of Cabs exhibit lots of berries, hints of spice and wood. Still, we go for the Zin; the Dickerson and Old Vine are among the best of the lot, with big berries and concentrated tannin—suitable for a long sleep. Prices are from $9 to the high teens.

Bartholomew Park Winery • T GTA ✗

◻ *1000 Vineyard Lane, Sonoma, CA 95476; (707) 935-9511. Daily 10 to 4:30; MC/VISA. Most varieties tasted. Wine history museum. Haraszthy villa open Wednesday, Saturday and Sunday noon to 4; shorter hours in winter. Some wine logo gift items in winery tasting room. Oak-shaded picnic area overlooking the vineyards; guided tours by appointment.* ◻

The "villa" catches your eye before you see the winery. It's a reconstruction of the Pompeiian mansion built in 1864 by Count Haraszthy. It has been furnished to the period and is staffed by a docent on Wednesdays, Saturdays and Sundays. Visitors are free to look around and admire the splendid old European furnishings, grand piano and crystal and brass chandeliers.

The winery and tasting room are just up the road—housed in a century-old Spanish-California structure that once served as a community hospital. Vineyards spill away from this wooded setting, and picnic areas occupy a park-like shaded slope.

News executive and international wine connoisseur Frank Bartholomew, who recycled Buena Vista Winery in 1943, established Hacienda as well—three decades later. It functioned for several years as Hacienda Winery under A. Crawford Cooley and his son Robert, then was purchased by the huge and fast-growing Bronco Wine Company in 1992. It has been converted into something of an historic shrine to both Haraszthy and Bartholomew. A Bartholomew foundation has been established to operate the historic facility; wine is no longer produced here.

A tasting room occupies one end of this grand old brick, stone and wooden structure. An excellent museum, completed in 1995, fills the rest of the old winery building. Your eye first catches an outstanding black and white photo display of contemporary Sonoma County grape growers, and then travels back through history to the 1850s when Haraszthy arrived to plant his vines here and establish the Buena Vista Winery nearby. Other exhibits trace the growth of the local wine industry. An 1800s wine picnic scene with a surrey and wicker picnic basket are a focal point.

Tasting notes: Bartholomew Park wine labels are attractive montages of Sonoma Valley wine history, although one doesn't buy these wines just for those labels. Those we tasted were quite good; they range in price from $10 to $14. A pair of Chardonnays displayed strong variety character with lots of fruit and a bit of spice; a five-year-old Zinfandel had a great raspberry nose that galloped into the taste; a three-year-old Merlot offered herbs and raspberries in the aroma and taste and a four-year old Cabernet Sauvignon was classic Cab—full- flavored and mellow with a light chili-pepper tang.

Buena Vista Carneros Winery • T & T$ GT & ST ✗ 📷

◻ *18000 Old Winery Rd. (P.O. Box 1842), Sonoma, CA 95476; (707) 938-1266. Daily 10 to 4:30; major credit cards. Most varieties tasted; some free, others for a $2.50. Extensive gift selection; specialty foods; art gallery. Self-guiding tours; historical presentations at 11:30 and 2 in summer, and at 2 p.m. only the rest of the year. Picnic areas in the courtyard, and terraced on a steep slope.* ◻

If any winery in America is steeped in antiquity, it is Buena Vista, one of California's oldest wine facilities, started by Haraszthy in 1857. It was restored by Bartholomew in 1943 and was owned by Youngs Market Company of Los Angeles until the Moller-Racke family of Germany purchased it in the

1980s. The word "Carneros" was added to the winery name recently to reflect the source of most of its grapes.

The original winery is shaped of rough blocks quarried from its own tunnels. Bunkered into a steep slope, shaded by giant eucalyptus, it exudes the mystique of a viticultural Mayan ruin. Peeking into the tunnels of the ancient winery or its next-door Press House, you can see the pick marks where Chinese laborers dug the tunnels. Stone blocks from the digging were then used to create the façades.

Self-guiding tours take you through the fountain courtyard and into the ancient recesses of the original wine cellars. (The cellars were closed for restoration in the mid-1990s.) Historical tours follow the trail of Agoston Haraszthy, which began in strife-torn Hungary and ended at this place.

The tasting room, in the Press House, is rimmed by a balconied art gallery, where works of San Francisco Bay Area artists are on display. The culturally conscious Moller-Racke family sponsors a fall Shakespeare Festival in the courtyard.

Tasting notes: Four gratis tastings are offered from a list that covers most varietals. Older reserve wines can be sampled for a fee. We liked the complex, buttery spiciness of the Carneros Chardonnay and the herbal flavor of a Sauvignon Blanc. The Carneros Cabernet Sauvignon also was herbal, with a soft finish. Buena Vista makes one of society's better cream sherries: velvety, nutty and lush. Prices range from $8 to the high teens.

Vintners choice: "We're known for our Chardonnay, Pinot Noir and Cabernet," said tasting room manager Jeri Wilson.

Gundlach-Bundschu Winery • T ✗

❑ *2000 Denmark St., Sonoma, CA 95476; (707) 938-5277. Daily 11 to 4:30; MC/VISA. Most wines tasted. Some wine related gift items. Picnic pavilion with a valley view.* ❑

Gundlach-Bundschu combines antiquity, a modern wine facility and hearty humor. There's a festive, laid-back Berkeleyian atmosphere to this ancient place; it's one of our favorite stops on the California wine tour. Lively contemporary music fed by an unseen CD fills the ancient cellars and the place is decorated with off-beat Gundlach-Bundschu advertising posters, which can be purchased. One shows a highway patrolman telling a motorist in an old Kaiser: "If you can't say *Gundlach-Bundschu Gewürztraminer*, you shouldn't be driving!" A sign invites wine enthusiasts to join the "Wine of the Moment Club."

Knowledgeable and gregarious tasting room personnel compliment this lively scene, with their casual attire, long curly hair and ear studs—and those are the guys!

This upbeat facility indeed is ancient. Jacob Gundlach started the winery in 1858 and was joined by Charles Bundschu, who married his daughter, in 1862. The 1906 earthquake destroyed their San Francisco warehouse and Prohibition closed the winery. However, the Bundschus continued growing grapes in the Sonoma Valley. Jim, great-great-great grandson of Charles, decided to re-open the ancient winery in the early 1970s.

Tasting notes: Jim Bundschu's winery produces the best Gewürztraminer in the valley, with a great crushed flower petal nose and taste. Yet the reds are the best product—when you can get them; they often sell out. Try the berry-rich, slightly spicy Bearitage, a blend of Cabernet Sauvignon, Merlot and Zinfandel; the label's great, too. The Pinot Nor was remarkably spicy for this variety, with the typical big berry taste. The Cabernet Sauvignon—a five-year-old version—was outstanding, inky black, rich and capably of hanging around for another decade or so. Prices range from $9 to the mid teens.

Vintners choice: "Reds, because," Jim said, flatly.

GLEN ELLEN-KENWOOD WINERY TOUR • From **Sonoma Plaza**, take Spain street west and go right onto State Highway 12 (the Sonoma Highway), headed northwest toward Santa Rosa. You'll pass the strung out, unplanned scatter of three communities—Boyes Hot Springs, Fetters Hot Springs and Agua Caliente. This is the least appealing area of the Sonoma Valley. As the names suggest, it was once a hot springs resort area. Boyes was spring training grounds for the old San Francisco Seals and Oakland Oaks. However, with the lone exception of beautifully refurbished Sonoma Mission Inn, this once glossy resort area is rather tarnished.

Once you clear Fetters, you enter open countryside and the prettiest part of the Sonoma Valley. Vineyards climb gentle slopes, nudging foothills of the Mayacamas Mountains to the east. Looking west, you see more vines scattered across the level valley floor; the Sonoma Mountains fill that horizon. Continue on Highway 12 to Madrone Road, turn left and you'll shortly encounter **Valley of the Moon Winery** on your right. Retrace your route back to Highway 12, turn left and you'll see the entrance to **B.R. Cohn Winery** on your left, after less than a third of a mile. From there, continue a brief distance to **Arrowood Winery,** up a vineyard slope to your right.

Continue northwest on Highway 12 for about two miles, turn left onto Arnold Drive and pass through the vintage hamlet of **Glen Ellen,** with its picturesque brick and wooden stores. Veer to the right onto London Ranch Road, which takes you to **Benziger Family Winery,** up the hill about half a mile and on your right. You'll likely want to continue on to **Jack London State Historic Park** up the road a bit. It preserves London's ranch, the ruins of his Wolf House stone mansion and the home of his wife, Charmian.

Return to Glen Ellen and follow Arnold Drive back to Route 12, headed for the town of **Kenwood,** about three and a half miles away, where many of the valley's wineries are clustered. You'll first see **Kunde Estate Winery** and in less than half a mile, **Kenwood Vineyards,** both uphill on your right. Entering the small town of Kenwood, you encounter three tasting rooms detached from their wineries, all on your left—**Smothers Brothers Wine Store, Stone Creek** and **Bandiera.** You next see **Château St. Jean Winery,** up a vineyard lane to the right. **St. Francis Winery** is on the left, almost directly across the highway. A bit farther along, at Highway 12 and Adobe Canyon Road, is **Landmark Vineyards**.

Valley of the Moon Winery • T ✗

◻ *777 Madrone Rd., Glen Ellen, CA 95442; (707) 996-6941. Daily 10 to 5; major credit cards. Selected wines tasted. Good selection of wine logo items and giftwares. Tree-shaded picnic area.* ◻

You first notice a no-nonsense collection of ranch buildings typical of pioneer family wineries. Then a giant bay laurel catches your eye; it's at least 400 years old. Crouched behind it, a mere century old, is a ruggedly handsome stone tasting room. In the wood-paneled interior, a family member likely will pour samples from the extensive list.

The winery was established in the 1800s and was operated at one time by Senator George Hearst. Closed by Prohibition, it came back to life in 1942 when Enrico Parducci, founder of the San Francisco Sausage Company, purchased the site. His son Harry, grandson Harry Jr., and assorted other family members operate the facility today. It's one of the oldest family-owned wineries in the Sonoma Valley.

Tasting notes: Valley of the Moon has long been noted for solid everyday wines, which still represent good buys. Very drinkable, full-flavored Private Stock red and white go for as little as $4 a bottle. The new generation has added premium varietals, and they've been winning their share of medals. The flavors of Chardonnay and Sauvignon Blanc are straight from the grape—fruity and full with nice acid finishes. A light and fruity Cabernet had a pleasantly herbal flavor, with a tiny hint of wood. Zinfandel, one of their best wines, was full of berries and peppery with a hint of oak. Premium varietals also are good buys, ranging from $7 to the mid teens.

Vintners choice: "Cabernet and Zinfandel are the best of our reserves," quoth Harry, Jr., "and I really like the Chardonnay."

B.R. Cohn Winery • T GTA ✕

☐ *15140 Sonoma Highway, Glen Ellen, CA 95442; (800) 330-4064 or 938-4064. Daily 10 to 4:30. Most varieties tasted; MC/VISA. Some wine logo gift items. Picnic area; guided tours by appointment.* ☐

Housed in neatly kept turn-of-the-century farm buildings, Cohn Winery crowns a hill shaded with olive trees, which is logical, since this originally was an olive ranch. The primly attractive tasting room, which once occupied a small cottage, was moved into the main ranch house in mid-1995.

Winery founder Bruce Cohn comes from a curious background for a vintner—TV, broadcasting and talent management. He discovered the Doobie Brothers in San Francisco and helped guide them to fame. However, he's not an entrepreneur who dabbles in wine as a second profession. He grew up in the Forestville area and has long been interested in wine. He bought his appropriately named Olive Hill Vineyard in 1974 and opened his winery a year later—while still keeping at least one finger on the pulse of the entertainment industry.

Tasting notes: Cohn is noted for his Cabernet Sauvignon and has won medals with several versions. They *are* excellent, often with firm tannins that encourage aging. However, we felt that his reserve Chardonnay was one of his best wines, with outstanding lush flavors and a soft touch of wood. Pinot Noir, the only other wine on his short list when we visited, was soft and drinkable with a slight hint of the barrel. Wine prices range from $12 to $20, with some of the Olive Hill Estate Cabernets going higher.

Arrowood Vineyards and Winery • GTA

☐ *14347 Sonoma Hwy. (P.O. Box 987), Glen Ellen, CA 95442; (707) 938-5170. Daily 10 to 4:30; MC/VISA. Small sales room; tasting sometimes available. A few wine related items. Guided tours by appointment.* ☐

Arrowood, housed in an appealing rural New England style structure, is tucked into a hillside vineyard. Wicker chairs on an vintage porch invite visitors to linger over the view. Arrowood doesn't always offer tasting, but if a bottle happens to be open, visitors are welcome to sample some of the valley's finest wines. They can be purchased in a cheery combination kitchen/sales room. It's presided over by co-owner Alis Demers Arrowood, whose eyes sparkle with enthusiasm for her husband's wines. She suggests that visitors call ahead for a tour of the small, well-appointed winery.

MEDAL, MEDAL, WHO'S GOTTA MEDAL?

As you visit assorted wineries, you'll note that many have walls full of ribbons. Does this mean that all their wines are wonderful? How can so many wineries win so many prizes? Doesn't anyone ever lose?

A gold medal doesn't mean that a wine won first place. It means that it scored high in a blind tasting, meeting all the criteria for that particular varietal. A medal—gold, silver or otherwise—is a *rating*. Several wines entered in a particular competition—or none—may be worthy of a gold.

To further cloud the issue of who won how many medals, some smaller wineries don't enter many competitions because they can't afford the gratis bottles that they're expected to provide. They may make wonderful wines, but have few medals to show for them.

Are we suggesting that medals aren't important; that just about any wine can win? What does all this medal business mean?

It means that California produces a lot of remarkably good wines, and that awards are *one* measure of their excellence, at least in the minds and taste buds of a particular tasting panel.

If you want to take this awards business seriously, look for wines with sweepstake or best of show awards, which *are* one of a kind.

What we seek, when we snatch up our MasterCard and go afield to replenish our wine cellar, are award-winning wines at modest prices. Yes, you can find them. A surprising number of inexpensive wines are bedecked with gold and silver tasting awards.

The best buys often are those from long established vintners such as Sebastiani, Pedroncelli, Fortino and Fetzer—family-owned wineries whose mortgages have long since been paid off. The newer wineries with smart young U.C. Davis graduates as winemakers certainly are capable of producing great wines, but they may have large debts to pay off, which is reflected in the price per bottle.

When all else fails, fall back on your one trusted authority—your taste buds.

Richard Arrowood made wine—and won medals—for several other vintners before he and Alis opened this facility in 1987. He buys grapes from several vineyards, produces and barrel-ages each batch separately, then skillfully blends them to create award-winning results.

Tasting notes: From Arrowood's short list, we tasted two exceptional wines. A Chardonnay Reserve was among the best we've sampled in the state—perfectly balanced, lush, spicy and silky with a crisp acid finish. A Cabernet Sauvignon, blended with Merlot, Cabernet Franc and Malbec, had a peppery, rich nose and a soft, spicy, berry-like flavor with a subtle touch of wood. Merlot also is available, but only when Dick can find exceptional grapes. Prices range from $19.25 to $27.

Benziger Family Winery • T GT & ST ✗ 🐚

☐ *1883 London Ranch Rd., Glen Ellen, CA 95442; (707) 935-3047. Daily 10 to 4:30; MC/VISA, DISC. Most varieties tasted. Good selection of wine logo and gift items. Informal self-guiding tours and conducted tours; picnic area in a redwood grove.* ☐

This is one of the wine industry's more startling success stories. In 1980, New York wine merchant Bruno Benziger started the Glen Ellen Winery here, buying grapes from more than 250 growers, and soon was shipping 3.7 million cases of wine worldwide. The Benziger family then sold the giant Heublein complex its Glen Ellen line of wines—which accounted for more than 90 percent of its production—while retaining the winery and starting a new label under its own name.

The facilities are located in a wooded vale surrounded by vineyards. It appears to be an old, well-maintained farmyard with its random scatter of neat white clapboard buildings, shaded by mature oaks. However, all except the original house are of recent vintage. The small Imagery Art Gallery near the tasting room displays original artwork and printed examples of the very creative Benziger labels.

Tasting notes: Fumé, Chardonnay, Pinot Blanc, Pinot Noir, Zinfandel, Merlot and Cabernet make up the Benziger list, plus a sparkling Blanc to Blanc and rich Muscat Canelli. Our favorite were a silky, spicy Chardonnay, a soft and mouth-filling Pinot Noir and a light and crisp Zinfandel. A second label called Benziger Imagery features small lots of lesser known varieties such as Viognier, Aleatico, Cabernet Franc and Syrah. Prices on both brands range from $8 to $20.

Vintners Choice: "The most popular Benziger wines are the Sonoma County Chardonnay, Cabernet Sauvignon and Merlot, but smaller production Zinfandel and Pinot also are enjoyable," said a winery source.

Kunde Estate Winery • T GTA ✕

◻ 10155 Sonoma Hwy. (Box 639), Kenwood, CA 95452; (707) 833-5501. Daily 11 to 5; MC/VISA, AMEX. Most wines tasted. A few wine logo items; shaded picnic area. Cave tours by appointment, Friday, Saturday, Sunday. ◻

A dramatic multi-gabled winery rising from the vineyards on an upslope from the highway marks this new facility. It was completed in the early 1990s by Bob Kunde, the fourth generation of a German immigrant family that has been growing grapes here since 1904. Grapes from Kunde's 3,000 acre ranch kept winning awards for other vintners, so he decided to pick up a few for himself, which he certainly has—particularly for his Chardonnays. It's definitely a family operation, with Bob's two sons, his sister and a cousin active in the winery.

The small tasting room occupies a corner of the impressive winery building. Even more impressive—and often open for special events—are aging cellars burrowed into an adjacent hill, with vines planted atop them.

Tasting notes: Kunde's list is short and excellent—full flavored Sauvignon Blanc, Merlot, Zinfandel, Cabernet Sauvignon and some interesting proprietary blends. Although we're red wine fans, we liked the fruity, flowery-nosed Magnolia Lane Sauvignon Blanc and lush, spicy reserve Chardonnay. Most of Kunde's reds are *big*, with tannins that want more sleep. A four-year-old un-fined and unfiltered Cabernet Sauvignon was one of the best we've tasted in the valley. A rich and spicy Rhône style blend, *Vallee de la Lune*, also exhibited a nice tannic finish.

Kenwood Vineyards • T ⬥

◻ 9592 Sonoma Hwy., Kenwood, CA 95452; (707) 833-5891. Daily 10 to 4; MC/VISA. Most varieties tasted. Good selection of wine related items and giftwares. ◻

Kenwood is located in a wood-sided ranch style structure amidst the vineyards, upslope from the highway. The grounds are carefully kept, with terraced gardens and fieldstone borders. The large, airy tasting room suggests an oversized chalet, with wood paneled walls and open beams. It's a nice example of rustic taste and style.

The facility came to being in 1970 when the Martin Lee family bought the old turn-of-the-century Pagani Brothers Winery, with an eye toward premium varietals. They've kept their focus, and Kenwood wines win a generous share of medals.

Tasting notes: Wines available for tasting are posted, and they represent a liberal portion of the list. Our favorite was a Beltane Ranch Chardonnay, barrel fermented with good fruit, spiciness and crisp acid. Jack London Pinot Noir was full flavored and berry-like with a soft drink-it-now finish. The Sonoma Valley Zinfandel had an herbal nose and taste and a crisp nip of tannin. Prices range from $7 to the mid teens, and go a bit higher for select reserves.

Vintners choice: "Sauvignon Blanc and Jack London Cabernet Sauvignon," spoke a voice from the winery.

Smothers Brothers Wine Store • T ✗ 📦

☐ 9575 Sonoma Hwy. (P.O. Box 789), Kenwood, CA 95452; (707) 833-1010. Daily 10 to 4:30; MC/VISA, AMEX. Three wines tasted from the list. Extensive wine logo, giftware and curio selection. ☐

This facility in a weathered wood storefront in downtown Kenwood is a blend of tasting room, wine store and curio shop. The musical-comedy brothers' winery is elsewhere. However, their presence is evident here, with assorted Smothers Brothers, a couple of their gold records adorning a wall and theme music from their old TV show in the background. It also has a nice selection of gift items.

Tasting notes: The Smothers' whimsy is evident in this souvenir shop kum tasting room, but their wines are fine, exhibiting strong varietal character. The Chards and Cabs were particularly pleasing; with good, spicy fruit in the former and big, full body in the latter. Naturally, their basic table wines are Mom's Favorite Red and White. Wine prices range from $10 into the teens and Mom's is yours for $7.

Vintners choice: "Tom Smothers takes his winemaking very seriously," said a winery spokesperson. "The Chardonnay, Cabernet Sauvignon and Merlot are quite pleasing, with spicy fruit in the Chardonnay and big, full body in the reds."

Stone Creek Tasting Room • T & T$ ✗

☐ 9380 Sonoma Hwy., Kenwood, CA 95452; (707) 833-5070. Daily 10 to 4:30; MC/VISA. Most varieties tasted; some free, some for a fee. Small but nice selection of wine logo items. Lawn picnic area. ☐

Stone Creek Winery is based in the Napa Valley and most of its wines come from there as well. This facility was opened recently to catch the growing wine tasting traffic through Kenwood. It's an appealing sipping stop, housed in a carefully restored 1890 home, complete with front porch swings and a white picket fence,

Tasting notes: Stone Creek's list runs the classic varietal gamut—Fumé Blanc, Chardonnay, Gewürztraminer, Merlot, Zinfandel and Cabernet Sauvignon. The style is soft and fruity for the whites; even the Gewürztraminer was pleasantly soft and dry without the typical pronounced floral favor. The Chard, with a lively fruity notes, was our favorite white. Of the reds, we really liked a light fruity Merlot. The Zin, four old, was soft and lush and ready to drink.

Bandiera Tasting Room ● T ✗

☐ *8860 Sonoma Highway (P.O. Box 1270), Kenwood, CA 95452; (707) 833-2448. Daily 10 to 4:30; MC/VISA. Most varieties tasted. Some wine logo items; a few picnic tables.* ☐

Bandiera Winery is a longtime fixture in Cloverdale to the north, where it has been a family operation since 1937. The firm decided to open a tasting room in Kenwood for the same reason that Stone Creek came to town; the traffic's better here. Grand Cru, one of several firms purchased by the Bronco Wine Company, was the original occupant of this little cottage. It was vacated because Bronco doesn't believe much in tasting rooms, except for its Bartholomew Park showplace.

The tasting room is a simple affair, trimmed with a few wine barrels and some wine logo items. A couple of picnic tables occupy the lawn out front. Incidentally, *bandiera* is Italian for banner or flag.

Tasting notes: Bandiera brought some very good prices when it came to Kenwood. Two quite tasty, spicy and ready-to-drink Cabernets were only $6.99 when we stopped by and a lush, fruity Sauvignon Blanc was a mere $5.50. Several vintage Cabs were offered—ranging as far back as eight years. Most were full flavored and nicely herbal with soft tannins; ready to drink. A 1990 was outstanding, the winner of seven gold medals. Cab prices ranged from $10 to $15.

Château St. Jean ● T ST ✗

☐ *8555 Sonoma Hwy., Kenwood, CA 95452; (707) 833-4134. Daily 10 to 4:30; MC/VISA, AMEX. Selected wines tasted. Some wine logo and giftware items; shaded picnic areas. Self-guided tours daily from 10:30 to 4.* ☐

St. Jean (as in denims) is a château in every sense of the word; it may be the valley's most attractive winery. Tasting room and offices are in the Spanish style manor house of a former country estate. The winery occupies a beige stucco creation with a distinctive witch's hat tower. The hat serves no purpose other than providing an awesome view of the countryside. The grounds, busy with lawns, fountains, patios and mature trees, are as carefully groomed as a proper English garden.

Self-guided tours take you through the towered structure too comely to be a winery. From carpeted hallways, you look down upon rows of stainless steel and tiers of French oak. Graphics along the wall offer a flash course in winemaking. A winding stairway leads to the medieval-style tower for a view of russet tile rooftops and the greater Sonoma Valley. Established in 1973, the winery was purchased in 1984 by Suntory International. It's corporate backing is evident in the careful grooming of this stylish facility.

Tasting notes: Selected wines are opened for tasting; only whites were available the day we visited. Fumé Blanc was flowery, soft and smooth with good acid; an Estate Chardonnay was buttery, complex and delicious; Gewürztraminer had the delectable nose and taste of crushed flower petals, with a crisp acid finish. A sparkling Brut was dry and fruity, with a bit of a grassy taste. The winery also produces Pinot Noir, Cabernet Sauvignon and Merlot. Prices range from $6.50 to $19; higher for some late harvest wines.

St. Francis Winery • T GTA ✕ ▨

 8450 Sonoma Hwy., Kenwood, CA 95452; (707) 833-4666. Daily 10 to 4:30. Most varieties tasted; choice of four from the list. Good giftware selection; sheltered picnic garden; tours by appointment.

Smaller than St. Jean but also well-groomed, neighbor St. Francis has an affluent rural European look, in a tree-shaded garden setting. The matched winery buildings have shingled roofs and cupolas, with burgundy awnings accenting the handsome oak tasting room.

The winery was started in 1972 by Joseph and Emma Martin. They have built a following for their Merlot and other ribbon-winning varietals, as they gradually built up their winery to its present attractive state.

Tasting notes: The Sonoma County Cabernet was our favorite, big and peppery, with nice oak tones; it was very drinkable, yet tannic enough for aging. A Zinfandel, from old vines and aged in American oak, was excellent as well, lushly berry-like and gently spicy. A Sonoma County Gewürztraminer had the proper flower petal aroma and flavor, and the Chardonnay was buttery and spicy. Prices range from $8 to the middle teens.

Vintners choice: "We're known for our Merlot," said tasting room manager Penny Cassina. "We also produce outstanding Cabernet Sauvignon and Chardonnay."

Landmark Vineyards • T GTA ✕ ▨

 101 Adobe Canyon Rd., Kenwood, CA 95452; (707) 833-0053. Daily 10 to 4:30; MC/VISA. Selected wines tasted. Good selection of wine related items and specialty foods. Picnic tables; guided tours by appointment.

This pleasing facility of beige stucco with shake roofs forms a large Spanish-style semi-courtyard. A tile-floored, vaulted-ceiling tasting room and a stylish gift and gourmet food shop occupy one wing. An imposing mural of the winery's premiere product, Chardonnay, dominates the wall behind the tasting counter.

Established in 1974, Landmark began operations northern Sonoma County near Windsor, then moved to this site in mid-1990. The winery's proprietor Damaris Deere Ethridge is great granddaughter of farm implement pioneer John Deere.

Tasting notes: Chardonnays dominate the short list and they're excellent. A Damaris Alexander Valley Reserve was rich and complex, and a Proprietor's Reserve Chard had a wonderfully nutty taste with a crisp yet silky finish. Landmark also produces a Brut sparkling wine and an Alexander Valley Cabernet Sauvignon. Prices range from $12 to $18.

Vintners choice: "Our award-winning premium Chardonnays," says winery president Michael D. Colhoun, Damaris' son. "They will cellar and age for a good amount of time."

THE BEST OF THE BUNCH

The best wine buys • Sebastiani Vineyards, Benziger Family Winery, Valley of the Moon Winery and Bandiera Winery.

The most attractive wineries • Viansa, Gloria Ferrer Champagne Cellars, Buena Vista Carneros, Kunde Estate Winery, Kenwood Vineyards, Château St. Jean and Landmark Vineyards.

The most interesting tasting rooms • Viansa, Sebastiani Vineyards, Buena Vista Carneros and Landmark Vineyards.

The funkiest tasting room ● Gundlach-Bundschu Winery.

The best gift shops ● Viansa, Sebastiani Vineyards, Buena Vista Winery and Landmark Vineyards.

The nicest picnic areas ● Viansa, Ravenswood, Bartholomew Park Winery, Buena Vista Winery, Gundlach-Bundschu Winery, Benziger Family Winery and Château St. Jean.

The best tours ● Gloria Ferrer Champagne Cellars (guided), Sebastiani Vineyards (guided), Buena Vista (historic; also self-guiding), Château St. Jean (self-guiding).

Wineland activities and such

Wineland events ● Heart of the Valley barrel tasting at eight Valley of the Moon area wineries, mid-March; (707) 833-5891. Sonoma Valley Wine Festival, mid-July; (707) 938-6800. Sonoma Valley Harvest Wine Auction, early September; (707) 935-0803. Valley of the Moon Vintage Festival, oldest in California with parade, grape stomps, wine tasting, late September; (707) 996-2109. California Wine Appreciation Week with special events and tastings at Sonoma Valley wineries; (707) 935-0803. Throughout the year, individual wineries also sponsor various events.

Winery maps and guides ● *Sonoma Valley Visitors Guide* is available at Sonoma Valley Visitors Bureau offices near Viansa Winery and on the Sonoma Plaza for $1.50. It contains winery maps and listings, plus listings of restaurants, lodgings, activities, services and annual events. The larger *Sonoma County Guide* has similiar information in a more elaborate format; $4.95 at various wineries and shops, or order it by mail for $7 from Vintage Publications, 764 Adobe Dr., Santa Rosa, CA 95404; (707) 538-8981. *Sonoma County Farm Trails* map and guide lists wineries and direct-to-consumer farm produce outlets. Pick up a free copy at member outlets or send a self-addressed envelope with 55 cents postage to: Sonoma County Farm Trails, P.O. Box 6032, Santa Rosa, CA 95406; for information call (707) 996-2154. Mattiololi's *In Your Pocket Guide* is a map directory to wineries, lodgings, services and attractions in the Valley of the Moon; on sale locally for $1.50; call (707) 965-2006.

Wine country tours ● Convertible Cruising offers chauffeured tours with picnics; (707) 935-0110. VinTours features personalized tours of smaller wineries in Sonoma and Napa counties; 536 Orchard St., Santa Rosa, CA 95404; (707) 546-9483. Sonoma Chardonnay Limousine Service offers wine country tours and airport transit; 22455 Broadway, Sonoma, CA 95476; (800) 232-7260 or (707) 938-4248. Pure Luxury Limousines has limo tours of the wine country; 5750-A Labath Ave., Rohnert Park, CA 94928; (800) 626-5466 or (707) 795-1615. Sonoma Thunder offers van tours and hot air balloon rides; 6984 McKinley St., Sebastopol, CA 95472; (800) 759-5638 or (707) 538-7359. VinTours does personalized tours of smaller Sonoma-Napa wineries; 536 Orchard St., Santa Rosa, CA 95404; (707) 546-9483.

BEYOND THE VINEYARDS

Sonoma is the historic focal point of the valley and you may want to spend considerable time here. Start at the eight-acre **Sonoma Plaza** with its 1906 mission revival **City Hall.** It was built with four matching "front entries" so none of the surrounding merchants would feel slighted. The **Bear Flag Monument** honoring California's brief tenure as a republic stands at the plaza's northeast corner. The plaza also has a playground, picnic tables and duck ponds.

The **Sonoma Valley Visitors Bureau** occupies an old Carnegie library building on the Plaza's east side; open daily 9 to 5. It faces the Italianate **Sebastiani Theatre,** a classic old movie house with a 72-foot tower. Boutiques, antique shops, restaurants and a startling number of bakery-cafés rim the plaza and more are tucked into little pedestrian malls. Various elements of **Sonoma State Historic Park** line Spain Street on the top side of the plaza—Mission San Francisco Solano, Sonoma Barracks, Toscano Hotel and the site of Casa Grande, once General Vallejo's home and headquarters.

A few blocks south on Spain Street, you'll encounter Vallejo's final home, a striking gingerbread Victorian called **Lachryma Montis,** Latin for "mountain tear." There's a small admission fee to some of the elements of the historic park. One same-day ticket is good for all, including Jack London State Historic Park and—over the mountains—Petaluma Adobe State Historic Park. Dozens of other yesteryear buildings occupy the streets of old Sonoma. To spot them, you can purchase a copy of the Sonoma League for Historic Preservation's *Sonoma Walking Tour* at the visitor's center.

In addition to wine, history and shopping, a fourth element helps draw Sonoma's nearly one million annual visitors—food. Since wining and dining are closely allied, the town has a reputation as a specialty food center. These places, most of them on or near the plaza, are worthy of a your attention:

Sonoma French Bakery, on the plaza at 470 First St. East, makes the best sourdough bread north of San Francisco, along with other baked goodies. Get there early, since the bread supply often runs out. Hours are Tuesday-Saturday 7:30 to 6 and Sunday 7:30 to 4; (707) 996-2691.

Sonoma Cheese Factory, on the north side of the plaza at Two Spain St., is a large deli and café specializing in local and international cheeses. Through a window, you can watch soft "jack" style cheese being made. Tables inside and under an outdoor vine-covered awning. Hours are 8:30 to 5:30 weekdays and 8:30 to 6 weekends; (707) 996-1931.

Vella Cheese Company, a block east of the mission, then a block north at 315 Second St., is Sonoma's other pioneer cheese-making firm, offering cheeses, picnic fare and specialty foods. Housed in a 1905 rough-cut stone brewery building, it's open Monday-Saturday 9 to 6 and Sunday 10 to 5; (800) 848-0505 or (707) 938-3232.

The Cherry Tree specializes in cherry juice, cider and other fruit juices and food items. Its main store is at 1901 Fremont Drive (Highways 12-121), just east of Broadway on the route to Napa. The smaller, original cherry tree stand is south on Highway 121, as you come in from the Bay Area. Hours are 6:30 a.m. to 8 p.m. at the Fremont Drive store and 9 to dusk at the stand; phone (707) 938-3480.

Wine Exchange of Sonoma at 453 First Street East compliments the specialty food outlets, offering dozens of wines local and from afar, 251 beers plus assorted wine and beer publications. Fee tastings of assorted wines and beers are available daily; (707) 938-1794.

SOUTHERN SONOMA COUNTY DRIVING TOUR ● This loop tour touches other points of interest in the southern half of the county. Assuming you visited Jack London State Historic Park during your winery prowling, we'll head you off in another direction.

From the Sonoma Plaza, drive south on Broadway, perhaps stopping for a choo-choo ride at **Train Town** on your left (see "Sonoma Valley activities" below). About a mile beyond Train Town, turn right onto Watmaugh Road, which crosses Arnold Drive, then swings left and blends onto Stage Gulch Road (Highway 116). This takes you into rolling hill country, thatched here and there with oak clusters and madrone groves.

Follow Stage Gulch 2.5 miles, turn left onto Adobe Road and follow it to **Petaluma Adobe State Historic Park,** a reconstruction of Vallejo's ranch headquarters. Continue on Adobe Road about a mile and a half, turn left onto Washington Street and take it into **Petaluma.** You'll cross U.S. 101 freeway and wind up in the heart of this old town with the funny name. It's noted for false front and rare iron front stores downtown, and for some attractive Victorian homes on its tree-lined residential streets. Petaluma has a couple of curious claims to fame. It's home to the World's Wristwrestling Championships and an annual ugly dog contest.

Once you've explored the town, follow D Street (lined with some fine old homes) until it becomes Red Hill Road. Drive nine miles to **Marin French Cheese Factory.** You can watch camembert and other smelly cheeses being made, then buy some cheese and wine and picnic beside a duck pond. You're now in Marin County, but never mind that. This route takes through some of the prettiest hilly landscape in all of northern California.

Stay on Red Hill (which becomes Petaluma-Point Reyes Road) until it intersects Highway 1 at **Tomales Bay**, about ten miles from the cheese place. Tomales is a narrow inlet formed by the famous San Andreas Fault—infamous if you're a fidgety California resident who fears earthquakes.

From here, you could stray completely off course by heading south to **Point Reyes National Seashore** on the Point Reyes Peninsula. Or bear with us and bear north on State Route 1 along the skinny bay's eastern shore, passing funky little **Marshall,** a town that seems transported from the New England seacoast. Continue to the equally rustic town of **Tomales**, seven miles north, then turn seaward and prowl the hideaway coastal hamlet of **Dillon Beach**. Press on north to **Bodega Bay,** a bucolic harbor town made famous by Alfred Hitchcock's film, *The Birds*. From here, you can head inland on the Bodega Highway to **Sebastopol**, then follow Highway 12 through **Santa Rosa** and back into the Valley of the Moon at Kenwood.

If you plan to travel from the Sonoma Valley to the Napa Valley, a dramatic and rarely used approach is over Trinity Grade, which branches eastward from Route 12 between Kenwood and Glen Ellen. It twists high into the evergreen reaches of the Mayacamus Mountains, offering views of the Valley of the Moon to the west and—once you start down the other side—the Napa Valley's green patchwork of vineyards. The road hits the Napa Valley's Highway 29 in Oakville and is known on this side as the Oakville Grade.

Sonoma Valley activities

Auto racing • Sears Point Raceway, auto and cycle races most weekends, Highway 37 at 121, Sonoma, CA 95476; (800) 870-RACE or (707) 938-8448.

Bike tours and rentals • Sonoma Valley Cyclery offers bike rentals and tour information; 1061 Broadway, Sonora, CA 95476; (707) 935-3377.

Farm products • For a map and guide to direct-outlet farms selling fresh and prepared fruits, vegetables, meats, dairy products and wines, pick up a

Sonoma County Farm Trails map, available at most member outlets. Or send a self-addressed envelope with 55 cents postage to: Sonoma County Farm Trails, P.O. Box 6032, Santa Rosa, CA 95406; for information call (707) 996-2154.

Hot-air ballooning ● Air Flamboyant, (800) 456-4711 or (707) 838-8500; Once in a Lifetime, (800) 799-9133 or (707) 578-0580. Sonoma Thunder, (800) 759-5638 or (707) 538-7359.

Horseback riding ● Guided trail rides through Jack London State Park and Sugarloaf Ridge State Park by Sonoma Cattle Company, (707) 996-8566.

Scenic flights ● Aeroschellville (open-cockpit biplane), 23982 Arnold Dr., Sonoma; (707) 938-2444.

Train rides ● Train Town, 20264 Broadway, Sonoma; (707) 938-3912. Daily 10:30 to 5 in summer; Friday-Sunday 10:30 to 5 October through May. Adult fare for 20-minute ride on elaborate miniature railroad setup $2.80; kids and seniors $1.90.

Walking tours ● One hour tours of Sonoma Plaza with interesting and humorous vignettes on its past and present; introduction by Marv Parker; $10. Monday, Friday and Saturday at 10 a.m. and 2 p.m. in front of Sonoma Valley Visitors Bureau, east side of the plaza, or by appointment. P.O. Box 15, Sonoma, CA 95476; (707) 996-9112.

Attractions

Jack London State Historic Park ● London Ranch Road, Glen Ellen; 938-5216. Daily 10 to 5; modest admission charge. Author's ranch, Wolf House ruins and wife's home.

Sonoma State Historic Park ● P.O. Box 167, Sonoma; (707) 938-1578. Daily 10 to 5; modest admission charge (one ticket good for all units of the park). Includes Mission San Francisco Solano, Sonoma Barracks, La Casa Grande and Toscano Hotel all on Sonoma Plaza and General Vallejo's Home, south of the plaza off Spain Street.

Spas, mineral springs ● Agua Caliente Mineral Springs, 17350 Vailetti Dr., Agua Caliente, CA 95416; (707) 996-6822. Morton's Warm Springs, 1651 Warm Springs Rd., Kenwood, CA 95452; (707) 833-5511. The Spa at Sonoma Mission Inn, P.O. Box 1447, Sonoma, CA 95476; (707) 938-9000.

WINE COUNTRY DINING

It will come as no gastronomic surprise that many of the Sonoma Valley's restaurants are of the Italian persuasion, although a good mix of *nouveau,* essential American, continental and Mexican fare can be found as well.

Babette's Restaurant & Wine Bar ● ☆☆☆☆ $$$

◻ *464 First Street East (in the alley), Sonora; (707) 939-8921. American nouveau; wine and beer. Daily 4 p.m. to midnight. MC/VISA.* ◻ One of wineland's better restaurants, with a weekly-changing *prix fixe* dinners around $30, offering savories such as yellowtail with sautéed vegetables in three sauces, plus creative soup and salad. It's served in a simple country Victorian atmosphere with plush velvet chairs and white nappery behind windows with vine covered lattice.

Café Citti ● ☆☆☆ $$

◻ *9049 Sonoma Highway, Kenwood; (707) 833-2690. Italian; wine and beer. Lunch and dinner daily 11 to 8:30. MC/VISA.* ◻ Attractive, cozy Italian *trattoria* in a cottage near the vineyards on the edge of Kenwood. Fresh pasta with a variety of sauces, plus classic cacciatoris, parmigianas and such; patio dining. Local and Italian wines by the glass; specialty foods for sale.

Coffee Garden and Gift Shop ● ☆ $

◻ *415 First Street West, Sonoma; (707) 996-6645. Bakery-café. Sunday-Thursday 6:30 a.m. to 10 p.m., Friday-Saturday 7 a.m. to 11 p.m.* ◻ Handy stop for a quite bite, housed in an 1836 adobe; it offers assorted coffees, espresso and such, pastries and muffins for breakfast, plus soups, salads and sandwiches. Sidewalk tables and dining patio; gift shop adjacent.

Della Santina Trattoria ● ☆☆☆ $$

◻ *101 E. Napa St. (opposite the plaza), Sonoma; (707) 935-0576. Italian; wine and beer. Daily 11 to 9:30. MC/VISA.* ◻ Cute and prim Italian restaurant tucked comfortably behind old cut stone walls, with white nappery and ceiling fans. The usual range of pastas, plus *rosticceria* (spit roasted) specialties such as Petaluma duck with wild rice and rabbit, chicken or turkey breast with herbs. Extensive wine list with 53 varieties; 21 by the glass.

Depot 1870 Restaurant ● ☆☆☆ $$

◻ *241 First St. West (Spain Street), Sonoma; (707) 938-2980. Northern Italian; wine and beer. Lunch Wednesday-Friday 11:30 to 2, dinner Wednesday-Sunday from 5. Major credit cards.* ◻ Chef-owned restaurant with dining at poolside in a landscaped garden, or in a country inn setting indoors. Fresh seafood and homemade pastas are a specialty, plus Northern Italian dishes such as *petto al paillard* (grilled chicken breast marinated in Italian herbs).

Eastside Oyster Bar & Grill ● ☆☆☆ $$

◻ *133 E. Napa St. (just off the plaza), Sonoma; (707) 939-1266. California nouveau and oyster bar; wine and beer. Lunch and dinner daily; Sunday brunch. Major credit cards.* ◻ Another trendy café residing in an old Victorian, with lofty ceilings, tile floors and white nappery. Typical of the fare is Mediterranean style grilled *tombo* tuna with black olives, artichoke broth and rosemary roasted potatoes; plus oysters and other shellfish; patio garden.

Fay's Garden Court Café & Bakery ● ☆☆ $

◻ *13875 Sonoma Highway, Glen Ellen; (707) 935-1565. Light American fare; wine and beer. Wednesday-Sunday 7 a.m. to 2 p.m. MC/VISA.* ◻ Appealing little breakfast and lunch stop in a tiny cottage on Highway 12 just beyond the Madrone Road turnoff. Breakfasts feature Italian sausage and eggs, assorted omelets, eggs Benedict, waffles and such. Assorted 'burgers, including a tasty meatless version and other sandwiches served for lunch.

Glen Ellen Inn ● ☆☆☆ $$

◻ *13670 Arnold Dr., Glen Ellen; (707) 996-6409. California cuisine; wine and beer. Lunch Tuesday-Saturday 11:30 to 2:30; dinner Tuesday-Sunday 5:30 to 9:30. MC/VISA.* ◻ Cute and cozy cafe in a Cape Cod cottage with an open kitchen. Typical offerings from the changing menu—with an emphais on fresh ingredients—might include breast of duck in Chinese orange dressing or pork loin in rosemary-burgundy sauce. Sonoma Valley wines featured; outdoor dining near an herb garden.

Kenwood Restaurant ● ☆☆☆☆ $$$

◻ *9900 Sonoma Highway, Kenwood; (707) 833-6326. French country cuisine; full bar service. Daily except Monday from 11:30 to 9. MC/VISA.* ◻ An open, cheerful place among the vineyards, with an outdoor dining patio if you want to get closer to the grapes. Changing menu with a strong *nouveau* tilt, featuring local fare such as roast Petaluma duck with wild rice and orange sauce and braised Sonoma rabbit with tomatoes and polenta.

La Casa ● ☆☆ $

◻ 121 E. Spain St. (opposite the mission), Sonoma; (707) 996-3406. Mexican; full bar service. Daily from 11:30 a.m. Major credit cards. ◻ Cheery little Latin place across from the mission, locally popular. Extensive menu features the usual Mexican specialties, singly or in *combinacións*. If you're feeling some south of the border patriotism, order the "Mexican flag"—three enchiladas draped with white sour cream, red ground beef and cheese, and green verde sauces.

London's Grill ● ☆☆ $$

◻ 13740 Arnold Drive, Glen Ellen; (707) 939-8084. American; full bar service. Lunch and dinner daily, Sunday brunch. MC/VISA. ◻ Creative, health-conscious country style fare served in a rustic setting overlooking Sonoma Creek. The menu focuses on traditional American dishes with some innovative sauces and seasonings. Good local wine list; outdoor patio near the creek.

Magliulo's Restaurant ● ☆☆☆ $$$

◻ 691 Broadway, Sonoma; (707) 996-1031. Italian-American; full bar service. Lunch daily 11 to 3, dinner 5 to 9. MC/VISA, DISC. ◻ Attractive, long-established place in an early American home with warm woods, iron-work and cut glass. Busy menu ranges from New York steak and rack of lamb to a full spectrum of Italian dishes. Lantern-lit dining garden.

Murphy's Irish Pub ● ☆☆ $$

◻ 464 First Street East (in the ally), Sonoma; (707) 935-0660. Irish-American; full bar service. Daily 11 to 11. MC/VISA. ◻ Guinness stout in the wine country? Sure, and why not? This lively pub, dressed up in Irish regalia, offers pub grub such as fish & chips, meat pies and Irish stew, served with an assortment of ales, pilsners, ales and stouts. Oh, yes—Sonoma Valley wines if you prefer. Live entertainment—often Irish—is featured frequently; an Irish gift shop is adjacent.

Pasta Nostra Restaurant ● ☆☆☆ $$

◻ 139 E. Napa St. (just east of the plaza), Sonoma; (707) 938-4166. Italian; wine and beer. Lunch Wednesday-Saturday 11:30 to 2:30, dinner Monday-Thursday 5 to 9, Friday-Saturday 4 to 10 and Sunday 4:30 to 9. MC/VISA, AMEX. ◻ Cheerful restaurant in a restored Victorian home. Pasta-focused menu, plus entrées such as veal piccata, marsala Milanese and chicken Sicilian with lemon, rosemary and garlic and a combined veal parmesana-scalloppini. Attractive dining patio in ivy draped courtyard.

Ristorante Piatti ● ☆☆☆ $$$

◻ 405 First St. West (in the El Dorado Hotel), Sonoma; (707) 996-2351. Regional Italian; full bar service. Daily from 11:30, various closing hours. MC/VISA. ◻ Lively *trattoria*, popular as a business lunch hangout. Open kitchen with wood-burning rotissiere; specialties include angel hair pasta, spaghetti with duck *ragout*, black and white pasta with fresh mussels and grilled seafoods. Tree-shaded dining patio.

Vineyards Inn ● ☆☆ $$

◻ 8445 Sonoma Highway (Adobe Canyon Road), Kenwood; (707) 833-4500. Spanish, Mexican, American; full bar service. Daily except Tuesday from 11:30, various closing times. MC/VISA. ◻ Mexican fare served in an early

American-style inn. Large menu also strays north of the border, offering gringo fare such as filet mignon, Enchiladas San Francisco with dungeness crab meat, and even lamb chops, plus Spanish dishes such as paella.

Zeno's Ristorante • ☆☆ $$

☐ *420 First Street East, Sonoma; (707) 996-4466. Traditional Italian; full bar service. Major credit cards.* ☐ Not at all trendy, Zeno's is an old fashion Italian restaurant with red checkered tablecloths, dark woods, bentwood chairs and tables topped with *raffia* bottles. A variety of sauces can be poured over spaghetti, linguine, angel hair or penna pastas cooked to order. Other *Italiano* standards are offered as well.

WINELAND LODGINGS

NOTE: Prices were provided by the establishments and are subject to change. Use the price ranges only as a rough guideline and call the places listed to confirm their current rates.

Even with the Sonoma Valley's popularity, motels are rather scarce. The area offers an assortment of bed & breakfast inns, historic hotels and—for those with a taste and budget for luxury—the Sonoma Mission Inn and Spa. Nearby Santa Rosa has scores of lodgings.

Wine Country Referrals is a reservation service for hotels, motels, inns, B&Bs and vacation homes in Lake, Mendocino, Napa and Sonoma counties; P.O. Box 543, Calistoga, CA 94515; (707) 942-2186, FAX (707) 942-4681. Also, the Bed and Breakfast Association of Sonoma Valley offers reservation service; call for lodging availability or a free brochure; (800) 969-INNS or (707) 938-9513.

Best Western Sonoma Valley Inn • ☆☆☆ $$$$$ ∅

☐ *550 Second St. West (a block west of plaza), Sonoma, CA 95476; (800) 528-1234 or (707) 938-9200. Couples and singles $105 to $149; off-season $75 to $100. Rates include complimentary breakfast and gift bottle of wine. Major credit cards.* ☐ Nicely appointed 72-unit motel with pool and spa. Rooms have TV movies, phones, refrigerators; most have fireplaces.

El Dorado Hotel • ☆☆☆ $$$$ ∅

☐ *405 First St. West (west side of plaza), Sonoma, CA 95476; (800) 289-3031 or (707) 996-3030. Couples $85 to $145. Rates include continental breakfast. MC/VISA, AMEX.* ☐ Refurbished 27-room mission-style hotel. Attractive rooms with terraces overlooking courtyard or plaza; continental furnishings with Spanish accents; swimming pool. **Ristorante Piatti** listed above.

Kenwood Inn & Spa • ☆☆☆ $$$$$ ∅

☐ *10400 Sonoma Hwy. (downtown), Kenwood, CA 95452; (800) 353-6966 or (707) 833-1293. Couples and singles $125 to $225. Rates include full breakfast. MC/VISA, AMEX.* ☐ An opulent Italian style villa with 12 rooms, all with private baths, Mediterranean furnishings, feather beds and other resort amenities; complimentary wine. Extensive landscaped grounds among the vineyards. Separate spa building offers massage, facial and body treatments; fitness workouts.

Sonoma Hotel • ☆☆ $$$

☐ *110 W. Spain St. (northwest corner of plaza), Sonoma, CA 95476; (800) 468-6016 or (707) 996-2996. Couples $75 to $120. Rates include continental breakfast and nightly bottle of wine. MC/VISA, AMEX.* ☐ Restored

1874 hotel; 17 rooms furnished with Victorian and early California antiques. Five rooms with private baths; others share. **Bistro Lunel** serves daily 11:30 to 10; European and "contemporary country" cuisine; dinners $10 to $17; full bar service.

Sonoma Mission Inn and Spa ● ☆☆☆☆ $$$$$ ∅

❐ *18140 Sonoma Highway, Boyes Hot Springs; mailing address P.O. Box 1447, Sonoma, CA 95476; (800) 862-4945 or (707) 938-9000. Couples and singles $110 to $375. Major credit cards.* ❐ Elegantly restored Mediterranean style resort on seven acres with a complete health spa, tennis courts and two natural hot artesian mineral water pools. The 170 beautifully appointed rooms have TV & VCRs, room phones and typical resort amenities. Two restaurants—**The Grille,** daily 11:30 to 2:30 and 6 to 9, California *nouveau,* dinners $25 to $40, overlooking pool and gardens; **Mission Inn Café,** 7 to 3 and 5:30 to 9:30, northern Italian, dinners $10 to $15; both smoke free.

Westerbeke Ranch ● ☆☆☆ $$$ ∅

❐ *2300 Grove St., (off Arnold Drive), Sonoma, CA 95476; (707) 996-7546. Rooms $60 to $80. MC/VISA.* ❐ Fifteen cabins and rooms, some with shared baths, in a wooded ranch retreat used both for conferences and individuals. Pool, sauna, hot tub, racquetball court. **Dining Room** serves California *nouveau* and vegetarian dishes, for guests only; Mexican décor.

Bed & breakfast inns

Beltane Ranch Bed & Breakfast ● ☆☆☆ $$$$ ∅

❐ *11775 Sonoma Highway (P.O. Box 395), Glen Ellen, CA 95442; (707) 996-6501. Couples and singles $95 to $125. Four rooms, all with private baths; full breakfast. No credit cards.* ❐ An 1892 Colonial style ranch house in a pleasant country setting. Tennis court, pleasant tree-shaded gardens, hammocks and hiking trails. Attractive rooms are furnished with American and European antiques.

Gaige House ● ☆☆☆ $$$$ ∅

❐ *13540 Arnold Dr. (half mile off Highway 12), Glen Ellen, CA 95442; (707) 935-0237. Couples $100 to $175; suite with whirlpool tub and private deck $195 to $225. Eight rooms with private baths; full breakfast. MC/VISA, DISC.* ❐ An 1890 Victorian restored and furnished with English and American antiques. Two units with fireplaces. Creekside setting; pool; short walk to town.

Glenelly Inn ● ☆☆☆ $$$$ ∅

❐ *5131 Warm Springs Rd. (off Arnold Drive), Glen Ellen, CA 95442; (707) 996-6720. Couples and singles $95 to $130. Eight rooms, all with private baths; full breakfast. MC/VISA.* ❐ A refurbished 1916 country resort in the French Colonial style. Rooms done in American and European antiques. One-acre landscaped grounds with spa and rose garden. Common room with stone fireplace.

Sonoma Chalet ● ☆☆ $$$$ ∅

❐ *18935 Fifth St. West (Verano Avenue), Sonoma, CA 95476; (707) 938-3129. Couples $75 to $135. Seven units, four with private baths; continental breakfast. MC/VISA, AMEX.* ❐ Nicely restored country-style complex with rooms in a farmhouse, plus private cottages. They're furnished with early American antiques; fireplaces, wood-burning stoves. Spa, bicycles, complimentary sherry.

Thistle Dew Inn ● ☆☆☆ $$$$$ Ø

◻ *171 W. Spain St. (a block west of plaza), Sonoma, CA 95476; (707) 938-2909. Couples and singles $100 to $140. Six rooms, all with private baths; full breakfast. MC/VISA, AMEX.* ◻ Lodgings in an 1869 Victorian and a 1905 early American home, furnished with turn-of-the-century antiques, decorated with arts and crafts. Spa, bicycles, afternoon *hors d'oeuvres.*

Trojan Horse Inn ● ☆☆☆ $$$$ Ø

◻ *19455 Sonoma Hwy. (between West Napa and Spain), Sonoma, CA 95476; (707) 996-2430. Couples $90 to $130. Six rooms, all with private baths; full breakfast. MC/VISA, AMEX.* ◻ Victorian style farmhouse with extensive landscaped grounds on banks of Sonoma Creek. Rooms furnished with English and American antiques; armoires, brass beds. One room with fireplace, one with spa. Pool, complimentary bicycles, evening cocktails.

Victorian Garden Inn ● ☆☆☆ $$$$ Ø

◻ *316 E. Napa St. (a block and a half east of plaza), Sonoma, CA 95476; (707) 996-5339. Couples $79 to $139. Four rooms, three with private baths, one cottage with fireplace; full breakfast. MC/VISA, AMEX.* ◻ An 1880 Greek Revival style home furnished with country antiques. Pool, landscaped grounds and patio; complimentary evening wine.

Sonoma Valley information sources

Sonoma State Historic Park, P.O. Box 167, Sonoma, CA 95476; (707) 938-1519.

Sonoma County Convention & Visitors Bureau, 5000 Roberts Lake Rd., Suite A, Rohnert Park, CA 94928; (800) 326-7666 or (707) 586-8100.

Sonoma County Wine & Visitors Center, 5000 Roberts Lake Rd., Rohnert Park, CA 94928; (707) 586-3795.

Sonoma Valley Chamber of Commerce, 645 Broadway, Sonoma, CA 95476; (707) 996-1033.

Sonoma Valley Visitors Bureau, 453 First St. East, Sonoma, CA 95476; (707) 996-1090 or (707) 966-1033.

"The amazing violet-spice complexity wrapped around a carload of ber-rylike, cherry-ish fruit plays tag with nuances of vanilla, toasted oak and faint cigar-box scents..."
— **Description of a Caymus Special Selection Cabernet Sauvignon**

Chapter Five
NAPA: DOWN VALLEY
The south end: Napa to Rutherford

Approached from the south, America's most famous wine valley appears to be more of a plain. The landscape, too gentle here to be called hilly, cradles the Napa River as it wanders aimlessly through a delta toward the San Pablo arm of San Francisco Bay.

From its outskirts, Napa—the valley's foundation city—seems little different from any other mid-sized American community. It could as well be Cedar Rapids, Iowa, or Boise, Idaho. Driving along the freeway portion of Highway 29, you see no clue to a fabled wineland, other than a purple grape cluster on the free-standing sign of the Napa Valley Center shopping complex.

Yet vineyards are all about you, crouching behind the subtly rolling terrain. The Carneros region is to the southwest, where the Napa and Sonoma valley flood plains merge at the edge of the bay. More vines garnish foothills of the Vaca Range to the northeast, shielded from view by spreading Napa suburbs. Other vineyards stride up the flanks of the Mayacamas Mountains to the northwest. None of these are apparant as you skirt the western edge of Napa. Then as the freeway portion ends and you pass through a stoplight at Redwood Road, grapes begin to appear, eventually covering the valley floor like green shag carpeting.

As you continue north on Highway 29, the two low mountain ranges draw near to create the vision of the Napa Valley so familiar to Americans. Ranks of vines march away from the highway like a retreating army in green camouflage. Ivy-walled wineries stand at roadside; mansions built by yesterday's wine barons sulk behind protective cloaks of trees. As you travel further into the valley toward Oakville, the great bulk of Mount St. Helena commands the northern horizon.

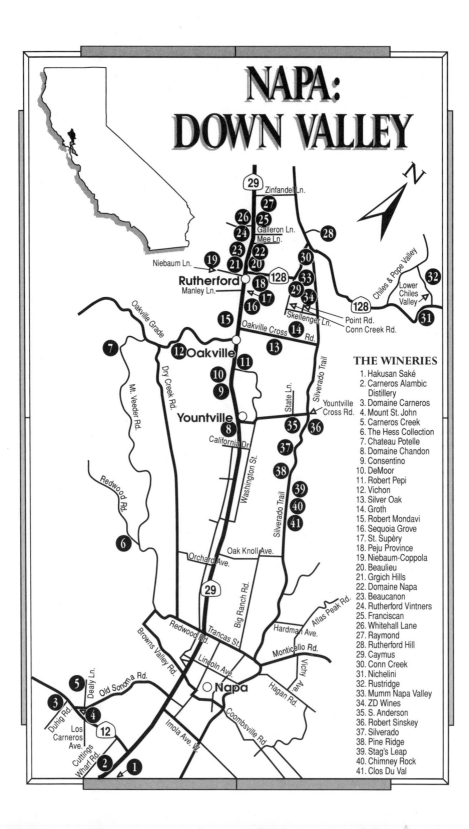

NAPA: DOWN VALLEY

THE WINERIES

1. Hakusan Saké
2. Carneros Alambic Distillery
3. Domaine Carneros
4. Mount St. John
5. Carneros Creek
6. The Hess Collection
7. Chateau Potelle
8. Domaine Chandon
9. Consentino
10. DeMoor
11. Robert Pepi
12. Vichon
13. Silver Oak
14. Groth
15. Robert Mondavi
16. Sequoia Grove
17. St. Supèry
18. Peju Province
19. Niebaum-Coppola
20. Beaulieu
21. Grgich Hills
22. Domaine Napa
23. Beaucanon
24. Rutherford Vintners
25. Franciscan
26. Whitehall Lane
27. Raymond
28. Rutherford Hill
29. Caymus
30. Conn Creek
31. Nichelini
32. Rustridge
33. Mumm Napa Valley
34. ZD Wines
35. S. Anderson
36. Robert Sinskey
37. Silverado
38. Pine Ridge
39. Stag's Leap
40. Chimney Rock
41. Clos Du Val

Two main routes, Highway 29 and the Silverado Trail, run roughly parallel along the valley's edges, linked by crossroads to form a crooked ladder. Vineyards line both main highways as well as the ladder-rung crossroads.

The Napa Valley is everything everyone says it is—only busier. Nearly 250 wineries dot the landscape; some of the larger ones draw more than 300,000 visitors a year. Tour buses may inundate tasting rooms without warning; insurance widows from Indiana will giggle nervously and ask for a sip of something sweet. Highway 29 can become traffic-tangled on summer weekends. Gimmicks such as the Napa Valley Wine Train, the "authentic" *City of Napa* sternwheeler and theme shopping centers lure visitor hoards.

Yet you can find picturesque, tucked-away wineries with tasting rooms that are rarely crowded, winding country lanes bereft of cars, and lonely ramparts with valley vistas to draw your breath away.

To avoid the mob, visit the Napa Valley on a weekday, when even the major wineries are uncrowded. If that's not practical (most of us work for a living), focus on wineries off Highway 29. The Silverado Trail, running through more attractive terrain in the Vaca foothills, entices only a fraction of the valley's visitors. Finally, get an early start. Yes, it may seem odd to drink before lunch, but you're here to taste and learn about wine. Most tasting rooms open at 10 a.m., yet crowds rarely peak until after noon. Consider retreating to your motel pool in the late afternoon—the busiest time of day for tasting rooms.

Many valley wineries charge for tasting, a practice which we approve, since it discourages those out for a free drinking spree. Tasting room folks scornfully refer to them as "recreational drinkers." Fees are nominal—two or three dollars to sample a variety of wines. Generally, you can keep the glass, which bears the winery's logo, or you can apply the charge toward a purchase. Glasses come in assorted sizes, so one winds up with a rather eclectic collection. (When we mentioned this to a tasting room host, he grinned and quipped: "Just come back eight times and you'll have a uniform set.")

We were impressed by the overall excellence of the wines as we visited the valley's tasting rooms. Despite its touristy reputation, the Napa Valley is home to serious vintners who produce some of America's finest wines. Not surprisingly, they're generally more expensive that similar varieties from other areas. Even unprocessed grapes command a higher price. They may be no better than comparable Sonoma or Mendocino fruit, but these are *Napa* grapes, thank you!

Incidentally, if you're biking through the Napa Valley, both Highway 29 and the Silverado Trail have bike lanes. The Silverado is more scenic and less crowded with traffic.

Even though the valley has two hundred-plus wineries, most are small. The ten largest control a third of the grape crop and produce 40 percent of the wine. The biggest is Christian Brothers, followed by Charles Krug, Robert Mondavi, Beringer and Beaulieu—all household names. Yet with all of the Napa Valley's vinicultural largess, this fabled Eden produces only two percent of California's wines. Most, about 85 percent, comes from the San Joaquin Valley.

California's most famous wine valley isn't its first. By the time Napa wine production began in earnest in the 1860s, vineyards around Los Angeles had passed their peak and Sonoma was regarded as the cradle of commercial viniculture. However, it now surpasses every wine producing area in America, not in overall wine production or vineyard acreage, but in the total number of wineries.

A hunter-gatherer Native American tribe variously called Wappo or Nappa inhabited the valley for nearly 4,000 years. "Nappa" may mean "bountiful place" or salmon or spear point or grizzly bear. We will never know, for the gentle Stone Age Wappo—victims of servitude, disease and bullets dealt by the Spanish and later American settlers—exist no more.

When Mission San Francisco Solano was established in Sonoma in 1823, the Napa Valley was seen as suitable only for grazing land. Huge chunks of it were granted to citizens of the newly-freed Mexico who had helped in its fight for independence from Spain. But for the most part it remained undeveloped—the domain of deer, grizzlies and wild oats.

The first outside settler was American frontiersman George Calvert Yount. After working for Sonoma's Mariano Vallejo, he was granted Rancho Caymus in the Napa Valley in the 1830s. The first American citizen to obtain a Mexican land grant, he planted vineyards and orchards near the town named in his honor. It's likely that he made a bit of wine from Mission grapes for his table and thus became one of the valley's earliest vintners.

Napa's first commercial wine production is attributed to John Patchett in 1858. Then came families whose names still ring in Napa Valley history books—Charles Krug in 1860, Jacob Schram of Schramsberg in 1862, the Beringer brothers in the 1870s, Gustave Neibaum of the former Inglenook in 1899 and Georges de Latour, who established Beaulieu at the turn of the century.

Others left their marks on the valley, as well. Flamboyant Mormon Sam Brannan, who had shouted out California's 1848 gold discovery in the streets of San Francisco, built the valley's first mineral springs resort in 1868. Styled after the grand Saratoga spa of New York, it was called by Brannan—perhaps in drunken jest—"the Calistoga of Sarifornia." During the summer of 1880, impoverished, ailing Scottish writer Robert Louis Stevenson and his bride Fanny spent their honeymoon in an old mining shack high in the flanks of Mount St. Helena. (See box in Chapter 6.)

Napa Valley's history pursued the typical pattern—the 1870s wine price crash, phylloxera, Prohibition, Repeal and a gradual rebuilding during this century's first half. The Christian Brothers came to the valley in 1930, Louis M. Martini established his winery in 1933 and Cesare Mondavi bought the Charles Krug facility ten years later. When Cesare died in 1959, it was passed to sons Peter and Robert. World War II slowed vineyard and winery growth. Life moved slowly in the idyllic valley for many quiet years.

Then, after a family spat said to be one of the seeds for TV's old *Falcon Crest* series, Robert Mondavi left Krug. In 1966, he opened the first "new" winery in the valley in several years. Indeed, it was a new concept—one of the first wineries designed for public tours, vineyard concerts and other spe-

---

WINERY CODES • **T** = Tasting with no fee; **T$** = Tasting for a fee; **GT** = Guided tours; **GTA** = Guided tours by appointment; **ST** = Self-guiding tours; **CT** = casual tours or a peek into the winery; ✕ = picnic area; 🎁 = Gift shop or good giftware selection. Price ranges listed in tasting notes are for varietals; jug wines may be available for less.

cial events. The energetic, outspoken Mondavi has become a leading defender of wine's public image and a foe of what he calls "neo-prohibitionists." Not surprisingly, he is one of the chief subjects in James Conaway's rather revealing book, *Napa: The Story of an American Eden.*

America's sudden "discovery" of wines in the late 1960s was both a boon and a menace to the Napa Valley. Vineyard acreage tripled and wineries multiplied; the valley became the target of every tour bus route. Many visitors put down roots and Napa's suburbs swelled northward, threatening prime vine land. A four-lane expressway bulled its way through the vineyards, seeking to alleviate Highway 29 congestion.

Vintners and other concerned citizens rushed to rescue their enchanted land. An agricultural preserve was established in 1968 to protect prime vineyards. The new highway was stopped at Yountville, so the rest of Highway 29 remains congested, particularly on weekends. Residents wisely decided that the cure would have been more painful than the illness.

Despite its growing popularity, the area still has its quiet moments and its quiet places. Early on a weekday morning, you can discover a Napa Valley much like that observed by Robert Louis Stevenson in 1880:

The stirring sunlight and the growing vines, and the vats and bottles in the caverns, made a pleasant music for the mind.

Since the valley has more wineries than any other area in America, we've divided it into two chapters. We use the local reference, "down valley" for the southern end and "up valley" for the north. In touring down valley, we'll divide it again, first visiting the Carneros and Mount Veeder areas near Napa, then the heart of the valley along Highway 29 and the Silverado Trail.

CARNEROS-MOUNT VEEDER WINERY TOUR ● As we mentioned earlier, the Sonoma and Napa valleys share the Carneros. Cooled by bay breezes, this gentle terrain is ideal for Chardonnay and Pinot Noir. Much of it goes into sparkling wines and three champagneries are located here. The tilted, rocky soils of nearby Mount Veeder in the Mayacamus range nurture exceptional Cabernets.

Napa's Carneros can be reached by two approaches from the Bay Area. From U.S. 101, turn east onto State Highway 37 north of Novato, then swing north onto Highway 29 in Vallejo. If you're following Interstate 80 north, take Highway 37 west through Vallejo, and then turn north onto Route 29. The first two wineries you will encounter are not wineries in the conventional sense. The first makes Japanese saké and the second produces French style pot still brandy.

Head north from Vallejo on Route 29 and, after about six miles, turn right onto Highway 12 at the Fairfield-Sacramento sign, and then go left at the first signal onto Kelley Road. You'll see the entrance to **Hakusan Saké Gardens** on the left. After visiting Hakusan, continue north on Kelly Road, since it merges back into Route 29/12. After a short distance, fork left to stay with Highway 29/12, then after two miles go west on Highway 121/12 (following the Sonoma sign) into the Carneros region. After a bit over a mile, turn left onto Cuttings Wharf Road and follow it a mile to **Carneros Alambic Distillery,** on your left.

Return to Highway 121/12, turn left and continue into the Carneros region. This is subtly rolling terrain, as softly contoured as a slender woman. Many vineyards but few winery tasting rooms occupy this area. You'll shortly encounter the palatial **Domaine Carneros** on the left at the Duhig Road junction. From here, you may want to follow Duhig into the Carneros terrain, enjoying vineyard vistas and distant blue slices of San Pablo Bay.

Return to Highway 121 from Domaine Carneros, fork left onto Old Sonoma Road and you'll soon see **Mont St. John Cellars** on your right. Now, continue on Old Sonoma a short distance to Dealy Lane and follow it just under a mile to **Carneros Creek Winery.**

Next, return to Old Sonoma Road and follow it into the city of **Napa**. Just short of the freeway, turn left at the Calistoga-San Rafael sign and drive a mile along a frontage road, past Napa Valley Center and a large **Napa Factory Stores** outlet center. Make a sharp right onto First Street, cross over the freeway and take a right-hand cloverleaf down to it. You're now headed north into the Napa Valley.

The freeway ends at a stoplight at the intersection of Redwood Road; go left onto Redwood and follow it west into the foothills of wooded Mount Veeder. After 4.3 winding and scenic miles, turn left at the junction of Redwood and Mount Veeder roads (staying on Redwood). The impressive **Hess Collection** winery is about a mile beyond, on your left.

Return to the junction and turn left onto Mount Veeder Road, following its route west along an attractive creek valley. It winds steeply into the Mayacamas, passing bearded oaks, pines and occasional redwoods. After seven

WINE TASTING

miles, you'll see a small sign to **Château Potelle,** reached by a steep and winding one-mile asphalt road. Stay alert, since it's easy to overshoot. (Note in the listing below that hours are limited; call ahead before making the climb.)

From Château Potelle, continue a bit over a mile downhill on Mount Veeder until it ends at Dry Creek Road. Go right, then right again after less than half a mile, staying on Dry Creek. After about ten miles, Dry Creek T-bones into Redwood Road; turn left and you're in Napa suburbs.

This route is more scenery than winery and we feel that the drive into the thickly wooded Mayacamas Mountains is worth the effort. If you don't care for excessive twisting and turning, you could skip Château Potelle and follow Redwood Road back to Napa.

Hakusan Saké Gardens ● T ST

☐ *Highway 12 at Highway 29 (One Executive Way), Napa, CA 94558; (707) 258-6160. Daily 9 to 6 in summer, 9 to 5 the rest of the year; MC/VISA. Saké samples tasted free, with a bit of sushi. Some gift items. Self-guiding tours; formal Japanese garden adjacent to tasting room.* ☐

Why not start your tour with the wine of another nation? Hakusan is the only saké (sakery) in the Napa Valley, producing Japanese rice wine from local rice—grown in California's Sacramento Valley. Sips of cold and warm saké and a sweet dessert wine are served in a large, airy tasting room done in Tokyo-modern style, furnished like a spacious Japanese restaurant. A hostess serves the saké and a sushi roll at a table, and invites you to watch a video about the history of saké and the establishment of Hakusan.

From here, you can walk past windows of the modern, warehouse-like distillery, whose stainless steel and ranks of pipes are suggestive of a conventional winery. Signs tell you what you're seeing. Your path then leads you through a tranquil (except for adjacent Highway 29 traffic) Japanese garden, back to the hospitality center. *Hakusan,* incidentally, means "white mountain."

Saké has been traced to 700 B.C., when it was called *kuchikami no saké,* which describes how it was made. Rice and chestnuts or millet were chewed into a wad, then spat into a wooden tub to ferment. Fortunately, today's production methods are a bit more clinical.

Tasting notes: Saké has a crisp pleasantly pungent apple or tropical fruit taste, a bit like a dry Sauvignon Blanc. The dessert saké is sweet yet crisp; think of a *very* light-bodied Muscat dessert wine. Prices are $5 for the saké and $6.25 for the dessert wine.

Carneros Alambic Distillery ● GT$ 🍷

☐ *1250 Cuttings Wharf Rd., Napa, CA 94559; (707) 253-9055. Daily 10 to 5 in summer and 10:30 to 4:30 the rest of the year; MC/VISA, AMEX. Tour of brandy distillery for $2, with "sensory evaluation," No tasting, since it's forbidden by federal law. Retail shop offering brandies and an extensive selection of logo items and giftwares.* ☐

Carneros Alambic Distillery makes brandy the old fashioned way—by burbling especially prepared wine it in copper kettles, capturing and condensing the alcohol and essence much the same way as Cognac is made in France. No surprise, since it is owned by *La Belle Françoise'* Remy Martín. Most American brandies are made in a "continuous column" device in which the vapors are captured at various levels. Brandy aficionados say the French "alambic" method produces a more full-flavored and complex brandy, while the American version is lighter and smoother.

A 30-minute tour of this sleek new tile roof facility reveals the simple yet technically sophisticated method of producing Cognac style brandy. It begins with an audio-visual demonstration employing a cleverly mechanized one-quarter scale model of an alambic disillery. Visitors adjourn to the still house to admire the full-scale handcrafted copper stills, then they inhale the heady aroma of aging brandies in the barrel room.

Sniffing notes: The tour ends in the library for a "sensory evaluation of Carneros Alambic's various products"—which means that you can only sniff. Several types of brandy and brandies in various stages of production can be swirled and inhaled from—well, nifters. These are not inexpensive products, beginning at $26 for a 350 milliliter pear liqueur and ascending from there. Further, they're available only at the distillery. After inhaling this heady ambrosia and taking home a bottle of the *pear de pear*, we think it's worth it.

Distillers choice: "Our eight-year-old RMS Special Reserve and our *Pear de Pear* rare liqueur," says Carneros Alambic's Lindsay Randolph.

Domaine Carneros • T$ GT

⌂ *1240 Duhig Rd. (at Highway 121; P.O. Box 5420), Napa, CA 94558; (707) 257-0101. Daily 10:30 to 6; MC/VISA, AMEX. Sparkling wines sold by the glass for $4 and $5. Some wine related gift items. Guided tours at 11, 1 and 3; between tours, a film concerning the winery is shown on request.* ⌂

This sparkling wine facility, an offspring of France's Champagne Tattinger, is among the valley's more elegant wine properties. Styled after the Tattinger family's 18th century Château de la Marquetterie in the French Champagne district, it is an imposing presence, crowning a low hill in the heart of the Carneros. It was completed in 1987.

After admiring the portrait of Madame Pompadour, the beaded glass chandeliers, high coffered ceilings and the view, you can seat yourself in a cane-backed chair at a brass and glass table. Here, you are served a current sparkling offering (for a fee), with *hors d'oeuvres*, of course. On warm days, you can adjourn to a view deck.

Tours, conducted thrice daily, are thorough and informative, amounting to a cram course in sparkling wine production. It begins with a nicely done multi-media show, presented in a fashionable little drawing room with a window into the winery. The tour then proceeds to a windowed gallery above the aging cellar and production floor.

Tasting notes: The Sparkling Brut, Domaine Carneros' primary product, was pleasantly complex and mouth-filling, with a nice crisp Chardonnay finish. Prices are in the mid teens.

Mont St. John Cellars • T GTA ✕

⌂ *5400 Old Sonoma Rd., Napa, CA 94558; (707) 255-8864. Daily 10 to 5; MC/VISA, AMEX. Most varieties tasted; no fee. Some wine logo gift items. A shaded public picnic grounds, plus a barbecue area available by reservation. Guided tours by prior arrangement.* ⌂

The Louis Bartolucci family has been making Napa Valley wines since the 1920s. Founder Andrea Bartolucci came to America from Italy in 1913 and started his first winery in 1922 in Oakville. Succeeding generations moved the operation to this small, attractive California mission style facility in the 1971, where they produce about 15,000 cases a year. In a separate "entertainment room," visitors can watch a film tracing the winery's production techniques from vineyard to bottle.

Tasting notes: Chardonnay, Sauvignon Blanc, Johannisberg Riesling, Gewürztraminer and Muscat di Canelli occupy the white list; Cabernet Sauvignon and Pinot Noir are the reds. The wines were uniformly good, with prices ranging from about $7 to the mid teens. A Chardonnay was exceptional and the Gewürztraminer was lush and rich without being sweet. Of the reds, we were impressed by the spicy-berry nose and complex flavor of the Pinot Noir.

Vintners choice: "Carneros is the ideal region for Chardonnay and Pinot Noir, and I would select those as our best wines," says the winery's Sue Bartolucci. "Our Pinot has won an international gold medal."

Carneros Creek Winery • T$ CT ✗

☐ *1285 Dealy Lane, Napa, CA 94558; (707) 253-WINE. Daily 9 to 4:30; MC/VISA. All varieties tasted for a $2.50 fee, which includes a logo glass. A few wine logo items. Picnic area under an arbor.* ☐

"We like to enter into a dialog with visitors," says Carneros Creek's sales manager Daniel Salinas. This small winery is serious about Pinot Noir and folks here like to talk with serious minded wine enthusiasts, even offering tastes of rare library selections. Established in this region in 1972, specifically to pursue the Pinot, it is a leader in clonal research and has won numerous awards for its noble Burgundian-style wines.

The appearance of the place belies its serious intent. It resembles a suburban home with an oversized garage. To reach the tiny tasting room, one drives across a set of truck scales and parks near a picnic arbor.

Tasting notes: The list, not surprisingly, is mostly Pinot Noir, accompanied by Chardonnay and Cabernet Sauvignon Cabernet. We particularly liked the Fleur de Carneros Pinot, light yet complex with a powerful berry focus brought about by cloning. A Signature Reserve Pinot was spicy, peppery and awesome. (It's not normally offered for tasting; try begging a little.) The barrel fermented Chardonnay was properly buttery and spicy, with a light finish. Prices start in the middle teens and go beyond for library selections.

The Hess Collection • T$ ST 🏛

☐ *4411 Redwood Rd. (P.O. Box 4140), Napa, CA 94558; (707) 255-1144. Daily 10 to 4; MC/VISA. Cabernet Sauvignon and Chardonnay tasted for a $2.50 fee. Good selection of gift and art items. Self-guiding tour of the art museum, with views into the winery. Periodic slide shows about the winery.* ☐

In a word or two, the Hess Collection is one of the most impressive inner spaces in California's wine country: a Château-like structure with an attractive island-counter tasting salon, windows peeking into the winery and an art gallery with dazzling white walls set against old stone. Despite the look of old world formality, however, staff members are friendly and helpful as they guide folks through tastings. Visitors may wander about the gallery on their own. The art? It's on the leading edge of the modern movement which, like a dry martini, is an acquired taste.

The ninth generation of a Swiss brewing family, Donald Hess inherited a small fortune and soon turned it into a large one. He diversified into mineral water, restaurants and vineyards. His American wife encouraged him to establish a winery in California and it was she who suggested combining it with an art gallery.

The original winery was built at the turn of the century by Oakland businessman Theodore Gier. Then the Christian Brothers, a Catholic teaching order, purchased it in 1932 and established an adjacent novitiate. It functioned as the Mont La Salle Vineyards until Hess acquired the property in 1986 and began an extensive renovation. The winery was re-opened to the public in 1989.

Tasting notes: The winery bottles only Cabernet Sauvignon and Chardonnay, offering them in two styles: the upscale Hess Collection, suitable for aging, and the moderately priced Hess Select. Prices range from $9.50 to the high teens. A Hess Collection Chardonnay was lush, nutty and silky; while a Monterey County Hess Select was fruitier and less complex yet quite tasty. The Hess Collection Cabernet, peppery and spicy with a nippy tannic finish, was exceptional.

Château Potelle • T GTA X

□ *3875 Mount Veeder Rd., Napa, CA 94558; (707) 252-0615. Weekends only from noon to 5, other times by appointment, closed from November through March. Select varieties tasted; no fee. Picnic tables on wooden deck with a view; tours by appointment.* □

Potelle is a château in name only. Scattered over wooded slopes, this small facility more resembles an American hill country farmyard than a French manor. It's an appealing place in a woodsy sort of way, with a barn of a winery and small tasting room in a clapboard cottage. A deck offers impressive views of tilted vineyards and the surrounding hills.

The Fourmeaux family, late of France, started their winery in Menlo Park south of San Francisco in 1983, then moved to this remote site toward the end of that decade.

Vintners choice: "Sauvignon Blanc, Chardonnay and Cabernet—all elegant and well balanced," insists the winery's Susan Dicks. Actually, she named the entire list. Prices range from $9 to the mid teens.

DOWN VALLEY WINERY TOUR • Finding wineries in this end of the valley requires no great navigational feat. They stand in ranks along Highway 29 and the paralleling Silverado Trail, or on the crossroads that connect the two.

We left you at the intersection of Redwood Road and Highway 29. Turn left (north) onto the highway, which is mostly a limited access expressway between here and **Yountville**. Shortly after it temporarily resumes full freeway status, take the Yountville exit and turn left onto Washington Street.

Within a couple of blocks, you'll see the Napa Valley **Tourist Information Center** on your right, at 6488 Washington. It's not an official tourist bureau but a no-fee booking agency for Napa Valley lodgings, tours, balloon flights and other activities, and it sells maps and guides to the area. It's open weekdays 9 to 5 and weekends 10 to 4; (707) 944-1557. The **Yountville Chamber of Commerce** is a bit beyond, on the right at a Y-intersection where Young Street splits off from Washington; it shares a shingle-sided building with the Yountville Community Center. The chamber offers the usual assortment of brochures, winery guides and such and it's open Monday-Saturday 10 to 3; closed Sundays.

You may want to explore the assortment of shops, boutiques and galleries in this tourist-oriented town. Many are in **Vintage 1870,** a former winery turned theme shopping center across Washington Street from the chamber.

Nicely done in old brick, the center has a wine-tasting facility offering six samples for $3, plus several restaurants. The **Yountville Pastry Shop and Deli** here, with a tree-shaded patio, is a handy stop for quick bites. Most Vintage 1870 shops are open 10 to 5:30; some restaurants remain open longer.

Having done with Yountville, go west under the freeway on California Drive, then follow signs to the right to **Domaine Chandon.** Then return to Highway 29 and continue north; it's no longer a freeway and the wineries present themselves in quick order, so keep a wary eye: **Cosentino Winery** on the left, just beyond the popular Mustard's Café, then **DeMoor Winery,** also on the left, a few yards beyond; and **Robert Pepi Winery,** about a quarter of a mile farther, up a vineyard lane to the right.

Now, turn left onto Oakville Grade in the tiny hamlet of **Oakville** and drive about a mile up to **Vichon Winery** in the Mayacamas foothills. Along the way, you might stop at the **Carmelite Monastery** and browse through its gift shop, in a clapboard building below the monastery (open Tuesday-Sunday 11 to 3:30); the chapel above is generally open to the public only during mass, at 8 a.m. weekdays and 9 a.m. Sunday; phone (707) 944-9408.

Return to Highway 29 and stop for a browse through the legendary **Oakville Grocery** on the corner of Oakville Cross Road. It's an old fashioned general store turned designer deli, with cheeses, meats, assorted olives, fresh pastas, breads, patés, prepared salads, a small produce section and a huge local wine selection. It's a one-stop picnic builder, although most items are a bit pricey. What's pricey? How about an eight-ounce package of *biscotti* for $7 and upscale cookies for $2 each.

From the grocery, follow Oakville Cross Road a mile east to **Silver Oak Wine Cellars**, up a lane to your right. (The sign is small; watch for an iron gate supported by decorative stone posts.) Continue briefly east on Oakville Cross to the new **Groth Vineyards and Winery,** on your left. Then retreat to Route 29, continue north and you'll soon encounter the Spanish mission style **Robert Mondavi Winery** on the right. Half a mile beyond is **Sequoia Grove Vineyards** on the right; just beyond are **St. Supéry Winery** and next-door **Peju Province.** As you approach the small town of **Rutherford**, look for Neibaum Lane on your left, leading up to **Neibaum-Coppola Estate Winery** (formerly Inglenook-Napa Valley). On the right in downtown Rutherford (what little there is of it), is **Beaulieu Vineyard**; **Grgich Hills Cellar** is just beyond, on the left.

A bit farther along, **Domaine Napa** and **Beaucanon** are across the highway from one another. To reach Domaine Napa, turn right onto a small lane, drive past a ranch complex and then turn right into the winery. Return to the highway and—when the busy traffic clears—shoot straight across to Beaucanon. Just up the highway, small **Rutherford Vintners** and large **Franciscan Vineyards** are across from one another—Rutherford on the left; Franciscan on the right. Briefly beyond is **Whitehall Lane,** on the left.

A few hundred feet from Whitehall, turn right onto Zinfandel Lane, stop at **Raymond Cellars** up a gravel lane on your right, then continue on to the Silverado Trail. Swing south on Silverado and watch for Rutherford Hill Road, leading to the left through the posh **Auberge du Soliel** resort to **Rutherford Hill Winery.** Continue a bit farther south on Silverado, then turn right onto Conn Creek Road and follow its twisting creekside course about half a mile to **Caymus Vineyards.** (At a T-junction where Highway 128 swings sharply to the right, continue straight ahead on Conn Creek Road;

Caymus comes up almost immediately, on your left.) From here, backtrack to the Silverado Trail, turn right and you'll immediately hit **Conn Creek Winery,** on your right.

If you'd like to venture into the mountains and discover a couple of tucked-away wineries, go north briefly and follow 128 east into; the route here is called Sage Canyon Road. (**Note:** Both wineries have limited hours, so this route is best run on weekends; see their listings below for specifics.) You'll pass **Lake Hennessey,** Napa's water supply, then wind steeply into the flanks of the Vaca Range to **Nichelini Winery,** perched precariously on the right edge of the highway. Drive a short distance beyond, turn left onto Lower Chiles Valley Road and follow it into the bucolic Chiles Valley. After about 2.5 miles, you'll see **Rustridge Winery,** part of a scattered ranch yard on your right.

Return to Silverado and continue south; you'll soon encounter **Mumm Napa Valley** on the right, with **ZD Wines** practically next door. You have about a two-mile breather, then turn right onto Yountville Cross and drive a short distance to **S. Anderson Vineyard** on the left. Back on Silverado, **Robert Sinskey Vineyards** occupies a ridge just across the highway.

Pressing south, you enter the Stags Leap district in the Vaca foothills, whose sloping, rocky soils produce some of Napa's finest wines. The name comes from a rocky promontory above. On the valley side of the highway, crowning a hill rising from the valley floor is **Silverado Vineyards,** then **Pine Ridge Winery.** Coming up on the left are **Stag's Leap Wine Cellars, Chimney Rock Winery** and finally, **Clos Du Val.**

Probably having grown weary of all this, you can stay on Silverado, which will take you back to Napa. It bumps into Trancas Street and a right turn will take you to Highway 29.

Domaine Chandon • *T$ GT* 🍷 *R*

☐ *One California Dr., Yountville, CA 94599; (707) 944-2280. Daily 11 to 6 (closed Monday-Tuesday November through April); MC/VISA, AMEX. Sparkling wine sold by the glass, $3 to $3.50. Extensive gift selection; champagne museum exhibits. Tours every half hour from 11 to 5; salon open until 6. Domaine Chandon Restaurant is listed under "Wine country dining."* ☐

Occupying a garden-like setting just below the Yountville Veterans Home, Domaine Chandon is the first of the Napa Valley's three French sparkling wine houses. It's owned by the Moët-Hennessey Louis Vuitton conglomerate and produces only sparkling wine by *méthode champenoise.*

It more resembles a country club than a winery, bunkered into the landscaped terrain, with barrel arched roofs over stone, rimmed by moats, fountains, and patios. All it lacks is a golf course.

Tours assemble in the entry corridor, where graphics and exhibits trace the process of sparkling wine from Dom Pérignon's accidental discovery three centuries ago. ("I am tasting stars!" he exclaimed, after his wine underwent a second fermentation in the bottle.) Tour groups stroll past giant bullet-nosed horizontal fermenting tanks, watch a gyro-riddler in action and follow the 17 steps required to conduct sparkling wine's disgorging and bottling process. You can get a glass of bubbly—for a fee—in the tasting salon or on a sunny patio. Thirsty souls can bypass the tour and go directly to the gift shop and salon.

Tasting notes: Our glass of Chandon Brut came with a plate of sourdough bread and cream cheese spread. All were excellent; we like the exploding effervescence of the brut and its lingering acidic finish. Domaine Chandon also produces Carneros Blanc de Noirs, Chandon Réserve, Club Cuvée and Étoile, with prices from $11.95 to $22. Two non-sparklers are Panache apéritif wine and Fred's Friends Chardonnay for $7.50 and $6.50.

Cosentino Winery • T$ CT

⊓ 7415 St. Helena Hwy. (P.O. Box 2818), Yountville, CA 94599. Daily 10 to 5:30; MC/VISA. Most varieties tasted for a $2 fee (which buys the glass or is applied toward wine purchase). A few wine related gift items. Group tours by appointment. ⊓

Built in 1990, Cosentino Winery suggests a cross between a château and a French military barracks, with its flat, rather austere façade with dormer windows. There's nothing austere about the wines, however. Founder Mitch Cosentino won 400 awards in just ten vintages, including many best of show and sweepstake medals. He was America's first vintner to produce a red Meritage, the Bordeaux-inspired blend of Cabernet Sauvignon, Cabernet Franc and Merlot. It earned the sweepstakes award over 1,900 National Wine Competition entries in 1990.

Cosentino started out in Modesto in 1981, then moved to the Napa Valley to get closer to the grapes which had been gathering all those medals.

Tasting notes: "The Sculptor" Chardonnay was exceptional—spicy, nutty and silky with a hint of wood and gentle acid finish. Cosentino's Pinot Noir was light and fruity—suggestive of a young Zinfandel, while the Cabernet Franc was peppery yet soft, with a delicate tannin. Cabernet Sauvignon displayed classic chili pepper and berry attributes, with hints of wood at the end. "The Poet," The Meritage was soft and spicy, deserving of its sweepstakes award. Prices range from $13 to $30. New on the Cosentino list are some Italian varietals including Sangiovese and Nebbiolo.

Vintners choice: "We're noted for our full bodied reds, such as Meritage, Cabernet Sauvignon, Cabernet Franc and Merlot," said a winery official.

DeMoor Winery and Vineyards • T$ ✗ 🌶

⊓ 7481 St. Helena Hwy., Oakville, CA 94562; (707) 944-2565. Daily 10:30 to 5:30 in summer and 10 to 5 the rest of the year; MC/VISA, AMEX. Most varieties tasted for a $2 fee (includes glass). Good gift and wine logo selection. Shaded picnic area amongst the vines; winery interior visible from the tasting room. ⊓

A tasting room in a yurt? Soft-spoken tasting host Michael Dobrich insists that it's a geodesic dome. Whatever its architectural pedigree, this is a pleasant, comfortably funky venue for sampling the fine DeMoor wines. The winery itself is more business-like, a large square structure just beyond the geodesic yurt. It was opened in 1976 and the first wines were produced five years later under the Napa Cellars label. It became DeMoor Winery in 1983.

Tasting notes: The wines exhibited an excellent overall quality. Sauvignon Blanc had a pleasant dusky nose and rich hint of raisins; Chenin Blanc was lush and fruity with a touch of acid at the end. Zinfandel was light and full of raspberries, unusually fruity for a Zin. The Cabernet was exemplary, big and complex with enough tannin for aging.

Robert Pepi Winery • T$

⊓ 7585 St. Helena Hwy. (P.O. Box 328), Oakville, CA 94562; (707) 944-2807. Daily 10:30 to 4:30; MC/VISA. All current releases available for tasting for a $2 fee (which buys the glass). ⊓

The Pepi Winery is a handsome Italianate stone and wood affair crowning a low hill above the vineyards. Carved doors beneath a stone arch lead into the tasting room and windows offer peeks into the winery. It's a pleasant spot—a welcome retreat from the din of Highway 29, and it offers nice valley views.

Robert and Ora Pepi, wanting to return to longtime winemaking traditions of their families in Lucca, Italy, purchased vineyards in the Napa Valley in 1966. They built their present winery in 1981, bringing his Italian heritage to its Mediterranean architecture. The small facility produces about 25,000 cases a year.

Tasting notes: Sauvignon Blanc has dominated production in this family-owned winery. Others on the brief and excellent list are Cabernet Sauvignon, Chardonnay and a reserve Sauvignon Blanc; all exhibit classic varietal characteristics. Pepi recently added Sangiovese Grosso, the traditional grape of Tuscany, a light yet full-flavored red. Prices range from $9 to the high teens.

Vichon Winery ● T & T$ GTA ✗

☐ *1595 Oakville Grade, Oakville, CA 94562; (707) 944-2611. Daily 10 to 4:30; MC/VISA, AMEX. Four wines tasted free; fee for older vintages. A few wine logo items. Picnic area with impressive valley view. Guided tours daily at 10:30 and 2; appointment required. In-depth tours at Robert Mondavi Winery followed by a picnic lunch at Vichon, are offered Wednesdays at 10, May through October. For reservations, call (800) 842-4661, extension 1619.* ☐

Robert Mondavi's offspring—Mike, Tim and Marica—purchased this small ten-year-old winery in the middle 1980s. Despite its youth, its pink stucco Spanish colonial architecture and ivy-covered façade give it a venerable look. Barrel-potted flowers add a touch of color. The site is impressive; the winery is notched into a steep slope off Oakville Grade in the Mayacamas foothills. Views from the winery and from a laurel and oak-shaded picnic area are elegant.

The tasting area forms a simple ante room to the main winery, with a tasting counter and small display of gift items. Visitors can peek into the winery through windowed doors.

Tasting notes: Vichon has won a generous share of awards for its select list, which includes Chevrignon (a Semillon and Sauvignon Blanc blend), Chardonnay, Cabernet Blanc, Cabernet Sauvignon and Merlot. The Cabs were particularly noteworthy—classic studies in the red wine art. A Stags Leap Cabernet offered tremendous body, spice and berries with a notable tannin finish. The winery also is noted for its full- bodied Chardonnays. Prices range from $7.50 to the middle teens, and beyond for a fine library of older vintages.

Vintners choice: The winery is particularly noted for its Chardonnays, available in several versions and vintages.

Silver Oak Cellars ● T$ GTA

☐ *915 Oakville Cross Rd. (P.O. Box 414), Oakville, CA 94562; (707) 944-8808. Monday-Friday 9 to 4:30, Saturday 10 to 4:30, closed Sunday; MC/VISA. Tasting for $5 fee (which buys the glass or is applied toward wine purchase). Guided tours by appointment at 1:30 weekdays.* ☐

Justin Meyer and Ray Duncan established Silver Oak in 1972; the present facility was completed ten years later. Their intent was to produce a single

WARNING: WINE MAY BE GOOD FOR YOU

"Prohibitionists say that drinking is bad for you, but the Bible says that Noah made wine and drank it, and he only lived to be 950 years old. Show me an abstainer who ever lived that long."— Will Rogers

Medical studies are confirming what Noah and Will knew all along, that moderate wine consumption is good for you. Not just harmless, but *beneficial.* This comes as bad news to neo-prohibitionists who have succeeded in having every winery tasting room, wine price list and bottle tattooed with federal warning labels.

A couple of decades ago, a major statistical survey revealed that moderate users of alcohol live longer than teetotalers. Subsequent studies have shown that wine consumption, particularly red wine, may help prevent heart disease.

Research reported in the early 1990s the *Journal of Applied Cardiology* showed that wine consumption increases high density lipoprotein (HDL) in the blood. That's the so-called "good cholesterol" which helps clear low density cholesterol from arterial walls. Since red wine is more effective than white, researchers think fruit-rich polyphenols—tannins—may play a major role.

An earlier Canadian study suggests that red wine may help counteract cancer. In laboratory tests, doses of gallic acid (a tannin component) prevented carcinogenic agents from mutating chromosomes. Such mutations are precursors to cancer. Although this hasn't yet been proven, most experts are confident that wine doesn't *cause* cancer. No study has found a positive link between moderate wine use and increased cancer rates. Laboratory rats kept constantly crocked have refused to become malignant. Despite this, wine's enemies want it labeled as a carcinogen, right up there with tobacco and burnt barbecued ribs.

Red wine plays another role, as an effective although short-lived disinfectant. In numerous tests, it has destroyed a variety of bacteria and viruses, including cholera and typhoid germs. It's not the alcohol, but the polyphenols, that kill the little critters. Ancient Greeks used wine as a disinfectant on combat wounds. Modern travelers add it to water in sanitation-poor countries to kill bacteria. Tests have shown that red wine concentrate can be effective against cold sores.

Louis Pasteur, noting that wine destroyed infection, called it "the most healthful and hygienic of beverages."

Statistics appear to confirm wine's role as a health aid. French and Italians, who drink nearly ten times as much wine as Americans, outlive us. Even poverty-level Italians live longer than the average American, despite poor medical care, sanitation and diet.

Other surveys show that people who get most of their spirits from wine have fewer heart attacks than those who drink mostly beer or hard liquor. Further, studies have found a positive link between exercise, moderate drinking and lowered cholesterol rates.

Writer Michael Brody speculated in an article in *Barons Weekly:* "This suggests that the best medicine for one's heart may be jogging from bar to bar—finally answering the question of how journalists manage to live so long."

and exceptional wine—Cabernet Sauvignon. Meyer, who guides the wine-making, obviously has exceeded, winning many award and expanding recently to a second winery in northern Sonoma County; see page 60.

A slender tree-lined lane leads through the vineyards to this comely Mediterranean style cut-stone winery, with a brown tile roof and dormer windows. The pleasant hospitality room inside is paneled with redwood from old wine tanks. An adjacent glass wine library contains every vintage produced by Silver Oak. Surprisingly, this fashionable facility is part of a made-over dairy barn.

Tasting notes: Silver Oak produces only 100 percent varietal Cab, drawing its grapes from Napa Valley and Sonoma's Alexander Valley. Interestingly, they're aged in American oak instead of the classic French, giving them a distinct spicy-soft finish with only subtle touches of wood. The Alexander Valley Cabernet, the only wine being tasted when we visited, was exceptional—gently complex and piquant with a light tannic finish. Prepare for sticker shock: Silver Oak's wines are in the $35 range and up. The glass—which you get to keep—is an impressively large thing, ideal for sloshing, sniffing and sipping.

Groth Vineyards and Winery • T$ GTA

☐ 750 Oakville Cross Rd. (P.O. Box 390), Oakville, CA 94562; (707) 944-0290. Monday-Saturday 10 to 4, closed Sunday; MC/VISA, AMEX. Guided tours by appointment at 11 and 2. All wines tasted for a $3. ☐

Dennis and Judy Groth have reversed their roles, both professionally and geographically. In past years, many wineries left the Santa Clara County to plant their vines elsewhere, crowded out by the growing "Silicone Valley" computer industries. Dennis did the reverse, leaving his Santa Clara valley post as CEO of the Atari computer firm to establish new vineyards in the Napa Valley. He crushed his first wine in 1982 and opened a handsome salmon colored California mission style winery and tasting room in 1990. Even though he now prefers planting grapes to planning computer games, he wanted to retain something of the Santa Clara Valley's Spanish architectural heritage.

The attractive tasting room and adjacent patio overlook those vines, and visitors can peek through Spanish arch windows into the main winery's barrel storage facility.

Tasting notes: The Groths produce select lots of Chardonnay, Cabernet Sauvignon and Merlot. The Cabernet reserve exhibits full body, a deep color, with a rich and earthy palate. The Merlot is unusually complex, with layered flavors and a silky texture. The Chardonnay exhibits those nutty undertones typical of this classic French white. Prices are $8 to $18, higher for a few limited production Cabernets.

Robert Mondavi Winery • T & T$ GT and GTA 🏠

☐ 7801 St. Helena Hwy. (P.O. Box 106), Oakville, CA 94562; (707) 259-9463. Daily 9 to 5:30 in summer and 9:30 to 4:30 November through April; major credit cards. Periodic guided tours followed by free tasting; fee tasting without tour, from $1 to $3 per sample. Separate gift shop with good selection. One-hour tours, conducted several times daily, do not require reservations, although they're recommended, particularly in the summer and on weekends. In-depth three-hour tours with tastings, scheduled Sunday and Monday at 10 a.m. May through October, do require reservations. For either tour type, call (707)

*226-1395, extension 4312. The winery also presents complimentary "essence"
tastings (call extension 4312); and wine and food seminars for $45 (extension
4566). In-depth tours followed by a picnic lunch at nearby Vichon Winery, are
offered Wednesdays at 10, May through October. For reservations, call (800)
842-4661, extension 1619.* ☐

The Mondavi winery has a mission-like quality, perhaps appropriate to
the owner's crusade to elevate wine's status and defend it from his "neo-prohibitionists." When he broke away from the family fold in the 1960s, he had
three goals—to produce exceptional wines, to build the first winery designed
for cultural offerings, and to enhance wine's public image. Along the way, he
has propelled his facility into the third largest producer in the Napa Valley.

Your Mondavi experience begins with a tour, first to the adjacent vineyards, then inside the winery, housed in a wing of this Spanish style facility.
It's designed as a shallow "V" that encloses a lawn area used for Mondavi's
popular summer concerts and other functions. The arched central entrance,
not accidentally, forms a natural podium for performers.

Tours end with a guide-conducted tasting of one white, one red and one
dessert wine. If you wish to bypass the tour, you can buy an assortment of
wines, by the glass, the bottle or the one-ounce sip.

Tasting notes: Mondavi was one of the first producers of Fumé Blanc,
a Sauvignon Blanc with a distinctive but subtle smoky flavor. Indeed, the
name translates as "white smoke." It's still one of our favorite Mondavi wines,
crisp and clean with that dusky finish. The Cabernet was excellent, peppery
with soft spices, good berries and a medium tannic finish. A Muscato D'Oro
dessert wine had a rich honey nose and a focused yet curiously light taste.
Other Mondavi wines include Chardonnay, Pinot Noir, a sweet Johannisberg
Riesling botrytis and Sauvignon Blanc botrytis. Prices range from $8 to the
twenties and well beyond for some reserve wines. Mondavi also markets a
selection of varietal jug wines, produced at another facility.

Sequoia Grove Vineyards • T & T$ ST ✕

☐ *8338 St. Helena Hwy., Rutherford, CA 94573; (707) 944-2945. Daily
11 to 5; MC/VISA, AMEX. Most varieties tasted free; $3 fee for some older
wines. A few wine related gift items. Small picnic area in front of the winery
and another near a stream below the tasting room. Tours at 2 and 4 p.m.; no
appointment necessary.* ☐

This small facility indeed sits in its own personal sequoia grove, a rustic
island in time and space among its larger, sleeker winery neighbors. But it's
big in reputation, having been picked a few years ago as the winery of the
year by the *International Wine Review*. Obviously, it wins a sizable share of
medals. A cozy tasting room is located in an 1860 weathered wood and
stone barn. From there you can stroll into the adjacent winery, of a much
more recent vintage. The operation was established in 1986 by James Allen.

Tasting notes: We were impressed by the low prices of the Allen Family label Chardonnay ($6.50), Gewürztraminer ($7) and a Napa Valley Cab
($10). All three were exceptional wines. A Carneros Chardonnay ($14) had a
nice mix of fruit, soft acid and spice, and an Estate Cabernet ($30) was ex-
ceptional with a great herbal nose, berry-like taste with a soft touch of wood
and enough tannin to suggest laying it away.

Vintner's Choice: "Our Cabs are more friendly, mellow and drinkable
now, yet with a big body that will improve with age," says assistant winemaker Michael Trujillo.

St. Supéry Vineyards and Winery • T$ GT & ST 🎁

⊡ *8440 St. Helena Hwy., Rutherford, CA 94573; (707) 963-4507. Daily 9:30 to 4:30; MC/VISA. Selected wines tasted for a $2.50 fee. Good assortment of wine logo items. Guided tours and self-guiding walks through the winery.* ⊡

Don't be put off by the exterior look of this low-slung winery, which has all the charm of a government office building. Inside you'll find bright, carpeted corridors lined with art, photos and wine displays. St. Supéry offers the most informative self-guiding tour in the Napa Valley and the winery properly calls itself a "wine discovery center." Large windows offer peeks into the working winery and graphics explain in detail what you're seeing. Charts and maps discuss wine production in the Napa Valley, America and the rest of the world. A unique "essence" station gives you exaggerated whiffs of the aromas you should seek in a good Cabernet Sauvignon and Sauvignon Blanc.

If you want to sip as well as sniff, purchase a ticket at the downstairs gift shop then adjourn to a tasting station upstairs. Wines also are available by the glass, to be sipped in a pleasant outdoor patio.

And who's Supéry? No saint, he was Edward St. Supéry, who owned a winery on this site in the last century. The present facility was launched by longtime valley winemaker Robert Broman in 1989. Despite its relative youth, it's the valley's seventh largest producer. A comely gingerbread Victorian home adjacent to the winery is now a period museum, which can be toured by appointment.

Tasting notes: The overall character of the wines is light, fruity and gently acidic. A Chardonnay was soft and fruity, with a hint of wood and a Cabernet Sauvignon was gently spicy and light, with a subtle tannic finish. A Muscato dessert wine had a good crushed flower petal nose and a rich yet light taste. Prices range from $8.50 to the low teens.

Peju Province • T$ ✗

⊡ *8466 St. Helena Hwy. (P.O. Box 478), Rutherford, CA 94573; (800) 446-7358 or (707) 963-3600. Daily 10 to 6; MC/VISA. Conducted tasting of select varieties for a small fee, which applies toward wine purchase. Limited but nice selection of gift items and good selection of wine and cook books. Arbor-shaded picnic area.* ⊡

This handsome Normandy style winery—stucco with stone corner accents—is one of the valley's newer additions, completed in the early 1990s. Owner Craig Peju has been around longer than that, however, operating a smaller facility in this area since the 1980s. His small, 8,000-case-a-year facility has made quite an impression, earning a winery of the year title from *Wine and Spirits* magazine in 1994 and winning numerous medals.

Peju has created an appealing showplace for his award-winning wines. As visitors approach the winery, they pass through formal gardens with modernistic sculptures, fountains, plazas and a picnic arbor. The tasting room, in the main winery building, has a high atrium ceiling with skylights to let the Napa Valley sun spill through. Potted plants, polished woods, works of art and twin tasting bars complete the pleasing interior picture.

Tasting notes: The two varietals we were offered in the conducted tasting—Chardonnay and Cabernet Sauvignon—were outstanding; the Chard was lush and spicy with a hint of wood and the Cab had a nice peppery nose and flavor and light tannin. Two proprietary wines also were tasty. The Karma, a blend of Cabernet, Chardonnay and French Colombard, tasted like a good French rosé. The Carnival was nice if you like slightly sweet wines; it's mostly French Colombard, soft and flowery. Peju also produces a late harvest Sauvignon Blanc and red Meritage of Cabernet, Merlot, Cabernet Franc and Petit Verdot. Prices range from $8.50 for Karma and Carnival into the $30s for the varietals and Meritage.

Neibaum-Coppola Estate Winery (formerly Inglenook) • T

☐ *1991 St. Helena Hwy., Rutherford, CA 94573; (707) 963-9099. Tasting and visitor facilities expected to open in late 1995; call winery for details.* ☐

Noted filmmaker Francis Ford Coppola purchased historic Inglenook just prior to this book going to press. Details of his plans were not yet available, although he intended to renovate the ancient winery. Public visitor and tasting facilities were to reopen after several months' work. In refurbishing the winery estate, Coppola will preserve its historic legacy, evidenced by the fact that he has included the name of its founder in its new name.

Finnish sea captain and fur trader Gustave Nybom (later spelled Neibaum) put down roots here in the 1880s and eventually built an impressive stone winery and elaborate Victorian mansion. Both survive today as keystones on the extensive grounds. One early-day writer described the courtyard as "large enough to accommodate several locomotives." Inglenook was part of the Heublein corporation before its recent purchase by Coppola.

Beaulieu Vineyard • T & T$ GT 🍷

☐ *1960 St. Helena Hwy., Rutherford, CA 94573; (707) 963-2411. Daily 10 to 5; MC/VISA, AMEX. Select wines tasted free; older wines tasted in the Private Reserve Room for a fee. Separate gift shop with good selection; periodic guided tours; audio-visual show.* ☐

Beaulieu's current corporate ownership hasn't dimmed its historic reputation for wines, established by legendary winemaker Andre Tchelistcheff. He guided Beaulieu's wine production for more than four decades until his recent death. The winery's Cabernets are among the most honored in the country, and are consistent medal winners. The winery dates back to the turn of the century, founded by Georges de Latour. The original structure survives, a great stone fortress-like affair covered with decades of ivy.

The adjacent hexagonal wood-paneled tasting room, recently remodeled, is one of the valley's more stylish. And it's wonderfully civilized. A smiling attendant hands you a sample of Chardonnay the moment you enter. You can seek more sips at a small tasting bar. An extensive gift and wine shop occupies a lower floor reached by a spiral stairway. An historical display tells the story of Beaulieu and its position in Napa Valley history. Twenty-minute tours are given periodically.

Tasting notes: Beaulieu's list is large, accommodating most of the premium varietals. We particularly savored a Carneros Chardonnay with a nutty, rich and buttery flavor. The Rutherford Cabernet had a spicy nose, fine berry-cinnamon taste and softly acidic finish. Equally appealing was a reserve Carneros Pinot Noir with nice berries in the bouquet and pleasing raspberry flavor. The Muscat de Frontignan dessert wine was cherry like, spicy and nutty—so intense it could pose as a liqueur. Prices range from $7.25 to the mid teens.

Vintners choice: "Georges de Latour private reserve," states marketing director Mark Koppen. "It's our finest Cabernet, produced at BV for more than fifty vintages."

Grgich Hills Cellar • T & T$ GT

◻ *1829 St. Helena Hwy. (P.O. Box 450), Rutherford, CA; (707) 963-2784. Daily 9:30 to 4:30; no credit cards. Most varieties tasted for no fee on weekdays; modest tasting fee on weekends. Small selection of gift items. Tours at 11 and 2 weekdays and 11 and 1:30 weekends.* ◻

Croatian Miljenko Grgich's name may be unpronounceable, but it's on the tongue of every serious wine aficionado in the country. His medium-sized winery is a consistent award winner; a Grgich Chardonnay once beat out serious French competition to be declared the world's best. Winemaker Grgich, who looks more like poet with a soft, round face topped by a beret, says simply: "I baby my wines."

Grgich Hills Cellar wasn't named for mountains. Mike Grgich and Austin Hills are its founders, establishing the facility on the Fourth of July, 1977. The vaguely Spanish-style structure, trimmed with ivy, houses a small, wood-paneled tasting room decorated mostly with press notices. It's easy to tour the winery visually, standing at the tasting counter, glass in hand. Or you can join a walking one, twice a day.

Tasting notes: We discovered one of our favorite Zinfandels here, from a Sonoma vineyard, naturally, with a luxuriously peppery aroma and wonderful berry flavor. The Napa Valley Cabernet had a great nose—a mixed banquet of spice, pepper, berries and soft wood, with a flavor to match. A Napa Valley Fumé Blanc was more flowery than smoky, with a buttery, almost Chardonnay-like taste. And the Chardonnay itself? Crisp, spicy, soft and silky. Prices range from $13 to $24; higher for library selections.

Vintners choice: The winery's Bob Hattaway's statement says nothing and therefore everything about the Grgich philosophy: "Each wine is treated as a special child—none better or less than the other."

Domaine Napa • T

◻ *1155 Mee Lane, St. Helena, CA 94574; (707) 963-1666. Daily 10 to 5; MC/VISA. Most wines tasted; no fee.* ◻

Genial Michel Perret, chewing on a toothpick, says he doesn't like too much wood in his wines. "A wine shouldn't make so powerful statement that it stands apart from the meal," he said with his rich French accent. "We use very little oak so the natural bouquet of the fruit will come forward."

A member of a longtime French winemaking family, Perret sold his winery in the Côtes de Provençe in 1980, deciding that France was too full of regulations. He came to California in 1977 and bought vineyard land in 1980, only to find that the Napa Valley, too, was riddled with regulations. Most of them involved the construction of his winery, and he agrees with the state's rules governing the quality of wine. They protect the product but don't inhibit creativity. "In France we follow tradition; in California, we create it."

His small 5,000-case winery occupies a basic stucco, metal-roofed building and the tasting room is a classic—several barrels standing on end. The only décor is an impressive array of ribbons on a wall. The tasting bar occupies a corner of the winery so a tour consists simply of glancing about at the stacks of French and American oak where Peret's wines rest.

Tasting notes: Peret's philosophy and that of his winemaker Grant Taylor are evident in the four wines they produce. The Sauvignon Blanc we tasted was flowery, fruit and crisp; the Chardonnay also was light on the tongue and yet very fruity and buttery. They preserved the spicy aroma and flavors of the Cabernet Sauvignon and Merlot while keeping both light on the woods. Curiously, the Merlot seemed to have more of a Cab flavor—full-bodied and peppery; it could easily pass for the classic varietal. Prices range from around $10 to the middle teens; a bit more for older Cabs.

Vintner's choice: "I like very much our Sauvignon Blanc and Cabernet. The Sauvignon Blanc stands up nicely to foods."

Beaucanon • T GTA

□ *1695 St. Helena Hwy., St. Helena, CA 94575; (707) 967-3520. Daily 10 to 5; major credit cards. Selected wines tasted; no fee. A few wine related gift items. Guided tours by appointment.* □

After two and a half centuries of practice, it's a safe bet that the de Coninck family of France knows how to make wines. Jacques de Coninck, who owns a large negociant in St. Emilion, established Beaucanon in 1986. It's operated by two of his children—Louis, the winemaker, and Chantal, who manages vineyard and winery operations.

Built in 1987, the winery is a simple, attractive Bordeaux style structure with a vaulted ceiling, which carries into the spacious, well groomed tasting room. As you enter, one of the first things to catch your eye is a sleek and shiny hotrod, one of Louis' toys. The tasting counter is set atop a row of old wine presses; beyond is a window into the main winery.

Tasting notes: The winery produces two types of wine—the more complex Beaucanon label that reflects is French heritage and the lighter, fruitier La Crosse label, more typical of California wines. We found the Beaucanon Chardonnay to be properly buttery and fruity with a soft tannic nip at the end. A side-by-side tasting of Cabernets revealed the two styles—the Beaucanon was spicier with a bit of tannin, while the La Cross was fruitier, even with a hint of pears. The balance of the short list consists of Merlot and a late harvest Chardonnay in the Beaucanon line and a La Crosse Chardonnay. Prices range from $7.50 to the mid teens.

Rutherford Vintners • T

□ *1673 St. Helena Hwy., (P.O. Box 238), Rutherford, CA 94573; (707) 963-7194. Daily 10 to 4:30; MC/VISA. Selected wines tasted; no fee. A few wine related gift items.* □

The Skoda family's small facility is a folksy island of intimacy afloat in a sea of larger-than-life wines and wineries. Evelyn Skoda herself, with a smiling face suggestive of Julia Childs, may stroll out of her cluttered office to pour the wines. The tasting room is a simple cottage-like affair; the Skodas decorate it mostly with medals they've won. The winery itself is back among the vineyards, basic and vine-covered.

Bernard Skoda grew up in Alsace-Lorraine, France, and brought his wine expertise to California in the 1950s. After working for others, he planted his own vineyards in 1968 and started Rutherford Vintners in 1976. He's been winning gold medals ever since.

Tasting notes: Rutherford's wines are good buys, ranging from $6.50 to the mid teens. A Johannisberg Riesling aged in German oak was soft on the palate, with a nice fruity nose and light finish. The Cabernet Sauvignon was subtly spicy, berry-like and full-flavored. A nice crushed flower petal aroma emerged from the Muscat of Alexandria dessert wine; the flavor was predictably intense. Incidentally, serious collectors can find select wines ranging as far back as 15 years.

Franciscan Vineyards • T$ GT & GTA 🎁

☐ *1178 Galleron Rd. (P.O. Box 407), Rutherford, CA 94573; (707) 963-7111. Daily 10 to 5; MC/VISA. Select varieties tasted for a small fee. Extensive gift shop selection. Guided tours three times a day on weekends and holidays; by appointment only on weekdays.* ☐

This appealing middle-sized winery, producing 120,000 cases a year, sits on landscaped grounds alongside Highway 29 (despite the Galleron Road address). It was started as a simple shed by Peter Eckes and Agustin Huneeus in 1973 and has since grown into a more picturesque redwood-sided structure.

Franciscan produces only estate wines, using traditional dry-farming techniques with no irrigation, and wild yeast fermentation in some of its vineyards. Coupling this with modern pruning and trellising techniques, it has earned considerable praise among wine aficionados.

Tasting notes: Franciscan's wines are uniformly excellent and modestly priced for the Napa Valley, ranging from $7 to the middle teens; a bit higher for library selections. The wines were light and palate-pleasing, focusing more on fruit than wood. Our agreeable samples included a gentle but intensely flavored Gewürztraminer, a good buy at $7; a light, subtly spiced Chardonnay priced at $12; a soft and herbal Cabernet Sauvignon and a peppery, raspberry-like Zinfandel with a good crisp finish.

Vintners choice: A winery source ticked them off without adjectives: "Meritage, Merlot, Cabernet Sauvignon, Chardonnay."

Whitehall Lane Winery • T$ GT

☐ *1563 St. Helena Hwy., St. Helena, CA 94574; (707) 963-9454. Daily 11 to 6; major credit cards. All varieties except reserves are tasted for $3 fee (in-*

MUSIC IN THE VINEYARDS

cludes logo glass). A few wine oriented gift items. Tours daily at 11 and 4; they include a barrel sampling of one of the aging wines. ☐

Originally opened in 1979 by architect-winemaker Art Finkelstein and his brother Allen Steen, Whitehall was purchased by an international wine conglomerate in 1988. Then the Leonardini family of San Francisco bought it in 1993, bringing it back into American ownership. With that has come an "Americanization" of wine style, producing fruitier and less woody wines aged in American oak.

Architect Finkelstein designed the simple convergence of lines, angles and geometric shapes that comprise this gray and beige winery alongside St. Helena Highway. The tasting room is a cozy space, decorated mostly with bottles, medals and a few wine logo items.

Tasting notes: Whitehall has won several awards with its balance of light, fruity wines. We liked the pronounced fruity varietal characters of its Chardonnay, Sauvignon Blanc, Cabernet Sauvignon and Merlot. Winemaker Gary Galleron, a Napa Valley native, also produces a full-flavored red Meritage. Prices range from $12 to $16, with reserve and library selections starting at $23.

Raymond Vineyard and Cellars • T & T$ GTA

☐ *849 Zinfandel Lane, St. Helena, CA 94574; (800) 525-2659 or (707) 963-3141. Daily 10 to 4; MC/VISA. Selected wines tasted free; fee for some reserves. Small giftware selection. Tours by appointment, usually at 11 a.m.* ☐

The Raymond family goes far back in Napa's winemaking history, although their modern winery dates from 1974. Right after Repeal, Roy Raymond started working at Beringer, where he met and married Martha Jane. Their sons operate things now, with Walter making wine and young Roy marketing it.

Raymond produces wines drawn from vineyards surrounding their winery, which is near the valley's geographic center. The winery is a comely lowrise structure—a modern oversized bungalow, painted green to blend in with the surrounding vineyards. An airy, open tasting room occupies one corner.

Tasting notes: The Raymond's brief lists consists of Chardonnay, Sauvignon Blanc and Cabernet Sauvignon. The Sauvignon Blanc was herbal and crisp with a nice tart finish and a three-year-old Chard was properly buttery and spicy, with a touch of oak. A Cabernet, two years in oak and two in the bottle, was smooth, complex with good berries and a touch of oak and tannin. Prices range from $10 to $17; higher for reserves.

Vintners choice: "Our Private Reserve Chardonnay and Cabernet; limited production; the best of each vintage," quoth the winery's Kas McGregor.

Rutherford Hill Winery • T$ GT ✕ ⌂

☐ *200 Rutherford Hill Rd., Rutherford, CA 94573; (707) 963-7194. Weekdays 10:30 to 4:30, weekends 10 to 5; MC/VISA, AMEX. Most varieties tasted for a $3 fee, including the glass and a cave tour with barrel tasting. Tours at 11:30, 12:30, 1:30, 2:30 and 3:30. Good choice of giftwares and wine logo items. Wooded picnic area with a valley view.* ☐

Rutherford Hill is a particularly striking facility, a monumental weathered wooden structure with flying buttresses, set in a wooded notch high above the valley. Tours take visitors through aging caves tunneled into the hillside, then into the state-of-the-art winery. Picnic areas are terraced and tree shaded, with valley views.

The weathered wooden winery and aging caves suggest antiquity, yet the facility dates from 1976, when it was founded as a limited partnership. Tunneled by modern machinery and coated with gunnite, the cave network covers nearly a mile; it's claimed to be the longest set of wine burrows in America. The tasting room is reached through tall cathedral-like doors at one end of the main winery. Heavy beams support the lofty ceiling. The atmosphere is that of a grand mountain ski chalet. Tours offer an interesting twist; after strolling through the pleasantly dim caves, visitors are offered a barrel tasting of one of the maturing wines.

Tasting notes: The lists consists of Chardonnay, Cabernet Sauvignon, Merlot, Gewürztraminer, Sauvignon Blanc and a Zinfandel port. Several versions of Chardonnay and Cabernet are available. We particularly liked the fruity, toasty Cellar Reserve Chardonnay and nicely balanced, berry-flavored Library Reserve Cabernet. The Merlot had a spicy, herbal nose and good berries in the taste, with an acid nip at the end. The Zinfandel port was nutty and berry-focused—an exceptionally rich sipping wine.

Vintners choice: A voice from within said: "We call ourselves the Merlot winery."

Caymus Vineyards • T$ ✕

☐ *8700 Conn Creek Rd. (P.O. Box 268), Rutherford, CA 94573; (707) 967-3010. Daily 10 to 4:30; MC/VISA. Most varieties tasted for a $2 fee (which buys the glass). A few wine logo items; picnic area.* ☐

Although this small winery was started in 1972, the founding Wagner family has been farming in this valley since 1906. They began making wine in 1915 and Charlie Wagner, Sr., boasts that they carried on right through Prohibition. "We had a large basement," he recalls.

The complex, at the intersection of Conn Creek Road and Highway 128, is housed in a new fieldstone winery, with an expanded tasting room off the barrel cellar that replaces the original cluttered tasting counter.

Wagner, somewhere beyond 80, is a crusty anomaly in this land of high-rollers, *nouveau* vintners and corporate giants—an outspoken, down-to-earth dirt farmer who's probably forgotten more about wine production than wet-behind-the-ears Davis graduates have ever learned. He and his wife of more than half a century can take it a bit easier now, since their son Chuck serves as president and winemaker.

Tasting notes: The *Wine Spectator* quotes Charlie as saying Caymus produces the "best damned Cabernet in California." After tasting this deep purple, intense, berry-rich and tannic wine, we agree. The family also produces a good, honest raspberry-tasting Zinfandel, a rich and fruity Sauvignon Blanc and a lush, complex and pleasantly herbal white called Conundrum, a blend of Sauvignon Blanc, Muscat Canelli, Chardonnay, Semillon and Viognier. (Work on the pronunciation before you drink it.) Prices are $7 to $20.

Vintners choice: Son Chuck Wagner likes his Caymus Cabernet for its "intense fruit character, medium tannin and rich, full taste with a long finish." Of course, those aren't the kind of words that his dad would use. As he said, it's damned fine wine.

Conn Creek Winery • T GTA 🍷

☐ *8711 Silverado Trail, St. Helena, CA 94574; (707) 963-9100. Daily 10 to 4; MC/VISA, AMEX. Most varieties tasted; no fee. Good gift and wine logo selection. Guided tours by appointment.* ☐

This prim little winery—established in 1974—would look at home in Madrid, with its white stucco and Spanish arches. The Mediterranean theme carries into the tasting room, accented with iron chandeliers, carved wooden furniture and a rough tile floor. Slices of the modern, efficient winery are visible through large windows.

Tasting notes: Meritage, Zinfandel, Merlot, Cabernet Sauvignon and a late harvest Sauvignon Blanc comprise the brief list. Prices wander from $8 to $20. Our favorites were a rich, raspberry accented Zinfandel and a fine Cabernet that was peppery, berry-like and velvety.

Vintners choice: "We're known as a Cabernet house," revealed the winery's Anne Salazar.

Nichelini Winery • T CT ✗

◻ 2950 Sage Canyon Rd., St. Helena, CA 94574; (707) 963-0717. Weekends only, 9 to 6 April-October and 9 to 5 November-March. MC/VISA. Most varieties tasted. Some wine logo gift items. Informal peeks into the winery; wooded picnic areas. ◻

This delightfully rustic winery seems to cling to the edge of the highway, threatening to topple into a wooded canyon. However, it has managed to hold on since 1890, when it was founded by Italian-Swiss immigrant Anton Nichelini. His descendants still run the place, using a mix of ancient and modern equipment to produce notable wines—mostly reds. There's nary a vine in sight, however; the winery is surrounded by trees. The grapes flourish in nearby Chiles Valley.

On nice days, tasting is conducted outdoors; you can settle onto a nearby bench to sip your wine and listen to the soft sounds of the forest. Picnic tables are terraced about this charmingly weathered winery complex.

Tasting notes: We particularly liked Nichelini's full-bodied, old vine Zinfandel, with a proper tannic nip at the end. The winery also does a Sauvignon Vert, a white Bordeaux varietal noted for its dry zesty flavor, plus full-flavored Chenin Blanc, Sauvignon Blanc, Chardonnay and Johannisberg Riesling. Prices are modest, starting well below $10, and not much beyond.

Vintners choice: "We pride ourselves in Zinfandel because our mountain-located vineyards produce excellent grapes," says Carol Nichelini.

Rustridge Winery • T ✗

◻ 2910 Lower Chiles Valley Rd., St. Helena, CA 94574; (707) 965-2871. Daily 10 to 4; call first on weekdays; MC/VISA, AMEX. Most varieties tasted. Some wine related gift items; shaded picnic area. ◻

You'll pass a ranch style bed and breakfast, a race horse paddock and a scattering of farm equipment and tired trucks to find the winery and tasting room. Both occupy a converted cinderblock hay barn with stainless steel fermenting tanks out front. The tasting room is a wide spot in the middle of the small winery, which produces only a few thousand cases a year.

This remote winery, part of a working ranch and horse farm, was established in 1985 by brothers Grant and Stan Meyer. Their sister Susan now runs the operation with her husband Jim Fresquez. They also run a bed and breakfast in their southwest ranch style home (see listing below). You won't always find the tasting room staffed, but yell or honk your horn and someone will come. A friendly farm hand climbed off a tractor to serve us.

Tasting notes: Chiles Valley's warm, breezy climate produces *big* reds. We liked a full-flavored Cabernet, nearly black in color and with enough tannin suitable for aging; and an equally hefty Zinfandel with nice berries and a tannic nip. Others on the list included a soft and silky Chardonnay with tropical fruit flavors and soft vanilla oak; and a silky smooth late harvest Riesling, rich with fruit yet with a surprisingly dry finish. Rustridge wines are produced from organically grown, pesticide free grapes. Prices range from $7.50 to $20.

Vintners choice: "Our special blend of Cabernet Sauvignon and Zinfandel," said Susan.

Mumm Napa Valley ● T$ GT 🎁

◻ *Five Silverado Trail (P.O. Drawer 500), Rutherford, CA 94573; (800) 686-6722 or (707) 942- 3434. Daily 10:30 to 6 (10 to 5 in winter); major credit cards. Sparkling wine by the glass, $3.50 to $4.50. Separate gift shop with good wine logo and book selection. Tours hourly from 10:30 to 6 in summer and from 11 to 3 in winter.* ◻

France's legendary Mumm set up shop in the Napa Valley in the mid-1980s, although the complex is now owned by the giant Seagram conglomerate. Officials still adhere to the French custom of avoiding the term champagne, unless it's from that particularly district in France. The Seagram-Mumm product is sparkling wine, if you please. Advance scouting for a Napa Valley site, cleverly called "Operation Lafayette," began in 1979, and the champagnery has grown in stages. The hospitality facility, a fashionable gift shop and airy tasting salon, was completed in 1990.

The structure is architecturally curious—a wood-sided creation suggestive of a king-sized California barn. It hovers low to the ground, and the guided tour reveals that much of it is underground, in true French champagnery fashion. The tour begins with an examination of a demonstration vineyard of Pinot Noir, Chardonnay and Meunier grapevines that are the basis for most premium sparkling wines. It then adjourns to the huge partly submerged facility, where 30,000 cases are produced each year.

Tasting notes: We sampled three sparkling wines and agreed with a recent edition of *The Wine Spectator,* which rated Mumm as America's best bubbly. The Vintage Reserve was crisply perfect with a splendid finish; the Winery Lake was explosively fruity and the Blanc de Noirs was soft with a strong hint of the parent Pinot Noir grape. Prices range from $14 to $23.

ZD Wines ● T$ GTA

◻ *8383 Silverado Trail, Napa, CA 94558; (707) 963-5188. Daily 10 to 4:30. Current releases tasted for a $3 fee (includes glass, or can be applied toward wine purchase). Tours by appointment, or brief ones can be arranged on the spot if staff members are available.* ◻

Originally housed in a modest vine-draped structure, ZD has expanded into a modern new winery with a roomy tasting room brightened by oversized windows. A fireplace sometimes crackles in a corner, inviting visitors to linger, sip wines and ask consequential questions such as: "What does ZD stand for?"

Former engineer Norman de Leuze and his wife Rosa Lee started their winery in Sonoma County more than a quarter of a century ago, and then shifted to the Napa Valley in 1979. The operation is mostly a family affair with Norman as CEO, eldest son Robert the winemaker, wife Rosa Lee and daughter Brett handling the marketing and daughter Julie as administrative director.

Winemaking started out as a hobby for Gino Zepponi and Norman de Luze in 1969. When wine critics began taking them seriously, they opened a full-time winery. And now you know what ZD stands for.

Tasting notes: It's a quick list: Chardonnay, Cabernet Sauvignon and Pinot Noir with prices ranging from $20 to $25. After tasting the wonderfully nutty-spicy Chard, the peppery berries of the Cab and the lushly herbal Pinot, we decided that they're worth it.

S. Anderson Vineyard ● T$ GT$

☐ 1473 Yountville Cross Rd., Yountville, CA 94599; (707) 944-8642. Daily 10 to 5. Five wines tasted for a $3 fee. Some wine logo items. Tours of wine caves daily at 10:30 and 2:30 for $3 per person; no appointment needed. ☐

Stanley and Carol Anderson started their vineyards in 1973, but didn't open their tasting room until 1990. It occupies a sort of glorified stone shed that once served as a pump house. More impressive are aging caves tunneled into a hill on the family estate. These stone rooms with lofty ceilings and cobbled floors are haven to nearly half a million bottles of sparkling wine and Chardonnay. The caves and adjacent winery can be visited on twice-daily tours. Visitors to the tiny tasting room can adjourn tables on a land-scaped terrace for more elbow room.

Tasting notes: Sparkling wine (which the Andersons dare to call Champagne) and Chardonnay make up the list. Prices range from $16 to $25. Our selection of five wines went thusly—A Stags Leap Chardonnay was spicy and balanced with enough acid for aging; Proprietor's Reserve Chardonnay was softer, more subtle and fruity with hints of oak; the Blanc de Noirs was surprisingly fruity and complex for a sparkling wine. The Brut Champagne had a nice grapey nose with a fruit-rich flavor and gentle acid finish; the Rose Champagne was strong on the Pinot Noir berries, a sparkling mouthful.

Robert Sinskey Vineyards ● T$ GTA

☐ 6320 Silverado Trail, Napa, CA 94558; 944-9090. Daily 10 to 4:30; MC/VISA. Most varieties tasted for a $3 fee (includes glass or credit toward purchase). Some wine related gift items. Guided tours by appointment. ☐

Like many Silverado wineries, Sinskey occupies an impressive vantage point in the flanks of the Vaca Range. The winery is architecturally intriguing, with a high, ridge-like wooden center flanked by low stone-trimmed wings. The parking area is rimmed by a lattice colonnade with fieldstone walls, and a deck off the winery invites one to lounge (but not picnic) and enjoy a stellar view of the Napa Valley.

The winery interior is a nice mix of wood and stone. The tasting room's high ceiling is held aloft by a web-work of finished rafters; French doors offer a view of vats, barrels and stainless steel. Tours take visitors to a grapevine "petting zoo," through the winery and into caves tunneled into a slope.

Opthamologist Robert Sinskey established the winery in the 1980s and completed the present facility in 1988. His son Rob is manager and marketing director. Tiny as Napa wineries go, with an output of 10,000 cases, it's nonetheless an attention-getter, having won numerous awards.

Tasting notes: Chardonnay, Pinot Noir, Merlot and a Bordeaux style Claret complete the Sinskey list. The Aries Chardonnay was light but complex and silky, with a soft finish. The Aries Pinot Noir was soft as well, almost like a tasty Beaujolais. The best of the lot was RSV Carneros Claret with

Chimney Rock is one of the Napa Valley's most attractive small wineries, with the elaborate facade of its distinctive South African Dutch architecture.

big berries, a nippy finish and enough tannin for aging. It should be good; the price tag read $28. Other wines range from $8 to the high teens.

Silverado Vineyards • T

◻ *6121 Silverado Trail, Napa, CA 94558; (707) 257-1770. Daily 11 to 4:30; MC/VISA. Most varieties tasted; no fee. Some wine related gift items.* ◻

Lillian Disney, widow of Mickey Mouse's creator, purchased several acres of Stags Leap vineyards in 1977, with her son-in-law and daughter, Ron and Diane Disney Miller. Construction of their winery followed in 1981. It was dedicated to the memory of Robert Louis Stevenson, who's *Silverado Squatters* inspired the name. Crowning a vineyard hill, Silverado is among the valley's more attractive wineries. Its fieldstone walls, ivy covered Spanish colonnade, arched windows and lofty ceilings give it the feel of an ancient abbey. The tasting room, occupying a portion of the main winery, is a study in old world refinement with a Spanish tile floor and wood panels.

Tasting notes: John Stuart won a "winemaker of the year" title in 1987 for his small lots of "hand-crafted" wines. His list consists of Sauvignon Blanc, Chardonnay, Cabernet Sauvignon and Merlot. Several vintages of most wines may be purchased. We were impressed with the barrel-fermented Chardonnay, full and complex with a crisp acid finish, and a classic Cabernet Sauvignon with a wonderful spicy bouquet and lush, complex flavor, tannic and suitable for aging. Prices range from $9 to the early twenties.

Pine Ridge Winery • T & T$ GTA ✕ 🍴

◻ *5901 Silverado Trail, Napa, CA 94558; (707) 253-7500. Daily 11 to 5; MC/VISA. Most varieties tasted free; some reserve wines tasted for a fee. Extensive selection of wine theme clothing and related items. Picnic area with barbecues and a swing set. Tours of winery and caves including barrel tasting, daily at 10:15, 1 and 3 by appointment.* ◻

Tucked into the pine-shaded hollow of a hill on the valley side of the highway, Pine Ridge presents a pleasing setting in which to taste some of its award winning wines. The facility has been dressed up considerably in recent years, with a flower-lined walkway leading to an expanded tasting room. From there, visitors can peek into the cellar and bottling area, or stroll into the underground aging caves.

Proprietor R. Gary Andrus, one of the valley's most respected winemakers, bought a vineyard in the Stags Leap district in 1978, added more vines, then released his first wines in 1981. In a decade, he won 114 medals, particularly for his Cabernet Sauvignon.

Tasting notes: The list is brief: Chenin Blanc, Chardonnay, Merlot and Cabernet. Every wine we tasted was excellent—a lush, silky and spicy Knollside Cuvée Chard; an herbal, softly acidic Stags Leap Vineyard Chard; a Selected Cuvée Merlot with a giant of a berry nose, full and complex and ready to age; and a Stags Leap Vineyard Cab with enough complexity and tannic power to carry into the next century.

Vintners choice: "We're well known for our vineyard designated Cabernet," said the winery's Nancy Andrus.

Stag's Leap Wine Cellars • T$ GTA ⚔

◻ *5766 Silverado Trail, Napa, CA 94558; (707) 944-2020. Daily 10 to 4; MC/VISA. Several varieties tasted for a $3 fee (includes glass). Wine oriented gift selection. Oak-shaded picnic area; guided tours by appointment.* ◻

Started in 1972 by Warren and Barbara Winiaraski, Stag's Leap has been growing by—forgive us—leaps and bounds. Starting with one small building, the Winiaraskis now have an extensive complex, with an attractive ivy-entwined Spanish style main winery and new white wine facility. Gnarled oaks enhance the setting.

The tasting room is a simple counter in one end of the main building. (A second counter is added when things get busy in summer.) From here, one can watch the business of winemaking. Tours are available by advance request. (When the couple started their winery, they added an apostrophe to separate it from the Stags Leap district, which is an AVA or Approved Viticultural Area. The winery is now designated as SLV.)

Tasting notes: The winery produces wines under two labels—Stag's Leap and a lighter, fruitier and modestly priced Hawk Crest line. From the Stag's Leap cellar list, we tasted an outstanding Cabernet, big and complex with a brisk tannic finish; and a couple of equally impressive Chardonnays, both spicy and silky with crisp finishes and hints of wood. Prices for the Stag's Leap label range from $10 to $28. The Hawk Crest wines are good buys. A peppery Cabernet, a spicy Chardonnay and a bright, light and fruity Sauvignon Blanc exhibited strong varietal character, all for under $10.

Vintners choice: "The Hawk Crest label features wines styled to be pleasant and accessible," says the Winiaraskis. They've priced their Hawk Crest Cabernet Sauvignon, Chardonnay and Sauvignon Blanc are "for everyday dining."

Chimney Rock Winery • T$ GTA

◻ *5350 Silverado Trail, Napa, CA 94558; (707) 257-2461. Daily 10 to 5; MC/VISA, DISC. Four wines tasted for $3 fee (includes glass, or applied to wine purchase). Small selection of gift items; guided tours by appointment.* ◻

With its ornate Dutch Colonial architecture, Chimney Rock is one of the valley's most striking small wineries. The two-building complex was fashioned after a winery in the Cape Colony of South Africa. Note the elaborate frieze on the main building, portraying Ganymede, cup bearer to Zeus and other Mount Olympus celestials. The tasting room and hospitality center is a study in old world elegance, with gleaming white walls, polished wood trim, a brass chandelier and 19th century furnishings. It's surrounded by manicured lawns and a protective ring of slender poplars which present a dazzling display of yellow in the fall.

All this is the creation of Sheldon and Stella Wilson, who purchased half of the Chimney Rock Golf Course in 1980 and converted it into a vineyard. The winery complex was completed in 1990. (The golf course, still in business, is now a nine-holer.)

Tasting notes: The intent here is to match wines with foods, making them soft, gentle and light on the wood, says winemaker Doug Fletcher. The Chardonnay is evidence of this philosophy—silky and almost honey-like, with only a slight hint of oak. We also tasted an herbal, complex and nicely balanced Cabernet Sauvignon and a bright, crisp Fumé Blanc with a great floral nose and just a hint of duskiness. Prices range from $10 to $25, more for some library wines.

Clos Du Val • T$ GT & GTA ✕

☐ 5330 Silverado Trail (P.O. Box 4350), Napa, CA 94558; (707) 252-6711. Daily 10 to 5; MC/VISA. Four wines tasted from the list of current releases for a $3 fee, which applies toward wine purchases. Selected wine oriented gift items including whimsical Ronald Searle posters and postcards. Oak-shaded picnic tables. Guided tours daily at 10:30, or by appointment. ☐

Sitting upslope in a wooded grove, cathedral-like Clos Du Val was established in 1972 by John Goelet and French winemaker Bernard Portet; they had in mind a noble yet rather simple château. Both men are still principals in the operation. The tasting room is a grand space—an imposing abbey-like affair with 50-foot ceilings, accented by ornate woods, conglomerate walls and tile floors. Lofty windows offer views into the working winery. In recent years, the ivy-entwined "abbey" has been dressed up with expanded landscaping and a bike path leading to the highway.

Tasting notes: A number of Cabernet vintages top the award-winning list, going back through several vintages. We tasted a complex and spicy eight-year-old Cab and one of Napa's better Zinfandels—herbal, peppery and tasty, with enough tannin to encourage aging. A Chardonnay was crisp, clean and pleasantly light. Merlot, Semillon and an inexpensive Le Clos White complete the list. Prices range from $10 to the mid-twenties. Buyers can select from a range of six or seven vintage years of most of the wines.

THE BEST OF THE BUNCH

The best wine buys • Mont St. John Cellars in the Carneros; Sequoia Grove Vineyards, Rutherford Vintners and Franciscan Vineyards along Highway 29, Stag's Leap on the Silverado Trail (Hawk Crest line) and Nichelini Winery in the Chiles Valley.

The most attractive wineries • Carneros Alambic and Domaine Carneros in the Carneros; The Hess Collection on Mount Veeder; Domaine Chandon, Robert Mondavi Winery, Peju Province on Highway 29; Rutherford Hill Winery, Silverado Vineyards, Chimney Rock Winery and Clos Du Val on the Silverado Trail.

The most interesting tasting rooms • Domaine Carneros in the Carneros; Domaine Chandon and Beaulieu Vineyard on Highway 29; Conn

Creek Winery, Rutherford Hill Winery, Silver Oak Cellars, Silverado Vineyards, Chimney Rock Winery and Clos Du Val on the Silverado Trail.

The funkiest tasting rooms • Nichelini Winery and Rustridge Winery in the Chiles Valley.

The best gift shops • The Hess Collection on Mount Veeder; Domaine Chandon, Robert Mondavi Winery, Beaulieu Vineyard and Franciscan Vineyards on Highway 29 and Mumm Napa Valley on the Silverado Trail.

The nicest picnic areas • Château Potelle on Mount Veeder; Vichon Winery on Oakville Grade; Rutherford Hill Winery, Pine Ridge Winery, Stag's Leap Cellars and Clos Du Val on the Silverado Trail; Nichelini Winery in the Chiles Valley.

The best tours • Carneros Alambic (guided) and Domaine Carneros (guided or self-guiding) in the Carneros; Hess Collection (self-guiding) on Mount Veeder; Domaine Chandon (guided), St. Supéry Winery (self-guiding) and Beaulieu (guided) on Highway 29; Rutherford Hill Winery (guided cave and winery tour) and Mumm Napa Valley (guided) on the Silverado Trail.

Wineland activities and such

Wineland events • Napa Valley Mustard Festival with wine tasting and food, photo contest and other activities, mid-March; (800) 919-NAPA. Taste of Yountville wine and food tasting, mid-March; (707) 944-0904. Art in the Carneros with art exhibits and wine tastings at Carneros district wineries, mid-April; (707) 996-7256. Napa Valley Wine Auction, first week of June; (707) 963-5246. Mondavi Pops Festival and Summer Music Festival, June-August; (707) 226-1395. Napa Town & Country Fair in Napa, featuring local winery exhibits, early August; (707) 253-4900. Harvest Crush celebration at Vintage 1870 featuring area winemakers, plus food and entertainment, September; (707) 944-2451.

Winery maps and guides • **Napa Valley Guide** with winery maps and listings of activities, restaurants and lodgings, available at many wineries and gift shops for $4.95 or $7 by mail from Vintage Publications, 764 Adobe Dr., Santa Rosa, CA 95404; (707) 538-8981. The **Silverado Trail** map produced by the Silverado Trail Wineries Association lists wineries on the "quiet side of the Napa Valley"; available free from member vintners along the Silverado Trail, or call (800) 624-WINE. Mattioli's **In Your Pocket Guide** to Yountville, Oakville and Rutherford lists wineries, lodging, shops, restaurants and recreation, $1.50, in gift shops and tasting rooms, or call 965-2006.

Napa Valley Wine Train • Three-hour 36-mile lunch, brunch and dinner rides through the Napa Valley in a handsomely restored early 20th century passenger train. Depot at 1275 McKinstry St., Napa, CA 94559; (800) 427-4124 or (707) 253-2111.

Wine country tours • VinTours features personalized tours of smaller wineries in Napa and Sonoma counties; 536 Orchard St., Santa Rosa, CA 95404; (707) 546-9483. Napa Valley Tourist Bureau creates personalized tours; (707) 944-1557. Wine Country Jeep Tours takes visitors through the Napa Valley's backroads; (800) 539-JEEP. Sonoma Chardonnay Limousine Service offers Napa and Sonoma wine country tours; 22455 Broadway, Sonoma, CA 95476; (707) 938-4248. Napa Valley Excursions offers personalized wine country tours, 1825 Lincoln Ave., Napa; (707) 252-6333. Winery and dining tours are offered by Wine & Dine Tours, 1250 Church St., St. Helena, CA 94574; (800) 946-3868 or (707) 963-8930. Guided wine country tours also are provided by Napa Valley Holidays, 1525 Andrea Circle, Napa, CA 94558, (707) 255-1050; and Wine Adventures Inc., 1258 Arroyo Sarco, Napa, CA 94558, (707) 257-0353.

BEYOND THE VINEYARDS

Wine's the thing in the southern end of the valley, but the area has a few other lures as well. The city of **Napa**, which we bypassed in our eagerness to reach the vineyards, offers several attractions. It's the valley's commercial center and home to 56,000 souls—half the county's population.

Although its suburbs are typical shopping center-service station Americana, the old fashioned downtown area shouldn't be overlooked. The small business district is well kept and attractive, with tree-lined streets, brick enhanced sidewalks and shops tucked into revitalized false front stores.

First and Main streets are the heart of old Napa; to reach it take the First Street exit east from Freeway 29. Carefully restored Victorian homes rim the downtown area. Many are concentrated along Jefferson, Clay and Polk streets, northeast of downtown. Also, visit the **Napa County Historical Society Museum** located in the Goodman Library building at 1219 First Street. For **walking tour maps** of historic Napa, contact Napa City Hall, Second and School streets (252-7711).

Mountains cradling the Napa Valley lure lovers of winding roads and solitude. Pick any east-west route and you'll soon be surrounded by silence, whispered through pine and redwood forests and oak groves clustered on tawny hillsides.

Oakville Grade offers a good excuse to wind among the heights on your way to neighboring Sonoma Valley, with splendid views back down to the Napa Valley as you climb. Pick it up in Oakville. (You went part of the way up in visiting Vichon Winery.) It crests the Mayacamus Mountains and becomes Trinity Road as it twists and winds downhill to Highway 12 near Glen Ellen. Highway 121 winding northeast of Napa takes you to **Lake Berryessa**, a large reservoir offering the usual boating, water-skiing, camping, swimming and fishing lures. You can check into one of several resorts, get provisions at lakeside marinas and rent houseboats, fishing boats and other water toys. Call (707) 966-2111 for details.

If you follow Highway 128 west from Berryessa, then turn right onto Lower Chiles Valley Road, you'll pass high meadows, forests and vineyards of the secluded **Chiles Valley**. Beyond that, you encounter **Pope Valley**, another prime vineyard area.

The tiny, prim Seventh-Day Adventist village of **Angwin** is home to **Pacific Union College** and a lot of good Christians. Interestingly, in this little hamlet in the hills above California's most famous wine country, one can't get a drink. Adventists forswear alcohol, tobacco and caffeine. Most are vegetarians and you'll find no meat or fish in the **College Market**. Its bulk food section, brimming with legumes, spices, whole-grain flour, dried fruits and candies is impressively extensive, however.

Down Valley activities & attractions

Bike tours and rentals ● Napa Valley Bike Tours and Napa Valley Cyclery at (800) 707-BIKE (California only) or (707) 255-3377; Bicycle Trax at (800) 859-2453 or (707) 258-8729; Getaway Wine Country Bicycle Tours at (800) 499-BIKE; or Napa Valley Bicycle and Canoe Trips at (707) 255-2224.

Boat tours • Napa Riverboat Company (sternwheeler), 1200 Milton Rd., Napa CA 94558; (707) 226-2648.

Boating at Lake Berryessa • Spanish Flat Resort with ski boat, patio boat, sailboard and jet ski rentals, (800) 966-7700; Lake Berryessa Marina Resort with ski boat, fishing and patio boat rentals, (707) 966-2365; Markley Cove, offering houseboat rentals, (800) 242-6287 or (707) 966-2134.

Bicycle rentals • Iggy's Bicycle Rental Company, 1527 Sage Canyon Rd., St. Helena, (707) 963-2585; Napa Valley Bicycle and Canoe Trips, 1370 Frances, Room 301, Napa, (707) 255- 2224; Napa Valley Cyclery, 4080 Byway East, Napa, (800) 707-BIKE; or St. Helena Cyclery, 1156 Main St., St. Helena, (707) 963-7736.

Scenic flights • Bridgeford Flying Service at Napa County Airport; (707) 224-0887.

Hot air ballooning • This is a great way to see the Napa Valley, which has the greatest concentration of hot air balloonists in California, maybe in the country. To take advantage of the still air, most balloonists launch early in the morning. For information and referral, contact Professional Balloon Pilots Association of Napa Valley, P.O. Box 2206, Yountville, CA 94599, (707) 944-8793.

Among Down Valley's operators are: Above It All, P.O. Box 2500, Yountville, CA 94599, (800) 226-8348; Above the West, P.O. Box 2290, Yountville, CA 94599, (800) NAPA-SKY or (707) 944-8638; American Balloon Adventures, 7321 St. Helena Hwy., Yountville, CA 94599, (800) 333-4359; Balloon Aviation of Napa Valley, P.O. Box 2500, Napa, CA 94559, (800) 367-6272 or (707) 944-4400.

Balloons Above the Valley, P.O. Box 3838, Napa, CA 94558, (800) 464-6824 or (707) 253-2222; Bonaventura Balloon Co., Caymus Inn, Rutherford, CA 94573, (800) 243-6743 or (707) 944-2822; Napa Valley Balloons, Box 2860, Yountville, CA 94599, (800) 253-2224 or (707) 944-0228; Napa Valley Drifters, 1106 Hardman, Napa, CA 94558, (707) 252-7210; and Napa's Great Balloon Escape, P.O. Box 4197, Napa, CA 94558, (800) 564-9399 or (707) 253-0860.

Napa County Historical Society Museum • In the 1901 Goodman Library Building at 1219 First St., Napa; (707) 224-1739. Tuesday and Thursday, noon to 4; local history exhibits.

WINE COUNTRY DINING

Since it draws hundreds of thousands of visitors including many San Francisco Bay Area regulars, the Napa Valley supports some of northern California's better restaurants. This list covers dining from Yountville south to Napa; those from St. Helena north are in the next chapter.

Ānestis Grill & Rotisserie • ☆☆ $$

◻ *6518 Washington St., Yountville; (707) 944-1500. Eclectic menu; wine and beer. Lunch from 11:30, dinner from 5. Major credit cards.* ◻ Simple, airy dining space opposite Vintage 1870, with an outdoor patio. The versatile menu ranges from grilled chicken pasta and garlic herb cheese tortellini to pesto chicken and mesquite grilled rack of lamb.

Café Kinyon • ☆☆ $

◻ *6525 Washington St. (in Vintage 1870), Yountville; (707) 944-2788. American; wine and beer. Lunch only, daily from 11:30. AMEX and personal checks.* ◻ Attractive café wrapped in old brick, with exposed heating ducts

THE WINE TRAIN: MOBILE VINELAND DINING

The Napa Valley Wine Train has finally become what San Francisco's Vince DeDomenico wanted in the first place. When the creator of Rice-A-Roni proposed running an excursion train through the Napa Valley a decade ago, some residents and vintners threw a collective fit. "Too disruptive!" they cried. "Too tacky!"

He got approval for his train, with the proviso that it wouldn't pause at wineries. It chugged non-stop from Napa to St. Helena and back, serving lunch or dinner on board—essentially a mobile restaurant.

However, as of 1995, it was permitted to make winery stops during its slow-motion amble through the valley. Now, after ten years, the maroon train with its 1920 style coaches has become a familiar—and non-threatening—sight as it moves alongside Highway 29.

We took the train when we wrote the original edition of this book, and then again for the revised edition—each time posing as tourists and paying our own way. We enjoyed it more the second time. The food had improved and the waitstaff was exceptionally friendly.

Question: Is it relaxed elegance on one of the world's most magnificent trains, as the brochure claims, or is it tacky?

Answer: "Magnificent" is an overstatement, although the refurbished coaches *are* handsomely appointed, with "polished mahogany, brass and etched glass," as the brochure states. Dining cars are set with fine silver, china and crystal over white nappery. But having your picture taken before boarding, to be purchased later? *That's* tacky.

Q: Is the meal "a deliciously crafted culinary & wine experience?"

A: It wasn't bad, considering that dozens of meals were served almost simultaneously. Most of the items are freshly prepared in a large kitchen right on the train. And here's a tip: ask for second seating, since you get to nibble *hors d'ouveres* in a rather handsome salon car, and then you can dine at a relaxed pace. The wine list is fine, although we felt it was overpriced. There's also a winetasting car on the train, offering samples from several Napa Valley wineries for a fee.

Q: Did you "glide gently past world famous vineyards?"

A: Gently and *slowly*. The train really pokes along, presumably to allow enough time for the two meal sittings. The railway parallels Highway 29, so passengers see the same vineyards and wineries that motorists see. They get something motorists don't—a running narrative about the valley, although passenger chatter tends to drown it out.

Q: Was it "an enjoyable and relaxed journey through California's historic and scenic wine country?"

A: Relaxing yes, since someone else was driving. And this wine valley is certainly historic. The train follows the route of the Napa Valley Railroad, which Mormon entrepreneur Sam Brannen built in 1864. However, it only goes half way—to St. Helena.

Q: Your summation?

A: It's a pleasant diversion, particularly if you like old trains. Some may feel it's rather expensive—$60 for the lunch run and $71 for dinner. However, that's comparable to other deliberately elegant tourist outings, such as San Francisco Bay dining cruises. Incidentally, the entire train is smoke free, a very nice feature.

and other rustic-modern touches. Luncheon fare includes assorted sandwiches and elaborate salads; we like the "Caesar was a Chicken" with romaine, red onion, breast of chicken and crumbled Parmesan cheese.

Compadres Bar & Grill • ☆☆ $$

☐ *6539 Washington St. (in Vintage Estate), Yountville; (707) 944-2406. Mexican; full bar service. Weekdays from 10 a.m., weekends from 9 a.m., various closing times. Major credit cards.* ☐ Lively cantina serving an interesting mix of Mexican fare ranging from fajitas, *Latino* spiced fresh fish and chicken *pollo borracho*. The look is bright, cheery upscale California-Mexican; patio dining.

Domaine Chandon Restaurant • ☆☆☆ $$$$

☐ *One California Drive, Yountville; (707) 944-2892. California-French; wine and beer. Open daily; lunch 11:30 to 2:30, dinner 6 to 9:30. Reservations essential; major credit cards.* ☐ At Domaine Chandon winery; one of the valley's more striking restaurants, with glass walls offering vineyard views. *Nouveau* menu ranges from roasted pork tenderloin with fava bean purée and sweet garlic to venison *tournedos* wrapped in pancetta with potatoes and Merlot-juniper essence. Extensive California wine list; smoke-free dining room.

The Fisherman • ☆☆☆ $$$

☐ *6534 Washington St.; 944-0170. American, mostly seafood; wine and beer. Dinner nightly from 5:30. MC/VISA.* ☐ Cozy little place in a brick building, with salmon colored walls and warm woods—kind of a European café atmosphere; outdoor patio. The predominately seafood menu offers prawns provençal, grilled filet of ahi tuna, crabcakes, lobster bisque and seafood pasta.

Frankie, Johnnie & Luigi Too! • ☆☆ $$

☐ *6772 Washington St., Yountville; (707) 944-0177. Italian; full bar service. Sunday-Thursday 11:30 to 10, 11:30 to 11 Friday-Saturday. Major credit cards.* ☐ More appealing than it's silly name, it's a cheerful family pasta and pizza parlor with blonde woods, ceramic tile floors and red checkered tables. Multi-course family dinners for six are about $37, or one can order assorted pastas, pizzas or typical Italian dinners such as chicken cacciatore, veal scaloppini or osso bucco. Large outdoor dining deck.

The French Laundry • ☆☆☆☆ $$$$

☐ *6640 Washington Street at Creek Street, Yountville; (707) 944-2380. Nouveau/French; four-course prix fixe dinners $46, five-course $49; wine and beer. Dinners nightly from 5:30. Reservations essential.* ☐ Fashionable French Country café in a century-old cut stone laundry building. The look is starkly simple, although the fare is legendary. The constantly changing menu features tasty fare such as avocado, honey tangerine and papaya salad with ginger; petrale sole medallion with a cassoulet of white beans and preserved lemon and for dessert—bruléed tapioca custard tart with orange-apricot glaze. The entrance is through a courtyard off Creek Street

Mustards • ☆☆☆ $$$

☐ *7399 St. Helena Hwy. (just north of Yountville), Napa; (707) 944-2424. California-American upscale grill; full bar service. Daily 11:30 to 10. Major credit cards.* ☐ California *nouveau* café with a designer American bistro look. Innovative and changing menu features offerings such as grilled chicken breast with black beans and papaya salsa, babyback ribs with cornbread and slaw and grilled Mongolian pork chops, plus some interesting sandwiches. All non-smoking; outdoor patio.

Napa Valley Grille ● ☆☆☆ **$$$**

◻ *6795 Washington St. (Washington Square), Yountville; 944-8686. California-Mediterranean; full bar service. Monday-Thursday 11:30 to 9:30, Friday-Saturday 11:30 to 10, Sunday 10 to 2:30 brunch and 4:30 to 9:30 dinner. Major credit cards.* ◻ Contemporary café with a "wine country look" of jewel-tone grape motif tapestry, wine rack room dividers and Napa Valley art. The frequently changing menu may feature grilled game hen with sweet onion potatoes, lamb loin in a bulgur wheat crust with sweet pepper and onion relish or grilled swordfish with banana curry rum sauce and papaya salsa. Extensive wine list; outdoor patio.

Ristorante Piatti ● ☆☆☆ **$$$**

◻ *6480 Washington St., Yountville; (707) 944-2070. Regional Italian; full bar service. Monday-Thursday 11:30 a.m. to 10 p.m., Friday 11:30 to 11 (closed 2:30 to 5), Saturday noon to 11, Sunday 11:30 to 10. MC/VISA, AMEX.* ◻ A branch of the Sonoma *trattoria* with bright, airy California décor and a versatile Italian menu. Specialties include linguine pasta with mussels, clams, shrimp, calimari and fish in wine sauce; and marinated chicken breast with garlic mashed potatoes and caramelized onions, plus grilled seafood and calzone. Outdoor tables; smoke-free dining room.

Red Rock Café ● ☆ **$**

◻ *At Vintage 1870, Yountville; (707) 944-2614. American; wine and beer. Daily 9 a.m. to 8 p.m. MC/VISA, AMEX.* ◻ Properly rustic and casual café in a 120-year-old brick railroad depot in front of Vintage 1870; indoor dining and outdoor deck. The fare is light and inexpensive—barbecued chicken, baby back ribs, 'burgers and such.

Rutherford Grill ● ☆☆☆ **$$$**

◻ *1180 Rutherford Crossroad, Rutherford; (707) 963-1792; American; full bar service. Daily 11:30 to 10. MC/VISA, AMEX.* ◻ Appealing restaurant in a modern fieldstone, shingle-roofed cottage rimmed by landscaping and vines, adjacent to Beaulieu Winery. Creative American nouveau fare with wine country accents. Extensive local wine list; wine tasting bar; outdoor patio.

Stars Oakville Café ● ☆☆☆☆ **$$$**

◻ *7848 St. Helena Hwy., Oakville; (707) 944-8905. American nouveau; wine and beer. Daily 10 to 3 and 5 to 9 (closed Tuesday-Wednesday in the winter).* ◻ Jeremiah Tower's now legendary Stars in San Francisco has opened this wine country branch in an old false-front store building beside Oakville Market, with a pleasing outdoor dining deck. The indoor look is fashionably rustic—bentwood chairs, track lighting, white nappery and mini flower vases on the tables. The menu changes frequently, featuring interestingly spiced versions of whatever's fresh and available.

WINELAND LODGINGS

NOTE: Prices were provided by the establishments and are subject to change. Use the price ranges only as a rough guideline and call the places listed to confirm their current rates.

Wine Country Referrals is a reservation service for hotels, motels, inns, B&Bs and vacation homes in Lake, Mendocino, Napa and Sonoma counties; P.O. Box 543, Calistoga, CA 94515; (707) 942-2186.

Resorts, hotels and motels

Although Napa has numerous motels and hotels, we're focusing primarily on those near the vineyards.

Auberge du Soleil ● ☆☆☆☆ **$$$$$** Ø

   ⌑ *180 Rutherford Hill Rd, Rutherford, CA 94573; (707) 963-1211). Couples $275 to $325, singles $275, suites $425 to $725, including continental breakfast. MC/VISA, AMEX.* ⌑ Opulent 50-unit Mediterranean style resort in a 33-acre olive grove; valley view suites in cottages with TV movies, room phones, wet bars, fireplaces and other amenities. Pools, health spa with masseuse and steam rooms, whirlpools and tennis. **Auberge du Soleil Restaurant** serves "California wine country cuisine"; breakfast 7 to 10:30, lunch 11:30 to 2:30, dinner 5:30 to 10:30; prix fixe dinner $52 or entrées from $23 to $30; full bar service. The restaurant is smoke-free.

Best Western Inn ● ☆☆☆ **$$$$** Ø

   ⌑ *100 Soscal Ave. (Imola Street), Napa, CA 94558; (800) 528-1234 or (707) 257-1930. Couples $69 to $99, singles $65 to $79, suites $119 to $149. Major credit cards.* ⌑ Attractive 68-unit motel with TV movies, phones, in-room coffee and balconies; some room refrigerators. Pool, spa. **Denny's Restaurant** adjacent; open 24 hours; dinners $6 to $12.

The Chablis Lodge ● ☆☆☆☆ **$$$$** Ø

   ⌑ *3360 Solano Ave. (Highway 29 at Redwood Road), Napa, CA 94558; (800) 443-3490 or (707) 257-1944. Couples and singles $75 to $100, kitchenettes $75 to $85, rooms with spa $90 to $100. Major credit cards.* ⌑ A 34-unit motel at the edge of the wine country; rooms with TV movies, phones, wet bars, refrigerators, coffee makers. Swimming pool and spa.

The Château ● ☆☆☆ **$$$$** Ø

   ⌑ *4195 Solano Ave. (Highway 29 at Wine Country Avenue), Napa, CA 94558; (800) 253-6272 in California only or (707) 253-9300. Couples $85 to $105, singles $85 to $95. Major credit cards.* ⌑ A well-situated 115-unit motel on the edge of the wine country. Rooms with TV movies and phones, some with refrigerators. Pool and spa.

Inn at Napa Valley ● ☆☆☆☆ **$$$$$** Ø

   ⌑ *1075 California Blvd. (at Highway 29), Napa, CA 94559; (800) 433-4600 or (707) 253-9540. All suites, $124 to $184, including full breakfast and afternoon cocktails. Major credit cards.* ⌑ A 205-room courtyard inn near the vineyards; nicely-furnished rooms with TV movies, phones, wet bars, refrigerators and microwaves. Indoor-outdoor pool, spa, sauna, sun decks, courtyard pond. **Caffé Napa** open for lunch, dinner and Sunday brunch; "Oriental-Italian" cuisine; full bar service.

John Muir Inn ● ☆☆ **$$$** Ø

   ⌑ *1998 Trower Ave. (Highway 29, near vineyards), Napa, CA 94558; (800) 522-8999 or (707) 257-7220. Couples and singles $75 to $95, suites from $105; rates include continental breakfast. Major credit cards.* ⌑ Attractively landscaped 60-unit inn with TV movies, room phones, in-room coffee; some with kitchenettes, refrigerators and wet bars. Pool and spa.

Napa Valley Lodge Best Western ● ☆☆☆ **$$$$** Ø

   ⌑ *Madison Street at Highway 29 (P.O. Box L), Yountville, CA 94599; (800) 368-2468 or (707) 944-2468. Couples $122 to $152, singles $115 to $142, suites and fireplace rooms $145 to $165; rates include breakfast. Major* *credit cards.* ☐ New 55-room lodge with TV, room phones, in-room coffee, refrigerators and patios. Pool, spa, sauna, exercise room.

Napa Valley Railway Inn ● ☆☆ **$$$** ∅
☐ *6503 Washington St. (adjacent to Vintage 1870), Yountville, CA 94599; (707) 944-2000. Units $65 to $115. Major credit cards.* ☐ Nine mini-suites cleverly built into several railroad cars. Units have TV and phones, with bay window alcoves to make them roomier.

Napa Valley Travelodge ● ☆☆ **$$$** ∅
☐ *853 Coombs St. (Second Street, downtown), Napa, CA 94559; (800) 255-3050 or (707) 226-1871. Couples $55 to $125, singles $50 to $125, suites from $125. Major credit cards.* ☐ A 44-room motel; TV, room phones; heated pool; morning coffee. Near Napa Valley Wine Train depot.

Sheraton Inn Napa Valley ☆☆☆☆ **$$$$** ∅
☐ *3425 Solano Ave. (Highway 29 at Redwood Road), Napa, CA 94558; (800) 333-7533 or (707) 253-7433. Couples $79 to $159, singles $69 to $149, suites $175 to $425. Major credit cards.* ☐ A 191-room courtyard inn on the edge of the wineland with country inn décor. Rooms have TV movies and phones; lighted tennis courts, spa and swimming pool. **Harvest Café** serves 7 a.m. to 10 p.m.; "Napa Valley cuisine"; dinners $8 to $29.

Silverado Country Club ● ☆☆☆☆ **$$$$$** ∅
☐ *1600 Atlas Peak Rd. (Monticello, above the vineyards), Napa, CA 94558; (800) 532-0500 or (707) 257-0200. Suites $175 to $235. Major credit cards.* ☐ Long-established luxury resort with two 18-hole PGA golf courses, 23 tennis courts, volleyball, cycling, jogging paths, spa and extensive conference facilities. Suites and cottages have kitchens, TV movies, phones and typical resort amenities. Three restaurants—**Vintners Court, Royal Oak** and **Bar and Grill**, with Pacific Rim and American regional cuisine and steak house; dinners $20 to $30; full bar service; All dining areas non-smoking.

Vintage Inn Napa Valley ● ☆☆☆☆ **$$$$$** ∅
☐ *6541 Washington St. (downtown), Yountville, CA 94599; (800) 351-1133 or (707) 944-1112. Couples $144 to $194, singles $134 to $194, suites $184 to $204; rate include continental breakfast. Major credit cards.* ☐ American country style resort with 80 rooms; wet bars, TV with VCR rentals, phones, in-room coffee and wine, spa tubs; rates include buffet breakfast. Adjacent to Vintage 1870, with several restaurants.

Bed & Breakfast Inns

Many area inns are members of the Bed & Breakfast Inns of Napa Valley, P.O. Box 3584, Yountville, CA 94599; (707) 944-4444. Call for lodging availability or a free brochure listing member inns.

Beazley House ● ☆☆☆ **$$$$$** ∅
☐ *1910 First St. (Warren), Napa, CA 94559; (800) 559-1649 or (707) 257-1649. Couples $105 to $185, singles $93.50 to $152.50. Ten rooms, all with private baths; full breakfast. MC/VISA, DISC.* ☐ Napa's first B&B in an historic landmark Edwardian mansion; rooms furnished with American and Victorian antiques; room phones available. Some rooms have fireplaces and spas. Extensive lawns and gardens.

Blue Violet Mansion ● ☆☆☆ **$$$$$** ∅
☐ *443 Brown St. (Oak and Laurel), Napa, CA 94559; (707) 253-BLUE. Couples $115 to $195. Six rooms, all with private baths; full breakfast.*

MC/VISA. ☐ Refurbished 1886 mansion listed on the National Register of Historic Places and winner of the 1993 Napa County Landmarks Historical Restoration Award. Nicely furnished rooms with early American and Victorian antiques. Afternoon tea, dessert buffet and wine tasting; private candlelight champagne dinners can be arranged in rooms.

Bordeaux House ● ☆☆☆ $$$$ Ø

☐ *P.O. Box 3274 (6000 Washington St.), Yountville, CA 94599; (707) 944-2855. Six rooms, all with private baths; continental breakfast. Couples and singles $95 to $120. MC/VISA.* ☐ Attractive brick complex built around extensive gardens. Italian contemporary décor; rooms have private patios, air conditioning and fireplaces; complimentary wine.

Burgundy House ● ☆☆☆ $$$$$ Ø

☐ *P.O. Box 3156 (6711 Washington St.), Yountville, CA 94599; (707) 944-0899. Five units with private baths; full breakfast. Couples and singles $110 to $125. MC/VISA.* ☐ Two-story 1874 fieldstone and river rock brandy distillery fashioned into a country inn. Antique country furnishings; landscaped garden. Decanter of local wine in rooms.

Churchill Manor ● ☆☆☆ $$$$ Ø

☐ *485 Brown St. (off Oak Street) Napa, CA 94559; (707) 253-7733. Couples and singles $75 to $145. Ten rooms, all with private baths and room phones; full buffet breakfast. Major credit cards.* ☐ An 1889 Victorian columned mansion, on the National Register of Historic Places. Some rooms with fireplaces or spa tubs; antique furnishings, chandeliers, oriental rugs, large veranda and solarium. Extensive gardens; evening wine and cheese.

Hennessey House Bed & Breakfast ● ☆☆☆ $$$$ Ø

☐ *1727 Main St. (downtown), Napa, CA 94559; (707) 226-3774. Couples $90 to $155. Ten rooms, all with private baths; full breakfast. MC/VISA, AMEX.* ☐ A Queen Anne Victorian with extensive grounds; on the National Register of Historic Places. Rooms in main house and carriage house; each with different decorator theme; canopy, brass or feather beds. Two rooms with fireplaces, four with whirlpool tubs. Belgian and English antiques. Sun porch and sauna; gardens and trellis.

La Belle Epoque ● ☆☆☆ $$$$$ Ø

☐ *1386 Calistoga Ave. (Seminary Street), Napa, CA 94559; (707) 257-2161. Couples $110 to $145. Six rooms, all with private baths, two with fireplaces; full breakfast. Major credit cards.* ☐ An 1893 Queen Anne Victorian with stained glass windows, antique furnishings; near "Old Town" Napa. Breakfast served in a formal dining room with fireplace or on a sun porch; wine cellar with evening tasting.

La Residence Country Inn ● ☆☆☆☆ $$$$ Ø

☐ *4066 St. Helena Highway (north of town, beyond Salvador Avenue), Napa, CA 94558; (707) 253-0337. Couples $90 to $235. Twenty rooms, all with phones, 18 with private baths, 15 with fireplaces; full breakfast. MC/VISA.* ☐ An 1870 French-style mansion with adjacent "barn." Guest rooms in both buildings; American and European antiques. Some rooms with honor bars and CD players. Two-acre landscaped grounds with a small vineyard, pool, spa, gazebo and brick patios.

Magnolia Hotel ● ☆☆☆ $$$$ Ø

☐ *6529 Yount St., Yountville, CA 94599; (800) 788-0369 or (707) 944-2056. Couples $89 to $169. Twelve rooms, all with private baths; full break-*

fast. No credit cards. ☐ Restored 1873 stone and brick hotel with Victorian antiques; five rooms with fireplaces. Gardens and decks with pool and spa.

Napa Inn ● ☆☆☆ **$$$$$** Ø

☐ *1137 Warren St. (between First and Jefferson), Napa, CA 94559; (707) 257-1444. Couples $120 to $170. Six rooms and three suites, all with private baths; full breakfast. MC/VISA.* ☐ Spacious bedrooms in an 1899 Queen Anne; furnished with turn-of-the-century antiques and collectibles. Formal dining room, parlor with fireplace; landscaped grounds.

Oleander House ● ☆☆☆ **$$$$$** Ø

☐ *7433 St. Helena Hwy. (near Mustards Grill), Yountville, CA 94599; (707) 944-8315. Couples $115 to $160. Four rooms, all with private baths; full breakfast. MC/VISA.* ☐ Contemporary country French style home with designer furnishings; high-ceiling rooms with fireplaces and private patios or balconies. Spa in landscaped patio garden.

Rustridge Bed & Breakfast ● ☆☆☆ **$$$$$** Ø

☐ *2910 Lower Chiles Valley Road, St. Helena, CA 94574; (707) 965-9353. Couples $100 to $155, singles $90 to $140. Three units with private baths; full breakfast. MC/VISA, AMEX.* ☐ Tucked-away retreat with a winery and horse ranch, in the mountain-rimmed Chiles Valley, off eastbound Highway 128. The renovated 1940s ranch house, with Southwest décor and antiques, has fireplaces in the master bedroom unit and living room. Facilities include a spa, sauna, tennis courts, hiking and biking trails and—of course—the adjacent winery with its tasting room.

Sybron House Bed & Breakfast ● ☆☆☆ **$$$$$** Ø

☐ *7400 St. Helena Way (1.5 miles from Yountville), Napa, CA 94558; (707) 944-2785. Couples and singles $120 to $160. Four rooms, three with private baths; expanded continental breakfast. MC/VISA, AMEX.* ☐ A new made-to-look Victorian home on a hilltop with an impressive valley view. Decorated with a blend of modern and antique furniture. Common room with a grand piano, fireplace, library and wet bar. Spa, tennis courts, nicely landscaped grounds.

Down Valley information sources

Napa Chamber of Commerce, 1556 First St., Napa, CA 94559; (707) 226-7455.

Yountville Chamber of Commerce, P.O. Box 2064 (6516 Yount St., Yountville, CA 94599; (707) 944-0904.

Napa Valley Tourist Bureau, 6488 Washington St., Yountville, CA 94599; (707) 258-1957 (A firm offering maps for sale, plus free reservation service for lodging and wine country tours).

"A broad wine, with enough maturity to drink now. Cedar, blackberry and herb flavors are supported by medium tannins and a decent acid balance, but a dusty, tired aroma holds it back."
— Description of an Iron Horse Sonoma County Brut

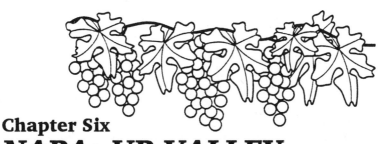

Chapter Six
NAPA: UP VALLEY
The north end: St. Helena to Calistoga

St. Helena is the maternity ward of the Napa Valley wine industry. The region's oldest wineries were born hereabouts and many still function. Among its 19th century dowagers are Charles Krug, Schramsberg, Inglenook and Beaulieu. However, not one is in the hands of a founding family, and some endured long periods of Prohibition-inspired dormancy. St. Helena's story, then, is one of history with hiccups.

Although several valley grape growing families go back many generations and some of their offspring have become vintners, the oldest family-owned operation is Louis M. Martini Winery. It dates back—appropriately—to 1933, the year of Repeal. Second and third-generation family members now operate it. The senior Martini was a giant among vintners, one of the movers and shapers of the valley's modern wine industry and a founder of the Wine Institute, the wine trade's leading watchdog organization.

Many of St. Helena's wineries are monumental structures, built when labor was cheap and owners had a sense of Victorian grandeur. Today, they are the state's most-visited wineries. As many as 300,000 tourists a year are processed by efficient and friendly guides, given quick doses of history and quick sips of wine at the end of the tour. Indeed, some of these are called "history tours," for they take visitors through outmoded stone wineries and grandiloquent mansions used now only for aging cellars and for show.

Sadly, the grandest of these, the former Christian Brothers Greystone Cellars, built in 1888 by California gold rush millionaire William Bowers Bourn, is closed to the public. It's now occupied by the Culinary Institute of America. Another popular St. Helena winery, whose history comes mostly from television, also has closed its tasting room. Spring Mountain Vineyards, portrayed

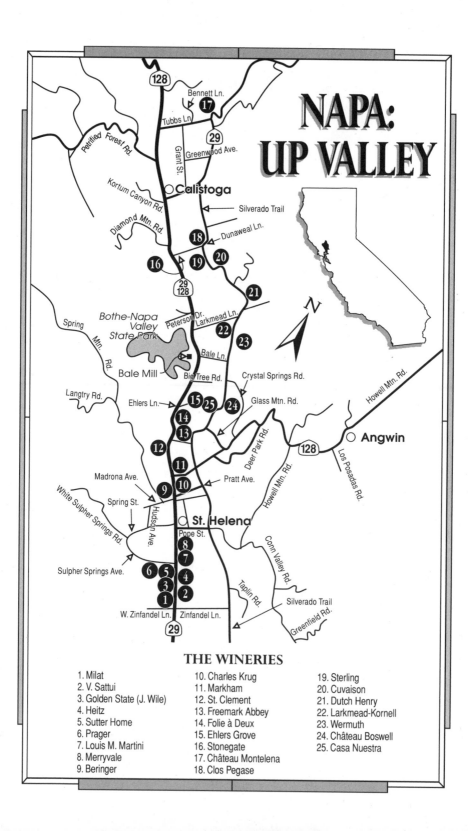

NAPA: UP VALLEY

128 Bennett Ln. **17**

Tubbs Ln

Petrified Forest Rd.

29 Greenwood Ave.

Grant St.

Kortum Canyon Rd.

○ **Calistoga**

Silverado Trail ←

Diamond Mtn. Rd.

18 ← Dunaweal Ln.

16 **19** **20**

29 128

Spring Mtn. Rd.

Bothe-Napa Valley State Park Peterson Dr. Larkmead Ln. **21**

22

23

Bale Ln.

Bale Mill Big Tree Rd.

Crystal Springs Rd.

Howell Mtn. Rd.

Langtry Rd.

Ehlers Ln. **15 25 24** Glass Mtn. Rd.

14

13 Deer Park Rd. ○ **Angwin**

12 **128** Los Posadas Rd.

11 Howell Mtn. Rd.

Madrona Ave. **10** ← Pratt Ave.

9

White Sulpher Springs Rd. Spring St.

Hudson Ave.

○ **St. Helena**

Pope St.

Sulpher Springs Ave. **8**

7

6 **5** **4** Conn Valley Rd.

3 **2**

1 Taplin Rd.

Silverado Trail

W. Zinfandel Ln. Zinfandel Ln.

Greenfield Rd.

29

THE WINERIES

1. Milat
2. V. Sattui
3. Golden State (J. Wile)
4. Heitz
5. Sutter Home
6. Prager
7. Louis M. Martini
8. Merryvale
9. Beringer

10. Charles Krug
11. Markham
12. St. Clement
13. Freemark Abbey
14. Folie à Deux
15. Ehlers Grove
16. Stonegate
17. Château Montelena
18. Clos Pegase

19. Sterling
20. Cuvaison
21. Dutch Henry
22. Larkmead-Kornell
23. Wermuth
24. Château Boswell
25. Casa Nuestra

as Falcon Crest on the TV series of that name, no longer hosts the public, although it remains a winery.

St. Helena is a picturesque country town that has become gentrified of late, with several tourist-inspired boutiques, galleries, upscale bakeries and of course, wine shops. The Napa Valley Wine Library is based here (see box on page 163) and shops and cafés are plentiful. However, this town of 5,100 residents tends to pull in its sidewalks early. When the last nearby tasting room has closed, most of the town's boutiques and galleries have closed as well. Restaurants remain open, of course, along with the ubiquitous Safeway and a good-ole-boy saloon called The Wine Cellar, smelling of stale cigarette smoke and yesterday's spilled beer.

The town's shops are worth a browse. We'd recommend breaking off from your winery touring with sufficient time to stroll its spotless sidewalks and nod pleasantly at the locals, who don't seem to mind all the hubbub. And certainly take time to visit the **Silverado Museum** which honors Robert Louis Stevenson's 1880 honeymoon stay and contains one of the world' largest collections of Stevenson lore. The **Napa Valley Museum,** focusing on the area's vinicultural history, also is worthy of pause. Both are listed below, under "Attractions."

After the shops have closed, use the last of the daylight to drive St. Helena's tree-lined residential streets. Admire handsome Victorian homes that speak of the days when adventuring Finnish sea captains, hard-working Italians and no-nonsense German immigrants built some of America's grandest mansions and wineries.

Calistoga, the other Up Valley community, is known more for mineral water and mud baths than for Merlot. The wineries are not far away, however, as new vineyards march ever northward. Founded as a resort by that capitalistic Mormon Sam Brannan, it wears its touristic mantle comfortably, quite pleased to be the Napa Valley's final visitor stop.

The town basks contentedly in the shadow of Mount St. Helena which, unlike its headline-making Washington state name-twin, is not volcanic. Its conical shape with a dip in the top has fooled many a brochure writer and author, including Stevenson. It is composed of faulted igneous rock, including silver-bearing cinnabar, but it never was a volcanic cone.

Like St. Helena, Calistoga is a comely little community, kept prim and prosperous by its place in tourism's limelight. It has the predictable assortment of boutiques, antique shops, restaurants and bed and breakfast inns. One can sink into a sensuously gooey mud bath or soar on wings of eagles from the Calistoga Glider Port (see box on page 173). Several attractions draw visitors to the area—a restored Sam Brannan resort cottage at Sharpsteen Museum, "Old Faithful" geyser on Tubbs Lane, the Petrified Forest and Robert Louis Stevenson State Historic Park, a few miles up the mountain.

The Up Valley winery tour is simple, since most of the tasting rooms stand alongside either Highway 29 or the Silverado Trail. A few are on crossroads between the two. We'll first send you up Highway 29 from St. Helena, and then down the Silverado from Calistoga.

HIGHWAY 29 WINERY TOUR ● We stopped at Zinfandel Lane just south of St. Helena in the last chapter. Your first tasting room encounter north of Zinfandel is **Milat Vineyards** housed on a small cottage style winery on your left. Big and bustling **V. Sattui Winery** is just beyond, on the right.

Then come **Golden State Vintners** (J. Wile) on the left, followed by **Heitz Cellars** on the right.

Sutter Home Winery arrives quickly on the left, and **Prager Winery and Port Works** is just beyond and behind Sutter Home, up narrow, tree-lined Lewelling Lane. Back on Highway 29, **Louis M. Martini Winery** is across the street. Then, after about a quarter of a mile, you reach **Merry-vale Vineyards** on the right, on the outer rim of St. Helena.

At the edge of town, turn right onto Charter Oak (at the old stone, vine-covered Tra Vigna restaurant building) and follow it two blocks to **Napa Valley Olive Oil Manufacturing Co.** Why? Because it's a wonderfully cluttered Italian deli, awash with the sights and smells of cheeses, spiced meats, fresh pasta and olive oil. The walls are papered with thousands of calling cards and the "cash register" is a rolltop desk, into which your money is casually tossed after you've made your purchases. It closes at 5, so end your wine tasting early if you want to stock up on Italian goodies.

Highway 29 becomes Main Street in St. Helena. On the left is the **Napa Valley Museum** at 473 Main, with changing exhibits on the valley's history, art and sociology. The **St. Helena Chamber of Commerce** is on the right, at 1080 Main Street, open weekdays 10 to 4. To reach the **Silverado Museum,** turn right at Adams, drive two blocks to the end, then go left on Library Lane.

Return to Main Street (Highway 29) and follow it through town and beyond; it travels under a sheltering canopy of Dutch elms as three of the valley's largest and most historic wineries—two active and one not—appear in quick succession. **Beringer Vineyards** with its fabled Rhine House and castle-like Greystone Cellars, still intact but no longer a winery, are on the left, and then **Charles Krug Winery** on the right. Just beyond Krug is **Markham Winery** on the right and then **St. Clement Vineyards** in an attractive Victorian just uphill on the left. **Freemark Abbey** comes next, a mile or so beyond on the right. It's in a busy complex, with a winery, two restaurants (listed below under "Wine country dining") and several shops. Beyond, up a narrow lane to the right, is **Folie à Deux Winery**.

Just beyond Folie à Deux, turn right onto Ehlers Lane and follow it about a quarter of a mile to **Ehlers Grove** winery in a splendid old fieldstone building on your left. Then return to Highway 29 and continue north. You'll soon encounter **Bale Grist Mill State Historic Park** and a couple of miles beyond, the entrance to **Bothe-Napa Valley State Park,** both on the left. Continue north and then dip briefly to the right onto Dunaweal Lane for **Stonegate Winery**. From Stonegate, you can see Sterling Vineyards, perched on a distant hilltop like a whitewashed Moorish monastary. We're saving it for the back nine, since it's closer to the Silverado Trail. From here north, the valley narrows and becomes even more beautiful as Highway 29 takes you into Calistoga.

WINERY CODES ● *T* = Tasting with no fee; *T$* = Tasting for a fee; *GT* = Guided tours; *GTA* = Guided tours by appointment; *ST* = Self-guiding tours; *CT* = casual tours or a peek into the winery; ✕ = picnic area; 🎁 = Gift shop or good giftware selection. Price ranges listed in tasting notes are for varietals; jug wines may be available for less.

Milat Vineyards • T$

◻ *1091 St. Helena Highway South, St. Helena, CA 94574; (800) 963-0168 or (707) 963-0758. Daily 10 to 6; major credit cards. All current releases tasted for $2 fee, which buys the glass or can go toward wine purchase. A few wine logo items; informal peek into the winery.* ◻

Housed in a cute little cottage style winery, Milat is a welcome haven from the bustle of its larger and more crowded winery neighbors. (It can get busy on weekends, since it sits on the main highway.) The hospitality room is a simple affair with tile floors and a small tasting counter. Walls are decorated with a few T-shirts and other wine theme apparel on sale.

Two brothers whose families have been growing grapes since 1949 established their winery in late 1986. Bob and Mike Milat and their wives Joyce and Carolyn have a few acres of classic varietals surrounding their small winery, which they can nurture and monitor carefully to produce the proper results in the bottle.

Tasting notes: What the Milats seek, as they baby their grapes and control every step of production, is a few wines with strong varietal character. They certainly have succeeded. Their Chardonnay is buttery yet crisp and clean, with a touch of wood from French oak aging. The Chenin Blanc has a light flowery nose and taste with a slight hint of sweetness and a proprietary blush wine called Zivio—a blend of Zinfandel and Cabernet—is light with a pleasant herbal nose and more character than a typical rosé. The Zinfandel had a nice dusky aroma and lush flavor—a really fine wine. The Cabernet was herbal and berry-like, with medium body, ready to drink. Their prices range from $6.95 for Zivio to $15 for a five-year old cab.

Vintners choice: The Milats like them all, "because we make them from our own estate vineyards," says Joyce. They're available only at the winery.

V. Sattui Winery • T ST ✗ ▣

◻ *1111 White Lane (Highway 29), St. Helena, CA 94574; (800) 799-8888 or (707) 963-7774. Daily 9 to 6 (closes at 5 November through February); MC/VISA, AMEX. Most varieties tasted, no fee. Extensive gift, wine logo, deli and specialty foods selection; picnic grounds surrounding winery. Self-guiding tour of the stone wine cellars.* ◻

In startling contrast to Milat, Sattui is a virtual supermarket of a winery and deli, with crowds thronging the tasting room and gift shop, and scattered about an extensive picnic area shaded by ancient oaks. On weekends, the winery even has parking lot attendants to help steer you to a vacant spot. They also hand you a flyer advising that Sattui wines are sold only at the winery, and that only Sattui wines may be consumed on the premises. More signs herald this information as you approach the attractive stone winery and adjacent tasting room. This "marketing outreach" obviously working. Sixty percent of Sattui's wines are sold here and the rest go by mail order.

One gets two quick impressions here, and they're both wrong. 1: The rugged stone castle-like tasting room and winery don't date back to King Arthur's day; they were built in 1976. It took $3 million and a lot of stone to make them look ancient. 2: This isn't a big corporate operation, but a family winery founded by Vittorio Sattui in to 1885. It was closed for several decades after Prohibition, then Vittorio's great-grandson Daryl got things rolling in the 1970s. With its extensive deli, large gift selection and unabashed self-promotion, the winery gets about a quarter of a million visitors a year. Perhaps it's the sight of all those happy picnickers that keeps drawing them in.

Tasting notes: A winery designed with tourists in mind doesn't necessarily make ordinary wine. The wines are quite good and Sattui has its share of medal winners. The list includes most of the white and red standard-bearers. We liked a soft yet crisp Chardonnay and an estate Zinfandel with a nice spicy nose and crisp medium flavor. The Cabernet Sauvignon also had medium body and a good berry nose and taste. Both were four years old and ready to drink. Prices start around $10—less for a couple of generics—and travel well beyond for the winery's extensive selection of older wines. Most of these are Cabernets.

Golden State Vintners (J. Wile Winery) ● T ✗ 📷

◻ *401 South St. Helena Hwy., St. Helena, CA 94574; (800) 755-2374 or (707) 963-7293. Daily 10:30 to 5:30; MC/VISA. Most varieties tasted; no fee. Nice giftware selection. Picnic tables with mountain and vineyard views.* ◻

This appealing winery with a modern Swiss chalet-style tasting room, originally a wine co-op under the Bergfeld banner, is now owned by Golden State Vintners. It may or may not have undergone a name change by the time you arrive, although you'll have no trouble spotting the large chalet tasting room with extensive lawns out front. The winery's roots go back to 1885; the Bergfeld name dates from 1891, when the facility was purchased by San Franciscan Robert Bergfeld. It became a co-op in 1935, and gone through various manifestations since.

The facility is bright and cheerful, with a shingled roof, cathedral ceiling, high arched windows, modern art on the walls and tiled floors. Picnic tables are in a park like setting, placed about the large lawn and on a back patio.

Tasting notes: Wines are produced under two labels, J. Wile and Monthaven. Prices are modest, some of the Napa Valley's better buys—particularly those under the J. Wile label, ranging from $6 to $8 a bottle while the Monthaven wines go into the early to mid teens. Those inexpensive J. Wile wines are fine, so you might want to move quickly. The Sauvignon Blanc displayed a nice herbal nose and softly fruity taste, and the Chardonnay was crisp and dry, with a flowery nose and flavor. The Cabernet was excellent, particularly for its $8 price—herbal, full-flavored and complex, with a light tannic finish.

Vintners choice: "Monthaven Napa Valley Cabernet, Chardonnay and Zinfandel, all from select Napa Valley apellations," says Nancy Wheeler.

Heitz Wine Cellars ● T GTA

◻ *436 South St. Helena Hwy., St. Helena, CA 94574; (707) 963-3542. Daily 11 to 4:30; MC/VISA. Selected wines tasted. Small wine logo selection; tours by appointment on weekdays.* ◻

Joe Heitz is a relative newcomer among the valley's veteran vintners, although he's been on the scene since 1961. The no-nonsense winemaker has made a name for himself as one of the area's premier producers of Cabernet Sauvignon, as well as award-grabbing Chardonnay and Zinfandel. The mid-sized facility, producing about 40,000 cases a year, is run by Joe, his wife Alice and their children David, Kathleen and Rollie.

Visitor facilities are rudimentary, consisting of a simple cottage near the winery, where visitors gather around a carved walnut table to sip Joe's latest offerings.

Tasting notes: Only two wines were open when we stopped by, and both were excellent. A three-year-old Chardonnay was lush, spicy and buttery with a soft finish; a four-year-old Zin was soft, lightly spiced with good berry flavor and subtle tannin. We know from previous tastings that the Cabernets are excellent, particularly from Heitz' Martha's Vineyard and Bella Oaks Vineyard. Prices range from $15 and go higher for older Cabs.

Sutter Home Winery • T ☎

☐ *277 South St. Helena Hwy. (P.O. Box 248), St. Helena, CA 94574; (707) 963-3104. Daily 10 to 4:30; major credit cards. Most varieties tasted, no fee. Extensive gift selection in new "Victorian Gallery."* ☐

You read the Bob Trinchero story in the rosé box in Chapter 3. He developed a blush version of Zin, called it white Zinfandel and catapulted Sutter Home from one of the valley's smallest to one of its largest wineries. Still dominating the white Zin market, it ships about five million cases a year. The winery gets its name from Lina Sutter Leuenberger, daughter of an early Napa Valley vintner; she and her husband Emil established Sutter Home at the turn of the century. The Trinchero family purchased it in 1947, and it's still a family-run operation.

Wine tasting occurs in a new Victorian-style hospitality center and mini-museum opened in mid-1990. Graphics, photos and old winery artifacts tell the Sutter Home story. Visitors can browse through assorted gift items and gather at an island tasting bar. The elaborate Victorian home of the original owners, purchased by the Trincheros in 1986, stands nearby on the immaculately landscaped grounds. It isn't open to visitors, but some of its original furnishings are on display in the Victorian Gallery.

Tasting notes: The fabled white Zinfandel *is* nearly white, unlike its pinker counterparts; it's crisp and light and we'd regard it as a good picnic wine. Hearty, full-bodied and serious Zinfandels emerged from here as well, produced mostly from Amador County grapes. We tasted a particularly berry-like and softly tannic four-year-old Amador County Reserve, priced at $9.75. A lighter Zin, which we often use as an everyday dinner wine, goes for around $4.50—a very good buy. Chardonnay, Chenin Blanc, Cabernet Sauvignon, Triple Cream Sherry and a sweet but light Muscat Alexandria complete the list. Most prices stay below $10.

Vintners choice: "Reserve Zinfandel and white Zinfandel," said the winery's Diana Panigazzi—not surprisingly.

Prager Winery and Port Works • T CT ✗

☐ *1281 Lewelling Lane, St. Helena, CA 94574; (707) 963-PORT. Daily 10:30 to 4:30; MC/VISA. Most varieties tasted; no fee. Some wine logo gift items. Informal tours, consisting of a "3.5 minute glance around the winery."* ☐

Bewhiskered Jim Prager, who needs only a bourbon complexion to resemble Ernest Hemingway (or perhaps Santa Claus), may greet you halfway up the walk when you approach his battered little winery. *If the tasting room isn't crowded—meaning there aren't more than three other people—he'll sit you down in one of four available chairs (unless it's occupied by a cat) and ply you with his Cabernets and ports. Between sips, you can admire a dusty corkscrew collection and old currency tacked on the walls.*

A former insurance broker, Prager began the winery in 1980 as his "mid-life crisis." He specializes in ports, 75 percent of his production, and he's grafted some traditional Portuguese vines onto a tiny vineyard in the front

Frederick Beringer's Rhine House is a splendid example of the early mansions built by Napa Valley wine pioneers. completed in 1883, it now houses the Beringer Vineyards tasting room and gift shop.

yard. His production is small, about 3,600 cases a year. He has been joined in the business by his son John, who is equally stocky and equally outgoing, but without the beard.

Tasting notes: Prager employs "native winemaking," using wild yeast, and adding no sulfites to his products. They are excellent and their prices, like their maker, are not modest—ranging from $30 to $35. Prager's not bashful about marketing: "How about two? One to kill and one to look forward to." Are the wines worth their lofty prices? Only your palate knows, and you can try before you buy. A five-year-old Cabernet Sauvignon, aged in American oak, was full flavored and spicy, fully capable of additional aging. The Royal Port, made from Petit Sirah grapes, was lush, nutty and mouth-filling and the tawny port, more than eight years old, had a beautiful caramel nose and deep rich taste with a lingering finish.

Vintners choice: "Our specialty is port," Prager said simply.

Louis M. Martini Winery • T & T$ GT ✕ 📷

⌂ *254 South St. Helena Hwy., St. Helena, CA 94574; (707) 963-2736. Daily 10 to 4:30; MC/VISA, AMEX. Most varieties tasted free; a $5 fee for a selection of reserve wines (includes glass). Good selection of wine logo items; picnic area; daily guided tours.* ⌂

As a teenager, immigrant Louis Martini peddled wines along with clams and mussels on the streets of San Francisco shortly after the 1906 earthquake. He and his parents rented a winery in Pleasanton in 1911, then Louis established a grape products company in the San Joaquin Valley in the middle of Prohibition. After Repeal in 1933, he opened his Napa Valley winery. A founder of the Wine Institute, the "grand old man" was a leading figure in California's wine history until his death in 1974 at the age of 87.

Still family-owned, the winery does about a quarter million cases a year. Louis' original ivy-covered red brick winery still stands alongside Highway 29. It shelters aging cellars and a simple wood-paneled tasting room, trimmed with family history exhibits. Picnic tables rest beneath ancient sycamores outside.

Tasting Notes: Several wines can be tasted free, but we recommend buying the $5 logo glass and doing a side-by-side sampling to compare regular releases with reserve wines. It's interesting to check the fruity, soft flavor of an inexpensive Louis M. Martini Chardonnay with the spicier, more complex and expensive Napa Valley Reserve Chardonnay. A smooth, berry-flavored seven-year-old Louis M. Martini Cabernet Sauvignon under $10 held up well beside a peppery, powerful eight-year-old Monte Rosso Vineyard Cabernet selling in the high teens. Although the winery has long been known for its reds, third-generation winemaker Michael Martini also earns recognition and medals for his whites. The list covers most popular varietals including a rarely-produced California Barbera, plus several sherries. Prices are modest for the quality, ranging from $7 to the high teens. Older vintages are available at higher prices.

Vintners choice "Our vineyard-designated selections: Monte Rosso Cabernet, La Loma Pinot Noir, Las Amigas Chardonnay and Los Vinedos del Rio Merlot," says the winery's Bobbie Vanderschoot.

Merryvale Vineyards • *T$ GTA*

◻ *1000 Main St., St. Helena, CA 94574; (707) 963-2225. Daily 10 to 5:30; major credit cards. Five varieties tasted for $3 fee. A few gift items. Saturday wine seminars by appointment for $5, which can be credited toward a wine purchase.* ◻

Old timers will remember this vine-entwined masonry building as Sunny St. Helena, the winery where Cesare Mondavi got his start shortly after Repeal. In 1986, William Harlan, John Montgomery and the late Peter Stocker, owners of the Napa Valley's posh Meadowood Country Club, bought the old place. They combined it with their already active Merryvale Vineyards.

The large tasting room, in the heart of the old winery, is one of the most esthetically pleasing in the wine country. It's softly lit by dozens of votive candles, perched on every available barrel head, niche, shelf and unoccupied wine bottle. Although it's above ground, it has the look, aroma and feel of an ancient wine cellar.

Tasting notes: Two labels are offered—moderately-priced Sunny St. Helena wines and the more upscale Merryvale Vineyards line. Tastings are intelligently conducted and, as at Louis Martini, one has the opportunity to compare two styles of the same varietal. Prices range from $7 to the low teens for Sunny St. Helena and $12 and up for Merryvale. In the "Sunny" line, we particularly liked a fruity and soft Gewürztraminer and a young Zinfandel with a proper berry nose and flavor and a crisp tannic finish. Others are Chardonnay, Chenin Blanc, Sauvignon Blanc, Cabernet Sauvignon, a *nouveau* and Muscat Canelli dessert wine. The Merryvale line consists of Chardonnay, Cabernet Sauvignon, Meritage White and some remarkably good red blends. A five-year-old Bordeaux style red was soft and full flavored, sort of a Meritage without portfolio. The Starmont Chardonnay was buttery and gently spicy and the Meritage White was medium-bodied, rich and nicely herbal.

Beringer Vineyards • T & T$ GT

◻ *2000 Main St., St. Helena, CA 94574; (707) 963-7115. Daily 9:30 to 6; 9 to 5 in winter; major credit cards. Free tasting following tour; tasting of reserve wines in Founders Room for a fee. Extensive giftware selection. Tours every half hour.* ◻

One of the valley's vintage landmarks, the winery was founded in the 1870s by immigrant brothers Frederick and Jacob Beringer. It remained in the family until Nestlé Chocolate (aka Wine World Estates) bought it in 1971. Its centerpiece is the stunning half-timbered Rhine House, an elaborate mansion styled after the brothers' German home. It now accommodates the gift shop and tasting room and it's easily one of the most gorgeous hospitality centers in all of California's wine country.

Tours begin near the original winery, an elaborate stone façade over caves dug by Chinese laborers into the steep slopes of Spring Mountain. They fill up quickly in the summer so get your wine label "ticket" as soon as you get there; it's free. The place lures more than 200,000 visitors a year.

Although most wine production occurs across the highway, an intelligent commentary provides a good understanding of the process as you tour the ancient cellars. Most of the caves have been shored up and gunnited; however, one has been left undisturbed since 1937. With lichen-stained ceilings and tiers of bottles covered with decades of dust and cobwebs, it suggests a wonderfully spooky Edgar Allan Poe scene.

Tasting notes: Three gratis samples are offered at the tour's end. We sipped a nice, fruit-busy Sauvignon Blanc; a five-year-old Cabernet Sauvignon that was a typical Bordeaux blend, with a good peppery nose, softly complex flavors and a hint of wood; and a fruity and slightly sweet but not sticky Gewürztraminer. The Beringer list covers most varietals, with prices ranging from $7.50 to the high teens. Serious sippers can taste reserves, mostly Cabernets, in the Founders Room for $2 to $3 per two-ounce sample.

Vintners choice: "Chardonnay and Cabernet, reserve and estate," says the winery's Bill Knox. "There's wonderful fruit in both."

Charles Krug Winery • T$ GT 🍷

◻ *2800 North St. Helena Hwy., St. Helena, CA 94574; (707) 963-5057. Monday-Thursday 10:30 to 5 and Friday-Sunday 10:30 to 6 in summer; Monday-Thursday 10:30 to 4:30 and Friday-Sunday 10 to 5 the rest of the year; MC/VISA, AMEX. Tour fee $1 per adult, including tasting; tasting without tour $3 (includes glass). Good giftware selection in separate gift shop. Tours at 11:30, 1:30 and 3:30 in summer; less often the rest of the year; call for hours. No tours on Wednesdays and tastings are free that day.* ◻

The venerable Charles Krug winery offers choices: You can take a tour, followed by a gratis tasting. Or you can march right through the large gift shop to the tasting room and sip wines for a fee. The glass you get to keep is a nice-sized one, incidentally. The tour is both historical and contemporary, including a walk through the massive old stone winery and into Krug's newer production facilities.

Despite the Krug name, the winery is the bastion of the Peter Mondavi family. It was established by Charles Krug in 1861 as the valley's first major winery, and it was operated by his heirs until Prohibition. Cesare Mondavi bought the empty facility in 1946 and ran it with his sons Peter and Robert until his death in 1959. After a family spat in the 1960s, Robert went his own way to start his down-valley winery; Peter is now Krug's president.

Tasting notes: The Mondavis pioneered cold fermentation and used the valley's first bladder press to produce crisp, fruity whites. It's evident in the citrusy, light and subtly acidic Sauvignon Blanc and fragrant, soft Chenin Blanc. A two-year-old Zinfandel was gentle with medium body, an herbal nose and light finish; a five-year-old Cabernet Sauvignon aged in American oak had a proper chili pepper nose and spicy, berry-like flavor with light tannin. Prices range from $5.50 to the mid teens; higher for the Vintage Select Cabernets.

Vintners choice: "The Vintage Select Cabernets are the benchmark of Charles Krug winemaking," says a spokesperson.

Markham Winery • *T ST* 🏠

□ *2812 North St. Helena Hwy. (P.O. Box 636), St. Helena, CA 94574; (707) 963-5292. Daily 11 to 5; major credit cards. Selected wines tasted, no fee. Good assortment of wine theme and other gift items; self guiding tours in balconies above the winery.* □

The ancient stone winery at Markham has a new look—about $12 million dollars worth. While preserving and restoring the original lava rock, quarried from nearby Glass Mountain, the owners added two wings to create a handsome courtyard effect, with extensive landscaping, pools and olive and eucalyptus trees.

The winery dates from 1879. French emigrant Jean Laurent came to California in search of gold, found none and began raising vegetables in the Napa Valley. He bought vineyard land in 1873 and started building the winery six years later. The operation later became a small co-op, then advertising executive Bruce Markham bought the crumbling old structure in 1978 and restored it. The facility is now owned by Mercian, Japan's largest wine company. Its president is Bryan Del Bondio, a Napa Valley native whose parents were longtime Inglenook Winery employees.

Tasting notes: "Overall excellent quality" reads the note on our wine-splotched tasting sheet. To be more specific: Sauvignon Blanc—fruity nose and taste, full-mouthed and crisp; Chardonnay—excellent, spicy, nutty with big grape flavor; Muscat Blanc—fruity nose, rich yet light; Cabernet Sauvignon—soft, spicy and pleasant, chili pepper nose and flavor, nippy tannic finish with a soft touch of wood. Prices range from $8 to the twenties.

St. Clement Vineyards • *T$ GTA*

□ *2867 North St. Helena Hwy. (P.O. Box 261), St. Helena, CA 94574; (707) 963-7221. Daily 10 to 4; MC/VISA, AMEX. All varieties tasted for a $2 fee. A few wine logo items. Guided tours by appointment and picnic area available by reservation.* □

An immaculately restored Victorian home with a witch's hat tower houses the tasting room of this old and new winery. Old because it was the eighth in the valley, bonded in 1879; new because it was re-opened by Dr. William Casey in the mid-1970s after a long period of dormancy. In the interim, the house served as a physicians' home and office.

Called the Rosenbaum house, the splendid structure originally had the winery in its basement. It's still used to age St. Clement wines, and the parlor—flawlessly restored—serves as the tasting room. The main winery, a rugged stone-faced affair, is tucked against the hill behind the house, reached by appointment-only tours.

Tasting notes: Prices range from $11 to $25 for St. Clement's short list. We tasted the lot and they were fine: Sauvignon Blanc—nice fruity-veggie nose, fruit-spice flavor, light acid; Chardonnay—very buttery, spicy-nutty, crisp finish; Merlot—lush, spicy nose, big berry flavor and tannic finish, to drink now or age; Cabernet Sauvignon (five years old)—wonderful nose, spicy and berry-like, soft tannins, to drink now or age.

Freemark Abbey Winery ● T$ P GT 🍷

   ☐ *3022 North St. Helena Hwy., St. Helena, CA 94574; (707) 963-9694. Daily 10 to 5 March through October and Thursday-Sunday 10 to 4:30 November through February; major credit cards. All current releases tasted for $5 fee (includes glass). Gift selection in tasting room; also gift shops nearby. Picnic area for winery patrons. Tours daily at 2 p.m.* ☐

One of the first tourist-oriented facilities in the valley, Freemark Abbey dates from the mid-1960s. The complex includes a gift shop, candle shop and two restaurants, the Abbey and Bravo Terrace (listed below under "Wine country dining"). This doesn't detract from the wine quality, or from its history. The original winery was built in 1886 by Josephine Tychson, California's first woman vintner. A seven-man partnership that re-established the winery in the 1960s. The restaurants and gift shops in this attractive, wooded complex are leased out to others.

Tasting notes: Current releases are Chardonnay, Johannisberg Riesling, Sycamore Vineyards Cabernet Sauvignon and Cabernet Bosché (from the John Bosché vineyard near Rutherford). The Chardonnay had a fruity aroma, with a very spicy nutty-wood flavor. A four-year-old Cab was medium-bodied, with a great peppery nose and light, spicy flavor. The five-year-old Bosché offered a nice balance of berries and wood, with gentrified tannin at the end. Prices run from $8.50 into the twenties; older Chardonnays and Cabs are available at higher prices.

Vintners choice: "Barrel aged Chardonnay and Edelwein Gold, a late-harvest, botrytized Johannisberg Riesling," says winemaker Ted Edwards.

Folie à Deux Winery ● T GTA 🍴

   ☐ *3070 North St. Helena Hwy., St Helena, CA 94574; (800) 473-4454 or (707) 963-1160. Daily 10 to 4; major credit cards. Selected wines tasted; no fee. A few giftware and logo items. Picnic tables near tasting room; guided tours by appointment.* ☐

Is it shared fantasy or pleasant reality? You're sitting in a comfortable chair, sipping good wine in a tasting room that more resembles an early American living room, being watched by a window-sitting cat with a Cheshire grin. You pick up the bottle and rotate it slowly in your hand. The label is an ink-blot test, suggesting dancing maidens in a scene from the fourth act of Shakespeare's *The Winter's Tale*. "I'll have another flagon of wine, please. Why is that cat staring at me? Am I in his chair?"

Folie à Deux was founded in 1981 by mental health professional Dr. Larry Dizmang. He bought an old sheep ranch with the intention of making wine, and two thoughts struck him at the time: **1.** A person has to be crazy to go into the wine business. **2.** Wine brings out the celebrative spirit in people. Folie à Deux, then, is not a name borrowed from a Bordeaux château; it translates as "a shared fantasy or delusion by two closely-linked people."

The tasting room in an old yellow cottage provides quiet escape from the busy Napa Valley, if not from reality. The grounds, shaded by oaks and poplars, still has that bucolic ranch feel. Fortunately, the sheep are gone.

Tasting notes: The Dizmang's winemaker crafts small lots of Chardonnay, Chenin Blanc and Cabernet Sauvignon. Specialties include a *methodé champenoise* sparkling wine called—what else?—Fantasie and a Blanc de Blanc blended from Chardonnay, Chenin Blanc and Muscat. A double award-winning Chenin was fittingly fruity, full-flavored and crisp.

Ehlers Grove • T ✕

□ *3222 Ehlers Lane (P.O. Box 545), St. Helena, CA 94575; (800) 946-3635 or (707) 963-3200. Daily 10 to 5; MC/VISA. Most varieties tasted; no fee. Picnic tables under olive trees, available by reservation.* □

A splendid square-shouldered fieldstone building dating from 1886 houses one of the valley's newest wineries. The structure was built by early winemaker Bernard Ehlers, an immigrant from Hanover, Germany. It went through assorted owners until it was purchased in 1968 by Mike and Lucy Casey. They still own the property, although they've leased the facility to others. Both Conn Creek and Vichon wineries got their start here. The newest manifestation began in 1993 when the Greenfield Wine Company moved in, completely restored the old building and began wine production.

This is a grand space. The tasting room consists of an L-shaped counter in a corner of the building, surrounded by aging barrels and ancient stone. Further, it's a peaceful retreat, just far enough from busy Highway 29 to be out of reach of most valley visitors and their noisy vehicles. It was uncrowded when visited and the tasting session—by Neil Murray—was unhurried and intelligently conducted.

Tasting notes: The wines are excellent overall and modestly priced for their quality, ranging from $7.50 to $15. They're bottled under two labels—Ehlers Grove and Cartlidge & Browne. A two-year-old Ehlers Grove Chardonnay was a classic of its type, lush and nutty with a slight hint of oak. The Ehlers Grove Sauvignon Blanc was so rich and silky that it *felt* like another Chardonnay, although the taste was Sauvignon-fruity. Two reds we tried, an Ehlers Grove Cabernet and Cartlidge & Browne Merlot were complex, full of berries and herbal; both great buys at around $10.

Vintners choice: "Chardonnay and Cabernet," says Murray. "We feel they offer good value and consistent quality."

Stonegate Winery • T & T$ GTA ✕

□ *1183 Dunaweal Lane, Calistoga, CA 94515; (707) 942-6500. Daily 10:30 to 4:30; MC/VISA, AMEX. Most varieties tasted free on weekdays, $1.25 fee on weekends and holidays (includes glass). A few wine related giftwares. Small picnic area; guided tours by appointment.* □

Jim and Barbara Spaulding started this small family winery in 1973 and have built up to a 14,000-case production. Son David is now involved in the operation as vice president and winemaker. Stainless steel tanks sit outdoors beside a vineyard; casks and other wine creating gear are tucked inside a modest winery structure.

The tasting room is reached via a small stone arch, which also appears on the label. It's friendly and cozy inside and not crowded—by design. A sign advises: "Limit 12 persons; if the door is locked, it should be a short wait." The picnic area consists of a single table.

Tasting notes: Cabernet Sauvignon, Merlot, Chardonnay, Sauvignon Blanc and a late harvest blend comprise the list. Prices range from $12.50 to $14. A five-year-old estate Cabernet had a spicy nose and subtly peppery taste, rich in berries with soft tannins. The Merlot, four years old, was full-flavored, dusky and mellow—the pleasant taste of an old wine cellar. The Late Harvest, a partly botrytised Sauvignon-Semillon blend, had a nice aroma of new mown hay and a honey-toasty flavor, sweet yet crisp.

CALISTOGA-SILVERADO TRAIL WINERY TOUR • Assuming you

returned to Highway 29 from Stonegate and continued north, you're now in **Calistoga**, trying to choose between a mud bath and yet another tasting room. Plan plenty of time in this neat old community at the foot of St. Helena, since it offers many diversions. We'll cover most of them in "Beyond the vineyards" below, after we've finished with the final string of Napa Valley wineries.

From the western edge of Calistoga, drive north on Highway 128 as if you're Geyserville-bound. After about 1.8 miles, turn right onto Tubbs Lane and follow it past **Old Faithful Geyser** (the signs won't let you miss it) and thence to **Château Montelena.** It's reached by a short, twisting drive that takes you quickly into a wooded thicket.

Continue a short distance on Tubbs Lane to Highway 29 and follow it south a mile, branching to your left onto the Silverado Trail. After a bit more than a mile, turn right onto Dunaweal Lane, then right again into the temple-like **Clos Pegase.** Just below, on the left, is **Sterling Vineyards,** crowning a hill and reached by a sky tram.

Return with us now to Silverado and you'll see Spanish-style **Cuvaison Winery** on the left. In less than a mile, you reach **Dutch Henry Winery,** up a rise to your left. A short distance below, turn right onto Larkmead Lane for **Larkmead-Kornell;** the road sign may still say Hanns Kornell Winery, since it changed hands recently. Back on the Silverado Trail, you'll soon reach tiny **Wermuth Winery;** look for the small sign on the left. Another mile or so takes you to the castle-like **Château Boswell,** on the left, and then **Casa Nuestra,** a bit off the highway on your right, tucked into a farm complex. Continuing south to Zinfandel lane to complete your loop, you'll pass through beautiful rolling vineyards and wooded meadowlands. A few more wineries stand alongside the Silverado Trail, but none with tasting rooms that keep regular hours.

Château Montelena Winery • T$ GTA

◻ *1429 Tubbs Lane, Calistoga, CA 94515; (707) 942-5105. Daily 10 to 4; MC/VISA. Selected wines tasted for $5 (credited toward wine purchase). Some wine oriented gift items. Guided tours by appointment at 11 and 2.* ◻

Sheltering trees, a mini-medieval castle and an Oriental lake provide one of the valley's most serene winery retreats. It's a place of discoveries, where visitors are invited to stroll the perimeter of Jade Lake, cross bright red arched bridges to tiny islands (when they're not occupied), converse with ducks, encounter stone knights guarding adjacent vineyard and pause under the quietude of Japanese maples.

Chateau Montelena's mixed heritage comes from two sources. In the 1880s, Alfred L. Tubbs, entrepreneur and state senator, hired a French architect to build a classic winery château, really more of a castle, with turrets and gun ports. Like many, it fell to ruin after Prohibition. The property was bought by a wealthy Chinese, Yort Franks, in the 1950s. He didn't revive the winery but he created an Asian showplace with a lake reminiscent of the old country. An investment group bought it in 1972 and resumed making wine.

Tasting notes: The wines were uniformly excellent. We tasted a fine two-year-old Chardonnay focused more on the fruit than spice and oak. A ten-year-old Cabernet Sauvignon was aged to near perfection, smooth yet peppery and complex, with a soft oak-tannin finish. A young Johannisberg Riesling, available only at the winery, was light and fruity with a hint of sugar. The Cabs and Chards have won scores of awards, including a Chardonnay victory over tough French competitors; it was so significant that it was reported in *Time Magazine.*

Vintners choice: Brazenly boasts winemaker Bo Barrett: "Our Chardonnay and Cabernet Sauvignon have been generally reckoned among the very best for two decades."

Clos Pegase • T$ GT

◻ *1060 Dunaweal Lane, Calistoga, CA 94515; (707) 942-4901. Daily 10:30 to 5. Selected wines tasted for $3 fee (includes glass). A few wine logo items. Guided tours daily at 11 and 3; wine and art lectures the third Saturday of each month, by appointment.* ◻

When multi-millionaire publisher Jan Shrem decided to build a shrine to wine and art in the 1980s, he sought logical sources. From Andre Tchelistcheff of Beaulieu fame he requested winemaking advice, and he asked the

San Francisco Museum of Modern Art to sponsor an architectural competition. Tchelistcheff recommended Bill Pease as a winemaker and the museum selected Princeton architect Michael Graves to design a "temple of wine." The result: Clos Pegase wines consistently win awards and Graves' impressive salmon-colored post-modern Greek-Roman-Aztec wine temple is the darling of new-wave architects. (Bob Masyczek is the current winemaker.)

Clos Pegase is at once imposing and stark—a towering, columnar presence enclosing a simple courtyard. Modern art "constructions" are placed about extensive lawns outside. A giant mural of Bacchus rises behind the counter in the large tasting room, taunting you to another sip. Although the huge winery appears to stand alone above the vineyards, it's actually built against a small, steep hillside with caves cut into the cliff. They can be seen on reservation-only tours.

Tasting notes: Clos Pegase offerings range from a Sauvignon Blanc with a fruity melon flavor and hints of oak to Hommage, a proprietary blend of Cabernet Sauvignon, Cabernet Franc, Merlot and Petit Sirah; it's similar to a Meritage in blend, with a smooth-full bodied taste. Others on the list are a Chardonnay finished in French oak, fruity and complex Merlot and a full flavored and herbal Cabernet Sauvignon. Prices range from $9.50 to $20.

Sterling Vineyards ● T$ ST ✕ 📷

☐ *1111 Dunaweal Lane (P.O. Box 365), Calistoga, CA 94515; (707) 942-4219. Daily 10:30 to 4:30; major credit cards. Tram ride $6 for adults and $3 (includes tasting of three wines; $2 on adult ticket credited toward wine purchase). Expect delays on the tram on summer weekends; the best bet is to arrive early in the day. Extensive gift and book selection; shaded picnic area with valley views; self-guiding tours.* ☐

Sterling gleams from a hillock among the vines hill like a misplaced Moorish monastery. It's reached in rather novel fashion: one buys a sky tram ticket and rides above tawny, tilted meadows and oak clusters to this "winery in the sky." Once there, the Moorish impression continues. Sterling is a gleaming collection of white stucco walls, sunny patios, stainless steel tanks and dimly-lit wine cellars that seem older than they are. The self-guiding tour is among the best of the California wine country, adorned with explanatory graphics, historic wine art reproductions and wonderful quotes about the grape. Never mind the sky bucket gimmick; once on top, the place exudes an aura of artistic class. The Napa Valley views are—sorry about this—sterling.

After touring, one adjourns to a spacious tasting room or outside terrace, where three wines are served. (The terrace may be closed in the off-season.) An adjacent gift shop offers a good selection of wineware, books and such.

The winery was created in 1969 by four owners of a San Francisco-based paper company, then it became part of the Coca-Cola Company's wine venture in 1977. It was sold in 1983 to Seagram Classics Wine Company, the present owners.

Tasting notes: Sauvignon Blanc, Chardonnay, Cabernet-blanc, Merlot and Cabernet Sauvignon comprise the list. Prices range from $8 to the high teens; more for reserve and some vineyard-designated wines. Our notes on the three tasted wines: Sauvignon Blanc—lush with soft fruit, almost a Chardonnay character, particularly with its herbal taste; Cabernet-blanc—light nose and flavor with a nice crisp aftertaste; Merlot—nice soft herbal nose with taste to match; good berry flavor and a light tannic nip at the finish.

Cuvaison Winery • T$ GTA ✕ 🍶

◻ *4550 Silverado Trail (P.O. Box 384), Calistoga, CA 94515; (707) 942-6266. Daily 10 to 5; MC/VISA, DISC. Most varieties tasted for $2.50 fee (includes glass). Good giftware selection. Shaded picnic area near tasting room; guided tours by appointment.* ◻

We've always regarded Cuvaison as the little jewel of the Napa Valley. It's a pleasing, Spanish mission-style winery with a matching tasting room, sheltered by ancient oaks. The tasting room is a comfortable space, trimmed in oak, roomy yet busy with bottles, cases and giftwares. A woodsy picnic area on a downslope offers views of vineyards and the distant Mayacamas Mountains.

Cuvaison, which comes from the French term for fermenting red wines on their skins, was started in 1969 by two engineers, with a small vineyard. They sold it to New York publisher Oakleigh Thorne in 1974. Five years later, the Schmidheiny family of Switzerland purchased the winery along with 400 acres of Carneros vineyard land.

Tasting notes: Cuvaison currently specializes in Chardonnay, Reserve Chardonnay, Cabernet Sauvignon and Pinot Noir. Winemaker John Thatcher creates well balanced wines; they all exhibit full fruity flavor, with enough intensity to encourage aging. Drink them now or lay them away, suggests Thatcher.

Dutch Henry Winery • T

◻ *4300 Silverado Trail, Calistoga, CA 94515; (707) 942-5771. Daily 10 to 5; MC/VISA, AMEX. All current releases tasted; no fee.* ◻

A small stucco building on a terraced slope marks one of the valley's smaller operations, with an output of about 2,000 cases—and growing. Dutch Henry, named for a ravine in the hillside behind it, emerged when Kendall Phelps and Scott Chafen took over a defunct winery in 1991. Members of valley grape growing families, they're learning the winemaking craft as they go, calling in friends to help with the crush and using basket presses and hand labeling. (Young Ken was a philosophy major in school, so he's rather philosophical about taking the gamble of starting a small business.)

The small winery is in a pleasant setting, shaded by gnarled madrones, oaks and eucalyptus, with vineyards tilted downhill to the Silverado Trail. The tasting room is a simple affair—a small counter occupying one end of the winery.

Tasting notes Scott and Ken are learning their craft well. All their varietals—Chardonnay, Sauvignon Blanc, Cabernet Sauvignon and Merlot—exhibited classic characteristics. They grow most of their own grapes and the style of their wines is attributable to their back-to-basics hands-on operation. The Chard was buttery and lush with a light finish; Sauvignon Blanc was light with a flowery nose and fruity crisp taste; the Cabernet was *big* with great berries and chili peppers, as was the Merlot. Prices range from $10 tothe high teens.

Larkmead-Kornell Cellars • T GT

◻ *1091 Larkmead Lane (P.O. Box 249), St. Helena, CA 95474; (707) 963-1237. Daily 10 to 4:30; major credit cards. Selected wines tasted after tour, no fee. A few wine logo items. Guided tours depart frequently, 10:30 to 3:45.* ◻

The Napa Valley lost one of its most remarkable individuals in 1994 when Hanns Kornell passed from the scene. He had fled from a Nazi concentration camp in 1939, arrived flat broke in America and—after years of saving and winemaking—opened his own sparkling wine facility in 1952, Hanns Kornell Champagne Cellars. He remained active in the business well into his 80s, then turned the operation over to his children. It's now owned by a Napa vintner Koerner Rombauer.

The winery's frequently-departing tours teach you everything you ever wanted to know about making sparkling wine. You then return to a simple, cottage style hospitality center to put to the taste what you've learned.

Tasting notes: We've long felt that Kornell's sparklers were among the best made for their price—mostly under $15. The Blanc de Noirs and Blanc de Blanc revealed good grape character and proper crispiness. Extra Dry (that wonderful winetalk antithesis) has a touch of sweet, while keeping the fruit flavor. A Muscat Alexandria dessert wine was rich and big-bodied, full of the grape with an almost liqueur character. Prices range from $12.75 to $17.75. Wines from Rombauer's Silverado Trail Winery also may be purchased here.

Wermuth Winery ● T CT ✕

☐ 3942 Silverado Trail, Calistoga, CA 94515; (707) 942-5924. Daily 11 to 5; MC/VISA. Most varieties tasted, no fee. Casual tours (a peek into the winery); small picnic area. ☐

This tiny operation is housed in a couple of pink corrugated sheds beside Ralph and Smitty Wermuth's home on the upside of the Silverado Trail. They started in 1981 and now produce about 4,000 cases a year, employing a classic Italian basket press and lots of personal attention.

Tastings are conducted in small cottage tasting room and pipe-smoking, soft-spoken Ralph, who started the winery about ten years ago, will sign your purchase. He'll also break into philosophical discussions at the slightest encouragement, so this is a good place to linger if you feel talkative. We wound up in a conversation about our company, and how the use of computers made small publishing enterprises possible.

Tasting notes: Prices are $8 to $10 for the wines on Ralph's short list. The dry Colombard was an improvement over earlier versions—herbal and fruity; a good picnic wine. His Zinfandel was light, yet with a pleasing and pronounced raspberry taste. The Gamay displayed surprisingly intense herbal flavor for a wine of this type, with a crisp, fruity finish. "It goes well with chocolates," Ralph said, offering a tin of chocolate bits. He was right. Then he pulled out a bottle of Zin, autographed it and presented it as a gift. (We never solicit, but we never turn down good Zin.) The inscription read: "Don't spill this on your computer."

Château Boswell ● T$

☐ 3468 Silverado Trail, St. Helena, CA 94574; (707) 963-5472. Friday-Sunday 10 to 5. Most varieties tasted for a $2 fee; $4.15 if you wish to keep the logo glass. ☐

There may or may not be anything to taste when you stop by this imposing mini-castle—or anything to buy, for that matter. If this occurs, we assume the fashionable wrought iron gates will be closed. Retired Southern California dentist built this cute little Arthurian hideaway on an upslope of the Silverado Trail in 1979, put a winery behind it, surrounded it with lush landscaping and parked a gleaming Rolls-Royce out front. Certainly the tools to draw in the curious.

When we were drawn to this curious castle, Boswell was selling off some fine old vintages and not producing new ones. He may resume production, the attractive hostess informed us. Then again, maybe not.

Tasting notes: Boswell's best and most affordable offering was a 1990 Chardonnay, barrel-fermented with big flavor and nice acid, for $15. The other wine being tasted, a 1984 Cabernet Sauvignon, was silky and soft, definitely at its peak and beginning to level off; price was $22.

Casa Nuestra ● T$ GTA ✕

◻ *3473 Silverado Trail, St. Helena, CA 94574; (707) 963-5783. Friday-Sunday 11 to 5 or by appointment; MC/VISA. Several varieties tasted for a $2 fee. A few wine related gift items. Picnic area; group tours by appointment.* ◻

This little yellow farmhouse is an inviting place to sip wine, with its fireplace, easy chairs and other properly weathered furnishing. The name, appropriately, is Spanish for "our house." A tree-shaded picnic area, complete with hammock, reinforces the laid-back, down-home impression.

The winery was bonded in 1980 by former civil rights attorney Gene Kirkham and his wife Cody. The San Francisco-born Kirkham became fed up with the pin-stripped city life, so he bought this small farm, grew a Mormon beard and started making wine. Learning the trade by trial and error, consulting county farm advisors and friendly neighbor vintners, he and his wife have become what the local paper once described as "happy farmers." These downhome folks make excellent wines.

Tasting notes: No, Tinto isn't the Lone Ranger's wimpy Indian companion. It's Casa Nuestra's red blend, made from a polyglot of grapes that grow in the same vineyard and are harvested together—Zinfandel, Cabernet, Gamay, Pinot Noir, Mondeuse, Carignane, Alicante and possibly Pfeffer. Our sample suggested a big Chianti, with lots of berries and spice yet curiously gentle; it has won a couple of gold medals. Others we sipped were a Chardonnay with an incredibly nutty and silky flavor; a crisp and lightly fruity Chenin Blanc and something called Quixote, an impressively lush Meritage style wine with a big yet soft berry flavor. Why Quixote? "Because selling a Meritage style wine at this place is an impossible dream," says Kirkham. Casa Nueva's prices range from $8.50 to $16.

THE BEST OF THE BUNCH

The best wine buys ● Sutter Home Winery, Louis M. Martini, Golden State Vintners, Charles Krug Winery, Freemark Abbey Winery and Casa Nuestra.

The most attractive wineries ● V. Sattui Winery, Beringer Vineyards, Château Montelena, Clos Pegase, Sterling Vineyards, Cuvaison Winery and Château Boswell.

The most interesting tasting rooms ● Golden State Vintners, Sutter Home Winery, Merryvale Vineyards, Beringer Vineyards, Folie à Deux Winery and Clos Pegase.

The funkiest tasting rooms ● Prager Winery and Casa Nuestra.

The best gift shops ● V. Sattui Winery, Sutter Home Winery, Beringer Vineyards, Charles Krug, Freemark Abbey Winery and Sterling Vineyards.

The nicest picnic areas ● V. Sattui Winery, Cuvaison Winery, Freemark Abbey Winery and Casa Nuestra.

The best tours ● Beringer Vineyards (guided), Larkmead-Kornell Cellars (guided, sparkling wine) and Sterling Vineyards (self-guiding).

Dr. Edward T. Bale's grist mill ground flower for the Napa Valley's earliest settlers. It's now a state historic park.

Wineland activities and such

Wineland events ● Napa Valley Wine Library Association courses (see box on page 163); (707) 963-3535. Napa Valley Mustard Celebration in early February in Calistoga; (707) 942-6333. Napa Valley Barbecue Festival, late May; (707) 942-6333. Napa Valley Wine Auction, first weekend of June; (707) 963-5246. Napa County Fair in Calistoga, with local winery exhibits, early July; (707) 942-5111. Beer and Sausage Fest at the Napa County Fairgrounds in Calistoga, early October; (707) 942-6333. Various wineries also sponsor various events throughout the year. Also see listings in Chapter 5.

Winery maps and guides ● *Napa Valley Guide* with winery maps and listings of activities, restaurants and lodgings, available at many wineries and gift shops for $4.95 or $7 by mail from Vintage Publications, 764 Adobe Dr., Santa Rosa, CA 95404; (707) 538-8981. The free *Silverado Trail* map produced by the Silverado Trail Wineries Association lists wineries on the "quiet side of the Napa Valley,"; it's available from member vintners along the Silverado Trail, or call (800) 624-WINE. Mattioli's *In Your Pocket Guide* to St. Helena and Calistoga lists wineries, lodging, shops, restaurants and recreation, $1.50; available in many gift shops and tasting rooms, or call (707) 965-2006.

Wine country tours ● VinTours features personalized tours of smaller wineries in Napa and Sonoma counties; 536 Orchard St., Santa Rosa, CA 95404; (707) 546-9483. Napa Valley Tourist Bureau creates personalized tours; (707) 944-1557. Wine Country Jeep Tours takes visitors through the Napa Valley's backroads; (800) 539-JEEP. Sonoma Chardonnay Limousine

Service offers Napa and Sonoma wine country tours; 22455 Broadway, Sonoma, CA 95476; (707) 938-4248. Napa Valley Excursions offers personalized wine country tours, 1825 Lincoln Ave., Napa; (707) 252-6333. Winery and dining tours are offered by Wine & Dine Tours, 1250 Church St., St. Helena, CA 94574; (800) 946-3868 or (707) 963-8 930. Guided wine country tours also are provided by Napa Valley Holidays, 1525 Andrea Circle, Napa, CA 94558, (707) 255-1050; and Wine Adventures Inc., 1258 Arroyo Sarco, Napa, CA 94558, (707) 257-0353.

BEYOND THE VINEYARDS

Up Valley offers more non-winery attractions than the lower end. They're focused mostly around Calistoga, which was a spa before the valley became America's best known wine producing region.

St. Helena has its share of lures as well, including the **Napa Valley Museum** and **Silverado Museum** (listed below). If you like scenery with a twist (in the roads), turn west onto Madrona Avenue (the last stop light on St. Helena's north side), follow it three blocks to Spring Mountain Road and turn right. It twists high into the thickly wooded Mayacamus Mountains, following a pretty little creek for much of the way. The route changes its name to St. Helena Road and, about 12 miles from town, it terminates at Calistoga Road. Turn right and follow that north; it blends into Petrified Forest Road and takes you into Calistoga.

In case you didn't visit **Angwin** in the previous chapter, take Deer Park Road east from St. Helena. It's a quaint little Seventh-Day Adventist town and home to **Pacific Union College.** You can get great health foods at the **College Market** but no wine; Angwin is a dry town. From here, continue north on Howell Mountain Road into bucolic **Pope Valley**, an hidden enclave of vineyards and high meadows rimmed by wooded mountains. Chiles-Pope Valley Road loops south and then west, back toward the Napa Valley.

As you follow Highway 29 north from St. Helena to Calistoga, visit the restored water wheel powered mill at **Bale Grist Mill State Historic Park.** Just above is **Bothe-Napa Valley State Park,** offering swimming, picnicking, camping and a good assortment of hiking trails. A particularly nice—if occasionally steep—hike is from the Bothe-Napa Valley picnic area to the Grist Mill; it's just under two miles.

Flamboyant Mormon entrepreneur Sam Brannan made Calistoga famous when he opened a spa, then he built a railroad to Napa to bring in the tourists. Those rails still exist (traveled part of the way by the Napa Valley Wine Train; see page 144), and the town continues to be a mecca for fans of mud baths and mineral water hot tubs. Resort operators tout the supposed therapeutic value of Calistoga's mineral water and they promote neck-deep mud baths and "European body wraps" to "purge your skin of toxins and restore its elasticin." Calistoga's spas are listed below, under "Up Valley activities."

If you'd rather drink mineral water than sit in it, two major bottling companies are located here, **Crystal Geyser** at 501 Washington Street and **Calistoga Mineral Water Company** on the Silverado Trail at the edge of town. They have no public facilities although their products—straight and fruit flavored—are available all over town. If you prefer more kick to your fizz, **Napa Valley Brewing Company** operates a micro-brewery in the old water tower of the Calistoga Inn at 1250 Lincoln Avenue (see listing under lodgings).

Calistoga is busy with shops and boutiques. Several are clustered in Sam Brannan's 1868 **Calistoga Depot**; some are housed in adjacent railroad cars. The Calistoga Chamber of Commerce is here, too, tucked into a cottage behind the depot. Other shops are strung along Lincoln Avenue, the main street. Also in town or nearby are the **Sharpsteen Museum and Sam Brannan cottage, Petrified Forest** and **Old Faithful Geyser.**

A seven-mile drive into the flanks of Mount St. Helena on Highway 29 takes you past the **Calistoga Glider Port** to **Robert Louis Stevenson State Park.** It's undeveloped, but fun to explore (see box on page 176). If you press north on Route 29, you'll witness impressive mountain scenery and eventually wind up in Lake County. It's home to huge Clear Lake and several wineries described in Chapter 2. Another pretty route out of Calistoga is Highway 128 northwest, which delivers you to Mendocino County.

Up Valley activities

Bicycle rentals and tours ● Getaway Wine Country Bicycle Tours, 1117 Lincoln Ave., Calistoga, CA 94515; (800) 499-2453 or (707) 942-0332. Palisades Mountain Sport, 1330-B Gerrard St., Calistoga, CA 94515; (707) 942-9687. St. Helena Cyclery, 1156 Main St., St. Helena, CA 94574; (707) 963-7736. Napa Valley Bike Tours and Napa Valley Cyclery; (800) 707-BIKE (California only) or (707) 255- 3377. Getaway Wine Country Bicycle Tours; (800) 499-BIKE. Napa Valley Bicycle and Canoe Trips; (707) 255-2224.

Glider rides ● Calistoga Gliders, 1546 Lincoln Ave., Calistoga, CA 94515; (707) 942-5000. Open daily from 9 a.m. (See box for prices and other details.)

Hiking, swimming ● Bothe-Napa Valley State Park, 3801 North St. Helena Hwy., Calistoga, CA 94515; (707) 942-4575. For campground reservations call (800) 444-7275.

Hot air balloon rides ● Once In a Lifetime Balloon Co., 1458 Lincoln Ave., Calistoga, CA 94515; (800) 659-9915 or (707) 942-6541.

Hot springs, mud baths & spas ● **With lodging:** Calistoga Spa Hot Springs at 1006 Washington St., (707) 942-6269; Calistoga Village Inn and Spa at 1880 Lincoln Ave., (707) 942-0991; Dr. Wilkinson's Hot Springs at 1507 Lincoln Ave., (707) 942-4102; Golden Haven Spa at 1713 Lake St., (707) 942-6793; Indian Springs Resort at 1712 Lincoln Ave., (707) 942-4913; Lincoln Avenue Spa at 1339 Lincoln Ave., (707) 942-5296; Mount View Hotel, 1457 Lincoln Ave., (800) 772-8838 or (707) 942-5789; Nance's Hot Springs at 1614 Lincoln Ave., (707) 942-6211; Pine Street Inn and Euro-spa, 1202 Pine St., (707) 942-6829; Roman Spa, 1300 Washington St., (707) 942-4441; and White Sulfur Springs Resort & Spa, 3100 White Sulfur Springs Rd, St. Helena, (707) 963-8588. **Without lodging:** International Spa at 1300 Washington St., (707) 942-6122; Lavender Hill Spa, 1015 Foothill Blvd., (707) 942-4495

Attractions
St. Helena

Bale Grist Mill State Historic Park and *Napa-Bothe State Park* ● Highway 29, three miles north of St. Helena; (707) 963-2236. Daily 9 to 5; admission fee. Restored grist mill built by Dr. Edward T. Bale in 1846 and adjacent recreational park with hiking, picnicking and camping.

ON WINGS OF EAGLES

The cool rush of wind through the vent reminds me that I'm simply a mortal, borne aloft not on wings of eagles or fantasies of Icarus, but on soft summer air, rising from the floor of the Napa Valley.

I am tucked under the Plexiglas dome of a Schweizer 2-32, sitting beside my son Dan who, at age 21, consists mostly of arms and legs. He is too absorbed in flight to notice that his right elbow seems intent on sinking my floating rib.

The two-passenger glider is a cozy fit, but neither my rib nor I notice. We are engaged in the purest form of flight, riding afternoon thermals that crawl invisibly up the flanks of Mount St. Helena like lazy, friendly ghosts. I have flown in most things with wings, several with rotors, one dirigible and three hot air balloons. Nothing matches the sensual, silent aerial ballet of a glider.

Our pilot Artie Sveum—who looks like the retired math teacher that he is, but seeks out thermals with the instincts of an eagle—puts his craft into a lazy spiral. The world rotates below; we are in perfect suspension, held in place by the gentle yaw of the glider. Then the left wing drops and the rocky crags of the Palisades rise up to greet us.

"Do you want to get closer?" Artie asks over his shoulder, noticing that I've unholstered my Nikon.

"Sure!" Dan answers before I can respond.

We sweep the face of the Palisades, then drift toward a ridge and lift effortlessly over it with all the grace and none of the noise of a helicopter. Later, after exploring the ramparts of St. Helena, Artie slips the glider off the afternoon thermals; the vineyards and glossy roofs of the Napa Valley sweep into view. Calistoga is an orderly grid, the glider port a streak of gray between the green fields and vines.

"Gliders use a steeper approach than airplanes," says Artie, who's been doing this for 25 years, in addition to teaching math.

The craft swoops downward like a fishhawk after a salmon, then levels off and scuttles across the asphalt. We jolt gently to a stop and Artie pops the canopy. Twenty minutes have passed in the blink of an eagle's eye.

Calistoga Gliders offers one and two-passenger flights daily from 9 a.m. until 6 or until sunset in summer. Rides are $79 for 20 minutes and $110 for 30 minutes for one person and $110 (20 minutes) and $150 (30 minutes) for two people. Morning trips are more smooth, while afternoon thermals provide a livelier ride. Generally, you can catch a flight on short notice during the week; it's best to make reservations on weekends. Contact Calistoga Gliders, 1546 Lincoln Ave., Calistoga, CA 94515; (707) 942-5000.

Napa Valley Museum • 473 Main St., St. Helena, CA 94574; (707) 963-7411. Weekdays 9 to 4, weekends 11 to 3. Historic museum in Vintage Hall, with permanent and changing exhibits of the valley's history and sociology.

Silverado Museum • 1490 Library Lane (P.O. Box 409), St. Helena, CA 94574; (707) 963-3757. Tuesday-Sunday noon to 4. Excellent collection of objects concerning Robert Louis Stevenson and his 1880 honeymoon visit.

Calistoga

Old Faithful Geyser • 1299 Tubbs Lane, Calistoga, CA 94515; (707) 942-6463. Daily 9 to 6 in summer, 9 to 5 the rest of the year; admission fee. Smaller than Yellowstone's but reasonably faithful, erupting about every 40 minutes; picnic area, gift and snack shop.

Petrified Forest • Petrified Forest Rd. (five miles west), Calistoga, CA 94515; (707) 942-6667. Daily 10 to 5:30 in summer, 10 to 4:30 the rest of the year; admission fee. A scattering of petrified trees, museum, gift shop and picnic area.

Robert Louis Stevenson State Historic Park • Seven miles above Calistoga on Highway 29. Site of the author's 1880 honeymoon; undeveloped, but with several hiking trails and a monument at the honeymoon cabin site.

Sharpsteen Museum and Sam Brannan Cottage • 1311 Washington St., Calistoga, CA 94515; (707) 942-5911. Daily 10 to 4 in summer, noon to 4 the rest of the year; free. Historic museum with a scale model of Sam Brannan's resort and a restoration of one of his cottages.

WINE COUNTRY DINING

St. Helena

Abbey Restaurant • ☆☆ $$

◻ *At Freemark Abbey Winery, 3022 N. St. Helena Hwy., St. Helena, CA 94574; (707) 963-2706. American-continental; full bar service. Lunch daily from 11:30, dinner nightly from 5. MC/VISA.* ◻ Housed in a handsome cutstone building, with curved booths and wrought iron chandeliers dangling from cathedral ceilings. Menu items include skewered prawns, Chicken breast Chardonnay with marinated tomatoes and mustard sauce and marinated spring lamb shish kabob.

Brava Terrace • ☆☆ $$$

◻ *3010 St. Helena Hwy., St. Helena; (707) 963-9300. French-American bistro; full bar service. Daily noon to 9 (closed on Wednesdays in winter). Major credit cards.* ◻ Charming bistro in an architecturally pleasing stone and wood A-frame, featuring local meats and produce and fresh pasta on its eclectic menu. Entrées vary from pan roasted chicken thighs with mushrooms and pistachio nuts to grilled ribeye steak.

Gillwoods Café • ☆☆ $

◻ *1313 Main St., St. Helena; (707) 963-1788. American; wine and beer. Daily 7 a.m. to 8 p.m. (closes at 3 Monday-Thursday in winter). MC/VISA.* ◻ Old fashioned American storefront café in downtown St. Helena with wainscotting and ceiling fans. It dishes up roasted leg of lamb, Yankee pot roast and other basic supper fare.

Pairs Parkside Café • ☆☆☆ $$

◻ *1480 Main St., St. Helena; (707) 963-7566. American-continental nouveau; wine and beer. Daily 11:30 to 3 and 5:30 to 9:30. MC/VISA, AMEX.* ◻

Exceptionally cute little windowbox café trimmed with modern art and wall sconces. Offerings include grilled curried and skewered prawns, cinnamon roasted duck breast and tarragon-dijon crusted chicken breast.

Showley's at Miramonte ● ☆☆☆ $$$

◻ *1327 Railroad Ave. (between Hunt and Adams), St. Helena; (707) 963-1200. California cuisine; wine and beer. Open Tuesday-Sunday 11:30 to 3 and 6 to 9:30; closed Monday. Major credit cards.* ◻ Housed the 1858 Miramonte building, one of St. Helena's oldest structures. with a blend of old fashioned and upscale décor. Creative California menu hops from grilled duck breast with green peppercorn sauce to salmon fillets in parchment with julienne vegetables. Outdoor dining.

Trilogy ● ☆☆☆ $$$

◻ *1234 Main St. (Hunt Street), St. Helena; (707) 963-5507. California nouveau; wine and beer. Lunch Tuesday-Friday noon to 2, dinner Tuesday-Saturday from 6 p.m. Reservations advised; MC/VISA.* ◻ Cozy little upscale bistro offering interesting fare from an often-changing *nouveau* menu, such as roasted duck breast with mission fig and port sauce, sautéed filet of beef thyme sauce and rack of lamb with olive sauce. *Prix fixe* dinners or one can order from the menu. Outdoor dining; large wine list featuring valley labels.

Calistoga

Alex's Restaurant & Pub ● ☆☆ $$$

◻ *1437 Lincoln Ave., Calistoga; (707) 942-6868. American-continental; full bar service. Tuesday-Friday 4 to 10, Saturday 2 to 10, Sunday 1 to 9. MC/VISA.* ◻ Small, simply-attired bistro with arched windows, ceiling fans, wall murals and white nappery; old fashioned pub adjacent. From the kitchen comes salmon marinated in olive oil, halibut with garlic and cream sauce, breast of chicken in white wine and herbs and assorted pastas and steaks.

Bosko's Ristoranti ● ☆☆ $

◻ *1364 Lincoln Ave., Calistoga; (707) 942-9088. Italian; full bar service. Daily 11 a.m. to 10 p.m. MC/VISA.* ◻ Old fashion Italian restaurant with fieldstone walls, warm woods, walnut chairs, exposed ceilings and drop lamps. The fare is inexpensive and essential Italian—assorted fresh pastas and pizza; a specialty is *varazze*, marinated chicken breast with bell peppers and broccoli in a tomato garlic sauce.

Café Sarafornia ● ☆☆ $$

◻ *1413 Lincoln Ave., Calistoga; (707) 942-0555. American; wine and beer. Daily from 7 a.m. MC/VISA.* ◻ Pleasantly funky place with ceiling fans, wall murals and small booths, popular with locals and handy for quick, light bites. Pastas, salads, 'burgers and other sandwiches make up the menu, along with a good variety of omelettes and other breakfast fare. The name comes from a legend that Calistoga founder Sam Brannan, in reference to New York's famous Saratoga mineral water spa, said after too many toasts: "I'll make this place the Sarafornia of Calistoga!"

Cinnabar Café ● ☆☆☆ $$

◻ *1440 Lincoln Ave., Calistoga; (707) 942-6989. American; full bar service. Daily 7 a.m. to 10 p.m. MC/VISA.* ◻ Appealing old fashion storefront café with *faux* Tiffany lamps, maple bentwood chairs and Victorian couches. It's popular for breakfast, including the "wake-up" version that includes

"...AND THE WINE IS BOTTLED POETRY"

A sign at the Napa Valley's entrance quotes a troubled, tubercular young Scottish writer who spent the summer of 1880 in the valley's upper end, seeking refuge from the damp fogs of San Francisco.

Robert Louis Stevenson had pursued Fanny Osbourne, a married American woman, from France to California, trying to convince her to leave her husband and marry him. She finally relented and they chose the Napa Valley for their honeymoon, accompanied by her son Samuel and their dog Chuchu. Not yet published, Stevenson was almost peniless, so they moved into an empty bunkhouse on the tailing dump of the old Calistoga Silver Mine on Mount St. Helena.

"The place was open like the proscenium of a theatre," he wrote, "and we looked forth into a great realm of air, and far and near on wild and varied country."

Stevenson, ever the poet, called their honeymoon haven Silverado. Traveling about the valley, they visited still-surviving landmarks such as Bale's Grist Mill, Schramsberg Winery and the Petrified Forest, where he found its owner, Charley Evans, to be a "far more delightful curiosity" than the stone trees.

Despite his illness, he hiked up Monitor Ledge to the top of the mine shaft to witness the stunning vista of the Napa Valley, often covered with a cottony fog blanket. "That vast fog-ocean lay in a trance of silence, nor did the sweet air of morning tremble with a sound."

Stevenson kept a diary called "Silverado Journal," and from this he compiled *The Silverado Squatters*, his first published work.

The honeymoon site is now part of Robert Luis Stevenson State Historic Park, reached by a seven-mile drive north from Calistoga on Highway 29. It's undeveloped, with no camping, water or other facilities. However, a few picnic tables sit near the concrete foundation of a former toll house below the mine. A one-mile hiking trail switchbacks up the mountain to the cabin site. The bunkhouse is gone; a monument erected by Napa Valley women's clubs marks the spot.

A difficult scramble over broken rock will deliver you to the mine, which is more of a slot cut into the silver-bearing ridge. A trail from the monument joins a forestry road that takes you to the top of the ridge. From there, you can enjoy Stevenson's dramatic Napa Valley view.

Memorabilia of Stevenson and his Napa Valley visit are preserved in the Silverado Museum at 1490 Library Lane, St. Helena, in the city library building. Hours are Tuesday through Sunday from noon to 4. Admission is free; phone (707) 963-3757.

Stevenson left his Silverado after two months. In renewed health and spirits, he became one of history's great authors. Sadly, he died just 14 years later. An inscription on the women's club monument, taken from one of his poems, marks his passage:

Doomed to know not Winter, only Spring,
A being trod the flowery April blithely for a while,
Took his fill of music, joy of thought and seeing,
Came and stayed and went, nor ever ceased to smile.

French toast, bacon or sausage, eggs, fruit and champagne. Dinner menu includes teriyaki steak, lemon chicken and such.

The Smokehouse ● ☆☆ $$

☐ 1458 Lincoln Ave. (in the Calistoga Depot), Calistoga; (707) 942-6060. American; wine and beer. Daily from 6 a.m. MC/VISA, DISC. ☐ The former Depot Restaurant has re-emerged as an informal café cleverly done up with waiting room benches for seats, slatwood walls, historic photos and a model train on a track above. "Full plate" dinners of pot pies, barbecued ribs or roasted fish come with vegetables, potatoes or slaw and cornbread.

Soo Yuan ● ☆☆ $

☐ 1354 Lincoln Ave., Calistoga; (707) 942-9404. Chinese; wine and beer. Daily 11:30 to 9:30 p.m. MC/VISA, AMEX. ☐ Cuter than the average Asian mom and pop café, Soo Yuan is a slender little diner with cane drop lamps, hanging ivy and bits of bright Chinese trim. The menu dances through most Chinese fare, from gentle Cantonese to spicy Szechuan; several combination dinners are available.

Triple S Ranch Restaurant ● ☆☆ $$

☐ 4600 Mt. Home Ranch Rd. (off Petrified Forest Road), Calistoga, CA 94515; (707) 942-6730. American; full bar service. Monday-Saturday 5 to 10, Sunday 4 to 10; closed Mondays in the winter. MC/VISA. ☐ Down-home atmosphere in a Western style family restaurant in the hills west of Calistoga. Menu with rural Americana tilt, leaning toward steak, chicken and ham, with a couple of seafood items; prime rib on weekends. At a family resort with wooded grounds, a pool and hiking trails.

WINELAND LODGINGS

NOTE: Prices were provided by the establishments and are subject to change. Use the price ranges only as a rough guideline and call the places listed to confirm their current rates.

Wine Country Referrals is a reservation service for hotels, motels, inns, B&Bs and vacation homes in Lake, Mendocino, Napa and Sonoma counties; P.O. Box 543, Calistoga, CA 94515; (707) 942-2186.

St. Helena

El Bonita Motel ☆☆ $$$ Ø

☐ 195 Main St., St. Helena, CA 94574; (707) 963-3216. Couples and singles $65 to $110; also kitchenettes and suites. Major credit cards. ☐ A 42-room art deco motel, recently remodeled, with landscaped grounds; on edge of St. Helena, near wineries. TV, room phones and some room refrigerators. Pool, spa, volleyball court.

Harvest Inn ● ☆☆☆☆ $$$$$

☐ One Main St., St. Helena, CA 94574; (800) 950-8466 or (707) 963-9463. Couples and singles $110 to $350. Major credit cards. ☐ Elegant brick Tudor style inn with elaborate landscaping, next to the vineyards on the edge of town. Fifty-four rooms, suites and cottages furnished with antiques, all with TV and phones; some fireplaces, wet bars and spa tubs. Two pools, wine bar, spa, rental bicycles.

Hotel St. Helena ● ☆☆☆ $$$$$

☐ 1390 Main St., St. Helena, CA 94574; (707) 963-4388. Couples and singles $130 to $180, Lily Langtry suite $150; rates include continental breakfast.

MC/VISA, AMEX. ☐ Cozily restored 1881 hotel in downtown St. Helena; some shared and some private baths; room phones, TVs available. All rooms have period décor. Lobby is a virtual museum of vintage dolls, toys and other antiques. Wine bar; garden patio.

Meadowood Napa Valley ● ☆☆☆☆ $$$$$

☐ *900 Meadowood Lane, St. Helena, CA 94574; (800) 458-8080 or (707) 963-3646. Couples and singles $245 to $385; some suites higher. Major credit cards.* ☐ Luxurious, secluded French country style resort with opulently furnished rooms with all amenities. Extensive landscaped grounds; golf, tennis, pool, spa and hiking trails. **Starmont Restaurant** features California cuisine; **Fairway Grill** is a bistro-style café; meal service daily from 11:30 to 10; dinners $23.50 to $35.50; full bar service; reservations essential; all non-smoking.

Wine Country Inn ● ☆☆☆ $$$$

☐ *1152 Lodi Lane (Highway 29), St. Helena, CA 94574; (707) 963-7077. Couples $92 to $188, singles $72 to $168, including continental breakfast. MC/VISA.* ☐ A 25-room inn fashioned like an elegant early American country home. Stylish rooms and common areas with wood paneling and print wallpaper; antique furnishings.

Calistoga

Calistoga Inn ● ☆ $$$

☐ *1250 Lincoln Ave. (Cedar), Calistoga, CA 94515; (707) 942-4101. Rooms $49 to $60; rates include continental breakfast. MC/VISA.* ☐ A venerable 17-room inn with shared baths and no-frills "American comfortable" furnishings; it dates from the turn of the century. **Napa Valley Brewing Company** microbrewery and restaurant are part of the rustic complex. Restaurant opens at 11:30 a.m. (various closing times), serving American fare; dinners $8 to $19; wine and beer, including—of course—its own microbrews.

Calistoga Village Inn & Spa ● ☆☆ $$$ Ø

☐ *1880 Lincoln Ave. (Silverado Trail), Calistoga, CA 94515; (707) 942-0991. Couples $65 to $175, singles $55 to $150. Major credit cards.* ☐ A 42-room inn with spa, featuring mud baths, mineral baths, massages and facials; swimming pool. Room have TV movies and phones.

Comfort Inn ● ☆☆ $$$ Ø

☐ *1865 Lincoln Ave., Calistoga, CA 94515; (800) 228-5150 or (707) 942-9400. Couples $90 to $120, singles $80 to $110. Major credit cards.* ☐ A 54-unit motel with landscaped grounds, mineral water pool and spa, plus a sauna and steam room. Rooms have cable TV and phones.

Dr. Wilkinson's Hot Springs ● ☆☆ $$$ Ø

☐ *1507 Lincoln Ave. (Fairway), Calistoga, CA 94515; (707) 942-4102. Couples $54 to $99, singles $49 to $89; kitchenettes $10 extra. MC/VISA, AMEX.* ☐ A 42-room motel and spa; TV and room phones. Full spa facilities with three mineral pools, massages, facials and mud baths. Two outdoor mineral water pools and indoor spa pool.

Golden Haven Spa & Resort ● ☆☆ $$$$

☐ *1713 Lake St., Calistoga, CA 94515; (707) 942-6793. Couples, singles and suites $59 to $115, kitchenettes $79 to $95. MC/VISA, AMEX.* ☐ A 26-room motel and mineral spa. TV, no room phones; some rooms have Jacuzzi tubs or saunas. Spa includes mud baths, massages, hot water mineral pool and Jacuzzi; swimming pool.

Hideaway Cottages ● ☆ $$$

⛶ *1412 Fairway (Lincoln), Calistoga, CA 94515; (707) 942-4108. Couples $47 to $94, singles $40 to $85; all units have kitchens. MC/VISA, AMEX.* ⛶ Seventeen individual cottages in a nicely landscaped setting with mature trees; mineral pool and spa; conference room.

Pine Street Inn and Spa ● ☆☆ $$$$

⛶ *1202 Pine St., Calistoga, CA 94515; (707) 942-6829. Couples and singles $75 to $125; rates include continental breakfast. MC/VISA.* ⛶ California ranch-style inn with 16 rooms; mix of antique and modern furnishings. Spa facilities including whirlpool, mud baths and facials.

Bed & breakfast inns

St. Helena and Angwin

Cinnamon Bear Bed & Breakfast ● ☆☆ $$$$ Ø

⛶ *1407 Kearney St. (Adams), St. Helena, CA 94574; (707) 963-4653. Couples $85 to $155. Four rooms with private baths; full breakfast. MC/VISA.* ⛶ Early 20th century redwood home with shady front porch. Former mayor's residence; furnished with antiques and early American arts and crafts; teddy bear theme. Comfortable living room with fireplace.

Forest Manor ● ☆☆☆☆ $$$$$ Ø

⛶ *415 Cold Spring Rd. (Deer Park Road), Angwin, CA 94508; (800) 788-0364 or (707) 965-3538. Couples and singles $105 to $239. Three rooms with refrigerators, coffee makers and private baths; full breakfast. MC/VISA.* ⛶ Striking English Tudor home on 20-acre estate, in the mountains above the Napa Valley. English antiques, Oriental art and Persian rugs; vaulted ceilings; verandas; billiard room; pool and spa. Large suites, some with fireplaces, one with spa.

Erika's Hillside ● ☆☆☆ $$$$ Ø

⛶ *285 Fawn Park (off Silverado Trail), St. Helena, CA 94574; (707) 963-2887. Couples $75 to $165, singles $55. Major credit cards.* ⛶ Three rooms with private baths; continental breakfast. Remodeled century-old Swiss chalet on wooded, landscaped three-acre estate; European furnishings and hand-painted rosemaling. Flower gardens between terraced rock walls, hot tub, valley views.

The Ink House ● ☆☆☆ $$$$$ Ø

⛶ *1575 St. Helena Hwy. (Whitehall Lane), St. Helena, CA 94574; (707) 963-3890. Couples and singles $125 to $165. Four rooms with private baths, TV and phones; continental breakfast. MC/VISA.* ⛶ Elegant 1884 Italianate mansion listed on the National Register of Historic Places. American and English antiques; 12-foot ceilings; large guest rooms and common rooms. Roof observatory with 360-degree valley view.

Shady Oaks Country Inn ● ☆☆ $$$$$ Ø

⛶ *399 Zinfandel Lane (Highway 29), St. Helena, CA 94574; (707) 963-1190. Couples and singles $135 to $175. Four rooms with private baths; full "champagne breakfast." No credit cards.* ⛶ Secluded inn on two acres with three units in a restored 1920s farmhouse and one in an 1887 fieldstone winery building. Rooms furnished with American antiques.

Calistoga

Calistoga's Wine Way Inn ● ☆☆☆ *$$$$* ∅

⊓ *1019 Foothill Blvd. (off Highway 29), Calistoga, CA 94515; (707) 942-0680. Couples $80 to $130, singles $75 to $125. Six rooms with private baths; full breakfast. MC/VISA, AMEX.* ⊓ A handsomely renovated early American home with multi-level decks, rimmed by a wooded yard. American antiques, leaded glass trim, fireplace in parlor. Gazebo with view of Calistoga.

Culver's, a Country Inn ● ☆☆☆ *$$$$$* ∅

⊓ *1805 Foothill Blvd. (Highway 128), Calistoga, CA 94515; (707) 942-4535. Couples and singles $105 to $115. Six room with shared baths; full breakfast. No credit cards.* ⊓ An 1875 Victorian with a mix of Victorian, art deco and art *nouveau*; fireplace and player piano in living room. Pool, spa and sauna. Afternoon *hors d'oeuvres* and sherry.

The Elms Bed & Breakfast ● ☆☆☆☆ *$$$$$* ∅

⊓ *1300 Cedar St., Calistoga, CA 94515; (800) 235-4316 or (707) 942-9476. Couples and singles $110 to $185. Seven rooms with private baths; five with fireplaces and TV; full breakfast. MC/VISA, AMEX.* ⊓ Elegant 1871 mansard-roofed Victorian, former judge's home, on the National Register of Historic Places. Nicely done rooms with European antiques; separate honeymoon cottage with kitchenette. Extensive landscaped grounds. Afternoon wine and cheese.

Larkmead Country Inn ● ☆☆☆ *$$$$$* ∅

⊓ *1103 Larkmead Lane (between Highway 29 and Silverado), Calistoga, CA 94515; (707) 942-5360. Couples and singles $125. Four rooms with private baths; continental breakfast. No credit cards.* ⊓ Imposing 1918 early California winery estate furnished with English antiques, Persian carpets and artwork. Extensive landscaped grounds with mature hardwoods.

Pink Mansion Bed & Breakfast ● ☆☆☆ *$$$$* ∅

⊓ *1415 Foothill Blvd., Calistoga, CA 94515; (707) 942-0558. Couples and singles $85 to $175. Five rooms with private baths; full breakfast. MC/VISA, AMEX.* ⊓ Handsomely restored 1875 mansion with a witch's hat tower; set against a wooded slope in the Mayacamas Mountains. Victorian and turn-of-the-century décor; valley or forest views from the rooms; indoor pool; afternoon wine tasting.

Silver Rose Inn ● ☆☆☆ *$$$$$* ∅

⊓ *351 Rosedale Rd. (Silverado Trail), Calistoga, CA 94515; (707) 942-9581. Couples $150 to $195. Nine rooms with private baths and TV; full breakfast. MC/VISA, DISC.* ⊓ Stylish modern-rustic country home on oak knoll with valley views from all guest rooms. Done in early American, Oriental and modern décor. Landscaped grounds with pool, flagstone paths and rock garden.

Up Valley information sources

Calistoga Chamber of Commerce, 1458 Lincoln Ave. (in the Calistoga Depot), Calistoga, CA 94515; (707) 942-6333.

Napa Valley Wine Library Association, P.O. Box 328, St. Helena, CA 94574; (707) 963-5145 or 963-5244.

St. Helena Chamber of Commerce, P.O. Box 124 (1080 Main Street), St. Helena, CA 94574; (800) 767-8528 or (707) 963-4456.

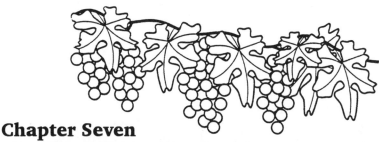

Chapter Seven
THE SOUTH BAY
Southern Alameda & northern Santa Clara counties

Silicon chips and suburbs have prevailed over Sauvignon Blanc and Semillon in much of southern Alameda and northern Santa Clara counties. 'Tis a pity, since these two wine producing areas southeast of San Francisco Bay appear on some of the earliest pages of California's history. Wineries such as Concannon, Wente and Mirassou date back more than a century. In fact, Mirassou is the oldest family-owned winery in California.

These venerable establishments and several newcomers are coping with the suburban spread in various ways. Some have set up shop in the foothills, or retreated even higher, particularly to Montebello Ridge of the Santa Cruz Mountains, southwest of San Jose. Others have remained firmly in place, with their wineries and tasting rooms surrounded by tract homes. They surrendered their vineyards to subdivisions and planted new vines in Monterey County to the south or Mendocino County to the north. A few, such as the long-popular Paul Masson facility in the heart of Silicon Valley, simply closed up shop and moved elsewhere.

A glowing exception to this suburban takeover is the Livermore Valley below Livermore and Pleasanton. Agricultural preserves have been established to protect vineyards that have occupied these gentle hills for more than a hundred years. Suburbia does nibble at the edges and highrises can be seen from venerable Concannon and Wente wineries. However, the relentless march of civilization has been stopped. Folks can still build homes in the vineyard areas although ingenious zoning laws require that parcels be a minimum of 20 acres—and 18 of those must be planted in vines! Owners of a new luxury home development, Ruby Hill, have agreed to plant 460 acres of vineyards, restore two historic wineries and contribute $8.5 million to a land trust.

181

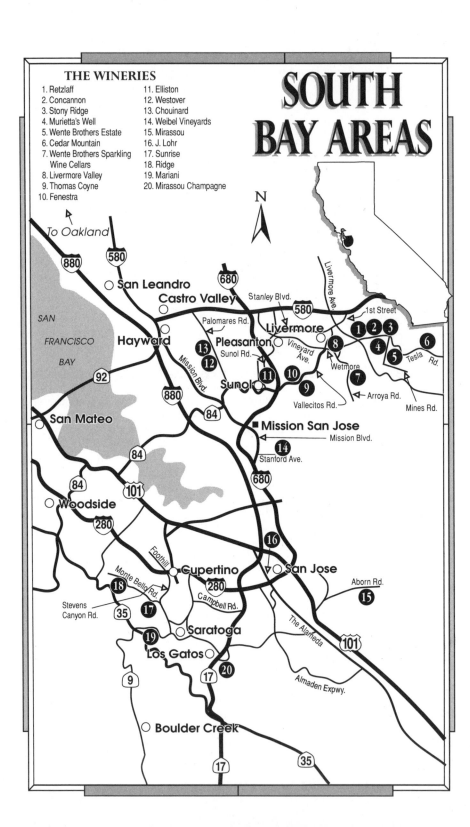

THE WINERIES

1. Retzlaff
2. Concannon
3. Stony Ridge
4. Murietta's Well
5. Wente Brothers Estate
6. Cedar Mountain
7. Wente Brothers Sparkling
   Wine Cellars
8. Livermore Valley
9. Thomas Coyne
10. Fenestra
11. Elliston
12. Westover
13. Chouinard
14. Weibel Vineyards
15. Mirassou
16. J. Lohr
17. Sunrise
18. Ridge
19. Mariani
20. Mirassou Champagne

SOUTH BAY AREAS

N

To Oakland

880
580

San Leandro

Castro Valley

Stanley Blvd.

Livermore Ave.

580
1st Street

680

Palomares Rd.

Livermore

① ② ③
⑧ ④
⑤
⑥

Hayward

Pleasanton

Sunol Rd.

Vineyard Ave.

Wetmore

⑦

Tesla Rd.

SAN
FRANCISCO
BAY

92

Mission Blvd.

⑬
⑫

Sunol

⑪ ⑩
⑨

Vallecitos Rd.

Arroya Rd.

Mines Rd.

880

84

San Mateo

Mission San Jose
Mission Blvd.

84

101

⑭

Stanford Ave.

680

Woodside

84

280

⑯

Foothill

Cupertino

San Jose

Aborn Rd.

Monte Bello Rd.

⑱

280

Campbell Rd.

⑮

Stevens
Canyon Rd.

35

⑰

Saratoga

The Alameda

⑲

Los Gatos

9

⑰ ⑳

101

Almaden Expwy.

Boulder Creek

17

35

Members of the Livermore Valley Winegrowers Association are promoting their area as an alternative to the Napa Valley, pointing out that it's less crowded, the wines are generally less expensive and it's closer to most of the San Francisco Bay Area's seven million residents than Napa or Sonoma.

The valley was settled by English sailor Robert Livermore, who picked up two Mexican land grants in 1830. He had grapes growing by the 1840s. Charles A. Wetmore, who served as California's chief viticultural officer, established Cresta Blanca Winery in 1882, followed by the arrival of Carl H. Wente and James Concannon the next year. At the turn of the century, the valley had 5,000 acres of vineyards and more than 50 wineries. Hit by phylloxera and Prohibition, the number had dwindled to six by the 1960s, although it's increasing again under the new agricultural zoning protection.

To the southwest, Santa Clara Valley's history also goes back well over a century. San Jose was born in 1777 as the state's first civil settlement; it served as California's first capital from 1849 to 1851. By the mid-1850s, San Jose was a major wine producer and its surrounding Santa Clara Valley was called the "Garden Spot of the World." French vineyardist Pierre Pellier started a winery here in 1854. His daughter married Pierre Mirassou in 1881, beginning the Mirassou wine dynasty that persists to this day. At the turn of the century, the Santa Clara Valley had more than 100 wineries and nearly 9,000 acres of vines. The double scourge of phylloxera and Prohibition closed all but the most obstinate of these early wineries.

The Santa Clara and Livermore valleys merge northeast of San Jose, near present-day Fremont. Here, Mission San José de Guadalupe was established in 1797 (to the confusion of those who assume the mission is in the city of San Jose). In 1869, railroad baron and politician Leland Stanford and his brother Josiah started a winery just east of the mission. The Swiss-born Weibels took over in 1940 and it's still a family enterprise.

Santa Clara County's Montebello Ridge wineries came along much later, beginning with the creation of Ridge Vineyards by three Stanford Research Institute couples in 1959. A few others have since settled in these steep, forested hills. Among them are Sunrise Winery, occupying the rustic site of the 1880s Picchetti Ranch winery.

Livermore and Santa Clara valleys, cooled by bay breezes, are known mostly for their whites; Cabernet Sauvignon and Petit Sirah are grown here as well. Montebello Ridge, higher but warmer, produces some excellent Zinfandels.

LIVERMORE VALLEY WINERY TOUR • It's best to plan this outing on a weekend since many of the smaller wineries are open Saturdays and Sundays only. Most folks get their bearings in **Livermore** at a couple of small swatches of green parkland in the old business district at the merger of Livermore Avenue and First Street. Coming from the Bay Area, take the Livermore Avenue turnoff and go south into downtown. Approaching from the east on I-580, First Street (State Highway 84 exit) will get you there. From the south, take route 84 (Vallecitos Road) east from I-680. You'll be backtracking along some of the winery route but for the sake of order, we're starting everyone at the same place.

From the old downtown area, follow Livermore Avenue south a bit over a mile until you see small **Retzlaff Vineyards** on your left. At this point you've shed most of Livermore's suburbia and are traveling through a mix of vineyards and farm fields. Tawny rolling hills stand on the horizon. Continuing southeast, the route swings to the left and becomes Tesla Road. Just beyond is **Concannon Vineyard** on the left and, less than a mile away, **Stony Ridge Winery**, also on the left. Immediately past Stony Ridge, turn right onto Mines Road for **Murietta's Well** winery; it comes up quickly on the right. Return to Tesla Road, continue eastward and you'll soon see the extensive complex of **Wente Brothers Estate Winery** on the right. Continue out Tesla about half a mile and small **Cedar Mountain Winery** arrives on the left; look for the wine barrel sign.

Now, retrace your path along Tesla Road and then, just beyond Concannon, turn left onto Wente Street. It curves to the right into Marina Avenue, which bumps into Arroyo Road. Go left and you'll soon pass, on the right, **Ravenswood Historical Site,** an elaborate country estate and former winery. It's now administered by the Livermore Area Recreation and Park District.

Continuing along Arroyo Road, you encounter the attractively landscaped grounds of **Wente Brothers Sparkling Wine Cellars** and Restaurant on the left. Reverse your route for about a mile, then take a left onto Wetmore Road and you'll soon see **Livermore Valley Cellars** on the right. Wetmore does a 90-degree right turn and becomes Holmes Street. Within a few hundred yards, turn left at a stop sign onto East Vallecitos Road (State Highway 84). You're now well into the country, taking a gentle roller-coaster ride through undulating hills.

After less than a mile, you see the new **Thomas Coyne Winery** on an upslope to the left and just beyond, **Fenestra Winery,** housed in a wonderful old tattered barn down on the right. Pressing on, you wind steeply over a set of low hills, then cross Interstate 680. To avoid blending onto I-680, fork to the right at the Sunol/Dumbarton Bridge sign just before passing under the freeway to stay with Highway 84; it becomes Niles Canyon Road.

After about a mile, veer to the right into the cute little community of **Sunol.** Just beyond its rustic false front business district, turn right onto Kilkare Road and follow it a short distance to the handsome cut stone **Elliston Vineyards** complex on the right. Return to Sunol, turn right to blend back onto Highway 84 and follow it through scenic, winding **Niles Canyon.** Its Alameda Creek waters offer a popular weekend retreat for locals. After about five miles, take a sharp right up Palomares Road; it's just beyond a railroad bridge overcrossing. Follow the road's steep, winding course uphill alongside a seasonal creek just under four miles to **Westover Vineyards.** Just beyond is **Chouinard Vineyards.** Both are on the left, tucked into the base of wooded hills.

From here, retrace your route to I-680, then go south about four and a half miles to the Mission Boulevard exit and take it east. You soon pass **Mission San José** and then Ohlone College. After another two miles or so,

WINERY CODES • *T* = Tasting with no fee; *T$* = Tasting for a fee; *GT* = Guided tours; *GTA* = Guided tours by appointment; *ST* = Self-guiding tours; *CT* = casual tours or a peek into the winery; ✕ = picnic area; 🎁 = Gift shop or good giftware selection. Price ranges listed in tasting notes are for varietals; jug wines may be available for less.

watch for small Stanford Road, near a Vintage Grove subdivision sign; a left turn on Stanford takes you up an olive tree lane to **Weibel Vineyards.** Few vineyards survive in this region; they're disappearing under spreading Fremont suburbs.

Retzlaff Vineyards • T ✕

◻ *1356 S. Livermore Ave., Livermore, CA 94550; (510) 447-8941. Monday-Friday noon to 2 and weekends noon to 5; MC/VISA. Most varieties tasted. A few wine logo items; shaded picnic area.* ◻

A gravel lane flanked by vineyards and pepper trees takes you to this small winery in a weathered farm complex. Park beside a lawn picnic area and stroll to the tasting room in a small cottage. It's likely that lively little Pi Matthews, sort of a mini-grandmother type, will serve you on a red-checker tablecloth tasting bar. Dried statice hanging from ceiling rafters gives the place a nice herbal aroma.

The winery was started in 1978 by home winemaker and chemist Bob Taylor and his wife Gloria Retzlaff Taylor. They began with the intention of selling grapes, then decided to produce their own wines, at the rate of about 3,000 cases a year.

Tasting notes: Sauvignon Blanc and Merlot have been added to the Retzlaff list, which originally was limited to Gray Riesling, Chardonnay and Cabernet Sauvignon. The Riesling had a nice herbal nose and it was soft and buttery on the palate; Chardonnay was very fruity and silky, with only a hint of wood and a two-year-old Cab offered a peppery nose, herbal flavor and soft finish. Prices start at a modest $7 ranging up to $35 for older wines.

Concannon Vineyard • T$ GT ✕ 📷

◻ *4590 Tesla Rd., Livermore, CA 94550; (510) 447-3760. Weekdays 10 to 4:30, weekends 11 to 4:30; MC/VISA. Five wines tasted. Good wine oriented gift selection. Nice picnic area; tours weekends at 1, 2 and 3 and weekdays on request. Horse carriage tours of vineyards for a $3 fee, by appointment.* ◻

The story goes that Irish immigrant Joseph Concannon, printer by trade, was asked by San Francisco Archbishop Joseph S. Alemany to make some good altar wine. Being a proper Catholic, Joe complied and thus started the first Gaelic winery in California. For generations, Concannons and Wentes were friendly rivals, making honest wines and sending their kids to the same schools. It remained thus until 1981, when Concannon was bought out by Deinhard and Partners, obviously non-Irish. Recently, the winery was purchased by a group called the Livermore Valley Wine Association, a group of investors that includes members of the Wente family. One Concannon, great-grandson Jim, is still involved with the winery, handling its public relations.

The tasting room is housed in one of the century-old winery buildings. It's all done up in brick and wormwood paneling, decorated by quilts hanging like rural tapestries.

Tasting notes: While most Livermore Valley wineries are noted for their whites, Concannon produces some fine reds, with strong varietal character, without excessive fining and filtering. A Pete Sirah, long a Concannon specialty, was big in flavor as always and tamed a bit with a splash of Zinfandel and Pinot Noir. A three-year-old Cabernet Sauvignon was light yet peppery and an Alicante Bouschet had a nice light Gamay flavor; good for drinking slightly chilled. The Chardonnay was outstanding, soft and toasty with a light acid finish. Others on the list are a proprietary blend of several whites called Assemblage, Sauvignon Blanc, Semillion, dry and sweet Muscats and a rich botrytised late harvest Johannisberg Reisling. Prices range from $7.50 to the middle teens.

Stony Ridge Winery ● T R

□ *4948 Tesla Rd., Livermore, CA 94550; (510) 449-0660. Monday-Saturday 11 to 5, Sunday noon to 5; MC/VISA, AMEX. All varieties tasted free; wine by the glass may be purchased. A few wine logo items available. Deli-restaurant liste below.* □

At first glimpse, this attractive Spanish style facility may more resemble a café than a winery, with an outdoor deck occupied by contented diners. It's both. A long tasting counter fills one side of the roomy, tile floor hospitality center, and a busy deli-café thrives at the other; see listing below. The combination is no surprise; the winery owners are Italian and their affair with wine and food is a family tradition.

Affable Anthony Scotto, who you may find pouring samples behind the counter or advising his sons on the finer points of winemaking, was born in Brooklyn; with shades of the accent are still evident. However, his roots and soul go back to the Bay of Naples, where for generations his family grew grapes and made wine. He ran a wine and liquor store in Brooklyn, then came to California in 1972 and owned a winery in Pleasanton until 1985. Now semi-retired, he's a major presence at Stony Ridge, which is owned by his three children, Dominic, Greg and Monica. Dominic is the winemaker, with able assistance from his father, and Greg is chef for the deli-café.

Stony Ridge, which the Scotto children bought in 1985, has grown quickly, to become the third largest in the Livermore Valley after Wente and Concannon, with an annual output of 20,000 cases.

Tasting notes: The Scotto list includes most of the classic varietals and it's excellent—Chardonnay, Sauvignon Blanc, Johannisberg Riesling, Merlot, Cabernet Sauvignon and Cabernet Franc, plus a white Zinfandel and Malvasia Bianca dessert wine. The Monterey Chardonnay had a flower petal nose, suggestive of a Sauvignon Blanc, yet with the crisp smoky character of a good Chard. Sauvignon Blanc was flowery as well, with pleasing citrus accents. Cabernets—several often are available—were soft, full flavored and ready to drink; some displayed enough tannin to encourage aging. Prices range from $7.50 to the early teens.

Stony Ridge Deli Café ● ☆☆ $

□ *Italian-American; wine. Monday-Saturday 11 to 5. MC/VISA, AMEX.* □

This appealing little deli-café in the Stony Ridge tasting room does a booming lunch business, with tables inside the tasting room and on a sunny deck with vineyard views. Offerings include Italian-American fare such as leg of lamb sandwiches, provolone terrine and an excellent Caesar salad served with a roasted garlic cluster.

Murietta's Well ● T

□ *3005 Mines Rd., Livermore, CA 94550; (510) 449-9229. Weekends 11 to 4:30.* □

Set back off the road a bit, this new winery occupies a small, modern barnlike structure, rimmed by trees and pasturelands at the foot of a low hill. Members of the Wente family (below) are among the owners and it's managed by Wente personnel, producing similar types of wines. (See the next listing.)

Wente Brothers Estate Winery • T GT ✕ 🎁

□ 5565 Tesla Rd., Livermore, CA 94550; (510) 447-3603. Monday-Saturday 10 to 4:30, Sunday 11 to 4:30; MC/VISA, AMEX. Most varieties tasted. Good selection of wine logo and specialty food items. Picnic area near tasting room. Tours Monday-Saturday at 10, 11, 1, 2 and 3; Sundays at 1, 2 and 3. □

The Wentes and Concannons started their wineries in 1883. After more than a century, fourth-generation Wentes are still at the helm. Only the Mirassou clan claims a longer uninterrupted California winery lineage. German emigrant Carl Heinrich Wente and his descendants have been and continue to be major forces in shaping the valley's wine industry. Carl purchased Wetmore vineyards in 1883 and started his winery. In 1918, brothers Ernest and Herman Wente purchased the vineyards and winery from Carl's estate, starting Wente Brothers Winery, which remains in the family. Jean Wente and her children Eric, Phil and Carolyn manage the operation today. In 1981, the family purchased Wetmore's old Cresta Blanca Winery and restored it as a sparkling wine facility; see below.

Although many of the vineyards have moved south to Monterey County and to the distant Livermore foothills, a few vines still embrace the neat, businesslike winery complex. The tasting room and adjoining gift shop are housed in an adobe block and wood double octagon. It's one of the more appealing winery structures in the area. Like their longtime Concannon neighbors, the Wentes sponsor frequent special events.

Tasting notes: Wente offers a very intelligent tasting form, useful in directing you and keeping track of your sips. The list covers most major varietals and side-by-side comparisons of similar varieties are possible. The wines are quite tasty and reasonably priced, ranging from $6.50 to the low teens; a bit more for reserves. The signature wine is Gray Riesling, named by the founder a century ago; it was fruity, light and dry—a good picnic wine. Sauvignon Blanc was oaky and spicy; Semillon had a herbal nose and flavor and a crisp, almost tart finish; the Estate Reserve Chardonnay was spicy and nutty with a soft touch of wood. A three-year-old Estate Cabernet Sauvignon offered a big bell pepper aroma, peppery-berry flavor and medium tannin.

Vintners choice: "We were the first producers of Chardonnay here, with more than 60 consecutive vintages," said a Wente source. "We offer a lot of different styles and prices."

Cedar Mountain Winery • T GTA ✕

□ 7000 Tesla Rd., Livermore, CA 94550; (510) 373-6636. Weekends noon to 4; MC/VISA. Most wines tasted; several wine logo gift items. Large picnic area. Tours by appointment or when someone is available. □

A large wine barrel out front, turned on end to make a sign, helps travelers find this new winery. The facility itself is housed in a classic old red barn. It was established in the early 1990s by Linda and Earl Ault, and it produces about 1,200 cases a year.

Vintners choice: "Our estate Cabernet Sauvignon has been getting ratings over 90 in *Wines and Spirits* and *The Wine Enthusiast magazine*," says Linda.

Wente Sparkling Wine Cellars • T GT R ✕ 🎁

□ 5050 Arroyo Rd., Livermore, CA 94550; (510) 447-3603. Monday-Saturday 10 to 5, Sunday 11 to 5; MC/VISA, AMEX. Several Wente sparkling and still wines tasted. Good selection of wine logo and specialty food items. Tours

Monday-Saturday at 10, 11, 1, 2 and 3 and Sundays at 1, 2 and 3. Restaurant adjacent; listed below. ⊓

The Wentes have blended history, architectural beauty and state-of-the-art sparkling wine making at this Spanish-style facility. Started in 1882 as Charles Wetmore's Cresta Blanca Winery, it was purchased by the Wente family in 1981. After extensive rehabilitation, it was reborn as a modern champagnery housed in glossy white stucco and tile-roofed buildings. The complex is accented by mature trees, lawns, gardens, cork trees and an herb garden. Here, chefs from the adjacent Restaurant pluck their seasonings.

The tasting room is housed in an enclosed former courtyard, with lofty coffered ceilings held up by imposing square columns. A small museum off the tasting room consists mostly of graphics tracing the history of the two founding families here—the Wetmores and the Wentes. Tours take visitors through the modern champagnery and into 650 feet of aging caves tunneled into a hillside. Re-excavated and gunnited by the Wentes, they still have that wonderfully musty mushroom farm smell of ancient caverns.

Tasting notes: Both Wente's still and sparkling wines are tasted here; and we tried the three sparklers. Wente Brut has won impressive awards, considering its modest $10 price. A typical blend of Pinot Noir, Pinot Blanc and Chardonnay, it was perfectly crisp, practically floating over the palate, with subtle flavors of the fruit. The Blanc de Blanc, which is 100 percent Chardonnay, was clean and dry, yet with the berry flavor still evident. Blanc de Noir was a nice, tasty rendition of a rosé sparkler.

The Restaurant ● ☆☆☆☆ $$$

⊓ *At Wente Sparkling Wine Cellars; (510) 447-3696. Regional American; wine and beer. Lunch Monday-Saturday 11:30 to 2:30; dinner Monday-Saturday 5:30 to 9:30, Sunday brunch 10:30 to 2:30 and dinner 5 to 9:30. Major credit cards.* ⊓ Stylish dining room with warm woods, cane-back chairs and linen nappery. Special events such as fixed price dinners with wine pairings are often scheduled. Among entrées on the frequently changing menu are smoked pork loin with roasted eggplant and peppers, grilled chicken breast with pepperjack cheese, and skillet roast salmon with mashed potatoes and pea-pancetta ragout. Smoke-free dining room; patio dining.

Livermore Valley Cellars ● T ✗

⊓ *1508 Wetmore Rd., Livermore, CA 94550; (510) 447-1751. Daily 11:30 to 5; MC/VISA. All varieties tasted. A few wine logo items; small picnic area.* ⊓

The smallest of the area wineries, Livermore Valley Cellars occupies a weathered farmyard up a graveled lane. Production was cut back during the long California drought because owners Chris and Beverly Lagiss are dry farmers and felt there wasn't enough water to bring in a crop. However, the little 2,000-case winery isn't out of business; son-in-law Tim Sauer has become their part-time winemaker and is creating some rather good products.

Tasting notes: Most of the older wines left over from the production lag were several years old and a bit tired. They're still drinkable and moderately priced, starting around $6. We found an eight-year-old Chardonnay to be very tasty, with nice spices and subtle oak. A new generation Chardonnay was nice as well, lush with strong varietal character; and a three-year-old Zinfandel had good berry flavor, medium body and a light tannin nip. One of Tim's new creations is Old Vine Cuvée, a blend of Chasselas, Muscat, Chardonnay, Gray Riesling and Colombard; it had lots of fruit in the taste and a nice herbal accent.

Pioneer George True's rough stone and wood barn near Livermore, built in 1889, provides properly rustic shelter for Fenestra Winery.

Thomas Coyne Winery • T CT ✕

☐ *51 E. Vallecitos Rd., Livermore; mailing address: 2162 Broadmoor St., Livermore, CA 94550; (510) 373-6541. Weekends noon to 5; MC/VISA, DISC. Most wines tasted. Picnic area; informal winery tours.* ☐

Thomas Coyne started his small family winery in the early 1990, and he has already won an imposing number of awards. The tasting room is a simple, neat affair adjacent to the winery, where visitors can peek in for a view of vats, stainless steel and oak. Considerably better is the view from the nearby picnic area, across the tawny hills of the Livermore Valley.

Tasting notes Coyne has quite a varied list for a small, new winery. Sauvignon Blanc is light and fruity with a touch of oak, Grenache California is a good sipping wine with a fruit bouquet, Sonoma County Zinfandel displays good oak character from 18 months on the wood, and two Merlots— one from the Livermore Valley and the other from Sonoma—are herbal with nice berry flavor. Coyne has several Cabernets Sauvignon, drawn from the Napa and Livermore valleys and one, with 40 percent Cabernet Franc, has won several major medals.

Vintners choice: "Merlot," Coyne says. "I get Merlot grapes from several appelations and they're all award winners."

Fenestra Winery • T ✕

☐ *83 E. Vallecitos Rd., Livermore; mailing address: P.O. Box 582, Sunol, CA 94589; (510) 862-2292. Weekends noon to 5; MC/VISA. Most varieties tasted. A few wine logo items; shaded picnic area.* ☐

All it lacks is a Mail Pouch tobacco sign painted on the roof. Fenestra Winery occupies one of the most wonderfully weathered old barns in California. Bunkered into a hollow, surrounded by gnarled oaks and wild oats, this concrete and wooded classic is a classic of American country Gothic. It was built in 1889 by a pioneer farmer named George True.

Inside, soft-spoken chemist Lanny Replogle makes wines while his wife Fran handles marketing. It's a weekend job, since Lanny teaches at San Jose State University; he started winemaking in 1976. On pleasant days, tastings are convened outside, beside the rustic oak-shaded picnic areas.

All this may be spruced up in coming years, since the area will be part of a large golf course, vineyard and housing complex called Signature Hills, headed by golfer Jack Nicholas. Developers promise to leave the historic barn intact. Hopefully, they it will leave it properly scruffy as well. Paint would ruin the effect.

Unless they decide to paint a Mail Pouch tobacco sign on the roof.

Tasting notes: When it comes to winemaking, Lanny the chemist is no mad scientist. His wines are straightforward, full bodied and excellent, certainly not test tube products. They've won a good share of medals. He produces most of the popular whites, plus Merlot and Cabernet Sauvignon. Our wines of choice were a nutty and spicy Semillon, an herbal and complex Pinot blanc, a Chardonnay with deep and intense buttery flavor, a young Merlot with rich berry flavor and a four-year-old Cab with a spicy nose and mellow berry-rich taste. Lanny's "user-friendly" everyday drinking wine has a great double *entendre* label to honor the barn-builder: True Red. Overall prices are modest, ranging from $6 to the low teens.

Elliston Vineyards ● T 🏠

☐ *463 Kilkare Rd., Sunol, CA 94586; (510) 862-2377. Weekends noon to 5 or by appointment on weekdays. Good selection of wine oriented giftwares. Winetasters dinners conducted monthly; contact the winery for details.* ☐

Your eye is first drawn to a grand cut stone château that seems to have been transported here from the Rhine. It's surrounded by lush landscaping and mature trees, with a few vines out front. The tasting room, carpeted and comfortable, occupies a small lattice covered cottage off to one side. The attractive complex is owned by Donna and Keith Flavetta.

The blue sandstone Victorian was built in 1890 by Henry Hiram Ellis and it contains some original furnishings, including a walnut bed shipped around the horn. Winery offices occupy the splendidly furnished mansion, and it's often used for weddings and other special events. The folks here probably won't mind if visitors take a brief peek when it's open and not in use.

Tasting notes: The list focuses mostly on whites, including a Pinos Gris that's quite lush and fruity. Generally, three Pinot Blancs and three Chardonnays are on the list; the blancs are surprisingly rich and most the Chardonnays have strong fruit character and a soft acid finish. A light bodied Pinot Noir and deep purple and intense Cabernet Sauvignon comprise the red side, along with Captain's Claret, a Bordeaux style blend. Completing the selections are a Chardonnay-Pinot Blanc-Pinot Gris blend called *Cuvée des Trois*, Elliston California Champagne, Rosé of Ruby Cabernet and Malvasia Bianca dessert wine. Prices range $9 into the teens; less for the rosé and Malvasia.

Westover Vineyards ● T ✗

☐ *34932 Palomares Rd., Castro Valley, CA 94546; (510) 537-3932. Weekends noon to 5, or by appointment; MC/VISA, AMEX. Most varieties tasted. Good selection of books and wine logo items. Picnic area; informal tours.* ☐

One of the most attractive wineries in this region, Westover is housed in a Spanish style complex of red tile roofs, beige stucco and Moorish arch windows. A picnic area occupies a sunny courtyard and mature trees, including some redwoods, complete this alluring creek canyon setting. Westover and neighbor Chouinard are high above the Livermore Valley—so high that they're in the Castro Valley postal zone

The setting is equally pleasant inside; the tasting room is like a casual living room, with a pool table, "foos" ball, a pinball machine and big screen TV. This family-owned winery, established by Bill and Linda Smyth, produces about 1,500 cases a year—and growing.

Vintners choice: "Our estate Chardonnay has a natural grapefruit flavor and our Zinfandel is from 70-year-old vines with lots of berry flavor," says Linda.

Chouinard Vineyard and Winery • T GT ✗

☐ *33853 Palomares Rd., Castro Valley, CA 94552; (510) 582-9900. Weekends and some holidays noon to 5; MC/VISA. Most varieties tasted. Some wine logo items. Shaded picnic area. Tours on request during tasting room hours.* ☐

Tucked into a wooded slope and housed in a bright red barn, Chouinard Winery could pose for a Grandma Moses painting. Its pleasant grounds and vineyards are terraced up a shallow ravine. The tasting room is in a cozy loft in the eaves of the red barn winery. Picnic tables rest beneath oaks, maples and redwoods nearby. We'd suggest arriving with a picnic lunch, buying a bottle of wine and spending a couple of hours in this pleasantly wooded mountain retreat.

Architect George Chouinard, his wife Caroline and their sons Rick and Daimian started their vineyards in 1978. They became intrigued with wine after living in France for several years. They opened their tasting room in 1985 and often host special events at this mountain retreat.

Tasting notes: Chardonnay, Semillon, Johannisberg Riesling, Gewürztraminer, Petite Sirah, Zinfandel, Cabernet Sauvignon and Granny Smith apple wine comprise the list. Prices range from $7 to $12.50. Wines are full-bodied, complex and quite tasty. Our choices included an 80 percent malolactic Chardonnay with a nutty aroma and nice spicy, buttery taste; a Johannisberg with a flower petal nose and fruity, crisp flavor; a young Zinfandel with a great raspberry nose and taste; and a powerful four-old Arroyo Seco Cab with a chili pepper nose and rich tannins—definitely one to age.

Vintners choice: "Chardonnay and our Granny Smith Apple wine; both are award-winners," says George.

Weibel Vineyards • T GT ✗ 🍷

☐ *1250 Stanford Ave. (P.O. Box 3398), Mission San Jose, CA 94539; (510) 656-2340. Daily 10 to 5; MC/VISA. Most varieties tasted. Gift shop with wine logo items; arbor-shaded picnic area. Tours on request from 10 to 3 weekdays.* ☐

After taking over the old Leland Stanford Winery in 1940, the Swiss family Weibel planted vineyards in these sunny, gently sloping hills. The winery is cradled between the Livermore and Santa Clara valleys, just east of Mission San Jose. The slopes are still sunny, but they're now covered with subdivisions instead of vines, with names like Vineyard Hills and Vintage Grove.

Most of Weibel's vines have been shifted north to Mendocino County, although some winemaking operations continue here. They can be witnessed during periodic tours. We've always liked the ruggedly handsome Spanish-style Weibel tasting room, called "The Hacienda." Its chapel-like architecture compliments old Mission San José, just down the road a bit.

Tasting notes: The Weibel family bottles half a million cases a year and the list includes most major varietals. Overall style is light and ready-to-drink. The Weibels also produce tasty and inexpensive sherries and ports. Overall wine prices are modest, ranging from $5 to $10. From the lengthy list, we particularly liked a light and fruity Chardonnay; a rich yet crisp and dry Gewürztraminer suitable as a good picnic wine; a three-year old Cabernet with a spicy nose, complex and soft flavor and low tannin; and a gentle ten-year Pinot Noir Reserve. The cream sherry and Rare Port were rich, lush and nutty, good buys at $8.

Vintners choice: "Sherry and ports are consistent gold medal winners," says Diana Weibel. "And we have very inexpensive sparkling wines."

SANTA CLARA VALLEY-MONTEBELLO WINERY TOUR ● One

of California's largest cities now stands where hundreds of acres of vines once flourished. San Jose is pushing a million population and its suburbs push far and wide into the Santa Clara Valley. Two wineries thrive here, however. Venerable Mirassou remains firmly rooted to the spot where it began more than a century ago. And latecomer Jerry Lohr decided to join the population swell instead of fighting it. He started a winery right in the middle of a San Jose industrial district.

The area's other wineries have found refuge on Montebello Ridge above San Jose, beyond reach of the commotion. Our tour thus takes you from thick civilization to thick forests. **Note:** The two valley winery tasting rooms are open daily, although some in the mountains are open on weekends only.

Mirassou is the first stop in this urban-mountain winery trek. From the Bayshore Freeway (U.S. 101), pass through the heart of San Jose and take the Capitol Expressway northeast for a couple of blocks. Go right on Aborn Road and follow it past shopping centers and subdivisions to the winery. (If you're continuing from the Livermore Valley tour, go south from the Weibel Tasting room on Mission Boulevard; it soon blends back into I-680. Follow it about a dozen miles until it intersects with U.S. 101 in San Jose, and then go south on 101 just over three miles to Capitol Expressway.)

From Mirassou, return to the Bayshore, go about six miles northwest to Interstate 880, then head southeast, following Santa Cruz signs. After about two miles, exit at The Alameda (State Route 82) and go left under the freeway, following it south. After a mile of pleasant older suburbs, you'll enter a commercial area. At the old Towne Theatre, turn left onto Lenzen Avenue and the **J. Lohr Winery** appears, in a brick building on your right.

Get back to I-880, continue south for just over a mile to the I-280 interchange and follow it right (west) through Cupertino. After about seven miles, take the Foothill Expressway exit and turn left under the freeway, following Foothill Boulevard. You'll quickly escape civilization and begin climbing into the Santa Cruz Mountain foothills.

This area offers more winding roads than wines, but it's a pretty drive and the wineries are interesting. Foothill Boulevard becomes Stevens Canyon Road, toiling through brushy slopes toward Stevens Creek Reservoir. Shortly after passing the dam, take a sharp right up Montebello Road, which twists and turns up to **Sunrise Winery.** It's on the historic Picchetti Ranch in the

Monte Bello Open Space Reserve. A graveled trailhead parking lot also provides parking for the tasting room.

Continue climbing and spiraling up Montebello Road, enjoying panoramic valley vistas if you dare look. You'll see more trees than vines here, although an occasional vineyard is spotted, clinging to these steep slopes. When it seems that you've climbed halfway to heaven, you see **Ridge Vineyards** crowning the ridge that provided its name. It's one of the most dramatically situated wineries in the country.

Retreat down Montebello to Stevens Canyon Road and turn right. After a couple of miles, fork to the left and upward onto Mount Eden Road. (Don't miss the fork; Stevens Canyon dead-ends into a wilderness.) You soon pass the mountain winery of Paul Masson. It's home to special vineyard events but is otherwise closed to the public. Its tasting room is in Chapter 10, at Monterey's Cannery Row.

Mount Eden blends into Pierce Road, which continues downhill and bumps into Congress Springs Road (Highway 9). Turn right and drive about a mile to **Mariani Winery**, up a steep, narrow lane to your left. If you were to continue up Congress Springs Road, you'd wind up in Santa Cruz County, whose wineries we cover in Chapter Nine. The *Wines of the Santa Cruz Mountains* map, available free at most wineries here, lists vintners on both sides of the slope; see below.

To continue this tour, reverse your route from Mariani Winery on Congress Springs Road (which becomes Big Basin Way) and follow it just over three miles to the wooded foothill community of **Saratoga.** En route, you'll pass the **Santa Clara County Arboretum** and **Hakkone Gardens**, both worth a browse. Also, you may want to explore a few Saratoga boutiques and shops before continuing.

Follow Saratoga-Los Gatos Road (still Highway 9) southeast to Los Gatos. Once there, turn right onto University Avenue (at a stoplight, just short of the Highway 17 freeway) and follow it about six blocks to Main Street. Go left on Main, cross the freeway and quickly turn right onto College Avenue (near a gray apartment building). College winds steeply into wooded hills, taking you to the **Novitiate of Los Gatos,** on whose grounds resides **Mirassou Champagne Cellars.**

Like Saratoga, Los Gatos is a lushly-wooded foothill town busy with boutiques, upscale shops and restaurants. You may want to explore its **Old Town** Spanish flavored shopping mall.

Mirassou Vineyards • T & T$ GT 📦

☐ *3000 Aborn Rd., San Jose, CA 95135; (408) 274-4000. Monday-Saturday noon to 5, Sunday noon to 4; MC/VISA, AMEX. Most varieties tasted; library reserves tasted at $1. Wine related gift selection. Tours Monday-Saturday at 1:30 and 3:30; Sunday at 1 and 3.* ☐

If you count in-laws, the Mirassou family traces its genealogical vines back to 1854, when Pierre Pellier planted grapes in the Santa Clara Valley, then married his daughter to a Mirassou. Their descendants still make wine on that plot of ground planted by Great, great-grandfather Pellier.

Most of the vines have shifted southward to Monterey County. Only 20 acres survive here, a small Cabernet vineyard forming a thin green line between the winery and encroaching subdivisions. The venerable winery grounds are stately, with weathered, properly ivy-covered buildings shaded by mature trees. The large and attractive tasting room is housed in one of the winery structures. Inside, you can peek through windows at redwood casks.

Tasting notes: We *like* the way Mirassou conducts tastings. You fetch a large tulip-shaped glass from a wall rack and walk past several tables, where samples of nearly everything on the lengthy list are poured. Nearly all popular California varietals are produced by Mirassou. Prices are modest, ranging from $6.50 to the middle teens; some library wines go higher. The Mirassou style is light, crisp and clean. Among our choices were a lightly spicy Chardonnay; a fruity and crisp Monterey Riesling; a spicy and medium bodied Cabernet Sauvignon, excellent for its $9.75 price; and young Pinot Noirs and Zinfandels, both refreshingly fruity with fine berry aromas.

Vintners choice: "Chardonnay, Pinot Noir, Pinot Blanc and Monterey Riesling," says publicity director Steve Wilson. "The cool climate of our Monterey County vineyards brings out the best in these grapes."

J. Lohr Winery ● *T GT* 🍷

◻ *1000 Lenzen Ave., San Jose, CA 95126; (408) 288-5057. Daily 10 to 5; MC/VISA. Most varieties tasted. Good selection of wine logo gift items. Tours Saturday and Sunday at 11 and 2.* ◻

Despite its industrial-strength location, Jerry Lohr's urban winery presents an attractive picture. Hedges and bushes grace the narrow space between the sidewalk and the square-shouldered brick winery. The redwood paneled tasting room is spacious and inviting; barrels, vats and other winery trappings are just beyond. In one corner, a video cassette recites the J. Lohr story.

That story began in 1974 when Jerry started making wine in this facility, which once housed the Falstaff and Fredericksburg breweries. Much of the winemaking occurs in the field, however. Lohr's crew has done much of the pioneering in night harvesting and field pressing to start the process when the juice is cool and fresh. Output has grown rapidly, now topping 300,000 cases a year.

Tasting notes: Lohr wines have won an array of medals, particularly the lush and fruity whites. They come in two labels—the modestly priced Cypress line, from $5 to $6.75 and the J. Lohr Estates wines, $7.25 to $12.25. We favored the nutty, spicy and silky Estates Riverstone Chardonnay, the Wildflower Monterey Gamay, with great raspberry nose and flavor (a major medal winner) and a lush, peppery Seven Oaks Cabernet. Of the Cypress line, we liked a fruity, crisp and light Fumé Blanc; spicy and subtly oaky Merlot and the Blush, with a brisk berry flavor. It's not a rosé, but a white-red blend, made with Chenin Blanc, Riesling, Petit Sirah and Merlot.

Vintners choice: "Our Chardonnays, Rieslings and Gamay from Monterey County and Paso Robles Cabernet Sauvignon," said a winery voice.

Sunrise Winery ● *T CT* ✗

◻ *13100 Montebello Rd., Cupertino, CA 95014; (408) 741-1310. Friday-Sunday 11 to 3; MC/VISA. Most varieties tasted. A few wine logo items. Picnic area near tasting room; informal tours.* ◻

From urban J. Lohr, the pendulum swings bucolic. Sunrise occupies old stone and wooden buildings at the Picchetti Ranch, where a pioneering family made wine more than a century earlier. Ronald and Rolayne Stortz started the present-day operation, moving from their Felton location in 1983. The setting is so oak-shaded rural Americana that it's often used as a movie location. It will remain unchanged, for the Picchetti Ranch is part of the Montebello Ridge Open Space Preserve.

The winery is reached by a farmyard lane from a large graveled parking lot that also serves as a trailhead for open space hikers. The tasting room, consisting of a small table and a few wine logo items, is a modest presence in a huge wooden-floored barn. This ample space is often used for weddings, private parties and such.

Tasting notes: Chardonnay, Pinot Blanc, Pinot Noir, Zinfandel and Cabernet comprise the list. We liked the nutty, lush flavor of the malolactic barrel-fermented Chardonnay and the herbal, grapey flavor of the Zin. A five-year old Pinot Noir was medium bodied with a nice berry flavor and tannin nip. A 12-year old Cabernet was lush, fully integrated and excellent, with chili pepper undertones. Prices range from $7.50 to $20.

Vintners choice: "Pinot Blanc, Pinot Noir and Estate Zinfandel" was Rolayne's roll call.

Ridge Vineyards • T ✕

☐ *17100 Montebello Rd. (P.O. Box 1810), Cupertino, CA 95015; (408) 867-3233. Weekends 11 to 3; MC/VISA, AMEX. Selected wines tasted. A few wine logo items.* ☐

Ridge, indeed. Several Stanford Research Institute scientists retreated to this lofty perch in 1959. They built an earthy yet technologically advanced winery and began producing some of the finest Zinfandels in California. Paul Draper, called by some the state's most intellectual winemaker, joined the crew in the late 1970s. He's still there, intellectually and poetically creating Zin—perhaps with a bit of Zen.

The Ridge structures are rudimentary, appropriate to this final base camp of the vintners' art. If the winemaking approach here is inward, the view is outward—spectacular and more than panoramic. On a rare clear day, when vehicle exhaust and silicon dust have settled in the valley below, one can see San Francisco's highrises, 40 miles away. There's a feeling of Oz about this place. It's like sitting on a vineyard in the clouds, peering down at a reality that can't touch you.

Bring lunch and buy a bottle. Picnic tables are at the highest point of Oz, sitting among 40-year old Cabernet vines, like gnarled old guardian angels. You won't want to leave.

Tasting notes: The original Zinfandel list has been expanded considerably to include Cabernet Sauvignon, Chardonnay, Merlot and Petite Sirah. Several vineyard designated and vintage year selections appear on the list, and a few are picked each weekend for tastings. We happened upon an incredibly lush and spicy eight-year-old Jimsomare Cabernet, a lush and nutty Santa Cruz Mountains Chardonnay and a raspberry-rich, mellow and subtly spicy eight-year-old Lime Kiln Zinfandel. A pepper-spice 10-year-old Petite Sirah completed our day on the mountain.

Mariani Winery • T GTA ✕ 📷

☐ *23600 Congress Springs Rd., Saratoga, CA 95070; (408) 741-2930. Daily 11 to 5; MC/VISA. Selected wines tasted. Good selection of wine logo and specialy food items; picnic area. Guided tours by appointment.* ☐

Far down from Montebello Ridge although still in a nice wooded setting, Mariani Winery occupies a sheltered hollow above Congress Springs Road. Redwoods and other conifers guard this little vineyard valley, reached by a short, tree-canopied drive. Vineyards tumble down a gentle slope and wine is made in a century-old concrete building farther up the hill. Tasting happens in an appealing old wood frame building with rough log rafters, which dates from 1912. The adjacent historic Villa de Monmartre is available for special occasions. (Incidentally, if you didn't do the ridge route, the winery is easily reached by a three-mile run from Saratoga on Congress Springs Road.)

Established by French immigrant Pierre Pourroy in 1892, the facility was reactivated by two local families in 1976 as Congress Springs Winery. Following a change of ownership in 1992, it's now owned by John and Maria Lisa (Mariani) Delmare and Vic and Mabel Erickson. The winery's name comes from Maria Lisa's side of the family, which goes back many generations in this area.

Tasting notes: The list is comprised of several renditions of Chardonnay plus Sauvignon Blanc, Johannisberg Riesling, Pinot Blanc, Semillion, Zinfandel, Merlot, Cabernet Franc and a red Meritage style called Trinity. We tasted two excellent Chardonnays—an estate bottled version done in French oak with a nice floral bouquet and great fruity-herbal taste; and an American oak Saratoga Vineyards version that was equally soft and fruity, with a lighter finish. A Zinfandel was medium-bodied, with good berries and spice in the taste. Prices range from $9 to the high teens.

Vintners choice: A winery source listed them simply: "Chardonnay, Cabernet Franc and Zinfandel."

Mirassou Champagne Cellars ● T GT 🏠

☐ *300 College Ave. (at the Novitiate of Los Gatos), Los Gatos, CA 95032; (408) 395-3790. Wednesday-Sunday noon to 5; MC/VISA, AMEX. Good selection of wine logo items. Guided tours at 1:30 and 3:30.* ☐

Like Wente, Mirassou found an historic site for its sparkling wine operation. It is leasing the 1888 Novitiate cellars, where Brother Corte produced memorable wines until a decade ago. The Novitiate of Los Gatos still owns the property; it has chosen to leave the winemaking to others.

This is indeed a handsome spot, tucked into a mountain shelf, half a mile above Los Gatos. Visitors enter through a formal gate and follow a tree-lined passage to the white-washed, tile-roofed Colonial Spanish complex. The tasting room, in a bold cut-stone building, is reached via a glowering stone archway right out of an Indiana Jones movie set. But the airy hospitality room is quite cheerful. Tours take visitors through the ancient winery buildings and pleasantly musty aging caves burrowed into surrounding hills.

Tasting notes: Mirassou produces four sparkling wines, all by *méthode champenoise*. We enjoyed a crisp and dry Au Naturel made from Pinot Noir and Chardonnay; a light, lean and clean Blanc de Noirs of 100 percent Pinot Noir; plus a Brut and Old Brut Reserve with just a hint of sweetness and a nice touch of the grape.

THE BEST OF THE BUNCH

The best wine buys ● Concannon Vineyard, Wente Brothers Estate Winery and Fenestra Winery in Livermore Valley; Weibel Vineyards at Mission San Jose; and J. Lohr Winery in San Jose.

The most attractive wineries ● Wente Brothers Sparkling Wine Cellars, Westover Vineyards and Chouinard Winery in Livermore Valley; Ridge Vineyards (for the setting) on Montebello Ridge; and Mirassou Champagne Cellars in Los Gatos.

The most interesting tasting rooms • Concannon Vineyard and Wente Brothers Estate Winery in Livermore Valley; Weibel Vineyards at Mission San Jose; J. Lohr Winery in San Jose; and Mariani Winery near Saratoga.

The funkiest tasting rooms • Retzlaff Vineyards, Livermore Valley Cellars and Fenestra Winery in Livermore Valley.

The best gift shop • Wente Brothers Estate and Wente Brothers Sparkling Wine Cellars in Livermore Valley.

The nicest picnic areas • Retzlaff Vineyards, Concannon Vineyard and Chouinard Winery in Livermore Valley; Ridge Vineyards on Montebello Ridge.

The best tours • Wente Brothers Sparkling Wine Cellars in Livermore Valley and Mirassou Champagne Cellars in Los Gatos.

Wineland activities and such

Wineland events • Monthly winetasting dinners at Elliston Winery, (510) 862-2377; summer vineyard concerts at Paul Masson's Mountain winery, (408) 741-5182; Wente Winery summer concert series featuring major stars, (800) 95-WENTE; various special events at Concannon Vineyard, (510) 455-7770; Harvest Celebration sponsored by Livermore Valley Winegrowers, Labor Day weekend, (510) 443-1500 or (510) 455-7770.

Winery touring maps • *Livermore Valley Winegrowers Map* and brochure is free at valley wineries or call (510) 447-9463. *Wines of Santa Clara Valley*, free at wineries or contact Santa Clara Valley Wine Growers Association, P.O. Box 1192, Morgan Hill, CA 95037; (408) 779-2145 or (408) 778-1555. The *Wines of the Santa Cruz Mountains* map and brochure includes several wineries on the Santa Clara County side of the mountains; it's available at member wineries or contact Santa Cruz Mountains Winegrowers Assn., P.O. Box 3000, Santa Cruz, CA 95063; (408) 479-WINE.

BEYOND THE VINEYARDS

As you have noted, the southern Bay Area is a mix of spreading suburbia laced with hide-away canyons, beige hills and wooded ridges of the Santa Cruz Mountains.

While in the Livermore Valley, you might take a break at **Del Valle Regional Park** at the end of Arroyo Road. It offers swimming, boating and picnicking. **Pleasanton,** Livermore's next-door neighbor, has a pleasing early American look to its downtown area, with some interesting boutiques. As you work southwestward in your winery quest, check out the **San Francisco Water Temple** just off Sunol Road at the head of **Niles Canyon** (if it's open to the public, which it often isn't). The canyon itself, as we noted earlier, has nice spots for picnicking, swimming and bank-sitting. **Mission San José de Guadalupe** in the Warm Springs district of Fremont is certainly worth a visit. The **San Jose-Santa Clara** area has several major attractions, ranging from **Great America** amusement park to museums and missions. Write to the sources at the end of this chapter for details.

If you've come here from the Bay Area and you aren't weary of winding roads, consider returning via the Coast Range's skyline ridge. **Skyline Boulevard** follows the ridgeline all the way to Belmont. There, you can pick up Highway 92 and go east to the Bayshore or west to U.S. Highway 1 and continue into San Francisco. To reach Skyline (Highway 35) take State Route 9 north from Saratoga; it intersects with Route 35 at Saratoga Gap.

Views to the east and west are impressive from this remote path high above the densely populated Bay Area.

South Bay attractions and activities

Hakkone Gardens • 21000 Big Basin Way, Saratoga; (408) 867-3438, ext. 43. Weekdays 10 to 5, weekends 11 to 5; donation requested. Formal Japanese gardens in 15-acre park.

Lawrence Livermore Laboratory Visitors Center • Greenville Rd., Livermore; (510) 422-9797. Weekdays 9 to 4:30, weekends noon to 5; free. Exhibits and slide show concerning the search for new energy sources.

Mission San José de Guadalupe • 43300 Mission Blvd., Fremont; (510) 657-1797. Daily 10 to 5; free. Mission chapel and museum with artifacts of California's Spanish settlement.

Villa Montalvo • Montalvo Road, off State Highway 9 southeast of Saratoga; (408) 741-3421. Weekdays 8 to 5, weekends 9 to 5, shorter hours for gallery; free. Lush gardens around a Mediterranean villa with an arboretum, art gallery and theater.

Farm products • Maps listing farms and wineries selling directly to the public. **Alameda County Farm Trails,** available at many wineries and farm trail participants, or send a stamped, self-addressed business-sized envelope to: Alameda County Farm Trails, 658 Enos Way, Livermore, CA 94550. **Country Crossroads,** listing outlets in Santa Clara and Santa Cruz counties; available at farm and winery members or send a stamped, self-addressed business-sized envelope to: Country Crossroads, Santa Clara County Farm Bureau, 1368 N. Fourth St., San Jose, CA 95112.

South Bay information sources

Since South Bay wineries are rather spread out, few lodgings or restaurants are within the vineyard areas, with the exceptions of the deli-café at Stony Ridge Winery and The Restaurant at Wente Sparkling Wine Cellars, listed above. There are, of course, hundreds of restaurants and lodgings in the communities of this thickly populated region. Sources below will happily provide long lists of them.

Livermore Chamber of Commerce, 2157 First St., Livermore, CA 94550; (510) 447-1606.

Pleasanton Chamber of Commerce, 450 Main St., Suite 202, Pleasanton, CA 94566; (510) 846-5858

Los Gatos Chamber of Commerce, 50 University Ave., Los Gatos, CA 95030; (408) 354-9300.

San Jose Chamber of Commerce, 180 S. Market St., San Jose, CA 95113; (408) 998-7000.

San Jose Convention & Visitors Bureau Tour and Travel Information Center, 333 W. San Carlos St., San Jose, CA 95110; (408) 295-9600.

Saratoga Chamber of Commerce, 20460 Saratoga-Los Gatos Rd., Saratoga, CA 95070; (408) 867-0753.

"A tough wine, but the focused cherry and raspberry flavors manage to make themselves heard above the tannic din."
— Description of a Parusso Barolo from Barbaresco, Italy

Chapter Eight

SOUTHERN SANTA CLARA
Friendly family wineries in garlic country

Southern Santa Clara Valley ranks with northern Sonoma County as one of our favorite touring areas. The wineries are easy to find, the folks are friendly and the wines are excellent and affordably priced. In fact, the area probably offers the best wine buys in California.

The region's focal point is Gilroy, a town of about 25,000 that's better known for garlic than for wine. Indeed, it produces a lot of both. Community leaders don't mind being kidded about Gilroy's garlicky reputation. In fact, they encourage it; highway signs proclaim the town to be the Garlic Capital of the World. It's a rightful claim, since 90 percent of America's garlic is produced thereabouts. If that statistic doesn't take your breath away, the aroma during the annual Gilroy Garlic Festival will.

"It's the only town in America where you can marinate a steak by hanging it on a clothesline," Will Rogers once quipped.

During the festival, in late July, citizens present their "scented pearls" in every conceivable format, from garnishes to garlands. Events include a *Tour de Garlique* bicycle run, Garlic Gallop, Garlic Squeeze Barn Dance and—hold your breath for the grand finale—the Great Garlic Cookoff. The *Los Angeles Herald Examiner* called it the "ultimate summer food fair."

You needn't wait for the festival to immerse yourself in the scented pearl—or the stinking rose, depending on your attitude regarding garlic breath. Two stores on U.S. 101 just south of town, Garlic World and The Garlic Shoppé, will sell you garlic-laced relish, mustard, marinade, jam, butter, ice cream and—good grief!—garlic wine. A new addition, in downtown Gilroy at Monterey and Fifth, is the Garlic Festival Store and Gallery.

With all that garlic and all that wine, can Italians be far behind? The list of wineries reads like a Milano phone book: Fortino, Conrotto, Rapazzini, Pedrizzetti and Guglielmo. Names like Kirigin, Kruse, Blocher of Live Oaks Winery, Vanni and Wilson of Solis and Inoue of Sycamore Creek have been blended in to create an international brew of winemakers.

Mostly they make red. The sloping hills and sheltering mountains provide the proper soils and warm climate for Zinfandel, Grignolino, Carignane, Petit Sirah, Cabernet and Merlot. You'll find fine whites as well, particularly more full-flavored types such as Chardonnay, Johannisberg Riesling and Sauvignon Blanc.

Wineries of the South Santa Clara region are conveniently packaged. Most stand alongside Hecker Pass Highway west of Gilroy. Others are in the Uvas Valley to the north and near U.S. 101 between Gilroy and Morgan Hill.

Despite their easy access, they're rarely crowded. On a typical day, you'll find few other visitors in the tasting rooms, and the person pouring your wine might be the one who made it. These are mostly family operations, ranging from third-generation vintners of Guglielmo Winery to the latter-day Dave Vanni of Solis.

Neither garlic nor Italians figure in the early history of this area. In 1813, a dour Scotsman named John Cameron went AWOL from a British ship in Monterey Bay and scampered northward. Using his mother's maiden name of Gilroy (presumably to avoid being hauled back to his ship), he befriended the Ortega ranching family, married daughter Clara and settled down. Local historians say he became the first permanent English speaking settler in California. The Ortega-Gilroys planted orchards and raised cattle, gradually forming the hub of a community.

Just up the trail, an Irishman named Martin Murphy acquired a chunk of Rancho Ojo de Agua de la Coche in 1845. In 1882, his granddaughter Diana married wealthy San Franciscan Morgan Hill, and they built a lavish ranch estate. Thus, the town bordering the northern edge of this wine country was named for a gentleman, not a mountain.

Hills do occur in abundance, however. The lower Santa Clara Valley is cradled between the Diablo Range to the east and the Madonna ridge of the Santa Cruz Mountains westward. Highway 152, slicing through this area, spirals over two noted passes---Hecker to the west and Pacheco to the east.

SOUTHERN SANTA CLARA VALLEY WINERY TOUR ● This is another area you might prefer to tour on weekends, since some of the wineries are only open then. A good number are open daily, however.

After going through urban San Jose and Montebello Ridge contortions in the previous chapter, this route is simple, and relatively flat. It's also relatively rural, since most of the area is still beyond the circle of suburbia that spreads like rings of disturbed water from greater San Jose.

Driving south on U.S. 101, you pass by checkerboard agricultural lands and an occasional vineyard. In **Morgan Hill**, take Dunne Road briefly east from the freeway, then swing back north by turning left onto Condit Road. Follow it less than a mile to a stop sign at Main Avenue. Turn right and you'll soon arrive at **Emilio Guglielmo Winery** (pronounced *Goo-YELL-mo*), just across the road from a high school. Obviously, Morgan Hill suburbia has encroached, but vineyards and farm fields still stretch to the east.

Re-trace your route down Main and go south on Condit beyond Dunne Road to San Pedro Avenue, the next cross street. A left turn brings you shortly to **Pedrizzetti Winery.** Return yet again to Condit, continue south

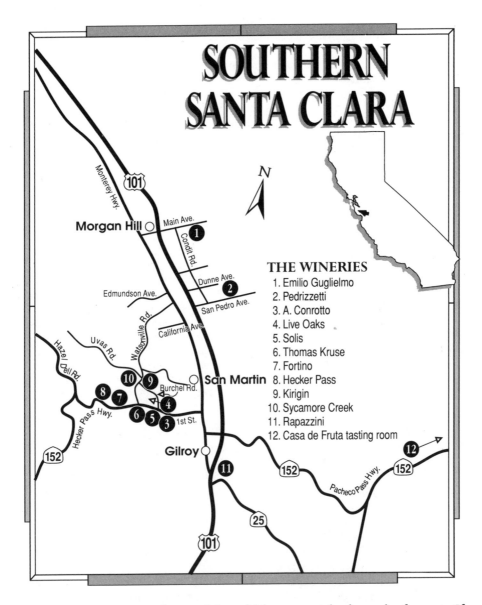

SOUTHERN SANTA CLARA

THE WINERIES

1. Emilio Guglielmo
2. Pedrizzetti
3. A. Conrotto
4. Live Oaks
5. Solis
6. Thomas Kruse
7. Fortino
8. Hecker Pass
9. Kirigin
10. Sycamore Creek
11. Rapazzini
12. Casa de Fruta tasting room

to Tennant Avenue and turn right, which gets you back on the freeway. If you want to visit **Casa de Fruta,** with its tasting room, kiddie zoo and extensive gift and wine selection, pick up eastbound Pacheco Pass Highway (Route 152) from downtown Gilroy.

You might want to continue into Morgan Hill. Its downtown area along Monterey Street is spruced up with landscaped sidewalks, brick crosswalks and street plantings. A few boutiques and antique shops may tempt you to explore. Most of Morgan Hill is contained between Tennant Road and Main Avenue. Until the freeway was completed a few years ago, U.S. 101 carried its heavy burden of traffic along Monterey Street through Morgan Hill, San Martin (pronounce it *Mar-TEEN*) and Gilroy. Freed from freight trucks and weekend traffic jams, the towns have redeveloped much of this stretch. There has been one casualty. San Martin Winery, a fixture in its namesake town since 1906, closed its tasting room doors after the new freeway took away its tourist traffic.

From Morgan Hill, stay on Monterey (if you don't mind a few stoplights), or continue south on U.S. 101 to **Gilroy** and take the Highway 152 exit to the right. It does one zig and one zag through town to put you on First Street; new signs pointing toward the wineries will help guide you. As you clear Gilroy's suburbs, First Street becomes Hecker Pass Highway, which delivers you to most of the area's wineries. It's one of southern Santa Clara County's nicest drives, passing vineyards, flower and tree nurseries and winding toward forested Madonna ridge, often capped with a soft halo of clouds.

Your first encounter is **A. Conrotto Winery** in an old farmyard on the left, just beyond Santa Teresa Boulevard. A bit farther is **Goldsmith Seeds, Inc.,** which presents a spectacular quilt of blooming flowers in summer. Visitors are welcome to stroll among its brilliant fields and admire its striking geometric floral displays. Take your camera. **Hecker Pass Family Park** is just beyond, slated for development into an amusement center. Next comes **Western Tree Nursery,** with great forests of potted pines and such.

The wineries now come thick and fast. You encounter **Live Oaks Winery** on your right and **Solis Winery** (*SOLE-lees*) right across the highway. Close by are Sarah's Vineyard (open by appointment only) on the right, and **Thomas Kruse Winery** on the left, opposite the Watsonville Road turnoff. The **Fortino** winery is just beyond, on the right. The final Hecker Pass facility, appropriately called **Hecker Pass Winery,** is next to Fortino, also on the right.

Backtrack briefly to Watsonville Road, turn left and you'll encounter **Kirigin Cellars** after about 2.5 miles; it's on the right, just beyond Day Road. A bit past Kirigin, fork left onto Uvas Road and you'll quickly see **Sycamore Creek Vineyards.**

Return now to downtown Gilroy and follow either Monterey Street or U.S. 101 south; they soon blend together. About two miles below town, take the Hollister/Pinnacles National Monument exit, cross east over the freeway, turn left toward a frontage road and you'll see **Garlic World**, then **Rapazzini Winery.** Just beyond the winery is **The Garlic Shoppé.**

Emilio Guglielmo Winery • T ✕ 📷

□ *1480 E. Main Ave., Morgan Hill, CA 95037; (408) 779-2145. Weekdays 9 to 5, weekends 10 to 5; major credit cards. Most varieties tasted. Good wine logo and specialty foods selection. Picnic patio near vineyards.* □

Immigrant Emile Guglielmo started making wines in 1925, and this handsome facility is the one of the Southern Santa Clara Valley's oldest wineries. However, that's rather recent in this family's time-line; Guglielmos have traced family winemakers back to the Roman era. The enterprise is presently run by Emilio's son George and his two sons, Gene and Gary, with yet another generation coming along.

The Guglielmo's combined tasting room and gift shop is an inviting space. Spanish style with thick tile floors, warm woods and brick trim. Picnic tables sit beside the vineyards on an attractive patio. A new addition is Villa Emile, a Mediterranean-style hospitality center among the vines, with a concert stage, outdoor wine bar and grassy seating area. It's used for concerts, winemakers dinners and other special events, and it can be rented for weddings and such.

Tasting notes: Guglielmo wines, straightforward and full bodied, have won a good share of awards. Issued under three labels—Guglielmo, Guglielmo Reserve and Emile's—they cover most of the red, white and blush spectrum. Our favorites were among the Guglielmo Reserve wines—a fruity, nutty flavored Chardonnay with a soft finish; a spicy and full-bodied Zinfandel and a big, peppery and herbal Cabernet Sauvignon. A Grignolino, rarely found as a varietal in California, had a lively berry nose and good spicy-fruity flavor. Prices are modest for the reserves, ranging from $8.25 to $12. The other lines are even less expensive, starting around $5 for regular Guglielmo varietals and as little as $3.75 for Emile's jug wines.

Pedrizzetti Winery • *T GTA* ✕

☐ *1645 San Pedro Ave., Morgan Hill, CA 95037; (408) 779-7389. Daily 10 to 5 (until 5:30 in summer), major credit cards. Most varieties tasted. A few wine logo items. Picnic area; guided tours by appointment.* ☐

This small family-run operation dates back to 1913, when it was established by Italian immigrant Camillo Colombano. John Pedrizzetti purchased it in 1945, and his son Ed and daughter-in-law Phyllis took over the operation in 1968. Ed and Phyllis make the wine, with Alan Kreutzer as their consulting enologist.

"Wine should be clean but not pristine," Kreutzer said. "Every time you fine a red, you take something out of it."

After tasting, it was evident that the Pedrizzettis and Kreutzer had put a lot of skill into these wines, and taken very little out of them.

The winery is a simple affair, housed in a basic masonry building. The tasting room is in a tiny space that more resembles a busy wine shop than a hospitality center; rows of bottles line several shelves. An attractive garden is used for group barbecues and it's open to casual picnickers. "All you have to do is show up with a basket and I'll throw on a cloth and leave you to a peaceful picnic," says Phyllis.

Tasting notes: Although it's a small operation, Pedrizzetti generates an impressive array of wines, including most of the varietals, several fruit wines, a sherry, port, brandy and sparkling wine. We particularly liked a full-bodied, spicy Chardonnay with a nice crisp finish; a peppery and light but complex Zinfandel; and a Cabernet Sauvignon with a great chili pepper nose and lush flavor with a nice tannic nip. A raspberry wine was delicious; it was like drinking crushed berries. Wines are very modestly priced, from $5 to $9.75.

A. Conrotto Winery • *T* ✕

☐ *1690 Hecker Pass Highway, Gilroy, CA 95020; (408) 842-3053. Weekends only 11 to 5 (11:30 to 5 in winter), MC/VISA, DISC. Reservations requested for groups or five or more. Most varieties tasted. A few wine logo items. Small picnic area.* ☐

Housed in a little red shed in an old farmyard, Conrotto's rustic tasting room looks out over an orchard, not a vineyard. A small planting of

---

WINERY CODES • ***T*** = Tasting with no fee; ***T$*** = Tasting for a fee; ***GT*** = Guided tours; ***GTA*** = Guided tours by appointment; ***ST*** = Self-guiding tours; ***CT*** = casual tours or a peek into the winery; ✕ = picnic area; 🏠 = Gift shop or good giftware selection. Price ranges listed in tasting notes are for varietals; jug wines may be available for less.

The Fortino Winery peeks through a veil of its own vineyards along Hecker Pass Highway west of Gilroy.

Symphony grapes up front reminds visitors that this is indeed a winery. This pocket-size, bucolic facility is one of the area's oldest, founded by Anselmo Conrotto in 1926. It's presently run by his two daughters and their husbands, Jim and Jean Burr and Gerald and Jermaine Case; they produce about 6,000 cases a year.

Tasting notes: The Conrotto list is small: Zinfandel, burgundy, chablis and rosé, all made in a hearty full-flavored Italian style. The burgundy is an excellent spaghetti wine, a blend of Grenache, Carignane and Barbara. Petit Sirah, Sauvignon Blanc and an award-winning cream sherry sometimes appear on the list. Prices are modest, staying well under $10.

Live Oaks Winery • T ✗

☐ *3875 Hecker Pass Highway, Gilroy, CA 95020; (408) 842-2401. Daily 10 to 5, major credit cards. Most varieties tasted. Picnic area near the tasting room.* ☐

Oak-shaded Live Oaks Winery began life in 1912 as the project of one Eduardo Scagliotti. His original winery, bunkered into the side of a hill, now houses the tasting room and aging cellars. Present-day owners are Richard and Barbara Blocher.

You must wander through an old farm yard and follow a gravel road down into a hollow to find the rustic little place. Once there, you step into a long, rudimentary tasting room whose walls are lined—not with wine—but with glossies of TV and movie stars. Tasting room manager Al Whitaker collects celebrity photos, claiming an accumulation of about 20,000. He sells them, along with wines, in the tasting room. If you need the latest pic of Lois (not Lewis) and Clark or Tom Cruse, or a vintage photo of ex-President Reagan as a drugstore cowboy, this is the place.

Tasting notes: Live Oaks offers several whites that lean toward the sweet side and some rather light reds. Of the whites, only Chenin Blanc and Chardonnay were dry; both were crisp with light finishes. A Zinfandel was subtly peppery and a Cabernet Sauvignon was gently herbal; both were light in tannin with rather veggie flavors. Prices are modest, ranging from $5.50 to $8.30.

Solis Winery ● T ✕

☐ *3920 Hecker Pass Hwy., Gilroy, CA 95020; (408) 847-6306. Open daily January to April and Wednesday through Sunday May to December, 11 to 5; major credit cards. Most varieties tasted. A few wine gift items. Picnic area with vineyard view.* ☐

This winery with an up and down history is up again. After a period of silence, it was dusted off and reopened in 1990 by Watsonville nurseryman Dave Vanni. Young U.C. Davis graduate Cory Wilson makes the wine and his wife Laura runs the business end. The facility dates back to 1917, when it was started by the Alfonso Bertrero family. It managed to survive Prohibition and Bertreros ran it until 1980, then it was operated by a corporation as Summerhill Winery before closing again.

Solis, which produces about 5,000 cases a year, has one of the most appealing tasting rooms in the area. A curved tasting bar is matched by a curving bay window that offers a CinemaScopic view of vineyards and distant forested ridges.

Tasting notes: Winemaker Cory likes to produce big fruit flavors with light woods. The list includes barrel fermented Chardonnay, Moscato Canelli, Riesling, Merlot and a proprietary red blend of Zinfandel, Carignane, Petite Sirah and Cabernet Franc called *Seducente*. Prices range from $6.50 to $12.50.

Vintners choice: "I always enjoy our Santa Clara Chardonnay and the Merlot and Seducente," says Cory. "Some of the vines used for the *Seducente* are more than 80 years old."

Thomas Kruse Winery ● T$ GTA ✕

☐ *4390 Hecker Pass Hwy., Gilroy, CA 95020; (408) 842-7016. Weekends 12 to 5; no credit cards. Most varieties tasted for $1 fee (refunded with purchase). Small picnic area. Guided tours by appointment or informal tours on the spot.* ☐

Tom Kruse is regarded as a renaissance man of the wine business. A laconic, philosophical muse, he started the winery in 1971, some years after fleeing the tumult of Chicago. He reactivated a facility originally built in 1910 by the Caesar Roffinella family; it had lain idle since 1946.

His wines and his operation are simple and forthright. Some of his labels are hand-written; one featured a detailed cost breakdown, from grape to foil cap, to suggest that some in the business are charging too much. His laid-

back wineyard is a casual scatter of rudimentary equipment—an old red tractor, plastic jugs and barrels for fermenting, a canoe paddle for stirring. Tastings occur on a plank inside a battered winery structure, or on a barrel head
outside. "No loose pets, ill behaved children, bicyclists or large groups of Re-
publicans," advises a sign.

Tasting notes: Kruse produces about 3,000 cases a year, focusing on
dry and crisp whites and reds that retain the fruity flavor of the grape. The
list is mostly red—Grignolino, Zinfandel, Cabernet Sauvignon, Pinot Noir,
Carignane and good old Gilroy Red. Its companion, Gilroy White, and Chardonnay cover the white side of the ledger, plus a bottle-fermented sparkling
wine aptly called Insouciance.

Vintners choice: "Inane question," he responded laconically.

Fortino Winery • T GTA ✕ 🍷

□ *4525 Hecker Pass Hwy., Gilroy, CA 95020; (408) 842-3305. Daily 9 to
6; MC/VISA, AMEX. Most varieties tasted. Gift shop with good selection of wine
related items and giftwares, plus imported and domestic specialty foods. Deli
with cheeses, sliced meats, salads and other fare; open in summers 11 to 4.
Guided tours by appointment. Shaded picnic area.* □

Fortino is the largest, busiest and most versatile of the Hecker Pass wineries. One can buy picnic fare from the Italian deli or have a hefty sandwich
constructed, pick out a bottle of wine or a soft drink, and adjourn to a tree-
shaded table beside a vineyard. The hospitality room is an appealing place,
with Tiffany style lamps and a long and roomy tasting counter. The deli is
adjacent.

Ernie and Marie Fortino created all this in two decades, after buying the
old Cassa Brothers Winery in 1970. Like many of his Italian neighbors, Ernie
is an immigrant from the old country, but one of recent vintage. Arriving in
1959, the amiable workaholic began building his version of the American
dream, working at other wineries and saving enough money to buy his own.
He and Marie have now decided to slow down a bit and enjoy the rewards of
their labors. The winery has been turned over to their son Gino, daughter
Terri and her husband Brian Dauenhauer. Gino is the winemaker—as he has
been for several years—while Terri and Brian manage other aspects of the
business. Of course, Ernie still keeps a hand in things at the winery, while
dabbling in other activities, such as a new import business to bring in special
Italian balsamic vinegar.

Tasting notes: The versatile Fortino list ranges from red and white varietals to sparkling wine and cream sherry. Winemaker Gino, like his father,
is noted for fine full-bodied reds and they've long been some of our favorite
wines. And they have won a good share of awards. Among our picks were a
rich, spicy and berry-like Petit Syrah; a Cabernet Sauvignon, soft and lush
yet with enough tannin to encourage aging; and a fine Zinfandel with a great
raspberry nose and taste. His Burgundy Reserve is one of our regular daily
wines. Of the whites, we liked a lush Chardonnay with a gentle nip at the
end and a Sauvignon Blanc with a wonderful floral nose and soft, crisp taste.
Prices are modest, ranging from $6 to $12.50; older "Cellar Selections" go
higher.

Vintners choice: We asked Ernie to pick his favorite from among son
Gino's wines. He flashed one of his impish grins and thought for a moment.
We could see that he didn't want to commit himself. "They're all good. What
can I say?" Gino wouldn't pick one, either.

Hecker Pass Winery • T GTA ✕

☐ 4605 Hecker Pass Hwy., Gilroy, CA 95020; (408) 842-8755. Daily 9 to 5; MC/VISA. Most varieties tasted. Some wine logo gift items. Picnic area; guided tours by appointment. ☐

Pardon the pun, but the Fortinos seems to have bottled up the western end of the Gilroy wine country. Ernie's brother Mario and his wife Frances opened their Hecker Pass Winery in 1972. The two brothers, both "back to basics" winemakers, engage in friendly competition. Like brother Ernie and nephew Gino, Mario is noted for his robust, full-bodied reds.

"Let the wine be wine," Mario said. "Chemists have no place in the wine business."

The tasting room is a simple affair, with wood paneling decorated mostly with award ribbons. A pleasant picnic area sits beside the vineyards, near the wooded slopes of Mount Madonna.

Tasting notes: Mario's reds dominate the list, and they're excellent—uniformly spicy and full-bodied; all are 100 percent varietal. The Zinfandel was nicely herbal with a good berry flavor and nippy tannic finish; Carignane had a spicy taste with big but not harsh tannins; and Petit Sirah had an appealing herbal-berry flavor. Of the more mellow wines, we liked Mario's Red Velvet, a "secret blend" that was soft, yet full flavored with a gentle finish. Blanc de Blanc, Grenache Rosé, Carignane Ruby, a generic burgundy and chablis, cream Sherry and Ruby Port complete the list. Prices are very modest, from $6 to $9.

Kirigin Cellars • T GTA ✕

☐ 11550 Watsonville Rd., Gilroy, CA 95020; (408) 847-8827. Daily 10 to 5; MC/VISA. All varieties tasted. Picnic area. Tours by appointment. ☐

The Gilroy countryside is populated by philosophical winemakers. "Dinner without wine is like a date without kissing," said Nikola Kirigin-Chargin, in his soft middle European accent.

Approaching 80, the owner of Kirigin Cellars claims to be semi-retired, although he makes 2,000 cases of wine a year and he still greets visitors in his pleasantly spartan tasting room. A good talker, he'll tell you that the wine industry and its writers and judges are too obsessed with the so-called attributes of wine. He refuses to enter competitions because he thinks judging is silly. "How can someone else judge your taste?"

From there, the discussion may progress to excessive government intervention, mandated warning signs, and a general American indifference to their country. There is good reason for his concern. He left his native Croatia in disgust after it became Communist Yugoslavia and the government took over his family winery. After working for several vintners in California, he bought the old Uvas Winery in 1976, at an age when most men are contemplating retirement.

He still talks about retiring, while continuing to host his tasting room visitors. He and his wife Biserka also make occasional trips to Croatia, deeply troubled by the ongoing crisis in their divided former homeland.

The Kirigin facility is quite appealing, built around a stylish old country home, with picnic tables under sheltering trees. The property was part of El Rancho Solis, an 1828 Mexican land grant, and the first winery was started here in 1887. Portions of the house dates back to 1833; it's one of the oldest in the county.

Tasting notes: Out of respect to Nikola, who dislikes winetasting verbosity even more than we do, we'll keep it simple: The list includes Sauvignon Blanc, Chardonnay, Sauvignon Vert, Gewürztraminer, Malvasia Bianca, Pinot Noir, Cabernet Sauvignon and Zinfandel. Whites are nice and full-bodied, not processed to blandness; reds are lush, tasting like the grapes they came from. Our favorites were Sauvignon Blanc, Chardonnay, Cabernet, Zinfandel and a delicious dessert wine called Vino de Mocca. It's made of wine, cocoa, chocolate and orange. Prices are modest, ranging from $5.50 to $8.50 and they haven't changed in six years. Is that simple enough, Nick?

Vintners choice: Nick looked at me as if I were crazy, then he smiled. "Why do you care what I like? You tell me what *you* like!"

Sycamore Creek Vineyards • *T* ✕

◻ *12775 Uvas Rd., Morgan Hill, CA 95037; (408) 779-4738. Weekends 11:30 to 5; MC/VISA, AMEX. Most varieties tasted. A few wine related gift items.* ◻

This small winery sits in a woodsy hollow, surrounded by vineyards and shaded by an assortment of mature trees. Neat white-painted outbuildings and trim landscaping give it the look of a prosperous, well-maintained old farm. The winery dates back beyond Prohibition, when it was started by the Marchetti family. Later abandoned, it was purchased in 1975 by Terry and Mary Kay Parks and rehabilitated.

A Japanese winemaking firm called Koshu Budoshu Honpo bought the facility from the Parks in 1989 and sent winemaker-manager Hideki "Mike" Yamaki to run things. Winemaking was no problem; he'd been doing that in Japan for more than a decade. He once told us the real challenge was to learn English. The company has since transferred him back to Japan (at his request; his English was doing fine) and American Barry Jackson is the new winemaker. Masao Inoue oversees the operation as winery president.

Tastings occur in a pleasing, country-style hospitality room with plank floors, wormwood walls and views of vines and trees.

Tasting notes: The Japanese like sweet wines and much of the production is sent back there, so Jackson has been following Yamaki's style. Although we prefer our wines dry, we liked the rich honey-like flavor of a semi-sweet Gamay Blanc and a perfumey and tasty Johannisberg Riesling; it was sweet but not sticky. The "Romeo and Juliet" dessert wine was so rich it was like drinking liquid fruit. Mike can make 'em dry, as well. We especially liked a spicy and fruity Sauvignon Blanc and a crisp, light Chardonnay. A selection of soft, flavorful reds—Carignane, Zinfandel, Cabernet Sauvignon and Pinot Noir—compete the list. Prices range from $6 to $15.

Rapazzini Winery • *T* 🍇

◻ *4350 Highway 101, Gilroy, CA 95020; (408) 842-5649. Daily 9 to 6 in summer and 9 to 5 the rest of the year; MC/VISA. Most varieties tasted. Extensive giftware and specialty food selection, with emphasis on garlic products.* ◻

It requires a good sense of humor to get serious about garlic, and Jon P. Rapazzini's family has done so. They opened their winery in 1962, and expanded to include a long list of garlic-laced specialty foods. "Mama Rap" Rapazzini has added the spicy pearl to just about everything imaginable: relish, sauces, mustards, mayonnaise, chips, dressings and yes—even chocolate, jelly and ice cream. Several of these items can be sampled at the tasting room and at the adjacent Garlic Shoppé.

Finally, are you ready for garlic wine? After sampling the products above, can you tell the difference? The wine is a French Colombard, which the family has courageously named *Château de Garlic*. It's crisp and subtly fruity with a lingering—*definitely* lingering—finish.

"It goes well with garlic-spiced foods," the tasting room host said with a straight face.

The hospitality room is quite handsome, made of cut stone, with a long copper tasting bar and a fireplace dominating one corner.

Tasting notes: Never mind Château de Garlic. The Rapazzinis make serious wines, with medals to prove it. The list includes Sauvignon Blanc, Chardonnay, a couple of blushes, Merlot, Cabernet Sauvignon, Petit Sirah, Zinfandel and some specialty dessert wines including a rich cream sherry. We liked a dry, subtly nutty Chardonnay; a Merlot with medium body, raspberry flavor and a hint of oak; a soft peppery Cabernet Sauvignon with light tannins; and a big Zinfandel, aged to perfection with a lots of berries and spice. Most of the reds are held six to ten years before release. Prices range from $6 to the middle teens; higher for a few old vintage wines. Take home *Château de Garlic* for a mere $6.

Casa de Fruta • T ✕ 🐓

⌂ *6680 Pacheco Pass Hwy., Holister, CA 95023; (408) 637-0051. Daily 9 to 8 in summer and 9 to 6 in winter; major credit cards. Most varieties tasted. Large complex with gift shops, restaurants, service station and RV park.*

The Zanger family, owners of local orchards since 1908, opened a small fruit stand near the top of Pacheco Pass in the 1940s. From this has grown a huge complex that includes a 24-hour restaurant, kiddie zoo, narrow gauge train and other rides, several gift galleries, a motel, RV park, service station and—oh, yes—a tasting counter. This isn't a winery, since the wines are made elsewhere.

Tasting notes: Most of the basic varietals are available, bottled for the Casa de Fruta label. They're quite good and competitively priced, from well below $10 to the early teens.

THE BEST OF THE BUNCH

The best wine buys • Southern Santa Clara wines are among the best buys in California; prices are very uniform among the various wineries. It was difficult to select overall "price leaders." So we didn't.

The most attractive wineries • Kirigin Cellars and Sycamore Creek Vineyards.

The most interesting tasting rooms • Guglielmo Winery, Solis Winery, Fortino Winery, Sycamore Creek Vineyards and Rapazzini Winery.

The funkiest tasting rooms • A. Conrotto Winery and Thomas Kruse Winery.

The best gift shops • Emilio Guglielmo Winery, Fortino Winery and Rapazzini Winery.

The nicest picnic areas • Emilio Guglielmo Winery and Kirigin.

Winery activities and such

Wineland events • Spring Wine Festival at Casa de Fruta Country Park, sponsored by the Santa Clara Valley Winegrowers Association, with tastings, dinner, music and games at various wineries, late April; (408) 778-1555 or (408) 842-9316. Gilroy Garlic Festival, mostly garlic but with winery participation, last full weekend of July, (408) 842-1625. Gilroy Wine Auction, October; (408) 842-3727.

Winery touring map • *Wines of the Santa Clara Valley* map is available from vintners or from the Santa Clara Valley Wine Growers Assn., P.O. Box 1192, Morgan Hill, CA 95037; (408) 779-2145 or (408) 778-1555.

BEYOND THE VINEYARDS

Wine is the main draw to this area, along with the seductive aroma of the scented pearl. However, the old historic district of downtown Gilroy is worth a pause. If you're returning from Rapazzini Winery, cruise along Monterey Street for a look at some of the old brickfronts; many are being refurbished. Particularly appealing is the delightful brick and cut stone 1905 **Gilroy City Hall** at Monterey and Sixth, with an ornate façade and fantasyland clock tower. It's now a restaurant (listed below). For still more garlic fare, pause at the **Garlic Festival Store and Gallery,** 7526 Monterey at Fifth; (408) 842-1625. Note the garlic mural on its side.

Neighborhoods near downtown have some fine old Victorian and early American homes. For a good selection, cruise along Eigleberry Street, a block west of and parallel to Monterey. The numbered streets through here also have some nice examples of old fashioned homes. To learn more about Gilroy, stop at the Chamber of Commerce at 7471 Monterey Street near Fourth or the Gilroy Visitors Bureau at 7780 Monterey, at IOOF Street between Second and Third.

Since this area is cradled between two mountain ranges, forests and their attendant hiking trails, campgrounds and picnic areas are but a short drive away. Pressing beyond the wineries on Highway 152, you'll climb Hecker Pass Highway into pine and redwood country. Near the pass is **Mount Madonna County Park** with beautiful redwood groves, camping, picnicking and hiking trails. It is, incidentally, one of the prettier mountain parks in northern California, and it's rarely crowded. Just beyond is **Mount Madonna Inn** (see dining listing below), a longtime landmark offering impressive views to the west. From here, you tumble down to Watsonville and—take your pick—the coastal resort communities of Santa Cruz to the north or Monterey to the south.

Heading inland on Route 152, you climb wooded **Pacheco Pass**, which takes you into the broad San Joaquin Valley. En route, you might like to pause at **Casa De Fruta**. Continue down to **San Luis Reservoir,** with boating, swimming, picnicking and birdwatching.

If you like wilderness areas, head east from Gilroy on Leavesley Road, following signs toward **Henry W. Coe State Park**. It's mostly undeveloped, with hiking trails and primitive camping. Once famous **Gilroy Hot Springs**, near the park entrance, is being restored to its former glory.

South Santa Clara County activities

Family parks • Casa de Fruta, 10031 Pacheco Pass Hwy., Hollister, CA 95023; (408) 842-9316. Gift shop, wine and cheese tasting, small zoo, ball fields, train ride, RV park and motel (wine tasting listed above). Hecker Pass Family Adventure, 3050 Hecker Pass Hwy., Gilroy, CA 95020; (408) 842-2121. Call for hours; admission fee. Train ride, zoo, water park, restaurant and such. Family amusement center slated for mid-1990s; under construction and open only to groups at press time.

Farm products • *Country Crossroads* map lists farms and wineries selling directly to the public. Available at farm and winery members or send a stamped, self-addressed business-sized envelope to: Country Crossroads, 136 N. Fourth St., San Jose, CA 95112; or 141 Monte Vista Ave., Watsonville, CA 95076.

Garlic shops • Garlic World, 4800 Monterey Hwy. (U.S. 101), Gilroy; (800) 537-6122 or (408) 847-2251. Garlic laced specialty foods, garlic souvenirs and a fruit and produce section. The Garlic Shoppé, 4350 Highway 101, Gilroy; 848-3646. Similar offerings as Garlic World. Garlic Festival Store and Gallery, 7526 Monterey at Fifth; (408) 842-1625. Garlic souvenirs, containers, garlic-based foods, cookbooks, plus other specialty foods.

Attractions

Gilroy Historical Museum • In the old Carnegie Library building at Fifth and Church Streets, Gilroy; (408) 848-0470. Open Monday-Friday 9 to 5 and some Saturdays 11 to 3. Early-day history exhibits, focusing on agriculture, wine and of course the garlic industry.

Goldsmith Seeds • In the wine country at 2280 Hecker Pass Highway; (408) 847-7333. Brilliant floral blooms, some in spectacular patterns during the May through August blooming season. Self-guided tours daily from dawn to dusk and guided group tours by appointment; call for details.

WINE COUNTRY DINING

Harvest Time • ☆☆☆ $$$

◻ *7397 Monterey St. (Sixth Street), Gilroy: (408) 842-7575. California-continental; full bar service. Lunch Monday-Saturday 11:30 to 3; dinner Monday-Thursday 4:30 to 9, Friday-Saturday 4:30 to 10 and Sunday 5 to 9. MC/VISA.* ◻ Stylish Victorian restaurant featuring local veggies—and garlic specialties, of course—from co-owner Don Christopher's ranch. Typical entrées are steak and mushrooms, sautéed chicken breast with mushrooms in wine and lemon sauce, veal and artichokes and egg-dipped calamari steak with lemon and tarter sauce. Patio service on weekends.

Mount Madonna Inn • ☆☆ $$ Y

◻ *1285 Hecker Pass Hwy., Watsonville; (408) 724-2275. American; full bar service. Lunch Friday-Sunday 11:30 to 3, Sunday brunch 10 to 3; dinner Thursday- Saturday 4 to 10 and Sunday 3 to 9. Major credit cards.* ◻ Long popular inn perched atop Hecker Pass, offering far-away views. Nights sparkle with the twinkle of a dozen cities. The menu ranges from pastas to assorted steaks, veal, chicken and seafood.

Old City Hall Restaurant • ☆☆ $$

◻ *7400 Monterey at Fifth, Gilroy; (408) 847-HALL. American-Italian; wine and beer. Lunch 11:30 to 2, dinner Tuesday-Saturday 5:30 to 8, Sunday brunch 10 to 2. Major credit cards.* ◻ The elaborate 1905 former city hall has been shaped into a restaurant that fits the period, with bentwood furniture, a Wurlitzer jukebox and an old fire department hose cart. Menu items include prime rib, Cajun red snapper, sautéed calamari and several Italian style veal dishes and pastas including—*naturellement*—garlic pasta primavera.

Station 55 Bar & Grill • ☆☆☆ $$

◻ *55 W. Fifth St.. Gilroy; (408) 847-5555. American; full bar service. Lunch Monday-Saturday 11 to 4:30, dinner Sunday-Thursday 4:30 to 9 and*

Friday-Saturday 4:30 to 10. Major credit cards. ☐ Appealing restaurant housed in an old brickfront fire station, dressed up in antique-modern décor with burgundies and greens, and oak furniture. Entrées include campi sautéed in garlic of course, grilled salmon and blackened prime rib.

Tassos' Old House ● ☆☆☆ **$$**

☐ *383 First St., Gilroy; (408) 847-7527. Eclectic menu; wine and beer. Monday-Saturday 11 to 10, Sunday 10 to 10. Major credit cards.* ☐ Busily decorated early American style restaurant in an old white clapboard house with an equally busy menu. It dances from Greek to American to Italian fare; from spiced lamb shank to pasta to basic steaks, chops and prime rib.

VINELAND LODGINGS

Best Western Inn ● ☆☆ **$$$** ∅

☐ *360 Leavesley Rd. (just off freeway), Gilroy, CA 95020; (800) 528-1234 or (408) 848-1467. Couples $48 to $62, singles $45 to $48; also larger family units. Major credit cards.* ☐ A 42-unit hotel with TV movies, room phones, refrigerators. Spa, pool, coin laundry.

Casa de Fruta Garden Motel ● ☆☆ **$$** ∅

☐ *10031 Pacheco Pass Hwy., Hollister, CA 95023; (408) 548-3813. Couples $55 to $59, singles $51 to $55; rates include continental breakfast. MC/VISA.* ☐ Country-style motel with TV, room phones and refrigerators; swimming pool. (Also see listing under "Family parks" above.)

Country Rose Inn Bed & Breakfast ● ☆☆☆ **$$$$** ∅

☐ *455 Fitzgerald Ave., Unit E (Monterey Road), San Martin (mailing address: P.O. Box 2500, Gilroy, CA 95021-2500); (408) 842-0441. Couples $89 to $169. Five rooms, all with private baths; full breakfast. MC/VISA, AMEX.* ☐ Restored Dutch Colonial home on landscaped grounds shaded by ancient oaks. Rooms are a nice blend of antique and modern décor. In a rural setting on the edge of San Martin.

Forest Park Inn ● ☆☆☆ **$$$** ∅

☐ *375 Leavesley Rd., Gilroy, CA 95020; (800) 237-7846 or (408) 848-5144. Couples $50 to $55, singles $38; also larger family units. Major credit cards.* ☐ Nicely-maintained 77-unit motel with TV movies, room phones, some refrigerators. Sauna, spa, pool. **Lyons Restaurant** serves American fare; open 24 hours; full bar service; non-smoking areas.

Sunrest Inn ● ☆☆☆ **$$** ∅

☐ *8292 Murray Ave., Gilroy, CA 95020; (408) 847-5500. Rooms $42.50 to $68.50. Major credit cards.* ☐ Attractive 65-unit motel with TV, fee movies, phones; some refrigerators and coffee makers. Pool, sauna, spa, laundry.

Super 8 Motel ● ☆☆ **$$** ∅

☐ *8435 San Ysidro (just off freeway), Gilroy, CA 95020; (800) 800-8000 or (408) 848-4108. Couples $40 to $49, singles $36 to $39, family units $41 to $53. Major credit cards.* ☐ A 53-unit motel with TV movies, room phones, some refrigerators. Continental breakfast, pool.

Southern Santa Clara Valley information sources

Gilroy Visitors Bureau, 7780 Monterey Rd., Gilroy, CA 95020; (408) 842-6436.

Morgan Hill Chamber of Commerce, 17875 Monterey Rd., Morgan Hill, CA 95037; (408) 779-9444.

"It lumbers rather than dances. Of marginal quality for a wine of this pedigree, but some may find its funkiness appealing."
— **Description of a Corton-Charlemagne white from Burgundy**

Chapter Nine
SANTA CRUZ COUNTY
Pinot in the pines

Santa Cruz County is one of the neatest little packages in California. In one small space, it offers miles of lonely beaches, miles of busy beaches, some remarkably charming little communities, an excellent university, silent redwood forests and some little jewels of wineries.

Although the county isn't far from the crowded San Francisco Bay Area, the thick wedge of the Santa Cruz Mountains keeps it relatively isolated. Fewer than 250,000 people live here and its largest city, Santa Cruz, numbers about 49,000. It's a popular tourist destination, although many visitors stay on Highway 101 and go shooting past, landing in easier-to-reach Monterey and Carmel.

The two are aquatic neighbors. Santa Cruz occupies the northern curve of huge Monterey Bay and Monterey has settled in the southern arch. This can cause confusion if you left your Boy Scout compass home and assume the ocean is west. Much of coastal Santa Cruz County faces south.

Because of its sheltered southward position, the popular Santa Cruz seaside resort is often fog-free while Monterey is veiled in the mists. Expect the beaches to be cheek-to-cheek bikinis on a summer weekend. You'd best stay to the high ground if you want to avoid Coney Island West.

Which is just fine, because the higher reaches of the county are where you'll discover most of the wineries and all of the vineyards. If you've come here looking for beaches and tawny young women and rustic piers and a great old art deco fun zone called the Santa Cruz Beach Boardwalk, you're in the the the right place but the wrong guidebook. Pick up a copy of our ***Northern California Discovery Guide.***

The sheltering mountains spared this area from much of California's tumultuous history. The Spanish, waving their crosses and crossbows, did take

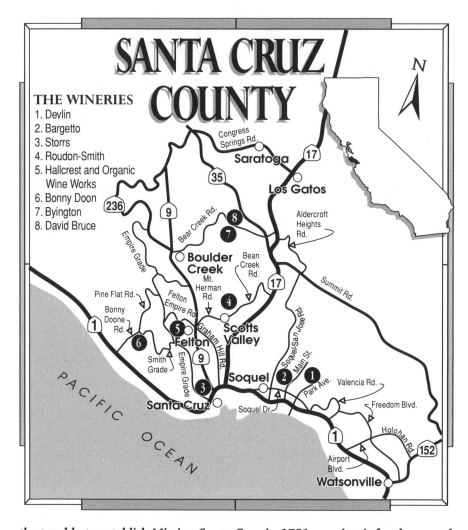

SANTA CRUZ COUNTY

N

THE WINERIES
1. Devlin
2. Bargetto
3. Storrs
4. Roudon-Smith
5. Hallcrest and Organic Wine Works
6. Bonny Doon
7. Byington
8. David Bruce

Congress Springs Rd.
Saratoga
17
35
Los Gatos
236
9
Aldercroft Heights Rd.
Bear Creek Rd.
8
7
Empire Grade
Boulder Creek
Bean Creek Rd.
Mt. Herman Rd.
17
Summit Rd.
Pine Flat Rd.
Felton Empire Rd.
4
Bonny Doone Rd.
1
5
Graham Hill Rd.
Soquel-San Jose Rd.
6
Scotts Valley
Felton
9
Smith Grade
Empire Grade
Main St.
Soquel
2
1
Park Ave.
Valencia Rd.
3
Santa Cruz
Soquel Dr.
Freedom Blvd.
1
Holohan Rd.
152
Airport Blvd.
Watsonville

P A C I F I C   O C E A N

the trouble to establish Mission Santa Cruz in 1791, naming it for the sacred cross. It didn't fare well, despite its access to fertile river delta croplands just to the south. Although it was out of the mainstream of Spanish California politics, it did have its own special set of troubles. A civil community populated with misfits and former convict was established nearby, and the unruly neighbors began harassing the padres and their Indian converts. In 1818, a pirate ship appeared offshore and the fathers fled inland to the mission at Soledad. The pirates didn't attack but during the padres' absence, members of the convict settlement pillaged and vandalized the mission. It never recovered. When Mexico took California from Spain and began closing the missions a few years later, Santa Cruz was among the first to go.

Americans came during and after the 1849 gold rush and did their best to rid the Santa Cruz Mountains of redwoods. That was the lumber of choice for booming San Francisco to the north. Fortunately, they missed a few and several stands are now preserved in large parks.

When California joined the Union, gringo farmers began clearing the flood plain around present-day Watsonville and vintners sought suitable vineyard sites in the mountains. Commercial winemaking began in 1863 but it never was a major enterprise. All of the county's small wineries perished during Prohibition.

One of the first to crop up after Repeal was Bargetto Winery in Soquel. It's alive and well, still run by Bargetto descendants. It had few immediate followers, however. Only three wineries were functioning by the 1960s. Then the wine boom of the '70s encouraged several solitude-seeking entrepreneurs to carve out vineyards in the steep slopes of the Santa Cruz Mountains. These heights offer cool micro-climates suited to Pinot Noir, Cabernet Sauvignon, Chardonnay, Gewürztraminer and Johannisberg Riesling. Today, nearly 40 wineries are tucked into these hills, although only a few have tasting rooms that keep regular hours.

Most Santa Cruz area wineries are small and virtually all are family owned, producing only a few thousand cases a year. They probably spill more wine than that at Gallo.

SANTA CRUZ COUNTY WINERY TOUR ● You have to work to tour the county's wineries, since most are scattered among the trees. But it's nice work, taking you to the coastal resort of Santa Cruz, then high into its namesake mountains. Further, you'll discover some exceptional wines. If possible, plan this outing for a weekend, since many of the wineries have limited weekday hours.

Pay attention now, because the mountain portion involves a lot of twisting and turning.

Since we left you in Gilroy in the last chapter, you may want to come on down by following Hecker Pass over the Mount Madonna ridge to **Watsonville**. To save a few miles after you've topped the pass and reached level ground, watch for a right turn onto Holohan Road at a sign indicating Santa Cruz. This bypasses the main part of Watsonville and hits Highway 1 farther north. You're traveling through the Pajaro River Delta—rich farming country and one of the few level areas in the county.

Pick up Highway 1 in Watsonville and head north past artichoke stands, through Aptos to **Capitola** and **Soquel**. The two small towns flank Highway 1, which is a freeway at this point. Take the Capitola/Park Avenue exit and follow Park Avenue north into the hills. The route quickly clears the suburban edge of Soquel and becomes a narrow lane, climbing steeply into wooded slopes. After less than a mile, swing left, pass through a gate and wind up in someone's yard. Fortunately, it's the **Devlins'** yard, and they operate a winery here. (Small Devlin Winery signs will keep you on course.)

Come back down Park Avenue (there's no alternative) and take a right onto Soquel Avenue at a stoplight, just short of the freeway. Drive north for less than a mile and turn right again onto Main Street (at a Unocal service station). This takes you to **Bargetto Winery,** just a few blocks up on your left. Retrace your route on Main Street; cross Soquel Avenue and stay aboard until Main curves into Porter Street. Go left, then quickly right and you're back on the freeway. Continue into **Santa Cruz,** staying to the left on Highway 1 at the Freeway 17 interchange. You'll sweep into a wide right-hand cloverleaf, then hit a stoplight at freeway's end.

This is River Street; turn left, then slant right onto Potrero Street after about three blocks. Within a block, you'll see a light industrial and shopping complex called **The Old Sash Mill.** Take the second right into the facility and you've found **Storrs Winery.**

From here, we offer two choices. If it's Saturday (the only day the next winery is open to the public), or if you'd like a scenic diversion, backtrack to Highway 17 and follow it about three miles north, then take the Mount Hermon Road exit into **Scotts Valley**. This hamlet sits on the edge of the wooded ramparts of the Santa Cruz Mountains. It's a pleasant region, interlaced with winding, redwood-canopied lanes. Don't expect a wilderness, however. Chalet-style homes, mountain lodges and RV parks poke through the trees every mile or so, but it's still a far cry from downtown Des Moines. Fork right onto Scotts Valley Road then after a block, turn left onto Bean Creek Road. A twisting two miles up Bean Creek takes you to **Roudon-Smith Vineyards,** on the left. Watch for the sign, which is quite small. Now, return to Scotts Valley and follow Mount Hermon Road to **Felton**.

If choose to bypass Scotts Valley and Roudon-Smith, simply follow River Street north into the mountains from Santa Cruz; it becomes State Highway 9 and takes you to Felton. This village of 5,000, scattered among the trees, still shows traces of its 1960s role as a hippie haven. However, boutiques now outnumber health food stores. At a stoplight, turn left onto Felton Empire Road. (If you're coming from Scotts Valley, Mount Hermon Road blends into Felton Empire at that signal.) After a quarter of a mile, you'll see **Hallcrest Vineyards** on your left. To reach the winery, drive through a residential parking area and drop downhill toward a vineyard.

From here, continue west on Felton-Empire, winding steeply upward. This is mostly mountainous woodland, but an occasional small vineyard will remind you of your purpose. After about three miles, you hit a stop sign at Empire Grade. Continue forward onto Ice Cream Grade and follow it about 2.5 miles until it deadends into Pine Flat Road. You're now in the hamlet of **Bonny Doon,** although you wouldn't know it. It's not a town with a business district, but a collection of hideaway homes tucked among the trees. Go left onto Pine Flat and follow it to its junction with Bonny Doon Road. **Bonny Doon Winery** is on your left, opposite the junction.

Our next destination is Boulder Creek. If you have a detailed map, you'll note that several roads wander vaguely in that direction. Some are startlingly steep and winding. For simplicity's sake, we'll return to Felton and press northward on Highway 9.

Once you pass **Ben Lomond** and achieve tree-sheltered **Boulder Creek**, drive through its small business district, then turn right onto Bear Creek Road. After what seems an eternity of winding, you see the striking château of **Byington Winery** on the right. It's about six miles from Boulder Creek. Half a mile beyond, on the left, is **David Bruce Winery,** terraced into a steep slope.

If you yen now for the flatlands, the quickest escape—albeit a twisting one—is to continue on Bear Creek Road, which winds down to Freeway 17 just south of Los Gatos.

WINERY CODES • *T* = Tasting with no fee; *T$* = Tasting for a fee; *GT* = Guided tours; *GTA* = Guided tours by appointment; *ST* = Self-guiding tours; *CT* = casual tours or a peek into the winery; ✕ = picnic area; 🎁 = Gift shop or good giftware selection. Price ranges listed in tasting notes are for varietals; jug wines may be available for less.

Devlin Wine Cellars ● T ✕

☐ *3801 Park Ave. (P.O. Box 728), Soquel, CA 95073; (408) 476-7288. Weekends noon to 5, MC/VISA. Most varieties tasted. Some wine logo gift items. Lawn picnic area.* ☐

Many California wines win sweepstakes awards, and some have the honor of being served to the President. But few small, new wineries reach these heights. U.C. Davis graduate Chuck Devlin and his wife Cheryl started their winery on a Soquel hilltop in 1978. They've since gathered a remarkable collection of major awards and their wines were among those selected to accompany former President Reagan on his China tour.

The Devlins' facility occupies a lofty hilltop perch. Wines are tasted in a small cottage beside their attractive but modest country home; the winery is just up the hill a bit. The front lawn serves as a picnic area, with a fine view down the valley.

Tasting notes: Devlin's prices are remarkably reasonable for such quality: $5 to $9.50. A four-year-old Beauregard Ranch Zinfandel had a nice spicy-berry nose, a pronounced raspberry flavor and light tannin finish. An award-winning six-year-old Central Coast Merlot was subtly dusky, complex and delicious, with a touch of oak. A three-year-old Chardonnay had a light floral nose, spicy and crisp flavor with soft tannins. The Devlins also do a Sauvignon Blanc, Chenin Blanc, Cabernet Sauvignon, Muscat Canelli, Gamay Beaujolais, a sparkling wine, Zinfandel and white Zinfandel.

Vintners choice: "Merlot and Cabernet; we've won sweepstakes for both," says Chuck.

Bargetto Winery ● T GT 🏠

☐ *3535 Main St., Soquel, CA 95703; (408) 475-2258. Tasting room also located on Cannery Row in Monterey. Monday-Saturday 9:30 to 5, Sunday 11 to 5; MC/VISA. Most varieties tasted. Good wine logo, gift and wine book selection. Tours daily at 11 a.m. and 2 p.m.* ☐

The Bargetto winery's neat and trim shingled structures appear to occupy a residential area. Step inside the tasting room, however, and you'll discover that the winery's backside borders the attractively wooded bank of Soquel Creek. The buildings shelter a cozy creekside courtyard, often used for art exhibits and sometimes as a tasting area. Visitors enter through a nicely-done gift shop and sales room, then step down to the handsome creek-bank tasting room. It's trimmed in barnwood and decorated with vintage winemaking tools. A large window offers creek views.

Philip and John Bargetto established the winery in 1933; John's son Lawrence and his family run things today.

Tasting notes: The Bargettos earned an early reputation for tasty yet light fruit wines and they still produce them. However, fine medium-bodied varietals are at the forefront of the list today. Our wines of choice were a dry and fruity Gewürztraminer, a spicy and light Central Coast Cypress Chardonnay and a three-year-old Central Coast Cypress Cabernet, with a nice spicy-oaky nose and medium rich berry taste. Several Cabs are on the list, along with Sauvignon Blanc, Gamay, white Zinfandel, Pinot Noir and a sparkling Brut. Fruit wines are raspberry (our favorite), olallieberry, apricot and Mead. A late harvest Riesling dessert wine was so rich it didn't need an accompaniment; it *was* dessert. Prices range from $6 into the middle teens; most current release varietals are under $10.

Vintners choice: "Our specialties are Santa Cruz Mountains Chardonnay, Cabernet and our fruit wines," says Beverly Bargetto.

Storrs Winery • T CT

◻ *303 Potrero St. (in the Old Sash Mill, #35), Santa Cruz, CA 95060; (408) 458-5030. Open Friday-Monday, noon to 5; major credit cards. Most varieties tasted. Informal tours on request.* ◻

Your first impression is that you've found one of those shopping center tasting rooms divorced from the main facility. However, Stephen or Pamela Storrs will happily show you their busy little winery. It's tucked into warehouse space behind the snug tasting room and spilling into a rear drive. Creatively cluttered, it's a marvel of compactness.

This is a husband-and-wife operation from crush to bottling; both are U.C. Davis graduates in enology and viticulture. They started their winery in 1988 to create Santa Cruz Mountain varietals. And create they have; the small 5,000-case winery has won an impressive array of awards.

Tasting notes: The Storrs specialize in *les méthodes anciennes,* classic European style winemaking, utilizing barrel fermenting and *sur lie* aging. The result: full-flavored wines with soft touches of oak. They focus on Chardonnays and the spicy, crisp Vanamanutagi Vineyards selection we tasted was exceptional. We also favored their lush and honey-like white Riesling and a soft Rhône-style San Miguel Petit Sirah with subtle tannins and wood. Prices range from $9 to $20.

Vintners choice: "Our Santa Cruz Mountains Chardonnays—filled with aromas of fruit and toasty oak," says Pamela. "We create four different vineyard-designated varieties."

Roudon-Smith Vineyards • T CT ✕

◻ *2364 Bean Creek Rd., Santa Cruz, CA 95066; (408) 438-1244. Saturday 11 to 4:30, Sunday by appointment; MC/VISA. Selected wines tasted. Small picnic area; informal tours.* ◻

This trim little wooden winery near Scotts Valley is tucked into a slope, encircled by sheltering trees. It's a bit hard to spot because of those trees and because of its small sign, so be watchful. It's probably best to call and get directions. Further, because it's a family operation, it may be closed on occasional weekends.

The double-joined name comes from Bob and Annamaria Roudon and Jim and June Smith. They started their small winery elsewhere in 1972 and settled here six years later. Production is about 10,000 cases.

Tasting notes: We especially liked the big, spicy reds, which the Roudon-Smiths let rest a few years before release. A four-year-old Santa Cruz Mountains Pinot Noir exhibited a nice berry nose and complex flavor. Of the whites, we tilted toward a nutty-silky five-year-old Santa Cruz Mountains Estate Chardonnay. Others on the list are Gewürztraminer, Petite Sirah and Zinfandel. Prices range from $8.85 to the mid teens, less for table winess.

Vintners choice: "Estate grown Chardonnay and Santa Cruz Mountains Pinot Noir," says Jim Smith. "And we add a touch of Chardonnay to our Petite Sirah to soften the tannins and add finesse to the wine."

Hallcrest Vineyards • T GTA ✕

◻ *379 Felton Empire Rd., Felton, CA 95018; (408) 335-4441. Daily 11 to 5:30; MC/VISA, AMEX. Most varieties tasted. A few wine logo and picnic items. Nice picnic area with a view of Felton.* ◻

The casually arrayed but neat buildings of Hallcrest occupy a wooded slope just above the town. A Riesling vineyard adds authenticity to the setting. The tasting room is a deliberately cute cottage with a schoolhouse-style bell tower. A grassy picnic area is just below; it's shaded by a huge gnarled oak right out of the forest scene from *Snow White*.

Hallcrest's career started in 1941 when it was established by Chaffe Hall. It functioned as Felton-Empire Winery in the late 1970s. Then, John and Lorraine Schumacher and John's sister Shirin bought the facility in 1987 and restored the original name. A U.C. Davis grad, John has been making wines since he fiddled with fermenting fruit from the family orchard as a teenager.

Tasting notes: The winery produces two lines, one under the Hallcrest Vineyards label and the other under Organic Wine Works. As you'll guess, the latter is made from organically grown grapes, and no sulfites or other preservatives are used in the production. They have a distinctive earthy taste and are becoming quite popular. We sampled a full flavored, herbal Semillion, a remarkably full flavored Grenache Rosé (remarkable because we don't

AN INFORMAL TOUR

care for pink wines) and an excellent big-bodied yet smooth Zinfandel. Others on the organic list are Fumé Blanc, Chardonnay, Pinot Noir, Merlot, Petite Sirah and a red blend called *Notre Terre*—appropriate since it means "To our earth." On the Hallcrest side are the usual varietals, all well prepared and quite tasty. Notables were a spicy-berry young Zinfandel and a rich, complex and gently tannic Cabernet Sauvignon. Prices range from $7.50 to the low teens for the organics and $8.50 to the early twenties for the Hallcrest line.

Vintners choice: "Hallcrest White Riesling, Cabernet Sauvignon and *Clos de Jeannine* red table wine that has won many medals," says Lorraine.

Bonny Doon Vineyard ● T GTA ✗

☐ *10 Pine Flat Rd., Bonny Doon; Mailing address: P.O. Box 8376, Santa Cruz, CA 95061; (408) 425-3625. Open noon to 5, daily from mid-April to mid-September, closed Tuesdays the rest of the year; MC/VISA, AMEX. Most varieties tasted. Wine logo gift items. Picnic area. Informal guided tours by appointment.* ☐

As long as you're making serious wine, you might as well have fun with the names. That appears to be the philosophy of Randall Grahm, owner of Bonny Doon Vineyard, whose blended wines have names such as Big House Red, *Vin de Glaciéres* (serve chilled), *Cigare Volant*, *Il Fiasco* and *Il Pescatore*, which goes well with fish. (*Fiasco* isn't funny if you're Italian, since it simply means flask.) His newsletters are both erudite and off the wall. A recent one bore the words to Grahm's "opera"—*Don Giovese in Bakersfield*, sort of an ode to Grignolino.

These serious wines with interesting names are tasted in a funkily pleasant wooden cottage at roadside in the Bonny Doon forest. The winery and a scatter of tree-shaded picnic tables are just upslope. The tasting room's best feature, in addition to its wines, of course—is its T-shirt collection. Many memorable Grahm labels have been captured for torso display.

Tasting notes: Behind Grahm's creative labels are several Italian varietals such as Malvasia, Sangiovese and Moscato, plus an assortment of creative blends. We found them to be excellent, for the most part. Prices are all over the court—$6.50 to $20. He also does fruit wines. *Vin Gris de Cigare* is a Rhône blend of Grenache, Pinot Noir and Mourvèdre and Pinot, a pink with more character and fruit than most blushers. We took heavily, perhaps too heavily, to *Clos De Gilroy*, a fruity and spicy Grenache that, says Grahm, is "exceptionally well suited to heavily garlicked preparations." Also on the list are several fruit wines and an Italian Grappa. Unfortunately, Bonny Doon no longer produces Chardonnay, so you'll miss this quote from an earlier tasting sheet: "There is a beautiful floral and tropical component to the wine buttressed by a rich, buttery nuance that makes it popular with *todo el mundo* and permits us to charge big bucks."

Vintners choice: "We specialize in Rhône style wines made from northern and central coastal California grapes and Italian varietals," says tasting room manager Sandra Mast.

Byington Winery and Vineyard ● T GTA ✗ 📸

☐ *21850 Bear Creek Rd., Los Gatos, CA 95030; (408) 354-1111. Daily 11 to 5; MC/VISA. Most varieties tasted. Giftware selection, mostly wine logo items. View picnic area with barbecue; tours by appointment.* ☐

Prepare for a double-take. After visiting quaint, prim and funky family wineries of Santa Cruz, you'll be pleasantly startled by the Italianate château

of Bill Byington. Tile-roofed and multi-gabled, it's the county's most imposing winery, occupying carefully-groomed grounds in a wooded knoll, amidst
young vineyards. The tasting room is a high-ceiling elegant space with tiled
floors and arched windows.

Tours, by appointment, take you into the cutting-edge winery and upstairs to opulent meeting and entertainment rooms, often the scene of weddings and other events. Views from the winery grounds are awesome, over
redwood forests to Monterey Bay and the Pacific. They're yours if you opt for
a picnic; the winery staff will even provide charcoal and a barbecue pit.

Byington, owner of the West Coast's largest steel treatment plant, bought
the land here in 1962, began producing wine in 1974, and completed his impressive facility in 1990. His winemaker is Alan Phillips, a U.C. Davis grad
and veteran of a score of harvests.

Tasting notes: The Byington list is short and selective: Fumé Blanc,
Gewürztraminer, Chardonnay, Cabernet and Pinot Noir. Phillips also produces white and red table wines and a sparkling wine. We favored the herbal
nose and spicy flavor of a San Luis Obispo Fumé Blanc and a complex, nutty
Santa Cruz Mountain Chardonnay. A Napa Valley Cabernet Sauvignon was
properly peppery, medium bodied and quite tasty. Prices range from $7.65 to
the middle teens.

David Bruce Winery • T ✕

⌂ 21439 Bear Creek Rd., Los Gatos, CA 95030; (408) 354-4212. Thursday-Sunday noon to 5; MC/VISA. All varieties tasted. Picnic area on a grassy
shelf overlooking the mountains. ⌂

Dr. David Bruce, noted for his medal-winning wines and no-nonsense approach to winemaking, has constructed a facility that matches his attitude.
The winery is a no-frills affair, where visitor amenities are secondary to wine
production. Tasting room décor consists of stacked boxes of wine; plain walls
exhibit the medals they've won. Classical music issues from a boom box stuck
in a corner. One thing *is* visually impressive: The winery is terraced into
steep slopes, surrounded by trees and its own vineyards, with views to the
far-away bay.

Bruce, a physician, was among the first new-generation Santa Cruz winemakers. He started his hillside facility in 1964 and gradually built it up to its
present output of 30,000 cases a year. "My life-long dream has been to concentrate on the wines of the Santa Cruz Mountains," he said. "We're on the
cool Chardonnay-Pinot Noir side of the hills and we focus with a vengeance
on these varietals."

Tasting notes: It is thus no surprise that Bruce's three single vineyard
Chardonnays—silky, lush and toasty—have won numerous medals; and the
San Francisco Vintner's Club selected his beautifully herbacious Estate Pinot
Noir as the best in America. He balances his list with five "flatlander" varie-
tals—Chardonnay, Pinot Noir, Cabernet Sauvignon, Zinfandel and Petite
Sirah. Prices range from $8.50 to $30.

THE BEST OF THE BUNCH

The best wine buys • Devlin Wine Cellars and Bargetto Winery.

The most attractive winery • Byington Winery.

The most interesting tasting rooms • Bargetto Winery and Byington
Winery.

The funkiest tasting rooms • Storrs Winery and Bonny Doon Vineyard.

The best gift shop • Bargetto Winery and Bonny Doon Vineyard (wine label T-shirts).

The nicest picnic areas • Devlin Wine Cellars, Hallcrest Vineyards, Byington Winery and David Bruce Winery.

The best tour • Bargetto Winery (guided).

Wineland activities and such

Wineland events • Santa Cruz County Vintners Festival, late June, (408) 479-WINE; Passport Saturday, with "passport" tickets to wine and foods at various wineries, late July, (408) 479-WINE; Capitola Art & Wine Festival, mid-September, 688-7377; Santa Cruz County Fair in mid-September, with a winegrowers booth and tastings, 425-1234; Wine & Roses benefit tasting for the Watsonville Community Hospital in the fall, (408) 724-3900.

Winery touring map • *Fine Wines of Santa Cruz* map/brochure, available at wineries and visitors bureaus or contact: Santa Cruz Mountains Winegrowers Assn., P.O. Box 3000, Santa Cruz, CA 95063; (408) 479-WINE.

BEYOND THE VINEYARDS

It's tempting to suggest that wine is the tip of the tail that wags Santa Cruz County's tourism dog. As we have seen, the area shelters some neat little wineries, but most folks come for the beaches and redwood forests. For more details on Santa Cruz County, pick up a copy of our *Northern California Discovery Guide*, available at bookstores everywhere, or it can be ordered directly from the source; see the back of this book.

Your trek to the wineries has taken you through its forested mountains. We'll now suggest a route that exposes its coastal lures. Begin at a familiar place—River Street and Highway 1. Drive south on River Street through the heart of Santa Cruz. You'll pass **Pacific Garden Mall,** devastated by the 1989 Loma Prieta earthquake and now mostly rebuilt, with a nice assortment of boutiques and restaurants.

River Street changes to Front Street and takes you to the primary Santa Cruz attractions—the **Municipal Wharf,** the **Beach Boardwalk** and of course, the beach. Head eastward from here (remembering that it's a south-facing beach), staying close to the shoreline. Follow Beach Street which turns into Riverside Avenue and swings inland, then turn right onto **East Cliff Drive**. This will keep you tucked close to the shore for the most part. You'll see fine old beachfront homes, lots of sand and seagulls and an occasional sea lion.

With luck, you'll reach **Capitola,** a cute little town of cliff-perched Victorian homes and beachside boutiques. A pedestrian path along Soquel Creek is quite pleasant. Park Avenue will return you to U.S. 1 freeway. From here, with the aid of a local map, you can work southwestward, dipping down to the bayfront where streets permit. An assortment of state and local beaches invite sunning and surf-sloshing.

If you prefer more beach and less congestion, go west (eventually north) on Highway 1 from our River Street starting point. (You might want to divert to the right onto Bay Street and follow signs to the forested campus of the **University of California at Santa Cruz.**) Back on U.S. 1, continue along the oceanfront, taking time for a stop at **Natural Bridges State Beach.** Other beaches will crop up frequently as you follow this relatively unspoiled coastal stretch toward San Mateo County.

Santa Cruz vineyard area attractions

Farm products ● Farms and wineries selling directly to the public are listed in Country Crossroads. It's available at farm and winery members or send a stamped, self-addressed business-sized envelope to: Country Crossroads, Santa Cruz County Farm Bureau, 600 Main St., Watsonville, CA 95076; (408) 724-1356.

Mystery Spot ● 1953 N. Branciforte Dr., Santa Cruz; (408) 423-8897. Daily 9:30 to 4:30; admission fee. It's one of those magnetic field places where folks seem to tilt at odd angles.

Redwood and other state parks ● **Big Basin Redwoods State Park,** north of Boulder Creek; (408) 338-6132; entrance fee. Camping, hiking and picnicking. **Henry Cowell Redwoods State Park,** off Graham Hill road near Felton; (408) 335-4598; entrance fee. Camping, hiking, picnicking, restaurant, snack bar and curio shop. **Forest of Nisene Marks**, Aptos Creek Road, Aptos; (408) 335-4598; no fee. Wilderness park with hiking and biking trails. **Wilder Ranch State Park,** 1401 Coast Rd., Santa Cruz; (408) 688-3241; entrance fee. Restored turn-of-the-century ranch.

Roaring Camp & Big Trees Railroad ● Graham Hill Road, Felton; (408) 335-4400. Various hours; admission fee. Steam train rides through the redwoods; also site of the Felton Covered Bridge.

Santa Cruz Beach Boardwalk ● At the beachfront; (408) 423-5590. Opens at 11 a.m. daily in summer, on weekends and holidays only the rest of the year. Free admission; fees for rides. Nicely restored old fashioned amusement park, one of the few beachfront fun zones left in America.

Santa Cruz Municipal Wharf ● Beach Street, Santa Cruz; (408) 429-3628. Busy, rustic wharf with restaurants, seafood shops and such.

Santa Cruz County information sources

The county offers scores of places to eat, sleep, swim, surf and play. The Conference and Visitors Council will happily provide you with pounds of information. Ask specifically for the *Santa Cruz County Visitor Guide, Accommodations Guide* and *Dining Guide.*

Santa Cruz Conference and Visitors Council, 701 Front St., Santa Cruz, CA 95060; (408) 425-1234.

For south county information, contact the **Watsonville Chamber of Commerce,** 318 Main St. (P.O. Box 470), Watsonville, CA 95076; (408) 724-3900.

"Assertive, tannic and flavorful, with weedy dill and slight menthol aromas and flavors that compete with the modest currant note."
— Description of a Joullian Carmel Valley Cabernet Sauvignon

Chapter Ten
MONTEREY COUNTY
Sun-soaked vines in Steinbeck Country

Noted primarily for tourism, Steinbeck novels and golf tournaments, Monterey County has a vineyard surprise. It contains nearly 30,000 acres of premium wine grapes, more than any California county except Napa and Sonoma.

They aren't all that evident. The visitor will find no great gathering of wineries, and the only concentration of tasting rooms is in that mother of all tourist traps, Cannery Row.

So, where's the grapes? Most are in the cool, flat and wind-brushed Salinas Valley below Salinas. A drive south on Highway 101 won't reveal many vines, although this is one of California's major agricultural areas. Grapes prefer the good drainage offered by slopes, so many of the vineyards are coved into the benchlands of the Gavilan Mountains to the east and the Santa Lucia section of the Coast Range to the west. A few vines also grow in the Carmel Valley, inland from Carmel.

Monterey County is rich with the lore of early California. However, it had nothing to do with wine, other than the usual mission grapes stomped by the padres for sacramental sipping. Father Junipero Serra started California's second mission near Carmel in 1770, and it served for decades as headquarters for the 21-mission chain. The only record of early grape planting was at Mission Soledad, established in the Salinas Valley in 1791. No trace of those vineyard remain.

It wasn't until 1960 that the Salinas Valley was seriously regarded as a premium wine producing area. Until then, it was thought to be too dry and windy. Aided by researchers from the University of California at Davis, growers solved the wind problem by planting grapes parallel to the prevailing breezes. Drilling proved that the Salinas Riverhad plenty of water, mostly un-

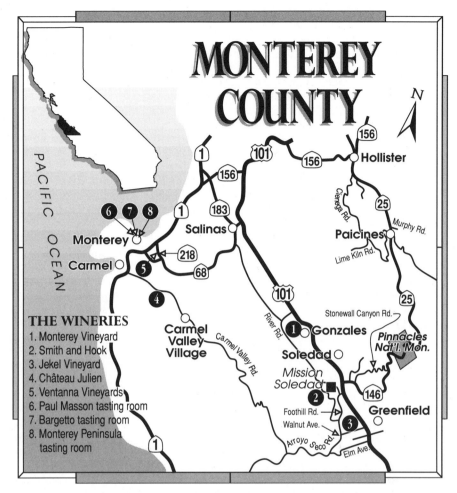

MONTEREY COUNTY

THE WINERIES
1. Monterey Vineyard
2. Smith and Hook
3. Jekel Vineyard
4. Château Julien
5. Ventanna Vineyards
6. Paul Masson tasting room
7. Bargetto tasting room
8. Monterey Peninsula
   tasting room

derground. This is a relatively cool area, kept that way by those winds, so it's ideal for whites, accounting for 75 percent of the plantings. Among those that thrive are Chardonnay (the most commonly planted variety), Sauvignon Blanc and Gewürztraminer. Cabernet Sauvignon is the most popular red; Zinfandel, Pinot Noir, Petite Sirah and Merlot are among its companions.

Despite its youth, this newcomer to the California wine world has won an impressive number of medals. Monterey County Chardonnays are particularly strong in competitions.

The first vintners were South Bay refugees such as the Wente, Mirassou, Alamden and Paul Masson, whose vines were being crowded out by subdivisions. Since they already had elaborate production facilities to the north, they planted grapes here but built no wineries. Monterey Vineyard was the first to build a large winery in the Salinas Valley. The doors to this attractive Spanish style winery and tasting room were opened in 1974.

MONTEREY COUNTY WINERY TOUR ● As we wrote this, only eight county vintners had tasting rooms that kept regular hours, and four of these are disconnecting from the wineries. The rest are in Monterey, which makes good business sense, since those areas attract hundreds of thousands of tourists a year—particularly Cannery Row.

Of the tasting rooms still married to their wineries, three are near U.S. Highway 101, south of Salinas. While this small number may not be worth a special trip from some great distance, it offers a nice diversion if you happen to be headed that way. Your tour thus begins somewhere on Highway 101, with your compass set for **Gonzales.**

A winery in Gonzales? Certainly.

Exit the freeway at Gloria Road just south of town, follow the frontage road north and you shortly arrive at the impressive structure of **The Monterey Vineyard.** From here, continue into Gonzales and turn left (west) onto Gonzales River Road. After 2.5 miles, you'll bump into River Road. Head south about six miles and fork to the right onto Foothill Road. Go another three miles, turn right and follow a road to **Smith and Hook,** cradled among vineyards in the Santa Lucia foothills.

Backtrack briefly on Foothill to Mission Road, turn right, follow it about a mile to Fort Romie Road and turn right again. You'll soon see the ruins of **Mission Soledad,** worth a brief perusal. Are you superstitious? It's interesting to note that this was the thirteenth California mission established, one of the least successful and one of the few that fell to complete ruin. Only fragments of adobe walls and a modern-day chapel mark this spot, now surrounded by farm fields.

From here, continue south on Fort Romie, following signs back to U.S. 101. Eight miles will fetch you into **Greenfield.** Ignore the first exit and take the second one right (west) onto Walnut Avenue and follow it a mile through vines and veggies to **Jekel Vineyard.**

You've now done the Salinas Valley vineyards. Four other tasting rooms are in or near Carmel and Monterey; they're easy to find once you're in the neighborhood. **Château Julien,** a winery still tied to its tasting facility, is about five miles inland from Carmel on Carmel Valley Road. Look for the castle-like structure on your right. (Pick up Carmel Valley Road from Highway 1.)

The **Ventana Vineyards** tasting room is at the junction of the Monterey-Salinas Highway (Route 68) and State Highway 218, about 2.5 miles from Highway 1 above Monterey. It's in the northwest corner of that junction, in a tree-sheltered fieldstone complex called the "Old Stone House," which contains a couple of other businesses.

The others are on Monterey's **Cannery Row**. We won't bother with driving instructions; just park and walk. If it's a weekend, get there early. Otherwise, you'll have trouble parking and you'll be lined up five deep at the tasting counters. **Paul Masson** and **Bargetto** tasting rooms are in an old pier piling cannery structure bearing a large "Paul Masson Museum" sign; it's opposite Steinbeck Plaza parking lot at Cannery Row and Prescott streets. From here, go one block up Prescott to Wave Street, turn right and walk a block to Irvin. **Monterey Peninsula Winery** tasting room is in an old Victorian cottage on your left.

WINERY CODES ● *T* = Tasting with no fee; *T$* = Tasting for a fee; *GT* = Guided tours; *GTA* = Guided tours by appointment; *ST* = Self-guiding tours; *CT* = casual tours or a peek into the winery; ✕ = picnic area; 🎁 = Gift shop or good giftware selection. Price ranges listed in tasting notes are for varietals; jug wines may be available for less.

The Monterey Vineyard • T GT ✕ 🍷

⊓ *800 S. Alta St. (P.O. Box 780), Gonzales, CA 93926; (408) 675-2316. Daily 10 to 5; major credit cards. Selected wines tasted. Good assortment of gifts, crystal, books and wine logo items and Ansel Adams photographic gallery. Frequent tours; landscaped picnic areas.* ⊓

The Monterey Vineyard's park-like facility is one of the most attractive in California's winelands. Geese glide along placid ponds, picnickers spread their fare on lawn tables and sippers sip in an opulent Spanish style tasting room. Tours depart frequently for close-ups of a state-of-the-art winery, in a Mediterranean-modern building.

A gallery features works of contemporary photographers and a permanent exhibit of Ansel Adams' black and white study, "Story of a Winery," which was commissioned by the Seagram Corporation in 1960. Most of the photos are of the Paul Masson winery. Why Paul? Because Seagrams Classics Wine Company owns the labels of both wineries (although not the physical properties).

Tasting notes: This is a fine place to sample Monterey County varietals because winemaker Phil Franscioni uses only local grapes. His list includes Johannisberg Riesling, Gewürztraminer, Chenin Blanc, Chardonnay, Cabernet Sauvignon, Gamay Beaujolais, Merlot and a brut sparkling wine. The Chardonnay and Chenin Blanc were full-bodied and complex with lots of fruit, and a five-year-old Cabernet was nicely mellowed, with hints of tannin still evident. The jug wines are quite good here. We especially liked the full flavor of Classic Red, a blend of Cab, Merlot and Pinot Noir. Prices are moderate, ranging from $6 to the late teens. Although Monterey Vineyard products are widely distributed, Johannisberg Riesling and Gewürztraminer are available only at the winery.

Smith and Hook • T CT ✕

⊓ *37700 Foothill Rd., Soledad, CA 93960; (408) 678-2132. Daily 11 to 4; MC/VISA. Most current releases tasted. A few wine logo items; picnic area.* ⊓

The Smith and Hook tasting room is particularly appealing, fashioned from an old redwood wine vat. The ranch-style winery sits in the Santa Lucia foothills, a refreshing escape from the flatlands of the Salinas Valley. You'll find no Smiths nor Hooks there today. The winery gets its name from owners of the former horse ranch that occupied this site. The Nicolaus Hahn family established the winery in 1979 and preserved much of the rustic look of the ranch.

Tasting notes: The Santa Lucia Highlands are warmer than the valley floor and thus ideal for reds. S&H has won scores of awards for its peppery, medium-bodied Cabernet Sauvignon and Cabernet Franc, among the best Monterey County reds we tasted. We also liked a three-year-old Merlot, so big and spicy it could have passed for a Cab. Heading the white side of the lis is a light, yet lush and fruity Chardonnay. Prices are moderate, ranging from $6 to the middle teens.

Jekel Vineyard • T GTA ✕

⊓ *40155 Walnut Ave. (P.O. Box 336), Greenfield, CA 93927; (408) 674-5522. Daily 10 to 5; MC/VISA. All varieties tasted. Picnic area beneath arbor; fair selection of wine related items. Tours by appointment.* ⊓

Upscale American Gothic might describe the trim, prosperous looking Jekel winery. The main facility is housed in a neat red barn with white trim.

The adjacent cheerful tasting room is sheltered by an arbor dripping with wisteria; an impressive array of medals add to the décor. All of this is accented by carefully tended landscaping. Surrounding vineyards complete this prim picture.

William and August Jekel built the winery in 1978, six years after planting their vineyards. It's now owned by a wine group that has expanded its vineyards and production.

Tasting notes: Chardonnay, a big award winner for Jekel, had a nice tropical fruit aroma and taste with an herbal accent. Pinot Noir was full flavored, with lots of berries and a pleasant hint of smokiness. Merlot, Cabernet Sauvignon and Riesling were all nicely crafted wines as well, displaying good varietal character. A soft and full flavored Meritage blend of Cabernet Franc, Petit Verdot and Malbec completes the list. Prices range from $6.50 to the middle teens.

Vintners choice: "The Sanctuary Estate reds are Jekel's pride and joy," says the winery's Dave Page. "In addition to the Merlot and Meritage, watch for limited releases of lesser known Bordeaux varieties."

Château Julien Winery • T GTA

⌑ *8940 Carmel Valley Rd. (P.O. Box 221775), Carmel, CA 93923; (408) 624-2600. Weekdays 8:30 to 5, weekends 11 to 5; MC/VISA, AMEX. Most varieties tasted. Wine oriented giftwares; guided tours at 10:30 and 2:30 weekdays by reservation.* ⌑

If King Arthur had yearned to make wine instead of fussing about Lancelot, he might have created Château Julien, a modern fairy castle set in affluent Carmel Valley. This Camelot is complete with a tower, but presumably no Repunzel resides therein. The tasting room is properly Arthurian, with a carved tasting table—not round but more or less oval—arched windows and a crackling fireplace.

A modern winery is sheltered within, which can be explored by reservation, followed by a tasting intelligently conducted by the tour host. All this opulence was conceived in 1983 by a corporation with a name no less modest than its creation—Great American Wineries, Inc.

Tasting notes: The list of medals is considerably longer than the roster of wines. Varietals are Chardonnay, Merlot, Cabernet Sauvignon, Sauvignon Blanc, Gewürztraminer and Johannisberg Riesling. They're full-bodied creations, often made *sur lie* to add to their complexity. We favored a young and spicy barrel fermented Chardonnay, a dry but fruit-filled *sur lie* Semillon and a soft, complex Merlot. A cream sherry was nutty and sensuously lush. Prices range from $6 for some of the whites to the high teens.

Vintners choice: "Chardonnay, Merlot and Cabernet Sauvignon, consistent gold and silver medal winners," says the corporation's Patricia Brower.

Ventana Vineyards tasting room • T ⌇

⌑ *2999 Monterey-Salinas Highway, Monterey, CA 93940; (408) 372-7415. Daily 11 to 5; no credit cards. Most varieties tasted. Sheltered picnic deck.* ⌑

Some years ago, former Vietnam fighter pilot J. Douglas Meador decided he wanted to go into the wine business. He cleared and planted a 400-acre vineyard in gravelly soil along the Arroyo Seco River, between Soledad and Greenfield. In 1978, when he began making his wines, perhaps even he was

Many tasting rooms in Monterey County are divorced from their wineries. Three are along Monterey's Cannery Row.

amazed. According to a winery source, Ventana has won more awards than any other single vineyard winery in America.

You won't see this remarkable vineyard, because the winery is elsewhere and it offers no tours. You can taste the wines in a handsome hospitality center in a rough-stone, vine covered complex called "the Old Stone House" just east of Monterey.

Tasting notes: Most premium whites appear on Doug's list, along with Cabernet Sauvignon, Syrah and a couple of dessert wines. His flagship Sauvignon Blanc was excellent, fruity and spicier than most Chardonnays; his barrel-fermented malolactic Chardonnay was—predictably—spicier still. Of the reds, we liked a rich, peppery young Cabernet Sauvignon with a typical Bordeaux blend of Cabernet Franc and Merlot; and a Pinot Noir Reserve rich with berries. Prices are modest for such award winners, ranging from $5 to the high teens.

Vintners choice: "Sauvignon Blanc, Chardonnay and Riesling," said a winery source.

Paul Masson tasting room • T 📷

☐ *700 Cannery Row, Monterey, CA 93940; (408) 646-5446. Daily 10 to 7 in summer, 10 to 6 the rest of the year. Most varieties tasted free; also wines by the glass at $3. Extensive wine logo, giftware and tourist souvenir selection.* ☐

We said earlier in this book that we prefer tasting rooms at the winery. Ambiance and all that sort of thing. We're ready to make an exception for the

Paul Masson Wine Tasting Room, Gift Shop & Museum. That's the full name, and it's all here.

The Masson facility occupies one of Cannery Row's best perches. On the second floor of an old cannery, reaching over the water on pilings, it commands a striking Monterey Bay view. One can sip Masson samples or purchase a glass of wine and snacks and relax in chairs before a window-wall to the bay. The gift area rivals the other Cannery Row curio shops in its selection of specialty foods, giftwares and tourist doodads. Soft classical music gives this glittering place a properly subdued aura. The museum portion contains old wine paraphernalia and photos tracing the history of the winery, which was founded in 1900 by rotund and robust Frenchman Paul Masson in the hills above Saratoga. An excellent film relates Masson's story, interlaced with rare historical footage of America and its wine industry.

Incidentally, the founder bears a resemblance—in circumference at least—to Orson Wells, who once advised us solemnly in his TV commercial that no Masson wine is sold before its time.

Tasting notes: From a list covering most premiums and a lot of specialty wines, we chose these for comment: A Sauvignon Blanc was light and crisp, yet with spicy overtones; a Pinot Noir had a pleasingly fruity nose and good berry flavor; a Cabernet Sauvignon was nicely tannic and peppery for its $9 price tag. Perhaps an even better buy was a fruity, soft $5 Zinfandel. To end this round, while watching a pair of pigeon guillemots on the railing outside, we sipped a rich, nutty Rare Cream Sherry, excellent at $7 a bottle.

Bargetto Winery tasting room • T 🐚

◻ *700 Cannery Row, Monterey, CA 93940; (408) 373-4053. Daily 10 to 5; MC/VISA. Most varieties tasted. Extensive wine logo, giftware, specialty foods and souvenir selection.* ◻

Bargetto's tasting room is on the ground floor of the building containing the Masson facility. It, too, offers a large gift selection, and a particularly good choice of specialty food items and cookware. Tasting notes and winery background are in the previous chapter, on page 217.

Monterey Peninsula Winery tasting room • T$ 🐚

◻ *786 Wave St., Monterey, CA 93940; (408) 372-4949. Monday-Saturday 10 to 5, Sunday noon to 5; major credit cards. Most varieties tasted for a fee; along with wines from several other Monterey County wineries. Wine oriented giftwares.* ◻

A pleasant old clapboard Victorian one block up from Cannery Row houses Monterey Peninsula Winery's offerings. Plans were afoot at this writing to include tastings from several other small area wineries, so you may have a multiple choice by the time you read this. The Monterey Peninsula Winery has never been far from its tasting room. Deryck Nuckton and Roy Thomas started the facility in the late 1970s in a structure at the Monterey County Airport. They moved in 1986 to a warehouse in Sand City, just up the beach from Monterey. Grapes, obviously, come from elsewhere.

Tasting notes: This outfit makes *big* wines. Whites were full-bodied and complex; many of the reds were husky and hearty, with enough tannin for aging. Both a Doctors Reserve Pinot Blanc and Sleepy Hollow Chardonnay were spicy, lush and subtly tart. Several Zinfandels occupy the red list, ranging in ages from four to ten years; all displayed strong varietal character and tannin accents. A Doctors Reserve Cabernet Sauvignon was herbal, complex and fruity and a non-vintage Black Burgundy had lots of pucker power; it was a Petite Sirah-Zinfandel blend. Prices range from $7 to the high teens for varietals; lower for blends.

Vintners choice: "Merlot, for which we've won numerous gold medals," said the winery's John C. Olds. "Also, our Barbera aged in oak and Pinot Blanc, fermented and treated like a Chardonnay." He had more to list, but we had to cut him off.

THE BEST OF THE BUNCH

The best wine buys ● The Monterey Vineyard, Smith and Hook, Ventana Vineyards and Paul Masson.

The most attractive wineries ● The Monterey Vineyard, Jekel Vineyard and Château Julien Winery.

The most interesting tasting rooms ● Smith and Hook, Ventana Vineyards and Paul Masson.

The best gift shops ● The Monterey Vineyard, Paul Masson and Bargetto Winery tasting room.

The nicest picnic areas ● The Monterey Vineyard and Jekel Vineyard.

The best tour ● Château Julien.

Wineland activities and such

Wineland events ● Masters of Food and Wine, Carmel Highlands in late February, (408) 624-3801; Monterey Wine Festival, mid-March, (800) 525-3378.

Winery touring guide ● Monterey Wine Country passport, Monterey Wine Country Associates; (408) 375-9400. A "passport," available from most wineries, will—when completed with stamps from participating tasting rooms—earn the bearer an invitation to a wine celebration.

BEYOND THE VINEYARDS

From a visitor standpoint, Monterey and Santa Cruz counties have much in common. Both have namesake cities bordering on huge, crescent shaped Monterey Bay and both are major tourist draws. The **Monterey Peninsula** is a playland for the rich, who tee off at Pebble Beach (now owned by a Japanese group), gallop their horses on the back trails of **Carmel Valley** and play tennis at luxury resorts. The wanna-be-rich shop the boutiques of **Carmel**, prowl **Fishermans Wharf** and **Cannery Row** in Monterey and hang out, scantily clad, at an assortment of beaches.

The more esoteric seek soulful peace on stormy strands and in the wilds of **Los Padres National Forest** to the south, particularly in the area with that mystical name, **Big Sur**. (Utter the phrase and you can almost see Liz Taylor in *The Sandpiper*, scuffing along the beach, eyes downcast.)

For more details on Monterey County—particularly historic Monterey, Carmel and Big Sur—pick up a copy of our ***Northern California Discovery Guide***. It's available at bookstores everywhere, or it can be ordered directly from the source; see the back of this book.

Monterey County attractions

Mission Nuestra Senora de la Soledad ● Fort Romni Road, Soledad; (408) 678-2586. Wednesday-Monday 10 to 4; donations asked. Fragments of original mission walls and a newer chapel with a museum.

Mission San Carlos Borromeo del Rio Carmelo • 3080 Rio Rd., Carmel; (408) 624-3600. Monday-Saturday 9:30 to 4:30, Sundays and holidays 10:30 to 4:30. Beautifully preserved former headquarters of the California missions, with a museum, chapel, courtyard and history exhibits.

Monterey Bay Aquarium • 886 Cannery Row, Monterey; (408) 648-4888. Daily 10 to 6; admission charge. One of America's leading aquariums with 23 habitat exhibits and tide pools.

Monterey State Historic Park • 20 Custom House Plaza, Monterey; (408) 649-2836. Daily 10 to 5 in summer, 10 to 4 in winter; admission charge, covers all exhibits and museums. A collection of historic structures tracing Monterey's history as the Spanish, then Mexican capital of California.

Point Lobos State Reserve • Four miles south of Carmel off Highway 1; (408) 624-4909. Daily 9 to 7 in spring and summer, 9 to 5 in fall and winter; modest admission charge. Wildlife preserve on a beautiful seacoast peninsula with beaches, picnicking and hiking.

Scenic drive • The Seventeen-Mile Drive takes visitors through the green and blue seacoast ramparts of the Monterey Peninsula's scenic tip, from Pacific Grove to Carmel; (408) 624-9585; toll charge.

Monterey County information source

Few lodgings and restaurants are near Monterey's wineries. For a comprehensive compendium of what to do and see, where to play, eat and sleep, get a copy of the *Monterey Peninsula Visitors Guide* from the **Monterey Peninsula Visitors & Convention Bureau,** P.O. Box 1770, Monterey, CA 93942; (408) 649-1770.

WINE TASTING IS SERIOUS BUSINESS

"Rich and highly extracted, with plum and chocolate flavors, but lacks acidity and lift and cruises to a listless finish of alcohol and wood."
— **Description of a Burgess Napa Valley Zinfandel**

Chapter Eleven
SOUTH CENTRAL COAST
San Luis Obispo and Santa Barbara counties

"Whaddya mean, our wines are as good as the Napa Valley's?" growled lanky Al Nerelli. It was his gruff way of agreeing with me. "Hell, we *are* the Napa Valley!"

I looked at him curiously.

"They've bought up half the damned area," he continued. "Bob Mondavi and those people. You drink Napa Valley wine, and it's a good bet you're drinkin' south coast wine!"

Nerelli, one of the owners of Pesenti Winery near Paso Robles, was right on target. "Those people" from Napa, Sonoma and other north coast wineries have discovered a new vineland, equal to their own. Robert Mondavi, Kendall-Jackson, the huge Wine World conglomerate and others have bought generously into Santa Barbara and San Luis Obispo counties.

Local folks have known for years what outsiders are now discovering: the south central coast provides ideal conditions for premium wine grapes. This is hill country, seamed by rough ridges that cradle river valleys leading to the sea. Cooling breezes and morning fogs temper the summer sun, creating a proper grape-growing climate. Chardonnay, Merlot, Cabernet Sauvignon and Zinfandel do exceptionally well here.

Geographic note: As we revised the first edition of this book, several San Luis Obispo and Santa Barbara county winery folks said this chapter should be called "Central Coast." This is the geographic term used locally, and it's part of the Central Coast AVA or Approved Viticultural Area, as designated by the federal Bureau of Alcohol, Tobacco and Firearms. However, the Central Coast AVA is much broader, extending all the way north to the Livermore Valley and southern Santa Clara County. The region covered by this chapter occupies the southern half of the Central Coast AVA. Further, it's

233

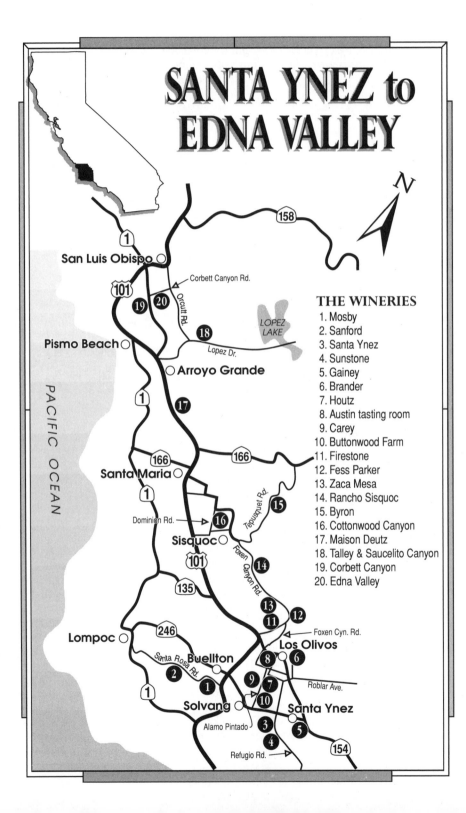

SANTA YNEZ to EDNA VALLEY

LOPEZ LAKE

PACIFIC OCEAN

San Luis Obispo

Corbett Canyon Rd.

Orcutt Rd.

Pismo Beach

Lopez Dr.

Arroyo Grande

Santa Maria

Dominion Rd.

Tepusquet Rd.

Sisquoc

Foxen Canyon Rd.

Lompoc

Santa Rosa Rd.

Buellton

Foxen Cyn. Rd.

Los Olivos

Roblar Ave.

Solvang

Santa Ynez

Alamo Pintado

Refugio Rd.

THE WINERIES

1. Mosby
2. Sanford
3. Santa Ynez
4. Sunstone
5. Gainey
6. Brander
7. Houtz
8. Austin tasting room
9. Carey
10. Buttonwood Farm
11. Firestone
12. Fess Parker
13. Zaca Mesa
14. Rancho Sisquoc
15. Byron
16. Cottonwood Canyon
17. Maison Deutz
18. Talley & Saucelito Canyon
19. Corbett Canyon
20. Edna Valley

twice as close to Los Angeles as it is to San Francisco. "South central coast" is a better geographic term. Sorry about that, folks.

The vines and wineries are focused in four areas, two in each of the counties. Santa Barbara's winelands are in the Santa Ynez Valley around Solvang and Buellton and in the Santa Maria Valley, east of the town by of name. Although most of the wineries are in the Santa Ynez Valley, 6,000 of the county's 10,000 vineyard acres are on the Santa Maria flood plain.

San Luis Obispo County's vinelands are concentrated in the Edna and Arroyo Grande valleys inland from Arroyo Grande, and the around the Templeton-Paso Robles area. Whites thrive in the cooler Santa Ynez, Santa Maria and Edna-Arroyo Grande areas while reds become big and bold in Paso Robles' summer warmth.

Compared with Sonoma and Napa, the south central coast became a major premium wine producer overnight. Among wineries open to visitors, only Pesenti and York Mountain date back more than 25 years. Most of the others have emerged since the late 1970s and new ones are blooming rapidly. This is particularly true in the Paso Robles region, where more than a dozen new wineries have opened in recent years.

All of this adds up to good tasting and uncrowded touring for the visitor. Although not tightly bunched like those in the Sonona-Napa areas, the wineries are easily reached and regional vintners' associations offer free maps. The facilities range from elegant to funky and they're tucked into some of the prettiest valleys and rolling hill country in California. This is a classic slice of the oak-chaparral woodland climate zone.

Manmade attractions abound as well. The Pacific coast provides an abundance of recreation, from clam-digging in Pismo to sunning off Santa Barbara. Los Padres National Forest lures hikers and reservoirs lure boaters. The region's five missions—Santa Barbara, Santa Inez, La Purísima Concepcion, San Luis Obispo and San Miguel—are havens of California history.

SANTA BARBARA COUNTY

Despite the youth of the county's wine industry, vines go deeply into its historic roots. The first cuttings likely were planted shortly after the founding of Mission Santa Barbara in 1786. Other vines followed with the establishment of Mission Santa Inez in 1804 in the Santa Ynez Valley.

Rancher Don Jose de Ortega pre-dates even the missions; he arrived in 1769 and built up the largest rancho in the county. During the late 1700s, he planted extensive vineyards and sold wine to his neighbors and to folks in the emerging pueblo of Santa Barbara.

The Santa Ynez Valley contained hundreds of acres of vines and several wineries until Prohibition shut them down. They weren't re-established after Repeal. Following an extended dry spell, the first major vineyards were planted by Richard Sanford in 1971, followed by Brooks Firestone in 1974. A member of the huge tire and rubber family, Firestone decided he'd rather make wine than whitewalls.

The Santa Barbara coastline is curiously shaped, taking a sharp right-angle turn at Point Conception to face south instead of west. This invites a west-to-east Pacific air flow that moderates the summer sun, providing proper temperatures for Chardonnay, Riesling, Merlot and other cool-weather grapes. The Santa Ynez Valley now has nearly 20 wineries; more than half host visitors.

However, more people come to see the deliberately cute Danish village of Solvang than to tour the wineries. A group of Danes arrived in 1910 to establish a colony and school beside Mission Santa Inez. The name of their hamlet is Danish for "Sunny Field." Since World War II, this collection of Scandinavian architecture has grown into one of the largest theme villages in America. Cross-timbered buildings abound and windmills creak in the wind, pumping nothing but atmosphere. Scores of shops sell import giftwares, restaurants serve *aebleskivers* and *smörgasbord*, and gas lamps flicker images of old Copenhagen.

The valley also is home to thoroughbred farms and elegant ranch estates with château-like mansions behind expansive lawns and neat white painted fences. Many of these shelter lifestyles of the rich and famous. Luminaries such as Ronald and Nancy Reagan, Bo Derek and Mike Nichols own ranches and horse farms here. Michael Jackson's Neverland and Fess Parker's estate are just down the road from one another. The Parker spread, however, is not a hideaway but a working winery open to the public.

Which brings us back to the subject of this book. Most of Santa Barbara County's wineries are in this fabled and affluent valley, while several others are spaced along scenic Foxen Canyon and the Santa Maria River flood plain to the north.

SANTA YNEZ VALLEY WINERY TOUR ● Begin not in Solvang but in **Buellton,** a neat and prim little town four miles west on Highway 101. Its primary presence is Anderson's, a large restaurant and gift shop. It dates back to 1924 when Juliette Anderson came up with a pretty tasty recipe for split pea soup. Anderson billboards, with Sweet-Pea and Ha-Pea splitting peas, are familiar sights throughout the state. A cellar tasting room offers samples of sweet fruit wines for small fee.

From Anderson's, head south on the town's wide Avenue of the Flags, which blends into Santa Rosa Road. As it swings sharply to the right, continue straight ahead into **Mosby Winery**, which is within sight of the freeway. About four miles beyond is **Sanford Winery**, on the left.

Now backtrack to Buellton and follow State Highway 246 to and through **Solvang.** Go about two miles beyond town and turn right onto Refugio Road at a traffic signal. **Santa Ynez Winery** soon appears on your right. Continue another quarter of a mile and you'll see the handsome Spanish adobe style **Sunstone Winery**, also on the right, just short of the Santa Ynez River bridge. Return to Highway 246 and continue east to **The Gainey Vineyard.** It's on your right, just short of the 246-154 junction.

Swing left onto State Highway 154 and drive about 3.5 miles to Roblar Avenue. Turn right and follow signs to **The Brander Vineyard.** Now, put it in reverse, cross Highway 154 on Roblar, then fork left onto Exterior Road and follow signs to **Houtz Vineyards,** up a narrow lane. To get back to Roblar, turn left just outside the Houtz lane, go a short distance to a stop sign and turn left again. Follow Roblar into the Victorian-style town of **Los Olivos**; the road makes a right turn into Grand Avenue. Among the avenue's 18th century buildings and storefronts, you'll find a pair of tasting rooms. Los Olivos Tasting Room offers sips—for a fee—from area wineries that have no tasting rooms. Just down the street is the tasting room for **Los Olivos Vintners/Austin Cellars**, a winery whose production facilities are elsewhere in the valley.

From Los Olivos head south on Grand Avenue, and then pick up Alamo Pintado Road by forking to the right and then turning left at a stop sign. Drive past oak woodlands, pasturelands, vineyards and ranch estates to **Carey Cellars,** on the right, about a mile from Los Olivos. Continue on Alamo Pintado for about a quarter of a mile and you'll encounter **Buttonwood Farm Winery** on your left. A mile beyond is State Highway 246 and a right turn puts you back in Solvang. You're probably ready to hit some gift shops and then graze through a *smörgasbord* in one of the town's many Danish restaurants. Incidentally, the Santa Ynez Winery has a tasting room in a cellar shop at 448 Alisal Road.

Mosby Winery ● T CT ✕

◻ *9496 Santa Rosa Rd. (P.O. Box 1849), Buellton, CA 93427; (805) 688-2415. Daily 10 to 4. All varieties except* grappa *tasted; MC/VISA, DISC. Some wine related gift items; a few picnic tables near the tasting room.* ◻

The Mosby Winery occupies an old red barn with an attractive little tasting room tucked into one end. The pleasantly scruffy farmyard and a peeling 1853 adobe transport you—metaphysically, at least—far from the freeway rumbling nearby. Bill and Jeri Mosby started *la petite* Vega Vineyards in 1979 and moved to this rustic spot a year later. Jeri may be running the tasting room, and she may permit a peek into the winery if things aren't too hectic.

Tasting notes: The short list tilts toward whites and the Mosby's produce some fine ones. Particularly interesting was the Mosby Chardonnay, deep straw colored, velvety and delicious. Several Rieslings were properly fruity and gentle on the acid and a lone red, Mosby Pinot Noir was mellow, low in tannin and very big on the berry. A powerful Italian cognac-style brew called *grappa* is sold at the winery but not tasted. Prices range from $9 to $14; a 375ml of *grappa* will set you back $25.

Sanford Winery ● T ✕

◻ *7250 Santa Rosa Rd., Buellton, CA 93427; (805) 688-3300. Daily 11 to 4; MC/VISA. Most varieties tasted. Picnic area beside a creek.* ◻

This mid-sized winery occupies a bucolic creek hollow, just uphill from Santa Rosa Road. Scattered winery buildings are deliberately rustic; some were fashioned of scrap lumber from dairy barns that once stood here. The tasting room is distinctively funky, with weathered wood siding and a twig-roofed *ramada* out front. Books about wine and other subjects share shelf space with some impressive wine awards. A pot-bellied stove and comfortable chairs occupy one area of the room and a sleeping pooch usually occupies the doorway. Richard and Thekla Sanford planted some of the valley's first grapes in 1971. They began making their own wine ten years later in San Luis Obispo County before moving to this part of the Santa Ynez Valley in 1983.

Tasting notes: The Sanfords' wines frequently gain *grand prix*, sweepstakes awards and platinum medals. The list is short and excellent: a flow-

A demonstration plot at Gainey Vineyard in the Santa Ynez Valley exhibits grape varieties and trellis styles. Gainey's Margo Alexander and co-author Betty Woo Martin discuss some of the finer points of Semillon.

ery, crisp Sauvignon Blanc; nutty-spicy and complex Chardonnay and a soft, lush and low tannin Pinot Noir. Prices are $5.50 for the Blanc, $16 for the Chardonnay and $14.50 for the Pinot.

Vintners choice: "Our Chardonnay and Pinot Noir have both received international awards," boasts the winery's Shelley Smith.

Santa Ynez Winery ● T ST ✕

☐ *343 N. Refugio Rd., Santa Ynez, CA 93460; (805) 688-8381. Daily 10 to 5; MC/VISA. Also a tasting room in Solvang at 448 Alisal Rd., and on Stearns Wharf in Santa Barbara. Most varieties tasted; major credit cards. Wine related items and specialty foods. Sheltered picnic area; self- guiding tours.* ☐

One can go on walkabout at the Santa Ynez Winery. A printed self-guiding tour explains what happens at the small facility, and helps the visitor identify varietal vines that fan out below the neat gray tasting room. Picnic tables on the vineyard-view porch offer an inviting rest stop.

This small facility, founded in 1979 as the Santa Ynez Valley Winery, is owned by the Doug and Candace Scott family. It occupies the site—and one of the cow barns—of a former dairy.

Tasting notes: The list is versatile, ranging from a sparkling wine through assorted varietals to a good jug red. The Sparkling Brut made of Chenin Blanc and Johannisberg Riesling had a nice touch of fruit. The Chardonnays were soft and pleasantly busy with light touches of oak. Among the reds, the Zinfandel was our favorite, with a peppery nose and taste and medium tannin. Cabernet-Merlot had a nice chili-pepper nose and a soft, low acid finish. Prices range from $8 to $15.

Vintners choice: "Johannisberg Riesling, Chardonnay and Merlot," said winemaker Mike Blom. "The east-west orientation of the valley provides a cooling effect from the ocean, ideal for these grapes."

Sunstone Vineyards and Winery • T$ GTA & CT ✕

☐ *125 Refugio Rd., Santa Ynez, CA 93460; (800) 313-WINE or (805) 688-WINE. Daily 10 to 4; MC/VISA, AMEX. Most varieties tasted for a $2 fee, which includes the glass. A few wine logo items; courtyard picnic area; tours of wine caves by appointment.* ☐

Developer Fred Rice and his wife Linda have created one of the valley's most striking new wineries on the banks of the Santa Maria River. It was completed in 1994 on land purchased in 1989, yet it appears to be two centuries old. The appealing facility has been fashioned as an early Spanish California *hacienda,* complete with adobe walls and a courtyard of hard-packed earth. Gnarled oaks, around which the winery was built, add to the sense of antiquity. Rough tiles form the floor of the tasting room and much of the attached winery has been bunkered into a low hill behind. Step into the earthen aging cellars and again you're transported back a couple of centuries. Even the pleasantly musty aroma is convincing. Out front, picnic tables in the courtyard offer views of the river and surrounding hilly countryside.

Tasting notes: Greg Brewer, like his predecessor Douglass Braun, likes to keep winemaking basic and simple, thus producing complex, full-flavored wines. Most Sunstone wines are unfined and unfiltered and organic grapes are used whenever possible. The result is pleasingly herbal wines with pronounced varietal flavors. From the brief list, we sampled a fruity and soft Chardonnay, an exceptional Merlot with a great herbal-spicy nose and taste, a big and complex yet soft Syrah and an outstanding Cabernet Sauvignon that was both mellow and yet with enough tannin to encourage aging. Prices range from the middle to high teens.

Vintners choice: "Merlot," said Brewer, a man of few words.

The Gainey Vineyard • T$ GT ✕

☐ *3950 E. Highway 246 (P.O. Box 910), Santa Ynez, CA 93460. Daily 10 to 5; MC/VISA. All varieties tasted in "flights" of four wines for $2.50 or seven wines for $3.50; both include a souvenir wine glass. Picnic tables in a vineyard garden. Guided tours on weekends at 10:30, 11:30, 12:30, 1:30, 2:30 and 3:30; on weekdays at 11, 1, 2 and 3.* ☐

This is a class operation. The winding, pepper tree-lined drive, the carefully landscaped Spanish style winery and its gleaming high-tech equipment speak of moneyed elegance. Wine columnist Robert Lawrence Balzer called Gainey "one of the most beautiful wineries in the world."

It also offers an excellent educational tour, starting with a small demonstration vineyard exhibiting different varieties of grapes and different styles of trellising. From there, visitors pass through the high-tech winery, then return to the refined tasting room—furnished with French antiques—for a personally conducted tasting. One can bypass the tour and go straight to the tasting counter, where flights are started every fifteen minutes. Visitors are conducted through three select wines.

The Daniel Gainey family, owners of a 2,000-acre Arabian horse ranch, created this artistic facility in 1984. Presumably, their investment has been returned, for their wines are winning a goodly share of awards.

Tasting notes: Herewith, the report on our flight: The Sauvignon Blanc was clean, crisp and wonderfully fruity. Chardonnay was spicy-nutty and lush with hints of oak. A Cabernet was full-bodied with strong tannin and a pleasant oak touch; suitable for laying away. Overall, the Gainey wines are excellent. Prices range from $8.75 to the early teens.

Vintners choice: "They're all great but our limited selection Pinot Noir is exceptional," exudes Karen Owens.

The Brander Vineyard • T GTA ✕

☐ *2401 Refugio Rd., Los Olivos, CA 93441; (805) 688-2455. Daily 10 to 5; MC/VISA, AMEX. Most varieties tasted. Some wine related gift items; small picnic area. Guided tours when time permits, or by appointment.* ☐

Fred Brander began planting his grapes in 1975, then he crushed his first wine—a Sauvignon Blanc—at a neighbor's winery. It won a gold medal at the Los Angeles County Fair and Fred knew he was on the right track. The present winery complex, including an Italianate château and a weathered barn, now produces about 8,000 cases of estate wines a year.

Tasting notes: Brander's wines are excellent, exhibiting strong varietal character and still winning medals. The Sauvignon Blanc is still the flagship wine, and Fred also produces Chardonnay, Cuvée Nicolas Reserve Sauvignon, Merlot, Bouchet (a blend of Bordeaux reds) and an Alsatian style Sauvignon Blanc called Cuvée Natalie.

Houtz Vineyards • T ✕

☐ *2670 Ontiveros Rd., Los Olivos, CA 93441; (805) 688-8664. Daily 10 to 4; MC/VISA. Selected wines tasted. Pleasant picnic area by a pond.* ☐

This inviting hillside winery, built around a pool and rose gardens above the vineyards, was opened in 1985. However, owners David and Margy Houtz have raised other crops on this picturesque place since the late 1970s. The winery occupies a redwood barn, where they produce about 3,000 cases a year. The family pours selections from its small list in the cheery little tasting room. Guests are encouraged to wander out to the gazebo, glass in hand, to survey this spot the Houtz' call Peace and Comfort Farm.

Tasting notes: The Chenin Blanc was rich and fruity, with a light acid finish; the Chardonnay had a proper nutty-fruity taste. Cabernet was soft and ready to drink, full-flavored with a slight touch of oak. Prices are modest, ranging from $6 to $11.

Los Olivos Vintners/Austin Cellars • T 📷

☐ *2923 Grand Ave. (P.O. Box 636), Los Olivos, CA 93441-0636; (800) 824-8584 or (805) 688-9665. Daily 11 to 6; MC/VISA, AMEX. Most varieties tasted. Good selection of wine related items and specialty foods; art gallery adjacent to tasting room.* ☐

Established in 1983 by Tony Austin, the fourth-generation son of a Sonoma Winemakers, this operation was purchased in 1992 by a corporation headed by Arthur and Nancy White. Initially, they commuted from the East Coast, where Art was in the computer business. How did the Whites, three thousand miles away, learn about Tony's winery? Nancy is a native of Santa Barbara and they were already fans of Austin wines. Why not, they reasoned, capture the source?

You'll sip fine wines in the pleasant environment of a refurbished turn-of-the-century cottage in their tasting room which, detached from its winery moorings, is in downtown Los Olivos.

The new owners have added a nice dimension to the wines and to the tasting room. Their labels are works of art—literally—reproductions of paintings that range from still life to portraits. The tasting room has been expanded to include an art gallery, which houses some of the original label paintings, plus works of other artists.

Tasting notes: Wines are now being marketed under four brands—the original Austin Cellars, with their artistic labels; Los Olivos Vintners for higher end reserve wines; Alisos Canyon for everyday inexpensive table wines; and *Mille Delices*, or "A Thousand Delights," for limited edition reserves. We sampled the Austin line, which continues the winery's tradition of producing tasty wines, inexpensive wines with good varietal flavor and nice herbal touches. The Chardonnays are rich and full bodied with vanilla hints of oak; several versions of Sauvignon Blanc also display lots of fruit and a touch of oakiness. Full bodied Pinot Noir and Cabernet comprise the red list. The Whites also produce three sweeter whites—a botrytis Sauvignon Blanc, white Riesling and Muscat Canelli. Prices range from $9 to the middle teens; a bit higher for the *Mille Delices* wines such as Cabernet.

Carey Cellars • T GT ✕

□ *1711 Alamo Pintado Rd., Solvang, CA 93463; (805) 688-8554. Daily 10 to 4; MC/VISA. Most varieties tasted. Wine related gift items; picnic deck with vineyard view. Tours on the half hour, by request.* □

Dr. J. Campbell Carey and his wife Mary Louise renovated an old dairy barn to create the winery in 1978. Then in 1987, Brooks and Kate Firestone of the nearby Firestone Vineyard purchased the facility. It's a handsome winery, housed in a weathered red barn tucked beneath giant oaks above hillside vineyards. A picnic deck off the tasting room offers valley views.

It isn't remarkable that the Firestones get a lot of press, since it's certainly a famous family name. Nor is it surprising that they had the means to purchase this facility, after developing their own Firestone Vineyard. What *is* remarkable is that Brooks and Kate are easy-to-meet, earthy people.

Kate, who manages Carey to keep its identity separate from Firestone Vineyard, is likely to pitch in at the tasting room when things get hectic. With her precise English accent and honest smile, the slender former ballerina talks enthusiastically of *her* winery. Then she may excuse herself and scamper away to complete preparations for an upcoming vineyard wedding.

Even if you don't meet Kate, you'll enjoy visiting this cute yellow and white trimmed cottage tasting room. Picnic tables occupy a deck shaded by a giant oak tree; the view down through the vineyards is a rural joy.

Tasting notes: Winemaker Allison Green focuses on upper end varietals. We tasted two Cabernets, found one soft, berry-like and ready to drink and another much heartier, higher in tannin and suitable for laying away. Two whites, Chardonnay and Sauvignon Blanc, were fruit-filled and perfectly balanced, and a Pinot Noir Blanc was surprisingly rich and fruity for a blush wine. Others on the list are Sangiovese, Merlot, Pinot Noir and a light Muscat dessert wine. Prices range from $8 to the middle teens.

Vintners choice: "We've been known for some of the best Cabernet Sauvignon in the area," says Kate. "We have two different vineyards which produce quite different styles. We're also known for our Sauvignon Blanc, Chardonnay and Merlot."

Buttonwood Farm Winery and Vineyard • *T$* ✗

◻ *1500 Alamo Pintado Rd. (P.O. Box 1007), Solvang, CA 93464; (805) 688-3032. Daily 11 to 5; MC/VISA. All varieties tasted for a $2.50 fee, which includes the glass. A few wine logo items, specialty foods and good selection of organically grown produce. Single picnic table near the tasting room.* ◻

A neat and prim gray cottage houses the combined Buttonwood tasting room and produce market, surrounded not by vineyards but by produce patches. The winery itself is up the hill a bit. This tidy facility represents an interesting transition for owner Betty Williams. She originally raised thoroughbreds here, then decided to shift to wines in the late 1980s and planted her first vineyards, along with several organic garden plots. The combined tasting room and produce market opened in early 1992. Her son-in-law Bret Davenport assists in this versatile operation, serving as winery president.

Tasting notes: Although not completely organic, the Buttonwood wines are mostly from pesticide-free grapes. They're made in the French style—earthy and herbal. One of the more interesting offerings is a Marsalle, a Rhône varietal rarely bottled in California. It's light and slightly herbal, with a subtle floral finish—a great sunny day wine with light foods. Others on the list are a lush and herbal Sauvignon Blanc that could almost pass for a Chardonnay; a soft and herbal Merlot; a light yet mouth-filling Cabernet Franc; and a big, dark and peppery four-year-old Cabernet Sauvignon. Buttonwood also produces a classic style Vintage Port, buttery and nutty, using a blend of three typical Portuguese varietals.

FOXEN CANYON-SANTA MARIA RIVER WINERY TOUR • From

Solvang, head north on Chalk Hill Road which blends into Ballard Canyon Road—an exceptionally scenic drive. The route crosses Highway 154 and cleverly becomes Foxen Canyon Road. A sign says you're on the Foxen Canyon wine trail. Continue for about four miles and take a hard left onto Zaca Mesa Road. This leads you to **Firestone Vineyard,** up a hill on your right. Return to Foxen and follow it a mile or so to the striking new **Fess Parker Winery** on the right; a short distance beyond is **Zaca Mesa Winery** on your left.

Following curving and somewhat bumpy Foxen Canyon Road beyond Zaca Mesa, you leave the Santa Ynez Valley and approach the broad **Santa Maria Valley**. About eight miles from Zaca, take a sharp right turn (just beyond an old twin steeple hilltop chapel) and follow a narrow road to **Rancho Sisquoc Winery.** The long lane into the winery complex is much smoother than Foxen Canyon Road, incidentally. From here, continue along Foxen Canyon for a mile, turn right onto Tepusquet Road and follow it across the usually dry river to **Byron Vineyard and Winery.** You'll note that the Santa Maria Valley has become a major vineyard area. Vines often extend from foothill to foothill on the broad, level floor of this flood plain.

From Byron, retrace your route to Foxen Canyon, continue west about four miles and turn left onto Orcutt-Garey Road. You'll shortly hit a stop sign at Old Dominion Road; go right for a quarter of a mile to **Cottonwood Canyon Vineyard** on the right. Continue on Old Dominion and you'll soon hit a stop sign, back on Foxen Canyon. Now well paved and smooth, passing through fertile farmlands, it blends into Betteravia, which returns you to U.S.

101 in **Santa Maria**. Head north across the Santa Maria River and you're in San Luis Obispo County.

Firestone Vineyard ● T GT ✕

☐ *5017 Zaca Station Rd., Los Olivos, CA 93441; (805) 688-3940. Daily 10 to 4; MC/VISA. Selected wines tasted. Selection of gift items; courtyard picnic area. Free tours available every 45 minutes, starting at 10 a.m.; reservations required for groups of 20 or more and there is a $2 per person charge.* ☐

In 1972, Brooks Firestone focused the wine world's attention on the Santa Ynez Valley when he and his father Leonard K. Firestone planted one of the first post-Prohibition vineyards in the county. For more than two decades, he has produced wines under the guidance of Alison Green, among the growing ranks of women winemakers in the industry.

The winery, an intriguing complexity of rooflines, is a large brown presence on an oak-studded knoll overlooking the vineyards. Tours through this facility provide dramatic views of a gallery of stainless steel tanks and a cellar filled with French and American oak barrels. Participants are then given a personal tasting in an attractive tile floor tasting room overlooking the vineyards and the Santa Ynez Mountains.

Tasting notes: The list includes Chardonnay, Sauvignon Blanc, Johannisberg Riesling, Gewürztraminer, Rosé of Cabernet Sauvignon, Merlot, Sauvignon Blanc and Syrah. The Rosé is one of the few pinks we like—rich and full lf flavor. The Chardonnay, Johannisberg Riesling and Sauvignon Blanc all displayed a nice crisp fruitiness with light acid. A Cabernet and Merlot were full flavored yet soft, with a gentle finish. Prices range from $7 to the early teens, going higher for some reserves.

Vintners Choice: "I'm extremely proud of all of our wines," says Brooks, "although in the last few years, our Chardonnay and Merlot have been particular favorites."

Fess Parker Winery ● T$ GT ✕ 🐾

☐ *6200 Foxen Canyon Rd. (P.O. Box 908), Los Olivos, CA 93441; (805) 688-1545. Daily 10 to 4; MC/VISA. Most varieties tasted for $2 fee, which includes the glass. Tours daily at 11, 1 and 3.* ☐

Television's Daniel Boone and Davy Crockett didn't swap his coonskin cap for a corkscrew. He's made the two work together at the most opulent winery on the south central coast.

Fess Parker's wholesome TV image carries into his real life; he's a down-to-earth family man who shed the trappings of Hollywood decades ago to return to the soil. He's also as down-home astute as the TV heroes he played. Early in his career, he began investing his Hollywood earnings in land, and he owns a couple of cattle ranches. He and his wife Marcie became interested in winemaking after visiting Napa's Silverado Vineyards, which was established by Lillian Disney, Walt's widow. It was Disney who started Parker's TV career by starring the tall Texan in *Davy Crockett: Indian Fighter.* In 1987, the Parkers bought their first vineyard land in the Santa Ynez Valley, where they'd been living since 1958. The first Fess Parker wines, complete with the coonskin cap on the label, were released in 1989.

The strikingly handsome winery and tasting room, suggestive of a huge pitched-roofed French château outside and an elegant hunting lodge within, was opened to the public in 1994. This is a family operation, with Parker—now 70-plus—as the mover, shaker and marketer. His son Eli is the winemaker, while wife Marcie and daughter Ashley help run the day-to-day operation. Fess doesn't hesitate using his TV hero image to promote his wines and yes, you can buy coonskin caps in the tasting room.

Tasting notes: Although Fess admits he's no wine expert, his son has learned the craft well, aided by consulting winemaker Jed Steele, who brought fame and awards to the Kendell-Jackson winery. We tasted a couple of fine, buttery and herbal Chardonnays; an excellent Merlot with good spice and berries; and a complex, full flavored Pinot Noir that won a recent best of class. A fruity Johannisberg Riesling and earthy-sweet Muscat Canelli complete the list. Prices range from $9 to the early twenties.

Zaca Mesa Winery • *T GT* ✗

☐ *6905 Foxen Canyon Rd. (P.O. Box 899), Los Olivos, CA 93441; (805) 688-3310. Daily 10 to 4; MC/VISA, AMEX. Most varieties tasted. Good selection of wine related giftwares and specialty foods. Tours every hour on the half hour 10:30 to 2:30.* ☐

Zaca Mesa's appealing cedar-sided barn of a winery sits in a hollow off Foxen Canyon Road. Here, the view is primarily inward. The building's elongated U-shape forms three sides of a courtyard; sheltering oaks provide the fourth. One can picnic at tables tucked under a roof overhang. A large, appealing hospitality room occupies one end of the winery, where sippers gather at one of three tasting areas. We settled before an oversized walnut banquet table to work through the small list of six wines.

Owned by John C. Cushman III, Zaca Mesa is one of the area's earlier wineries, dating from 1978; the first vineyards were planted in 1972. Tours take visitors through the busy but well organized facility, from modern cluster presses to ranks of French oak.

Tasting notes: All wines are estate produced and vineyard designated. Two Chardonnays showed markedly different styles, although both were excellent. The Zaca Vineyards Chardonnay was fruity, fresh and crisp while the Chapel Vineyard Chardonnay was more complex, nutty and buttery. A Sierra

PICKNICKING AMONG THE VINES

Madre Vineyard Pinot Noir was soft and berry-like. Currently, the winery is focusing on some Rhône varietals—Syrah, Grenache, Mourvèdre, Viognier and others. Zaca Mesa's prices range from $6 to $16.50.

Vintners choice: "Vineyard designated Chardonnays and Pinot Noirs are our best wines," says Zaca's Jim Fiolek. "They're our focus varietals."

Rancho Sisquoc • T ✗

☐ *6600 Foxen Canyon Road, Santa Maria, CA 93454; (805) 934-4332. Daily 10 to 4; MC/VISA. All varieties tasted. Picnic tables on a lawn area.* ☐

A long lane into Rancho Sisquoc delivers you to a large, neatly maintained farmyard, the work center of a 38,000 acre cattle ranch and winery. The tasting room is easy to spot—a somewhat weathered brown shed that stands in contrast to the prim white farm buildings. San Franciscan James Flood started this ruggedly handsome, hidden-away winery in 1977, and it's owned by the Flood Ranch Company, Inc. The surrounding cattle ranch hearkens back to Spanish days.

Tasting notes: Most of winemaker Stephen Bedford's products are aged in wood, giving even the whites a nice complexity. Barrel-fermented Sauvignon Blanc and Chardonnay were delicious, with nice spicy-fruity flavors. A Sylvaner, uncommon in this area, was crisp yet fruit-rich. Merlot and Cabernet Sauvignon had powerful peppery bouquets and flavors; both were big wines suitable for putting away. Others on the list are Johannisberg Riesling, a rich late harvest Riesling and Cellar Select Red that's a blend of Cabernet Sauvignon and Franc and Merlot. Prices range from $8 to $15.

Byron Winery • T GT ✗

☐ *5230 Tepusquet Rd., Santa Maria, CA 93454; (805) 937-7288. Daily 10 to 4; major credit cards. Wine related gift items and picnic fare. Picnic tables overlooking Tepusquet Creek. Guided tours on request.* ☐

Byron represents Robert Mondavi's entry into the south central coast wine area. However, founder and managing partner Byron Ken Brown still runs the operation and makes the wine. It was established by Brown and several partners in 1984, and later purchased by the Mondavi family.

The winery is among the most dramatically situated in the county. Surrounded on three sides by vines, it perches on the wooded rim of a small ravine. Tepusquet Creek rustles beneath the trees, 50 or so feet below. It's an appealing facility, a stylish wood sided barn with vague Spanish-Oriental lines. The tasting room, tucked under a balcony at one end, is done in knotty pine. A landscaped picnic area on the edge of the ravine is a great spot for a lunch break; you can buy the wine and nibbles inside.

Tasting notes: Normally, a good bottle of wine shouldn't cost more than a good bottle of Scotch, but we'd pay the $22.50 for Byron's silky, buttery Chardonnay Reserve. The 1988 version was voted best in the American Wine Competition. A Sauvignon Blanc was fruity and complex while the Pinot Noir had a pleasant peppery nose and gentle berry flavor. The Cabernet Sauvignon was a typical Bordeaux, well-rounded and full flavored with gentle hints of wood. Prices range from $7.50 to $22.50.

Vintners choice: The focus is on premium Burgundian varietals—Chardonnay and Pinot Noir, according to a winery source.

Cottonwood Canyon Vineyards • T$ ✗

☐ *3940 Old Dominion Rd., Santa Maria (mailing address: P.O. Box 3459, San Luis Obispo, CA 93403-3459); (805) 937-9063 or (805) 549-WINE. Daily*

10:30 to 5:30; MC/VISA, AMEX. Most varieties tasted for a $2 fee, which includes glass and can be applied toward purchase. A few wine logo gift items; small picnic area. □

We caught Cottonwood Canyon's new facility the day after it had opened. By the time you get there, expect more than a spartan tile floor tasting room in a basic metal sided winery building. The winery perches on a shelf above a vineyard valley, and a planned landscaped picnic area will offer a view.

That's just the beginning. San Luis Obispo winemaker Norman Beko bought 78 acres in the Santa Maria Valley in 1988 and planted Chardonnay and Pinot Noir to produce estate wines. The new winery was completed in 1995 and future plans call for wine caves, a restaurant, bed & breakfast inn and special event facility. First, of course, he must sell a lot of wine. "It cost about four times as much as we expected to get the new winery going," he said. "It's tough when you have to spend $20,000 for a tank you use only three weeks a year." He said his simple, attractive label of surrealistic cottonwood trees represents "my design and a low cost artist."

Tasting notes: Norman probably will sell a lot of wine. His Chardonnays—several are usually available for tasting—were lush, herbal and buttery; some were fruity while others exhibit vanilla accents from barrel finishing. The Pinot Noir had a big berry flavor with a soft, complex finish and a slight tannic nip; a typical Burgundian style. Prices range from $12.50 into the early twenties.

SAN LUIS OBISPO COUNTY

With a wider climatic range than Santa Barbara, San Luis Obispo County vineyards produce hearty, award-winning reds as well as whites. The Edna-Arroyo Grande valley area, open to Pacific breezes, is noted for its premium whites and full-flavored Pinot Noir. The Paso Robles-Templeton-San Miguel area is sheltered by the Coast Range, providing warmer climates for outstanding Zinfandel and Cabernet.

Edna-Arroyo Grande valleys

These wineries are new kids on the block. This area northeast of Arroyo Grande shelters eight wineries with the oldest dating back to the 1980s; the first vines were planted here in 1972. Pacific breezes provide natural summer air conditioning that's ideal for Chardonnay and Pinot Noir. Six vintners offer their products for sampling, with two of these sharing one tasting room.

EDNA-ARROYO GRANDE WINERY TOUR ● Picking up from the end of the Foxen Canyon-Santa Maria River Valley tour, drive about 14 miles north of **Santa Maria** on U.S. 101. Just south of Arroyo Grande, you'll see the modern **Maison Deutz** winery sprouting among hillside vineyards on your right, reached by a short uphill lane. Continue north on U.S. 101, take the Grand Avenue exit and drive east into the old fashioned business district of **Arroyo Grande**. You might want to pause and browse through the shops tucked behind false front and brick façades in the prim, well-maintained downtown area.

Heading east from town, you'll go through several street name changes although it's easy to stay your course by following signs toward **Lopez Lake**. Clearing the suburbs, you enter bucolic **Edna Valley**, rimmed with softly contoured hills. They're green velvet in spring and French-bread beige in summer and fall. An occasional vineyard climbs toward the low horizon. After a couple of miles on Lopez Drive, you'll encounter **Talley Vineyards,** up a vine-covered rise to your left. It also houses the tasting facilities of **Saucelito Canyon Vineyard.** Retrace your route briefly on Lopez Drive and turn right (north) onto Orcutt Road. Drive a short distance, turn left onto Tiffany Ranch Road, drive about a mile past some elegant country spreads, and go right onto Corbett Canyon Road. Within about half a mile, **Corbett Canyon Vineyards** crests a hill to the left. Continuing north, Corbett Canyon Road blends into Edna Road (State Route 227); turn right onto Biddle Ranch Road and you'll see, within a quarter of a mile, **Edna Valley Vineyard** on the right. Continue northwest on Edna Road, which blends into Broad Street and takes you into the heart of **San Luis Obispo**, with its nicely restored mission. If you prefer to avoid downtown, stay with State Route 227, which swings to the left on Buckley Road and delivers you back to Highway 101.

Maison Deutz ● T$ ST & GTA ✕

◻ *453 Deutz Dr., Arroyo Grande, CA 93420; (805) 481-1763. Daily except Tuesday 11 to 5; MC/VISA. Glass of Brut Cuvée and snack plate, $3.75; or sparkling wines by the glass from $3.75 to $5. Some wine related gift items; small picnic area. Guided tour by reservation.* ◻

Since this château style hillside sparkling wine cellar doesn't open until 11, consider making it a lunch stop. The "tasting" consists of a glass of Brut Cuvée served with a plate of cheese spread, crackers, fruits, pistachios and other goodies. During the crush, you can nibble on freshly-picked wine grapes and perhaps sip a bit of free-run juice that, without your intercession, would have become fine sparkling wine.

A joint venture of the 150-year-old Champagne Deutz of France and America's Wine World, Inc., the facility was built in 1983. It's an impressive complex, emerging from its own vineyards above the highway. From the stylish cathedral-ceiling tasting room, one can see the Pacific, whose breezes create a the ideal habitat for grapes that go into Deutz' sparkling wine. Barstools at the tasting counter and small tables in the spacious tile-floored room invite you to linger. You can study the huge wooden *Coquard* French basket wine press in the adjacent crush room; it's the only one of its kind in America. Then, stroll down to a lower winery building cantilevered into the hillside for a peek through a window at the riddling racks and *triage* of sleeping sparkling wine. Call ahead if you'd like a detailed tour.

Tasting note: The primary product is Brut Cuvée ($12), rated by wine judges among California's finer sparkling wines. After letting its tiny bubbles tickle our nose and enjoying its crisp, complex flavor, we agree. The tasting room also has Brut Reserve ($23), Brut Rosé ($20) and Blanc de Noir ($12) available.

Talley Vineyards and Saucelito tasting room ● T ✕

◻ *3031 Lopez Dr., Arroyo Grande, CA 93420; (805) 489-0446. Noon to 5, daily in summer and Thursday through Sunday the rest of the year; MC/VISA. Most varieties tasted. Wine logo gift items and specialty foods. Picnic tables in a gazebo and on a lawn near the tasting room.* ◻

A square-shouldered, two-story brown farmhouse first catches your eye. It stands, almost arrogantly, above the surrounding vineyards, without need of shielding vegetation. Closer scrutiny reveals that it's an ancient adobe, now impeccably restored. El Rincon Adobe was built in 1863 as headquarters of a 4,000-acre rancho. It houses the offices of Talley Vineyards, and tasting facilities for Talley and Saucelito Canyon Vineyard. The Saucelito winery is located farther up the valley, beyond Lopez Lake. El Rincon is a mini-museum as well as a tasting facility. An exhibit room has been furnished with Spanish and early American antiques.

The Talley family has owned this land for 40 years. The winery dates back to the late 1980s when Don and Rosemary and their son Brian began producing a select list of whites and a Pinot Noir. Saucelito Canyon is owned by Bill and Nancy Greenough; they do about 2,500 cases a year.

Tasting notes—Talley: We sipped an excellent Chardonnay, full of buttery fruit, with a hint of oak, and a soft and fruity Sauvignon Blanc; both were barrel-aged. A Riesling was crisp and fresh, done in stainless steel. The lone red is a Pinot Noir, spicy and berry-like with a medium body and light tannin. Prices range from $9 to $20. **Tasting notes—Saucelito Canyon:** This winery focuses on Zinfandel. The 1988 version we tasted was excellent, berry-like and peppery with a subtle hint of wood.

Vintners choice—Talley: "Our Chardonnay and Pinot Noir, both from the family vineyards," says Michele Good. **Vintners choice—Saucelito Canyon:** "We specialize in Zinfandel from our 110-year-old dry-farmed vineyard. Our wines are intense but drinkable on release," quotes Nancy .

Corbett Canyon Vineyards ● T GT ✕ 🎁

☐ *2195 Corbett Canyon Rd. (P.O. Box 3159), San Luis Obispo, CA 93403: (805) 544-5800. Monday-Friday 10 to 4:30 and weekends 10 to 5; MC/VISA, AMEX. Selected varieties tasted; usually six. Good assortment of gift items and wine related books. Picnic area near the tasting room. Guided tours on weekends only, at 11, 1 and 3.* ☐

There's no denying that this is a winery—one of the more handsome in the south coast area, in fact. However, there's not a vineyard in sight; they're elsewhere in the county. Built in 1978 as the Lawrence Winery, it is now owned by the Wine Group, a partnership that has spent time and money upgrading the facility. It also has won more than its share of awards; *Wine and Spirits* and *Vanity Fair* have praised its wines.

The stucco Spanish style building is almost mission-like, with a tile roof and arched entry. The large tasting room is bright and cheery, done in salmon stucco, with a latticed skylight and colonnades. Picnic tables sit beneath an arbor; the entire facility is nicely landscaped. It's no surprise that a local newspaper voted this as the county's most attractive winery.

Tasting notes: Corbett's list is larger than most in this area. We were struck by the fresh, fruity varietal flavor of the whites—a Coastal Classic Sauvignon Blanc, Chardonnay and Reserve Chardonnay. A Coastal Classic Pinot Noir was light and soft yet pleasantly spicy. The Merlot was equally spicy, more complex with a nice tannic finish. Prices are modest here, ranging from $4.25 to $8.50.

Vintners choice: Our tasting hostess informed us that they're particularly proud of their reserve Chardonnay and Pinot Noir.

Edna Valley Vineyard ● T CT ✕

☐ *2585 Biddle Ranch Rd., San Luis Obispo, CA 93401: (805) 544-9594. Daily 10 to 4; MC/VISA, AMEX. Most varieties tasted. Small picnic area; casual tours.* ☐

From showy, we come to austere. However, Edna Valley's wines don't play second fiddle to its more glitzy neighbor. Although the winery is rather rudimentary, the wines are excellent. One enters through a roll-down door and passes through a roomy emptiness that suggests this facility was built for expansion. The tasting area is a simple counter and stacked boxes form a working background. The area is brightened, however, by a couple of vases of flowers on the counter.

Nearby is an ancient cellar where this mid-sized winery's 58,000-case production matures. Guided tours, available by prior arrangement, will get you there. Further, you'll learn that this "roomy emptiness" is state of the art, with the proper facilities for producing Burgundian style wines. The winery is operated as a partnership between Paragon Vineyard, the valley's largest grower, and Chalone Wine Group, which also owns Chalone Vineyard, Acacia Winery and Carmenet Vineyard.

Tasting notes: Chardonnay topped our list; it was buttery, spicy and crisp. A rarely-seen Pinot Noir Vin Gris was pleasantly tart and fruity. The Pinot Noir was lush, complex and rather light on the finish while the Cabernet Sauvignon had a proper spicy nose, boldly complex flavor and a nice tannin finish. Edna's Sparkling Wine, five years in the making, was full flavored and smooth. Prices range from $6.50 to the middle teens, going higher for some reserves.

Vintners choice: "Chardonnay and Pinot Noir," says the winery's public relations director Pam Biggs. "We are growing some of the best fruit available to produce superior wines."

Paso Robles and environs

In contrast to Edna and Arroyo Grande region, the Paso Robles area has a long history in the wine business. And we aren't just referring to the usual practice of Spanish padres sticking cuttings into the ground.

Indeed, founders of Mission San Miguel Archangel near Paso Robles *did* plant vines around 1797. In 1882, Andrew York established the York Mountain winery, followed by Adolph Siot's winery in 1890, which was purchased by the Rotta family in 1907. Both survived Prohibition; some of the Rotta vineyards are being worked by grandson Mike Giubbini and York still hosts visitors. Another old-timer is Pesenti Winery, started by Frank Pesenti in 1934 and still owned by the family.

This area contains the most wineries on the south central coast. In fact, it's the fastest growing wine region in the entire state—not in vineyard acreage but in individual wineries. More than a dozen new ones have cropped up in the last few years, bringing the total count to nearly 30, and most have tasting rooms. They're in and around Templeton, above and below San Miguel and east and west of Paso Robles.

Why the rapid winery growth? "Local growers got tired of selling their grapes to Napa Valley wineries and seeing them win all those medals," a new winery owner told us. "So we decided to keep our grapes and win some for ourselves."

This is primarily red wine country, and vintners produce outstanding Zinfandel, Pinot Noir and Cabernet. White wine enthusiasts needn't stay away; award-winning Chardonnay and exceptional Sauvignon Blanc is created here as well. This region's somewhat scattered wineries are in three separate areas, so we'll divide it into a trio of tours.

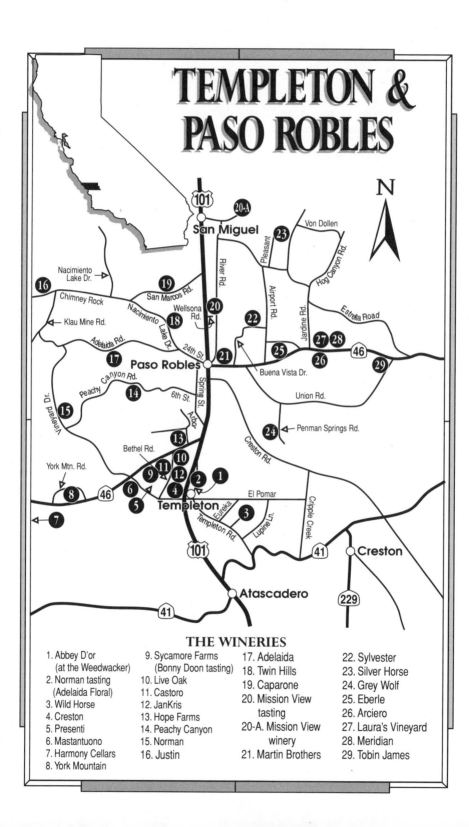

TEMPLETON &
PASO ROBLES

N

101
20-A
San Miguel
Von Dollen
23
Nacimiento
Lake Dr.
16
Chimney Rock
19
San Marcos Rd.
River Rd.
Pleasant
Airport Rd.
Hog Canyon Rd.
Nacimiento Lake Dr.
Wellsona Rd.
20
18
22
Jardine Rd.
Estrella Road
27
28
Klau Mine Rd.
Adelaida Rd.
17
24th St.
21
25
46
26
29
Paso Robles
Buena Vista Dr.
Peachy Canyon Rd.
14
6th St.
Spring St.
Vineyard Dr.
15
Arbor
Union Rd.
York Mtn. Rd.
13
24
Penman Springs Rd.
Bethel Rd.
10
9
11
Creston Rd.
8
46
6
12
2
1
5
4
El Pomar
7
Templeton
Eureka
3
Cripple Creek
Templeton Rd.
Lupine Ln.
101
41
Creston
Atascadero
229
41

THE WINERIES

1. Abbey D'or (at the Weedwacker)	9. Sycamore Farms (Bonny Doon tasting)	17. Adelaida	22. Sylvester
2. Norman tasting (Adelaida Floral)	10. Live Oak	18. Twin Hills	23. Silver Horse
3. Wild Horse	11. Castoro	19. Caparone	24. Grey Wolf
4. Creston	12. JanKris	20. Mission View tasting	25. Eberle
5. Presenti	13. Hope Farms	20-A. Mission View winery	26. Arciero
6. Mastantuono	14. Peachy Canyon	21. Martin Brothers	27. Laura's Vineyard
7. Harmony Cellars	15. Norman		28. Meridian
8. York Mountain	16. Justin		29. Tobin James

TEMPLETON AREA WINERY TOUR • This will be a loop, taking you into Templeton, west to the Pacific Ocean and then back along State Highway 46 to U.S. 101. The tour begins with an appropriately named road—Vineyard. From the Vineyard Drive interchange on U.S. 101, go east briefly, turn north onto Main Street and drive into **Templeton.** It's a handsome town of 2,900 folks that has preserved its distinctive old west look. Brick and false front buildings house restaurants, trendy shops, galleries and a couple of tasting rooms.

The **Abbey D'or** tasting room shares a small space with the busy Weedwacker coffee house and deli at Main and Sixth streets. Three blocks beyond, the Adelaida flower shop at Main and Third functions as a tasting room for **Norman Vineyards.** The winery itself is west of Paso Robles, open to visitors on weekends; we'll steer you to that later.

Return to Vineyard Drive from downtown, turn left (east) across the Salinas River Bridge, then take a quick right onto Templeton Road. After two miles, a sign directs you to the left up a narrow lane to **Wild Horse Winery.** Now, return to Templeton, cross over the freeway on Vineyard Drive and head west, but not very far. Make a quick right to the **Creston** tasting room, within sight of the freeway. As you continue west on Vineyard, you'll pass upscale horse farms and fancy country homes similar to those in the Santa Ynez Valley. Some of California's finest breeding stables are hereabouts. You'll soon find **Pesenti Winery** on your right and then the château-shaped **Mastantuono Winery,** on the left; it shows up about the time Vineyard blends into Highway 46.

Now, settle back for a 20-mile drive on Route 46, through a parade of picturesque country images. You'll pass a pleasing mix of meadows, pasturelands, clumps of oaks and madrones; stay alert and you can catch an occasional glimpse of the distant Pacific. Vineyards appear now and again to remind you that this is wine country. Forested hills of the Lucia mountains of the Coast Range cradle this area, marking the horizon on every side. Then you'll quickly break free of the rolling hills and hurry downhill to the green headlands above the Pacific.

At Highway 1, turn left and drive about a mile to a tiny nest of rustic charm called **Harmony.** Once a busy dairy complex, this 130-year old hamlet tucked into a green hollow now boasts a population of 18. The weathered buildings—all five of them—are occupied by artists, boutiques and one good restaurant (listed below). The tasting room for**Harmony Cellars** occupies a hill overlooking the town.

Retrace your route on Highway 46; after about 12 miles, turn left at York Mountain Road to visit **York Mountain Winery.** Continue eastaard on York Mountain since it loops back to the highway. After five miles or so, just beyond the Oakdale Road junction, you'll see a **Sycamore Farms** sign on the right, with a reference to **Bonny Doon Vineyards**. This isn't a winery but a large herb and specialty foods outlet in a well-tended old farm complex, with a Bonny Doon tasting room. A mile beyond, you'll encounter a cluster of three wineries near Highway 46 and Bethel Road. **Live Oak Vineyards** occupies a restored Victorian school at the corner of Route 46 and Bethel. A short distance up Bethel are **Castoro Cellars** in the vineyards off to the right and **JanKris Winery** in an attractive ranch yard on the left. A bit farther along on Highway 46 is **Hope Farms Winery** on the left. Another mile takes you to Highway 101 between Templeton and Paso Robles.

Abbey D'or • T GTA R

❑ *Tasting room at 590 Main Street, Templeton; (805) 434-3257; winery at 4620 Hog Canyon Rd., San Miguel; (805) 467-3248. Daily noon to 5 in Templeton; no tasting room at winery; MC/VISA. Most varieties tasted for $2 fee, which includes the glass. Weedwacker coffee house and deli adjacent. Tours of the winery by appointment.* ❑

Affable Joe Farley, who owns an area vineyard in partnership with his father Al, honed his winemaking skills at Martin Brothers Winery in Paso Robles for a couple of years, and then opened his own winery in 1987. The name comes from an abbey in his ancestral village in Ireland. He "went public" with his downtown Templeton tasting room in the spring of 1995. Earlier, this spot was occupied by Templeton Corner, a tasting room that sampled and sold the products of small regional wineries.

"They sold so much of my wine out of here that when they closed and the lease came up for this place, I grabbed it," he said.

Tasting notes: Joe's brief list is excellent and reasonably priced. A rich, almost buttery Chenin Blanc goes for a mere $6.25 and his Red Table Wine—actually a tasty Rhône style blend of Gamay and Pinot Noir—is $8.50. Others—priced into the early teens—are a lush, fruit and soft Chardonnay, full-bodied Cabernet that's capable of aging nicely and a spicy, soft Syrah. Coming soon is a Zinfandel.

Vintners choice: "Our barrel fermented Chardonnay, Cabernet, late harvest Zinfandel—" We had to stop him before he named the whole list.

Norman Vineyards tasting room • T 📷

❑ *At Adelaida Floral, Main and Third, Templeton; (805) 434-2997. Monday-Saturday 10 to 5. Most varieties tasted.* ❑

Folks at this small flower shop manage to find room at the cluttered counter to offer samples of Norman Vineyards wines. For specifics on the wines and winery, see listing below.

Wild Horse • T$ ✕

❑ *1437 Wild Horse Winery Ct. (P.O. Box 910), Templeton, CA 93465; (805) 434-2541. Daily 11 to 5; MC/VISA. Selected wines tasted. Small, select assortment of wine logo gift items; attractive courtyard picnic area.* ❑

A narrow lane delivers you to an appealing collection of white tile-roofed buildings rimmed by new vineyards and trimmed by carefully manicured landscaping. A picnic area occupies a courtyard accented by a gurgling fountain. The tasting room is a bright and cheery space with Spanish tile floors and open beam ceilings. The overall impression at Wild Horse is prosperity, well maintained.

Winery owner Ken Volk's beginnings were a bit more plebeian. While a student at Cal Poly in nearby San Luis Obispo, he used a baseball bat and a trash can to crush some grapes from the campus vineyard. He hasn't missed a vintage since. He'd intended to become an orchard manager, but the idea of producing something from perishable fruit and having in improve with age fascinated him. He began "working the industry" in 1981 and produced his first commercial crush in 1983. His marriage in 1986 to chef and cooking instructor Tricia Tartaglione produced a perfect pairing of wine and food enthusiasts, and they often sponsor epicurean events at the winery.

Tasting notes: A Burgundian style Pinot Noir is Wild Horse's signature wine, and it has won numerous awards. The rendition we sampled was full of fruit and clean, with an exceptionally smooth finish. Our other favorites list were *Bella Notte,* a Malvasia Bianca fermented dry to create a fruity and crisp wine; a spicy and smoky full flavored Syrah and an "Unbridled" Zinfandel that was big and full flavored with a great spicy berry taste. The list also includes Chardonnay, Pinot Blanc, a pink *Vin Gris* produced from Pinot Noir, Merlot, Cabernet Franc and Cabernet Sauvignon. Prices range from $7 into the middle teens.

Creston Vineyards ● T ✕ ⬛

◻ *Highway 101 at Vineyard Dr. (P.O. Box 577), Templeton, CA 93465; (805) 434-1399. Daily 10 to 5; MC/VISA, AMEX. Most varieties tasted. Good selection of gift and wine logo items. Picnic area near the tasting room.* ◻

Creston's tasting room occupies a prim little French-windowed cottage. It's been on this spot since the mid-80s, luring travelers off nearby Highway 101. Visitors can picnic under the shade of the cottage eaves.

The vines and winery are about ten miles inland, near the town of Creston northeast of Atascadero. Creston Vineyards was established in 1981 by Larry and Stephanie Rosenbloom. It's now owned by TV personality Alex Trebek.

Tasting notes: Creston's list includes Chardonnay, Cabernet Sauvignon, Pinot Noir, Semillon, Merlot, Zinfandel and white Zinfandel. The Chard was properly fruity and silky with a nice acid nip to the finish; two Cabernets—the Creston Vineyards and the Winemakers Selection—were complex and mildly peppery, with enough tannin to encourage putting them down for a few years. The Pinot Noir was softer, ready to drink and the white Zin revealed a nice flowery palate. Prices range from $6 to $11.50.

Vintners choice: Chardonnay, Merlot and Cabernet Sauvignon, said the tasting room host.

Pesenti Winery ● T GTA ⬛

◻ *2900 Vineyard Dr., Templeton, CA 93465; (805) 434-1030. Monday-Saturday 8 to 5:30 and Sunday 9 to 5:30; no credit cards but out-of-town checks accepted. Most varieties tasted. Extensive giftware and wine logo selection. Guided tours by appointment.* ◻

Venerable Pesenti Winery's tasting list reads like a vintner's catalog. We counted 44 items! Everything from premium varietals to jug wines to hard cider to fruit and berry wines. The tasting room resembles a well-stocked wine shop, with shelves running from floor to ceiling. In the early days, according to local legend, the Pesenti family would leave a few bottles and a sampler jug out front. If you liked the wine, you left a dollar and took a bottle home.

Pesenti is still a popular place to stop by for a bottle or two. The prices have increased, but not all that much, when adjusted for inflation. Frank and Caterina started growing grapes here in 1923, even though it was during Prohibition. When Repeal came in 1933, they started building their winery, which opened a year later. Son Victor, his sister Sylvia and her husband Al Nerelli have been running things since the 40s. They're assisted now by younger Pesenti and Nerelli members; Al's son Frank is the winemaker

Tasting notes: Still using the no-frills approach initiated by the founders, Pesenti offers some of the best wine buys south of Sonoma. Maybe south of Seattle. Most of their reds are big and lusty, and the whites are classic examples of fresh fruitiness. A grand national champion Cabernet Sauvignon goes for $9.95, and a national champ Gray Riesling, their best seller, is yours for $5.95. An exceptional Zinfandel, winner of national and international medals, sells for $6.95. Other premium varietals are priced between $5 and $10; quite drinkable blends drop below $5. And don't forget that hard cider; take it home for $4.

Vintners choice: Al thought for a moment, then issued his list: "Cabernet Sauvignon, Zinfandel, Gray Riesling and Johannisberg Reisling."

Mastantuono Winery • T ✕ 📷

☐ *100 Oak View Rd. (Route 2), Templeton, CA 93465; (805) 238-0676. Daily 10 to 6; MC/VISA. Most varieties tasted. Extensive selection of giftwares, stemware and deli foods. Picnic area.* ☐

Step inside Pat Mastantuono's wonderfully overdone tasting room and you expect to see jolly knights thumping their flagons on the bar, demanding refills. From afar, the place looks like a cross between a château and a castle. From within, it might be a Bavarian hunting lodge, with game trophies glaring from their wall mounts.

"*Italian* hunting lodge," corrected the gregarious founder of this place. Between sips of wine as robust as their creator, we get the Pasquale Mastantuono story. "I started a furniture business in L.A. With these hands; tool box and the whole thing. I wanted to make a million so I could retire at 39. So that's what I did."

With an exaggerated sweep of his left hand, he gestured around the tasting room. "*This* is my retirement. This is fun!"

Pat started having fun in 1976 when he began making wine commercially. His Italian forbearers had been doing it for three generations, so he figures it was in his genes. Actually, he says he doesn't make wine; he only guides it along.

"The wine is made in the vineyard," he said, in refreshing contradiction to the modern school of test tube winemakers.

Tasting notes: Mastantuono's philosophy practically jumps from the glass. His reds are dry-farmed, unfined and unfiltered. The Zinfandels run a tasty gamut from light and berry-like to powerful and robust. A six-year-old Zin, aged three years in oak, was one of the best we've tasted. Chardonnays were crisp and spicy with a hint of wood and a Cabernet was rich and aged to smoothness. Also on the list were a fruity white Zin, a soft but nippy Carminello (from the Carmine grape, a U.C. Davis hybrid of Cabernet, Merlot and Carignane) and a silky, full flavored port. Prices range from $6 to $20.

Vintners choice: The license plate on Pat's flashy boat-tailed vintage Auburn sports car displayed out front says it: "ZINMAN 1."

Harmony Cellars • T ✕ 📷

☐ *Harmony Valley Road (P.O. Box 2502), Harmony, CA 93435; (805) 927-1625. Daily 10 to 5; MC/VISA. Most varieties tasted. Wine logo and specialty food items; view picnic area.* ☐

This small family-owned winery is tucked into a hillside with a splendid view of Harmony and the rolling headlands of the Pacific Coast. The tasting room, once in the tiny hamlet of Harmony, has moved up to the winery, where sippers can enjoy that great view. The site also includes a picnic area with access to that vista.

Tasting notes: Winemaker Chuck Mulligan likes a lot of fruit in his wine. The Chardonnay and Johannisberg Riesling displayed pronounced varietal character, strong on berries, light on wood, with a crisp acid finish. The Pinot Noir was pleasantly herbal with a spicy nose and a good taste of berries while the Cabernet was lighter and somewhat herbaceous. A Zinjolais, a blend of Zinfandel and Beaujolais, was light yet rich with the flavor of the grapes, with a gentle acid finish. Prices range from $5.75 to $12.25.

Vintners choice: Mulligan's favorite is Zinjolais, and the grapes are hand picked right into a fermentation tank, where they're chilled with dry ice to retard fermentation and retain the fruity flavor.

York Mountain Winery • T CT ✕ 🍶

◻ York Mountain Road (Route 2, Box 191), Templeton, CA 93465; (805) 238-3925. Daily 10 to 5; MC/VISA. All varieties tasted; most free, $4 for samples of five reserves or 50 cents a sip. Good wineware selection, books and specialty foods. Tours by appointment, or one can peek into the winery. ◻

York Mountain is aging gracefully. The venerable winery occupies an early American farmyard fringed by trees and vineyards high on the flanks of the Santa Lucias. The vine entwined tasting room has the look of an old general store, with a wide selection of gifts, specialty foods and books. It's one of wineland's more intriguing tasting rooms, with a beamed ceiling, craggy stone fireplace and a 1910 New Era motorcycle parked along one wall.

As far as we could determine, York Mountain is the oldest surviving winery in all of southern California, dating from 1882, when it was established by Andrew York. Present owner Max Goldman bought it from the York family in 1970.

Tasting notes: York's busy list ranges from red and white jug wines and classic varietals to a sparkling wine and dry sherry. The Zinfandel, Pinot Noir and Cabernet Sauvignon were hearty and full-bodied with a strong taste of the grape. Chardonnay, the only varietal white, was crisp and light, while the jug white was nicely acidic—one of the better we've tasted. Sherry, made from Chenin Blanc and French Colombard, was properly nutty. Prices range from $4.50 for the blends to the mid teens for high end varietals.

Vintners choice: "We're in a red area," said Goldman simply.

Bonny Doon tasting room at Sycamore Farms • T 🍶

◻ Sycamore Farms, 2485 Highway 46 West (P.O. Box 49-A), Paso Robles, CA 93446; (805) 239-5614. Most varieties tasted, including glass. ◻

Sycamore Farms is a large natural herb and produce outlet in an attractive old fashioned green and white farm complex. Bonny Doon Vineyard of Santa Cruz, noted for its fine wine blends and hilariously campy labels, started a tasting facility here in 1994. If you haven't or don't plan to visit the winery in the Santa Cruz Mountains, this provides an opportunity to sample Vin Gris de Cigare, Clos de Gilroy and Ca'del Solo Big House Red. And yes, the wines are serious. For specifics, see the Bonny Doon listing in Chapter 9, page 220. Sycamore Farms also sells an array of specialty foods, cookbooks, gardening books and American folk crafts.

Live Oak Vineyards • T$ ✕ 🍶

◻ 1480 N. Bethel Rd., Templeton, CA 93465; (805) 227-4766. Daily 10 to 6; MC/VISA. Most varieties tasted for $2 fee. Good selection of wine logo and gift items. Two picnic areas. ◻

Completing a game of musical wineries, Live Oak set up shop in early 1995 in the 1880 Bethel Road School previously occupied by Castoro. The year before, Castoro had moved to new quarters across Bethel Road.

Jane and Bill Alberts own this corner property, which includes the nicely restored old schoolhouse and other early American structures. After the Castoro operation moved, they had problems finding a new tenant, so they decided to set up their own winery. Bill's wine interests go back to his youth when he worked at his aunt's Zinfandel vineyard in Alexander Valley. However, he chose a round-about path, first serving as a naval aviator and then as an optometrist in Lodi, another vineyard area. He and Jane, a former dental hygienist, established a winery in northern Sonoma County in 1972, and then moved to the Paso Robles area in 1981.

The tasting room is a splendid space within the refurbished white clapboard school house, with polished tile floors, select antique furnishings and an inviting fireplace. Ancient oaks and landscaped gardens accent the ranch yard, with vineyards just beyond.

Tasting notes: Sauvignon Blanc, Chardonnay, Zinfandel and white Zinfandel, Merlot and Cabernet Sauvignon comprise the Alberts' list. The overall style is a nice balance between fruitiness and oak. We were partial to a crisp, citrus-accented Sauvignon Blanc; a buttery and soft Chardonnay and an excellent Zinfandel with lots of spice and berries. Prices range from $7 to the early teens.

Vintners choice: Our tasting room hosts liked the Merlot and Zinfandel "because they're very soft and mouth filling."

Castoro Cellars • T$ ✗ 👜

☐ *1315 N. Bethel Rd., Templeton, CA 93465; (805) 238-0725. Daily 11 to 5:30; MC/VISA, AMEX. All varieties tasted for $2 fee, including logo glass. Good selection of wine related giftware and specialty food items. Picnic area near the tasting room.* ☐

Castoro Cellars began across Bethel Road as a joint venture, with Niels and Bimmer Udsen producing the wines and Dawn and John Hawley providing the tasting room. Their operation moved to the old El Paso de Robles Winery in 1994, although you'll not think of it as "old." It has been handsomely renovated into a Spanish mission style complex reached by a colonnade walkway. Picnic tables occupy a lawn area. The tasting room interior is even more impressive—a grand open space with a cathedral ceiling held up by huge trusses. A fireplace, tile floor and replica of a Loire Valley tapestry of winemaking complete this appealing setting. (A similar tapestry occupies Live Oak, signaling the former connection between the two.)

The Udsen's family winery produces about 15,000 cases a year. Most varieties are available at the tasting room. The Hawleys intend to produce their own wines as well, sometime in the future.

Tasting notes: The Castoro Fumé Blanc, one of the few produced on the south central coast, was crisp and light with a nice acidic finish. A light touch of oak accented the Chardonnay. Of the reds, the Pinot Noir was full and complex yet soft. The Zinfandel also was on the light side, with typical raspberry flavor. A pretty cranberry-colored Gamay Nouveau had nice strawberry taste. Cabernet Sauvignon, a rich late harvest Zinfandel, white Zin and Muscat Canelli complete the list. Prices range from $7 to the mid teens.

Vintners choice: "What we're really known for is our reds, especially our Zin and Cab" commented winemaker Niels.

JanKris Vineyard • T$ CT R ✗

☐ *Bethel Road (Route 2, Box 40), Templeton, CA 93465; (805) 434-0319. Daily 11 to 5:30; MC/VISA, AMEX. All varieties tasted for a $2 fee, which includes logo glass. Picnic area; informal self-guiding tours. Wine logo and spe-*

cialty food items. Deli restaurant offers light lunch fare, serving daily 11 to 3 weekdays; sometimes longer on weekends. ☐

A fairly recent arrival on the local wine scene, JanKris occupies an elegantly restored century-old gray and white Victorian farm house. The café is a sunny space behind French windows, with the attractive picnic area is just below, in a glass wall gazebo. It's all part of a ranch complex that includes a barn-turned-winery, corrals with livestock and surrounding pasturelands and vineyards. This facility once was home to Farview Farms Winery.

Although they aren't old enough to drink what's inside, the profiles of January and Kristin Gendron appear on the JanKris labels. Obviously, this is a family operation; it involves Jan and Kris' parents Mark and Paula, and Mark's father Ernie and brother Kelley.

Tasting notes: "Fruity and soft" describes the JanKris wine style, although some of the reds are—well—assertive. We liked a smooth, mouth-filling Chardonnay, herbal and fruity Pinot Blanc and a Pinot Noir with a gentle, spicy nose and a pleasing buttery taste. The Zinfandel and Syrah were big wines, complex and full of berries. A light Gamay and gentle, fruity Merlot completed the list. Prices range from $8 to the middle teens.

Hope Farms Winery ● T$ ✕ 🍶

☐ *2175 Arbor Rd., Paso Robles, CA 93446; (805) 238-6979. Daily 11 to 5; MC/VISA. All varieties tasted. Extensive gift and specialty food selection; free food samples. Picnic area in a gazebo.* ☐

The sparkling Hope Farms tasting room is a study in 19th century rural elegance, with a stained glass entryway, coffered ceilings, Casablanca fans and lively fruit print wallpaper. Dishes of cheeses, sauces, mustards and dips arrayed along the tasting counter are yours for sampling. You can buy what you like, both food and wine, and adjourn to a picnic area in a gazebo furnished with white wrought iron. Arbor Inn, a new bed and breakfast is adjacent; it's listed below under "Wineland lodgings." Two Hope couples, Chuck and Marilyn and Paul and Janet, planted vineyards in this area in 1978, then they opened their middle American country-style winery a decade later.

Tasting notes: The Hope Farm list consists of five varietals and a white Zinfandel. The Chardonnay was light yet complex, Sauvignon Blanc was fruity and crisp with a nice acid finish and the white Zinfandel was soft with a hint of sweetness. Both the Zinfandel and Cabernet Sauvignon were very berry, soft and ready to drink. The sixth entry, Muscat Canelli, is a sweet dessert wine, rich enough to sip slowly or pour over fruit. Prices are modest, ranging from $6 for the white Zin to $12.95 for the Cab.

WEST PASO ROBLES AREA WINERY TOUR ● Six wineries with tasting rooms are scattered in the Santa Lucia Range west of Paso Robles and south of the twin reservoirs of San Antonio and Nacimiento. Four are so remote that they call themselves "The Far Out Wineries of Paso Robles," and they've issued a brochure to help folks find them. Actually, none of the six are all that difficult to locate and the scenery is splendid in this area. Narrow lanes wind beneath moss-draped oaks, through thickly wooded foothills. Vineyards appear as occasional patchworks, terraced up steep slopes and mounded over high ridges. **Note:** This tour is best done on a weekend since two of the wineries, Peachy Canyon and Norman, are only open then.

The route begins and ends in Paso Robles. Follow Spring Street (which is the town's main drag, paralleling Highway 101) to Sixth Street and turn west. Go through a couple of stop signs, then swing right onto Olive and left onto Pacific. This soon becomes Peachy Canyon Road, which takes you on a winding course through this wooded foothill wine country. The first four wineries you'll encounter are—well—really far out.

About 5.5 twisting and scenic miles delivers you to **Peachy Canyon Winery,** perched high atop a ridge and reached by a narrow uphill lane. Continue another five miles on Peachy Canyon Road to Vineyard Drive; turn right and you'll shortly see the Romanesque **Norman Vineyards** on your right. Continue north on Vineyard Drive about three miles until it ends at Adelaida Drive. Turn left and then, at a stop sign, go right on Klau Mine Road briefly to Chimney Rock Road. A left turn takes you very quickly to the imposing **Justin Winery.** The final facility in the far out group is **Adelaida Cellars,** named for the country road it occupies. From Justin, retrace your path back to Adelaida Road and follow it just under four miles to the winery.

Continue eastward on Adelaida for 5.3 miles until it ends at Nacimiento Lake Drive; turn left and you soon see **Twin Hills Winery** on your right. A couple of miles beyond, turn right onto San Marcos Road for a mile or so to **Caparone Winery** on the left. From here, you can backtrack to Nacimiento Lake Drive and follow it into Paso Robles, or continue northeast on San Marcos Road, which hits Highway 101 just below San Miguel.

Peachy Canyon Winery • T GTA ✕

◻ *4045 Peachy Canyon Rd., Paso Robles, CA 93446; (800) 315-7908 or (805) 237-1577. Weekends 11 to 5; MC/VISA. Most varieties tasted. A few wine logo items; mountain-view picnic area. Guided tours by appointment.* ◻

Peachy Canyon Winery perches atop a high ridge, offering splendid views of the tumbled Santa Lucia mountains. Owners Doug and Nancy Beckett and sons Josh and Jake occupy a square shouldered colonial style home here, and the well-kept barn style winery is just beyond. Vineyards tilt steeply downhill, sharing the slopes with groves of trees. The simple tasting room is decorated with watercolors, an antique cash register and Wurlitzer jukebox.

Doug, who once taught school in San Diego and dabbled in real estate, started the winery in 1987 after working for another vintner, and opened the tasting room in 1994. Wife Nancy operates the Class Act dance studio in Paso Robles and helps with the winery operation. A third member of the team, who stopped by years ago to lend a temporary hand and never left, is part-time vineyard manager Bunny Quinn. She also produces the Coneja (Lady Rabbit) line of red and white wine mustards, which is sold in the tasting room and distributed elsewhere.

Tasting notes: *Bon Appetit* once picked the Becketts' Zinfandel Especial as one of the best reds in America. After sampling their full-flavored wines, it's easy to agree. Four Zinfandels currently are produced—a soft and fruity version from a young vineyard and two hearty numbers from ancient vines. The forth is the non-vintage Incredible Red, a blend from several Zin vineyards. A complex and full bodied Cabernet Sauvignon and spicy-fruity Merlot complete the list. Prices range from $9.50 to $20.

Norman Vineyards • T GTA ✕

◻ *7450 Vineyard Dr., Paso Robles, CA 93446; (805) 237-0138. Weekends 11 to 5:30 or by appointment; wines also tasted at Adelaida Floral, 300 Main Street in Paso Robles Monday-Saturday 10 to 5. Major credit cards. Most varieties tasted. Some wine logo items; view picnic deck.* ◻

Norman emerges as a stucco and masonry Romanesque structure with columns and curved roof lines, bunkered into to a hillside and surrounded by woods, vines and lawns. It's of the more attractive of the west Paso Robles wineries. The tasting room is as comfortable as a living room, with overstuffed furniture, ceiling fans and exposed beam ceilings. A picnic terrace offers an exceptional view of surrounding hills and vineyards.

The winery is the work of Art and Lei Norman, native Californians who planted their first vines on this scenic slope way back in 1971. The imposing Italianate winery-tasting room was completed more than two decades later.

Tasting notes: The Normans believe in letting nature produce their wines, minimizing the use of pesticides and fertilizers. The results are evident in the clean, straightforward taste of their wines. The Chardonnay was light and crisp; almost flinty while the Cabernet Franc had an earthy spicy nose and nice herbal flavor. Cabernet Sauvignon was light yet full flavored and peppery and the Zinfandel was the best of the lot, with a big spicy nose, nice full berry taste and crisp tannic finish. A late harvest Zinfandel and white Zin complete the list. Prices range from $10 to $15, with the white Zin down around $6.

Justin Vineyards and Winery • T CT ✗

☐ *11680 Chimney Rock Rd., Paso Robles, CA 93446; (805) 238-6932. Daily except Monday, 10 to 6; MC/VISA, AMEX. Most varieties tasted. Garden picnic area; tours if someone is available.* ☐

What's this? A French château in the Santa Lucia wilds? This grand symbol of affluence rises in striking contrast to its bucolic surroundings. Architecture of the multi-gabled wooden winery appears to be a mix between French manor house and a California seacoast hideaway. It's rimmed by formal English gardens, with picnic tables beneath an arbor. The tasting room features thick ceiling beams, rough terrazzo floors, an iron chandelier dangling above a glass-topped tasting table, a grand piano and walls of—uh—simulated marble. The winery complex also has a new bed and breakfast, the Just Inn, listed below under "Wineland lodgings." Former investment banker Justin Baldwin established the winery in 1987. He produces small lots of carefully crafted estate bottled wines.

Tasting notes: Justin's wines, which win numerous medals, often sell out. The Chardonnay was a classic—nutty, buttery and crisp. The Meritage, labeled Isosceles, was lush and berry like, with a pleasant nip of tannin. Others on the select list are Merlot, Cabernet Franc, Cabernet Sauvignon, sparkling Blanc de Noir, Orange Muscat and a rich Port style Cabernet. Prices range from $15 to $22.50.

Adelaida Cellars • T$

☐ *5805 Adelaida Rd., Paso Robles, CA 93446; (800) 676-1232 or (805) 239-8980. Open 11 to 5 weekdays and 11 to 6 weekends, then daily 11 to 5 in winter; MC/VISA. The "price of indulgence" is $2; most varieties sampled. A few wine logo items and—good grief!—Lava Lamps.* ☐

The Adelaida tasting room occupies a kind of corral space at one end of a pleasantly cavernous winery—corralled in by a low wall of barrels and wine boxes, which are hung with artwork and draped with wine logo T-shirts. Several Lava Lamps wriggled, blobbed and glowed as we entered; soft music issued from unseen speakers. (I always think of a Lava Lamp as a cross between a belly dancer and an amoeba.)

"This place needs a little Clannad," I told pretty young tasting room manager Jennifer Lippeatt.

"Clannad?" She looked puzzled. I went back to Ickybod, our on-the-road home and mobile office, and then returned with my favorite disk by the new wave Irish group. She installed it on the CD and I was right. The spiritually melancholy melodies were ideal for this grand, dim space and its wriggling Lava Lamps. Jennifer appeared unconvinced.

Adelaida Cellars, with its atmospheric tasting corral, is the kind of place that a couple like John and Andree Munch would create. He grew up on a banana plantation in Central America and she was raised in a hamlet in the French Alps. Seeking a site to produce French style wines, the international pair came to the foothills of the Santa Lucia Range. They decided that it reminded them of the Rhône Valley and started their winery in 1981.

Tasting notes: The winery produces outstanding reds. The Zinfandel was round and lush and full of berries and the Cabernet was spicy and complex, with tannin to invite aging. The Chardonnay was excellent as well. An "extended lees reserve" had a great nutty flavor with a soft, lush finish. Two sparkling wines complete the brief list. Prices range from $12 to the middle twenties; higher for some library wines.

Vintners choice: "The Zinfandel; it's always been my favorite wine," said Jennifer. She obviously prefers it to Clannad.

Twin Hills Winery • T GTA ✕ 🔯

◻ *2025 Nacimiento Lake Dr., Paso Robles, CA 93447; (805) 238-9148. Daily 11 to 5; MC/VISA. All current releases tasted. Good selection of wine logo items; art gallery and banquet facilities; shaded picnic area.* ◻

Twin Hills' copper roofed, cross-timbered tasting room is a curious—and pleasant—blend of Spanish and French, with touches of the plantation South. The winery builder used bricks and beams from an anti-bellum mansion in its construction. Inside is a comfortable living room setting of bentwood chairs, couches before a fireplace that sometimes crackles, and potted ivy perched on high shelves.

Established in 1982 by aerospace executive Jim Lockshaw, Twin Hills was purchased in 1992 by husband and wife Glenn Reid and Caroline Scott, who own an engineering consulting firm in Menlo Park. Both amateur winemakers, they decided to switch from Lockshaw's light, European style and make their reds big and hearty—working them by hand and using no pesticides.

Tasting notes: The reds live up to their billing, from a robust old vine Zinfandel to a nicely balanced 100 percent varietal Cabernet Sauvignon. Also on the list are a barrel fermented reserve Chardonnay and cold fermented Chardonnay, both soft and silky, with a touch of oak in the reserve version; a rosé, white Zinfandel and Johannisberg Riesling. They also make two fine dessert wines—a classic Solera process sherry using Spanish Palomino grapes and a rich Zinfandel Port. Wine prices range from $6.50 to $12.50.

Vintners choice: "Our big reds—Zinfandel and Cabernet," said owner and winemaker Caroline.

Caparone Winery • T CT

◻ *2280 San Marcos Rd., Paso Robles, CA 93446; (805) 467-3827. Daily 11 to 5; no credit cards, checks accepted. All varieties tasted.* ◻

Don't be put off by the austere brown prefabricated metal shed that houses M. David and Mary Caparone's winery. The surprise is inside: an assortment of excellent red wines at affordable prices. Dave makes only reds and he makes them powerful, lush and high in tannin. Drink them now or lay them away. He racks his wines instead of filtering them to preserve their complexity to "let the big fruit come forward." Like Mastantuono, he feels the foundation for the wine is laid down in the vineyard.

A tour here consists of a glance around the cozy 4,500-case winery. The tasting room host likes to guide visitors through a vertical tasting, including some barrel samples.

Tasting notes: Dave's big reds are easy on the wood, full flavored and lush with berries. The Zinfandel was predictably bold and fruity and the Cabernet was complex and tannic yet surprisingly soft. Merlot rounds out the short list; it exhibited a nice peppery nose and flavor, with a tongue-tickling tannic finish. Among their current releases are Brunello and Nebbiolo. Prices are $8 to $10.50. The Caparones also have yearly releases of ten-year-old wines, at higher prices, of course.

ESTRELLA RIVER VALLEY WINERY TOUR • This is shallow, softly contoured countryside, not as striking as the Nacimiento area with its steep oak-thatched hills and tilted meadows. You will be rewarded, however, with fine wines and some impressive looking wineries.

From Paso Robles, head north on U.S. 101 to one of two destinations. The last time we looked, **Mission View Estate** winery operated a tasting room in a former colonial style restaurant on the east side of the highway, about three miles north of Paso. There was talk, however, of returning the sipping facility to the winery, which is on a benchland above San Miguel. If you drive north and don't find a tasting room at U.S. 101 and Wellsona Road, continue another four miles to **San Miguel.** Either way, the village is worth a look, since it's home to the wonderfully weathered **Mission San Miguel.** Take the first San Miguel turnoff and follow the sleepy old town's main street to the mission. To reach Mission View Estate winery, continue on Main Street and turn right onto River Road, about half a mile beyond the mission. It winds up into vineyard benchlands above the town and shortly reaches the winery.

Return to Paso Robles, either from San Miguel or from Mission View's Highway 101 tasting room, and take the eastbound Highway 46 exit. The next winery comes up within a mile: **Martin Brothers** on your left, at Buena Vista Drive. From here, continue north on Buena Vista about three miles, through several rural right-angle turns. As the road swings eastward, the new **Sylvester Winery** might appear among the vineyards on your left; it was scheduled to open in the middle 1990s. Continue on Buena Vista for a mile to a stop sign at Airport Road, turn left and follow Airport about three miles to another stop at Estrella Road. Turn right, go less than a mile and turn left onto Pleasant Road. Another mile takes you to **Silver Horse Vineyards,** up a slender lane to your right.

Return to Airport Road, follow it 5.6 miles back to Highway 46 and turn right (west). Take the next left and then another quick left to get onto Union Road. Follow it 2.5 miles to Penman Springs Road, turn right and you'll see the small **Grey Wolf Cellars** on a ridge above, to your right. Return to Highway 46, continue eastward and the remaining Estrella River Valley wineries will present themselves without further search. **Eberle Winery** is on the left, elegant **Arciero Winery** appears on the right and the simple tasting room of **Laura's Vineyard** is directly across the highway. After a short drive, you'll see **Meridian Vineyards** on the left. A mile or so beyond, turn right from Route 46 onto the eastern end of Union Road for—last and in no way least—**Tobin James.**

Mission View Vineyards • T GTA ⛩

❑ *Tasting room at Highway 101 and Wellsona Road, between Paso Robles and San Miguel. Winery at 13350 N. River Rd., San Miguel, CA 93451; (805) 467-3104. Tasting room open daily 10 to 5; MC/VISA. All wines available for tasting. Good selection of wine logo wares and gift items; antique doll museum and shop next door; not connected to Mission View. San Miguel winery open by appointment only.* ❑

Mission View, perched atop a benchland above the mission at San Miguel, has moved its tasting room to this highway-side colonial style structure, although—as mentioned above—there is talk of returning it to the winery. The carpeted tasting room, with an American colonial look left over from a previous restaurant occupant, offers a few wine logo items and books and a long tasting counter. The Helen Moe antique doll museum and shop shares the same building.

Corporate-owned Mission View Vineyards was established in 1979. The winery in San Miguel was completed in 1985 and currently bottles about 2,000 cases.

Tasting notes: Mission View produces full flavored reds with lots of fruit and a subtle oak background. We particularly favored a Zinfandel with smoky raspberry flavors and a Cabernet Sauvignon with that good chili pepper taste. Chardonnay, fermented and aged in barrels, had a complex nutty flavor. The Sauvignon Blanc, also barrel-aged, displayed an ideal balance between fruit and crisp acidity. Others on the list are Pinot Noir, Merlot, white Zinfandel and Muscat Canelli; prices range from $8 to $13.50.

Vintners choice: "The Paso Robles area is noted for its Cabernet and Zinfandel and Mission View is no exception," said winery marketing director Chris T. Land. "The Sauvignon Blanc is also well received and it's a fabulous picnic wine, too!"

Martin Brothers • T GTA ✗ ⛩

❑ *Highway 46 at Buena Vista Drive (P.O. Box 2599), Paso Robles, CA 93447; (805) 238-2520. Daily 10 to 6 in summer, 10 to 5 the rest of the year; MC/VISA, AMEX. All varieties tasted. Gift items, books, specialty foods and wine accessories; view picnic patio. Guided tours by appointment at the winery, a mile away on Buena Vista Drive.* ❑

Nick and Tom Martin are Irish, although they specialize in Italian-style wines. They've planted such old world varieties as Nebbiolo, Vin Santo and Aleatico. These can be sampled, along with others, at their neat gray and white-trimmed tasting room set in a formal garden. The airy, color-coordinated interior provides a pleasing sipping setting.

The brothers established their winery in 1981 and produce about 15,000 cases a year. They're so focused on their Italian wines that they open a booth each year at VinItaly, Verona's noted international wine trade show.

Tasting notes: The list also contains traditional white and red varietals that show strong varietal character; they're light and ready to drink. We were particularly interested in the Italian entrées. Nebbiolo is a crisp, tannin-rich red with a nice berry flavor. Vin Santo and Aleatico are dessert wines;

the first with sweet apricot aroma and taste and the second a rich Muscat style. Prices range from $6.50 to the mid teens. A Grappa de Nebbiolo goes for $40 and, understandably, isn't available for tasting.

Sylvester Winery • T ✗

☐ *5115 Buena Vista Dr., Paso Robles, CA 93446; (805) 227-4000. Daily 10 to 5; MC/VISA, AMEX. Most varieties tasted; some wine related gift items and picnic area.* ☐

This new winery was planned for completion in the mid-1990s, so it may or may not be here when you pass by. If it arrives on schedule, you may see some old Pullman railroad cars as part of the complex—a trademark of Austrian businessman Sylvester Feichtinger. Among his many successful enterprises is a railcar restaurant in the Los Angeles area. He has owned 93 acres of vineyards on this bend in Buena Vista Drive for several years, and he's currently producing Chardonnay and Cabernet at Castoro Cellars, with Merlot to be added soon.

Silver Horse Vineyards • T ✗

☐ *2995 Pleasant Rd. (P.O. Box 2010), Paso Robles, CA 93447-2010; (805) 467-WINE. Thursday-Monday 11 to 5; MC/VISA. Most varieties tasted. A few wine logo and specialty food items; picnic area near a pond.* ☐

A straightforward industrial style building houses this new winery on a knoll above the surrounding countryside. The tasting room, brightened by big windows, consists of planks laid across wine barrels—a nice touch. The grounds and adjacent horse farm are tidily kept, and the complex is reached by a narrow lane rimmed by pasturelands and new vines.

This 3,000-case winery was established in 1993 by Rich and Kristen Simons. They were absentee grape growers for several years, commuting from their home in Del Mar above San Diego to their vineyard near San Miguel. Sluggish economy slowed their real estate development business so they decided to make this area their permanent home and start making wine as well as growing grapes.

Tasting notes: The list is brief and quite good. A Zinfandel, in fact, was excellent—peppery nose, lush herbal taste and a nice smooth finish. A five-year-old Cabernet was spicy and herbal, with a bit of oak; and the Chardonnay was medium-soft and fruity with a bit of oak. Also on the list are a white Zinfandel and Pinot Noir. Prices are $11 to $12; the white Zin is $6.50.

Grey Wolf Cellars • T ✗

☐ *1985 Penman Springs Rd., Paso Robles, CA 93446; (805) 237-0771. Daily 11 to 5:30; MC/VISA. Small picnic area; a few wine logo items.* ☐

This small winery in an cottage-style structure on a ridge above the vineyards is operated as a partnership between longtime local vineyard manager Gary Porter, who handles production, and Joe Barton, who runs the tasting room operation. Barton's background is in teaching and construction, and he hopes to have his own wine label in the coming years. Both of their wives, Becky Porter and Shirlene Barton, are Bakersfield teachers and they'll sign on full time "when we can afford for them to stop working," says Joe. The winery was purchased in late 1994 from former Los Angeles fireman Tom Baron and his wife Sharon, who had begun growing grapes here in 1981.

Tasting notes: Only Chardonnay and Zinfandel were in the bottle when we arrived, and both were quite tasty. The Chard was light, crisp and fruity with a pear-apple flavor and the Zin was spicy with a big berry taste and enough tannin to age a bit. Coming soon are a Merlot, Cabernet Sauvignon, Sauvignon Blanc and Muscat Canelli. Prices range from $7 to $12.

Eberle Winery ● T GTA ✕ 🏠

◻ *P.O. Box 2459 (Highway 46 East), Paso Robles, CA 93447; (805) 238-9607. Daily 10 to 5, until 6 in summer; MC/VISA. Most varieties tasted. Good selection of giftwares and books. Picnic tables on a view terrace; guided tours by appointment.* ◻

This attractive cedar, shake-roofed winery sits on a rise above its own vines, commanding a wide-angle view of the shallow river valley. The tasting room suggests a nicely furnished modern home with beamed ceilings, fabric walls and a fireplace. Formal landscaping completes a pleasant setting.

W. Gary Eberle established the winery in 1982. A "pioneer" in this young area, he studied winemaking at U.C. Davis and settled here in 1973, working initially with Estrella River Vineyards. He was named Central Coast Winemaker of the Year in 1990. The much traveled young wine pioneer also holds a master's in zoology and he was a defensive tackle for Penn State; he has the barrel chest to prove it.

Tasting notes: The Eberle wines we tasted were uniformly excellent. The Chardonnay was crisp, buttery and spicy, while the Cabernets were light yet lush with a peppery nose and nicely complex flavor. Zinfandel was powerful and fruity; peppery with strong tannic accents, it will improve greatly with aging. For chuckles, Gary has created "Eye of the Swine," a pink blend of Cabernet, Zinfandel, Muscat Canelli and Chardonnay. This is no wimpy rosé; think of it as a blush wine with the heart of a defensive tackle. A recent edition is Viognier, a white French varietal rarely bottled in California; it had a nice herbal nose and taste—kind of a cross between a Chardonnay and Sauvignon Blanc.

Arciero Winery ● T ST ✕ 🏠

◻ *Highway 46 at Jardine Road (P.O. Box 1287), Paso Robles, CA 93447; (805) 239-2562. Daily 11 to 5 (until 6 on summer weekends); MC/VISA, AMEX. Select varieties tasted. Extensive gift, wineware and deli selection. Self-guiding tour; racing car display.* ◻

This is how you build a family winery if you happen to be a family of millionaires. Visually, Arciero is one of America's great wine châteaux—a study in tile-roofed Italian elegance set into a vineyard slope. A juniper-lined drive, extensive lawns, lavish landscaping and umbrella picnic tables create a setting of moneyed country refinement. The high ceiling tasting room is accented with glossy tile, chandeliers and a fireplace. A horseshoe-shaped tasting counter is its focal point. Excellent graphics take you on a self-guiding tour through the winery. Bunkered into the hillside, it rivals the luxury of the tasting room, with carved oaken doors, a brass chandelier in the entry and carpeted corridors. View windows allow peeks into the winery operations.

Brothers Frank and Phil Arciero made their fortunes in southern California construction, and ran a stable of racing cars as a pastime. Three of their cars, including an Indy Super Vee flown by Phil Hill, Dan Gurney and Al Unser, are displayed in the tasting room.

Tasting notes: Like the winery, the wines are uniformly upscale. Yet they're modestly priced, ranging from $3.69 for good serviceable red and white table wines to $10.50 for excellent varietals. The Chardonnay was full bodied and nutty, with a nice hint of oak. Chenin Blanc was fruity and sweet;

good if you like sweeter whites. Cabernet Sauvignon, Zinfandel and Petite Sirah were full flavored and robust, suitable for immediate sipping or putting down. A current addition to the list is Italian-based Nebbiolo.

Laura's Vineyard • T ✗ 📷

□ *5620 Highway 46 East, Paso Robles, CA 93447; (805) 238-6300; mailing address: P.O. Box 304, San Miguel, CA 93451. Daily 10 to 6; MC/VISA. All varieties tasted. Good selection of giftwares, specialty foods and wine logo items. Shaded picnic area.* □

Who says you can't turn a doublewide into an appealing wine tasting rooms? Perched on a knoll above the vineyards, this space is a busy blend of great nibblies, assorted gift items, good wines and lively chatter with hosts George and Betty Cazaly. Try the chocolate coated coffee beans between sips; they don't clear the palate, but who cares? They're absolutely addictive.

The winery was started a few years ago by Cliff Giacobine, longtime local winemaker and formerly a principle at Estrella River Winery. Who was Laura? A remarkable lady and mother of two Estrella Valley vintners—Cliff and his half-brother Gary Eberle.

Tasting notes: The Cabernet was excellent—well balanced, soft and lush; and the Chardonnay was smooth and spicy, the result of sleeping in both American and French oak. Cabernet Franc, blended with a bit of Petite Sirah and Cabernet Sauvignon, displayed a spicy, herbal flavor. We were even convinced to try a nip of white Zinfandel, which had a touch of Muscat to bring up the flavor. Not bad, although we preferred the chocolate-covered coffee beans. Prices range from $8 to $18—the wine, not the beans.

Meridian Vineyards • T ✗

□ *Highway 46 East (P.O. Box 3289), Paso Robles, CA 93447; (805) 237-6000. Daily except Tuesday 10 to 5; MC/VISA. Most varieties tasted. Wine related gift items. Picnic area near winery.* □

Starting from a small but well-financed base, Meridian is emerging as another major Paso Robles wine estate. Nestle's Wine World division built this facility, which crests a hill with a fish-eye view of its own vineyards. It's an impressive affair—a large U-shaped complex with stone facing, a landscaped courtyard and other amenities. Most of its grapes are drawn from three vineyards owned by Meridian in Santa Barbara County; others are maturing right at the new winery's doorstep. The facility was started in 1988 and the tasting room opened in 1990, with other embellishments added later.

Tasting notes: The winery likes to focus on central coast grapes. Both the Santa Barbara County and Edna Valley Chardonnays were excellent, fruity and toasty with crisp finishes and hints of oak. The Pinot Noir had a berry-like nose and taste; light in body and mouth-filling. Paso Robles Syrah was big, oaky and peppery; excellent if you like assertive wines. The Cabernet was softer, complex and spicy with a light tannin finish. Prices range from well under $10 to the mid teens.

Tobin James Cellars • T GTA ✗

□ *8950 Union Rd., Paso Robles, CA 93446; (805) 239-2204. Daily 10 to 6; MC/VISA. Most varieties tasted. A few wine logo items; picnic area. Tours by appointment.* □

In the wine country, you don't often hear the expression "Belly up to the bar, boys," so you probably haven't been to Tobin James. And what a great bar it is—an elaborately carved structure more than a century old, complete with a mirrored backbar. Tobin found it in an old saloon in Overton, Missouri—back there in Jesse James country. In fact, there's a couple of James Gang posters in his tasting room—stuck on the walls near the farm implements. In the background, you'll hear Garth Brooks wailing about being a misfit and bustin' up his former girlfriend's wedding party.

Are we still in the wine country?

If you think all this is improbable, how about an 18-year-old Cincinnati kid with no money deciding that he wanted to own a winery, and then actually doing it? This unlikely chain of events started when Tobin James Shumrick—working in a wine shop in Cincinatti—met Gary Eberle, then a partner and winemaker at Estrella River Winery. Tobin offered to follow Gary back to Paso Robles and work for no pay. Less than 15 years later, working hard, having fun and often laboring for free just to learn, Tobin had his own winery. He opened his cellars with its old Western saloon motif in 1994. Why the Western look?

"We wanted a place where people could feel comfortable," Tobin told us. "Sometimes, the wine industry takes itself too seriously."

Tasting notes Tobin *is* serious about making wine, particularly big and hearty reds—and "the medals just keep rockin' in," he said. A James Gang Reserve, big, lush and spicy was as good as Zinfandel gets. The Sure Fire Zinfandel was almost as great—spicy, peppery and raspberry. The Blue Sky Cabernet was complex and full of berry flavor, big enough to face off any entrée. "A charbroiled steak would be lost without it," according to the tasting notes. Barrel fermented Sundance Chardonnay was lush, silky and toasty. Prices range from well under $10 to the middle teens. Perhaps the best buy is a $7.50 blend of Gamay, Syrah and Pinot Noir that's soft, herbal and complex. It's called *Chateau le Cacheflo*.

We said he was serious about *making* wines, not about naming them.

Vintners choice: "My favorite? Whatever we have the most of."

THE BEST OF THE BUNCH

The best wine buys ● Houtz Vineyards and Los Olivos Vintners/Austin Cellars in Santa Ynez Valley; Corbett Canyon Vineyards in Edna Valley; Abbey D'or tasting room, Pesenti Winery and Hope Farms in the Templeton area; and Arciero Winery and Tobin James in the Estrella River Valley.

The most attractive wineries ● The Gainey Vineyard and Sunstone in Santa Ynez Valley; Fess Parker Winery in Foxen Canyon; Corbett Canyon Vineyards in Edna Valley; Justin Winery east of Paso Robles; and Arciero Winery in the Estrella River Valley.

The most interesting tasting rooms ● Sanford Winery east of Buellton; the Gainey Vineyard and Sunstone Winery in Santa Ynez Valley; Fess Parker Winery in Foxen Canyon; Mastantuono Winery, Castoro Cellars and Hope Farms in the Templeton area; Norman Vineyards and Twin Hills east of Paso Robles; and Laura's Vineyard and Arciero Winery in the Estrella River Valley.

The funkiest tasting room ● Tobin James in the Estrella River Valley.

The best gift shops ● Buttonwood Farm (with its wine, produce and specialty foods blend) in the Santa Ynez Valley; Mastantuono Winery, York Mountain Winery and Hope Farms in the Templeton area; and Laura's Vineyard and Arciero Winery in the Estrella River Valley.

The nicest picnic areas ● Houtz Vineyards, Carey Cellars and Firestone Vineyard in Santa Ynez Valley; Byron Winery in Santa Maria Valley; Harmony Cellars above Harmony; JanKris Vineyard and Hope Farms in the Templeton area; Norman Vineyards and Justin Cellars west of Paso Robles; and Arciero Winery in the Estrella River Valley.

The best tour • The Gainey Vineyard (guided), in Santa Ynez Valley.

Wineland activities and such

Winery touring maps • Santa Barbara County Wineries, available at area wineries or from the Santa Barbara County Vintners' Association, P.O. Box 1558, Santa Ynez, CA 93460-1558; (805) 688-0881. **Wineries of the Edna Valley and Arroyo Grande Valley**, available at area wineries or from: Edna Valley Arroyo Grande Vintners, P.O. Box 159, Arroyo Grande, CA 93420; 541-5868. **Wine Tasting in Paso Robles**, available at area wineries or from: Paso Robles Vintners and Growers, 1225 Polk St., Paso Robles, CA 93446, or call the Paso Robles Chamber of Commerce at 238-0506.

Wineland events • SANTA BARBARA COUNTY: Santa Barbara County Vintners' Festival, barrel tastings and other events various wineries in the Santa Ynez Valley, late April; (800) 218-0881 (805) 688-0881. Danish Days in Solvang includes some winery events, late September; (805) 688-3317.

SAN LUIS OBISPO COUNTY: Zinfandel Weekend with Paso Robles area wineries saluting the "mystery grape," mid-March; (805) 239-8463; Paso Robles Wine Festival, mid-May; (800) 549-WINE or (805) 239-8463. Central Coast Winetasting Classic, San Luis Bay Inn, Avila Beach, July; (805) 544-5229 or (805) 543-1323. Central Coast Wine Festival, Mission Plaza, San Luis Obispo, September; (805) 543-1323. Individual wineries also sponsor events throughout the year.

BEYOND THE VINEYARDS

The south central coast was a popular tourist area before the first Pesenti squeezed his first grape, and certainly before the new crop of high-tech wineries arrived. Without all those tasting rooms, tens of thousands still would come to prowl through the missions, poke about Solvang's shops and toast themselves on Pacific beaches. Just over the ridge, architecturally gorgeous, tile-roofed Santa Barbara is one of California's major tourist lures.

Starting from **Solvang**, we'll suggest driving tours that will carry you to the area's touristic highlights. First, you'll likely want to go "shop-about" in Solvang, stuff your little faces with Danish pastries, ride the horse-drawn streetcar and perhaps catch a play at the **Festival Theater.** A repertory group performs summer-long in this outdoor playhouse. **Elverhoy Museum** in a Scandinavian-style building at 1624 Elverhoy Way (Second Street) recalls Solvang's Danish heritage and the **Hans Christian Andersen Museum** above the Book Loft on Mission Street has exhibits concerning the legendary storyteller. You'll also want to investigate the museum and ancient adobe halls of **Mission Santa Inez.**

From Solvang, head south on Alisal Road, which coils through some of Santa Ynez Valley's prettiest oak woodlands. Pause at lushly wooded **Nojoqui Falls County Park** for the short hike to the waterfalls, which may or may not be falling, depending on the season. Continue on Alisal Road to U.S. 101; you can follow it south to **Gaviota State Beach** and on to alluring **Santa Barbara**, or head north to **Buellton** of pea soup fame.

We'll focus on the northern route, which is closer to the vinelands. From Buellton, take State Highway 246 west to **La Purísima Mission State**

Historic Park near Lompoc. It's the most authentically restored of California's 21 missions, having been rebuilt as a WPA project during the Depression. Workers used the same tools as those originally employed by the Indians. The Lompoc area also is famous for its glittering Technicolor **flower fields** in spring and early summer. **Vandenberg Air Force Base,** noted for its missile launches, is out this way but not open to casual visitors.

From Lompoc, head north on one of America's most scenic byways, State Highway 1. It will take you to the wide sandy beaches of **Oceano, Grover City** and clam-famous **Pismo Beach**. At the Grover City-Oceano section of **Pismo State Beach,** you can drive right along the surf, just like they do in the TV commercials—if your car has the proper tires. Be careful you don't get stuck; ask the ranger at the gate if the sand's firm enough for your vehicle.

Highway 1 rejoins U.S. 101 in Pismo, but avoid that and follow the ocean-front drive through **Shell Beach** to wonderfully funky old **Avila Beach.** It's a resort town right out of the Thirties with tiny stucco cottages and a beach walk. Just beyond, weathered **Port San Luis Pier** is host to a good seafood restaurant (listed below), a fish market, uncounted seagulls and an occasional visiting sea lion.

Return to U.S. 101 and explore tidy and well-kept old **San Luis Obispo.** Its visitor offerings include **Mission San Luis Obispo;** several boutiques, restaurants and antique shops in SLO's clean- swept downtown area, just below the mission. Nearby is the comely campus of **California Polytechnic State University,** or simply Cal Poly. (Noted for its high-tech agricultural courses, it's sometimes unkindly called "Cow Piley.")

From SLO, take State Highway 1 northwest to **Morro Bay,** a seaside charmer with dome-shaped **Morro Rock** as its centerpiece. Two state parks, **Morro Bay** and **Montaña de Oro,** preserve slices of rocky beaches, windy headlands and lush forests. Driving north on Highway 1, you'll skim the rough-hewn coastline and pass **Harmony,** the dairy town turned art colony. From here, you can continue north to aquatically rustic **Cambria**. Just beyond is **Hearst San Simeon State Historical Monument**, the lavish castle-home of the late newspaper baron William Randolph Hearst.

If you head south from Solvang, you'll want to visit Santa Barbara's many attractions. On the don't-miss list are **Mission Santa Barbara,** the **County Courthouse** with its lavish Spanish- Moorish architecture, **El Presidio de Santa Barbara State Historic Park** for the flavor of early Mexico, old **Stearns Wharf** and the city's excellent expanse of beaches.

A nice approach to Santa Barbara from Solvang is on State Highway 154. It carries you past **Lake Cachuma County Park** with boating, fishing, hiking, camping, and picnicking; across the dizzying **Cold Spring Bridge,** one of the highest single-arch spans in America, thence over **San Marcos Pass** through the rugged Santa Ynez Mountains. As you spiral down from the hills into Santa Barbara, you'll enjoy impressive city and ocean views.

Santa Ynez Valley activities & attractions

Boating, swimming • Cachuma Lake Recreation Area; (805) 688-4658.

Elverhoy Museum • 1624 Elverhoy Way, Solvang, CA 93463; (805) 686-1211. Friday 11 to 4, weekends 1 to 4. This small museum focuses on Solvang's Scandinavian heritage.

Hans Christian Andersen Museum • Above the Book Loft and Coffee House on Mission Street in Solvang. Open daily from 9, various closing hours. Exhibits concerning the life of storyteller Hans Christian Andersen, plus vintage books for display and sale.

La Purisima Mission State Historic Park • Lompoc, CA 93436; (805) 733-3713. Daily 9 to 5; modest admission charge. A faithful WPA reconstruction of an early California mission.

Mission Santa Inez • 1760 Mission Dr., Solvang, CA 93463; (805) 688-4815. Weekdays 9 to 5, Saturdays 9 to 4:30 and Sundays noon to 4:30. Restored early California mission; self-guiding tour and museum.

Santa Ynez Valley Historical Society Museum and Carriage House • 3596 Sagunto St., Santa Ynez, CA 93460; (805) 688-7889. Museum open Friday-Sunday 1 to 4 and carriage house Tuesday-Thursday 10 to 4 and Friday-Sunday 1-4. Exhibits on local history and the Chumash Indians.

Theater • Solvang Theaterfest, June-September, outdoors in the Solvang Festival Theater; (805) 922-8313. Pacific Conservatory of the Performing Arts Theaterfest, Allan Hancock College, Santa Maria; (805) 922- 8313.

San Luis Obispo County attractions

Mission San Luis Obispo • Chorro and Monterey streets, San Luis Obispo, CA 93405; (805) 543-6850. Daily 9 to 5. Restored early California mission, self- guiding tours, museum.

San Luis Obispo County Historical Museum • 696 Monterey St., San Luis Obispo, CA 93405; (805) 543-0638. Wednesday-Sunday 10 to 4. Historical exhibits in restored Carnegie Library.

WINE COUNTRY DINING
Santa Barbara County

A.J. Spurs • ☆☆☆ *$$$*

☐ *350 E. Hwy. 246 (just east of the freeway), Buellton; (805) 686-1655. Western barbecue-style fare; full bar service. Dinner nightly 4 to 9:30. MC/VISA, AMEX.* ☐ Housed in an oversized log cabin, abrim with Old Western atmosphere, contrived but nicely done. Cowboy curios, game trophies and geegaws to study while you chew. The menu is as Western as John Wayne's drawl—barbecued steaks, ribs and chicken, served with soup, salsa and tequila beans. Live music Friday and Saturday.

Bit O' Denmark • ☆☆ *$$*

☐ *473 Alisal Rd. (Mission Drive), Solvang; (805) 688-5426. Danish-American; full bar service. Daily 8 a.m. to 9 p.m. Major credit cards.* ☐ Popular Danish restaurant featuring breakfasts with a variety of pancakes; a full *smörgasbord* for lunch and dinner, plus *frikadeller* (meatballs with sweet and sour red cabbage). Local wines and international beers.

Cold Spring Tavern • ☆☆☆ *$$$*

☐ *5995 Stagecoach Rd. (half an hour uphill from Solvang on Highway 154), Santa Barbara; (805) 967-0066. American; full bar service. Lunch daily 11 to 3, dinner Sunday-Thursday 5 to 9 and Friday-Saturday 5 to 10, breakfast weekends only, 8 to 11. Reservations essential on weekends; MC/VISA.* ☐ Century-old stage stop tucked into the bottom of a ravine; a setting that's at once dramatic, romantic and rustic. Wagon wheel chandeliers, kerosene lamps and the like. Varied menu with large portions—steak, pasta, chop, venison, rabbit and chicken, with interesting seasonings and sauces. Smoke-free; live music on weekends.

Danish Inn Restaurant ● ☆☆ $$

⊡ *1547 Mission Dr., Solvang; (805) 688-4813. Danish-continental; full bar service. Daily 11:30 to 10. Major credit cards.* ⊡ Scandinavian in architecture and menu, styled as an old world wayside inn. *Smörgasbord* and assorted continental entrées. Family owned restaurant since 1973. Piano bar nightly in lounge.

The Hitching Post ● ☆☆ $$$

⊡ *406 E. Hwy 246 (half mile east of the freeway), Buellton; (805) 688-0676. Western barbecue; full bar service. Daily 5 to 9:30; MC/VISA.* ⊡ Long established, locally popular place featuring barbecue specialties: steak, baby back pork ribs, grilled quail, chicken or duck and seafood. Décor is austere rural American.

The Little Mermaid ● ☆☆ $$

⊡ *1546 Mission Dr. (Fourth Place), Solvang; (805) 688-6141. Danish-American; wine and beer. Lunch noon to 4, dinner 7:30 a.m. to 8 p.m. MC/VISA, AMEX.* ⊡ Cute Scandinavian-style café featuring puffy round pancakes called *aebleskivers*. The "skiver-maker" works in full view, observable from within or without the restaurant. Breakfasts feature *aebleskivers* with a dollop of jam and a large Danish sausage. Also Danish and American lunches and dinners.

Massimi Ristorante ● ☆☆ $$$

⊡ *1588 Mission Dr. (Petersen Village Square), Solvang; (805) 688-0027. Italian; wine and beer. Daily except Monday, 5:30 p.m. to 9 p.m. MC/VISA, AMEX.* ⊡ Pleasingly decorated Italian chef-owned restaurant featuring fresh pastas, Osso Buco, seafood, chicken, veal and in-house desserts.

Mattei's Tavern ● ☆☆☆ $$

⊡ *Highway 154 (Grand Avenue), Los Olivos; (805) 688-4820. American; full bar service. Monday- Thursday from 5:30, Friday-Sunday from noon. Reservations advised on weekends; MC/VISA.* ⊡ An 1886 stage stop, refurbished and furnished with antiques and western America artifacts. Menu ranges from prime rib and steaks to fresh seafood and pastas.

Moellerkrohn ● ☆☆ $$

⊡ *Alisal Ave., Solvang; (805) 688-4555. Danish-American; wine and beer. Lunch and dinner daily. Major credit cards.* ⊡ Another of Solvang's Danish style restaurants, serving a complete *smörgasbord* dinner, plus Danish sausage and meatball entrées for dinner, and open faced sandwiches for lunch.

Mustard Seed ● ☆☆ $$

⊡ *1655 Mission (First), Solvang; (805) 688-1318. American rural; no alcohol. Breakfast and lunch daily from 7:30, dinner Tuesday-Saturday 5:30 until 9. MC/VISA.* ⊡ American country restaurant in a Danish style cottage, featuring rural fare such as breaded veal cutlets, sautéed beef liver and southern fried chicken.

Pea Soup Andersen's ● ☆☆ $$

⊡ *376 Avenue of the Flags, Buellton; (805) 688-5581. American; full bar service. Daily 7 a.m. to 10 p.m. MC/VISA.* ⊡ Historic restaurant started in 1924, based on Juliette's recipe for split pea soup. It's still the most interesting thing on the menu, which features Americana steaks, chops and pot roast. Complex includes gift shops, fruit wine tasting and a mini-museum offering a quick study of Anderson family history.

Royal Scandia Restaurant ● ☆☆ $$$

☐ *420 Alisal Rd. (downtown), Solvang; (805) 688-8000. American-continental; full bar service. 7 a.m. to 9 p.m. daily. Major credit cards.* ☐ Danish-style restaurant with Scandinavian entrées, plus other European and American fare such as chicken marsala, chardonnay seafood pasta and teriyaki sirloin. Buffet breakfast daily; brunch on Sunday. Scandinavian interior with open beam cathedral ceiling; Outdoor patio.

The Viking Garden ● ☆☆ $

☐ *446-C Alisal Rd. (Copenhagen), Solvang; (805) 688-1250. Danish, German, American and Mexican; wine and beer. Breakfast, lunch and dinner daily. MC/VISA.* ☐ Small restaurant that looks more Italian than Danish, with red checkered tablecloths. The menu is eclectic and inexpensive, and includes "early bird" Danish dinners such as *Karbonander* (breaded pork patties and red cabbage) and *kassler rippchen* (smoked pork chops with sauerkraut and potato pancakes). Indoor and outdoor dining.

San Luis Obispo County

A.J. Spurs ● ☆☆☆ $$$

☐ *508 Main St., Templeton; (805) 434-2700. Western barbecue; full bar service. Daily 4 to 9:30. Major credit cards.* ☐ See description under Santa Barbara County.

Berardi's Italian Restaurant ● ☆☆ $$

☐ *1202 Pine St., Paso Robles; (805) 238-1330. Italian; wine and beer. Dinner nightly 5 to 9:30. Reservations essential on weekends; MC/VISA.* ☐ Local hangout housed in a narrow, century-old brick store; busy and noisy most nights. Some interesting dishes include chicken *saltimbucca* topped with prosciutto and cheese and calamari *Diablo* with sweet peppers and onions. Customers select their own local or imported wine from wine racks.

Chelsea Book and Café ● ☆ $

☐ *Spring and Sixth streets (Valley Oak Plaza), Paso Robles; (805) 237-2464. Light fare; no alcohol. Weekdays 8 a.m. to 9 p.m., Saturday 8:30 to 10, Sunday 11 to 6. MC/VISA.* ☐ Attractive new bookstore-café with comfortable couch seating amidst oak book shelves; salads, sandwiches and specialty coffees; oatmeal cookies are a popular item.

Ian McPhee's ● ☆☆☆ $$$

☐ *416 Main Street, Templeton; (805) 434-3204. American; full bar service. Lunch weekdays from 11:30 to 2:30, dinner nightly from 5. Major credit cards.* ☐ Appealing old style restaurant with a contemporary menu—lemon pepper boneless chicken, grilled veal chops, New York pepper Steak and barbecued duck. The look is early Americana, with cane back chairs, coffered ceiling and old fashioned bar.

Joshua's Restaurant and Vineyards ● ☆☆☆ $$$

☐ *13th and Vine streets, Paso Robles; (805) 238-7515. American; full bar service. Lunch Monday-Friday 11:30 to 2:30, dinner Monday-Sunday from 4, Sunday brunch 10 to 2. MC/VISA, AMEX.* ☐ Very appealing restaurant, fashioned into a century old Catholic church building; spacious interior with the original stained glass. Menu focuses on steaks, sweetbreads, prime rib, chicken, baby back ribs, seafood and pastas. Periodic "Meet the Winemaker Dinners," with five courses and five local wines. Live entertainment Friday and Saturday nights.

Old Harmony Pasta Factory and Saloon ● ☆☆ $$

◻ *Two Old Creamery Rd., Harmony; (805) 927-5882. Italian-Californian; wine and beer. Lunch in the saloon 11 to 5, dinner nightly from 5, Sunday brunch 9:30 to 2. Reservations advised; MC/VISA, AMEX.* ◻ Cute old place done in rural Americana, in the old Harmony creamery complex. Italian menu, with assorted home made pastas, pork and chicken dishes, plus seafood with California accents. Outdoor dining.

Olde Port Inn ● ☆☆☆ $$$

◻ *Port San Luis Pier; (805) 595-2515. American, mostly seafood; full bar service. Lunch and dinner daily, from 11 and 5:30. Reservations essential on weekends; MC/VISA.* ◻ Cheerfully rustic fish house perched on the Port San Luis Pier, with views of sand, sea and headlands. Daily seafood specials are fresh, often just off one of the restaurant's boats. The spicy *bouillabaisse* is excellent. Live 50s and 60s music on weekends.

Paso Robles Inn ● ☆☆ $$

◻ *1103 Spring St. (Eleventh Street), Paso Robles; (805) 238-2660. American; full bar service. Daily 7 a.m. to 9 p.m. Reservations advised; major credit cards.* ◻ Turn-of-the-century dining room in Paso Robles' landmark multi-gabled brick hotel. The menu fits the mood—steak, prime rib, chicken and chops, with a focus on local wines. Veranda dining; live music on weekends.

This Old House ● ☆☆☆ $$$

◻ *740 W. Foothill Blvd. (west on Los Osos from freeway), San Luis Obispo; (805) 543-2690. Western barbecue; full bar service. Monday-Friday from 5, Saturday-Sunday from 4. Reservations advised; major credit cards.* ◻ Some folks say this 1917 house is haunted, that chairs move by themselves. Perhaps it's merely hungry diners reaching for another brace of ribs or a barbecued chicken wing. In a rural setting at the end of Foothill Boulevard, decorated with old photos, Indian sketches and Western regalia.

Weedwacker Coffee House ● ☆ $

◻ *590 Main St., Templeton; (805) 434-3865. Deli; wine and beer. Daily 7 a.m. to 7:30 p.m. MC/VISA.* ◻ Busy little deli offering soups, sandwiches, pastries, bagels and specialty coffees; adjacent to Abbey D'Or tasting room; small sidewalk patio.

WINELAND LODGINGS
Santa Barbara County

The Ballard Inn ● ☆☆☆☆ $$$$$ ∅

◻ *2436 Baseline (Alamo Pintado Road), Ballard, CA 93463; (800) 638-BINN or (805) 688-7770. Rooms $160 to $195. MC/VISA.* ◻ Comfortably elegant 15-room Victorian inn, furnished with antiques. Individually decorated rooms stocked with cheese, crackers and fruit; some rooms with fireplaces. Full cooked-to-order breakfast, afternoon wine with *hors d'oeuvres.*

Danish Country Inn ● ☆☆☆ $$$ ∅

◻ *1455 Mission Dr., Solvang, CA 93463; (805) 688-2018. Units $62 to $77; rates include continental breakfast. Major credit cards.* ◻ Danish-style 82-room motel with TV-VCRs, phones and refrigerators; swimming pool.

Meadowlark Motel ● ☆☆ $$

◻ *2644 Mission Dr. (near Refugio Road), Solvang, CA 93463; (805) 688-4631. Couples $45 to $55, singles $40 to $50, kitchenettes $55 to $68. Major* credit cards. ⬜ A 19-room motel on two acres just east of Solvang; TV, phones; pool; nicely landscaped grounds.

Svendsgaard's Lodge ● ☆☆ $$$ ∅

⬜ *1711 Mission Dr. (Alisal Road), Solvang, CA 93463; (800) 733-8757 or (805) 688-3277. Couples $50 to $80, singles $45 to $75, kitchenettes $90, suites $75 to $90. Major credit cards.* ⬜ Danish-style 48-room motel with remote TV, room phones; free continental breakfast, swimming pool.

Solvang Royal Scandinavian Inn ● ☆☆☆ $$$$ ∅

⬜ *400 Alisal Rd. (P.O. Box 30), Solvang, CA 93464; (800) 624-5572 or (805) 688-8000. Couples and singles $95 to $135, suites from $135. Major credit cards.* ⬜ Attractive 133-room resort; TV movies, room phones, Danish-American décor. Pool, spa, fireplace in lobby, dancing in Valhalla lounge. **Royal Scandia restaurant** serves from 7 a.m. to 9 p.m.; California-continental with Danish specialties; dinners $15 to $21.50; full bar service.

Tivoli Inn ● ☆☆☆ $$$$$

⬜ *1564 Copenhagen Dr. (Atterdag Avenue), Solvang, CA 93463; (800) 266-1484 or (805) 688-0559. Rooms and suites $125 to $250; rates include continental breakfast. Major credit cards.* ⬜ Nicely appointed 29-room Danish inn. TV, phones, fireplaces and mini-bars in rooms; swimming pool. **Restaurant** serves seafood and California *nouveau*, lunch and dinner, full bar.

San Luis Obispo County

San Luis Obispo, Morro Bay and Pismo Beach have dozens of motels. Our list here covers only communities next door to the vineyards: Paso Robles, Arroyo Grande and Templeton.

Adelaide Motor Inn ● ☆☆ $$ ∅

⬜ *1215 Ysabel Ave. (Highway 46 exit), Paso Robles, CA 93446; (800) 549-PASO (California) or (805) 238-2770. Couples $47 to $50, singles $36 to $47, suites $72 to $81. Major credit cards.* ⬜ Nicely-appointed 67-unit motel; TV movies, video rentals, phones, radios, refrigerators. Heated pool; laundry.

Arbor Inn ● ☆☆☆☆ $$$$$ ∅

⬜ *2175 Arbor Rd., Paso Robles, CA 93446; (805) 238-6979 (the number for adjacent Hope Farms Winery). Units $95 to $215. Major credit cards.* ⬜ Beautiful new multi-gabled eight-room inn opened in 1995. It's adjacent to Hope Farms Winery, with the same elegant country home style. Rooms furnished with English antiques. Full or continental breakfast and late afternoon snacks with wine.

Arroyo Village Inn Bed & Breakfast ● ☆☆☆ $$$$ ∅

⬜ *407 El Camino Real (Brisco or Halcyon exits), Arroyo Grande, CA 94320; (805) 489-5926. Couples $95 to $110, singles $85 to $155, suites $125 to $179. Major credit cards.* ⬜ Seven rooms in a replicated Victorian farmhouse, all with private baths; TV and VCRs available. Full breakfast, afternoon wines and cordials. Early American country décor with Laura Ashley prints and antiques.

Best Western Black Oak Motor Lodge ● ☆☆☆ $$$ ∅

⬜ *1135 24th St. (Highway 46 exit), Paso Robles, CA 93446; (800) 528-1234 or (805) 238-4740. Couples and singles $48 to $68. Major credit cards.* ⬜ A 110-unit motel with TV, radios, phones and refrigerators. Swimming and wading pools, spa, sauna, coin laundry. **Black Oak Restaurant** serves 7 a.m. to 10:30 p.m.; American; dinners $10 to $18; full bar service.

Best Western Casa Grande Inn ● ☆☆☆ $$$ Ø

☐ *850 Oak Park Rd. (Oak Park exit), Arroyo Grande, CA 93420; (800) 528-1234 or (805) 481-7398. Couples $63 to $95, singles $58 to $88; kitchenettes and suites available. Major credit cards.* ☐ A 114-unit motel with TV movies, phones, some rooms with refrigerators, some efficiency units. Pool, spa, sauna, game room, small exercise room, coin laundry. Free continental breakfast, beer and wine. Adjacent **Lyon's Restaurant** serves 7 a.m. to 11 p.m.; American; dinners $7 to $11; full bar service.

Country House Inn ● ☆☆☆ $$$$ Ø

☐ *91 Main St. (Vineyard Drive), Templeton, CA 93465; (800) 362-6032 or (805) 434-1598. Couples $75 to $95, singles $70 to $90. MC/VISA, DISC.* ☐ Bed and breakfast inn with six rooms; four with private baths. Full breakfast. An 1886 Victorian with country French furnishings, landscaped gardens.

Econo Lodge ● ☆☆ $$$

☐ *611 El Camino Real (Halcyon Road exit), Arroyo Grande, CA 93420; (805) 489-9300. Units $55 to $100; rates include continental breakfast. Major credit cards.* ☐ A 42-unit motel with TV, room phones; pool.

Just Inn ● ☆☆☆☆ $$$$$ Ø

☐ *At Justin Winery, 11680 Chimney Rock Rd., Paso Robles, CA 93446; (805) 238-6932. Three suites, $195 each; $155 for Justin wine club members (membership is free). MC/VISA, AMEX.* ☐ Opulent French château style inn with luxuriously furnished three-room suites with decks; overstuffed tapestry-covered furniture, down comforters, ceiling murals and marble bathrooms with hydro-tubs. Full breakfast, evening wine; pool, spa and bicycles.

Madonna Inn ● ☆☆☆ $$$$ Ø

☐ *100 Madonna Rd. (just off freeway), San Luis Obispo, CA 93405; (800) 543-9666 or (805) 543-3000. Couples and singles $82 to $170, suites $130 to $170. Major credit cards.* ☐ Legendary for its whimsical, gaudy architecture, the inn has 109 rooms, all decorated differently. Many travelers stop just to check out the architecture in the lobby, restaurant and even the restrooms. Rooms have TV, phones and flashy décor. **Dining room** serves from 5:30 to 10 p.m. (coffee shop from 7 a.m. to 9 p.m.); American; dinners $16 to $30; full bar services. Dining areas are smoke free.

Paso Robles Travelodge ● ☆☆ $$ Ø

☐ *2701 Spring St., Paso Robles, CA 93446; (800) 255-3050 or (805) 238-0078. Couples $38 to $48, singles $34 to $48. Major credit cards.* ☐ Thirty-one rooms; TV movies, room phones, refrigerators; pool.

South central coast information sources

Arroyo Grande Chamber of Commerce, 150 W. Branch St., Arroyo Grande, CA 93420; (805) 489-1488.

Paso Robles Chamber of Commerce, 1113 Spring St., Paso Robles, CA 93446; (805) 238-0506.

San Luis Obispo Chamber of Commerce, 1039 Chorro St., San Luis Obispo, CA 93401; (805) 781-2777.

Solvang Chamber of Commerce, 1511 Mission St., Solvang, CA 93463; (805) 688-3317. (Visitor information booth on Copenhagen near first, adjacent to small downtown park.)

"It has flavors of blackberry-like fruit with hints of fresh plums, spice, cassis and beeswax with a cigar box quality."
— **Description of a Santino Amador County Zinfandel**

Chapter Twelve
THE GOLD COUNTRY
Bottled bullion from the Sierra foothills

No region looms larger in the history of California than the foothills of the Sierra Nevada. Here, the discovery of gold in 1848 catapulted a remote Mexican outpost into the most populous and prosperous state in the Union.

This also was the one of the state's first major wine producing areas. There were, after all, a lot of thirsty miners in those hills! When the gold ran out in the late 1800s, most of the people ran out, too, and wineries began closing. Prohibition finished off all save one. Today, the wineries and the people are coming back, and this region of the Sierra Nevada foothills called the "Gold Country" is one of California's most diverse and scenic winelands.

The Sierra foothills wine country is focused in three counties in the heart of the Gold Country—El Dorado, Amador and Calaveras. Early Spanish miners called this region *La Veta Madre*. We know it by the more familiar "Mother Lode."

During the rush to riches, towns germinated overnight, then they faded as the gold was depleted. In the fading, they left a treasure trove of sturdy brick buildings, grand balconied hotels and Victorian homes. These now house antique and curio shops, museums and bed and breakfast inns. The area has more state historic parks than any other region of California. All of this yesterday lore is set in scenic foothills of oak clusters, pine forests and tawny meadows.

Vineyards are here, too—draped over ridges, terraced up steep slopes and tucked into hidden canyons. They merge with woodlands, pastures and an occasional Christmas tree farm to create a rumpled green patchwork quilt. Sierra foothills tasting rooms are inviting places, often in intriguing settings. Some are in log or rough stone cellars dating back to the gold rush. Others are in modern structures perched on high knolls, offering a panorama of the hilly countryside.

275

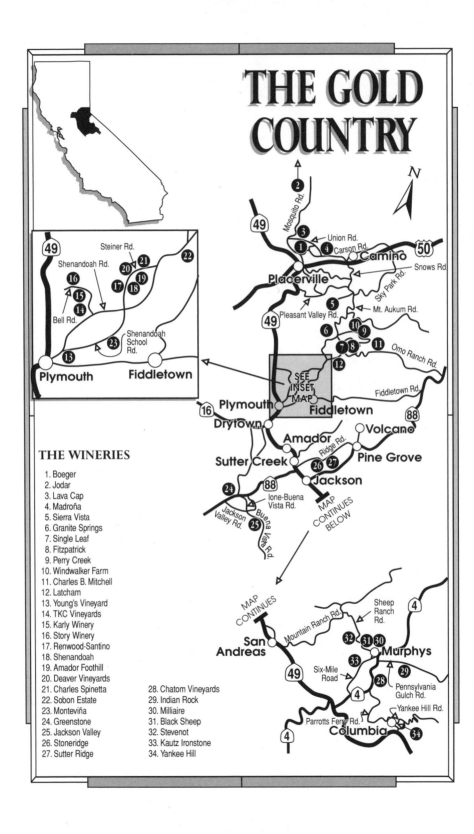

THE GOLD COUNTRY

THE WINERIES

1. Boeger
2. Jodar
3. Lava Cap
4. Madroña
5. Sierra Vista
6. Granite Springs
7. Single Leaf
8. Fitzpatrick
9. Perry Creek
10. Windwalker Farm
11. Charles B. Mitchell
12. Latcham
13. Young's Vineyard
14. TKC Vineyards
15. Karly Winery
16. Story Winery
17. Renwood-Santino
18. Shenandoah
19. Amador Foothill
20. Deaver Vineyards
21. Charles Spinetta
22. Sobon Estate
23. Monteviña
24. Greenstone
25. Jackson Valley
26. Stoneridge
27. Sutter Ridge
28. Chatom Vineyards
29. Indian Rock
30. Milliaire
31. Black Sheep
32. Stevenot
33. Kautz Ironstone
34. Yankee Hill

As further incentive to visit this region, the wines are excellent, winning a goodly share of medals, and they're remarkably inexpensive. This is primarily red wine territory. The area's Zinfandels are legendary, and account for more than half the total vineyard acreage. Sierra foothills reds are typically robust, spicy and full-flavored, without a lot of filtering and fining. They're straightforward and hearty, like the people who settled this land. Some excellent whites are made here as well, in the higher, cooler elevations.

There is no best season to tour the Gold Country's wine country. In winter, one can sip a bit of Zin after hitting the ski slopes a few miles above the vineyards. In spring, summer and fall, these mountains and their running streams lure hikers, campers, white-water enthusiasts and fisherfolk. Dams, thrown across the rivers to form reservoirs and quench flatlanders' thirst, form dozens of reservoirs that draw the boating set.

These streams ran unchecked for millions of years, leaching gold from the great granite *massif* of the Sierra Nevada—Spanish for snowy peaks. As they reached the foothills, the streams slowed their flow, depositing their valuable cargo in their gravelly beds.

On January 24, 1848, an itinerant carpenter named James Wilson Marshall had the dumb luck to find a bit of this gold in the tailrace of a sawmill. He'd been hired by John Sutter, a flamboyant Swiss entrepreneur, to build the mill on the American River. Sutter had conned 50,000 acres of land from officials of Mexican California, and he needed lumber to create a new empire. Checking his tail race one morning, Marshall saw something glitter. He bent down and picked up two tiny nuggets, about "half the size and of the shape of a pea." The rest is epic.

Most of the hundreds of thousands of gold seekers drawn by Marshall's discovery found nothing but frustration. Many moved down into the valley to start farms and to finish building the hastily assembled cities of San Francisco, Stockton and Sacramento.

A few, mostly Italians, stayed in these sun-warmed hills and planted grapes. They figured their brethren still laboring in the mines would work up a mighty thirst. Soon, thousands of acres of vines thrived in the foothills of El Dorado, Amador and Calaveras counties. Zinfandel was then—as it is now—the wine of choice. By the 1880s, a hundred wineries were operating.

They were never very large and all save one was closed, either by dwindling population as the gold ran out, by phylloxera or by Prohibition. Only D'Agostini Winery (now Sobon Estate) traces its roots to the gold rush. It was founded in 1856 by Adam Uhlinger who, like Sutter, was Swiss.

In the 1970s, U.C. Davis researchers found that the soil and terrain in some of the foothill areas provided ideal conditions for Zinfandel. Hot summer afternoons, cool alpine nights and tough granite soil produce high-sugar, high-acid grapes that ripen late, sometime between deer season and the first rains.

A few early foothill growers had retained their vineyards after the wineries closed, selling their grapes to vintners in Napa and Sonoma. Observers noted that many award-winning Zins bore curious names like Amador, Grandpère and Fiddletown. Soon, a new gold rush began in these hills—quieter this time, and from a different direction. Between 1970 and 1995, the number of wineries increased from one to nearly fifty.

Amador County is the Sierra foothills's best known wine producing area because of its Zinfandel reputation. Most of its vineyards and wineries are concentrated in the Shenandoah Valley east of Plymouth. The counties above and below Amador are gaining in vinicultural stature, as well. El Dorado County to the north has some of the world's highest vineyards, approaching 3,000 feet. These elevations offer suitable climate for Chardonnay, Sauvignon Blanc, Cabernet Sauvignon, Merlot and other cool-weather types. El Dorado's wineries are focused in two areas—the Apple Hill region north of Placerville, and the Somerset-Fairplay area to the south.

Calaveras County, just below Amador, is the Gold Country's newest wine region, boasting several hundred acres of grapes and six wineries with tasting rooms. They're around Murphys, uphill from Angels Camp. South across the Stanislaus River in Tuolumne County, a single winery-tasting room operates near Columbia State Historic Park.

Frost is an ever-present danger in the foothills, so vines often are located in pocket canyons, or on wind-graced ridges. Another problem, faced by few other California grape growers, is hungry deer. You'll note eight to ten-foot fences around many vineyards.

We'll divide our Gold Country winery tour into its three major county areas. Assuming that you plan to approach them one at a time, we'll suggest the most logical routes from the San Francisco Bay Area for each. Some wineries in this region are open only on weekends, so plan accordingly. Most of these, however, will offer tastings and informal tours on weekdays if you call ahead.

EL DORADO COUNTY WINERY TOUR ● If you've ever been lured by the cool scenery and hot dice of south shore Lake Tahoe, you have passed this way, driving eastward on U.S. Highway 50. Let the dice cool this time and get off in Placerville, where the dry Central Valley begins to rumple into the Sierra foothills.

The freeway ends in Placerville and then resumes about a mile further up. You might like to detour through the old downtown area. Main Street, paralleling U.S. 50, offers an interesting mix of brick front, cut stone, Art Deco and modern store fronts, sheltering assorted shops, boutiques cafés and antique stores. Check the beautifully restored **Cary House** hotel, on the right as you enter town.

Near the Greek federalist style **El Dorado County Courthouse,** turn left onto Bedford Avenue to re-join Highway 50 and continue north. After about a mile, exit on Schnell School Road, go left under the freeway, drive uphill a few blocks to Carson Road, and turn right. This takes you into **Apple Hill,** a high, rolling ridgeline area noted for its orchards, fruit stands, Christmas tree farms and wineries.

During autumn, tens of thousands of visitors swarm over ribboned country lanes to buy apples, home-baked pies and other apple goodies from dozens of fruit stands, packing sheds and seasonal café-bake shops. Some

---

WINERY CODES ● T = Tasting with no fee; *T$* = Tasting for a fee; *GT* = Guided tours; *GTA* = Guided tours by appointment; *ST* = Self-guiding tours; *CT* = casual tours or a peek into the winery; ✕ = picnic area; 📻 = Gift shop or good giftware selection. Price ranges listed in tasting notes are for varietals; jug wines may be available for less.

operate the year-around. This is exceptionally pretty country. It's a patch-work of orchards, vineyards and evergreens—both Christmas tree farms and forests *au natural*. Clusters of cottonwoods and poplars provide dazzling bursts of yellow in autumn.

Weekdays are best for an autumn visit to Apple Hill, since both the fruit stands and the tasting rooms can be rather busy during weekends, and most of the wineries are open daily. On the other hand, most of the Somerset-Fair-play wineries are open only on weekends.

Climbing into the pine belt on Carson Road, you encounter your first win-ery within a quarter of a mile, **Boeger,** down in a little hollow to your left. The next winery, **Jodar Vineyards,** is a bit of a challenge to reach, albeit a *scenic* challenge. (Passenger cars can make it easily, although the route isn't recommended for large RVs or trailer rigs.) Head north from Boeger (passing Perron Orchards, one of the few apple hill outlets that's open all year) and turn left onto Union Ridge Road, just beyond Abel's Apple Acres. After 1.5 miles, go right onto Mosquito Road. You'll twist and wind through thick for-est and down into a dramatic, rocky ravine, then cross a skinny one-lane ca-ble suspension bridge. After a corkscrew climb up the other side, you'll pass through high country forest. Fork left onto La Paz Road and go quickly left again onto Mosquito Cutoff Road. After about a mile, it's left yet again, onto Rock Creek Road and then right onto Gravel Road (in name and in fact). This takes you along a high ridgeline to the winery.

After successfully unraveling this complex course (worth it for the views), return to Union Ridge, go left and—just before you hit Carson Road—go left again onto Hassler Road. Take it a short distance to Fruitridge Road, turn left and you're at **Lava Cap Winery** on the right. Leaving Lava Cap, continue northward on Fruitridge, past the **U.S. Forest Service tree nursery** with its great swatches of tree seedlings, so small they look like coarse grass. Fruitridge soon bumps into North Canyon Road; go right and you'll return to Carson. Pressing northward for a mile, turn left and follow signs to **Madroña Vineyards**.

Continue north on Carson Road and you'll pass another all-year fruit and produce place, Boa Vista, on your right. Just beyond, Carson carries you into the cute little wood frame town of Camino. Turn right onto Snows Road at the "Pleasant Valley" sign and drop down under the Highway 50 freeway (there's no interchange here). A twisting, up and down four miles gets you to Newtown Road; go left and follow it to Pleasant Valley Road and go left again. Drive a bit over half a mile and turn right up Leisure Lane in down-town Pleasant Valley. Two upward miles take you to **Sierra Vista Winery,** occupying a knoll with an impressive view of the Sierra Nevada. This is one of the few foothill perches where you see the granite ridge itself, since lower mountains generally block your view.

Retreat from these heights, continue half a mile on Pleasant Valley Road and turn right onto Mount Aukum Road. You're headed for a cluster of win-eries surrounding a wooded hamlet with a great name left over from the rush to riches, Fairplay. Follow Mount Aukum about 6.5 miles, turn left onto Fairplay Road and drive 1.5 miles to **Granite Springs Winery** at the end of a narrow lane to your left. Just beyond, up another narrow lane is the new **Single Leaf Vineyards,** on your right. About a mile beyond, up another gravel lane to the right, **Fitzpatrick Winery** occupies a bluff with an awe-some vineyard and mountain view. A short distance beyond Fitzpatrick, in the one-store hamlet of **Fairplay,** turn left onto Perry Creek Road. Follow it a but under two miles and go right up a narrow lane to the imposing new **Perry Creek Vineyards.** Immediately beyond is **Windwalker Farm**; also on your right.

Now, retrace your route to Fairplay, turn left onto Fairplay Road and follow it briefly to **Charles B Mitchell Vineyards,** up a lane to your left. Just beyond, Fairplay bumps into Omo Ranch Road; turn right and within about three miles, **Latcham Vineyards** appears on your left, tucked behind its own vineyards.

This ends the El Dorado segment. If you continue west on Omo Ranch Road and follow it to Mount Aukum Road, you'll wind up in the Shenandoah Valley, home to Amador County wineries.

Boeger Winery • T CT ✕

☐ *1709 Carson Rd., Placerville, CA 95667; (916) 622-8094. Daily 10 to 5; MC/VISA. All varieties tasted. Some wine logo gift items. Casual tours on request; attractive picnic facilities.* ☐

This rustic ranch style winery has two links to the past. Although the present facility dates from 1972, it was established on the site of the Fossati-Lombardo Winery, hearkening back to the 1870s. Further, founder Greg Boeger is the grandson of Anton Nichelini, who started the still-operating Nichelini Winery high above the Napa Valley in 1890. The Boegers and Nichelinis still share close ties, swapping grapes and probably stories of the old days. For a period, Greg served as the Nichelini winemaker.

The tasting room is in a rough-cut stone structure that housed the original Fossati-Lombardo facility. It's listed on the National Register of Historic Places as one of America's oldest winery structures. The family lived upstairs and stomped the grapes there; juice flowed down through wooden chutes to fermenting vats in the cellar. Those chutes are still in place, hanging above the tasting counter.

Pear trees, vines and flowers share the busy farmyard with winery buildings. Several picnic tables are tucked into assorted shady spots; some are on a shady terrace above a pond.

Tasting notes: Boeger produces a Chardonnay, Sauvignon Blanc, a couple of Zinfandels, Barbera, Merlot, Cabernet Sauvignon, Cabernet Franc a table wine with a great name—Hangtown Red. Our favorites were a nutty-fruity Chardonnay; El Dorado Zinfandel with a great peppery taste; and Hangtown Red, much better than a mere table wine with Cab, Barbera and Petite Sirah. Prices range from $7 to the mid teens. Recently added to the list is Greg Boeger's "M Series": Meritage, an Italian blend called Migilóre, a Spanish blend Milagro and a French Rhône blend, Majeure.

Vintners choice: Greg's wife Sue read them off: "Merlot, Cabernet Sauvignon, Barbera and Cabernet Franc. Our elevation, climate and soil are excellent for the reds."

Jodar Vineyards • T ✕

☐ *2393 Gravel Rd., Placerville, CA 95667; (916) 626-4582. Weekends only, noon to 5, or by appointment; major credit cards. Most tasted; small picnic area with valley views.* ☐

The Jodar winery operation is in a simple metal building, with a modest tasting room occupying one corner, and a picnic table or two down the slope a bit. Although the winery isn't visually impressive, its hilltop perch offers one of the most imposing vistas in the county. Green-blue waves of mountains fall away to the horizon; new vineyards spill their orderly rows down from this steep ridge. The winery complex, brand new and rather spartan when we visited, may be more elaborate by the time you arrive.

Byron and Sherril Jodar and Byron's brother Vaughn opened this tiny winery in 1992, and their production has increased significantly, to 3,000 cases a year. They own 40 acres of this mountain top and plan to have more than half of this in grapes. Three different careers are represented by the team. Byron was a geologist employed by the federal government, Sherril is an accountant and Vaughn is a public health worker. They aren't amateurs, however; they've been making wine at home for 20 years.

Tasting notes: Initially, the Jodars produced only Cabernet Sauvignon and Chardonnay, plus a nicely flavored salmon-colored Cabernet Blanc and two table wines, American River red and white. Zinfandel and others may be added by the time you climb their mountain. Prices range from $10.50 for the Cab to $5 for the table wines.

Lava Cap Winery • T GTA & CT ✕

☐ *2221 Fruitridge Rd., Placerville, CA 95667; (800) 475-0175 or (916) 621-0175. Daily 11 to 5; MC/VISA. Most varieties tasted. Some wine logo items. Picnic deck; casual peek into the winer; guided tours by appointment. Food and wine appreciation classes conducted in summer, by reservation. ☐*

Housed in a modern barn-like structure, Lava Cap Winery sits among its own vineyards in the heart of Apple Hill. The curious name comes from the cap of volcanic ash and lava that once covered the area's gold-bearing quartz. David Jones, who opened the winery in 1987, teaches at U.C. Berkeley; not surprisingly, geology is a favorite subject. He and his wife Jeanne are primarily weekend vintners; their sons pretty much run things. Tom is the winemaker and Charlie tends the vineyards.

Tastings happen in a pleasant redwood paneled room. One set of windows opens into the winery and another looks over vineyards, orchards and the distant American River Canyon. That same view can be enjoyed from a picnic deck just off the tasting room.

Tasting notes: Wines are estate-bottled and the overall style is soft and lush, with lots of fruit. A Chardonnay Reserve was outstanding, full flavored with subtle spice; the Sauvignon Blanc had a nice herbal nose that carried into the crisp, fruity flavor; a three-year-old Zinfandel exhibited nice berries, spice and a light finish. Fumé Blanc, Muscat Canelli, Merlot, Barbera, Cabernet Blanc and a white Zin complete the list. Prices are $8 to $15.

Vintners choice: "Our Chardonnays are coming on strong and we've won lots of medals with our Sauvignon Blanc," said Dave.

Madroña Vineyards • T CT ✕

☐ *High Hill Road (P.O. Box 454), Camino, CA 95709; (916) 644-5948. Daily 11 to 5; MC/VISA. Most varieties tasted. A few wine logo items. Casual tours by request. Picnic tables are placed about a surrounding glen. ☐*

Madroña occupies a shady retreat beneath the cinnamon-barked trees that inspire its name. Vineyards and orchards are just beyond. The neat wood-sided winery looks deceptively small from the front; it's a two-story affair built into a downslope behind the tasting room. Several picnic tables are tucked beneath the madrones, black oaks and pines.

Dick and Leslie Bush planted vines in a section of the High Hill apple ranch in 1973, then opened their winery seven years later. Like those at neighboring Lava Cap, their wines are all estate bottled.

Tasting notes: Madroña produces two distinctive styles—light, dry whites and hearty, full-flavored reds. The wines include Chardonnay, Gewürztraminer, Johannisberg Riesling, Zinfandel, Cabernet Franc, Merlot, Cabernet Sauvignon, plus late harvest Zinfandel and Riesling. We favored a peppery, spicy six-year-old Zin; an herbal, full-flavored Merlot; and a rich late harvest Zin that would be great for fireplace snuggling.

Vintners choice: "It depends on the year," says Dick, "although our Cabernet Franc, Gewürztraminer and late harvest Riesling are always among the tops."

Sierra Vista Winery • T GTA ✕

⊡ *4560 Cabernet Way, Placerville, CA 95667; (916) 622-7221. Daily 11 to 4; major credit cards. Most varieties tasted. Some wine logo gift items. Tours and weekday tasting by appointment. Picnic area with spectacular view.* ⊡

Visitors here get twin views of the distant Crystal Range of the Sierra Nevada. The dramatic peaks are visible from the winery and picnic area, and they grace the wine labels. This lofty ridge—rimmed in vineyards—is one of California's most dramatic winery perches, and one of the highest, at 2,900 feet. John and Barbara MacCready were among the first of El Dorado's modern-day vintners, buying their property in 1972 and starting the winery five years later. They've since shed their respective careers as a university professor and computer programmer to devote full time to vinting. They've built a simple, attractive wood-sided winery from their own pines, and increased their output from a handful of cases to 9,000 a year.

Tasting notes: Sierra Vista has been an El Dorado County leader in developing Rhône varietals. Among its plantings are Syrah, Grenache, Cinsault, Mourvèdre, Viognier, Fleur de Montagne and a cuvée called Lynelle (a blend named for daughters Lynette and Michelle) are used in the "Rhône program." The winery also produces excellent Cabernet Sauvignon, barrel-fermented Chardonnay, Fumé Blanc and Zinfandel.

Vintners choice: "Since we're Rhône rangers, we tend to favor our Châteauneuf-du-Pape style reds and Viognier (a Rhône Valley white)," says Barbara.

Granite Springs Winery • T CT ✕

⊡ *6060 Granite Springs Rd., Somerset, CA 95684; (916) 620-6395. Weekends 11 to 5. Most varieties tasted. A few wine logo items; shaded picnic area near a pond. Informal tours on request.* ⊡

The austere bungalow tasting room and simple, barn like winery belie Granite Springs' success. It's one of America's most award-winning wineries. Not only have its wines been served in the White House, but its Chenin Blanc has been poured as the official reception wine there for several years.

Les and Lynne Russell planted their vines in a stubborn granite slope in 1980, then they blasted away additional granite to plant their winery against a hillside, The first crush was in 1981. Since then, Granite Springs wines have won more than a hundred medals. They hang by the cluster, like golden grapes, from the beams of the tasting room.

After Lynne passed away in 1994, Les sold the winery to his neighboring vintner Frank Latcham, although he stayed on for a year to continue his skills as a winemaker.

Tasting notes: Although we rarely comment on jug wines, we found one worthy of special note—the $5.50 Sierra Reserve Red, mostly Zinfandel, with a typical Gold Country spice overlaying a nice raspberry nose and flavor. Granite Springs' varietals are great buys, ranging from $5.50 to $14.50. A three-year-old Zinfandel displayed a great peppery nose and herbal-berry flavor. Higgins Zinfandel, also age three, was even heartier, with more tannin. A three-year-old Petite Sirah was a classic black wine, bold in color, with a light nose yet big pepper-berry flavor. Also on the list are Chardonnay, that White House Chenin Blanc (crisp, touch of sweetness), Cabernet Sauvignon, Vintage Port and Black Muscat Port.

Single Leaf Vineyards • T CT ✕

◻ *7480 Fairplay Rd., Somerset, CA 95684; (916) 882-8701. Weekends only 11 to 5. Most varieties tasted; MC/VISA. A few wine logo items; view picnic area. Self guiding tours.* ◻

This small family-owned winery occupies an attractive redwood structure on a slope among the trees and vineyards. Picnic tables on a concrete deck offer lunch with a view of the valley. Single Leaf was established in 1993 by Scott and Pam Miller of Carson City, Nevada. They've been farming the area since 1988.

The Millers bring interesting—and somewhat appropriate—backgrounds to the wine business. Scott, a biologist by profession, is administrator for the Nevada State Museum in Carson City and Pam is a marketing specialist. They operate the winery on weekends, commuting over the Sierra Nevada from their Carson City home. And the winery's unusual name? The source is a bit esoteric. The single-leaf piñon is the Nevada state tree and Scott, stepping out of his house one day, saw a single oak leaf on the ground. That leaf now resides on the winery label.

Tasting notes: This is Zinfandel country and it's a specialty of the Single Leaf house; the Zins are hardy and spicy. Others on the list are a full-flavored Chardonnay, soft and lush Sauvignon Blanc, a white Zinfandel, Cabernet Sauvignon, a Cabernet Port and Signature Red—a table wine that's half Zin and half Cab. Prices range from $6 to the early teens, with the Port fetching $15.

Vintner's choice: "We're best known for our reds and we pride ourselves in producing big, robust Zinfandels," said Scott.

Fitzpatrick Winery and Lodge • T CT ✕

◻ *7740 Fairplay Road, Somerset, CA 95684; (916) 620-3248. Weekends 11 to 5; MC/VISA. Most varieties tasted. Picnic deck with valley view. Plowman lunch served in the lodge on weekends. Rooms available; see listing under bed & breakfast inns. Casual winery tours on request.* ◻

A combined lodge and winery, Fitzpatrick occupies a high bluff with a stellar view of the surrounding hills. It's an imposing structure of heavy logs, with a rustic tasting room. A picnic deck offers vistas of vineyards and an occasional Christmas tree farm. Well-kept and tidy, with lawns and landscaping, it's among the more appealing of the Sierra foothill wineries.

Brian and Diane Fitzpatrick began their operation on Fairplay Road in 1980 near their Famine's End nursery; it was the first winery in the Fairplay area. Later, they moved two miles uphill to build—mostly by hand—their impressive tasting room and lodge, which looks like it was spirited away from Yosemite Valley. The winemaking operation is a few hundred feet away.

Tasting notes: The list is typical of hearty Gold Country wines—a fruity Chenin Blanc; a spicy and full-flavored Cabernet Sauvignon; a light and crisp Chardonnay; an herbal Sauvignon Blanc; and a spicy, raspberry flavored Zinfandel. Prices range from $6 to the early teens.

Vintners choice: "We specialize in wines made from organically grown grapes," says winemaker Brian, declining to pick a favorite child.

Perry Creek Vineyards • T ✗ 🖼

☐ *7400 Perry Creek Rd. (P.O. Box 304), Somerset, CA 95684; (800) 880-4026, (916) 620-5175. January through October—weekends only 11 to 5; November and December—Wednesday through Sunday 11 to 5; MC/VISA. Good specialty foods and wine oriented gift selection. Patio picnic facilities; antique car collection.* ☐

The most striking of El Dorado County's wineries, this tile roof mission style complex occupies an upslope among the trees. Colonnade arches, patios, hand carved doors and a friendly fountain help transport the visitor from the Sierra foothills to a Spanish villa. The handsome tile floor tasting room with blonde wood furnishings and tasting counter complete this appealing picture. An unexpected bonus for visitors is a small collection of classic cars, a hobby of owners Mike and Alice Chazen, who completed this imposing complex in 1991.

"They say you can make a small fortune in the wine business, as long as you start with a large fortune," mused wealthy garment importer Chazen. He and his wife are the accidental tourists of the Gold County wine industry. They were driving from Beverly Hills to Reno, taking the back roads so they could relax, when they saw a "for sale" sign on a piece of pastureland. They impulsively bought this 155-acre tract, planning to build a cabin as an escape from the rat race of international trading. Instead, a few months and a considerable sum of money later, they were owners of the foothills most opulent winery. A New Yorker who moved to Beverly Hills after "doing very well" contracting for the overseas manufacture of mens' sweaters, he has now forsaken both cities for the laid back Levi lifestyle of the foothills.

Tasting notes: The Perry Creek label covers the classic varietals and the new facility has already won many medals under the hand of winemaker Nancy Steel. Among the selections, all well-crafted wines displaying good varietal character, are Sauvignon Blanc, Chardonnay, Johannisberg Riesling, Zinfandel and white Zin, Merlot, Cabernet Sauvignon and Cabernet Franc. Prices range from $6 to the mid teens.

Windwalker Farm • T CT ✗

☐ *7360 Perry Creek Rd., Somerset, CA 95684; (916) 620-4054. Weekends 11 to 5 or by appointment; MC/VISA. All varieties tasted. A few wine logo items. Informal tours on request. Shaded picnic deck.* ☐

Perry Creek's next door neighbor vintners also came here by chance. Arnold and Paige Gilpin were vacationing in nearby Arnold in 1992 when they saw a "winery for sale" add in the local newspaper. Why did they decide to buy it? Because their son Rich happened to be a graduate of UC Davis with a degree in Enology. He had worked at other wineries for seven years and the idea of being the winemaker for his own family was obviously appealing. It is indeed an all-family venture; Rich's wife Siri handles marketing and sales.

The winery's name and impressionistic horse logo come from previous owners Gaylene and Ken Bailey of Sacramento, who had a combined winery and Arabian horse ranch here. The horses are gone and the Gilpins are brightening up this attractive ranch style complex with added lawns and a gazebo. The winery and matching house are of Pennsylvania Dutch architecture, with double-pitched roofs. A picnic deck sits under sheltering oaks, offering views of vines and the valley below.

Tasting notes: Four classic varietals occupy the Windwalker list. The Chenin Blanc is cold fermented dry in stainless steel to give it a crisp, clean flavor; and Chardonnays are aged *sur lie* in French oak after barrel fermentation, for a rich and spicy taste. The reds are an estate grown Cabernet Sauvignon with deep colors and full body; and a nicely balanced Zinfandel with lots of fruit and typical Gold Country spiciness. Prices range from $5 to $14.

Charles B Mitchell Vineyards ● T GT ✕

◻ *8221 Stoney Creek Rd., Somerset, CA 95684; (916) 620-3467. Weekends 11 to 5; MC/VISA, AMEX. Most varieties tasted. Wine logo items and specialty foods. Large lawn picnic area under oaks; tours by request.* ◻

This small winery and its vineyards are off the highway, tucked into an upslope among oaks, blackberry vines, sheep pastures and other things rural. Expect to be greeted by an occasional squirrel and scolded by a Steller Jay as you prowl about or picnic on its pleasantly wooded grounds. The tasting room occupies a cheerful little cottage with white trim and the sipping counter is a simple affair, laid across barrel heads and wine racks. However, a comic wooden statue of an early-day pilot—complete with silk scarf—and a couple of splendid examples of hand-carved European furniture suggest that the winery owner isn't as bucolic as the setting.

In 1994, Charles B Mitchell, wine broker and columnist, amateur pilot and admitted Mammoth Lakes ski bum, purchased this small winery, which had been established in 1981 by Vernon and Marcia Gerwer. He hired U.C. Davis graduate Mark Foster as a consultant, took some Davis courses himself, bought the best grapes he could find and started making wines. His first releases began winning gold medals, and the wines continue to do so.

"I'm the winemaker, although I've certainly learned a lot from Mark," he said. "As a winemaker, I'm more of a philosopher than a technician and it seems to be paying off. Wine is more art than science."

Tasting notes: A Chenin Blanc was dry and crisp, a good lunch wine. Fumé Blanc had an incisive nose with a full fruity taste and nice acidic nip. A second Fumé done in stainless steel was surprisingly soft and buttery. The Zinfandel was excellent, spicy and lush while the Cabernet was light and herbal. A Port made from traditional Portuguese grapes was rich and lush— an fine dessert wine. Others on the list include Semillon, Chardonnay, Johannisberg Riesling, a sparkling wine and a light table wine called Monsieur Omo's Red Sunshine. Prices range from $6 for Sunshine to the low teens for the varietals; the port fetches $22.50.

Vintners choice: "Cabernet and its Bordeaux relatives are my favorites," he said. "My daughter attended the American University in Paris and we spent a lot of time touring the Bordeaux region, getting to know the wines and learning the winemakers' philosophy."

Latcham Vineyards ● T CT ✕

◻ *2860 Omo Ranch Rd. (P.O. Box 80), Mount Aukum, CA 95656; (800) 750-5591, (916) 620-6834 or (916) 620-6642. Daily 11 to 5; MC/VISA, AMEX. Most varieties tasted. Wine logo items. Informal tours; picnic areas.* ◻

A courtliness in his manner and a neatness to his dress tells you that Frank Latcham, aged 70-plus, isn't an ordinary sodbuster. He's a retired San Francisco attorney, fulfilling an urge to get closer to the land. He and his wife Patty bought this land in 1980 and opened their winery ten years later. Although he still does consulting with his old firm, Frank likes to roll up his white sleeves and get involved in the wine business. The Latchams' son and daughter-in-law, Jon and Joyce, complete the cast of this family operation. Frank recently purchased Granite Springs Winery and its founder, master winemaker Les Russell, keeps a hand in things at both facilities.

A weathered old barn housing the winery operation is matched by a new Midwestern style farm home. A small shed built off the barn serves as a tasting room, where sippers can relax in chairs. Vineyards and trees rim the neat, orderly complex.

Tasting notes: Chardonnay, Sauvignon Blanc, Cabernet Sauvignon, Cabernet Franc, Petit Sirah, Zinfandel and a couple of generics comprise the list. Good hearty, spicy flavors in the Sauvignon Blanc, Zinfandel, Cabernet and Petit are typical of these mountain-grown grapes. The Cabernet Franc was spicy with a nice tannic nip and a four-year-old, full bodied medal-winning Zin was outstanding. Prices are modest for the quality, ranging from $6.59 to $10.50 for varietals, and down to $4.50 for blends.

AMADOR COUNTY WINERY TOUR • The Shenandoah Valley, home to most of Amador's wineries, is one of the few relatively level areas in the foothills. We did say "relatively;" it gently pitches and rolls like a green ocean of vineyards, pasturelands and oak groves. The valley was settled in the 1850s by folks seeking farm and ranch land, not gold. Many Shenandoah settlers were "Downeasters" and Southerners (thus, the valley name). There's still an eastern American air about its neat farms and occasional red barns.

If you continue westward from Frank Latcham's place, you'll wind up in the back end of this valley. However, after all of those El Dorado tasting rooms, you've probably saved Amador for a different trip. The logical access is from Highway 49, in the small hamlet of Plymouth.

Approaching on Highway 49 either from the north or south, turn eastward at a sign indicating the Shenandoah Valley, opposite Plymouth's main street. After a few hundred yards, fork left onto Shenandoah Road. The right hand fork leads to Fiddletown, home to some noted vineyards but no tasting rooms. Your first winery, **Young's Vineyard,** arrives quickly, on your right. Continue a few miles and turn left onto Bell Road, which takes you to three wineries. A long lane leading to **TKC Vineyards** comes up almost immediately. After less than half a mile, watch for a sign directing you to the left to **Karly Winery,** reached by a pleasantly winding drive through vineyards and pasturelands. Continue on Bell road until it ends, then turn left and follow a fragmented bit of pavement about half a mile to **Story Winery.**

Return to Shenandoah Road, turn left (east) and go about a mile before turning left again onto Steiner Road. About a mile up Steiner, several wineries are grouped together, almost within walking distance of one another: **Renwood-Santino** on the left at Steiner and Upton Road, and then **Shenandoah Vineyards** and **Amador Foothill Winery,** both uphill and above the vineyards, to your right. Just beyond is **Deaver Vineyards** and then **Charles Spinetta Winery and Wildlife Gallery** down in a hollow; both are on the left.

Steiner Road curves back into Shenandoah Road, so stay with it. Then continue east on Shenandoah about a mile and a half to **Sobon Estate,** on your right. Now, reverse yourself on Shenandoah Road for a mile or so, turn left onto Shenandoah School Road and follow it to **Monteviña Winery** on your left. Continue on Shenandoah School Road, which curves back to Shenandoah Road for a return to Plymouth.

We didn't cover four Amador wineries outside the Shenandoah Valley, although they're worth a visit if you're in the area around Sutter Creek or Ione. **Greenstone Winery** (Wednesday-Sunday 10 to 4; 274-2238) is on Highway 88, the main route from the San Joaquin Valley to Amador County. Look for it on the left, just beyond the Jackson Valley Road below **Ione**. Turn right onto Jackson Valley for about a mile, and then right again onto Buena Vista Road at the cute and rustic town of **Buena Vista**, and drive a mile to **Jackson Valley Vineyards** on the right (daily 11 to 4; 274-4721). The other two are on Sutter Ridge Road east of Sutter Creek. **Stoneridge Winery** is at 13862 Ridge (weekends noon to 4; 223-1761) and **Sutter Ridge Vineyards** is a bit farther up at 14110 Ridge Rd. (Thursday-Sunday 11 to 4; 267-1316). Get specifics on these from the Amador Vintners Association, listed under "Winery maps" below.

Young's Vineyard • T CT ✕

◻ *10120 Shenandoah Rd., Plymouth, CA 95669; (209) 245-3198. Weekends 10 to 5 or by appointment; MC/VISA. Most varieties tasted. A few wine logo items; casual tours. Picnic area by a duck pond.* ◻

Established in 1979 as Kenworthy Vineyards, this winery was reopened in 1995 by the Young family—Steven, his Dutch bride Annette and Steve's father Stell. Dad, a former military test pilot and head of the California Air National Guard, is the winemaker and Annette helps run the business end of things. Steve, who travels abroad for a company that makes specialty tools for nuclear and industrial plants, lends an occasional hand. (Steve and Annette met on one of his trips to Europe.)

The family has spruced up the once weather-worn Kenworthy Ranch, refacing and painting the buildings and repairing an ancient Chinese-built rock wall that rims a duck pond and picnic area.

Tasting notes: Stell likes to hand-craft his wines, evident in the strong varietal character of the estate Cabernet Sauvignon and Zinfandel. They're aged in French oak to add complexity. Muscat Canneli completes the short list and prices range from $9 to $12.

TKC Vineyards • T

◻ *11001 Valley Drive, Plymouth, CA 95669; (209) 245-6428 or (916) 933-3088. Saturday 11 to 4 and Sunday 2 to 4, or by appointment; MC/VISA. Most wines tasted.* ◻

This small winery dates from 1981 when Harold and Monica Nuffert started buying and crushing grapes to make "big, non-wimpy reds." To assure a reliable source, they began planting their own grapes in 1994. The operation is small, with an annual output of 1,000 cases. Tastings occur in a simple space at one end of their modest winery.

Harold came to the wine business by way of the aerospace industry. After years as an engineer, he decided that the business was suffering from "technology stagnation," so he sought a new and different kind of challenge and one that was more creative than technological—making wines.

Tasting notes: Only two varieties occupy the TKC list, Cabernet Sauvignon and Zinfandel and they are indeed non-wimpy, full bodied with lots of fruit and enough tannin to age for eight to ten years. The Zins range from $5 to $10, with Cab in the middle teens.

Karly Winery ● T GTA ✕

☐ *11076 Bell Rd., Plymouth, CA 95669; (209) 245-3922. Daily noon to 4; MC/VISA. Most varieties tasted. Some wine logo gift items. Snacks served with wine samples. Small picnic area; guided tours by appointment.* ☐

You may go to Karly for the wines, but you may return for *her* snacks. Lawrence (Buck) Cobb makes full-bodied wines, and his wife Karly serves oven-warm homemade bread and bits of cheese to weekend tasters. This happens in a neat tasting room that's also a kitchen, which is certainly appropriate. A full set of appliances is installed behind the counter. The winery is a modern metal structure, bunkered unobtrusively into a slope, surrounded by vineyards. It's all in a small hollow, a short drive off Bell Road.

The Cobbs were drawn to this area to escape from the corporate rat race in 1980. Earlier, Buck served as an Air Force fighter pilot in Korea, and he now flies a high performance stunt plane.

Tasting notes: Buck likes a touch of oak in his wines; we found them to be quite tasty. Our picks were a silky Chardonnay with a bit of wood; a soft yet spicy and full-bodied three-year-old Zinfandel and a *big* two-year-old Zin that should be kept around for a bit. Others on the list are the county's only Petit Sirah, plus Sauvignon Blanc, the requisite white Zinfandel and a tasty, sweet Orange Muscat. They've recently added Mourvèdre, Syrah and Grenache. Prices range from $8.50 to the mid teens; some library wines are available as well.

Story Winery ● T GTA ✕

☐ *10525 Bell Rd., Plymouth, CA 95669; (209) 245-6208. Weekdays noon to 4, weekends 11 to 5; MC/VISA, DISC. Select varieties tasted. Picnic area with valley view; tours by appointment.* ☐

Following a narrow lane past ancient gnarled vines toward Story, you don't realize that you're approaching a crest with a striking view. The old farmyard winery sits on the rim of the Consumnes River Canyon, with a sweeping vista of vineyards, oak clusters and pine forests. The tasting room in a weathered barnboard cottage perches on this knoll, beside a casually kept lawn. Picnic tables entice one to linger for the view.

Founded early in the 1970s by the late Eugene Story and now owned by Bruce and Jan Tichenor, this is one of the foothills' oldest wineries. In classic Gold Country fashion, it focuses heavily on Zinfandel, since Eugene had the good fortune to find a ranch with some old vines still in place.

Tasting notes: Several Zins occupy the list and a tasting consists of a vertical sampling of wines ranging from light fruity to big and boisterous. White wines include an estate Chenin Blanc and an Amador County Sauvignon Blanc, both light and fruity, yet with distinctly different characteristics. A white Zinfandel and a dessert wine made from old Mission vines on the property complete the list.

Renwood-Santino Winery ● T GTA ✕ 📷

☐ *12225 Steiner Rd., Plymouth, CA 95669; (800) 348-8466 or (209) 245-6013. Daily 11 to 4:30; MC/VISA. Most varieties tasted. A few wine logo items. Guided tours by appointment, for a fee. Shaded picnic areas.* ☐

The multi-layered look of the Gold Country's wine country—old vines, distant hills and a peaceful pond. This scene is in the Shenandoah Valley.

Folks who haven't visited Santino lately will find several changes, starting with the new double-jointed name. Scott Harvey, who had been Santino's winemaker since it was started by Matt and Nancy Santino in 1979, purchased the winery in partnership with Boston stockbroker Robert Smerling in 1994. Scott has been for years owner of the legendary 125-year-old Grandpère Zinfandel vineyard, the oldest in California. Although there are no more Santinos at the winery, the name will remain as one of two labels. Santino will be the main line of table and dessert wines, while Renwood labels go on higher end varietals and special select wines. Of course, they're all made by Harvey, who has won scores of medals.

The other changes are physical—additional vineyard plantings and an enlarged and brightened tasting room in aCalifornia-Spanish tile roofed building. An accent wall in the tasting room, fashioned from the curved slats of an ancient wine vat, cleverly hides the potties.

Tasting notes: Zin's the name of the Renwood-Santino game, and Harvey's are excellent—particularly the delicious, full bodied Grandpère. However, other grapes are joining the new partnership, such as Viognier, Barbera, Sangiovese and Nebbiolo. (Retail sales manager Jerry Budrick took us outside—his excuse to light a roll-your-own cigarette—and showed us the new plantings.) The Renwood Barbera Reserve was lush, spicy and delicious, and the Santino White Harvest was one of the few white Zins we've liked; it has won several golds. The list includes—from new and old plantings—Renwood Syrah, Viognier and Sangiovese, plus Santino Fumé Blanc, Satyricon (a Rhône blend), Port, Moscato del Diavolo and late Harvest Riesling and Zinfandel. Prices range from $6 for the white Zin to $20 for varietals, and higher for a few reserves.

Vintners choice: "We are a Zinfandel house," said Scott, getting right to the point. "We're also known for our Barbera and dessert wines."

Shenandoah Vineyards • T ✖

☐ *12300 Steiner Rd., Plymouth, CA 95669; (209) 245-4455. Daily 10 to 5; MC/VISA. Most varieties tasted. Some wine logo items and art gallery; small picnic area.* ☐

Leon and Shirley Sobon claim to be risk-takers, although their timing appears to be good. When the aircraft industry slowed in 1977, Leon left his engineering job at Lockheed Sunnyvale, bought a piece of land with a handsome fieldstone house and started Shenandoah Vineyards. Three years later, they sold a chunk to Ben Zeitman (who started Amador Foothill Winery) at a tidy profit. Their wines have caught on quickly, winning numerous awards; their production has leaped from a few cases to 35,000. In 1989, they bought the defunct D'Agostini Winery, one of California's oldest and turned it into Sobon Estate, a satellite winery and site of the Shenandoah Valley Museum (see below).

Shenandoah is an appealing complex, with a modern fieldstone winery fashioned to match the house. The tasting room is a delight—part rustic with log beam ceilings, and part art gallery, with rotating exhibits among barrels of aging wines.

Tasting notes: The Shenandoah list is predominately red, typical for Amador, although the winery produces an excellent full-bodied Sauvignon Blanc. Our favorite reds included a rich and mellow Zingiovese (obviously a Zinfandel Sangiovese blend), a spicy five-year-old Zinfandel Reserve and a three-year-old mellow and tasty Cabernet Sauvignon. A late harvest Zinfandel-Sirah, vintage Port, black Muscat and "Old Cream Muscat" complete the list. Prices range from $5.50 to the early teens.

Amador Foothill Winery • T CT ✖

☐ *12500 Steiner Rd., Plymouth, CA 95669; (209) 245-6307. Weekends and most long holiday weekends noon to 5; MC/VISA. Most varieties tasted. Casual tours of the winery, adjacent to the tasting room. Picnic area with valley and mountain views.* ☐

When we wrote **The Best of the Gold Country** several years ago, we conducted a blind tasting among knowledgeable friends to pick the area's best Zinfandel and white Zinfandel. To our surprise and Ben Zeitman's pleasure, his Amador Foothill wines won both. Ben and his wife Katie Quinn's Zins also win in arenas much more prestigious than ours.

A former NASA chemist, Ben started the winery in 1980. Then in 1986, he had the good sense to marry Katie, who brought with her a master's degree in Enology from U.C. Davis. The winery is simple but on the leading edge of technology—a glossy white passive solar structure equipped with the best of the winemaking art and science. All this is visible from the tasting counter, on a gallery above the main part of the winery. A tour thus consists of looking over your shoulder, glass in hand.

Tasting notes: Zinfandel, of course, dominates the list and it has won many of the awards that decorate the walls. A three-year-old Grandpère

Vineyards was herbal and full-bodied, one of the best we've tasted. A three-year-old Fiddletown displayed nice raspberries and a two-year old Ferraro exhibited lots of fruit and tannin; a fine candidate for aging. The list also includes a nice complex and crisp Fumé Blanc, a tasty version of the requisite white Zin and Sangiovese. Prices range from $8.50 to a bit over $10.

Deaver Vineyards ● T ✕ 🏚

☐ *12455 Steiner Rd., Plymouth, CA 95669; (209) 245-5512. Friday-Monday 11 to 5; MC/VISA. Most wines tasted; good selection of gift, wine logo items, books and specialty foods. Picnic area near a lake.* ☐

One of the Shenandoah Valley's newest winery complexes traces its roots back to the Gold Rush—in a sense. John Davis came to California in search of gold in 1850. Finding none, he became a cooper in the foothill wine country and some of his barrels still exist at Sobon Estate. He adopted young Kenneth Deaver, and members of the Deaver family has been in the valley since. The present generation began making wine in 1985 and opened a sales outlet in 1988. The Deavers completed a handsome new winery and tasting room in 1994, with the equally attractive Amador Harvest Inn adjacent. (See "Wineland lodgings" below, on page 305.)

The tasting room is an appealing space, bright and airy, with tile floors and oak wood trim. Samples from an extensive selection of specialty foods are offered, along with sips of wine. Outside, well-tended lawns and a picnic area border a lake, where several affable ducks have taken up residence.

Tasting notes: The Deaver list is brief and quite good. We sampled a soft, fruity Chardonnay, crisp and spicy Zinfandel with medium body and a late harvest Zinfandel that was so rich that it could have passed for a Port. Others on the list are white Zin and white and red table wines. Prices are modest, ranging from $6 to the early teens; more for some library wines.

Charles Spinetta Winery and Wildlife Gallery ● T ✕ 🏚

☐ *12557 Steiner Rd., Plymouth, CA 95669; (209) 245-3384. Tuesday-Friday 8 to 4 and weekends 10 to 4:30; closed Monday; MC/VISA. Selected wines tasted, plus wines by the glass for under $5. Wine logo items and extensive wildlife art collection; frame shop. Large picnic area.* ☐

This square-shouldered masonry block building, rather austere from without, is a surprise package within. Visitors step into a huge, high-ceiling tasting room with an L-shaped counter. Wildlife scenes fill the redwood paneled walls and scores more occupy a mezzanine gallery above. Bronzes and other sculptures complete the collection. It's all for sale and generally affordable, since most are prints of works by leading artists. Another element of the facility, unique to the wine country, is a picture framing shop.

The operation is an all-family affair. Charles, whose background is forestry management, bought the vineyards in 1979 and completed the winery-gallery about ten years later. Wife Laura runs the frame shop and has framed the more than 250 prints on the walls. Son Jim manages the vineyards, Tony is into marketing and Michael, the youngest, has joined the operation. Not surprisingly, there's always a Spinetta on hand to greet visitors. Each fall, the family hosts a harvest party that sounds like fun, crushing grapes with ancient equipment that has been in the family for generations. Call the winery for details.

Tasting notes: Wines are made by a nearby facility under the Spinettas' direction and cellared here, with prices ranging from $6 to $15. The Zins were our favorites, unfiltered and full-flavored. We tasted a mellow nine-year-old Eschen Vineyard entry from 80-year-old vines and a lighter five-year-old Amador Zinfandel. Zinetta is a rich appetizer wine with big flavors of berries and cherries. Also on the list are white Zinfandel, Heritage Red table wine, sweet and dry Chenin Blancs, Chardonnay, Cabernet, Merlot, a sweet Muscat Canelli and a rich, ice-wine style Frost Chenin Blanc.

Sobon Estate • T ST ✕ 🏠

□ *14430 Shenandoah Rd. (mailing address: 12300 Steiner Rd.), Plymouth, CA 95669; (209) 245-6554. Daily 10 to 5; MC/VISA. Most varieties tasted. Good giftware selection, deli and picnic fare. Self-guiding tour of the Shenandoah Valley Museum. Shaded picnic area.* □

D'Agostini winery—California's fourth oldest—is in good hands. Since buying the facility in 1989, Leon and Shirley Sobon have installed the Shenandoah Valley Museum in the main cellar, thus preserving this state historical landmark. Exhibits focus on the gold rush, Shenandoah Valley pioneers and early farming and wine production. It also captures that wonderful musty-grapy-old library smell typical of ancient wineries. The large tasting room, in another of the old buildings, fits the historic theme, with heavy ceiling beams and barnwood paneling. It offers one of the better selections of gift and specialty food items of the foothill wineries.

Tasting notes: Many Sobon Estate wines use grapes from the old D'Agostini vineyards, although they're produced mostly at the family's Shenandoah facility. Selections vary. When we visited, we sampled a Fumé Blanc with a spicy-herbal flavor; a complex and fresh young Chardonnay; a light, berry-filled Pinot Noir; a tasty herbal Zinfandel and a Cabernet Sauvignon with a big chili pepper nose and herbal-berry flavor. Prices range from $9 to the early teens.

Monteviña Winery • T ✕

□ *20680 Shenandoah School Rd., Plymouth, CA 95669; (209) 245-6942. Daily 11 to 4; MC/VISA. Most varieties tasted. Good selection of wine logo items. Large, landscaped picnic area.* □

Bob Trinchero of Napa Valley's Sutter Home Winery was among the first to call attention to Sierra foothill grapes. He won scores of awards with his hearty Amador County Zinfandels in the 1970s. It seemed logical, then, to move closer to the source, so he bought Monteviña Winery in 1988. He operates it as a separate entity.

Monteviña was among the first of the post-Prohibition Gold Country facilities, established in 1970. It's a handsome complex—a Spanish-California structure rimmed by vineyards and landscaped grounds. Artwork and photos accent the spacious, cathedral ceiling tasting room. A picnic area occupies a paved courtyard beneath a shady arbor.

Tasting notes: The wines are fine, displaying an overall light and fruity style. Varietals include Chardonnay, Fumé Blanc, Zinfandel and Cabernet Sauvignon. And of course, there's a Monteviña version of white Zin, the Trinchero wine that put Sutter Home on the map. A three-year-old Zinfandel was soft for an Amador wine, with a nice raspberry nose and flavor, while a three-year-old Cab was pleasantly peppery with lush berries and a soft tannin finish. Trinchero also has planted Italian classics and is releasing blends and varietals such as Matrimonio, Montanaro, Sangiovese and Aleatico. Wine prices range from $6.50 for the white Zin to the early teens for the others.

Vintners choice: "Zinfandel," said general manager Jeffrey Meyers, uttering Trinchero's favorite word. "It's rich, with aromas and flavors of berries and cedar."

CALAVERAS-TUOLUMNE WINERY TOUR ● The southern most wine country in the Gold Country also is the newest. Of Calaveras County's six tasting rooms, four opened in the decade of the Nineties. All are in or near the appealing old mining town of Murphys. Neighboring Tuolumne County's only winery-connected tasting room, near Columbia State Historic Park, goes back a bit further, to 1970.

As you tour this southern reach of the Gold Country's wine country, you will see new wineries a-building and new vines a-growing. You'll be rewarded with considerable variety as well, from funky tasting rooms to modern wineries with aging caves. You will note, as you explore, that the area abounds with other attractions as well, from limestone caverns to restored mining towns and gold rush museums.

The most direct route to Murphys is via State Highway 4 from **Stockton**. You can pick it up from Interstate 5 or U.S. 99 and follow it through **Angels Camp**. Another approach, used by many Bay Area visitors, is via I-580 to I-205 past **Tracy**, then State Highway 120 through **Manteca**. Follow signs to and through **Sonora** on Highway 49, then drive 17 miles north to Angels Camp and turn right onto Route 4. For a more scenic variation, fork to the right onto Parrotts Ferry Road about four miles north of Sonora; this takes you past **Columbia State Historic Park**. Beyond this restored mining town, Parrotts Ferry Road spirals down to the Stanislaus River Canyon, now filled with New Melones Reservoir. You'll cross the big pond and enter Calaveras County, climb out of the canyon, pass the **Moaning Cavern** limestone cave, then hit a stop sign at Route 4. Go right to reach Murphys, about four miles up the highway.

Using any of these approaches, you'll encounter the first wine sipping stop before you reach Murphys—the stylish new winery and tasting room of **Chatom Vineyards** on your right, near the hamlet of **Douglas Flat**. Continue a couple of miles to Murphys and turn right onto Pennsylvania Gulch Road. A winding one-mile drive into pleasant oak woodlands takes you to **Indian Rock Vineyard.**

Return to Highway 4, go east for a few hundred feet and follow signs (a left and a quick right) into the business district of **Murphys.** Shaded by huge locust and elm trees, it's one of the Gold Country's more charming towns, with a nice collection of old brick and false front stores. Driving along Main Street, watch for **Milliaire** (*millie-AIR*) winery on your right. It's easy to spot, since it's housed in a former service station. Continue through and beyond the business district to **Black Sheep Vintners,** in a weathered structure on your right at Main and Murphys Grade. Now, backtrack briefly on Main and turn left onto Sheep Ranch Road at the Olde Timers Museum (look for a black and orange Mercer Caverns sign). This lane seems too narrow to be a serious road, but it quickly takes you out of town, into pine and oak woodlands. Considerable twisting and turning delivers you to **Mercer Caverns,** another limestone cave attraction. The road then swings right and spirals down into a hideaway canyon, green with pines and vines, home to **Stevenot Winery.**

Return to Main Street and head southwest on Algiers Street beside the venerable Murphys Hotel. You may not see the small street sign, although you will see a sign to your next destination—**Kautz Ironstone Vineyards.** Algiers takes you past the neat little city park and soon ends at a stop sign, where you turn right onto Six Mile Road. After a mile of oaks and pasturelands, you'll see Kautz Ironstone on your right, just beyond Hay Station Ranch. From Kautz, reverse your route to get back to Murphys, or continue down Six Mile Road and you'll hit Highway 4, headed for Angels Camp.

Before or after your Calaveras winery tour, you may want to take time to explore Murphys' shops and boutiques, as well as next-door Columbia State Historic Park and nearby Yankee Hill Winery. Columbia is a restored 1851 mining town with time-worn but carefully preserved buildings housing boutiques, curio shops, restaurants and gold rush hotels. The only traffic on Main Street is an occasional stagecoach or string of horses, hauling grinning tourists. This once was the "gem of the Mother Lode," one of the largest and most prosperous of the foothill mining towns.

To reach **Yankee Hill Winery,** go east past the Columbia post office on Jackson Street. It becomes Yankee Hill Road and delivers you to the winery after less than a mile; it's up a lane to the right. (Pine Cone Press also is located on Yankee Hill Road, although we don't do tours or tastings.)

Chatom Vineyards • T ✕

◻ *1969 E. Highway 4, Douglas Flat; mailing address: P.O. Box 2730, Murphys, CA 95247; (800) 435-8852 or (209) 736-6500. Daily 11 to 4:30; major credit cards. All varieties tasted. A few wine logo gift items. Landscaped picnic area under arbor.* ◻

Gay Callan, daughter of a long line of growers and ranchers, planted vineyards in a sheltered valley near Calaveras County's San Andreas in 1980. She started making wines five years later. After winning a number of awards, she "went public," opening a striking new winery and tasting room on the highway to Murphys in 1991.

The structure, part masonry and part vertical wood slat, is something of a blend between French country and early American railroad station, which is more appealing than it sounds. The tasting room is light and cheerful, trimmed with oak and artwork. A picnic area is particularly inviting, with bentwood lounges as well as tables. It's sheltered by a sturdy arbor which, as the seasons pass, is becoming entwined with vines.

Tasting notes: Light, fruity and crisp are proper adjectives for the Chatom wine list. It includes a Semillon, Sauvignon Blanc, Chardonnay, reserve Sauvignon Blanc, Merlot, Sangiovese, Zinfandel and Cabernet Sauvignon. Our picks were a dry, subtly spicy Chardonnay; a full-flavored four-year-old Cab with a soft tannin finish; a full-flavored four-year-old Merlot and a four-year-old Zinfandel with a raspberry nose and flavor. Prices are $7 to $14.

Indian Rock Vineyard • T CT ✕

◻ *1154 Pennsylvania Gulch Rd. (P.O. Box 1526), Murphys, CA 95247; (209) 728-2266. Weekends 10 to 5; no credit cards. All varieties tasted. Pleasant picnic area on lawn beside a lake. Casual tours on request.* ◻

Boyd Thompson and his son Scott have teamed up to become the newest members of the Calaveras County wine clan. Boyd, who was CEO of a major medical care group, longed to pursue a more bucolic life, so he bought an historic dairy ranch. Scott, who has been making wine since he was a kid, happily signed on as winemaker. They started planting in 1985, began producing wine three years later and opened the winery in 1991. They plan to burrow aging caverns in a nearby hillside. The family also is developing a luxury subdivision adjacent, with homes on two to three-acre parcels.

In a sense, Boyd's arrival in Murphys was a homecoming, since his father I.B. Thompson once ran a small hospital there. Indian Rock occupies an idyllic glen among the pines and oaks just east of Murphys. Old pasturelands have become new vineyards and the tiny tasting room is housed in an ancient whitewashed milk barn. On chilly days, a fire crackles in an old cast iron stove. Picnic tables are placed about a grassy lawn beside a pond. Sitting under a shady oak, sipping a bit of Chardonnay, listening to the birds and squirrels discussing important issues, one is reluctant to leave this spot.

Tasting notes: Scott had released only one wine when we visited, a classic buttery and spicy Chardonnay, which sells for $12. By the time you visit, selections will include Cabernet Sauvignon, Merlot and Charbono.

Milliaire Vineyard Selections ● T

◻ *276 Main St. (P.O. Box 1554), Murphys, CA 95247; (209) 728-1658. Daily 11 to 4:30 in summer, Friday-Monday 11 to 4:30 the rest of the year; MC/VISA. Most varieties tasted. A few wine logo items.* ◻

"Fill 'er up" takes on a new meaning when you visit Milliaire. It may be America's only winery operating in a former service station. The overhang that once sheltered Flying A gas pumps is still in place, although the pumps themselves are gone. "We'd love to find one of those old gravity feed gas pumps for color," Liz Millier mused.

The ancient little building began as a carriage house, then served as a livery stable and service station before assuming its new role. The tasting room, with a simple plank over a barrel head, occupies the store portion of the station, where you once paid for your gas and picked out a new set of wiper blades. Wine ages in the garage portion, where grease racks once stood.

Steve and Liz Millier started their winery in 1983 and moved to their unique quarters in 1990. *Milliaire,* derived from Steve's family name, means "milestone" in French. A Fresno State University grad, he served as winemaker at David Bruce Winery in the Santa Cruz Mountains, then locally at Stevenot, Kautz and half a dozen other wineries. Then he decided it was finally time to put his own labels on his wine; he now produces about 1,500 cases a year. Liz runs the business end and is active in local affairs; she's past president of the Calaveras Wine Association.

Tasting notes: Milliaire reflects the big, spicy character of Gold Country wines. We liked all the varietals—a fruity and herbal Sauvignon Blanc; spicy and buttery Chardonnay; Zinfandel with a great herbal-berry flavor; a full-bodied, oak-finished Cabernet Sauvignon; and a spicy Merlot. Three dessert wines were rich but not yucky-sweet—a late harvest Zinfandel, orange Muscat and Zinfandel Port. Prices range from $7.50 to the middle teens.

Black Sheep Vintners ● T CT

◻ *Main Street at Murphys Grade (P.O. Box 1851), Murphys, CA 95247; (209) 728-2157. Weekends noon to 5 or by appointment; MC/VISA, DISC. All varieties tasted. A few wine logo items. Informal tours.* ◻

Black Sheep *looks* like a Gold Country winery, occupying a weather-textured wooden building with a rusting corrugated roof, at the far end of Murphys' gold rush era Main Street. Inside, rough-cut boards hold up the ceiling; tasting occurs in a small space shared by tiers of sleeping wines. A collection of sheep figurines, given by friends to honor the winery name, clutters a shelf behind the rustic tasting bar. Dave and Jan Olson bought the old Chispa Cellars in the mid-1980s. They'd been farming near the hamlet of Sheepranch in the hills above Murphys, so they decided to use a woolly reference for their winery name. They were the black sheep of the business, Jan recalled, when they decided to turn home winemaking into a profession. They weren't greenhorns, however, since Dave had worked for Stevenot earlier, and received some of his winemaking training from Steve Millier.

Tasting notes: Black Sheep Zinfandel is one of our standards—typically spicy with big berry flavors. Other wines we sampled were equally tasty—a five-year-old Cabernet Sauvignon with lots of berries and a touch of oak and tannin at the end; and a full-flavored Sauvignon Blanc with Semillon added for complexity. To honor nearby Angels Camp's annual frog-jumping celebration, the Olsons created "True Frogs." It's a light, fruity white with a great label—two grinning croakers enjoying a lily pad picnic. Prices range from $6.50 for the euphoric frogs to $13 for the top varietals.

Vintners choice: "Our Zinfandel—very peppery with nice berry flavors," says Jan. "It's our hallmark wine."

Stevenot Winery ● T CT ✕ 🌣

⊡ *2690 Santo Domingo Rd., Murphys, CA 95247; (209) 728-3436. Daily 10 to 5; MC/VISA, DISC. Most varieties tasted. Good wine related gift selection and picnic fare. Arbor picnic area; tours on request.* ⊡

Sitting at the bottom of a deep draw, walled by pines and limestone slopes, Stevenot occupies one of the California wine country's prettiest settings. This scene is further enhanced by the "Alaska House," a sod roofed log cabin that seems to have sprouted from the earth in centuries past. It serves as a warm and cozy tasting room and gift shop. A vine-entwined picnic arbor and lawn invite visitors to linger. Old ranch buildings sheltering modern winery equipment and several acres of vineyards complete this idyllic setting.

The first Stevenots came to the Sierra foothills seeking gold in 1849 and stayed on as ranchers and farmers. Fifth-generation Barden started planting vineyards at the historic Shaw Ranch in 1974 and turned the hay barn into a winery in 1977. Newer facilities have been added. It's the county's oldest winery and the largest in the foothills, producing about 50,000 cases a year.

Tasting notes: Stevenot wines have won many awards for their spicy, fruity foothills style. Typically, Zinfandel monopolizes the list. A three-year-old Grand Reserve aged in American oak was spicy-herbal with a nice tannic nip; and a two-year-old late harvest Zin displayed huge flavors and spices. Also on the list were a crispy and light Chenin Blanc; a medium-bodied and spicy Chardonnay; a bigger, more buttery Chardonnay Grand Reserve; an herbal, subtly tannic Merlot; and a complex, tasty Cabernet Sauvignon with an oak touch. Late harvest Zinfandel dessert wine and the requisite white Zinfandel complete the list. Prices range from $6 to the mid teens.

Vintners choice: "Reserve Chardonnay, Cabernet Sauvignon and Merlot," says winemaker Chuck Hovey.

Kautz Ironstone Vineyards ● T ✕ 🌣

⊡ *Six Mile Road (P.O. Box 2263), Murphys, CA 95247; (209) 728-1251. Daily 11 to 5; MC/VISA. Most varieties tasted. Deli and wine logo giftwares. Tours of winery caverns at noon, 1:30 and three weekends, less often weekdays. Shaded picnic area, plus tables inside tasting room and on a winery deck.* ⊡

Kautz Ironstone is housed in an imposing twin-gabled wood-sided structure with a tasting room, deli and visitor facility above and winery below. Fitted into a gentle slope, shaded by ancient oaks and rimmed by terraced landscaping, it's easily the most attractive winery in Calaveras County, and one of the most appealing in the entire state. A massive four-way fieldstone fireplace with a barbecue for special cooking events commands one end of the vaulted-ceiling tasting room. Old farm implements and trophy heads decorate display balconies. Deli and wine purchases can be fashioned into lunch, and visitors can eat at tables inside, outside deck or a picnic area.

John Kautz, a successful Lodi grower and vintner, began planting vines near Murphys' historic Hay Station Ranch in 1988, then he had tunnels bored as his first "buildings" and aging cellars in 1991. Tastings were held in the tunnels until the main winery and tasting room were completed. Tours take visitors through these caves and to an underground spring that was discovered during the "mining."

Tasting notes: The Kautz list focuses on Chardonnay, Merlot, Cabernet Franc, Merlot, Cabernet Sauvignon, Shiraz and the U.C. Davis hybrid Symphony. Some Bordeaux blend reds are coming in the future. We sampled a crisp and clean barrel-stainless fermented Gold Canyon Chardonnay, a more lush barrel-fermented and oak aged library collection Chard, an herbal and peppery Cabernet Franc and a crisp and spicy Triune Cabernet Sauvignon. The Symphony "Obsession" is a semi-dry sipping wine with an apple-flower petal nose and taste. Prices range from $10 to the mid teens. The winery also produces grape and apple brandy and Italian-style grappa.

Yankee Hill Winery • *T CT* ✕

◻ *11755 Coarsegold Lane (P.O. Box 330), Columbia, CA 95310; (209) 533-2417. Daily 10 to 5; MC/VISA. All varieties tasted. Some wine related gift items and picnic fare. Shaded picnic area with barbecue; informal tours on request. Personalized imprinted labels available.* ◻

Ron and Gudrun Erickson's simple masonry block and wood winery is terraced into an oak-covered slope, reached by a gravel lane off Yankee Hill Road. A few tables and a barbecue occupy a deck just off the small tasting room, inviting visitors to lounge in this wooded setting. You'll see no vineyard here; the Ericksons buy their grapes, usually from other Gold Country vineyards. Yankee Hill is old by foothills standards, dating back to 1970. Ron, who has dabbled in an assortment of businesses and presently teaches courses at nearby Columbia College, bought it in 1977. The Ericksons also conduct summer cooking schools at their winery.

Tasting notes: The list is quite versatile for a small winery—Chardonnay, Chenin Blanc, several proprietary blends, Cabernet Sauvignon, Barbera, an Extra Dry sparkling wine, a Spumante, California Port and cream sherry and five fruit wines: apple, red currant, blackberry, loganberry and raspberry. We favored the buttery, crisp Chardonnay aged in toasted barrels, a fruity yet dry Rhine blend and the nutty cream sherry, made in the classic solera style. Fruit wines were very tasty, rich but not sticky-sweet. Wine prices are modest, ranging from $4.50 to $11.

THE BEST OF THE BUNCH

The best wine buys • Sierra foothills vintners consistently offer some of California's best premium wine buys. We found little price difference, winery-to-winery.

The most attractive wineries ● Monteviña Winery and Perry Creek Vineyards in El Dorado County; Renwood-Santino Winery and Sobon Estate (with its museum) in Amador County; Chatom Vineyards, Kautz Ironstone Vineyards and Stevenot Winery (for its setting) in Calaveras County.

The most interesting tasting rooms ● Boeger Winery, Fitzpatrick Winery, Perry Creek Vineyards and Charles B Mitchell Vineyards in El Dorado County; Renwood-Santino Winery, Charles Spinetta Winery, Shenandoah Vineyards, Deaver Vineyards and Sobon Estate in Amador County; Kautz Ironstone Vineyards and Stevenot's "Alaska House" in Calaveras County.

The funkiest tasting rooms ● Story Winery in Amador County; Indian Rock, Milliaire Winery and Black Sheep Vintners in Calaveras County.

The best gift shops ● Perry Creek Vineyards in El Dorado County, Charles Spinetta Winery and Wildlife Gallery, Deaver Vineyards and Sobon Estate in Amador County; Stevenot Winery and Kautz Ironstone Vineyards in Calaveras County.

The nicest picnic areas ● Boeger Winery, Madroña Vineyards, Sierra Vista Winery, Fitzpatrick Winery and Charles B Mitchell Vineyards in El Dorado County; Monteviña Winery and Story Winery in Amador County; Chatom Vineyards, Kautz Ironstone Vineyards and Stevenot Winery in Calaveras County and Yankee Hill Winery in Tuolumne County.

The best tours ● Sobon Estate (self-guiding tour of winery museum) in Amador County; and Kautz Ironstone Vineyards (guided tour of wine caves) in Calaveras County.

Wineland activities and such

Wineland events ● A Taste of Amador in February, wine and food event sponsored by Amador County vintners; (800) 400-0305 or (209) 223-0350. El Dorado Wine Passport, last weekend of March and first weekend of April; (800) 306-3956 or (916) 446-6562. Sierra Showcase of Wine with auction and tasting, early May, Amador County Fairgrounds in Plymouth; (209) 267-5978, extension 50 or (209) 245-6921. Amador County Grape Growers Wine Festival in June, Amador County Fairgrounds; (209) 245-6119, Fairplay Wine Festival, June; (916) 245-3467. El Dorado County Harvest Faire, September; (916) 621-5885. El Dorado County Wine Appreciation Week with barbecue, music, tours and tasting; (800) 306-3956 or (916) 446-6562.

Amador County Fair in Plymouth in late July; (209) 245-6921; and El Dorado County Fair, August, (916) 621-5885 feature local wine displays.

Winery touring maps ● These map-brochures cover the Gold Country's three major wine producing regions: *Beautiful El Dorado Wine Country Tour,* El Dorado Vintners Assn., P.O. Box 1614, Placerville, CA 95667; (800) 306-3956 or (916) 446-6562. *Amador County Wine Country*, Amador Vintners Assn., c/o the Amador County Chamber of Commerce, P.O. Box 596, Jackson, CA 95642; (209) 223-0350. *Calaveras, the Other Wine Country*, Calaveras Wine Association, P.O. Box 2492, Murphys, CA 95247; (800) 225-3764; maps also available at the Calaveras County Visitors Center at highways 49 and 4 in Angels Camp; P.O. Box 637, Angels Camp, CA 95222; (800) 225-3764 or (209) 736-0049.

Wine country tours ● Abacus Luxury Limousine at (916) 756-0162 has tours of wineries in Amador County and the Napa Valley. Wagon & Wine tour of historic Murphys with stops at several wineries; Big Trees Carriage Company, P.O. Box 977, Murphys, CA 95247; (209) 728-2602.

BEYOND THE VINEYARDS

Like Monterey and Santa Cruz, the Sierra foothills are more famous for tourism than for wineries—although those citadels of Zinfandel are quickly gaining fame. We only touch on the central Mother Lode's highlights here. For more detail, pick up a copy of our other books, *The Best of the Gold Country* and *Northern California Discovery Guide,* available at book stores everywhere, or they can be ordered directly from the source; see the back of this book.

The favored route for exploring the Sierra foothills is Highway 49, named in honor of the peak year of the gold rush. Call the "Golden Chain," it meanders for 310 miles through the full length of the Sierra Nevada mining area, from Vinton in the north to Oakhurst in the south. It's a popular vacationers' route; some folks spend days wandering its serpentine course. As we have noted, only its central area offers functioning wineries. Using each of the three wine producing areas as a base, we'll suggest some driving tours that take you past other Sierra foothill attractions.

El Dorado County

Placerville was so rowdy in its early days that it was initially called Hangtown in honor of a frequent method of discipline. Later, more sedate citizens changed the name. After exploring its lures, you can continue east to south shore **Lake Tahoe** with its famous glitter—coming both from the lake and its surrounding casinos. This was the route of the **Pony Express** and markers chart its progress through the Sierra Nevada.

If you follow the twisting course of State Highway 193 fifteen miles north of Placerville, you'll encounter **Georgetown,** one of the best-preserved of the old mining towns.

A short, winding drive northwest on Highway 49 will take you to **Marshall Gold Discovery State Historic Park** in **Coloma**, where James Marshall found his pea-sized nuggets that started all this business. Beyond, you'll travel through the ruggedly imposing **American River Canyon** and arrive in **Auburn,** which has a funkily attractive Old Town section.

Amador County

Little remains of Plymouth's glory days, although **Drytown, Amador City** and **Sutter Creek,** south on Highway 49, have preserved much of their yesterday charm. They're noted for boutiques and antique shops and they offer several bed and breakfast inns, handy stops for Shenandoah Valley wine country visitors.

Sutter Creek-Volcano Road heading northeast from Sutter Creek leads through one of the prettiest creek valleys in the foothills, ending at the rustic mining town of **Volcano.** Just above is **Daffodil Hill,** where acres of daffodils blossom every spring; call (209) 223-0608 for bloom times. Just below is **Indian Grinding Rock State Park,** preserving the history of the area's earliest residents.

Calaveras-Tuolumne counties

Several historic hamlets draw visitors to Calaveras County, most notably **San Andreas,** where stage coach bandit Black Bart was jailed, and **Angels Camp,** made famous by Mark Twain's frog-jumping yarn. Both have historic districts with the requisite boutiques and antique stores.

You already know that an uphill drive on Highway 4 takes you to the wine country around Murphys. Stay on the highway and you'll reach the high Sierra and the famous **Bear Valley** summer and winter resort. On the way, you'll pass **Calaveras Big Trees State Park,** whose giant sequoia groves are definitely worth a stop.

Neighboring Tuolumne County brims with gold rush lore, most notably **Columbia State Historic Park.** Just south on Highway 49, **Sonora** and **Jamestown** are treasure-troves of early California architecture and memorabilia. Much of downtown Sonora has been renovated of late, with boutiques and restaurants occupying ancient storefronts. **Railtown 1897 State Historic Park** is "Jimtown's" premier attraction. A drive north from Sonora takes you to the piney wood hamlets of **Twain Harte** and **Pinecrest,** popular Sierra retreats.

Drive east from Jamestown on Highway 49, then Route 120, and you'll climb up to the neat old mining town of **Groveland** and then to the Sierra Nevada's most famous attraction, **Yosemite National Park.**

Gold Country activities

Cave tours • Three limestone caverns are located near Calaveras County's wine country: California Caverns at Cave City above San Andreas and Moaning Cavern near Murphys, both (209) 736-2708; and Mercer Caverns above Stevenot Winery, (209) 728-2101. Admission charge at each.

Farm products • For a map and guide to farms selling fresh and prepared fruits, vegetables and wines (including Apple Hill Growers), contact El Dorado County Farm Trails Assn., P.O. Box 542, Camino, CA 95709; (916) 621-4772 or the El Dorado County Chamber of Commerce, 542 Main St., Placerville, CA 95667; (800) 457-6279 or (916) 621-5885. Apple Hill Growers also produces a brochure, with a map locating direct-to-consumer orchard and farm product sales, baked goods and specialty foods, along with wineries in the area. See below, under "Gold Country attractions.

Gold country tours • Gold Rush Tours, 5580 Tosca Court in Placerville, (800) 787-4246 or (916) 677-4316, offers tours of Coloma State Historic Park, the Gold Bug Mine, Apple Hill and other sites in El Dorado County. Mother Lode Tours has two to five-day excursion in the Gold Country, Murphys, (209) 728-1190. Hidden Treasure Mine, Columbia State Historic Park has a short tour of a working gold mine, (209) 532-9693.

Gold panning • Appropriate to the area, one can pan for gold at: Columbia State Historic Park, (209) 532-9693; Jensen's Pick & Shovel Ranch, Vallecitos, (209) 736-0287; and Gold Prospecting Expeditions, Jamestown, (209) 984-GOLD.

White-water rafting • Rivers that once carried gold from the Sierra Nevada now carry rafters splashing through their rapids. For lists of river-runners, contact the chambers of commerce listed at the end of this chapter.

Gold Country attractions

Amador County Museum • 225 Church St., Jackson; (209) 223-6386. Wednesday-Sunday 10 to 4; modest admission charge. Relics of early Amador County; mine exhibit and mining gear.

Angels Camp Museum • 753 S. Main St., Angels Camp; (209) 736-4444. Daily 10 to 3; modest admission charge. Historic relics and old farm and gold-mining equipment.

Apple Hill • Nearly 50 Apple Hill growers offer direct-to-consumer products, particularly apple goodies, between Labor Day and Thanksgiving. A few remain open the year-around. For a guide map, contact Apple Hill Growers, Inc., P.O. Box 494, Camino, CA 95709; (916) 644-7692.

Calaveras County Museum and Archives • 30 N. Main St., San Andreas; (209) 754-4023. Daily 10 to 4; modest admission charge. Pioneer museum in old Hall of Records building; original Black Bart jail cell out back.

Chaw'se Indian Grinding Rock State Historic Park • 14881 Pine Grove-Volcano Rd., Pine Grove, CA 95665; (209) 296-7488. Museum open weekdays 11 to 3 and weekends 10 to 4; day use fee for park. Reconstructed Miwok village, museum and huge Indian grinding rock; campgrounds.

Columbia State Historic Park • Parrotts Ferry Road (P.O. Box 151), Columbia, CA 95310; (209) 532-4301. Most museums and shops open 10 to 5 daily; free. Restored gold mining town that once was the gem of the Mother Lode. Stage coach rides, horseback rides, gold panning, Hidden Treasure Mine tour, costumed docent tours; hotels, restaurants.

El Dorado County Historical Museum • 100 Placerville Dr., Placerville; (916) 621-5865. Wednesday-Saturday 10 to 4, Sunday noon to 4. Free, donations appreciated. Artifacts of early-day Hangtown and El Dorado County.

Gold Bug Park and Mine • 549 Main St., Placerville, CA 95667; (916) 642-5232. Daily in summer; weekends only mid-March through April and mid-September through October; closed November through mid-March. Gold mine, stamp mill and other mining artifacts.

Marshall Gold Discovery State Historic Park • P.O. Box 461, Coloma, CA 95613; (916) 622-3470. Museum open daily 10 to 4:30 Memorial Day through Labor Day, 11 to 5 the rest of the year; day use fee. Historical buildings and exhibits, reconstruction of Sutter's Mill gold discovery site.

Old Timers Museum • 470 Main Street at Sheep Ranch Road, Murphys; (209) 728-2607. Thursday-Sunday 11 to 4; small admission charge. Early-day mining relics and reconstructed blacksmith shop.

Railtown 1897 State Historic Park • Fifth Avenue, Jamestown; (209) 984-3953. Gift shop and roundhouse open daily 10 to 5 (shorter hours in off-season), free admission; train rides weekends 10:30 to 3; fee charged. Old time steam trains, roundhouse and rail memorabilia.

Tuolumne County Museum and History Center • 158 W. Bradford Ave., Sonora; (209) 532-1317. Daily 9 to 4:30; donations accepted. Gold rush and pioneer relics, old jail cells, gold nugget exhibit.

WINE COUNTRY DINING

El Dorado County

The Apple Cellar • ☆ $

□ 325 Main St., Placerville; (916) 642-1700. American; no alcohol. Weekdays 7 to 5, weekends 9 to 5. MC/VISA. □ Cute American contry style place decorated with rural artifacts, serving hearty breakfasts and light lunch entrées. Try the specialty breads such as pesto pine nut and jalapeño cheese.

Buttercup Pantry • ☆☆ $$

□ 222 Main Street (at Highway 49), Placerville; (916) 621-1320; American; wine and beer. Daily from 6 a.m. MC/VISA. □ Cheerful early American café with print curtains, drop lamps, wood trim and ceiling fans. Earthy American fare includes Texas barbecue, assorted chickens and steaks.

Cable House Restaurant ● ☆☆ $$

◻ *4110 Carson Rd., Camino; (916) 644-1818. American; no alcohol. Monday-Saturday 6 a.m. to 3 p.m., Sunday 8 to 3. MC/VISA.* ◻ Small café tucked into a wood frame cottage, serving hefty breakfasts and "cookhouse lunches" of fried chicken or steak, plus sandwiches. Woodsy interior with slant-board walls hung with whipsaws and other lumbering gear. The restaurant's name comes from a suspension cable carriage that once hauled lumber across the American River gorge.

Café Sarah ● ☆☆ $$

◻ *301 Main St., Placerville; (916) 621-4680. Country American; wine and beer. Lunch and dinner daily. MC/VISA.* ◻ Pleasing rural American café with a white embossed tin ceiling, maple chairs, potted palms and modern art, giving it a kind of Berkeley-in-the-Gold-Country feel. Sandwiches and elaborate salads for lunch, typical American fare with interesting seasonings for dinner.

Smith Flat House Restaurant ● ☆☆☆ $$

◻ *2021 Smith Flat Rd., Smith Flat; (916) 662-0471 or (916) 621-0667. American; full bar service. Lunch Tuesday-Friday 11 to 2 daily, dinner Tuesday-Thursday 5 to 9 and Friday-Saturday 5 to 10, Sunday brunch 10 to 3. Major credit cards.* ◻ Generous portions of pioneer history come with the menu of steak, chicken or seafood. The 1850 structure was a hotel, restaurant, wagon and stage stop, dance hall, Pony Express stop, post office and general store. A mine shaft leads from the old fashioned saloon to the Blue Lead Channel, which yielded $18 million during the rush for gold.

La Casa Grande ● ☆☆ $

◻ *251 Main St. (at Spring, just off Highway 50), Placerville; (916) 626-5454. Mexican-American; full bar service. Sunday-Thursday 11 to 8:45, Friday-Saturday 11 to 9:45. MC/VISA, AMEX.* ◻ Family-style Mexican café housed in a pair of 1896 storefronts in the historic area of Placerville. Large *Latino* menu has typical tortilla-wrapped fare, plus specials such as enchilada verde, chicken chimichangas and pork in molé sauce.

Powell Brothers Steamer Company ● ☆☆☆ $$

◻ *425 Main St., Placerville; (916) 626-1091. Seafood; full bar service. Daily 11 to 10. MC/VISA.* ◻ Lively place with "old wharf atmosphere" in one of downtown Placerville's store fronts. The menu features oysters, *cioppino*, scampi and New York pan roast oysters, shrimp or combo. Extensive Gold Country wine list.

Amador County

Bar-T-Bar ● ☆☆ $$

◻ *Highway 49 (just south of town), Plymouth; (209) 245-3729. American; full bar service. Daily 11 a.m. to 9 p.m (to 9:30 Friday and Saturday). MC/VISA* ◻ A likable roadhouse that dishes up hearty fare at modest prices; steak, seafood, ribs and chops dinners include soup and salad, potatoes or rice and hot bread. American country décor with warm wood paneling, ceiling fans and maple furnishings. Amador County wines featured.

Bellotti Inn ● ☆☆ $$

◻ *53 Main St., Sutter Creek; (209) 267-5211. Italian-American; full bar service. Sunday-Monday and Wednesday-Thursday 11:30 to 9, Friday-Saturday 11:30 to 10, closed Tuesday. MC/VISA.* ◻ Gold Rush style restaurant in an

1858 hotel with attractive although spartan 19th century décor. Usual pastas plus specials such as breast of chicken Parmesan, calamari steak and some American steak and prime rib dishes.

Imperial Hotel Restaurant ● ☆☆☆ $$$

◻ Main Street, Amador City; (209) 267-9172. Continental; full bar service. Nightly 5 to 9, Sunday brunch 10 to 2. Major credit cards. ◻ Attractive old style restaurant in an 1879 brick Gold Country classic. High backed fabric chairs, ceiling fans and white nappery in the cozy little dining room. Menu items include filet Diane, pork loin in rhubarb sauce, bleu cheese chicken, prawn and scallop scampi and several low fat-low cholesterol entrées. Western style saloon adjacent to dining room.

Pelargonium ● ☆☆☆ $$$

◻ One Hanford St. (Highway 49 North), Sutter Creek; (209) 267-5008. Contemporary American; wine and beer. Dinner Tuesday-Saturday from 5:30. Reservations recommended on weekends. No credit cards; checks accepted. ◻ Eye-appealing restaurant in a Victorian house all gussied up in geranium wallpaper and Americana frills. Locally popular place, offering a daily-changing menu with attractively presented entrées such as gallantine of chicken, pork loin, crepes Florentine and red snapper amondine.

Ron and Nancy's Palace Restaurant ● ☆☆☆ $$$

◻ 76 Main St., Sutter Creek; (209) 267-1355. Continental; full bar service. Lunch daily 11:30 to 3, dinner nightly 5 to 9. Reservations suggested on weekends; major credit cards. ◻ Sutter Creek's most attractive restaurant; a study in Victorian elegance, housed in an 1896 building that began life, appropriately, as a restaurant and saloon. Entreés are a mix of Continental standards such as calamari amondine and American fare such as prime rib and steaks. Good local wine list.

Calaveras-Tuolumne counties

City Hotel Restaurant ● ☆☆☆☆ $$$$

◻ Main Street (Jackson), Columbia State Historic Park; (209) 532-1479. California-continental; full bar service. Multi-course prix fixe dinners Tuesday-Sunday from 5, Sunday brunch 11 to 2. Reservations essential on weekends; MC/VISA, AMEX. ◻ Splendid Victorian dining room in restored gold rush hotel; considered by many as the Sierra foothills' finest restaurant. Entrées on the ever-changing menu may include baked rack of lamb with pine nut and garlic crust, rabbit braised in wine with pearl onions, or poached salmon with sautéed spinach. Good foothills wine list; all smoke-free.

Columbia House Restaurant ● ☆☆ $

◻ Main and State streets, Columbia State Historic Park; (209) 532-5134. American; wine and beer. Breakfast-lunch weekdays 8 to 3 and weekends 8 to 5. MC/VISA. ◻ Hearty breakfasts plus lunches of sandwiches, sirloin steak, chicken breasts and pasties, a meat pie specialty of Cornish miners, served in a gold rush café whose roots date back to 1850 (although the original was in a tent). Country décor with wainscoting, print wallpaper and quilt panels. Smoke-free.

Lickskillet Café ● ☆☆ $$

◻ 11256 State St., Columbia; (209) 536-9599. American-continental; wine and beer. Lunch and dinner daily from 11:30 in summer and Wednesday through Sunday the rest of the year. Major credit cards. ◻ Cute early American style café (despite its unfortunate name) just off Main Street in historic Columbia. Fare is "country international," such as lamb eggplant ragout with Middle Eastern spices, rosemary roasted chicken and rock shrimp scampi with green onion *focaccia* bread. All non-smoking; good foothills wine list. Outdoor tables on a porch and lawn.

Murphys Hotel Restaurant ● ☆☆☆ $$$

◻ *457 Main Street (Algiers Street), Murphys; (209) 728-3444. American-continental; full bar service. Sunday-Thursday 7 a.m. to 8:30, Friday-Saturday 7 to 9:30. Major credit cards.* ◻ Victorian style restaurant in 1856 hotel (listing below), featuring fare such as steaks, prime rib, pastas and seafood, with homemade desserts and a good selection of Amador wines. Elaborate period décor includes hurricane ceiling lamps, pioneer photos and relics.

Nugget Family Restaurant ● ☆ $$

◻ *Main and Scott streets, Murphys; (209) 728-2608. American; full bar service. Breakfast and lunch daily from 6:30 a.m., dinner nightly except Tuesday- Wednesday, MC/VISA.* ◻ Rustic diner with red checkered tablecloths, ceiling fans and a few old movie posters. The menu tilts strongly toward basic American steak, plus pork chops, chicken and lobster.

Peppermint Stick ● ☆☆ $

◻ *454 Main St. (downtown), Murphys; (209) 728-3570. American; no alcohol. Monday-Friday 11 to 5, Saturday 10 to 9, Sunday noon to 5 (hours may be longer in summer). MC/VISA.* ◻ Cute old fashioned fountain in a century-old building with white wrought iron chairs, folk art décor. Light lunch and dinner fare, including unusual "miners chili" and "old timers beef stew" served in a hollowed-out bread loaf. Slurp the soup and eat the bowl.

WINELAND LODGINGS

NOTE: Prices were provided by the establishments and are subject to change. Use the price ranges only as a rough guideline and call the places listed to confirm their current rates.

El Dorado County

Best Western Placerville Inn ● ☆☆☆ $$$ Ø

◻ *6850 Greenleaf Dr. (Highway 50 at Missouri Flat), Placerville, CA 95667; (800) 854-9100 or (916) 622-9100. Couples $64 to $75, singles $59 to $69. Major credit cards.* ◻ Attractive 105-room motel with Southwest décor. TV movies, phones, some fireplaces. Pool, spa. **Eppie's Restaurant** serves 24 hours; American, dinners from $9; full bar service.

Chichester-McKee House Bed & Breakfast ● ☆☆☆ $$$$ Ø

◻ *800 Spring St., Placerville, CA 95667; (800) 831-4008 or (916) 626-1882. Couples $75 to $85. Three rooms, all with half-baths; full breakfast. Major credit cards.* ◻ Nicely furnished 1892 Queen Anne Victorian home with Victorian, American and country antiques. Conservatory, landscaped garden, porch with old fashioned swing, fireplaces in parlor and lobby.

Fitzpatrick Lodge ● ☆☆ $$$ Ø

◻ *7740 Fairplay Road, Somerset, CA 95684; (916) 620-3248. Couples $79 to $99. Four rooms, all with private baths; full breakfast. MC/VISA.* ◻ Handsome log chalet with hilltop view of mountains and valleys; part of Fitzpatrick Winery. Comfortable country-style furnishings; all rooms with view decks. Chalet-style sitting room with fireplace; afternoon wine and snacks.

Gold Trail Motor Lodge ● ☆ $$ Ø

□ *1970 Broadway (Point View), Placerville, CA 95667; (916) 622-2906. Couples $41 to $46, singles $36 to $41. Major credit cards.* □ A 32-room motel on landscaped grounds with picnic area, pool. TV, room phones, some room refrigerators and hair dryers.

Mother Lode Motel ● ☆ $$ Ø

□ *1940 Broadway (Point View), Placerville, CA 95667; (916) 622-0895. Couples $39 to $51, singles $34 to $48. Major credit cards.* □ A 21-unit motel with pool, lawn area. Rooms have TV movies, phones; some refrigerators.

The Seven-Up Bar Guest Ranch ● ☆☆☆ $$$$ Ø

□ *P.O. Box 304 (8060 Fairplay Rd.), Somerset, CA 95684; (916) 620-5450. Couples $95 to $115, singles $85 to $105. Six units with private baths; ranch style breakfast. MC/VISA, DISC.* □ A 1930s dude ranch bought by Alice and Michael Chazen of Perry Creek Vineyards and spruced up as a Western-style B&B. Log cabin accommodations have contemporary Western furnishings. Activities include hiking, fishing and treks to an ancient Native American archeological site.

Amador County

Amador Harvest Inn ● ☆☆☆ $$$$ Ø

□ *12455 Steiner Rd. (Shenandoah Valley), Plymouth, CA 95669; (209) 245-5512. Couples and singles $85 to $110. Four rooms with private baths; full breakfast and afternoon snacks. MC/VISA.* □ Beautifully restored historic farm house adjacent to Deaver Vineyards tasting room, with views of vineyard and a lake. Victorian and early American décor; comfortable living room with fireplace. Near Shenandoah Valley wineries.

Gold Quartz Inn ● ☆☆☆ $$$$ Ø

□ *15 Bryson Dr., Sutter Creek, CA 95685; (800) 752-8738 or (209) 267-9155. Couples and singles $75 to $125, including full breakfast and afternoon tea. MC/VISA, AMEX.* □ Nicely maintained 24-room Queen Anne style inn. Rooms furnished in period décor with American and Victorian antiques; TV, phones, sitting porches and private entrances.

Imperial Hotel ● ☆☆☆ $$$$ Ø

□ *14202 Highway 49 (P.O. Box 195), Amador City, CA 95601; (209) 267-9172. Rooms $65 to $95, including full breakfast. Major credit cards.* □ Nicely restored brick 1879 hotel; six individually decorated rooms with period furnishings and modern private baths. **Restaurant** and bar are listed above.

The PictureRock Inn ● ☆☆☆ $$$$ Ø

□ *55 Eureka St., Sutter Creek, CA 95685; (800) 399-2389 or (209) 267-5500. Couples and singles $80 to $105. Six rooms, all with private baths; full breakfast. Major credit cards.* □ Nicely restored two-story 1914 Craftsman bungalow between Sutter Creek's historic Main Street and the Knights Foundry visitor center. Rooms individually furnished with vintage European or early American themes. Comfortable living room; nice art collection of oils, watercolors and sculpture.

Shenandoah Inn ● ☆☆☆ $$$ Ø

□ *17674 Village Dr., Plymouth, CA 95669; (800) 542-4549 or (209) 245-4491. Couples and singles $50 to $59, suites $75 to $95; prices include continental breakfast. Major credit cards.* □ Attractive Spanish style inn with 47 rooms; TV movies, phones, in-room coffee. Pool, spa, landscaped grounds. Near turnoff to Shenandoah Valley wine country.

Sutter Creek Inn ● ☆☆☆ $$$ Ø

◻ 75 Main St. (P.O. Box 385), Sutter Creek, CA 95685; (209) 267-5606. Couples $50 to $97, singles $42 to $92, including full breakfast. No credit cards; checks accepted. ◻ A 19-room inn fashioned from an 1850s Greek revival house; furnished with a blend of antique and contemporary. Some rooms with fireplaces, all with private baths. Landscaped grounds with hammocks; afternoon refreshments.

The Foxes ● ☆☆☆☆ $$$$$ Ø

◻ 77 Main St. (P.O. Box 159), Sutter Creek, CA 95685; (209) 267-5882. Couples $100 to $145, singles $95 to $135. Six rooms, all with private baths; full breakfast. MC/VISA, DISC. ◻ Beautifully appointed inn fashioned from an early day merchant's home. Period furnishings with fox decorator theme; radio/tape players in rooms, some rooms with TV. Landscaped grounds, gardens and covered porches.

The Hanford House ● ☆☆☆ $$$$ Ø

◻ 61 Hanford St. (P.O. Box 1450), Sutter Creek, CA 95685; (916) 267-0747. Couples $85 to $110, singles $75 to $105. Eight rooms, all with private baths; expanded buffet breakfast. MC/VISA, DISC. ◻ A stylish brick inn fashioned around a 1920s home. Large rooms furnished with early California antiques; fireplace in honeymoon suite. Large parlor, sun deck and patio.

The Heirloom Bed & Breakfast Inn ● ☆☆☆ $$$$ Ø

◻ 214 Shakeley Lane (Preston Avenue), Ione, CA 95640; (209) 274-4468. Couples $60 to $92, singles $55 to $87. Six rooms, four with private baths; full breakfast. Major credit cards. ◻ An 1863 antebellum brick mansion listed as a Native Sons of the Golden West "Dedicated Historical Site." Rooms done in American and Victorian antiques and art works; three with fireplaces or wood burning stoves. Convenient to Ione-area wineries.

Indian Creek Bed & Breakfast ● ☆☆ $$$ Ø

◻ 21950 Highway 49 (three miles north), Plymouth, CA 95669; (800) 24-CREEK or (209) 245-4648. Couples and singles $70 to $95; all units $50 Monday-Thursday. Four rooms, all with private baths; full breakfast. MC/VISA, DISC. ◻ Restored log home on ten wooded acres; decks, lodge-style living room with fireplace. Furnished with a mix of antiques, pine and country crafts.

Mine House Inn ● ☆☆☆ $$$ Ø

◻ 14125 Highway 49 (P.O. Box 245), Amador City, CA 95601; (800) 646-3473 or (209) 267-5900. Couples $65 to $90; $15 less Monday through Thursday. Eight rooms, all with private baths; expanded continental breakfast. MC/VISA. ◻ Attractive inn fashioned from an 1880 mining office building, overlooking Amador City and the Keystone mine headframe. Rooms with Victorian antiques; sitting room, art gallery and swimming pool.

Calaveras-Tuolumne

City Hotel and Fallon Hotel ● ☆☆☆☆ $$$ Ø

◻ P.O. Box 1870, Columbia, CA 95310; City Hotel—(209) 532-1479, Fallon Hotel—(209) 532- 1470. Couples $44 to $85, singles $50 to $80, one suite for $115; rates include continental breakfast. MC/VISA, AMEX. ◻ Impeccably restored gold rush hotels in the heart of Columbia State Historic Park. Furnished in the style of the 1860s and 1870s. Wainscoting, print wallpaper, Victorian and American antiques; service staff in period dress. Some half-baths and shared showers. **City Hotel Restaurant** listed above.

Columbia Gem Motel ● ☆ $$

□ *22131 Parrotts Ferry Rd. (P.O. Box 874), Columbia, CA 95310; (209) 532-4508. Couples $45 to $70, singles $25 to $40. MC/VISA.* □ Well-kept vintage "auto court" style motel with 12 units in individual cottages. TV, in-room coffee. Near Columbia State Historic Park.

Dunbar House, 1880 ● ☆☆☆ $$$$$ ∅

□ *271 Jones St. (P.O. Box 1375), Murphys, CA 95247; (209) 728-2897. Couples $105 to $145, singles $100 to $140. Four rooms, all with private baths; full breakfast. MC/VISA, AMEX.* □ Imposing Italianate home furnished with country and Victorian antiques. Rooms have wood-burning stoves and refrigerators stocked with a bottle of local wine. Two-room suite with spa tub. Afternoon refreshments; country-style gardens.

The Harlan House ● ☆☆☆ $$$ ∅

□ *22890 School House St. (P.O. Box 686), Columbia, CA 95310; (209) 533-4862. Doubles $75 to $130. Three rooms, plus a cozy cellar suite, all with private baths; full breakfast. MC/VISA.* □ Handsome two-story Victorian perched on a slope above Columbia State Historic Park; nicely appointed rooms feature a mix of Victorian and American antiques. Shady porch and garden patio. Free shuttle to Columbia airport.

Murphys Hotel ● ☆☆☆ $$$$

□ *457 Main St. (P.O. 329), Murphys, CA 95247; (800) 532-7684 or (209) 728-3444. Couples and singles $70 to $95; rates include continental breakfast. MC/VISA, AMEX.* □ National historic landmark hotel, handsomely refurbished in Victorian style. The Presidential Suite, where Ulysses S. Grant once slept, is particularly opulent. Nine rooms in the 1856 hotel have share baths; 20 rooms in adjacent lodge wing have TV, phones and private baths.

Gold/wine country information sources

Amador County Chamber of Commerce, P.O. Box 596, Jackson, CA 95642; (209) 223-0350.

Calaveras Lodging and Visitors Association, P.O. Box 367 (1211 S. Main St.), Angels Camp, CA 95333; (800) 225-3764 or (209) 736-0049.

El Dorado County Chamber of Commerce, 542 Main St., Placerville, CA 95667; (800) 457-6279 or (916) 621-5885.

Sutter Creek Visitor Center, 80 Eureka St. (in Knights Foundry), Sutter Creek, CA 95685; (800) 400-0305.

Tuolumne County Visitors Bureau, 55 Stockton St. (at Washington), Box 4020, Sonora, CA 95370; (800) 446-1333 or (209) 533- 4420.

"This lively, intense wine is light enough on its feet to let the grapefruit, nutmeg and vanilla flavors extend over a long finish."
— Description of a Markham Napa Valley Chardonnay

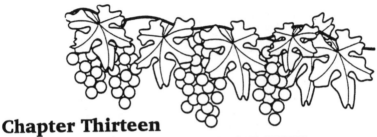

Chapter Thirteen
TEMECULA VALLEY
Chardonnay in a Southland suburb

During California's formative years, its population was centered in the north central area, drawn by the gold discovery in the Sierra Nevada foothills. Wine production, however, began in the south, since that's where most of the mission vineyards were located. The state's first commercial planters were drawn to southern California as well.

Today, of course, both conditions are reversed. Most of the people live in the south and most of the premium wine production is in the north central area. In fact, the Southland's only major vineyard area is quite new.

Pioneer planters such as Jean-Louis Vignes and William Wolfskill made Los Angeles the center of the state's commercial wine industry in the 1830s. Later, a utopian colony of Germans planted tens of thousands of vines in Anaheim, not far from the land now ruled by Mickey Mouse.

Urban growth pushed the vines eastward from Los Angeles and Anaheim toward Cucamonga, where a dozen or so wineries functioned from the 1930s until the 1960s. New population surges and the popularity of orange groves put the squeeze on the grapes again and they shifted southward.

In the 1970s, a new home was found for Southern California's wine country, the Temecula Valley between Los Angeles and San Diego. Although a few wineries are scattered elsewhere about the Southland, Temecula offers the only concentration of vineyards and vintners. It's in southern Riverside County, about fifteen miles from the Pacific, close enough to benefit from temperate ocean air.

Those cooling breezes, morning fogs and a 1,300-foot elevation provide suitable climate for premium whites. Chardonnay and Sauvignon Blanc are the most popular, and we found some excellent specimens here. Some reds also do well, and growers are beginning to make room for Cabernet, Merlot and Petit Syrah.

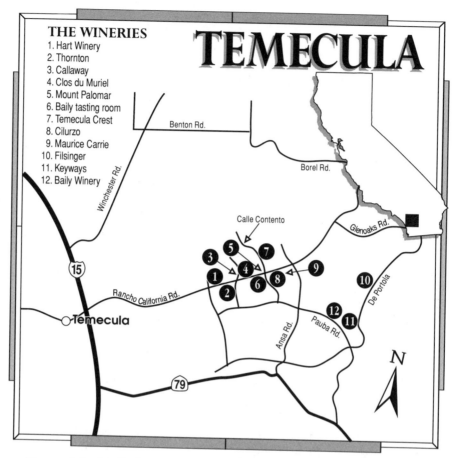

THE WINERIES

1. Hart Winery
2. Thornton
3. Callaway
4. Clos du Muriel
5. Mount Palomar
6. Baily tasting room
7. Temecula Crest
8. Cilurzo
9. Maurice Carrie
10. Filsinger
11. Keyways
12. Baily Winery

TEMECULA

Benton Rd.

Winchester Rd.

Borel Rd.

Calle Contento

Glenoaks Rd.

15

Rancho California Rd.

Temecula

De Portola

Ansa Rd.

Pauba Rd.

79

N

Temecula's vineyards aren't exactly sheltered from the Southland's population sprawl. In 25 years, the town has rocketed from a quiet cowboy hamlet into a semi-planned community of nearly 40,000. One sees a virtual explosion of planned residential areas, shopping centers and business parks. According to the most recent census, this area is one of California's fastest-growing regions.

However, the vines are in a protected agricultural zone, to the east of the mushrooming city. Here, they share dry, sandy hillocks with avocado and citrus groves, fancy horse ranches and a remarkable tally of luxurious country estates. The area's architectural look—apparently by some silent dictate—is Spanish Southwest. From business parks to ranch mansions to shopping centers to winery tasting rooms, the rule is beige stucco, pink tile and Spanish arches, with salmon and turquoise accents. The effect is quite pleasing.

Temecula began as a genuine cowtown, laid out in 1884 to serve the commercial needs of the huge Vail Ranch, which filled most of the valley. The town consisted of the Longbranch Saloon, the Stables Bar, a folksy restaurant called the Swing Inn, and a couple of stores. Real cowboys and Indians, most employed on the ranch, strolled about the streets. Passersby called the place quaint. The name is quaint, too. "Temecula" is an Indian word for "Valley of Joy."

In the late 1960s, it became just that, at least for land speculators. The ranch was sold to Kaiser Development Company, and the planned community of Rancho California began taking form. The die was cast for the pink tile and turquoise Temecula of tomorrow. Old Town sought refuge in boutiques and antiques. It survives today as a resolutely Western shopping and dining area.

Vineyard growth has nearly out-paced the spread of tile roofs. The Temecula wine industry emerged in less time than it takes a newborn infant to reach drinking age. A dozen vintners now exist where only one, Callaway, stood in 1974. The first vineyard was planted in 1967 by Vincenzo Cilurzo, who started his winery in 1978. More than 4,000 acres of vines now thrive in the shallow valley. Still, many winemakers have to import their grapes from other areas. Most reach northwest, toward the central coast.

TEMECULA VALLEY WINERY TOUR ● The area offers a pleasing assortment of wineries and tasting rooms, from family funky to corporate opulent. Most are clustered along Rancho California Road east of Temecula.

Winery touring is relatively simple. Approach Temecula on Interstate 15, take the Rancho California exit and head toward the sunrise. The first two miles carry you through new shopping centers and monotonously attractive tile-roofed housing tracts. After one final subdivision, appropriately called Chardonnay Hills, you enter real Chardonnay country. A locator map at roadside points you to the wineries.

Small **Hart Winery** is on your left, up a narrow lane; the imposing **Thornton Winery** is just beyond, on the right. Practically across the road from Thornton is **Callaway Vineyard and Winery.** Just beyond are **Clos du Muriel** and **Mount Palomar Winery**, on the left.

Baily Winery's tasting room is perched on a nearby knoll on the right, at Rancho California Road and Calle Contento. Turn left onto unpaved but reasonably smooth Calle Contento and you'll find **Temecula Crest Winery,** at the end of a country lane. Now, reverse yourself on Calle Contento, cross Rancho California and you encounter **Cilurzo Winery** (*chee-LURE-so*), about a third of a mile up, on your left. Return to Rancho California, turn right and you quickly see the fanciful **Maurice Carrie Winery,** on the right, just beyond Calle Contento.

The remaining wineries require a short looping drive around the valley, providing an excuse to admire some of the opulent estates perched on the knolls. From Carrie, continue a bit more than a mile on Rancho California and turn right onto Glenoaks Road. Follow Glenoaks 2.7 miles to a stop sign at De Portola and turn right. After two miles, you'll see the small Spanish-style tasting room of **Filsinger Vineyards and Winery**, on your right.

Another two miles takes you to **Keyways Vineyard,** also on the right and also Spanish style. A short distance beyond, turn right up unpaved Pauba Road and follow its sandy course about half a mile to **Baily Winery**. (This is winery that belongs to the tasting room we encountered earlier.)

WINERY CODES ● *T* = Tasting with no fee; *T$* = Tasting for a fee; *GT* = Guided tours; *GTA* = Guided tours by appointment; *ST* = Self-guiding tours; *CT* = casual tours or a peek into the winery; ✕ = picnic area; 🐚 = Gift shop or good giftware selection. Price ranges listed in tasting notes are for varietals; jug wines may be available for less.

To get back to Temecula, retreat down Pauba, turn right and continue on De Portola until it bumps into Anza Road. Go left and you will soon encounter State Highway 79. A right turn will return you to I-15 and Temecula.

Hart Winery • T ⚔

☐ *32500 Rancho California Rd. (P.O. Box 956), Temecula, CA 92593; (909) 676-6300. Daily 9 to 4:30; MC/VISA, AMEX. Most varieties tasted for a $2 fee, which includes a wine logo glass. A few wine related items for sale. Small picnic area.* ☐

This small barnboard winery started as a weekend venture by Travis (Joe) Hart, who taught school weekdays in Carlsbad, a coastal town northwest of here. He planted vineyards in 1974 and built his winery six years later. His son Bill helps out, mostly in the business end. The winery is nearly a full-time activity now. The tasting room is a small, cozy place where you'll be hosted by one Hart or the other while sipping their sturdy, tasty wines.

"Dad's a seat-of-the-pants winemaker, mostly self-taught," Bill said. "He started out making wine as a hobby, then took a few courses at Davis."

Tasting notes: The Harts among the few area winemakers focusing on reds as well as whites. Their three-year-old Cabernet Sauvignon was properly peppery, with medium tannin, and a Cabernet blanc displayed good spicy varietal character. The Harts also do a full bodied yet mellow and exceedingly tasty Merlot. A light, crisp Sauvignon Blanc and a dry, nippy Chenin Blanc complete the list. Prices range from $7 to $9.75 for the whites; the Cabernet sells for $14.

Vintner's Choice: "Our Sauvignon Blanc is consistently good," said Bill. "And we we're happy with our Cabernet Sauvignon and Merlot."

Thornton Winery • T$ GT R 🏮

☐ *32575 Rancho California Rd., Temecula, CA 92591; (909) 699-0099. Champagne Bar tasting room and gift shop open daily from 10; MC/VISA. Two sparkling and two still wines tasted for $6; wines also sold by the glass. Tours weekends only; hourly from 10 to 5 Saturday and 10 to 4 Sunday. Extensive giftware selection. Café Champagne adjacent; see listing under "Wine country dining" on page 318.* ☐

The Thornton champagnery and winery is one of the more opulent of the Temecula Valley facilities. It's a French style château done in textured stone and brick, built around a courtyard and fountain. An herb garden greets visitors as they enter the complex. On weekends, you can join hourly tours, followed by a sit-down tasting of three sparkling wines for $6. During the week, tastings are conducted in the stylish Champagne Bar, which adjoins a large gift shop. You can buy wine by the glass or bottle here, along with some interesting appetizers, and adjourn to indoor or outdoor tables.

John and Martha Culbertson began making wine at their home in nearby Fallbrook in 1981. They opened this Temecula facility in 1988 as the Culbertson Winery, producing *méthode champenoise* sparkling wines. Their partners, the Thornton family, bought them out in 1993, renamed the facility and added a line of still wines to its list.

Tasting notes: The Culbertson label remains on the sparkling wines, while the new line of table wines are labeled *Brindiamo*, an Italian toast to the good life. The non-vintage Brut had a nice herbal nose and taste with a soft yet crisp finish. Blanc de Noir is a gentle pink wine, dry with a very berry finish. Both were wonderfully complex for sparkling wines. Of the new table

In the aging cellars of California's wineries, tomorrow's wines sleep to soften their tannins and absorb a touch of oak. Although wineries have modernized, they still use the ancient ritual of wood to finish many of their wines.

wines, we tasted a Brindiamo Chardonnay and Cabernet Sauvignon. The white was fruity and mellow, with a hint of oak and a curiously strong vanilla finish. The Cab was complex yet mellow, drinkable now and with enough character to stay around for a few years. Others among the table wines are white Zinfandel, a sweet Muscat Canelli and Rosso Vecchio, a Rhône style red. Prices range from $8 to the early teens for still wines and $12.50 to $28 for the sparklers.

Vintner's Choice: A winery spokesperson insists that the sparkling wines are on a par with dry French Champagnes, and who's to argue? They've been among the state's most award-winning sparkling wines.

Callaway Vineyard & Winery • T$ GT ✕ 🍴

◻ *32720 Rancho California Rd., Temecula, CA 92589; (909) 676-4001. Daily 10:30 to 5; MC/VISA, AMEX. Four varieties tasted for $3 fee (includes logo glass). Arbor picnic area. Extensive gift, wine logo, deli and specialty foods selection. Tours hourly from 11 to 3 weekdays and 11 to 4 weekends.* ◻

Callaway is the oldest and by far the largest of Temecula's wineries, with an output of 225,000 cases. Ely Callaway started the facility in 1974, expanded quickly and sold to the Hiram Walker combine in 1981.

Those hundreds of thousands of cases emerge from a facility that resembles a light industrial park, crowning one of the valley's sandy hillocks. The large tasting room and gift shop are more attractive, with vine-covered exterior walls and big windows offering pleasing valley views. Picnic tables are sheltered under vine-entwined arbors near the vineyards.

Tasting notes: Our ritual began with a "Calla-Lees" Chardonnay, aged on its yeast cells to give it a hearty flavor. Fumé Blanc, barrel fermented in French and American oak, had a hint of that wood with a complex, crisp taste. Our favorite was Sauvignon Blanc, with a nice pepper-herbal smell and taste and a soft finish. Morning Harvest Chenin Blanc had a light nose and flavor and light acid; suitable for picnics. White Riesling, Muscat Canelli and Cabernet Sauvignon complete the list. Prices range from $6 to $14.

Clos du Muriel Vineyards and Winery • T$ CT ✗

◻ *33410 Rancho California Rd., Temecula, CA 92390; (909) 676-5400. Daily 10 to 5; MC/VISA. Any of ten wines tasted for a $4 fee, which includes a wine logo glass. Small picnic area. Informal tours. Wine related gift items.* ◻

Earlier Temecula Valley visitors will remember this as the Piconi facility, opened in 1982 by Dr. John Piconi. Then, in a game of musical wineries, it was taken over in the early 1990s by Clos du Muriel, which originally had a winery and tasting room on nearby Calle Contento. That facility was, in turn, purchased by the Baily winery people and some other investors, and reopened as Temecula Crest.

The Clos du Muriel winery is a simple Spanish style affair, occupying a high ridge with 360-degree views of the valley. One gets a quickie tour while in the small tasting room, for it's perched above the winery's stainless steel and wooden tanks. Outside, a small picnic area sits in the shade of the tile-roofed building.

Tasting notes: Like Hart Winery, Clos du Muriel focuses on reds as well as whites. Cabernet comes in two styles—a light and drinkable non-vintage version, and a reserve with Napa Valley roots, which displayed a berry and nippy pepper flavor with light tannins. Merlot is rich and full-bodied. Of the whites, the Chardonnay was dry with pleasing touches of spice and fruit, while the Sauvignon Blanc had a light, crisp flavor and a gentle spicy touch. Prices range from under $10 to the early teens.

Mount Palomar Winery • T P ▥

◻ *33820 Rancho California Rd., Temecula, CA 92591; (909) 676-5047. Daily 9 to 5; MC/VISA. Most varieties tasted. Good selection of giftwares, specialty foods, picnic fare and deli items. View picnic area.* ◻

One of Temecula's earliest wineries, Palomar was established by John Poole; it has won an impressive number of awards since its creation early in the 1980s. It's an attractive place, on a ridge and tucked behind a hill, out of sight of the busy Rancho California corridor. A multi-gabled Spanish façade hides the business-like winery, and picnic tables have been placed under just about every available tree. The tasting room is done up in white stucco and barn board—a nice effect.

Tasting notes: Whites dominate the list, and we found most to be full bodied with nice herbal undertones. Among the reds were a young and

drinkable Cabernet, a soft blend called Sonrisa and a light Italian style Sangiovese, bottled under the Casteletto label. A solera-style cream sherry was
rich and nutty, among the better we've tasted. Prices range from $6 to $10.

Baily Tasting Room • T & T$ ✕

☐ *33833 Rancho California Rd., Temecula, CA 92589; (909) 676-9463.
Daily 10 to 5; MC/VISA. Most varieties tasted free; a small fee for some. Fair
selection of wine logo items. View picnic area.* ☐

Housed in a hilltop bungalow, this tasting room was opened in late 1990
by Phil and Carol Baily. They wanted to spare visitors the bumpy drive to
their winery on Pauba Road, whose small tasting room is open on weekends
(see listing below). A picnic area under a patio cover near the tasting room
takes advantage of the valley view.

Tasting notes: The brief Baily list consists of Chardonnay, a Sauvignon
Blanc-Semillon Montage, Riesling, Cabernet Blanc and Carmine. We preferred the fruity, nutty Chardonnay with a nice crisp finish; the Montage,
with its interesting herbal-dusky flavor; and a spicy, complex dry Mothers'
Vineyard Riesling. Prices range from $6 to $10.

Vintners choice: "Our two styles of Riesling—dry and off-dry, and our
Montage," says Carol Baily.

Temecula Crest Winery • T$ GTA 🏠

☐ *40620 Calle Contento, Temecula, CA 92591; (909) 676-8231. Daily 10
to 5; MC/VISA. Five wines tasted for a $2.50 fee, which includes the glass. A
fair selection of wine logo and gift items. Picnic area; group tours available by
appointment.* ☐

As noted above, this was Clos du Muriel Winery until its recent purchase
by the Baily family and some investing friends. For history buffs, it started in
1984 as Britton Cellars. The new name is certainly appropriate, since Temecula Crest occupies a ridge high above the valley's vines and dry meadowlands. The structure is one of the valley's most appealing spaces, inside and
out. It's a large designer barn, accented by bits of Bacchus in leaded glass
windows. The interior is a great open space of massive laminated beams and
winery paraphernalia. The tasting room and gift shop blend into one end,
with no partitions to clutter the open feeling. Gift items are scattered about
on barrel heads, drawing browsers into the winery. To shop is to tour.

Tasting notes: You won't taste typical Baily wines when you visit Temecula Crest. These are a bit more complex and woody. The focus is on
whites, including a Chardonnay with pleasing oak touches and a nice acid
finish, an herbal and crisp Sauvignon Blanc and a fruity Riesling with a hint
of the sweet. A white Zinfandel offered a bit of character, created by the addition of 25 percent Cabernet blanc. The Cabernet Sauvignon was young yet
willing, smoothly drinkable, with the slightest hint of oak and vanilla. Prices
are quite modest, from $7 to $13.

Cilurzo Vineyard and Winery • T ST ✕ 🏠

☐ *41220 Calle Contento (P.O. Box 775), Temecula, CA 92592; (909) 676-
5250. Daily 9:30 to 5; MC/VISA. Most varieties tasted for $1 fee, which is ap-
plied to a wine purchase. Giftwares and a good selection of specialty foods and
picnic fare. Self-guiding tours. Picnic tables near winery.* ☐

Vincenzo and Audrey Cilurzo are the senior members of this relatively
new group of Temecula vintners. They planted their vines in 1967 and have
raised both grapes and children here. This is a world apart from the glitter of

Hollywood, where Vince worked for decades as a highly respected lighting director. He has an Oscar to prove his skill, and the tasting room walls are papered with photos of stars who've been placed in his limelights. In true Hollywood fashion, he and Audrey met on the set of the Roy Rogers show.

The rambling winery, tasting room and gift shop run together in a pleasantly inviting scatter. Visitors are encouraged to follow a self-guiding tour for one-on-one encounters with filters, vats and barrels.

Tasting notes: Tastings are conducted in a sit-down classroom style, often by son Vinnie. The Cilurzos produce the best reds in the valley—unfiltered, with big body and complex flavors. We liked a lush, herbal Merlot with a soft finish; a peppery medium bodied Cab with a nice tannic nip at the end; and an outstanding six-year-old Petit Syrah, a bold and black wine with enough tannin to carry it into the next century. Sauvignon Blanc, a nice barrel-fermented Chardonnay, Chenin Blanc, Muscat Canelli and a rich, late harvest Petit Syrah complete the list. Prices range from $6.50 to the mid teens.

Vintners choice: "We're particularly noted for our full bodied Petit Syrah," says Vinnie.

Maurice Carrie Winery • T ✗ 🏠

◻ *34225 Rancho California Rd., Temecula, CA 92591; (909) 676-1711. Daily 10 to 5; major credit cards. Selected wines tasted. Extensive giftware and specialty food assortment. Picnic area and children's playground.* ◻

The Maurice Carrie complex is both imposing and cheerful, an intriguing mix of French country manor and upscale American farm architecture, with an old-fashioned windmill for good measure. A gazebo, rose garden, picnic areas and even a kiddie land complete this inviting picture. The cheery tasting room is accented with beam ceilings, French windows and café curtains.

It's a safe bet that Gordon and Maurice Carrie Van Roekel are the only vintners who entered to this profession on roller skates. They retired to the valley in 1984 after successful careers as skating rink operators, then they soon became bored. They bought a vineyard in 1985, and completed their elaborate winery and hospitality center two years later. A banquet and reception room were added in 1990, popular with locals for weddings.

Tasting notes: Following current trends toward light, crisp whites, Maurice Carrie has won a fair stack of awards for a young winery. Their wine list, originally small, has grown in recent years to include three varieties of Chardonnay that range from light and fruity to rich and complex, a crisply dry Chenin Blanc, a fruit-focused Johannisberg Riesling and a sweet Muscat Canelli. On the red side of the ledger are mellow and dry Cabernet Sauvignon and Pinot Noir, an Italian Nebbiolo, soft and drinkable Merlot and Syrah, and Cody's Crush, a very light Gamay-style blend. Prices range from $5 to $13.

Filsinger Vineyards • T GTA ✗

◻ *39050 De Portola Rd., Temecula, CA 92592; (909) 676-4594. Weekends 10 to 5; MC/VISA, AMEX. Most wines tasted free; $1 for sparkling wines. Wine logo gift items. Guided tours by appointment. Attractive picnic gazebo.* ◻

The Filsingers' cottage-style tasting room is one of the coziest in the Southland, an inviting Spanish colonial space with ceramic tile floors, a carved tasting counter and lazily-turning ceiling fans. A nearby picnic area is equally appealing, housed within a large gazebo. The plain, business-like winery is a discreet distance away.

This pleasant enclave is the handiwork of physician Bill Filsinger and his wife Kathy. In fact, they built much of it with their own hands. They planted vines in 1972 and started making wine eight years later. Son Eric now has a hand in things as well, as assistant winemaker.

Tasting notes: Dr. Filsinger's wines are full-flavored and complex, with the medals to prove it. He makes one of the few Gewürztraminers in the valley and it's properly herbal and rich. Others we liked were a piquant, fruity and crisp Chardonnay; a lush and complex Chenin Blanc; a spicy buttery Fumé Blanc; and a fine medium-bodied Cabernet Sauvignon, aged in American Oak. Three *méthode champenoise* sparkling wines were tasty as well. The good doctor also produces a white Zinfandel that we actually liked. The addition of small amounts of Gewürztraminer, Muscat and Cabernet give it a complexity rarely found in this infamous picnic wine. Prices are modest, from $7 to the early teens.

Keyways Winery & Vineyard • T$ ✗

◻ 37338 De Portola Rd., Temecula, CA 92592; (909) 676-1451. Weekends 10 to 5; MC/VISA, AMEX. All varieties tasted for $1 fee. Some wine related gift items and picnic fare. Exhibit of Americana antiques; small picnic area. ◻

This medium-sized Spanish-style facility is an interesting blend of winery, tasting room, art gallery and American folk museum. An impeccably restored Model-A Ford sits opposite the tasting counter; an electric train rustles overhead on a circular track. A pot-bellied stove, antique kitchenware and a copper-topped tasting bar complete an American Gothic image. From an art gallery loft, one can peer into a cellaring facility; wines are made elsewhere.

Carl Key is one of those people who has a problem with retirement. After succeeding rather handsomely in the restaurant and liquor business, he built an elegant Spanish style mansion in this valley. Getting restless, be began growing grapes and producing wines in the 1980s, then he opened this facility in 1989. "I keep retiring, but it never seems to work out," he grinned.

Tasting notes: Light and soft describes the Keyways style. Prices also are soft, from $7 to $13. The list includes a crisp, clean Chardonnay; a dry and fruity Sauvignon Blanc and a delicate, medium-acid Johannisberg Riesling. A Cabernet Sauvignon with hearty yet soft varietal character is the list's red wine representative. Misty Key is one of the more interesting wines, a dusky-fruity blend of Gewürztraminer and Emerald Riesling.

Baily Vineyard and Winery • T CT ✗

◻ 36150 Pauba Rd., Temecula, CA 92592; (909) 676-WINE. Weekends 10 to 5. Most varieties tasted. Some wine related gift items. Informal tours; small picnic area. ◻

This attractive little gray stucco facility is tucked into a hillside hollow above the Temecula Valley floor. A walk to the tasting room is a trip through the winery, since an open passageway leads past stainless steel vats and other vinting devices. Once in the small, inviting tasting room, you can take your selection to café-style seating and enjoy a valley view. Outside, a shaded picnic area also takes advantage of this Temecula Valley vista.

Most Baily patrons sample the wines at the new visitor center on Rancho California Road. However, we feel it's worth the additional drive, including half a mile of sandy bumps, to see this appealing Spanish-California style winery where they're made.

Tasting notes and Vintners choice: See tasting room listing above.

THE BEST OF THE BUNCH

The best wine buys ● Mount Palomar Winery, Temecula Crest Winery, Baily Winery, Maurice Carrie Winery, Filsinger Vineyards and Keyways Winery & Vineyard.

The most attractive wineries ● Thornton Winery, Maurice Carrie Winery and Temecula Crest Winery.

The most interesting tasting rooms ● Cilurzo Vineyard & Winery, Temecula Crest, Filsinger Vineyards and Keyways Winery & Vineyard.

The best gift shops ● Thornton Winery, Callaway Vineyard & Winery, Mount Palomar Winery, Maurice Carrie Winery and Temecula Crest Winery.

The nicest picnic areas ● Callaway Vineyard & Winery, Mount Palomar Winery, Maurice Carrie Winery and Filsinger Vineyards.

The best tours ● Thornton Winery (guided tour with wine tasting) and Cilurzo Vineyard & Winery (self-guided).

Wineland activities and such

Wineland events ● Temecula Valley Vintners Association Barrel Tasting, early February, (909) 699-3626; Temecula Valley Balloon and Wine Festival, mid-May, (909) 676-5090; Nouveau Wine and Food Tasting, third weekend in November, (909) 676-5090. Individual wineries also sponsor events. Thornton Winery is particularly active, with a summer and fall concert series, wine dinners and other activities; call (909) 699-3021.

Winery touring map ● *Temecula Valley Wine Country*, available at area wineries or contact: Temecula Valley Vintners Association, P.O. Box 1601, Temecula, CA 92593-1601; (909) 699-3626.

BEYOND THE VINEYARDS

What lies beyond Temecula's vineyards is the whole of Southern California, one of America's leading vacation destinations.

An hour's drive south on I-15 gets you to **San Diego,** where you can soak in the sun at the beaches, visit California's first mission, its oldest park, with a fine collection of museum, and the state's finest zoo. An hour and a half north delivers you to the **Anaheim-Los Angeles** area, with multitudinous touristic offerings.

Temecula's immediate surrounds provide a few vineyard distractions as well. **Murietta Hot Springs** just to the north is a family resort offering mud and mineral baths. **Lake Skinner** county park, immediately northeast of the vineyards, offers water sports, fishing and camping. **Lake Elsinore** to the northwest, off I-15, and **Lake Perris,** north off State Highway 215, are major water sports areas with shoreside resorts. Beyond Elsinore, State Route 74 wanders through the oaks, pines, campsites and hiking trails of **Cleveland National Forest.** It ends at the Pacific, just beyond **San Juan Capistrano,** home to the mission of the swallows.

A more direct route to *El Pacifico's* beaches is State Highway 76, reached via I-15 about 12 miles south of Temecula. The approach takes you through the wooded **San Luis River Valley,** past **Mission San Luis Rey** to the coastal towns of **Oceanside** and **Carlsbad.** Both have extensive public beaches and Carlsbad is home to the famed **La Costa** resort.

If you head inland on Highway 76, you'll encounter **San Antonio de Pala,** the only California mission still fulfilling its original role—serving Native Americans. It's on the Pala Indian reservation. Beyond is **Palomar Mountain State Park** and the famed **Palomar Observatory** with its giant 200-inch telescope.

Temecula area activities

Hot air ballooning • Dae Flights, P.O. Box 1671, Temecula, CA 92593, (909) 676-3902; Sunrise Balloons, (800) 548-9912.

Water sports • Lake Elsinore resorts, (909) 674-3171; Lake Perris resorts, (909) 657- 0676; and Lake Skinner County Park, (909) 926-1541.

Attractions

Old Town Temecula Museum • 28670 Front St., Temecula; (909) 676-0021. Wednesday-Sunday 11 to 4; donations requested. Exhibits of Temecula's early Indian, Spanish and American ranching days.

Pala Mission • Off Route 76 in Pala; (619) 742-3317. Tuesday-Sunday 10 to 3; mission free, small charge for museum. Mission-era relics and mineral exhibit.

Palomar Observatory museum and gallery • In Palomar Mountain State Park; (619) 742-3476; free. Astronomy museum open daily 9 to 4:30; Hale 200-inch telescope visitors gallery open 9 to 4.

WINE COUNTRY DINING

Most restaurants are clumped in two areas in Temecula: the old town section, and Rancho California Town Center just east of the freeway interchange, off Rancho California Road. We list three in Old Town—The Bank, Rosa's Cantina and Swing Inn; and two in Town Center—Baily Wine Country Café and the Claimjumper. You'll find the Steak Ranch off Rancho California, just west of the freeway, and Café Champagne at the Thornton Winery.

Baily Wine Country Café • ☆☆☆ *$$*

☐ *27644 Ynez Road (Town Center); (909) 694-6887. American; good local wine list, plus a variety of domestic and imported beers. Tuesday-Thursday 11:30 to 3 and 5 to 9, Friday 11:30 to 3 and 5 to 9:30, Saturday 11:30 to 9:30, Sunday 11:30 to 9. Reservation recommended Friday and Saturday nights. Major credit cards.* ☐ Very appealing café with white nappery and modernistic wrought iron grape clusters on the walls. The fare tilts toward *nouveau*, ranging from chicken breast stuffed with leeks to a two-course presentation of duck leg salad and grilled duck breast with Cabernet demiglacé; plus a fresh daily catch. Smoke-free dining room.

The Bank of Mexican Food • ☆ *$*

☐ *28645 Front Street (Main street); (909) 676-6760. Mexican; wine and beer. Daily 11 to 9. MC/VISA.* ☐ Basic smashed beans and rice place in an interesting setting—the 1912 Temecula Bank building, called "The Pawn Shop" by its rancher board of directors. High ceilings; large open space brightened by a few Mexican artifacts.

Café Champagne • ☆☆☆ *$$$*

☐ *At Thornton Winery, 32575 Rancho California Rd.; (909) 699-0088. California nouveau; extensive local wine list. Daily from 11. Reservations essential for weekend lunches; MC/VISA.* ☐ Stylishly modern restaurant with dishes designed to match Temecula Valley wines, such as baked pecan chicken and mesquite grilled salmon. Herbs are plucked from a nearby garden to season this *nouveau* fare. Dining indoors or on an attractive patio with vineyard views.

The Claimjumper ● ☆☆☆ $$

⊓ *29370 Rancho California Rd. (Town Center); (909) 694-6887. American; full bar service. Sunday-Monday 11 to 10, Tuesday-Thursday 11 to 11, Friday-Saturday 11 to midnight. Reservations accepted; recommended Friday and Saturday nights. Major credit cards.* ⊓ New but made to look old; cleverly fashioned western style restaurant with brick interior walls, simulated Tiffany and pressed tin ceilings. Rural American menu ranges from hickory smoked prime ribs to assorted chickens and chops. Large beer selection.

Rosa's Cantina ● ☆ $

⊓ *28636 Front St. (Main); (909) 695-2428. Mexican; wine and beer. Daily 11 to 9 with weekend breakfast 8 to 11:30. MC/VISA, DISC.* ⊓ Simple Mexican take-out dressed up with *faux* adobe and bright Mexican doodads. Patio dining is appealing on a sunny afternoon or warm summer evening. While not gourmet, the food is priced right; many entrées are under $5.

Steak Ranch Restaurant ● ☆☆☆ $$

⊓ *28910 Rancho California Rd. (at I-15 interchange); (909) 676-6788. American; full bar service. Daily 7 a.m. to 10 p.m. Reservations accepted. MC/VISA.* ⊓ Attractive designer-Western restaurant with booths, ceiling fans and leaded glass. Prime rib, steak, seafood with an oyster bar, and an occasional pasta.

Swing Inn ● ☆ $$

⊓ *28676 Front St. (Third); (909) 676-2321. Rural American; wine and beer. Daily 5 a.m. to 10 p.m. MC/VISA.* ⊓ The sign says "World famous" and it is if Temecula is your world. Swing Inn has been getting up with the roosters and feeding folks breakfast, dinner and supper since the last century. An authentic slice of the Old West, updated with 1950s Formica. Steaks, chops, chickens and even chicken fried steak; generous portions and cheap prices.

WINELAND LODGINGS

Best Western Country Inn ● ☆☆☆ $$$ Ø

⊓ *27706 Jefferson Ave. (at I-15 Winchester exit), Temecula, CA 92590; (800) 528-1234 or (909) 676-7378. Couples $48 to $62, singles $39 to $47.50, suites $85 to $115. Major credit cards.* ⊓ A 74- unit motel with TV movies, room phones and refrigerators; some in-room spas. Pool, outdoor spa, fireplace lounge; microwave available.

Best Western Guest House Inn ● ☆☆ $$$ Ø

⊓ *41873 Moreno Rd., Temecula, CA 92591; (909) 676-5700. Couples $49 to $64, singles $43 to $46. Majot credit cards.* ⊓ A 24-room motel with TV movies and phones. Pool, spa, restaurant adjacent.

Embassy Suites ● ☆☆☆ $$$$ Ø

⊓ *29345 Rancho California Rd. (at the I-15 interchange), Temecula, CA 92591; (800) 362-2779 or (909) 676-5656. Couples and singles from $89. Major credit cards.* ⊓ Attractive resort complex with pool, spa and other amenities. All two-room suites; 136 units with TV movies, VCR, room phones, microwaves and refrigerators; complimentary evening beverages. **Restaurant** serves from 6:30 a.m. to 9:30 p.m.; American fare; dinners $9 to $17; full bar service.

Loma Vista Bed and Breakfast ● ☆☆☆ *$$$$$ Ø*

□ *33350 La Serena Way (off Rancho California), Temecula, CA 92591; (909) 676-7047. Couples $95 to $125; lower midweek rates. Six rooms, all with private baths; champagne breakfast. MC/VISA.* □ Handsome Spanish mission-style inn on a bluff overlooking vineyards of Callaway Winery. Rooms nicely done in early American and California style.

Temecula Creek Inn ● ☆☆☆☆ *$$$$$ Ø*

□ *44501 Rainbow Canyon Rd. (Highway 79), Temecula, CA 92592; (800) 962-7335 or (909) 694- 1000. Couples and singles $115 to $150. Major credit cards.* □ Opulent Southwest theme resort with 27-hole golf course, tennis courts, pool and spa. Eighty-four rooms with TV, phones, safes, honor bars, refrigerators and balconies or patios. **Temet Grill** serves weekdays 6:30 a.m. to 10 p.m., weekends 6 to 10; dinners $16 to $25; full bar service.

Temecula area information source

Temecula Valley Chamber of Commerce, 27450 Ynez Rd., Suite 104, Temecula, CA 92591; (909) 676-5090. Send a stamped, self-addressed business size envelope for an information packet. The chamber is located in the courtyard of Town Center Corporate Plaza, just east of the freeway at Rancho California Road and Ynez Road.

LEARNING ABOUT WINE

"The finish is long with the opening fruit tones looping back at the end to complete a rich cyclic experience." — **Description of a Beaulieu Cabernet**

Chapter Fourteen
AFTERTHOUGHTS
Serving & storing tips; a winetalk lexicon

Now that you have completed your rich cyclic experience through this book, we shall loop back to the end with a few items of useful information. As we said at the beginning, wine is neither an enigma or something to be revered. It is merely a tasty and relaxing beverage best enjoyed with food—and sometimes on a hot August afternoon with nothing at all, if it's white or maybe even pink and properly chilled.

Thus, our rules have to do with practicality, not with mysticism. We begin with the basics: serving and storing wine.

Pulling the cork on food & wine rules

Wine is the only adult beverage created primarily to be consumed with food—with the exception of iced-down beer at a Texas chili cook-off. It is therefore helpful to determine which works with what. For many of us, wine *is* food, as much a part of the evening meal as the meat and veggies.

Unfortunately, some wine writers and winery brochures complicate a simple issue with a lot of specific rules about wine and food combinations. One suggestion, for instance, is that Zinfandel should be served with game. But Zinfandel can range from a light and soft young wine to bold, high-tannin, industrial strength stuff from century-old vines. A Chenin Blanc can be fruity and lush with a touch of sweetness, or dry and crisp. Do you really want sweet, fruity wine with filét of sole?

So, you wonder as you wander through this wilderness of wines, what rules *does* one follow. The rules are simple. Both of them.

1. Match the wine to the strength of the food. Bold wines are best with highly-spiced meat and pasta dishes; delicate wines work well with mildly flavored dishes. The idea is to balance the two, so the flavor of one doesn't overwhelm the taste of the other.

321

CONQUERING WINE LIST PANIC

You and your archrival, Watercooler Willie, are being considered for that vice presidency slot. Your boss invites you and your wife out to dinner; you just *know* he's testing your social graces. He's a wine aficionado but you wouldn't know a Cabernet from a cantaloupe. A guy with a spoon hanging from his vest hands your boss the wine list and—*omygawd*—he passes it over to you! It flashes through your mind that you have four choices:

1. Hand it back.

2. Smile naively at the waiter and say: "It's difficult to pick from such a wonderful selection. What would *you* suggest?"

3. Order white Zinfandel.

4. Go for it.

You didn't become manager of the Vertical Flange Department through timidity, so you decide to go for it.

Here are the five essential steps to bluffing your way through a wine list:

1. Thumb—casually—to the California wine section. It's easier to pronounce Zinfandel than *Côtes de Provence Sociéte Civile des Domaines Ott Frères*.

2. Remember that—as a general rule—white wines are more suitable with subtly-flavored foods such as poached fish or mildly-seasoned fowl. The flavor of heartier reds will stand up to red meats, highly-spiced dishes and just about anything Italian, up to and including Gina Lolabrigida.

3. Poll your table to see what's been ordered. If it's a mix of fish and red meat, go for a light red such as a young Merlot, or for a more complex white like aged Chardonnay. Resist the temptation to order rosé. Make major points by suggesting that the Chardonnay shouldn't be *too* cold, lest it mask that wonderful spicy aroma. Or be Joe Cool and order a sparkling wine—to celebrate your coming promotion? (If it's from California, don't call it Champagne.)

4. When the wine arrives, the waiter or *sommelier* will unplug the thing and hand you the cork. F'gawdsake, don't sniff it! Check its little bottom to see if it's damp (meaning it was properly stored), then place it on the table.

5. Now, here's where you nail down that vice presidency. Swirl the wine vigorously, keeping the base of the glass on the table so you won't shower the boss. (If you ordered a sparkling wine, you *don't* swirl it, of course.) Then sniff the wine with one long, dramatic inhalation, purse your lips thoughtfully and—don't sip it!* Nod knowingly to the waiter and tell him it's fine.

*If it's a bad wine, you can tell by the smell—a pungent vinegary or sour aroma. You should refuse a wine only if it's spoiled; not because you chose poorly and don't care for it. Besides, it's really cool just to sniff the wine.

2. If both spicy and subtly flavored dishes are being served (he ordered pepper steak, she 's having scallops), try a light yet lively wine. This is where rosés, sparkling wines and young reds are useful.

Serving temperatures

Here's a rule that may be *too* simple: Experts tell us to serve white wines chilled and reds at room temperature. But chilling can muffle the bouquet and flavor of a lush and spicy, barrel-fermented Chardonnay. At room temperature—particularly if it's August in Tucson—a delicate young red may lose its fresh berry taste. Our rules? We serve crisp whites, rosés and sparkling wines at about 50 degrees, full bodied whites and some young reds at 55 to 60, and heartier reds around 65 degrees.

The story on storing wine

So you've really gotten into this thing and you want to build your own wine cellar. But suppose you don't have a cellar? Maybe your house is on a concrete slab, or you live in a 12th floor condo. You could spend a few thousand dollars on a temperature and humidity controlled wine mausoleum, which will certainly impress your friends. Or you could use that money to send your kids to college, and still create a safe place for your wines.

Bottles should be stored on their sides to keep the corks moist. They should be in a dark, cool place with little day-to-day temperature variation. Extreme changes cause expansion and contraction, pushing wine out through the cork and drawing in air. Remember, wine plus air equals expensive vinegar. A dark closet on the north side of the house will provide proper protection for your precious wine caché. If your house is on a raised foundation with a crawl space, tuck those puppies down there. An old refrigerator or freezer can serve as a good, inexpensive wine vault. Don't plug it in! You just want to take advantage of its insulation.

It's wise to peel the lead foil caps off the bottles, so you can keep an eye on the corks. If you see discoloration—a sign of leakage—you'd better schedule that bottle for tonight's dinner.

Coming home: Protecting your investment

It's not difficult to protect your wine at home, since it's an environment you can control. However, getting it there in good health may be a challenge. You may be touring the wine country on a hot August day and—while you sampled wines in a cool cellar—the greenhouse effect elevated the temperature in your car to 120 degrees. You may be far from home, and transport may involve several thousand miles of flying.

When you go shopping among the vinelands on a summer day, take a cooler along so you can moderate their temperature changes. Remember, it's sudden and extreme changes that can damage a wine. If you've flown in and are renting a car, pick up one of those inexpensive styrofoam coolers. Also, keep your wine in the vehicle's trunk. Because of that greenhouse business, it's cooler than the passenger compartment. And—oh yes—don't set it in the area of the trunk that's over the tailpipe.

If you're flying home, make your new wine purchase part of your carry-on luggage. After all, what's more precious—a suitcase full of wrinkled shirts or six bottles of awesome Zinfandel? Most wineries can provide handy six-pack carriers and you can slip a couple of them under your seat. Wine bottles of course are fragile, and the wine within shouldn't be subjected to unpredictable temperatures and pressure changes in a cargo compartment. If you must check it, ask the winery tasting room folks if the have styrofoam "over-shippers" which come in six and twelve bottle sizes.

If you've gotten carried away and purchased several cases of wine, the winery will offer to ship it. Some states have funny laws about incoming wine, and the U.S. Postal Service refuses to touch the stuff. Other shippers will handle it and they can be discreet about restrictive state laws.

What price wine?

Someone once said that a good bottle of wine shouldn't cost more than a good bottle of Scotch. Wine is less complicated to produce, and it's taxed at a much lower rate. So why are $35 Chardonnays, $45 Cabernets and $125 *Louis Jadot Chevalier-Montrachet Les Demoiselles* on the market? Because people will pay for them. We don't question their motives, but guidebook authors—even clever ones—can't afford such extravagance.

If you follow winetasting results, you'll often note little similarity between quality and price. We regularly discover fine wines for under $15, and often for under $10. Only by sampling a variety can you determine which is best for you and your budget. That's one of the great advantages of wine country tasting. Come to think of it, isn't that why you bought this book?

The great house wine heist

Do you often order house wine because you're dining alone or your partner doesn't drink, and you don't want a full bottle? You probably aren't getting your money's worth, particularly if you desire two glasses to get through a meal. House wine is the single greatest profit item of many restaurants.

Perhaps the place pours one of the better jug varietals—an August Sebastiani or Fetzer. These aren't bad wines, but the restaurant probably paid $4 to $6 wholesale, and it's nicking you $3.50 a glass. A 1.5-liter bottle contains 52 ounces, from which the establishment can get 13 four-ounce servings. Multiply that by $3.50 and you've got $45.50. Not a bad return on the restaurant's investment, but a lousy bargain for you. And if it's pouring Grace L. Furguson burgundy and charging $3.50 a pop—try not to think about it.

You're better served, literally, by ordering half bottles if the restaurant offers them. That gives you about two and a half glasses of decent wine. If the restaurant sells premium wines by the glass, they may be a better buy than the overpriced jug stuff, although by-the-glass varietals often are overpriced.

In California and a few other civilized states, the law allows you to take unfinished wine home, so go for a regular bottle and ask for a brown paper doggie bag. Full bottles generally are marked up three to five times over wholesale. That's still rather steep, and we think restaurants in general charge too much for their wine. But it's better than the eight to ten-fold mark-up on a jug. And you'll be getting a better quality wine.

A WINETALK LEXICON

As in most professions and avocations, wine world participants and enthusiasts have their own language. What follows is a glossary of vintners' and wine enthusiasts' shoptalk.

Acid — The grapes' tartaric and malic acid that give a wine its crisp after-taste.

Appellation — The term describing a legally defined grape growing area in the winelands of the world. In America, it's called an Approved Viticultural Area (AVA) and it's administered—gawd knows why—by the Bureau of Alcohol, Tobacco and Firearms. For an American label to bear an appellation designation, 85 percent of its grapes must come from that area, and the wine must be "fermented, manufactured and finished" there. Dry Creek, Carneros, Chalk Hill and Shenandoah Valley are typical California appellations. The first appellation designations came in France decades ago, called *Appellation d'Origine Contrôlée* (AOC), which dictates the types of grapes that can be grown in each area as well as how it is labeled. American AVA rules don't address grape types.

Aperitif (*a-PERI-teef*) — A drink taken before a meal as an appetizer; often a full flavored but dry wine like vermouth or dry sherry.

Aroma — The smell of the grape from which the wine was made.

Balance — A catch-all term describing a wine in which nothing is out of balance: not too acidic, not too sweet, not too high in tannin.

Berry — To a vineyardist, grapes are berries; berry-like describes the flavor of the fruit in wine.

Big — No, it's not a large bottle. "Big" in winetalk refers to a wine with strong, complex flavor, full bodied and often high in alcohol. Tasters use the expression "big nose" to describe a wine with a strong aroma and bouquet.

Binning — Storing wine away, or "putting it down" for aging.

Blush — A term to describe a pink wine made from red grapes, usually Grenache, Zinfandel, Cabernet Sauvignon or Pinot Noir.

Body — The fullness of a wine, sometimes—but not always—referring to the viscosity or alcoholic content. A thin and watery wine lacks body.

Bordeaux (*bor-DOE*) — A large area of France that produces some of the world's finest red wines, usually blends of Cabernet Sauvignon, Merlot, Cabernet Franc, Malbec, Petit Verdot and Carmenere.

Botrytis cinerea (*bo-TREET-is sin-AIR-e-ah*) — A mold that wrinkles ripening grapes, causing a concentration of sugar and flavor that produces a rich, full-bodied wine. Called "noble mold" by romantics and "noble rot" by cynical romantics.

Bottle sick — The condition of a wine immediately after bottling, when it has been filtered, shaken and otherwise abused. The condition passes after the bottle has rested a few weeks.

Bouquet — The often complex smell of wine that comes from fermenting and aging, as opposed to aroma, which is the smell of the fruit.

Breathing — The practice of letting a wine stand open so it absorbs oxygen, supposedly to enhance its aroma and taste. Experts disagree on its usefulness, but it's a harmless gesture to let your wine catch its breath.

Brilliant — Not a measure of the winemaker's cleverness, but the clarity of the wine. All good wines should be brilliant. So should a good winemaker, for that matter.

Brix — The measure of sugar content in a grape, which will determine its alcoholic level upon fermentation.

Brut (*brute*) — One of the driest of champagnes.

Bulk process — Cheap method of making sparkling wine by fermenting it in large sealed tanks to capture the bubbles.

Cap — Layer of skins, pulp and other grape solids that floats to the top of a fermenting vat of grapes. The winemaker "punches it down" or pumps the wine over itself to keep it broken up.

Cave (*Kahv*) — French for cellar; "Cava" in Spanish.

Chai — French word for a small building, usually above ground, for aging wine in small oak barrels. Some California wineries now use the term.

Champagne — Specifically, it refers to a sparkling wine produced in France's Champagne district although some countries—notably ours—use the term to describe any effervescent wine. The use of the French term is becoming less common here, however.

Character — Term used to describe the good qualities of a wine. A poor wine, like a poor citizen, "lacks character."

Charmat (*SHAR-mahn*) — French term for bulk process champagne-making; named for the Frenchman who developed it.

Château — Not necessarily a house, "château" is commonly used in France to describe a particular vineyard operation.

Claret — Usually referring to a Bordeaux in England, but used to describe just about any red wine in the rest of the world.

Coarse — A full-bodied wine, but with ragged edges and perhaps a harsh aftertaste; no finesse.

Cooperage — Wooden wine containers—barrels, vats and such.

Corky — A wine that has been invaded by a disintegrating cork, giving it a bad flavor.

Crush — It's often used as a noun in winetalk, referring to the harvest and subsequent crushing of wine grapes. "We had a good crush this year," a winegrower might say.

Cuvee (*Coo-VAY*) — A specific blend of wine, as in the "cuvee" used for a champagne. Also a vat or tank used for blending or fermenting wine.

Demijon — A large and rather squat wine bottle, sometimes covered with wicker.

Demi-sec — Sparkling wine with rather high residual sugar content; sweeter than sec.

Disgorging — Removing sediment that has settled in the neck of a bottle of sparkling wine; most of it is trapped in a small plastic *bidule*, placed there for that purpose

Dosage (*Do-SAJ*) — The mix of sugar syrup, wine, brandy or other product added to sparkling wine to make it less dry.

Dry — Crisp and not sweet or sour. In winetalk, it has nothing to do with lack of wetness.

Enology — Winemaking science; one who makes wine is an enologist. Classic spelling is *oenology*.

Estate bottled — A wine in which all the grapes came from the vintner's "estate" or vineyards.

Fermentation — The reason for all this—the wine industry, winery touring, this book in your hand. It's the process of converting sugar in grape juice into alcohol and carbon dioxide by the addition of yeast.

Fining — Clarifying wine to remove the solids, usually by adding an agent such as egg white that collects them.

Finish — The aftertaste of a wine, created primarily by the acid. A crisp, properly balanced wine will have a "long, lingering finish." A thin, wimpey one won't.

Flowery — The aroma of a wine more akin to blossoms than to grapes.

Fortified — A wine whose alcoholic content has been increased by the addition of brandy or other high-alcohol beverage.

Fruity — The flavor of a wine that comes from the grape.

Generic — A wine of no particular pedigree. In countries other than France, it is sometimes named for a wine region, like Burgundy or Chablis in France and Chianti in Italy.

Grapey — A wine that tastes too much like grape juice (think of Welsh's). The grape taste should be subtle and is often described, particularly in reds, as berry-like.

Grassy — A subtle grass-like flavor, sometimes found in reds; sort of herbal without the herbs. Not necessarily unpleasant.

Green — A wine not ready to drink; too young; harsh and raw tasting.

Haut (*oh* or *auh*) — French for "high" or "upper," referring to wine producing regions. Haut-Sauternes is a general term applied to a sweet white wine from upper Sauternes; the name has no bearing on quality.

Hock — Generic term for white wine, usually used in England.

Horizontal tasting — No, it doesn't mean you've sampled too many. It's a comparative tasting of the same wine varietal from different vineyards. Vertical tasting is sampling the same wine from different vintages.

Jerez (*hair-eth*) — A city and a wine producing region of Spain; the birthplace of sherry.

Jeroboam — Wine jug holding the equivalent of six .75 liter bottles.

Late harvest — A wine made from grapes left on the vine until their sugar content was unusually high. It produces a full-bodied, high-alcohol wine—and sometimes a very sweet one if the fermentation is interrupted to leave some residual sugar.

Lees — Dead yeast cells and other sediment cast off by a young wine as it's being aged.

Magnum — A container twice the size of a normal wine bottle.

Maceration — A method of softening red wines after fermentation by letting them sit with their skins and seeds in sealed tanks for several weeks.

Malolactic fermentation — A secondary fermentation that occurs in wine, converting malic acid into milder lactic acid and carbon dioxide. This action, often occurring in reds, helps reduce their youthful harshness to create a softer, more complex wine.

May wine — Sweet white wine, sometimes flavored with leaves or herbs; of German origin.

Meritage — A term adopted by several California wineries to designate red or white premium wines blended from classic French grape varieties. Red Meritage seems to be more common. A winery must join the Meritage Association and meet strict blending criteria in order to use the label. Many California wineries now do similar blends—particularly reds—without calling the wine Meritage.

Méthode champenoise (*me-thoad sham-pen-WAH*) — The classic French method of making sparkling wine, in which it is produced and aged in the same bottle.

Methusalem — King-sized glass wine container, holding the equivalent of eight ordinary bottles.

Micro-climate — Specific climatic conditions in a small area—a sheltered valley or exposed knoll—that make it ideal for a particular grape.

Must — The liquid of crushed grapes, en route to becoming wine.

Nature — The driest of sparkling wines; in other words, one that is natural, supposedly with no sweetner added, although a very light *dosage* usually is.

Negociant — A winery that owns no vineyards, but buys grapes from selected growers. Advantages are that it permits flexibility and—if the wines are selling well—rapid expansion.

Noble grapes — The term, given somewhat arbitrarily, to the Cabernet Sauvignon of Bordeaux, Pinot Noir and Chardonnay of Burgundy and Riesling of Germany.

Nose — The aroma and bouquet of a wine.

Oakey — Wine with a strong flavor of the wood in which it was aged.

Off — Slang taster's term, meaning that a wine is "off base"; not "on."

Off-dry — A wonderfully silly winetaster's redundancy for slightly sweet.

Ordinaire (*or-dee-nair*) — French for ordinary. *Vin ordinaire* is a basic table wine; in America, a jug wine.

Oxidized — A wine that has been exposed to air, and is starting to become vinegary.

Phylloxera (*fill-LOX-er-ah*) — Nasty little plant louse, 1/25th of an inch long, which destroys grapevines by attacking their roots. It raised havoc in America late in the last century and destroyed 75 percent of France's wine crop. The scourge was stopped by grafting European varietals onto phylloxera-resistant native American root stock. However, it's back on the attack in some California vineyards.

Proof — Measurement of alcohol by volume, in which the proof number, for some odd reason, represents half the alcohol content. A hundred-proof whisky is half alcohol. The term isn't used in winemaking; its measure is "percentage of alcohol"—by volume, not by weight.

Proprietary wines — Special names given to a wine by the proprietor, usually reflecting place names or some pet fetish. They're almost always blends. "Riverside Farms White" or "Workhorse Red" are examples.

Pulp — A grape's fleshy part.

Punch down — The process of breaking up the thick layer of solids that float to the top when a wine, particularly a red, is fermenting.

Racking — Clarifying a wine by drawing off the clear liquid from one cask or vat to another, leaving the lees and sediment that has settled to the bottom.

Residual sugar — The sugar that remains in a wine to give it sweetness, usually measured by percentage. In table wines, fermentation is stopped by lowering the temperature to kill the yeast cells, thus leaving residual sugar. In dessert wines, brandy is added, which pickles the yeast.

Riddling — Periodically turning and gently bumping champagne bottles to work the sediments into the neck. It can be done by hand or with automatic riddling racks.

Sack — Elizabethan term for sherry; thus "Dry Sack."

Schloss — "Castle" in Germany, synonymous with France's "château" in describing a winery.

Sec — French for dry (not sweet), yet it describes a sweeter style of Champagne—and yes, it doesn't make sense.

Secondary fermentation — Creating a sparkling wine by injecting sugar and yeast in a still wine and keeping it sealed (in the bottle or other closed container) so the carbon dioxide bubbles can't escape.

Sekt — German for sparkling wine.

Set — The appearance of berries after a vine has finished flowering.

Soft — A wine lacking harshness or rough edges.

Solera — The process of blending wines of different ages but the same type to achieve a consistency of style. This practice is commonly used to produce sherries. *Solera* refers not to the sun; it comes from *suelo*, the Spanish word for "floor," since the wines usually are blended from tiers of barrels, from top to bottom.

Stemmy — An unpleasant veggie flavor to wine, as if stems were left in during fermentation.

Still wine — Any wine that isn't sparkling.

Sulfuring — Sterilizing wine casks or barrels to kill harmful bacteria, and dusting vines with sulfur to eliminate fungus.

Sur lie aging — The technique of letting white wines rest on their yeast lees (and sometimes other solids) for months, causing the release of amino acids, esters and other compounds. This adds to the wine's complexity.

Tannin — Organic acids found in most plant matter. In wines, it comes primarily from the skins and seeds of grapes. Reds are higher in tannin because they're usually fermented with their skins. Tannin adds complexity, and an acidic "bite" to wine. Aging mellows these tannins while leaving the full, complex flavor. Don't be alarmed, but tannic acid is used to treat leather, thus the word "tan."

Tartar — Those sparkly little crystals you may see on the underside of a cork are tartaric acid, which occurs naturally in wine and settles out during aging. If the wine is stored upside down, which it should be, the crystals settle onto the cork. Don't worry; they're harmless.

Tirage (*tee-RAJ*) — French word with three definitions: 1. The sugar-syrup yeast mixture added to still wine (*liqueur de tirage*) to begin secondary fermentation; 2. Drawing off wine, usually from a barrel into a bottle; 3. *En tirage* indicates bottles stacked for aging.

Vermouth — Yes, that stuff that adds zing to your martini is a wine. Vermouth originated in Germany and is flavored with assorted herbs and spices. The word comes from *wermut* or wormwood, whose flowers are used to add aroma. Both sweet and dry Vermouths are produced in California. In Europe, sweet Vermouth is usually made in Italy and dry Vermouth is associated with France.

Vertical tasting — Sampling several wines of the same variety from different vintages, usually from the same winery. Horizontal tasting is sampling the same variety of wines from different wineries.

Viniculture — The science of growing grapes for wine production.

Vintage — The year in which grapes of a particular wine were harvested. In California, a wine bottle can be "vintage dated" only if 95 percent of the grapes therein were harvested in that year. The harvest itself is sometimes called the "vintage."

Viticulture — The science of grape-growing in general.

Vineyard designated wine — A varietal named for the vineyard where the grapes are grown; 95 percent of the grapes must be from there.

Vitis labrusca — The American grape, found growing wild and used unsuccessfully in early attempts at winemaking. Its rootstock, however, proved resistant to deadly phylloxera, so it became the base for many premium grapes, both in Europe and America.

Vitis vinifera — The source of most premium grapes; the vine grew wild in Asia Minor and likely was one of mankind's first cultivated crops. The Crusaders probably brought cuttings back to Europe.

INDEX: Primary listings indicated by *bold face italics*

REMARKABLY USEFUL GUIDEBOOKS
from *PINE CONE PRESS*

Critics praise the "jaunty prose" and "beautiful editing" of Pine Cone Press guidebooks by Don and Betty Martin. In addition to being comprehensive and "remarkably useful," their books are frank, witty and opinionated. They're available from book stores, or by direct order from the publisher.

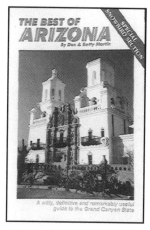

THE BEST OF ARIZONA
One of our best sellers, this detailed guide covers attractions, dining, lodgings and campgrounds in the Grand Canyon State. It also features maps, hikes and scenic drives. A special "Snowbird Directory" helps retirees plan their winters under the Southwestern sun. — *336 pages; $12.95*

THE BEST OF THE GOLD COUNTRY
It's a remarkably useful guide to California's gold rush area in the Sierra Nevada foothills and old Sacramento. This comprehensive book covers attractions, historic sites, dining, lodging and camping. — *240 pages; $11.95*

THE BEST OF NEVADA
This guide covers all of Nevada, with a special focus on gaming centers of Las Vegas, Reno-Tahoe and Laughlin. A special section advises readers how to "Beat the odds," with casino gambling tips. — *352 pages; $12.95*

THE BEST OF THE WINE COUNTRY
Where to taste wine in California? More than 250 wineries are featured, along with nearby restaurants, lodging and attractions. Special sections offer tips on selecting, tasting, serving and storing wine. — *320 pages; $13.95*

COMING TO ARIZONA
This is an all-purpose relocation guide for job-seekers, retirees and winter "Snowbirds" planning a move to Arizona. It provides essential data on dozens of cities, from recreation to medical care. — *232 pages; $12.95*

INSIDE SAN FRANCISCO
It's the ideal pocket guide to everybody's favorite city. This difinitive little book covers attractions, activities, shopping, nightlife, restaurants and lodging. Maps help readers find their way around the city. — *248 pages; $8.95*

More books and ordering information on the next page

NORTHERN CALIFORNIA DISCOVERY GUIDE

Our new Discovery Guide series focuses on driving vacations for motorists and RVers. We steer our readers to popular attractions and little-known jewels, along with great places to play, eat and sleep. — *356 pages; $12.95*

OREGON DISCOVERY GUIDE

From the wilderness coast to the Cascades to urban Portland, this book takes motorists and RVers over Oregon's byways and through its cities. It's another in the Martins' new Discovery Guide series. — *352 pages; $12.95*

SAN FRANCISCO'S ULTIMATE DINING GUIDE

The authors surveyed the *real* experts to compile this upbeat guide to 300 area restaurants: chefs, concierges and critics. — *224 pages; $9.95*

THE ULTIMATE WINE BOOK

It's the complete guide for wine enthusiasts, covering the subject in three major areas: wine and health, wine appreciation and wine with food. Written with candid humor, it pokes fun at wine snobs while providing reams of useful information for the serious wine lover. — *176 pages; $8.95*

UTAH DISCOVERY GUIDE

This remarkably useful driving guide covers every area of interest in the Beehive State, from its splendid canyonlands to Salt Lake City to the "Jurassic Parkway" of dinosaur country. — *360 pages; $13.95*

WASHINGTON DISCOVERY GUIDE

This handy book takes motorists and RVers from one corner of the Evergreen State to the other, from the Olympic Peninsula and Seattle to Eastern Washington's wine country and great rivers. — *372 pages; $13.95*

If you can't find your selection in a book store, ask a clerk to order it. Or you can order directly from the publisher. Include $1.05 postage and handling for each book; California residents add sales tax. Please give a phone number with your address, in case there's a question about your order.

Send your order to: Pine Cone Press

P.O. Box 1494, Columbia, CA 95310

THE MARTIN TRAVEL GUIDES
ARE AVAILABLE AT MOST BOOK STORES